An Arkansas History
For Young People

An Arkansas History
For Young People

Shay E. Hopper

T. Harri Baker
Jane Browning

Fourth Edition

The University of Arkansas Press • Fayetteville • 2008

Copyright © 2008 by The University of Arkansas Press

All rights reserved
Manufactured in the United States of America

ISBN-10 1-55728-845-3
ISBN-13 978-1-55728-845-5

11 10 09 08 07 5 4 3 2 1

Cover photo, Hawkbill Crag at sunrise, by TimErnst.com

The paper used in this publication meets the minimum requirements of the American National Standard for Permanence of Paper for Printed Library Materials Z39.48-1984.

AN ARKANSAS HISTORY FOR YOUNG PEOPLE, 4TH EDITION is supported in part by funds from the Arkansas Humanities Council and the National Endowment for the Humanities. Any views, findings, conclusions, or recommendations expressed in the textbook do not necessarily reflect those of the National Endowment for the Humanities.

Special thanks to Tyson Foods and the Tyson Family Foundation whose generous support made this publication possible.

In creating this textbook, we worked to make it true to Arkansas, all her people, and wonders. We worked with only Arkansas teachers, professors, and consultants, and we would like to offer our most heartfelt "thank you" to our educational and historical partners. Without you, this project would not have been possible.

Additional thanks go to senators Blanche L. Lincoln and Mark Pryor, former Governor Mike Huckabee, and Governor Mike Beebe for their contributions.

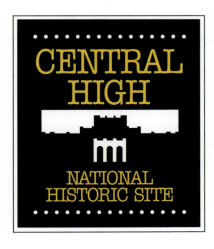

★ Authors and Textbook Consultants ★

Shay E. Hopper, MAT

Woodland Junior High School, Fayetteville
Washington County
Director of Textbook Development for
   Arkansas History
University of Arkansas Press, Fayetteville

Shay Elizabeth Hopper teaches eighth-grade Arkansas history, introduction to journalism (a course which she developed and instituted for her school), and ninth-grade yearbook at Woodland Junior High School in Fayetteville, Arkansas. She is a native of Conroe, Texas, and comes from a long line of teachers. Both of her grandmothers, her mother, and her sister are, or were, educators in the areas of history, civics, English, journalism, and family and consumer sciences.

Mrs. Hopper has a bachelor's degree in journalism with an emphasis in advertising and public relations from the University of Arkansas, Fayetteville. She has a master's degree in secondary education, also from the University of Arkansas. She holds certifications in secondary social studies and journalism. She is a member of her district's vertical team and curriculum committees, advanced-placement (AP) certified, Literacy Lab trained, on the board of the Arkansas Council for Social Studies, and a member of the National Council for Social Studies, and the Journalism Education Association and has participated in the Northwest Arkansas Writing Project. She has had lesson plans published in the *Arkansas Historical Quarterly* and has been a frequent presenter at the Arkansas Curriculum Conference in Little Rock.

Prior to entering the teaching field, she worked in marketing, advertising, community relations, and corporate staff training and development and as a national education director for VisionAmerica in Memphis and McDonald Eye Associates in Fayetteville. She is certified by the National Board of Opticianry.

Mrs. Hopper has lived in northwest Arkansas for fifteen years and is married to a native of Lee County, Arkansas.

T. Harri Baker

T. Harri Baker (1933–2004) was a history professor and administrator at the University of Arkansas at Little Rock for twenty-seven years. Prior to that, he worked as a journalist, then taught history at the University of Texas and at Mississippi Women's University. He spent a year in Washington, D.C., as a research associate for the Lyndon B. Johnson Oral History Project, conducting numerous interviews. Among his many projects in Arkansas, Dr. Baker was a founder of the UALR History Institute and a coeditor of a historical newspaper for fifth graders, the *Arkansas News,* published by the Old State House. Dr. Baker always believed that if the young people of the next generation knew and understood Arkansas history, they would love and appreciate Arkansas as much as he did and would have pride in their own history.

Jane Browning

Jane Browning is the executive director of the International Community Corrections Association in Washington, D.C. Previously executive director of the Learning Disabilities Association of America, Ms. Browning also served in the Clinton administration as executive director of the President's Committee on Mental Retardation and was director of Membership Services and Publications at the National Association of Social Workers and director of Program Development for The Arc of Maryland. In addition, Ms. Browning was executive director of the Arkansas Endowment for the Humanities throughout the 1980s.

★ Arkansas History Teacher Consultants ★

University of Arkansas Press Consultant

Brent E. Riffel, PhD
University of Arkansas, Fayetteville
Washington County
Director of Research and Photography, Textbook Development for Arkansas History
University of Arkansas Press, Fayetteville

A native of Little Rock, Brent Riffel is a graduate of Hendrix College in Conway. He holds a master of arts degree and a doctorate in history from the University of Arkansas, where he specialized in the civil rights movement, as well as southern labor and economics.

His work has appeared in, among other publications, the *Arkansas Historical Quarterly* and the *Encyclopedia of Arkansas*.

The following, all of whom teach Arkansas history and/or social studies, participated in regional roundtable sessions to contribute lesson ideas, strategies, and content to both the student and teacher editions of *An Arkansas History For Young People*.

Sherry Allen
DeWitt Middle School, DeWitt
Arkansas County
Southeast Arkansas Teacher Roundtable, Stuttgart

Madelyn Brown
Harrison Junior High School, Harrison
Boone County
Northwest Arkansas Teacher Roundtable, Fayetteville

Ruth Brown
Marvell High School, Marvell
Phillips County
Southeast Arkansas Teacher Roundtable, Stuttgart

Ethel Butler
Brinkley Middle School, Brinkley
Monroe County
Southeast Arkansas Teacher Roundtable, Stuttgart

Cherokee Cole
George Junior High School, Springdale
Washington County
Northwest Arkansas Teacher Roundtable, Fayetteville

Carleta Currie
Oakdale Junior High School, Rogers
Benton County
Northwest Arkansas Teacher Roundtable, Fayetteville

Paul Davenport
Jasper Schools, Jasper
Newton County
Northwest Arkansas Teacher Roundtable, Fayetteville

Richard Davis
Brinkley Middle School, Brinkley
Monroe County
Southeast Arkansas Teacher Roundtable, Stuttgart

Kimble Edwards
Resource
Jacksonville Middle Boys' School, Jacksonville
Pulaski County
Central Arkansas Teacher Roundtable, Little Rock

Debi Ewing-Hight
Washington Junior High School, Bentonville
Benton County
Northwest Arkansas Teacher Roundtable, Fayetteville

Diann Fancher
Gifted and Talented, Administration
Green Forest Schools, Green Forest
Carroll County
Northwest Arkansas Teacher
Roundtable, Fayetteville

Margret Grimes
Conway Public Schools, Conway
Faulkner County
Central Arkansas Teacher Roundtable, Little Rock

Mike Hemme
Mountain Home Junior High School, Mountain Home
Baxter County
Northeast Arkansas Teacher Roundtable, Jonesboro

Stephanie Hoops
English as a Second Language
Woodland Junior High School, Fayetteville
Washington County
Northwest Arkansas Teacher Roundtable, Fayetteville

Christina Hostetter
Barton Junior High School, El Dorado
Union County
Southwest Arkansas Teacher Roundtable, El Dorado

Lisa Huelle
Dardanelle Middle School, Dardanelle
Yell County
Central Arkansas Teacher Roundtable, Little Rock

Philita James
Henderson Middle Magnet School, Little Rock
Pulaski County
Central Arkansas Teacher Roundtable, Little Rock

Willette Jeffers
Palestine/Wheatley Junior High School, Wheatley
St. Francis County
Southeast Arkansas Teacher Roundtable, Stuttgart

Marian Jimerson
Malvern Junior High School, Malvern
Hot Spring County
Central Arkansas Teacher Roundtable, Little Rock

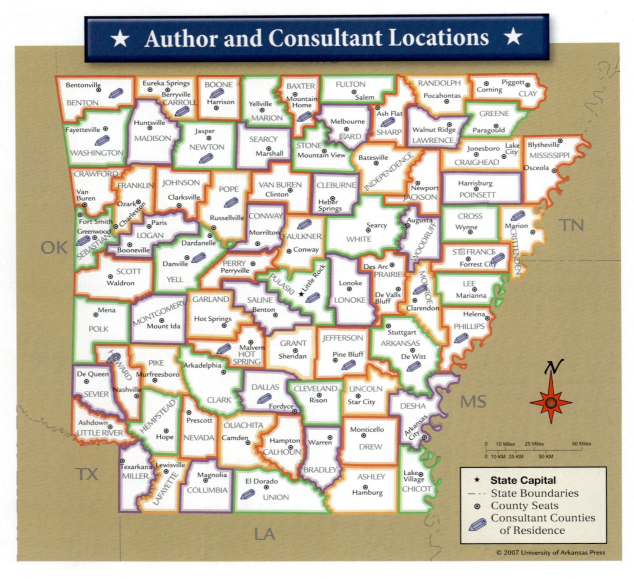

Adrian Knapper
Barton Junior High School,
El Dorado
Union County
Southwest Arkansas Teacher
Roundtable, El Dorado

Jerry Langston
Strong-Huttig Schools
Union County
Southwest Arkansas Teacher
Roundtable, El Dorado

Carole Provin
Northwood Middle School, North
Little Rock
Pulaski County
Central Arkansas Teacher Round-
table, Little Rock

Paula Roberts
Dover Middle School, Dover
Pope County
Central Arkansas Teacher Round-
table, Little Rock

Robert E. Rose
Williford High School, Williford
Sharp County
Northeast Arkansas Teacher Round-
table, Jonesboro

Joshua Shepherd
Marion Middle School, Marion
Crittenden County
Northeast Arkansas Teacher Round-
table, Jonesboro

Donald E. Smith
Darby Junior High School,
Fort Smith
Sebastian County
Northwest Arkansas Teacher
Roundtable, Fayetteville

Annette Sparkman
Resource
Palestine/Wheatley Junior High
School, Wheatley
St. Francis County
Southeast Arkansas Teacher Round-
table, Stuttgart

Wilma Sutton
Mann Magnet Middle School, Little
Rock
Pulaski County
Central Arkansas Teacher Round-
table, Little Rock

Lisa Taylor
White Hall Junior High School,
White Hall
Jefferson County
Southeast Arkansas Teacher Round-
table, Stuttgart

Roland Womack
Sparkman High School, Sparkman
Dallas County
Southwest Arkansas Teacher
Roundtable, El Dorado

▲ **Northeast Arkansas Teacher Roundtable, Jonesboro**
Left to right: Mike Hemme, Joshua Shepherd, and Robert E. Rose.

▲ **Central Arkansas Teacher Roundtable, Little Rock**
Left to right: Paula Roberts, Lisa Huelle, Carole Provin, Philita James, Kimble Edwards, Margret Grimes, Marian Jimerson, Wilma Sutton, and Kathleen Pate, of the Clinton Library.

◀ **Central Arkansas Teacher Roundtable, Little Rock**
Left to right: Kimble Edwards, Philita James, and Carole Provin.

▼ **Southwest Arkansas Teacher Roundtable, El Dorado**
Left to right: Roland Womack and Adrian Knapper.

▲ **Central Arkansas Teacher Roundtable, Little Rock**
Left to right: Lisa Huelle, Paula Roberts, and Margret Grimes.

▶ **Southwest Arkansas Teacher Roundtable, El Dorado**
Standing: Adrian Knapper. *Seated, left to right:* Jerry Langston, Christina Hostetter, and Roland Womack.

◀ **Northwest Arkansas Teacher Roundtable, Fayetteville**
Standing, left to right: Paul Davenport, Cherokee Cole, Stephanie Hoops, Debi Ewing-Hight, Madelyn Brown, and Donald E. Smith. *Seated:* Diann Fancher and Carleta Currie.

Arkansas History Teacher Contributor

Carolyn Anderson
Ramay Junior High School, Fayetteville
Washington County
Consultant

Content Consultants

The content consultants reviewed manuscript for content accuracy.

Economics
David Gay, PhD
Department of Economics
University of Arkansas, Fayetteville
Washington County

Geography
Fiona M. Davidson, PhD
Department of Geosciences
University of Arkansas, Fayetteville
Washington County

History
Patrick Williams, PhD
Department of History
Editor, *Arkansas Historical Quarterly*
University of Arkansas, Fayetteville
Washington County

Political Science
Janine Parry, PhD
Department of Political Science
University of Arkansas, Fayetteville
Washington County

Literacy Consultants

The literacy consultants reviewed the manuscript for appropriate word choice, sentence structure, comprehension level, and clarity.

Mary Beth Cox
North Little Rock High School, North Little Rock
Pulaski County
English Department Chair
AP Certified

Connie Echols
Nashville High School, Nashville
Howard County
English Department Chair
AP Certified
Certified Administrator
State ELA Frameworks Committee Member

Debbie Kamps
Highland High School, Hardy
Sharp County
English and Social Studies Teacher
AP Certified

Sharla Keen-Mills
Woodland Junior High School, Fayetteville
Washington County
English Department Head
AP Certified
National Board Certified Teacher
National Writing Project Consultant
Literacy Lab Trained

Cartography

Maps by *Map Ink,* Norman, Oklahoma, (405) 831-3858

Text design, cover design, and page composition

by SettingPace, Cincinnati, Ohio.
www.settingpace.com

Thanks to Mrs. Hopper's 2006–2007 eighth-grade Arkansas-history classes at Woodland Junior High School in Fayetteville for reviewing portions of the manuscript and offering feedback.

★ Selected Student Bibliography ★

Books
Bednarz, Sarah, Catherine Clinton, Michael Hartoonian, Arthur Hernandez, Patricia Marshall, and Pat Nickell. *Explore Arkansas* (Boston: Houghton Mifflin, 1997).

Boehm, Richard, David G. Armstrong, and Francis P. Hankins. *Geography: The World and Its People* (New York: Glencoe-McGraw-Hill, 2002).

Bowman, Ann O'M, and Richard C. Kearney. *State and Local Government* (Boston: Houghton Mifflin Company, 1999).

Coleman, George, Marisha Coleman, and Dee Ann Holt. *Celebrating Arkansas: Teacher's Supplement* (Upper Saddle River, NJ: Prentice Hall, Inc., 2002).

Di Piazza, Domencia. *Hello USA: Arkansas* (Minneapolis, MN: Lerner Publications, 2002).

Garcia, Jesus, Donna M. Ogle, Frederick M. Risinger, Joyce Stevos, and Winthrop Jordan. *Creating America: A History of the United States Beginnings Through Reconstruction* (Evanston, IL: McDougal Littell, 2002).

Gill, John P. *The Crossroads of Arkansas* (Little Rock: The Butler Center For Arkansas Studies, 2001).

Greer, Tom, and Lavell Cole. *Arkansas: the World Around Us* (New York, MacMillan McGraw-Hill School Publishing, 1991).

Heinrichs, Ann, C. Fred Williams, Nadyne Aikman, and Robert L. Hillerich. *America the Beautiful: Arkansas* (Chicago: Children's Press, 1989).

Johnson, Ben F., III. *Arkansas in Modern America: 1930–1999* (Fayetteville: University of Arkansas Press, 2000).

Marsh, Carole. *My First Pocket Guide: Arkansas* (Peachtree City, GA: Gallopade International, 2001).

Olien, Rebecca, and C. Fred Williams. *Arkansas* (Mankato, MN: Capstone Press, 2003).

Paulson, Alan C. *Roadside History of Arkansas* (Missoula, MT: Mountain Press Publishing Company, 1998).

Roach, Patricia. *Arkansas Resource Book* (Westerville, OH: Glencoe/McGraw-Hill, 1997).

Stroud, Hubert B., and Gerald T. Hanson. *Arkansas Geography: The Physical Landscape and Historical-Cultural Setting* (Little Rock: Rose Publishing Company, 1981).

Whayne, Jeannie, M., Thomas A. DeBlack, George Sabo III, and Morris S. Arnold. *Arkansas: A Narrative History* (Fayetteville: The University of Arkansas Press, 2002).

Magazine Articles
"Looking Back at the Sultana Steamboat Explosion: An Interview with Jerry O. Potter, Author of *The Sultana Tragedy*." *National Board Bulletin,* Summer 2000, 16–23.

Potter, Jerry O. "A Tragic Postscript." *American History,* December 1996, 16–20, 58–61.

Partner Organizations and Their Websites
Arkansas Department of Parks and Tourism
http://www.arkansas.com

Arkansas History Commission
http://www.ark-ives.com

Encyclopedia of Arkansas History and Culture
http://www.encyclopediaofarkansas.net

Little Rock Central High School National Historic Site, U.S. National Park Service
http://www.nps.gov/chsc

University of Arkansas Special Collections
http://www.libinfo.uark.edu/specialcollections/arkansaslinks.asp

William J. Clinton Presidential Library and Museum
http://www.clintonlibrary.gov

Websites for Additional Arkansas Information
Anything Arkansas Directory
http://www.anythingarkansas.com/arkapedia/pedia/timeline

Arkansas Department of Economic Development
http://1-800-arkansas.com

Arkansas Highway and Transportation Department
http://www.ahtd.state.ar.us
http://www.arkansashighways.com

Arkansas Historic Preservation Program
http://www.arkansaspreservation.org

Arkansas Secretary of State
http://www.sosweb.state.ar.us.educational.html

Arkansas State Parks
http://www.arkansasstateparks.com

Arkansas Stories, Arkansas Studies—Association of Arkansas Counties
http://www.arcounties.org

Butler Center for Arkansas Studies
http://www.cals.lib.ar.us/butlercenter

Department of Arkansas Heritage
http://www.arkansasheritage.com

Historic Arkansas Museum
http://www.arkansashistory.com

KidsKonnect Arkansas
http://www.kidskonnect.com/Arkansas/ArkansasHome.htm

Old Statehouse Museum
http://www.oldstatehouse.com

Other Websites
Brown v. Board of Education National Historic Site, National Park Service
http://www.nps.gov/brvb

Economic History Services
http://www.eh.net/hmit

National Archives and Records Administration
http://www.archives.gov/presidential_libraries

General Reference Websites
Dictionary.com
http://www.dictionary.com

Google Earth
http://earth.google.com

History Channel World Timeline
http://www.history.com

Maps.com
http://www.maps.com

Merriam-Webster Dictionary Online
http://www.merriamwebster.com

National Atlas of the United States
http://www.nationalatlas.gov

U.S. Census Bureau
http://www.quickfacts.census.gov

Wikipedia
http://www.wikipedia.org

Other Sources
Arkansas Atlas and Gazetteer, 2nd edition. (Yarmouth, ME: DeLorme, 2004).

Arkansas Highway and Transportation Department. State Highway Tourist Map (Little Rock, 2004).

★ Dedication and Recognitions ★

I would first like to thank Lawrence Malley, director and editor of the University of Arkansas Press, for giving me this once-in-a-lifetime opportunity. Larry was willing to take a risk on an outspoken teacher who said, "Sure we can do this!" He listened to all my ideas and plans, regardless of how unorthodox they might have seemed, and allowed me to explore and challenge traditional conventions to create a book that, I hope, will serve all of our Arkansas students and teachers well in their quest to know our amazing state.

I would like to thank the Fayetteville Public School District (Dr. Bobby New, Superintendent) and my building administrators (Dr. Anita Lawson, principal; Mr. Byron Zeagler, assistant principal) for affording me this opportunity. Thanks to my University of Arkansas intern, Josh Worthy, for graciously taking care of our class in my absence.

Brent, there are no words to adequately express my gratitude. I have so enjoyed getting to know you as a friend and colleague. You brought so much to the table. Your knowledge and work ethic are unsurpassed. I hope that your talents are appropriately recognized and rewarded. Thank you for your humor, conversation, CDs, and ideas—without you, well, I could not have done it.

Thank you to all the Arkansas history teachers across the state who contributed to this project. Your advice and ideas were invaluable. I hope I represented you well.

Thank you to Laura Miller and Spirit Trickey at Central High School National Historic Site, Nathania Sawyer at the Encyclopedia of Arkansas Culture and Heritage, and Kathleen Pate at the William J. Clinton Presidential Library and Museum, administered by the National Archives and Records Administration, as well as Robert Holified in Senator Lincoln's office and Zac Wright in Governor Beebe's office, and Tom Dillard and the phenomenal staff of U of A Special Collections—it was a joy to work with each of you, and I so appreciate your support.

I would like to recognize my family, the one to whom I was born and the one that I married into—Mother, Daddy, Lindsay, Jacob, Moona, Dadah, Meme, Pops, Patsy, Glenn, Scott, Dean, Mark, and John. Thank you for my heritage, curiosity, drive, ability to learn and share, and your support. I will always work to honor you, to continue to earn your respect, and to make you proud through my life and work.

I admire and thank my wonderful friends who are such remarkable, impressive women and great role models: Karen, Beth, Shirley, Lisa, Sonya, and Ashley. You are my cheerleaders and a trusted outlet to "vent." You have celebrated me, as I do each of you.

A big thanks also goes to DavidO, James, Jay, Mike, Doug, Paul, Morgan, Matt, Kathy and Joel, Big Shirl and Rich, Lolo and Bob, Toppy and Paula, Ronnie and Wayne and countless other friends and well-wishers for their thoughts and encouragement.

Sharla, I cannot tell you how much your guidance and mentorship has helped me as a teacher and a writer. I could not have done this without knowing you were there as a trusted and valuable resource, and as a supporter.

To all my students—thank you for letting me teach you, learn from you, challenge you, and get to know you. Each of you has brought something to my life and something to this book.

Finally, I must thank my husband. Without your calm, loving spirit and unwavering faith in me, I would not succeed. You are my world and I love you. You have patiently lived with me through many late and sleepless nights, tears, deadlines, and "projects"—this, the greatest thus far. Thank you for sharing "your" Arkansas with me. We can do anything together, C & D.

Thank you,
—S. E. H.

Table of Contents

Authors and Textbook Consultants vi
Arkansas History Teacher Consultants vii
Content Consultants. xi
Literacy Consultants. xi
Cartography. xi
Selected Bibliography. xii
Dedication and Recognitions xiii
Textbook Tour
Tools for Easy Reading About Your Arkansas Adventure!. . . xxx
Before You Read xxx
After You Read xxxii
While You Read xxxiii
Special Features xxxiii
Ask Yourself! xxxiv
Before You Begin Each Chapter of Your
Adventure through Arkansas xxxv
Are You Ready? Let's Go! xxxv

UNIT 1 **Young Arkansans Exploring Arkansas**
Road Trip! 2

Chapter 1 **Welcome to Arkansas!**
Introduction 4
Big Picture Questions 5
Section 1 Defining Ourselves 6
Guide to Reading 6
Being an Arkansan 6
Defining and Defying Stereotypes 6
Defining our State Image and Reputation 7
Section 2 The Souvenir Shop 8
Guide to Reading 8
Why Our State Is Called "Arkansas". 8
State Symbols 9
State Seal 11
The State Flag 13
Chapter Reflection 15

Table of Contents

Chapter 2 Geography—Let's Take a Road Trip! 16
    Why Do We Study This? 17
    Big Picture Questions 17
    Section 1 Ready, Set, Explore! 18
    Guide to Reading 18
    What Is Geography? 18
    How Does Geography Affect History? 18
    How and Why We Use Maps and Globes 18
    Section 2 Our Place in the World 22
    Guide to Reading 22
    Location, Arkansas: Finding Arkansas's Place in the World . . 22
    The Six Geographic Regions of Arkansas 22
    Arkansas's Natural Resources and Land Use 25
    Arkansas's Climate and Unique Geographical Features 26
    The Impact of Geography on Arkansas and Arkansans 27
    Chapter Reflection 29
    Reference Atlas 31

Chapter 3 State and Local Government—How We Govern Ourselves 52
    Why Do We Study This? 53
    Big Picture Questions 53
    Section 1 Our National and State Governments 54
    Guide to Reading 54
    On the National Level 54
    On the State Level 55
    Section 2 Arkansas Governors 58
    Section 3 Our Local Governments 68
    Guide to Reading 68
    On the County Level 68
    On the Municipal Level 68
    Chapter Reflection 72

Chapter 4 Economics and Tourism—Where We Learn, Work, Live, and Play 74
    Why Do We Study This? 75
    Big Picture Questions 75

xv

Table of Contents

Section 1 Arkansas's Economy 76
Guide to Reading 76
An Overview 76
Section 2 Where We Learn 78
Guide to Reading 78
  Arkansas's Schools 78
    Arkansas's Colleges and Universities 78
    Arkansas Museums 80
    Section 3 Where We Work 82
    Guide to Reading 82
    Big Business, Entrepreneurs, and Transport 82
Agriculture 84
Section 4 Where We Live 88
Our Communities 88
Population Trends 89
Section 5 Where We Play 90
Taking a Vacation Right in Your Own Backyard 90
The Ozarks 90
The Arkansas River Valley 92
The Ouachitas 94
The Gulf Coastal Plain 95
The Mississippi Alluvial Plain 96
Crowley's Ridge 98
Central Arkansas 100
Chapter Reflection 102

UNIT 2 **Our State's History Through Discovery, Exploration, and Settlement, The Beginning to 1803** 104

Chapter 5 The First Arkansans, The Beginning to 1540 106
Timeline 106
Why Do We Study This? 107
Big Picture Questions 107
Section 1 What Is History? 108
Guide to Reading 108
History: How Do We Know What We Know? 108
BC, AD, and the Passage of Time: What Does It Mean? 109

Table of Contents

Section 2 The First People 110
  Guide to Reading 110
  The Paleo-Arkansans Arrive, 11,500 BC to 9,500 BC 110
  The Archaic Tradition Begins, 9,500 BC to 1000 BC 112
  The Woodland Tradition Begins, 1000 BC to 950 AD 113
  The Mississippian Tradition Begins, 950 AD to 1541 AD .. 114

Section 3 The Historic Indians 116
  Guide to Reading 116
  The Caddos 117
  The Quapaws 118
  The Osages 119
  Chapter Reflection 120

Chapter 6 Discovery, Exploration, and Settlement, 1541–1802 122
  Timeline 122
  Why Do We Study This? 123
  Big Picture Questions 123

Section 1 The First Explorers 124
  Guide to Reading 124
  Europeans in the Americas 124
  De Soto Comes to Arkansas 125
  The French in Arkansas 130

Section 2 Arkansas Post 134
  Guide to Reading 134
  De Tonti 134
  John Law 135
  Daily Life at Arkansas Post 138
  Revolution 141
  Chapter Reflection 142

UNIT 3 Nineteenth-Century Arkansas—The Territorial Period, Statehood, and Slavery, 1803–1860 144

Chapter 7 Jefferson's Louisiana and the Exploration of a Rugged New Land, 1803–1812 146
  Timeline 146
  Why Do We Study This? 147
  Big Picture Questions 147

xvii

Table of Contents

Section 1 The Journey Began In Arkansas 148
The Louisiana Purchase and President Jefferson 148
Section 2 Ready, Set, Explore! 150
Guide to Reading 150
Lewis and Clark 150
    Dunbar and Hunter and the Forgotten Expedition . . . 152
    Schoolcraft and Nuttall 152
Section 3 Life in the Rugged New Land 154
    Guide to Reading 154
    Early Settlements 155
    Early Agriculture 156
    The New Madrid Earthquake and the Sunken Lands . . . 158
Chapter Reflection 160

Chapter 8 **Growing Pains: Territorial Power, Politics, and Compromise, 1803–1835** 162
Timeline 162
Why Do We Study This? 163
Big Picture Questions 163
Section 1 Territorial Power 164
Guide to Reading 164
  The First Governments 164
    Slavery and the Missouri Compromise 165
    The New Territory 168
  Section 2 Politics, People, and
  the Challenges of Progress 170
    Guide to Reading 170
    The "Family" 170
  Indian Removal 172
Progress toward Statehood 176
Chapter Reflection 178

Chapter 9 **Statehood and Slavery, 1836–1860** 180
Timeline 180
Why Do We Study This? 181
Big Picture Questions 181
Section 1 The Decision for Statehood 182

Table of Contents

Guide to Reading 182
The First State Constitution. 184
The New State Government 184
The State Banks. 186

Section 2 Agricultural Life
and Society. 188
Guide to Reading 188
The Yeoman Farmers 188
The Life of the Planters, Their
Plantations, and Their Slaves 189
Black Arkansans and the Slave Codes. 190

Section 3 Daily Life in the Fledgling State 194
Guide to Reading 194
Town Life 194
Religion in Arkansas .197

Section 4 Expansion. 198
Guide to Reading 198
Manifest Destiny. 198
Mountain Meadows Massacre 200
Looking Back at Pre–Civil War Arkansas 202
Chapter Reflection 204

UNIT 4 The Civil War, Reconstruction, and the New South,
1861–1899 208

Chapter 10 Secession and Civil War, 1861–1865 210
Timeline 210
Why Do We Study This? 211
Big Picture Questions. 211

Section 1 War Looms. 212
Guide to Reading 212
The Union Trembles. 212
   The Election of 1860. 212
   A Nation Breaks Apart—Secession 214

   Section 2 War Arrives 216
   Guide to Reading 216
      Pride and Glory. 216
      Who's Who in the Civil War . . . The Generals. . .217

xix

Table of Contents

The Battle of Pea Ridge	220
War Marches through Arkansas	222
The Battle of Prairie Grove	223
Steele's Southern Campaign	224
Women and Blacks in the War and at Home	227
The Emancipation Proclamation: "Then, Thenceforward, and Forever Free"	230
War Ends	232
Chapter Reflection	233

Chapter 11 **The Politics of Rebuilding,** 1866–1899 236
- Timeline 236
- Why Do We Study This? 237
- Big Picture Questions 237
  - **Section 1** Lincoln, Johnson, and Their Impacts on Arkansas . 238
  - Guide to Reading 238
  - "Charity for All": Lincoln's "Soft" Reconstruction Plan . . . 238
  - Lincoln's Assassination Sequence of Events 238
  - President Andrew Johnson 239
  - **Section 2** Government Muscle 240
  - Guide to Reading 240
    - Things Get Radical 240
    - The Republicans 242
    - Political Chaos 244
- The Constitution of 1874 246
- The Democrats 246
  - **Section 3** Power to the People 248
  - Guide to Reading 248
  - Farmers' Political Organizations 248
- Chapter Reflection 252

Chapter 12 **Something Old, Something New**—Society, the Economy, and Race in Reconstruction-Era Arkansas, 1866–1899 254
- Timeline 254
- Why Do We Study This? 255
- Big Picture Questions 255
  - **Section 1** Picking Up the Pieces 256
  - Guide to Reading 256

xx

Table of Contents

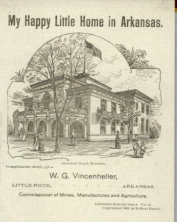

Physical Damage and Human Agony	256
The New South	257
Section 2 Opportunity Knocks	260
Guide to Reading	260
New Responsibilities for Women	260
The Establishment of the University of Arkansas–Fayetteville	261
Opportunities for African Americans	263
Section 3 The Challenge of Change	266
Guide to Reading	266
Sharecropping	266
The Beginning of Jim Crow in Society and the Rise of the Ku Klux Klan	267
Arkansas at the End of the Century	269
Chapter Reflection	272

UNIT 5 Early Twentieth-Century Arkansas: A New South— Progression, War, and Depression, 1900–1939 274

Chapter 13 Progressing into the New Century, 1900s–1920s 276

Timeline	276
Why Do We Study This?	277
Big Picture Questions	277
Section 1 Progressing with Spirit	278
Guide to Reading	278
The Progressive Era	278
Politics, Policy, and State Government in Progressive-Era Arkansas	279
Progressive Politicians	281
Prohibition and Suffrage	282
A More Active State Government	283
Section 2 A Poor State Continues the Struggle for Progress	286
Guide to Reading	286
Improvements in Education	286
Arkansas Takes to the Road	289
A Healthier State	291
Section 3 New Developments in Industry	294
Guide to Reading	294

xxi

Table of Contents

Lumbering and Mining	294
Tenant Farming	297
New Developments in Agriculture	298
Chapter Reflection	300

Chapter 14 **Wars and Wonderment,** 1914–1928 302

- Timeline 302
- Why Do We Study This? 303
- Big Picture Questions 303
- **Section 1** Wars with the World 304
  - Guide to Reading 304
    - Arkansas and the First Great War: World War I 304
    - **Section 2** Wars with Weapons and Words 306
    - Guide to Reading 306
    - The Elaine Race Riot 306
    - **Section 3** Wonderment 310
    - Guide to Reading 310
    - The Prosperity of a Nation and the Beginning of a Modern Arkansas 310
    - Electrification 312
  - The Oil Boom 313
  - **Section 4** War Against Change 316
  - Guide to Reading 316
  - The Resurgence of the Ku Klux Klan—Weapons and Words of War 316
  - A War of Words Over Evolution 317
  - Chapter Reflection 320

Chapter 15 **Hard Times—The Great Depression,** 1927–1939 322

- Timeline 322
- Why Do We Study This? 323
- Big Picture Questions 323
- **Section 1** Nature's Wrath 324
- Guide to Reading 324
- The 1927 Flood 324
- The Drought and the Dustbowl 327
- **Section 2** The Great Depression 330
- Guide to Reading 330

Table of Contents

    Black Tuesday 330
    The Plight of Arkansans. 330
    The State Government in Turmoil 331
    Social Unrest 332
    Section 3 A Hero With a Plan. 334
    Guide to Reading 334
    The New Deal and Franklin D. Roosevelt. 334
    The New Deal's Impact on Agriculture. 336
    The Southern Tenant Farmers' Union 337
    The State Government and the New Deal 341
    Chapter Reflection 342

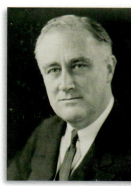

UNIT 6 Mid-Twentieth-Century Arkansas: The Great War, Recovery, and Prosperity, 1940–1966 344

Chapter 16 World War II and the Postwar World. 346
    Timeline 346
    Why Do We Study This? 347
    Big Picture Questions. 347
    Section 1 War and Peace 348
    Guide to Reading 348
    The Axis Powers 349
    The United States Enters the War. 350
    Arkansans Serving in World War II 351
    Section 2 Economy and Equality. 353
    Guide to Reading 353
    Wartime Economy and Education 353
    The Changing Agricultural Economy. 355
    Women in Wartime. 357
    African Americans in Wartime 358
    The Internment Camps and New Wartime Prejudices. 362
    Chapter Reflection 366

Chapter 17 From Fulbright to Faubus—
    Representation and Circumstance,
    1942–1966. 368
    Timeline 368

xxiii

Table of Contents

Why Do We Study This? 369
Big Picture Questions 369
Section 1 The Election of 1944 370
Guide to Reading 370
The G.I. Revolt 370
McMath Takes a Stand 371
Korea 372
McCarthyism 373
The Recovery Process 374
Section 2 The Rise and Demise of Orval Faubus 376
Guide to Reading 376
Chapter Reflection 380

UNIT 7 **The Cycle of Conflict and Change, 1955–1991** 382

Chapter 18 Separate and Unequal, 1955–1965 384
Timeline 384
Why Do We Study This? 385
Big Picture Questions 385
Timeline—The National Civil Rights Movement and the Central High Crisis 386
Who's Who in the Little Rock High School Crisis ... 389
Section 1 Crisis in the Schools: The End of Segregation ... 390
   Guide to Reading 390
   Separate and Unequal No More 390
   Brown v. the Board of Education, 1954 390
     September 1954: Charleston and Fayetteville ... 392
     September 1955: Hoxie 392
     Little Rock Central High School 393
       The Crisis 396
       "The Lost Year" 400
       Where Are They Now? 403
       Central High Today 406
Section 2 The National Civil Rights Movement in Arkansas ... 408
Guide to Reading 408
Local Power 408
Section 3 Life in the 1960s 410

Table of Contents

    Guide to Reading 410
    Counterculture and Music. 410
    Vietnam and Antiwar Protests 411
    Lyndon B. Johnson 412
    Arkansas in the 1960s. 412
    Chapter Reflection 414

Chapter 19   **Defining Ourselves,** 1966–1991. 416
    Timeline 416
    Why Do We Study This? 417
    Big Picture Questions. 417
    Section 1   The New Faces of Arkansas Politics. 418
    Guide to Reading 418
    Rockefeller, Fulbright, and Wallace 418
    Bumpers and Pryor 420
    Other Major Events of the Late 1960s and
    Early 1970s in Arkansas 422
    Section 2   The Arrival of Clinton 426
    Guide to Reading 426
    Car Tags and Cubans 426
    Being Governor Is Better the Second Time Around. 427
    The Economy and Developing Big Business 428
    The Rise of the Poultry and
    Agricultural Industries 429
    Achievements in Public
    Education. 431
    The Newspaper War. 431
    Chapter Reflection 434

UNIT 8   **A Global, Modern Arkansas,
1992–** 436

Chapter 20   The White House, Arkansas on the National Stage, and the
Future, 1992– 438
    Timeline 438
    Why Do We Study This? 439
    Section 1   The Presidency 440
    Accomplishments of the Clinton Presidency 441

Table of Contents

Controversies..442
The End of an Era......................................442
The National Archives and Presidential Libraries......444
What is the National Archives and
Records Administration?................................444
What is a Presidential Library?........................444
Welcome to the Clinton Library.........................446
Section 2 Following in the Footsteps...............448
Mike Huckabee..448
Diversity and the Changing Face of Arkansas............449
Mike Beebe...449
Section 3 You Are Arkansas's Future—The Crystal Ball...450
Chapter Reflection.....................................452
I Am an Arkansan Index.................................453
Index..466
Photo Credits..489

List of Maps

Author and Consultant Locations viii

Chapter 1
Arkansas State Symbols 10

Chapter 2
Arkansas Geographic Regions 23
Arkansas Geographic Regions 23
Arkansas Average Precipitation 24
Arkansas Average Temperatures 25
Arkansas Mineral Resources 26
Average Annual Tornado Incidence 26

Reference Atlas
World Physical 32
World Political 34
North America, Physical 36
North America, Political 37
United States, Physical 38
United States, Political 40
United States, Land Use 42
Arkansas, Neighboring States 44
Arkansas, Physical 46
Arkansas, Political 47
Arkansas, Population 48
Arkansas, Land Use 49
Arkansas, Rivers and Lakes 50

Chapter 3
Arkansas's US Congressional Districts, 2006 57

Chapter 4
Arkansas College & Universities 79
Arkansas Museums 81
Arkansas's Largest Employers 83
Major Municipal Airports 83
Rice Producing Counties 84

xxvii

List of Maps (continued)

Major Turkey Producing States 2005 86
Agricultural Products 86
Arkansas Population Centers 89
Arkansas Festivals 90
Arkansas State Parks 99
Arkansas Federal Lands 100

Chapter 5
Indian Tribal Areas 116

Chapter 6
De Soto Expedition 129
Marquette and Joliet Explore the Mississippi 131
La Salle Explores the Mississippi 132
Catfish Production 140

Chapter 7
The Louisiana Purchase – 1803 149
Louisiana Purchase Explorations 150
Early Settlements, 1810 156
New Madrid Earthquake Impact Zones 158

Chapter 8
Arkansas Counties from Territory to State 166
The Missouri Compromise 167
Diminishing Lands of the Quapaw 173
Indian Tribal Lands Ceded by Treaty 174
The Trail of Tears 175
Major Roads & Trails, 1830 176

Chapter 9
Slave Population, 1850 189
Plantation Counties – 1860 191
African American Population Concentration, 1860 193

List of Maps (continued)

Chapter 10
Secession of the Southern States, 1861 214
The Union & the Confederacy, 1861 218
Civil War Battles in Arkansas 220

Chapter 11
The Reconstruction 241

Chapter 12
Arkansas Railroads, 1900 258

Chapter 13
Women's Suffrage, 1915 283

Chapter 14
Wars and Wonderment, 1914–1928 311

Chapter 15
Flood of 1927 325
The Dust Bowl, Early 1930s 328

Chapter 16
Important Locations WWII 360

Chapter 18
Segregation in the Public Schools, 1954 391
Significant Moments of the Civil Rights Movement 392

Textbook Tour

Tools for Easy Reading about Your Arkansas Adventure!

This textbook was designed by Arkansas history teachers from all across our state and was tested with middle-level and junior high school students just like you. We hope that we have provided you with fun and interesting information that will help you learn and understand the geography, economics, history, government, culture, people, and heritage of Arkansas.

Before You Read . . .

Table of Contents

Consider this a "ladder" to help you climb through the information. Use it as an organizational tool and an easy way to locate information.

Unit Opener

Information has been organized into groups of information with a similar theme or time period. These groupings are called "units." Each time you come to a new set of topics, you will see the unit opener that will introduce you to what you are about to explore.

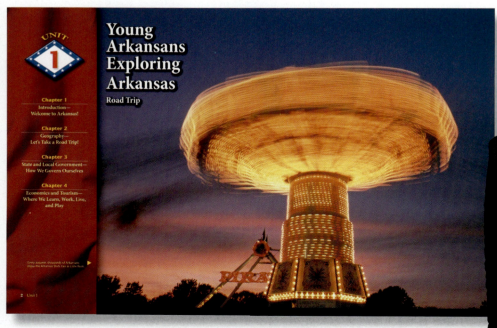

Textbook Tour

Chapter Opener

Within each unit, you will find chapters. These are smaller groupings of information. At the beginning of each chapter, as well as within the body of the chapter, you will find several tools to help you successfully manage new topics. Chapters are also subdivided into sections for easier reading.

Why Do We Study This?

This section tells why it is important to study the information contained in the chapter. It also tells you what it has to do with you and modern times and why it matters in the scheme of life.

Big Picture Questions

Big picture questions are thinking questions or guiding questions. You may not know the answers to the questions before you read the chapter. Keep these questions and ideas in mind as you read to help you better understand the material.

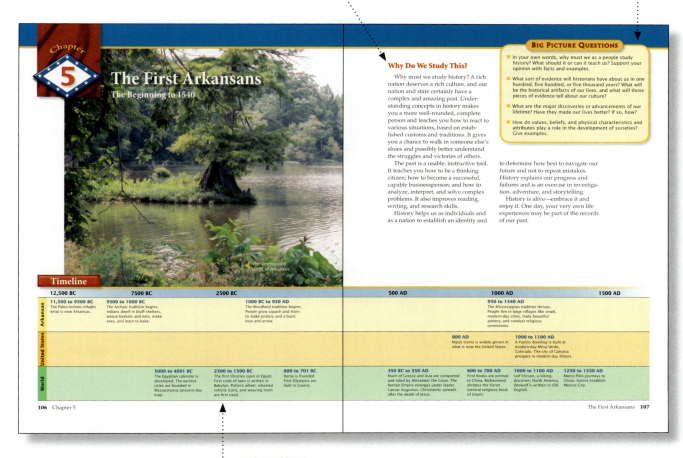

Timeline

Beginning in chapter 5, you will see a historical timeline on the chapter-opener pages. The timelines help you to understand the chronology of the major events of the period being studied in that chapter. They also give you an overview of the information you are preparing to study.

xxxi

Textbook Tour

Guide to Reading

Several times throughout each chapter, at the beginning of each new section, you will find a list of terms. These are important words, phrases, names, places, and events that help you comprehend new material. These definitions also help you correctly pronounce new or difficult terms. They have been divided into four categories: terms, events, people, and places. Your teacher will let you know which of these terms you will be tested on or if you only need to be familiar with a term.

Terms, people, places, and events in blue letters are defined in the margins of the chapter. So, as you are reading, you can glance over and learn the definition, pronunciation, or importance of a new term, person, place, or event.

After You Read...

Chapter Reflection

At the conclusion of each chapter, you will find exercises in a section called "Chapter Reflection." This section helps you recall and review what you have learned, analyze and apply new information, and connect it to what you learned previously and what you will learn in the future. Each Chapter Reflection is unique and includes a variety of fun and challenging activities: you might be asked to draw, role-play, write a poem, or read a journal entry from real people from Arkansas's past.

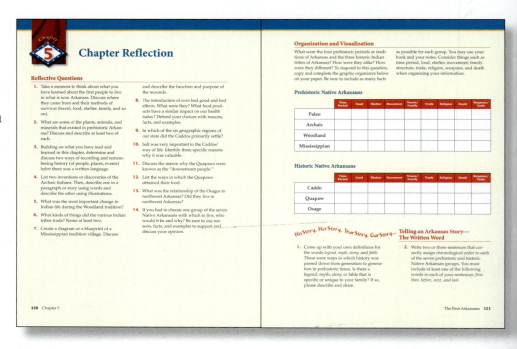

Textbook Tour

While You Read...

Photos, Graphs, Maps, and Charts

Each chapter contains a wide range of illustrations and graphics to help you better understand the material. Each has a heading or caption that provides you with valuable information and unique facts.

Special Features

County Quest

Each chapter contains a feature called "County Quest." In this section, you can see the location of an Arkansas county on a map of the seventy-five Arkansas counties and learn some unique and interesting facts about its people, history, or economy.

I Am an Arkansan

This fun and interesting feature profiles some of the many notable or famous residents and citizens of our state.

Only in Arkansas!

The features in many chapters called "Did You Know?" or "Only in Arkansas!" provide unusual facts and stories about Arkansas events, places, oddities, and tall tales.

Did You Know?

The features in many chapters called "Did You Know?" or "Only in Arkansas!" provide unusual facts and stories about Arkansas events, places, oddities, and tall tales.

A Day in the Life

This feature transports you back in time to a day in the life of a historic or well-known Arkansan, using primary or secondary sources and photos and documents.

Index

This section serves as a reference to help you quickly locate names, events, places, or other topics.

Textbook Tour

◄ "Mrs Hopper's 8th grade students read and study Arkansas History. *Left row, front to back:* Tyler Washabaugh, Rachel Roenfeldt, Tate Wingo. *Right row, front to back:* Gerald Carthan, Hope Cavell, Dakota Sloan.

Ask Yourself

Who?

In this chapter, for whom am I reading? Am I reading for myself to learn, enjoy, and make personal connections; am I reading for my teacher to answer questions, interpret and analyze information, and participate in class discussions; or am I reading for the textbook author to learn to interpret directions and assemble facts?

What?

What is the point of reading this Arkansas history textbook? The purpose when reading *An Arkansas History For Young People* is to learn about your state's history and your responsibility as a citizen and to have a better understanding of and appreciation for your own culture and heritage.

Your purpose is also to prepare to discuss and assess the information you have learned and to acquire knowledge, read and interpret instructions, and respond to "Big Picture Questions" and "Chapter Reflection" questions.

How?

How will I understand and use what I read? In each chapter, you will be determining what is important by processing new vocabulary terms; participating in related classroom note taking and discussions; studying maps, graphs, charts, illustrations, and photos and their captions; using your own background knowledge to make personal connections to historical events and people; and responding to "Big Picture Questions."

Textbook Tour

Before You Begin Each Chapter of Your Adventure Through Arkansas

Do a Little Research!
Scan all titles, section headings, terms, photos, captions, maps, charts, graphs, and questions. Look at items that are in bold or in color. Make sure you understand the main idea of the chapter.

Introduce Yourself!
Read the first one or two paragraphs of the chapter; then immediately read the last paragraph of the chapter—this way you have "introduced" yourself to the material.

Check Your Reflection!
Before you begin your reading journey, review the questions and activities in "Chapter Reflection." This review will draw your attention to new or challenging information that you need to focus on while reading.

Prepare for Your Journey!
Making a quick outline of key themes of the chapter or making a list of its main ideas also helps you categorize information.

All of these strategies will help you read, enjoy, and easily understand new ideas.

Are You Ready? Let's Go!

UNIT 1

Chapter 1
Introduction—
Welcome to Arkansas!

Chapter 2
Geography—
Let's Take a Road Trip!

Chapter 3
State and Local Government—
How We Govern Ourselves

Chapter 4
Economics and Tourism—
Where We Learn, Work, Live, and Play

Every autumn, thousands of Arkansans enjoy the Arkansas State Fair in Little Rock.

Young Arkansans Exploring Arkansas
Road Trip

Chapter 1

Welcome to Arkansas!
Introduction

▲ The Arkansas state flag.

Defining Ourselves

You are about to embark on an amazing journey through the wonderful places and stories of your state and its people. You are lucky enough to live in a state with a diverse cultural heritage, a thrilling history, and unique characters.

On this journey, you will explore everything from how your state got its name and what it means to be a modern-day Arkansan, to the big businesses of Arkansas, to the fun outdoor adventures in the state, and to sports. You will travel through time to better understand the experiences of the American Indians who were the first Arkansans. You will go on a journey with explorers and walk in the shoes of powerful politicians and in those of women finding their place and making their mark. You will find your way through the darkness of slavery to emerge in a fast-paced, modern society.

Your Arkansas journey will take you through the development of flavorful foods and music that tells stories. You will feel poor and rich as our state struggles to find new economic opportunities. You will survive wars and mourn those who were lost proudly fighting for their land and homes. You will see the dreams of your ancestors be washed away in raging floodwaters, and then crumble into dust. You will conquer fear and hate with the Little Rock Nine and help build the largest corporation in the world. You will share in the spotlight of a native son's presidency. You will see Arkansas and Arkansans continue with pride and dignity through challenge after challenge, victory after victory.

The future is yours to define. You will make the history. Be responsible and proud as you remember your state. Arkansas and Arkansans are unique—the state's history, its people, the land, the failures, and successes make us that way. Continue the traditions and honor those who came before you.

BIG PICTURE QUESTIONS

- Why do cities, states, and countries have symbols?
- How is a reputation or image established? Are they important? Why or why not? Are they easy to change? Why or why not? Are they accurate or unfair? Why?
- What are some examples of traditions in your culture? What is something that is a true part of your heritage? Give specific examples.

County Quest

Arkansas

Named after: Arkansas Native American settlement
Chief Source of Income: Manufacturing
Seat: DeWitt and Stuttgart

Arkansas County was established in 1813 by the Territorial Legislature of Missouri after annexation and was one of the state's first counties. The White and Arkansas rivers flow through this county. Its first European settlement was the French outpost of Arkansas Post in 1686. In 1819, Arkansas Post was named the territorial capital of Arkansas and remained so until 1821. William Woodruff printed the first newspaper in Arkansas, the *Arkansas Gazette*, there in 1819.

Riceland Foods, the largest rice miller, seller, and distributor in the world, is headquartered in Stuttgart and was established there in 1921. Stuttgart also hosts the annual Duck Gumbo Cook-off Festival and is known as the "rice and duck capital of the world."

Stuttgart is home to the Harry K. Dupree National Aquaculture Research Center, which is commonly known as the "Federal Catfish Lab." It studies aquaculture farming, feed, diseases, and bird control on fish farms.

Welcome to Arkansas!

Section 1: Defining Ourselves

Guide to Reading

Terms

citizen
culture
heritage
image
pride
reputation
stereotypes

Being an Arkansan

What does it mean to be an Arkansan? It means many things. It means being a **citizen** of your community, state, nation, and the world. It means having **pride**. It means being aware of and understanding your history.

Being an Arkansan can mean being a student, farmer, lawyer, politician, banker, fisherman, nurse, truck driver, teacher, mother, child, father, riverboat captain, factory worker, inventor, public servant, poultry processor, a Razorback fan, artist, environmentalist, Democrat, Independent, Republican, black, white, Indian, Latino, Asian. It means being an American—period.

Defining and Defying Stereotypes

Sadly, because of conflicts and fear, some people use **stereotypes** when they talk about other people or places. Arkansas, like several other rural and southern states, has long suffered from stereotypical comments and unfair judgments. Many times those who pass judgment have not even been to our state! It is our job as proud Arkansans not only to learn our history and **heritage** but also to learn from past mistakes. It is our duty to become achievers who give back to our state, to triumph over these unfair stereotypes. We as Arkansans should define ourselves, rather than allowing others to define us.

citizen a person who has the right to live in a country because of birth or because they have legally applied for and been granted citizenship by that country.

County Quest

Lawrence

Named after: Capt. James Lawrence, commander of the vessel Chesapeake in the War of 1812

Chief Source of Income: Agriculture

Seat: Powhatan and Walnut Ridge

Lawrence County was established in 1815 along the Black and Spring rivers. Hoxie, Lynn, Walnut Ridge, Powhatan, Imboden, Black Rock, Clover Bend, and Strawberry are communities within the county. There was a World War II flying school at Walnut Ridge, and it is now a museum. Despite tremendous opposition from regional, state, and national influences, the town of Hoxie was one of the first towns in Arkansas to voluntarily desegregate the town's public schools in the mid-1950s. Today, the county is home to Williams Baptist College.

It is referred to as the "Mother of Counties" because thirty-one counties were carved out of Lawrence County.

Defining Our State Image and Reputation

To define ourselves, we must convey a positive image of our state and citizens that will continue to improve our reputation. With the incredibly successful businesses and industries in our state, the many outdoor and recreational adventures our state offers, the respected and accomplished politicians who represent us, a multi-faceted culture that is everchanging and becoming diverse and worldly, and the beautiful land, water, and nature in our state, it is an easy job to show our pride when we define ourselves as Arkansans.

pride a respect for the importance and value of yourself, your accomplishments, your representative group, or your state.

stereotype a very simple, basic image or idea about someone or something, often a misconception.

heritage legacy; inherited customs; traditions passed down in families.

image a representation, impression, or idea of someone or something; a perception.

reputation widely held viewpoint or opinion about someone or something and typically shared by others.

culture customs; way of life; background.

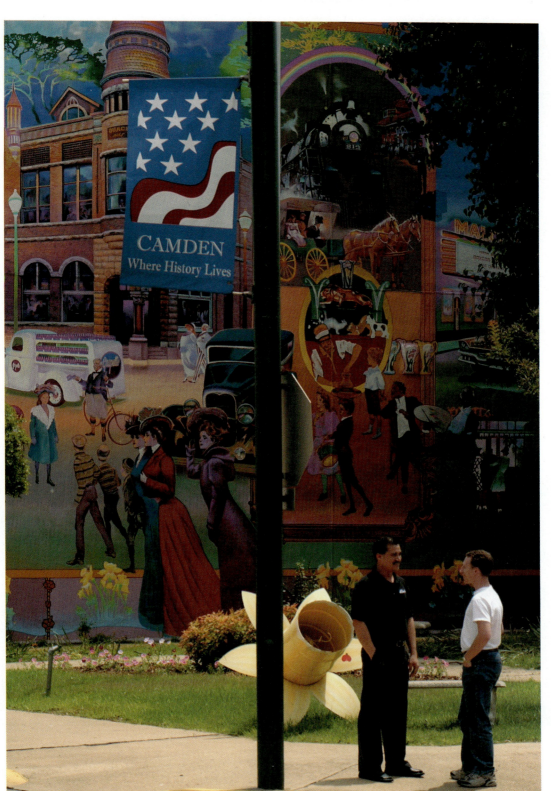

◀ Downtown Camden (Ouachita County). Does your city or town display or celebrate its history in any way? If so, how?

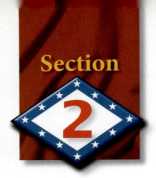

Section 2

The Souvenir Shop

Guide to Reading

Terms
creed

People
Eva Ware Barnett
Col. Sanford Faulkner
Willie Kavanaugh Hocker
Wayland Holyfield
Gary Klaff
Terry Rose
Dortha Scott

Why Our State Is Called "Arkansas"

The name of our state came originally from the Quapaw Indians by way of the French. When Father Jacques Marquette and Louis Joliet (whom you will learn about in chapter 6) visited the Quapaws in 1673, their interpreter was a young man living with the Quapaws who spoke the languages of both the Quapaw and the Illinois Indians. When Marquette asked who these people were, the interpreter translated from the Quapaw language to Illinois and then to French. Marquette recorded the answer in his journal as "Arkansea," which may have been the Illinois translation of the Quapaw for "down-river people." Some accounts say that translated it means "people of the south wind."

Other sources say the Quapaw called themselves the "Ugakhpah" which, in French, roughly translated to "down-stream people." Further accounts say that the word "Arkansas" came from the French word for "bow," which is *"arc,"* combined with the Quapaw word *"ansa,"* which loosely translates to "people of the south wind" to create the name "Arcansa."

Because spelling was not as standardized then as it is now, people tended to write words the way they sounded to them. So there came to be many ways of writing the word, perhaps as many as

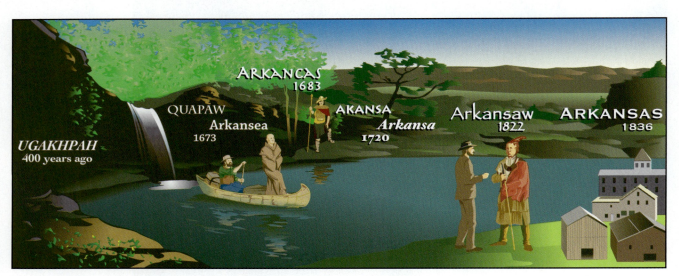

8 Chapter 1

seventy, including "Akamsea," "Acansa," "Arkansa," "Arkanssas," "Axkanzas," "Arkinsaw," and "Arkansaw."

A congressional act in 1819 that officially created the Territory of Arkansas used the spelling "Arkansaw." Eventually "Arkansas" became the accepted version for both the land and its major river partly because the *Arkansas Gazette,* established in 1819, consistently used that spelling.

Thus began a debate on how to say or pronounce the name. The accepted version came to be "AR-kan-saw," "AR-kun-saw," or "AR-ken-saw," which is probably similar to the way the French heard it from their interpreter. (French speakers do not pronounce the "s" sound at the end of a word.) It is a bit confusing that the name Kansas, which looks similar, is pronounced "KAN-zuhss," but the state of Arkansas is never "Ar-KAN-zuhss."

The Arkansas River, which runs from the Rocky Mountains to the Mississippi River, is pronounced "AR-kan-saw" in Arkansas but "Ar-KAN-zuhss" (like the pronunciation for "Kansas") in most of the other states it runs through.

To make things even more confusing, there has always been a debate on what to call the people who live in Arkansas. The most widely accepted form is Arkansans (in this form it is pronounced "Ar-KAN-zans" or "Ar-KAN-zuhnz"), but on a rare occasion, Arkansians ("Ar-KAN-zee-uhnz") and Arkansawyers ("Ar-KAN-saw-yurz") have been used.

State Symbols

Arkansas has many unique symbols that represent many areas and stories of our state. A traveler in our state could see these symbols firsthand during an Arkansas journey.

If you traveled through the northwestern part of the state, you might encounter our state flower, the apple blossom, adopted in 1901. Northwest

◀ "Mockingbird," by Fayetteville artist James Kunzelmann.

Arkansas once produced large quantities of apples, but now most are grown in Washington state. While in the apple orchards, you might look overhead and see our state bird, the mockingbird, flying from tree to tree. It was adopted as the official state bird in 1929. Mockingbirds mock or copy other bird songs they hear.

If mockingbirds need a place to roost in the southwestern or eastern parts of Arkansas, they might roost in our state

Clark

Named after: William Clark, governor of the Missouri Territory

Chief Source of Income: Manufacturing

Seat: Arkadelphia

Formed in 1818, Clark County, in southwest Arkansas, was one of the first counties in Arkansas. Its largest towns are Arkadelphia and Gurdon. Tourists and locals alike enjoy Lake De Gray State Park, and Henderson State and Ouachita Baptist universities draw students from all over the nation.

The Concatenated Order of Hoo-Hoo, a fraternal organization of lumbermen, was established in Gurdon in 1892. The order's museum is also located in Gurdon, and in 2004 the group had 3,500 members.

Welcome to Arkansas!

Arkansas State Symbols

tree, the pine. It was officially adopted by the state legislature in 1939. The loblolly and short leaf pines are the two most common varieties found in Arkansas. A traveler might spot our state mammal—the white-tailed deer—leaping among the pines. Adopted in 1993, the white-tailed deer is common in many regions of our state. What is that buzzing sound? It's our state insect, the honeybee!

If you are hungry or thirsty on your journey, Arkansas has something for you! Arkansas's state beverage, milk, was adopted in 1985 because dairy farming contributes to Arkansas's agricultural economy. For a snack, you might try the south Arkansas vine-ripe pink tomato, the state's official fruit and vegetable, adopted in 1987. If you want to cook your dinner the old-fashioned way, try the Arkansas state cooking vessel, the Dutch oven—a sturdy metal cooking pot, with a tight-fitting lid, sometimes having three legs or a handle with which to hang it over a campfire.

After you've had an old-fashioned dinner, you might be ready for a song and dance around the campfire. The square dance is our state's official folk dance, and the fiddle is our official state instrument. Arkansas is known as the Folk Music Capital of the World.

If you have a shovel with you on your journey, you are in luck! Arkansas has many treasures buried beneath the earth like our state rock, bauxite, which is used to produce aluminum and which was adopted in 1967. Historically, Arkansas has had some of the nation's largest bauxite deposits (in Saline County). You might also dig up a sparkly quartz crystal, our state mineral, which was adopted in 1967 and is used in computers or sold as souvenirs. However, the greatest treasure to unearth is our state gem, the diamond! The Crater of Diamonds State Park is located in Murfreesboro (Pike County), and tourists and locals have discovered over seventy thousand diamonds.

◀ Quartz crystal is Arkansas's state mineral.

State Seal

If you visit the state capitol of Arkansas, you will see our state seal. The Great Seal of Arkansas has a steamboat (representing rivers and industry), a plow (agriculture and economy), a beehive (agriculture), a sheaf of wheat (agriculture and economy), an angel of mercy, the goddess of liberty, and a bald eagle. The symbols represent our state and our country, and the seal was adopted in 1907. In the bald eagle's beak is a scroll that reads "Regnat Populus," which is Latin for "The People Rule," our state motto.

Like our other symbols, Arkansas has several official state songs that represent our heritage and culture: "The Arkansas Traveler," music by **Col. Sanford Faulkner**, 1850 and lyrics by the Arkansas State Song Selection Committee, 1947; "Arkansas" by **Eva Ware Barnett**; "Arkansas (You Run Deep in Me)" by **Wayland Holyfield**; and "Oh, Arkansas" by **Terry Rose** and **Gary Klaff**. All the state songs were officially adopted in 1987. Arkansas also has a state **creed**, adopted in 1972.

▼ People can dig for diamonds and keep what they find at the Crater of Diamonds State Park in Murfreesboro (Pike County).

Col. Sanford Faulkner composer of the state song "The Arkansas Traveler."

Eva Ware Barnett composer of one of the official state songs, "Arkansas," which was composed in 1916. She attended Ouachita Baptist University and later lived in Little Rock.

Wayland Holyfield songwriter born in Mallettown, Arkansas. He attended Hendrix University and the University of Arkansas and now lives in Nashville, Tennessee. His songs have been recorded by George Strait, Reba McEntire, Tammy Wynette, Conway Twitty, Charley Pride, and the Judds. He performed at the 1992 Clinton inauguration.

Terry Rose writer, with Gary Klaff, of "Oh, Arkansas," which was officially adopted as a state song in 1987.

Gary Klaff writer of "Oh, Arkansas" with Terry Rose, which was officially adopted as a state song in 1987.

creed a statement of belief; pledge; doctrine.

Welcome to Arkansas!

The Arkansas State Creed

I believe in Arkansas as a land of opportunity and promise.

I believe in the rich heritage of Arkansas and I honor the men and women who created this heritage.

I believe in the youth of Arkansas who will build our future.

I am proud of my state. I will uphold its constitution, obey its laws, and work for the good of all its citizens.

Official State Song
Arkansas (You Run Deep In Me)
By Wayland Holyfield

October morning in the Ozark Mountains,
Hills ablazing like that sun in the sky.
I fell in love there and the fire's still burning
A flame that will never die.

Chorus
Oh, I may wander, but when I do
I will never be far from you.
You're in my blood and I know you'll always be.
Arkansas, you run deep in me.

Moonlight dancing on a delta levee,
To a band of frogs and whippoorwill
I lost my heart there one July evening
And it's still there, I can tell.

Repeat Chorus

Magnolia blooming, Mama smiling,
Mallards sailing on a December wind.
God bless the memories I keep recalling
Like an old familiar friend.

Repeat Chorus

And there's a river rambling through the fields and valleys,
Smooth and steady as she makes her way south,
A lot like the people whose name she carries.
She goes strong and she goes proud.

Repeat Chorus

Source: Arkansas Secretary of State, (http://www.sosweb.state.ar.us/educational_activity_book.html), September 22, 2004

Arkansas

By Eva Ware Barnett

I am thinking tonight of the Southland,
Of the home of my childhood days,
Where I roamed through the woods and the meadows,
By the mill and the brook that plays;
Where the roses are in bloom,
And the sweet magnolia too,
Where the jasmine is white
And the violets are blue,
There a welcome awaits all her children
Who have wandered afar from home.

Chorus
Arkansas, Arkansas, 'tis a name dear,
'Tis the place I call "home, sweet home";
Arkansas, Arkansas, I salute thee,
From thy shelter no more I'll roam.

'Tis a land full of joy and of sunshine,
Rich in pearls and in diamonds rare,
Full of hope, faith and love for the stranger,
Who may pass 'neath her portals fair;
There the rice fields are full,
And the cotton, corn and hay,
There the fruits of the field,
Bloom in winter months and May,
'Tis the land that I love, first of all, dear,
And to her let us all give cheer.

Repeat Chorus

Source: Arkansas Secretary of State, (http://www.sosweb.state.ar.us/educational_activity_book.html), September 22, 2004. "Arkansas" was initially adopted as the official state song of Arkansas by Senate Concurrent Resolution No. 6 on January 12, 1917. By 1949, a copyright dispute broke out and "Arkansas" was replaced by "The Arkansas Traveler." In 1963, "Arkansas" was restored as the official state song and served as such until 1987 when it was designated as the Official State Anthem.

Also in 1987, the General Assembly named "The Arkansas Traveler" the official state historical song and "Arkansas (You Run Deep In Me)" and "Oh, Arkansas" official state songs.

The State Flag

Our state flag is also a symbol rich in meaning and history. The colors of the Arkansas flag are red, white, and blue because we are a part of the United States. The three stars below the word *Arkansas* represent the three nations under which Arkansas has been ruled: Spain, France, and the United States. The large star above the word *Arkansas* represents our state's four years as a member of the Confederate States of America, from 1861 to 1865. Arkansas was the twenty-fifth state to enter the Union in 1836, so there are twenty-five stars around the diamond shape surrounding our state name.

Miss **Willie Kavanaugh Hocker** designed the flag in the early 1900s in a

Willie Kavanaugh Hocker the designer of the Arkansas state flag.

Welcome to Arkansas! 13

▲ The Arkansas State quarter designed by Dortha Scott of Mt. Ida. Which of the six geographic regions of Arkansas are represented by the images on the quarter?

Dortha Scott a self-taught artist from near Mount Ida in Montgomery County who designed the official Arkansas state quarter.

design contest sponsored by the Pine Bluff chapter of the Daughters of the American Revolution (DAR). In 1912, the DAR was going to present a "stand of colors" to the battleship USS *Arkansas*. An Arkansas flag was to be included. The group learned that Arkansas did not have an official state flag and held the design contest. Hocker's design was officially adopted as the state flag in 1913.

In 1998, the U.S. Mint began a program to create unique quarters to represent each of the fifty states. In 2001, Governor Huckabee created a quarter-design contest. Over nine thousand entries were received, and after receiving approval from the mint, Gov. Mike Huckabee chose the design by **Dortha Scott** of Mount Ida (Montgomery County). A launch party was held to reveal the quarter at the Crater of Diamonds State Park in Murfreesboro in 2003. It was the fifth and final quarter to be released that year and the twenty-fifth in the fifty-state series. The quarter's design includes a mallard flying over a Grand Prairie lake, rice stalks, and a diamond. In the background are a grove of trees representative of the various forests in our state.

Your journey through the symbols of Arkansas should help you understand a little more about your heritage and culture. As you read, study, and reflect upon all of the other stories about Arkansas in this book, consider how they apply to you as a student, a citizen, and an Arkansan. Who or what symbolizes you? How are you defined? What will you add to the story?

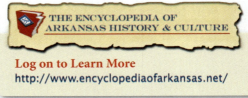

Log on to Learn More
http://www.encyclopediaofarkansas.net/

Hempstead

Named after: *Edward Hempstead, first delegate in U.S. Congress from the Missouri Territory*

Chief Source of Income: *Manufacturing*

Seat: *Hope*

Hempstead is one of five counties created when the area was still a part of Missouri. The county has agricultural land and timber and is also a center of the poultry industry. The largest alligator found in the state, Big Arkie, was found in floodwaters near Hope. Hope is also the birthplace of former president Bill Clinton and hometown of former governor Mike Huckabee and his wife Janet. Each year, Hope hosts its annual Watermelon Festival.

Chapter Reflection

Reflective Questions

1. In your own words, describe what it means to be an Arkansan.

2. It what ways do Americans and/or Arkansans display their pride? What activities do they participate in, what symbols do they display or wear, and so on?

3. What are some of the stereotypes have you heard people use? In your opinion, why do people make such general judgments about others, especially those they might not know?

4. Describe some of the traditions or customs shared or passed down in your family and explain what they mean to you.

5. In what ways can Arkansans define themselves and the state in a positive light? What symbols, places, and activities can be showcased to create the best image possible? Defend your choices with specific reasons, facts, and examples.

6. From what Native Arkansan and European languages did the name of our state originate?

7. Why do states, and sometimes countries, have symbols? What is the purpose or value of such items and images?

8. What is our state bird?

9. What is our state tree and in what area of the state might a traveler discover it?

10. What is our state vegetable? What is your favorite way to eat this vegetable?

11. Name three uses for the state gem of Arkansas.

12. List the seven symbols on the state seal of Arkansas.

13. After learning about the Arkansas state quarter, what other different or additional state images or symbols would you have chosen for the design? Describe and explain your answer using specific detail.

14. Who is the person who designed the state quarter and what city is he or she from?

15. What do the four stars in the center of the Arkansas flag represent?

16. What is our state beverage? Why? If you were to choose a new state beverage, what would it be and why?

17. In your opinion, what is Arkansas's image or reputation? Why? Does it need to be changed? Why or why not? If so, to what?

HisStory, HerStory, YourStory, OurStory...

Telling an Arkansas Story— The Written Word

Imagine that you have been asked by the governor of Arkansas to write a new state song. What lyrics (words) would you write and why? On your own paper, write two verses of the new Arkansas state song that you would submit to the governor. Remember that songs are poetry set to music—consider Arkansas's natural beauty, state symbols, people, places, and events when crafting your masterpiece.

Chapter 2

Geography
Let's Take a Road Trip!

◀ Motorcyclists enjoy the scenery on Arkansas Scenic Highway 7. This beautiful roadway allows motorists to drive from northern Arkansas through the Ozarks and Ouachitas south to the Louisiana border. Did you know that if a highway is numbered with an odd number, it is typically a north-south roadway and even-numbered roads usually run east-west?

Why Do We Study This?

Geography is a subject that has connections to many other topics and themes in social studies including economics and trade, production of goods, weather, population, environmental issues, wars, political systems, natural resources, recreation, and shelter. The study of geography helps to create an awareness of other cultures and regions. It also promotes respect for other people and boundaries and helps to promote the idea of a successful, interdependent, global community. Our planet is constantly changing, and knowledge acquired through the study of geography provides good citizens with tools to help manage the global challenges of the future.

Big Picture Questions

- What are some current challenging global situations or crises in which geography is playing a role? Use specific examples and locations in your answer.
- How does the geography of your hometown affect you and your family on a daily basis? Consider travel, food, weather, and jobs in your answer.
- Does geography have an impact on the way people speak, the words they use, the clothes they wear, the houses they build, the food they eat, or their transportation? Why or why not? If so, how?
- How does geography highlight unique or different characteristics in people that distinguish one group from another?

County Quest

Pulaski

Named after: Count Pulaski

Chief Source of Income: Service industry and state and federal governments

Seat: Little Rock

Pulaski County was created in 1818 (making it one of the original five counties) and was named in honor of Count Pulaski, a Revolutionary War hero. The largest city in Arkansas and the state capital, Little Rock, is located in the county. Today, it is home to many museums, cultural attractions, and schools, including the University of Arkansas at Little Rock and the Clinton Presidential Library and Museum.

The Old Mill in North Little Rock appeared in *Gone With the Wind*. Jacksonville Air Force Base is also located in Pulaski County. The county is also the vicinity in which three of Arkansas's six geographical regions converge: the Arkansas River Valley, the Mississippi Alluvial Plain (the Delta), and the Ouachita Mountains.

Geography 17

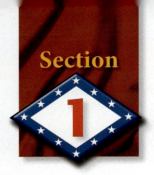

Section 1

Ready, Set, Explore!

Guide to Reading

Terms
- absolute
- adapt
- five themes of geography
- geography
- globe
- hemispheres
- human environmental interaction
- interdependent
- latitude
- location
- longitude
- map
- modifying
- movement
- place
- region
- relative

People
- geographers

Places
- Arkansas River Valley
- Crowley's Ridge
- equator
- Gulf Coastal Plain
- Mississippi Alluvial Plain
- Ouachita Mountains
- Ozark Mountains
- prime meridian

---

geography the study of the human living trends and physical characteristics of the Earth.

globe a model or map of the Earth that is spherical in shape.

latitude imaginary lines on the globe that run from east to west to measure distances north or south of the equator.

longitude imaginary lines on the globe that run north and south, which are measures of distance east or west of the prime meridian.

What Is Geography?

Geography is the study of the Earth, the places on the Earth, the people who live in these places, and their interactions. We study two broad types of geography—physical and human. Physical geography is the study of subjects like climate, landforms, and plant life. In human geography, we study where people live, why they live there, and how human presence has affected the land and environment.

How Does Geography Affect History?

Arkansas's geography has had an impact on its history. Throughout time, man has fought to control and make use of geographic features: rivers or other bodies of water used for drinking, growing food, transport, and exploration; mountains, which can provide shelter and protection; prairies, grasslands, and fields, which can be used for planting and harvesting crops; and the land's natural resources like oil, timber, or wildlife, which can be hunted and killed for food. Geography may also determine the way someone fights and what types of weapons are used.

Geography can also dictate what types of homes people build, the jobs they have, the foods they eat, or even the music they listen to and the clothes they wear. Many places in the world are complex and crowded, and in some places, people must also fight for their own space—their privacy and safety—on a planet becoming more crowded every day.

How and Why We Use Maps and Globes

To study geography, we must have some important tools—those most commonly used are globes and maps. A globe is the most realistic representation of the Earth. It is spherical in shape and is marked with lines of latitude and longitude to indicate the location of a place. A

18 Chapter 2

globe is divided into two **hemispheres**, the northern and southern. An imaginary line called the **equator** circles the Earth and divides it in half to create northern and southern hemispheres. Vertical lines called the **prime meridian** and the international date line divide the Earth into eastern and western hemispheres. A globe shows features like oceans, continents, and countries.

The second common tool used to study geography is a **map**. There are thousands of different types of maps. Maps can show tourist attractions, lakes, historical events, regions, hiking trails, restaurants, ghost towns, malls, libraries, and theaters. Maps are portable and can be more detailed than a globe. It is easier to measure and determine distance from one point to another on a map as opposed to a globe.

Geographers use globes and maps in their work. They also use modern, technological tools such as a global positioning system (GPS) to locate people, places, and landforms. They also use another set of tools known as the **five themes of geography** to categorize and analyze information. (See graphic 2.1 on page 21.) The five themes are

1. Human Environmental Interaction
2. Location
3. Movement
4. Place
5. Region

An example of **human environmental interaction** (HEI) in Arkansas is Arkansas Post (which you will study in chapter 6) having to be relocated several times because of floods and disease-carrying mosquitoes. Humans were forced to **adapt** to the environment. Another example of HEI in Arkansas is farmers in east Arkansas building levees and drainage systems to manage rains and irrigate crops. This is an example of people **modifying** environmental conditions to better their lives or promote success. HEI can be both positive and negative. Humans have developed new medicines based on resources discovered from the earth, but pollution and overdevelopment are destructive by-products of human progress.

Location has two primary elements. Location can be **relative** or **absolute**. If a tourist were to ask a local Arkansan where Fountain Hill, Arkansas, is, the answer might be, "It is in far south Arkansas," or "In deep southeast Arkansas," and that would be its relative location. However, if the answer were to be something like "It is on U.S. Highway 425 at the intersection of State Highway 8," that would be an absolute location. If you were to give the exact latitude and longitude of Fountain Hill (33° 21′ 27.29″ N 91° 50′ 58.63″ W), that would be an absolute location. If someone asked you where you live and you said "My house is behind Wal-Mart," that would be a relative location. If you responded by saying, "My house is at 123 Arkansas Road, Small Town, Arkansas," that would be an absolute location.

Movement is a very important theme in geography. Without it, we would not have the diverse products, traditions, cultures, and heritages that are present today. The sharing of knowledge, goods, and experience is critical to the survival and success of humans—we are **interdependent**. However, movement, like HEI, can have negative impacts as well. People are not instinctively territorial, but when one person attempts to share in or take what others consider their land or resources, conflict can result. Examples of movement in Arkansas are everywhere. From trucks and trains, which move goods and products; to public schools and universities, which

hemispheres divisions of the globe using either a northern and southern division or an eastern and western one.

equator the imaginary line that divides the Northern and Southern hemispheres.

prime meridian starting point from which longitude is measured.

map a flat drawing or illustration of an area.

geographers scientists who study geography.

five themes of geography methods or tools that geographers use to classify and organize information.

human environmental interaction used when discussing human impact on Earth and the environment.

adapt to change or modify conditions to suit surroundings.

modifying adjusting slightly or changing to achieve a result.

location the point of existence of a place on Earth.

relative referring to a location that is approximate.

absolute referring to the precise location of a place.

movement one of the five themes of geography used when discussing the exchange or development of ideas, goods, and/or people.

interdependent relying on help from someone or something else to exist or survive.

Geography 19

place one of the five themes of geography used when discussing the personality or unique and distinguishing features of a location or region.

region one of the five themes of geography used when discussing the common characteristics of an area; that is, political or physical, as the six geographic regions of Arkansas.

Ozark Mountains flat-topped plateau mountains of northwest Arkansas, eastern Oklahoma, and southwestern Missouri. The steepest portion is the Boston Mountains of northwest Arkansas.

Arkansas River Valley a series of valleys between the Ozark and Ouachita mountains through which the Arkansas River flows.

Ouachita Mountains (WASH-ih-taw) a unique mountain range that is folded, with long east-west ridges running throughout.

I Am an Arkansan

Tim Ernst (1955–)

Tim Ernst is one of the most respected outdoor photographers in Arkansas. His striking images are also some of the most recognizable photographs of the state. Ernst has been hiking through the Ozark Mountains for most of his life. His photographs of the region have appeared in dozens of publications, including *National Geographic, Audubon, Backpacker, Outside, Outdoor Photographer, Natural History,* Sierra Club and Hallmark calendars, National Park Service and U.S. Forest Service maps and brochures, Readers Digest books, and the *New York Times.* He also teaches photography workshops from his cabin near the Buffalo National River. He is the founder and president of the Ozark Highlands Trail Association, and he and his many volunteers have logged thousands of hours working to preserve and protect this rugged, beautiful highlands trail. In fact, his volunteer work has garnered him awards and commendations from the White House as well as from former Arkansas governor Jim Guy Tucker.

Not only is Tim Ernst a noted backpacker, teacher, conservationist, and photographer, he is also a widely respected author. His magazine articles have drawn high praise, and his many books of photography, including *Arkansas Portfolio: Twenty Years of Wilderness Photography* (1994) and *Wilderness Reflections: An Intimate Look at Wild Places in America* (1996), have brought considerable attention to outdoor life both in Arkansas and around the nation—particularly in Wyoming, where Ernst conducts workshops and volunteer projects.

To learn more, visit Mr. Ernst's web site, cloudland.net.

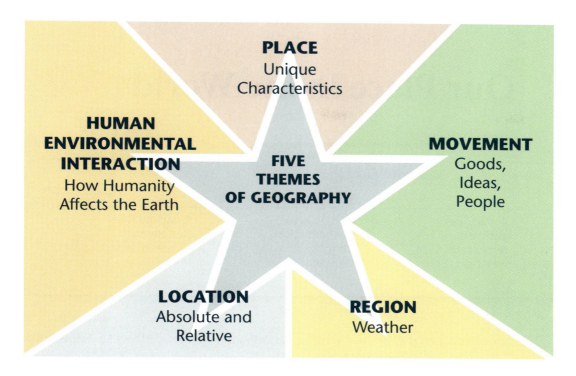

Gulf Coastal Plain the area of southwest Arkansas that, fifty million years ago, was covered by waters from what is now the Gulf of Mexico. The area is rich in bauxite, clay, salt, and petroleum deposits as well as pine forests.

Mississippi Alluvial Plain one of the six geographic regions of Arkansas, also known as the Delta, that is made up of flat, rich farmland and extends along the eastern border of the state. The eastern border of the Delta is the Mississippi River.

Crowley's Ridge hills on the Mississippi Alluvial Plain that are from one to twelve miles wide and about two hundred miles in length, running from Missouri to Helena, Arkansas.

move ideas; to airplanes and cars, buses, and trains, which move people, movement is a part of daily life.

Daily life is also something that contributes to the next theme of geography, **place**. Place is the unique or distinctive human and physical features that give character to the land. The ways in which people live and work, their faith and belief systems, music they listen to, languages they speak, foods they eat, clothes they wear, and even who they vote for contribute to the uniqueness of a place. The mountains, lakes, rivers, native plants, and animals are important features of a place. Place is the personality of an area. Downtown Little Rock is a place characterized by the River Market, the capitol, and the Clinton Presidential Center. Garland County is characterized by the naturally occurring hot springs found there. These are some home-state examples of place.

The final tool a geographer would use from the five themes of geography is the concept of **region**. Arkansas has six geographical regions: the **Ozark Mountains**, the **Arkansas River Valley**, the **Ouachita Mountains**, the **Gulf Coastal Plain**, the **Mississippi Alluvial Plain** (Delta), and **Crowley's Ridge**. Regions are used to organize geographical information.

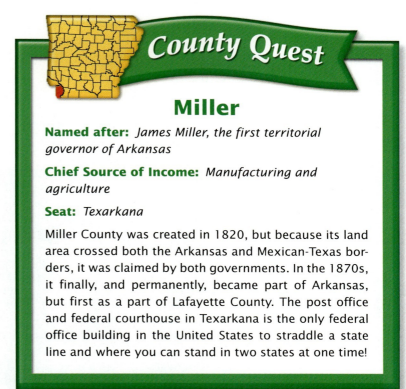

County Quest

Miller

Named after: *James Miller, the first territorial governor of Arkansas*

Chief Source of Income: *Manufacturing and agriculture*

Seat: *Texarkana*

Miller County was created in 1820, but because its land area crossed both the Arkansas and Mexican-Texas borders, it was claimed by both governments. In the 1870s, it finally, and permanently, became part of Arkansas, but first as a part of Lafayette County. The post office and federal courthouse in Texarkana is the only federal office building in the United States to straddle a state line and where you can stand in two states at one time!

Geography 21

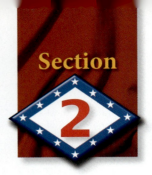

Section 2

Our Place in the World

Guide to Reading

Terms
- bromine
- chert
- climate
- loess
- natural gas
- novaculite
- petroleum
- temperate
- weather

Places
- Buffalo River
- Cache River
- Kings River
- L'Anguille River
- Ouachita River
- Red River
- Saline River
- White River

To understand geography and what it means to us as Arkansans, we have to find Arkansas's place in the world. Who and what is around us?

Location, Arkansas: Finding Arkansas's Place in the World

Arkansas is in the south-central region of the United States, on the North American continent, in the Northern and Western Hemisphere. Arkansas is bordered by six states: to the north, Missouri; to the east, Tennessee and Mississippi; to the south, Louisiana; to the southwest, Texas; and to the west, Oklahoma. The Mississippi River forms our largest water border and runs almost the entire length of the eastern border. The St. Francis River flows along the Missouri and Arkansas line and the Red River separates Texas and Arkansas.

The Six Geographic Regions of Arkansas

In the northern and western portions of our state are the uplands, which include the Ozark Mountains, the Arkansas River Valley, and the Ouachita Mountains. The southern and eastern lowlands include the

▼ Calico Rock in north central Arkansas offers visitors a chance to experience Arkansas's natural wonders.

▲ Old Town Lake in Phillips County is located on the Great River Road National Scenic Byway. What is a scenic byway?

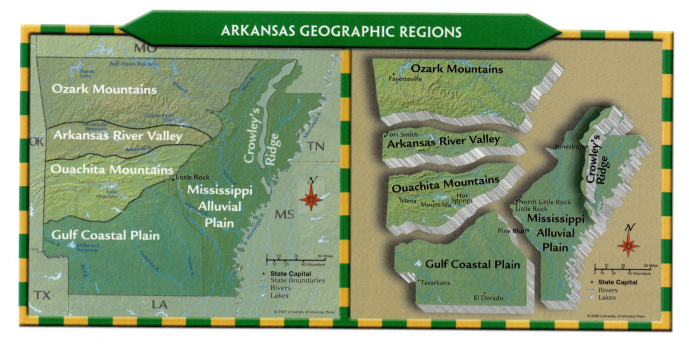

ARKANSAS GEOGRAPHIC REGIONS

Gulf Coastal Plain, the Mississippi Alluvial Plain, and Crowley's Ridge.

Almost all of northwestern Arkansas occupies the southern portion of the Ozark Plateau, which stretches into southwestern Missouri. This is the oldest landform in the state. On the Ozark Plateau region are the rugged and beautiful Boston Mountains. The **Buffalo**, **Kings**, and **White rivers** flow through the Ozark Plateau, where they have created fertile river valleys.

To the south of the Ozarks are the Ouachita Mountains, among the oldest mountains in North America. When they were new, they were possibly as tall and craggy as the Rocky Mountains are now. Millions of years of water and weather have worn them down and smoothed their edges. Several rivers run through these mountains, including the Maumelle, the Fourche LaFave, and the Ouachita rivers. The Ouachita Mountains are rich in underground mineral resources. The Indians knew how to quarry one of these minerals, called **chert**, for making spear points, arrowheads, and other tools. An unusual rock is **novaculite**, which the native Arkansans also used for making tools and which is still used for sharpening metal tools and knives. The **Ouachita River** is the largest in this region.

Crossing the state from northwest to southeast is the mighty and beautiful Arkansas River, one of America's major rivers. The Arkansas River begins high in the Colorado Rocky Mountains and travels across a third of the continent to

▼ Canoeists paddle the Mulberry River in Franklin County.

Only in Arkansas!

Arkansas has towns named Turkey Scratch, Possum Trot, Hog Jaw, Bug Scuffle, Grubb Springs, Fifty-Six, Number Nine, Figure Five, Eleven Point, Goobertown, and Forty-Four!

Buffalo River the 150-mile-long river is the nation's first nationally protected river and runs through Newton, Searcy, and Marion counties.

Kings River the approximately eighty-mile free-flowing river that runs through Madison and Carroll counties.

White River after the Arkansas River, the state river with the greatest volume.

chert a silica rock that is used in road surfacing and for gravestones and is found in the Ouachitas.

novaculite found in the Ouachitas, a mineral that is used as a sharpening stone.

Ouachita River (WASH-ih-tah) a river that flows through the Ouachita Mountains.

Saline River a river flowing through the Ouachita Mountains.

Red River a river that forms the border between northeast Texas and southwest Arkansas.

Cache (CASH) River runs through Craighead, Jackson, Poinsett, Woodruff, and borders Prairie and Monroe counties and flows into the White River.

L'Anguille River (lan-geel) a St. Francis River tributary.

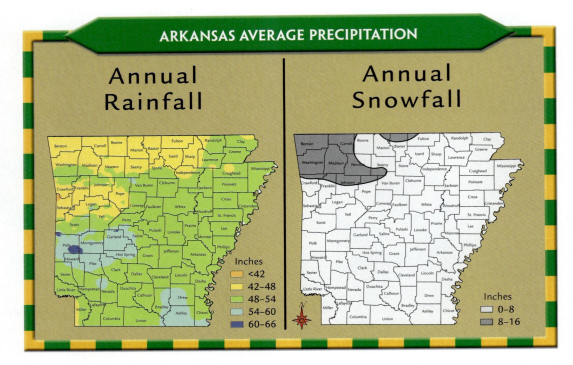

join the Mississippi River in the southeast corner of Arkansas. The Arkansas River has brought prosperity and hardship to Arkansans. Its long valley contains good farmland, but it can also flood frequently. Before the railroad and the automobile, the river offered the primary avenue of travel into the state.

Across the southern part of the state is the flat area called the Gulf Coastal Plain. Several rivers, including the Ouachita, **Saline**, and **Red rivers**, all flowing toward the south, cross this area. The river valleys create narrow strips of rich, fertile soil, which is suitable for farming, but much of the rest of the Gulf Coastal Plain is timberland. Pine forests grow there, but it has poor soil for farming. Million of years ago, this area was covered by the waters of what now is the Gulf of Mexico. The waters receded and left salt and oil deposits deep in the dirt.

All along the eastern part of Arkansas is the Mississippi Alluvial Plain, a broad, flat area of rich soil. This is the area often called the Mississippi Delta, or the Delta, because it was formed by the waters of the Mississippi River. Almost all flat, the Delta is some of the best farmland in America. Part of it, the Grand Prairie between the White and St. Francis rivers, is natural grassland. This is the location of what are now Prairie and Arkansas counties. The **Cache** and **L'Anguille rivers** also flow through the Delta.

Phillips

Named after: Sylvanus Phillips, a settler in the 1790s

Chief Source of Income: Agriculture

Seat: Helena

Phillips County, located in the fertile lands of the Arkansas Delta, was established in 1820. The county offers abundant farmland. In 1919, deadly race riots took place in the small town of Elaine in the far-eastern reaches of the county, near the Mississippi River.

The King Biscuit Blues Festival is a nationally known music festival held annually in Helena, and the Delta Cultural Center is a regional attraction focusing on the history, culture, and music of the area.

Running north to south in the upper part of the Delta is a long, narrow area of high ground called Crowley's Ridge. Long ago, the Ohio River flowed down one side of Crowley's Ridge, and the Mississippi River flowed down the other side. The water washed away the soil of the river valleys, but left the tall ridge in the middle. The ridge is covered by wind-blown dirt, which is called loess. Crowley's Ridge offers high ground, safe from the Mississippi River floods that can put the Delta land under water.

Arkansas's Natural Resources and Land Use

For a state with a relatively small land area, Arkansas has abundant natural resources. Our state is one of the only diamond-producing states in the nation, and the top three minerals naturally produced in Arkansas are petroleum, bromine, and natural gas. Natural gas has had a recent boom in central and eastern Arkansas. Arkansas once provided the majority of the nation's bauxite, which is used to make aluminum. Arkansas has abundant forests for timber and some coal. There are sand and gravel (also considered mineral resources) deposits in fifty Arkansas counties. Land in Arkansas is used for farming, mining, forestry, transportation, and recreation. Our homes are on residential lands, and our government buildings and schools are on public lands.

County Quest

Crawford

Named after: *William Crawford, U.S. secretary of war in 1815*

Chief Source of Income: *Manufacturing*

Seat: *Van Buren*

Created from parts of Pulaski County, Crawford County was formed in western Arkansas in 1820. When Crawford County was originally formed, it contained much of modern-day Oklahoma. The county seat of Van Buren has a well-known historic district with shopping and train rides. Alma claims to be the "Spinach Capitol of the World," and the Mulberry River is a popular area for canoeists.

loess (LOH-uhs) wind-borne soil.

petroleum a dark liquid, crude oil, that is found beneath the Earth's surface.

bromine a chemical element processed in compounds used as gasoline additives and in dyes, medicines, sanitizers, and brominated vegetable oil, which is found in some soft drinks.

natural gas an explosive, naturally-occurring chemical, also called methane, used for home heating and cooking.

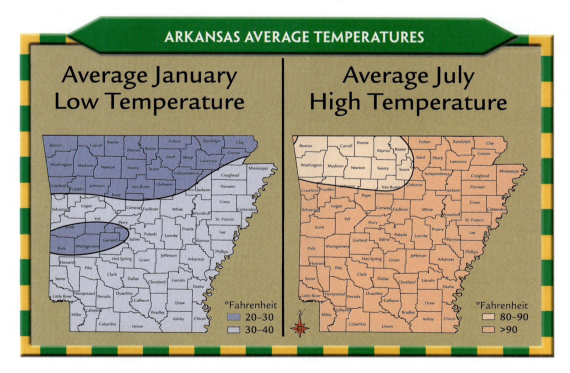

ARKANSAS AVERAGE TEMPERATURES

Average January Low Temperature — °Fahrenheit 20–30, 30–40

Average July High Temperature — °Fahrenheit 80–90, >90

Geography 25

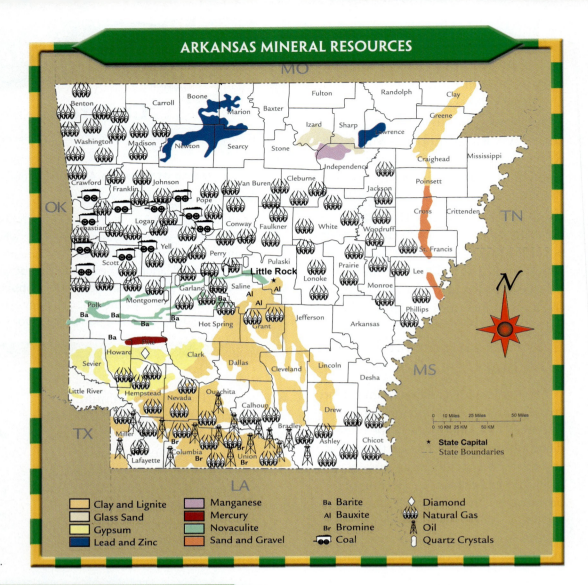

climate the long-term predictable weather patterns of an area.

temperate mild or moderate, not extreme.

weather measured atmospheric conditions such as wind, precipitation, and/or temperature.

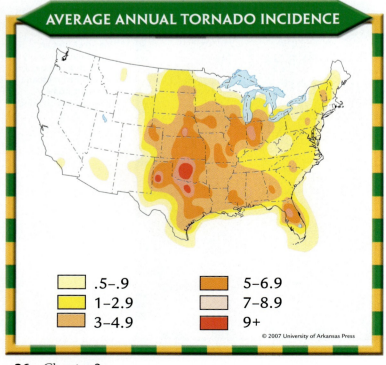

Arkansas's Climate and Unique Geographical Features

Overall, Arkansas's **climate** is **temperate**, with warm summers and mild winters. Technically, it is classified as a humid subtropical climate. Typically, the Ozarks receive the most annual snowfall, and the Ouachitas and parts of the lower Mississippi Alluvial Plain receive the most rain. In 1905, Benton County recorded Arkansas's coldest temperature on record, minus 29 degrees Fahrenheit. Arkansas's hottest day was recorded in Ozark (Franklin County) in 1936—it was 120 degrees Fahrenheit! Arkansas's **weather** varies across the state as well, ranging from tornadoes to floods and drought, to snow, wind, and ice.

Within its diverse terrain, Arkansas has several unique geographical features, like caverns and springs. Blanchard Springs Caverns in Stone County are a series of underground caves with stalactites and hidden waterways deep inside the Ozark Mountains. Mammoth Spring in Fulton County is an underground spring that flows out through a cavern to form a sixty-four-foot-deep pool, which is the headwaters of the Spring River.

The geographic center of the state is in Pulaski County, approximately twelve miles due north of Little Rock. The state's lowest geographic point is near Felsenthal at only 54 feet above sea level, along the Ouachita River in Union County. The highest point is Mount Magazine at 2,753 feet in Logan County. Arkansas is 53,187 square miles in area and ranks twenty-seventh in land size of all fifty states.

The Impact of Geography on Arkansas and Arkansans

Arkansas's geography is dramatic, rich, diverse, and powerful—just as the state and its people are. The geography of our state has long influenced our history, economy, lifestyles, politics, image, reputation, and citizens. Agriculture is our main

▼ The Lost Valley Trail takes hikers through part of the Ozark National Forest.

▼ Hikers examine the natural underground formations at Blanchard Springs Caverns.

DID YOU KNOW?

Wacky Weather

Arkansas snowfall records were noted on January 10–12, 1918, in northern Arkansas, when thirty inches fell. Another snowfall event that was in the record books was on December 8–9, 1917, in Yell County. Twenty-one inches dropped in two days.

Fayetteville had a record one-day snowfall of eleven and one-half inches on February 16, 1993. The deepest snow depth for Fayetteville at one time was twenty-three inches on January 21, 1918. The most tornadoes ever for Arkansas in one year were in 1999 when 107 tornadoes touched down. Most of these tornadoes occurred on one day in central and northeast Arkansas on January 21. This was the biggest one-day outbreak for tornadoes in Arkansas's history. The previous record for the most tornadoes in one year was 78 set back in 1982.

County Quest

Independence

Named after: The spirit of the Declaration of Independence

Chief Source of Income: Timber, poultry, and agriculture

Seat: Batesville

Created in 1820, Independence County is considered a "mother county" because it once contained all or part of fifteen modern counties. The Black and White rivers run through the county, and there is a great deal of rich delta farmland in the area. Batesville is home to Lyon College and the University of Arkansas Community College at Batesville. Well-known NASCAR driver Mark Martin is a native of the area, and there is a new racetrack in the Locust Grove area that has drawn much positive attention.

economic industry because of the makeup of our land. Racial inequalities seemed to be more pronounced because of the geographic regions of our state. Statewide population shifts occurred because of geography. Geography's effect on Arkansas's historical events will be seen throughout your studies. You will see limits and advantages resulting from our geographical diversity. Understanding that Arkansas's geography is unique and powerful, more so than in many other states, will help you better understand the state's development.

▼ The downtown Little Rock skyline and the Arkansas River sparkle at night.

▼ Atop Calico Rock in Izard County, hikers gaze down at the White River.

◄ A fisherman tries his luck at Lake Chicot in Chicot County.

► Mount Magazine, Arkansas's highest point, is located in Logan County.

► Swampy land dominates McGehee City Park in Desha County.

Chapter Reflection

Reflective Questions

1. In what region of Arkansas do you live? What are three natural features of your area?
2. What are the six geographic regions of Arkansas? After naming the six, list one distinctive characteristic of each.
3. Considering land size, which geographic region is the smallest? The largest?
4. Choose a different region than the one in which you live and explain how its lifestyle, jobs, recreation, transportation, neighbors, and travel might be different than those of where you live now.
5. When you look at the effects of pollution, traffic, the construction of new subdivisions and office buildings, and oil consumption, you are working with which of the five themes of geography?
6. Why is the Delta soil good for growing crops?
7. What is a negative aspect of living in lowland, river-bottom regions?
8. Why are the Ozarks not a large-scale farming area?
9. What are the primary rivers in Arkansas? What benefits or resources do these rivers provide for our state and its people?
10. The Ouachitas are primarily known for what two major naturally-occurring unique resources?
11. When considering the five themes of geography, driving a truck with a load of goods going to a grocer, teaching at a university, and piloting a cargo barge on the Arkansas River all apply to which theme?

You Don't Say!

On your own paper, write *TRUE* beside the number of any true statement or *FALSE* beside the number of any statement that has untrue or incorrect information.

1. Geography has no connection to or impact on any other area in social studies.
2. Globes, maps, and the five themes of geography are all important tools in studying the Earth and where and how we live.
3. Millions of years ago, what is now Arkansas was covered by the salty waters of the Gulf of Mexico.
4. Place has to do with the weather patterns of an area.
5. Sugarloaf and Petit Jean mountains are the highest points in Arkansas.

Geography **29**

Prove It!

Look back at the statements from the previous section, **"You Don't Say!"** Using what you read and learned in the chapter, rewrite each statement that you said was false into a true statement.

Compare and Contrast

Region	Rivers	Natural Resources	Weather	Major City or Town
Ozark Mountains				
Arkansas River Valley				
Ouachita Mountains				
Gulf Coastal Plain				
Mississippi Alluvial Plain				
Crowley's Ridge				

Unlock the Meaning . . .

The *Key* to new *Terms* from the chapter . . .

Look at the vocabulary terms in blue throughout the chapter. Choose four that are brand new to you. Write and number them 1, 2, 3, 4 on your paper. Then, on your own paper, copy or trace the diagram below. Then . . .

1. In the section of the state where the coldest Arkansas temperature was ever recorded, write two synonyms for the first term you chose.

2. In the section of the state where the Lake Chicot is located, write a sentence that uses your second term correctly and conveys its meaning.

3. In the Jonesboro area, write the third term.

4. In the Texarkana area, define the fourth term using your own words.

Reference Atlas

Contents

The World, Physical	32
The World, Political	34
North America, Physical	36
North America, Political	37
United States, Physical	38
United States, Political	40
United States, Land Use	42
Arkansas, Neighboring States	44
Arkansas, Physical	46
Arkansas, Political	47
Arkansas, Population	48
Arkansas, Land Use	49
Arkansas, Rivers and Lakes	50

Reference Atlas

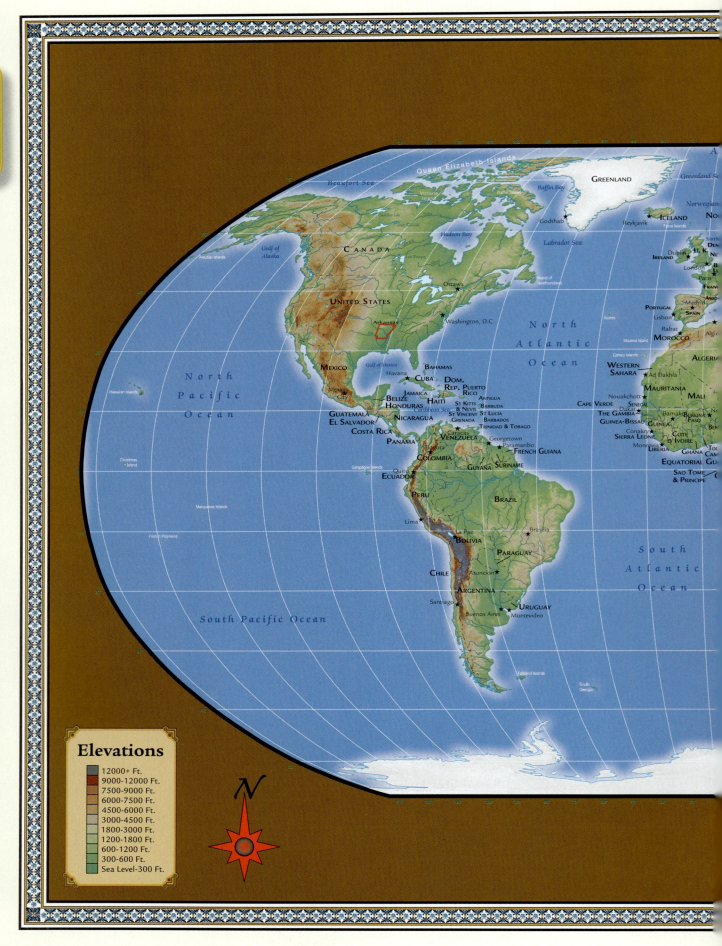

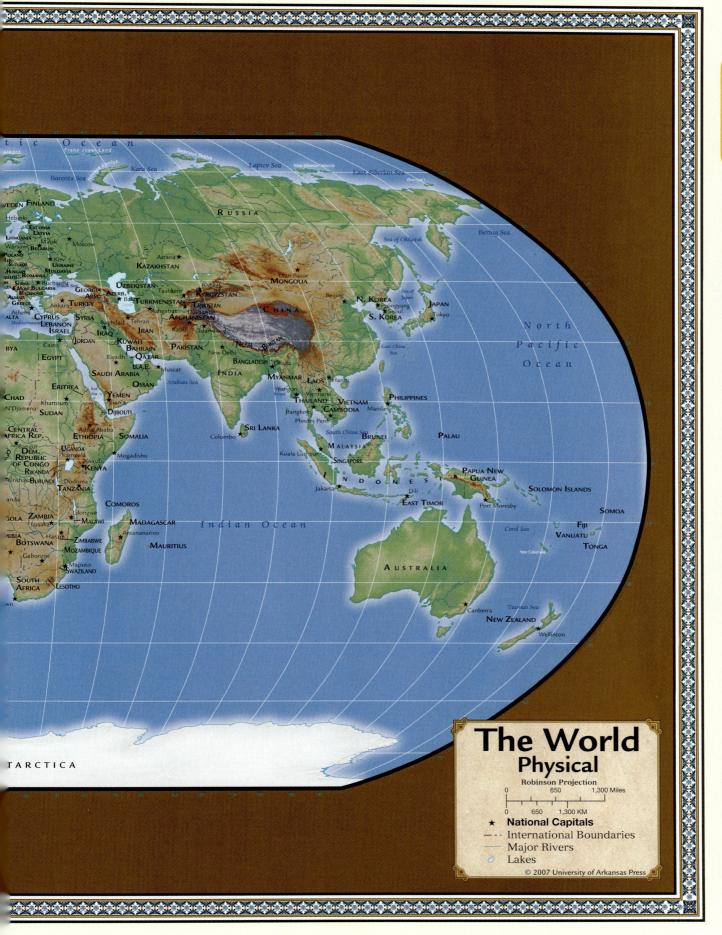

Reference Atlas

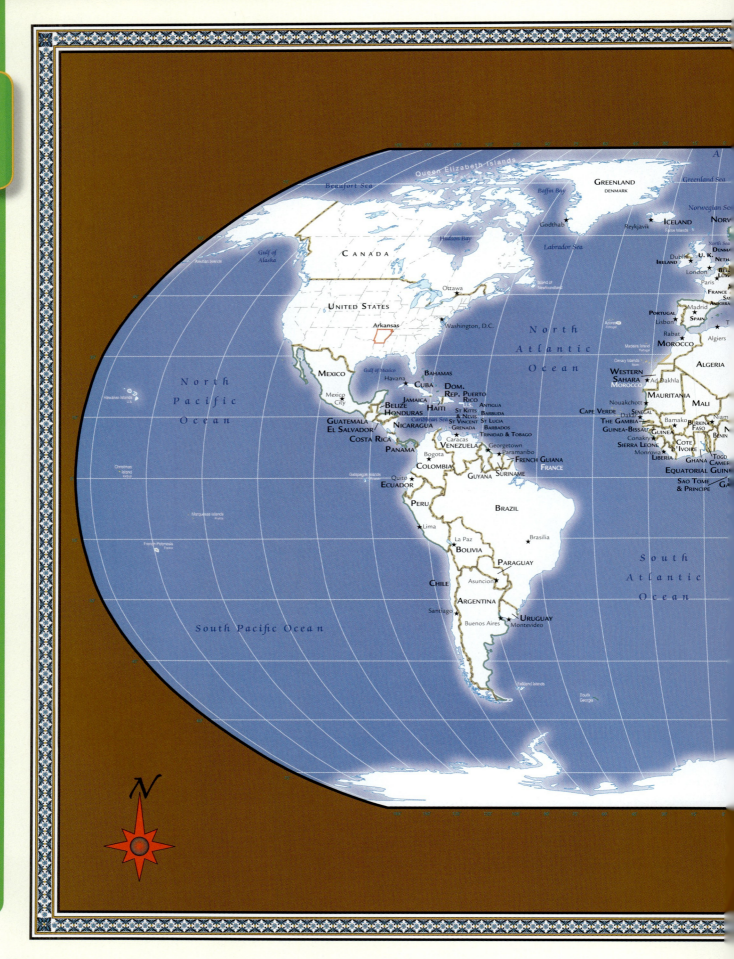

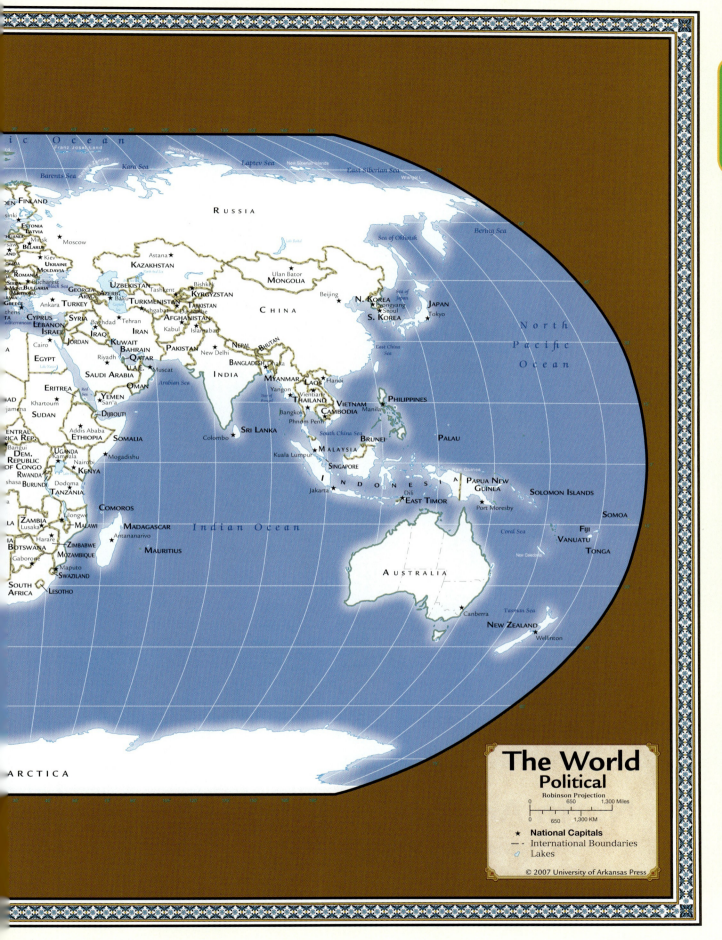

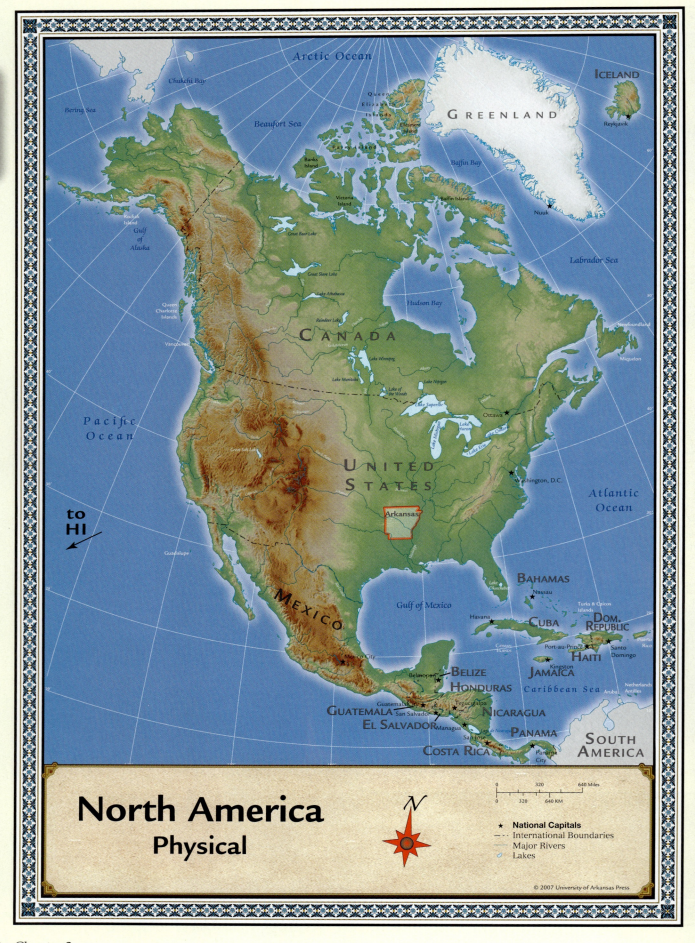

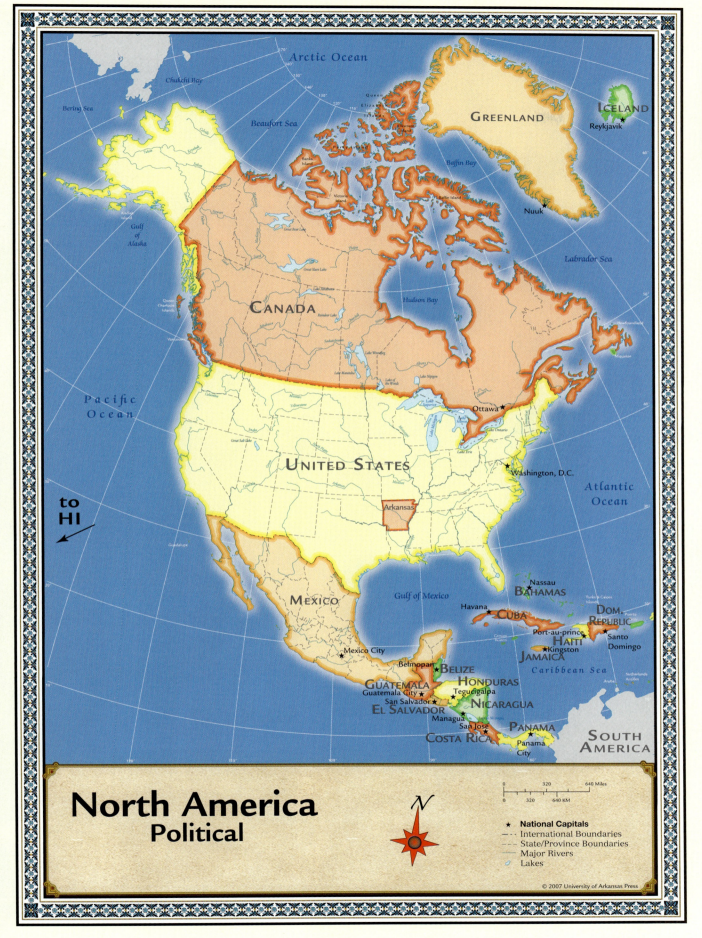

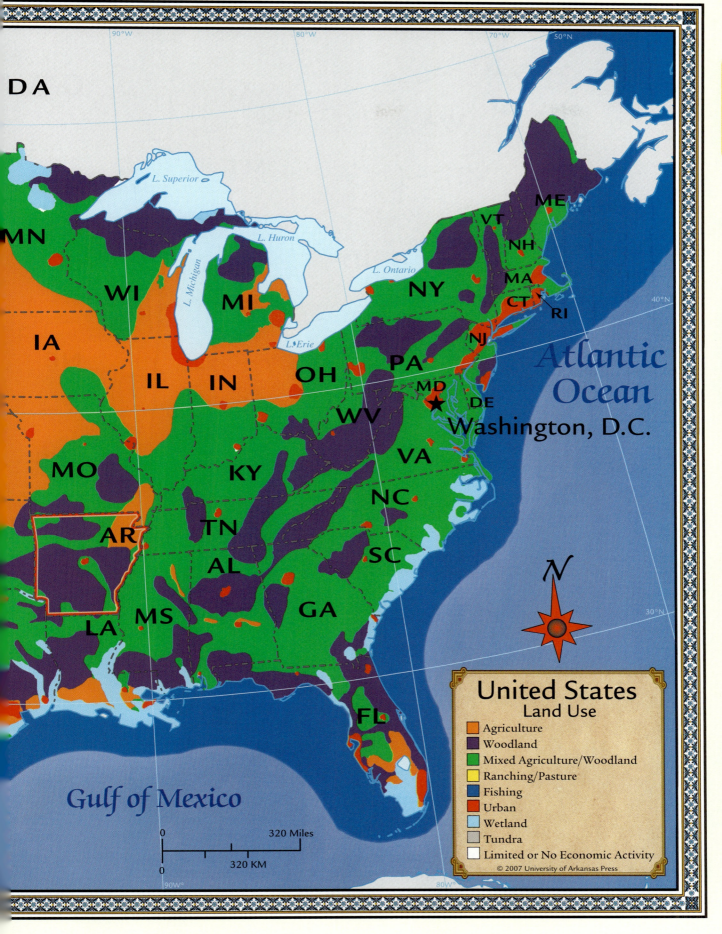

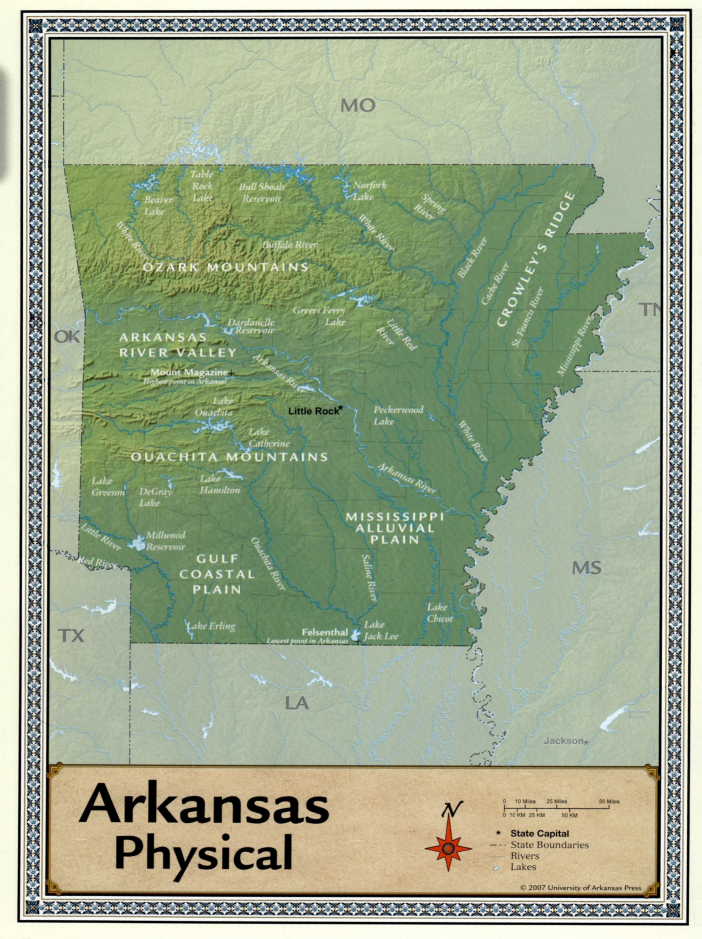

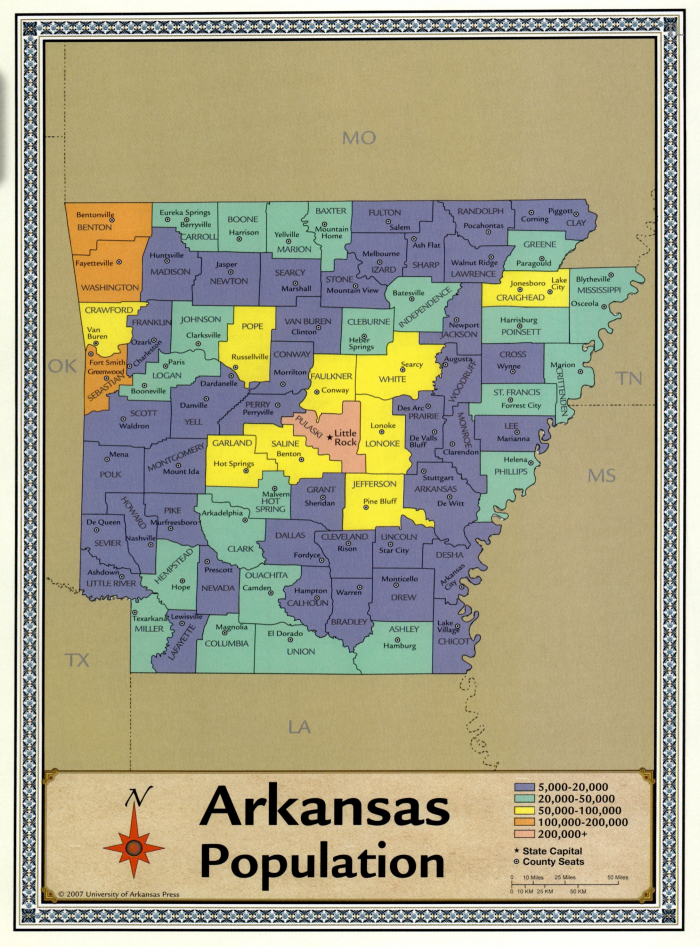

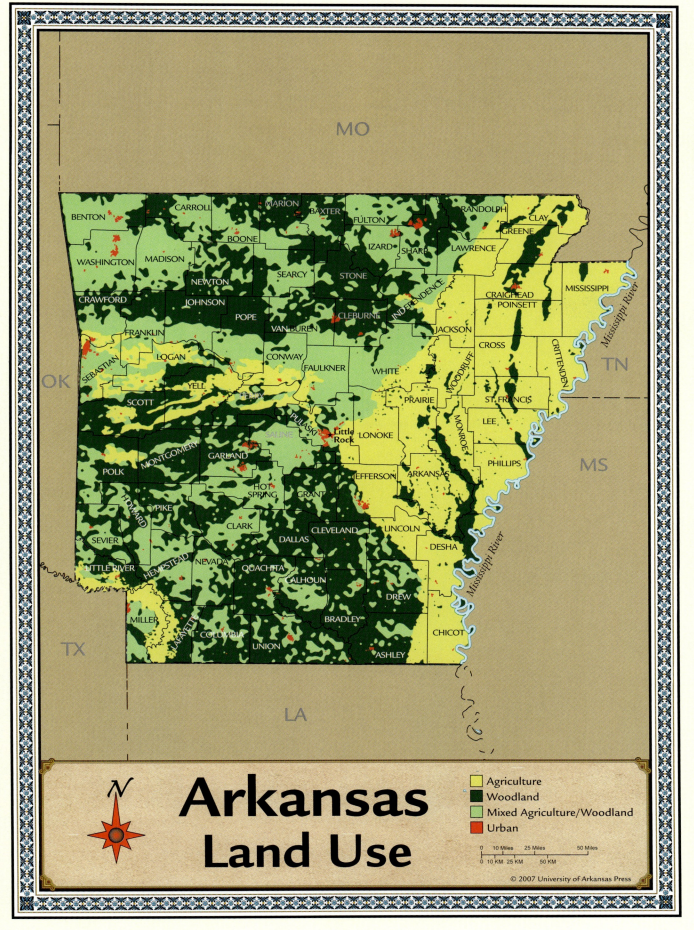

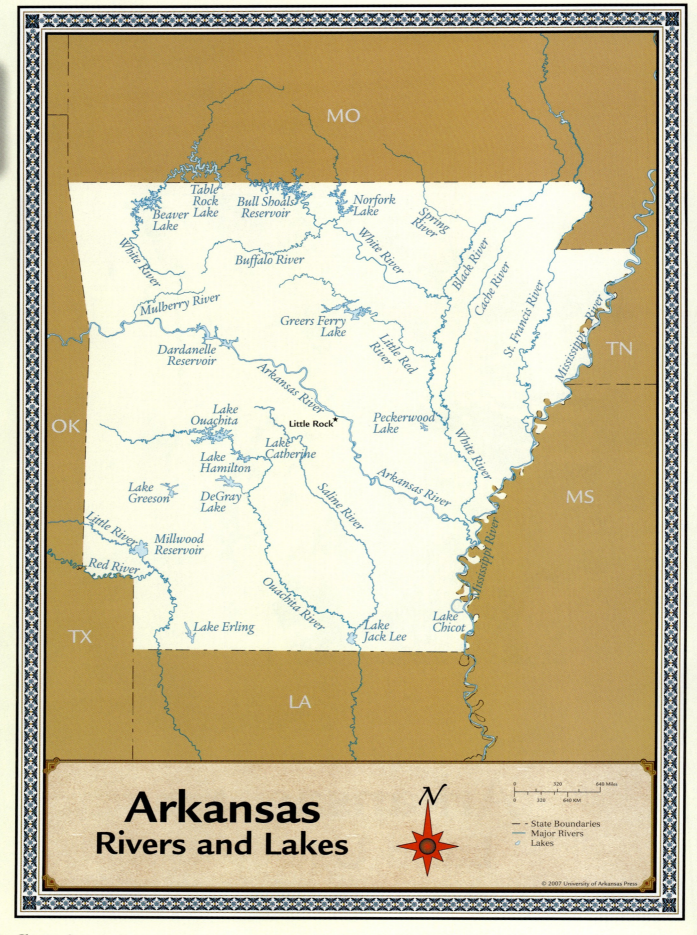

Chapter 3
State and Local Government
How We Govern Ourselves

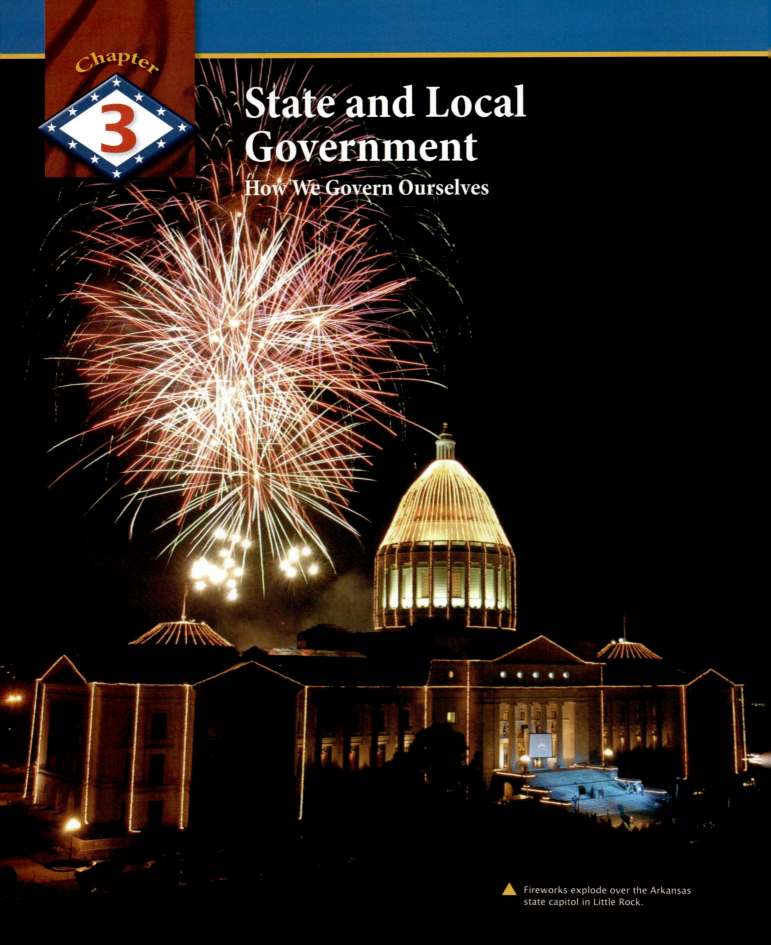

▲ Fireworks explode over the Arkansas state capitol in Little Rock.

Why Do We Study This?

Learning who you are and where you came from is an essential lesson for you as a citizen. It helps prepare you for your life-long citizenship responsibilities and challenges. To make the world in which you live a better place and to participate as a valuable contributor to society, you should have pride in your state, know your culture and heritage, and respond positively to your **inherent** civic duties. You should pride yourself on being a good ambassador for your state and representing your state well to others as you travel and meet citizens from other states and nations.

> ### Big Picture Questions
> - The United States operates under a democratic system of government. What other types of governmental structures exist in today's world? Why are there numerous types of governments? What are the advantages and disadvantages of each? Why?
> - How do citizens express their opinions in a democratic society? Why is it important to express opinions?

inherent something that is natural or that a person is born with.

I Am an Arkansan

J. William Fulbright (1905–1995)

James William Fulbright served as a U.S. senator from 1945 to 1975. He was the youngest person to serve as president of the University of Arkansas, taking the post in 1936, at the age of thirty-four. During his long career, he became one of the most prominent members of the U.S. Senate.

He was born in Missouri, but when he was young, his family settled in northwest Arkansas. In 1925, he earned a bachelor's degree in political science from the University of Arkansas. He was a Rhodes Scholar, studying at Oxford University in England. He received a law degree from George Washington University in 1934.

For the next two years, he served as U.S. attorney in Washington, D.C., returning to Fayetteville (Washington County) in 1936. In 1942, he was elected to the U.S. House of Representatives, and in 1945, won a Senate seat. In the Senate, he rose to become one of the most powerful senators in American history. His views were respected on a variety of issues, particularly in matters of foreign policy.

During the 1960s, he became an outspoken critic of the Vietnam War. He also became famous throughout the world for his efforts in establishing the Fulbright Fellowships, which have provided funds for thousands of students and scholars from across the globe to study in foreign countries. He died in 1995 and is buried in Fayetteville.

THE ENCYCLOPEDIA OF ARKANSAS HISTORY & CULTURE

Log on to Learn More
http://www.encyclopediaofarkansas.net/

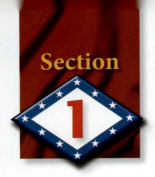

Section 1

Our National and State Governments

Guide to Reading

Terms

- appeals
- bench
- bills
- cabinet
- circuit
- constituents
- democratic
- district
- executive
- federal
- General Assembly
- judicial
- legislative
- legislature
- ordinance
- override
- principles
- tax
- veto
- vice versa

---

democratic of or run by the people through representation and vote.

tax monies collected by a government from citizens.

federal at a national or centralized level.

executive branch the area of government in which a president, governor, attorney general, cabinet members, and so on carry out the laws.

legislative branch the part of the government that writes or creates the laws.

judicial branch the system of courts and judges.

cabinet an advising council.

veto to override, terminate, or stop.

bills ideas for new laws or proposed laws.

principles basic beliefs

On the National Level

Our nation is governed by a **democratic** system. We elect those who represent us, and the voice of the people is the ultimate authority. Our government is funded by a **tax** collection system. Taxes pay for the operational costs and social programs of our nation as well as the salaries of those whom we elect to represent us.

Our national or **federal** government has three branches: the **executive**, the **legislative**, and the **judicial**. The executive branch includes the president, the vice-president, and all the members of the **cabinet**, such as the secretary of state, the secretary of homeland security, the secretary of defense, the attorney general, and others. The legislative branch includes those who serve in the U.S. House of Representatives and the U.S. Senate, which make up the two chambers of Congress. Finally, the U.S. Supreme Court heads the judicial branch.

The members of the executive branch work to ensure the safety and progress of our nation and make sure that laws are carried out properly. The president serves as commander in chief of the military and has the power to **veto** legislation or **bills** brought forward by Congress. The main responsibility of the legislative branch is to make our nation's laws. These laws are made by one hundred elected senators (two from each state) and 435 members of the House of Representatives. The number of elected representatives from each state to the House is based upon that state's population. The job of the judicial branch is to interpret and explain the laws made by the legislative branch and determine if an act is unconstitutional, which means that it would violate the founding **principles** of our nation. There are nine justices who serve on the Supreme Court **bench**, who once appointed by the president typically serve for life unless they chose to retire. The decisions made by the Supreme Court are final—no court can **override** their ruling.

Arkansans are represented in Washington, D.C., our nation's seat of government, not only by the president but also by two senators and four representatives. Senators are elected

54   Chapter 3

◀ The Arkansas state capitol building in downtown Little Rock. Who works in this building?

every six years, and members of the House of Representatives are elected every two years. Their job is to listen to the voices of the Arkansans who elect them and speak for their needs, concerns, and interests.

On the State Level

Our state has its own governmental structure as well, which is somewhat similar to that of our national government's. The federal government has the most authority, followed by state and local governments; and even though the federal government has the greatest burden of responsibility, and therefore more power, there are specific tasks that the state is responsible for, that the federal and local governments cannot influence, and **vice versa**. For example, it is the responsibility of the national government to declare war, while it is the responsibility of the state government to ensure good conditions in state prisons and to establish licensing

bench the office of the judge as well as where he or she presides in the courtroom.

override to exercise the right or authority to vote against.

vice versa reversed in order; interchangeable.

▼ The bridges shown connect Little Rock and North Little Rock.

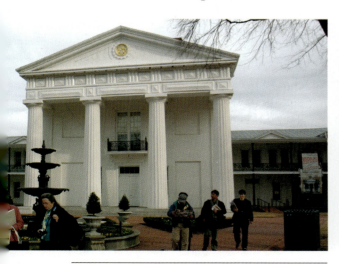

▲ The Old State House in Little Rock was once the home of Arkansas's state government. It is now a museum and meeting hall.

State and Local Government 55

▲ The Arkansas state capitol is modeled after what well-known capitol building?

ordinance a municipal (or city) regulation or guideline.

legislature a body of elected representatives that has the power to make laws.

General Assembly in Arkansas, the legislative branch of the government, the state congress, made up of the state senate and house of representatives.

requirements for teachers. It is also the responsibility of local governments to issue building permits for new community businesses, install stop signs, or create an **ordinance** that would limit the height and size of roadside signs.

The executive, legislative, and judicial branches make up Arkansas's state governmental structure. The executive branch is led by the governor. Other state officials who serve in the executive branch of Arkansas's state government are the lieutenant governor, the secretary of state, the attorney general, and other state officers such as the treasurer, auditor, and land commissioner. The state **legislature** or **General Assembly** has two chambers: the senate and the house of representatives. Their meetings to make and revise laws are held in Little Rock. Thirty-five senators and one hundred representatives meet every other year for a regular legislative session. State law limits Arkansas state senators to serving only two four-year terms. Based on recent state population estimates, it can be determined that each senator serves over seventy-five thousand Arkansans. Representatives each serve over twenty-five thousand. State representatives are limited to three two-year terms in office. The judicial branch of the state government includes five court systems—the Arkansas State Supreme Court, the Arkansas Court of **Appeals**, **circuit courts**, **district** courts, and city courts—and is responsible for making sure laws are carefully followed and interpreted correctly. The seven state-supreme-court justices are each elected for eight-year terms.

One of the most important jobs a senator or representative has is to listen to the needs and concerns of his or her **constituents** and determine if a bill needs to be created, written, proposed, and passed. These are the *basic* steps in this process:

- A citizen has an idea for a law, and he or she contacts his or her representative.
- The representative researches the situation and drafts a bill.
- The bill is assigned a number and read by the sponsoring representative to the other members of the senate or house.
- The bill is assigned to a committee for further research, debate, and presentation to the public or other representatives.
- The committee votes to pass, amend the bill, or not recommend the bill.

County Quest

Chicot

Named after: Point Chicot, on the Mississippi River

Chief Source of Income: Agriculture

Seat: Lake Village

Chicot County was created in 1823 and today harvests large amounts of cotton and soybeans. Lake Chicot is the state's largest natural lake and the continent's largest oxbow lake, which was formed from the Mississippi River.

The county was the area over which Charles Lindbergh made his first nighttime flight, and somewhere near Lake Village is rumored to be the burial site of Spanish explorer Hernando De Soto.

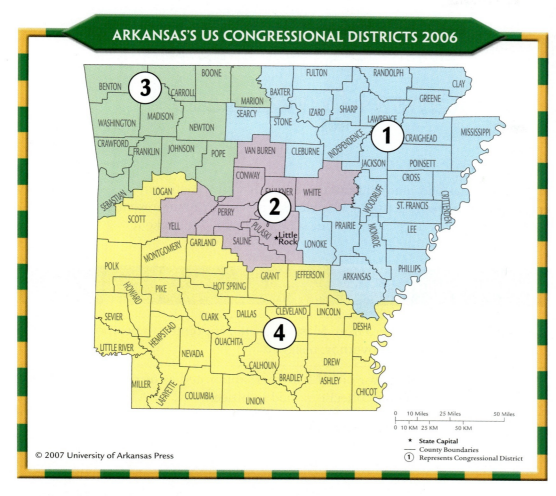

appeal to ask to be heard or reviewed again. An appellate court or court of appeals is where cases are heard or tried once more.

circuit court a court that is mobile and is held at multiple locations within one judicial district.

district court an administrative unit based on territorial division to manage courts or groups of schools.

constituents members of a population or citizenry; voters represented by an elected official.

- The bill is read again on the house or senate floor, and a vote is taken. A simple majority must occur for the bill to pass.
- After approval by both houses, the governor must sign or veto the bill within five days of receipt.
- If it is signed by the governor, it becomes law. If it is vetoed, the legislature has an opportunity to vote again and have a simple majority to override the veto. If there is a majority vote, the bill becomes a law.

Every branch of our national and state governments has many critical responsibilities and, most importantly, must serve and protect the people. Like that of the U.S. president, the office of the governor is the most powerful in our state's political structure and has the greatest burden of responsibility.

County Quest

Lafayette

Named after: Marquis de Lafayette, a French general in the American Revolution

Chief Source of Income: Agriculture, poultry, and timber

Seat: Lewisville

Poet Maya Angelou spent some of her childhood living in Stamps, a community in this county. Located in Arkansas's Gulf Coastal Plain/Timberlands region, the county was established in 1827 and is home to Lake Erling. Lafayette County has excellent agricultural lands used for raising livestock and crops, and the Red River forms the western county border. Arkansas's first governor, James Sevier Conway, was from Lafayette County, and residents and tourists can enjoy festivities at the Governor Conway Days in Bradley.

State and Local Government

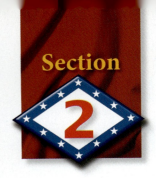

Section 2
Arkansas Governors

Arkansas has had many influential, colorful, and sometimes controversial governors from the territorial period through present day. Their legacies have changed our state and helped to make it what it is today.

Name	Served	Quick Facts
James Miller	1819–25	military hero from Massachusetts; appointed to position of territorial governor; resigned.
George Izard	1825–29	served in War of 1812; lawyer; appointed as territorial governor; had a razor collection; died in office.
John Pope	1829–35	lost one arm in a farm accident; Kentucky lawyer; appointed to office by President Jackson; eventually won a U.S. Congress seat from Kentucky.
William Fulton	1835–36	lawyer; appointed by President Jackson; governor of territory and when Arkansas became a state chosen as one of Arkansas's first U.S. senators.
James Sevier Conway	1836–40	owned a cotton plantation along the Red River; worked to improve education and state banking and to establish a federal arsenal.
Archibald Yell	1840–44	lawyer; war hero; worked to control state banks and improve education; he was killed leading Arkansas troops in the war for Texas's independence in the battle of Buena Vista, Mexico, in 1847.
Thomas S. Drew	1844–49	schoolteacher; postman; farmer; had personal financial problems; supported education and attempted to improve state finances; resigned because of the poor salary of the governor's office.
John S. Roane	1849–52	lawyer; won special election after Drew's resignation; supported education; later served in Civil War.
Elias N. Conway	1852–60	brother of Arkansas's first governor; improved state roads; secured land grants for railroads and improved state-prison conditions; reorganized state finances. His death in 1892 ended the dynasty of the "Family."

58 Chapter 3

Name	Served	Quick Facts
Henry Rector	1860–62	U.S. marshal; served in state senate; lawyer; served on state supreme court; cooperated with secessionists; served in Civil War; cotton farmer.
Harris Flanagin	1862–64	teacher; lawyer; fought in the Battle of Pea Ridge; served as Confederate governor; supported aid to soldiers' families and tried to suppress illegal liquor making.
Isaac Murphy	1864–68	lawyer; teacher; served in General Assembly; Union governor during Civil War; only man to vote against secession for Arkansas.
Powell Clayton	1868–71	served in Civil War; helped to start the Arkansas Republican Party; declared martial law to suppress Ku Klux Klan in Arkansas; accused of being dishonest in state railroad aid program; later served as U.S. senator from Arkansas; ambassador to Mexico.
Ozra Hadley	1871–73	farmer; storeowner; served in Arkansas state senate and as senate president; acting governor after the resignation of Powell Clayton.
Elisha Baxter	1873–74	merchant; served in state legislature; involved in political war, the Brooks-Baxter War, where he was declared the winner by the state legislature, but was accused of fraud; temporarily removed from the office but returned after President Ulysses S. Grant reviewed the situation and declared him the winner.
Augustus Garland	1874–77	lawyer; served in Confederate Senate and House of Representatives; as governor, helped to create black teachers' training college; supported schools for blind and deaf; served in U.S. Senate; as U.S. attorney general, argued cases before the U.S. Supreme Court, where he died during a trial.
William Miller	1877–81	the first man who was born in Arkansas to be elected governor; supported education; worked on improving the state financial situation; later served as state treasurer and auditor.

State and Local Government

Name	Served	Quick Facts
Thomas Churchill	1881–83	farmer; postmaster; war veteran; state treasurer; established state board of health while governor; was investigated for and convicted of stealing money while state treasurer.
James Berry	1883–85	lawyer; teacher; lost right leg while fighting in Civil War; served in state house of representatives; during term as governor, reduced state debt and prevented racial lynchings; later filled the seat of Augustus Garland in the U.S. Senate when he resigned; served as commissioner of the Arkansas History Commission from 1910 to 1913.
Simon Hughes	1885–89	sheriff; lawyer; abolished public executions and established the State Debt Board while governor; later served on Arkansas State Supreme Court.
James Eagle	1889–93	sheriff; served in Civil War; Baptist minister; served in Arkansas legislature and as speaker of the house; as governor, supported railroad regulation and education but also supported the Arkansas Separate Coach Law, which forced black people to ride in separate train cars.
William Fishback	1893–95	lawyer; organized a Unionist newspaper; served in Arkansas state legislature; while governor, organized levee districts and promoted industrial growth and the national image of Arkansas.

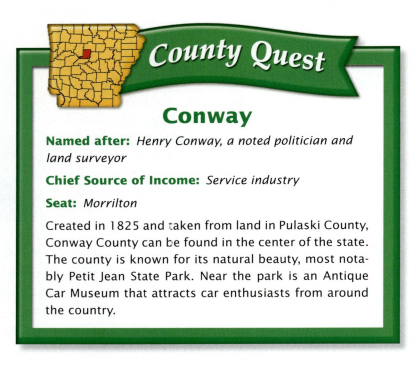

County Quest

Conway

Named after: Henry Conway, a noted politician and land surveyor

Chief Source of Income: Service industry

Seat: Morrilton

Created in 1825 and taken from land in Pulaski County, Conway County can be found in the center of the state. The county is known for its natural beauty, most notably Petit Jean State Park. Near the park is an Antique Car Museum that attracts car enthusiasts from around the country.

Name	Served	Quick Facts
James P. Clarke	1895–97	lawyer; served in Arkansas house of representatives and the state senate; while governor, regulated railroads and worked with federal government to relieve Arkansas's state debt; later served in U.S. Senate.
Daniel Jones	1897–1901	Civil War veteran; lawyer; served in Arkansas house of representatives; supported education and created state railroad commission while governor; secured money for new state capitol building during second term.
Jefferson Davis	1901–07	lawyer; first governor to serve more than two consecutive terms, during which he established guidelines for salaries for state legislators, opposed convict leasing, and was known for being a segregationist; later served in U.S. Senate.
John S. Little	1907	lawyer; served in Arkansas house of representatives and U.S. Congress; two days after being elected governor, suffered a mental and physical breakdown. He later died in a state mental hospital.
John I. Moore	1907–08	acting governor
X. O. Pindall	1908–09	acting governor
George W. Donaghey	1909–13	teacher; carpenter; building and road contractor; as governor, improved healthcare, roads, and education and oversaw the completion of the new state capitol and the Booneville sanatorium; eliminated convict-lease system. Schools that would later become Arkansas Tech University, University of Arkansas at Monticello, and Arkansas State University were organized during his terms.
Joseph T. Robinson	1913	lawyer; served in Arkansas house of representatives and U.S. Congress; resigned office of governor to serve in U.S. Senate. During gubernatorial term, state flag was adopted and highway commission was formed.

Name	Served	Quick Facts
George W. Hays	1913–17	lawyer; judge; supported road improvement; vetoed legal betting in Hot Springs.
Charles H. Brough	1917–21	professor; public speaker; reformer; while governor, established laws to require school attendance and to allow women to vote and aid programs for mothers and the needy. He was able to quickly restore order after the Elaine race riot and then worked to promote stable, peaceful race relations.
Thomas McRae	1921–25	lawyer; banker; served in Arkansas house of representatives; created a personal income-tax law and tobacco tax for school funding while governor.
Thomas J. Terral	1925–27	lawyer; served Arkansas as a state leader in education administration and as assistant secretary of the state senate before becoming governor who created Arkansas's first state park, Petit Jean Mountain.
John Martineau	1927–28	lawyer; served in Arkansas house of representatives; as governor, served as president of tri-state flood board (after floods of 1927) and created a lasting road program, the Martineau Road Plan; served as a judge until his death.
Harvey Parnell	1928–33	bookkeeper; farmer; merchant; served in Arkansas house of representatives and senate and as lieutenant governor; supported school and highway improvement while governor.
Junius M. Futrell	1933–37	lawyer; teacher; farmer; judge; served in Arkansas house of representatives; while governor, legalized gambling on dog and horse races and established the Department of Public Welfare.
Carl E. Bailey	1937–41	bookkeeper; lawyer; served as Arkansas attorney general; while governor, created a free public-library system and made all state-owned bridges toll free.
Homer M. Adkins	1941–45	pharmacist; World War I veteran; sheriff; during term as governor, created state financial surplus; obtained more energy for northeast Arkansas, restructured state highway debt, fought against WWII Japanese Internment camps being built in Arkansas.

Name	Served	Quick Facts
Benjamin Laney Jr.	1945–49	Navy veteran; store owner; real-estate investor; mayor of Camden; during gubernatorial service, consolidated public services and helped gain approval for the building of War Memorial Stadium in Little Rock and the new governor's mansion; often identified with the racist movement.
Sidney S. McMath	1949–53	lawyer; World War II hero; as governor, authorized funds for new medical center in Little Rock and highway construction and increased the minimum wage; forward-thinking in regard to race relations, appointing blacks to state boards and supporting state antilynching law and repeal of poll taxes.
Francis Cherry	1953–55	lawyer; judge; served in the Navy during World War II; first to use radio effectively to win political race; formed new department of finance and administration and made reforms to the highway commission while in the governor's office.
Orval Faubus	1955–67	raised in a log cabin; teacher; farmer; lumberjack; World War II veteran; postmaster; his controversial actions as governor during the Little Rock Central High School crisis gained national attention in 1957.
Winthrop Rockefeller	1967–71	World War II Army hero; chairman of Arkansas Industrial Development Commission; first Republican governor since Reconstruction; while governor, stopped illegal gambling in Hot Springs, worked to reform state prisons, and appointed many African Americans to state boards, commissions, and other jobs.

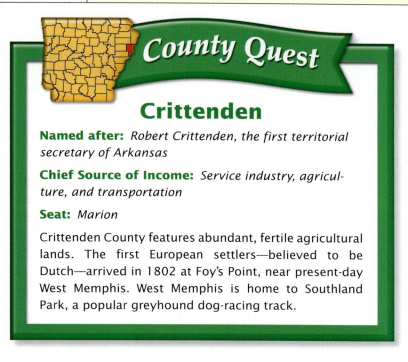

County Quest

Crittenden

Named after: *Robert Crittenden, the first territorial secretary of Arkansas*

Chief Source of Income: *Service industry, agriculture, and transportation*

Seat: *Marion*

Crittenden County features abundant, fertile agricultural lands. The first European settlers—believed to be Dutch—arrived in 1802 at Foy's Point, near present-day West Memphis. West Memphis is home to Southland Park, a popular greyhound dog-racing track.

State and Local Government

Name	Served	Quick Facts
Dale Bumpers	1971–75	World War II veteran; lawyer; store owner; farmer; served on local school boards, as city attorney, and on the Arkansas Supreme Court before being elected governor; as governor, raised teacher salaries and continued to develop state parks, increased aid to education, and abolished the trusty program in the state's prisons; went on to serve in the U.S. Senate.
David Pryor	1975–79	lawyer; newspaperman; served in Arkansas house of representatives and U.S. House; as governor, appointed many women and African Americans to state boards, was conservative in state spending, supported education and the elderly, and fought for fair local taxation.
William J. Clinton	1979–81, 1983–93	lawyer; professor; state attorney general; as governor, improved teaching standards, state economic and industrial development, and road construction but was affected by many controversies including increasing car-tag license fees and allowing Cuban refugees to be housed at Fort Chaffee during his first term as well as accusations of personal misconduct. Clinton would later go on to serve two terms as president of the United States, the only president from Arkansas.
Frank White	1981–83	served in the Air Force; stockbroker; banker; served as director of the Arkansas Industrial Development Commission; created controversy while governor for requiring the teaching of creationism in Arkansas schools. The law was later ruled unconstitutional in the U.S. Supreme Court.
James "Jim Guy" Tucker	acting 1991–93 1993–96	lawyer; state attorney general; served in U.S. House of Representatives; Arkansas lieutenant governor and acting governor when Clinton left office to run for president in 1991; cut state spending and reformed the juvenile justice system while in governor's office; convicted of illegal activity related to Whitewater real-estate transaction (for which the Clintons were also investigated) for which he paid large fines but served little jail time.

Name	Served	Quick Facts
Mike Huckabee	1996–2007	Baptist minister; Arkansas lieutenant governor; assumed office upon Tucker's resignation; as governor, enacted wide reforms to education, including the creation of many new charter schools, increasing college scholarships, and establishing the Smart Start and Smart Step math- and reading-improvement programs; also generated funds for state highway improvements and chaired a regional board to study and reduce poverty in poverty-stricken Delta counties; signed legislation to improve school lunches as part of a statewide health initiative and supported the statewide ban on smoking in all public places in Arkansas. Controversies surrounding his service included his wife running for Arkansas secretary of state and the possibility of the receipt of gifts he did not officially report to the state. Presidential candidate in 2008.
Mike Beebe	2007–	lawyer; Army reservist; served in Arkansas state senate and as attorney general; while in office, worked as an advocate for victims of crime and to prevent Medicaid fraud and began a mentor program for the youth of Arkansas.

It is very important for our nationally elected representatives, governors, and local governments to work together to form a secure, comprehensive network of agencies and representatives to ensure the prosperity and safety of the citizenry. To support the state and national structures, we also have local offices to serve the voters. Many governors, senators, members of Congress, and even presidents have first worked in local offices or as local and community activists.

State and Local Government

STATE OF ARKANSAS
MIKE HUCKABEE
GOVERNOR

July 12, 2006

To the students of Arkansas:

You are about to embark on an exciting journey that will take you deep into the past of our great state. Through the pages of this history book you will come to understand the sacrifices our founding fathers made in order to ensure the freedom and liberty you enjoy every day. You'll learn of their call to action and the citizenship they demonstrated that was necessary to establish the pillars of our government.

Citizenship is social responsibility in action. This means doing your part for the common good, serving your community, and helping make our democracy work.

We, as citizens, have a responsibility to participate in the political process by registering and voting in elections. Serving on a jury is another responsibility of citizenship. It is by participating in your community that you truly exercise your rights as an American.

I encourage you to get involved in the workings of state government. Write letters to government officials or newspapers to advocate your opinions on public issues and policies. Don't sit on the sidelines – develop a voice and let it be heard!

Enjoy this next year as you travel back in time and celebrate the rich history of Arkansas. Be diligent in your studies and take pride in your past – take pride in your future.

Sincerely yours,

Mike Huckabee

MH:gs

State Capitol Building, Suite 250 * Little Rock, AR 72201 * mike.huckabee@state.ar.us
501-682-2345 * Fax 501-682-1382 * TDD 501-682-7515

▲ A letter from former governor Mike Huckabee to the students of Arkansas. Mr. Huckabee ran for president in 2008.

STATE OF ARKANSAS
MIKE BEEBE
GOVERNOR

To the Future of Our State:

You are about to take the first steps on a journey of discovering the foundations of our Nation and of our State. I hope that, as you are introduced to many of our nation's greatest leaders in this book, you will develop a true understanding of their selfless character and unparalleled leadership. These are the men and women who created the process of our democracy and expanded the rights and freedoms we enjoy today.

As you read these pages, you will discover the value of leadership, and I want you to realize that you are our future leaders. I urge you to delve into history and apply the concepts that you learn to your own life, so that you can become an involved and knowledgeable contributor to our society, as these leaders before you have done.

I come from humble beginnings, like many of you. I was raised by a single mom, who worked to raise me on her tips as a waitress. She taught me the value of an education, because she knew that knowledge would provide the opportunity for me to have a better life. Now, as our State's Governor, I have the ability to help make our State the best it can be. You, too, have this same opportunity.

Use the lessons in this book to develop into productive citizens of our country. Starting today, learn about the issues we face as a State, write to your state legislators, and let your voices be heard. One person really can make a difference.

I hope that this is the beginning of a journey toward leadership for each of you and that you will become inspired by the people you will learn about in this book.

Sincerely yours,

Mike Beebe

STATE CAPITOL, SUITE 250 • LITTLE ROCK, AR 72201
TELEPHONE (501) 682-2345 • FAX (501) 682-1382
INTERNET WEB SITE • www.governor.arkansas.gov

▲ A letter from governor Mike Beebe to the students of Arkansas.

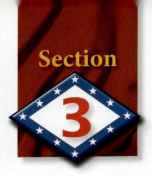

Section 3: Our Local Governments

Guide to Reading

Terms

counties
county seat
municipal
quorum court
rural

---

counties governmental subdivisions within a territory or a state.

quorum court in Arkansas counties, the branch responsible for making laws.

county seat a town that houses county management operations, such as the courthouse and the tax collector.

On the County Level

As the United States is divided into fifty states, Arkansas is divided into seventy-five **counties**, each with its own governmental structures. Counties have two branches of government: the executive and legislative. The executive branch is headed by a county judge who is not a judge in the usual sense, but more a county manager with responsibilities similar to that of the governor. The legislative branch of county government is known as the **quorum court**. This body is not a typical court, but an elected group that determines county laws and regulations. There are also tax collectors, sheriffs, and clerks within the county-government system. The center of county operations is typically the largest city or town in the county and is called the **county seat**.

On the Municipal Level

Within counties are often cities, towns, and small or **rural** communities. City or town governments are called **municipal** governments. These city organizations are headed by an elected mayor (executive branch) and governed by a city council (legislative branch). Some cities have a city manager, who is chosen by the elected city council, rather than a mayor. City and county governments provide a variety of necessary services to the citizens: water and sewage treatment, police and fire protection, conducting elections, garbage collection, snow and ice removal, traffic safety, animal control, and much more.

Izard

Named after: George Izard, Arkansas's second territorial governor

Chief Source of Income: State prison and tourism

Seat: Melbourne

Izard County was created in 1825, making it one of the first counties in the state. The White River scenic waterway lures fishermen from all over the state to the county, as it offers some of the best fishing in Arkansas. Elwin Charles "Preacher" Roe, an all-star major-league baseball pitcher (Brooklyn Dodgers and Pittsburgh Pirates, 1938–54), was reared in Izard County. In Horseshoe Bend, residents and guests alike can enjoy swimming and fishing in the Strawberry River and any of the many golf and tennis facilities.

I Am an Arkansan

Mark Pryor (1963–)

Mark Pryor, the son of former U.S. senator and governor of Arkansas David Pryor, was elected to the U.S. Senate in 2002. He was born in Fayetteville on January 10, 1963, and spent much of his childhood in both Arkansas and, because his father was a senator, the Washington, D.C., area. He studied history at the University of Arkansas and went on to get his law degree from there as well. Pryor worked as a lawyer for over a decade until he decided to follow in the family tradition of politics. (After all, his grandmother Susan Pryor was a pioneering female politician in Arkansas and a key influence on David Pryor's political career.) A Democrat, he was a member of the state house of representatives from 1991 to 1994 and served as attorney general of Arkansas from 1999 to 2002.

Among other committee assignments, he is a member of the Armed Services Committee. This makes him a very important member of the Senate, as he has a say in many military matters. He is generally known as a moderate, which means that although he is a Democrat, he sometimes sides with Republicans.

Log on to Learn More
http://www.senate.gov/~pryor

rural in the country as opposed to the city; less populated; having to do with farming.

municipal of or having to do with a city, community, or town government.

MARK PRYOR
ARKANSAS

UNITED STATES SENATE
WASHINGTON, D.C. 20510

September, 2006

Dear Students:

You are about to embark on a wonderful journey through the history of one of America's greatest states—the State of Arkansas. You will meet many heroes along the way, and read about great individuals whose intelligence, courage, ingenuity and thoughtfulness changed lives for the better and whose actions and adventures ultimately affected the quality of life that we enjoy today. As you read through the pages of this book, I hope you will discover some of these heroes, learn from the examples that they set, and, in turn, become better citizens and contributors to your community, your state, and your nation.

Sincerely,

Mark Pryor

Mark Pryor

State and Local Government

The structure of our government is essential to our success as citizens and as a nation. It also ensures our rights as citizens—the rights that our forefathers granted us in the U.S. Constitution. As citizens, we have a right to life, liberty, the pursuit of happiness, a fair and speedy trial, and fair and just representation, among other things. As citizens, it is our responsibility and privilege to exercise our rights and use our voice responsibly through the systems of our national, state, and local governments.

I Am an Arkansan

Blanche Meyers Lambert Lincoln (1960–)

United States senator Blanche Meyers Lambert Lincoln is the first woman to be elected to the Senate from Arkansas since Hattie W. Caraway in 1932, who was the first female ever elected to the U.S. Senate. At age thirty-eight, Lincoln was also the youngest woman ever elected to the Senate. She was born on September 30, 1960, in Helena (Phillips County) into a farm family that has called Arkansas home for over seven generations.

After attending the University of Arkansas, Fayetteville and Randolph Macon College in Virginia, she moved to Washington, D.C., where she worked as an aide to Arkansas congressman Bill Alexander. Later she worked as a lobbyist. Returning to Arkansas in 1992, she ran successfully against Alexander for his seat in Congress. She served in the U.S. House of Representatives until 1998, when she decided to run for the U.S. Senate after Senator Dale Bumpers made the decision to retire from service.

She has a reputation for working towards bipartisan solutions to many of the issues our nation faces. She once remarked, "I am not normally a betting person, but I say that putting your money on the American people is about as close to a sure bet as you are going to get."

She and her family, which includes her husband Steve, who is a physician, and their two sons, Reece and Bennett, reside in the Washington, D.C., metro area.

Read more about the women of the Senate in the book *Nine and Counting: The Women of the Senate* (by Barbara Mikulski and published by William Morrow and Company in 2000), to which Senator Lincoln is also a contributor.

THE ENCYCLOPEDIA OF ARKANSAS HISTORY & CULTURE

Log on to Learn More
http://www.senate.gov/~lincoln
http://www.encyclopediaofarkansas.net/

BLANCHE L. LINCOLN
UNITED STATES SENATOR
ARKANSAS

Dear Young Arkansan,

As one of Arkansas's two U.S. Senators and a member of a seventh generation Arkansas farm family, I take enormous pride in our state's heritage. In fact, when I'm asked to sign photos I always write, "With Arkansas Pride, Blanche Lincoln."

The contents of this textbook provide many examples of why Arkansas is such a special place. One of my favorite things to share with non-Arkansans is the natural beauty that our state offers citizens and visitors alike — from the Ozark Mountains in the Northwest corner to the numerous lakes and nature reserves scattered throughout the state. Additionally, as Arkansans we can be proud of our state's contribution to the world; Arkansas is home to some of the world's largest companies, boasts a nationally recognized university that conducts state-of-the-art research, and grows crops that provide food to countries across the globe.

Women have also played a significant role in our state's history. Just as they have nationally, women in Arkansas have broken the glass ceiling to lead companies, win elections and conduct groundbreaking medical research. One of the most inspiring facts, and one that has had a tremendous impact on my life, was the election of Hattie Caraway to the U.S. Senate on January 12, 1932. Senator Caraway, a native of Jonesboro, became the first woman in our nation's history elected to the U.S. Senate in her own right. I'm reminded of the significance of her election everyday when I pass her portrait which is prominently displayed just outside the door of the Senate Chamber. Her contribution to Arkansas and U.S. history continues to give me inspiration and a great sense of pride.

I commend your study of Arkansas's history and consider it a great honor to serve our state in the U.S. Senate.

With Arkansas Pride!
Blanche L. Lincoln

NOT PRINTED OR MAILED AT GOVERNMENT EXPENSE.

Chapter 3

Chapter Reflection

Reflective Questions

1. How many of our state governors were lawyers?
2. How many of our state governors were women?
3. Who was the longest serving governor? Who served for the shortest length of time?
4. What were some of the most common policies or programs that the governors spent money on or tried to improve? Why? Is there a pattern? Why or why not?
5. How many of our governors served in the military?
6. Suppose you were running for governor of Arkansas. Write a short paragraph explaining what you would tell citizens during your campaign. What is your platform (issues, problems you hope to correct)? How will you raise money? What would be your plan of action to make our state better if you won? Be sure to include who, what, when, where, why, and how when crafting your answer.

THE OL' FILLIN' STATION

On your own paper, copy the sentence and then write the word or phrase that best completes each sentence.

1. The _____ branch is the part of the government that carries out the laws.
2. If you request a second trial so a different judge can hear your case, you will go to _____ court.
3. Our society is _____ , which means that the people are free to vote and elect representatives of their choice.
4. The city passed a tree _____ requiring that the owner must leave 23 percent of the original tree canopy.
5. A U.S. senator who represents Arkansans in Washington, D.C., is a part of the _____ branch of government.
6. There are _____ justices on the U.S. Supreme Court.
7. When the president appoints the secretary of state, the secretary of education, and the secretary of defense, he or she is appointing members of the _____ .

Picture It!

Suppose you are running for governor of Arkansas. Design your campaign slogan, poster, bumper sticker, or campaign button. What is your platform (issues, problems you hope to correct, how you will raise money, etc.)? What would be your plan of action to make our state better if you won? What do you want the voters to learn about you when they catch a quick glimpse of your poster, bumper sticker, slogan, or button? Be sure to include who, what, when, where, why, and how when creating your poster, bumper sticker, slogan, or button.

Chapter 4

Economics and Tourism
Where We Learn, Work, Live, and Play

▲ Hang gliding off Mt. Nebo in Yell County.

Why Do We Study This?

Economics, like geography, is a very important area in social studies. Trade, money, commerce, and prosperity all dramatically affect our society and livelihoods. Therefore, it is critical to have a basic understanding of the way our economic system functions and how Arkansas's geography, history, culture, and economy are all connected and all affect one another. It is also the responsibility of citizens to make a valuable contribution to the state's economy through working, buying and selling goods, accessing services, and attending college or vacationing in Arkansas.

Big Picture Questions

- What are the economic systems of other states? Other nations? How are they similar or how do they differ from our own? Why are there different systems?

- Why is there not one global economic system? One type of money? Would a global economic system be successful? Why or why not? If so, how? If not, why not?

- What business or industry has had the biggest impact on Arkansas? Why? How? Be sure to consider jobs, charitable donations, community impact, and effects on the land and environment when crafting your answer. Be sure to use reasons, facts, and examples to support your opinion.

DID YOU KNOW?

In 1952, the largest alligator ever caught in the western hemisphere up until that point was Big Arkie. He was caught in waters just outside of Hope and was thirteen feet long and weighed nearly five hundred pounds! The southern United States and the Yangtze River Valley in China are the only two places in the world where alligators are found. Big Arkie died in 1970.

THE ENCYCLOPEDIA OF ARKANSAS HISTORY & CULTURE

Log on to Learn More
http://www.encyclopediaofarkansas.net/

Economics and Tourism

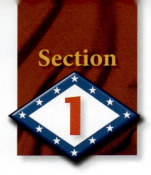

Section 1

Arkansas's Economy

Guide to Reading

Terms
capitalism
goods
gross state product
resources
scarcity
sectors
surplus

goods products or items that have economic value or satisfy a want.

resources available items or goods or a naturally occurring supply such as petroleum.

scarcity the quality of being rare or difficult to obtain.

surplus abundance, excess, or leftover goods or money.

capitalism a financial system in which goods, products, and many services are privately owned and operated (not by government) and in which businesses, trade groups, and organizations are encouraged and expected to compete for consumers and profit.

gross state product the total amount of money or revenue created in a state each year or the whole value of the state's production of all goods and services each year.

sectors portions, areas, parts, or subdivisions of a group or workforce.

An Overview

Economics is the study of how a state or nation distributes and consumes **goods**, **resources**, and services and how value is created. Many times, a society demands more goods, resources, or services than are available, and that creates **scarcity**. However, some goods are abundant or there is a **surplus**, like air. It is not considered scarce. For an economic system to be successful, there must be growth, employment, and stable prices. Arkansas's economic system is based on **capitalism** as is the United States', and our **gross state product** is contributed to each year by service-oriented businesses (such as hotels and restaurants), the financial and real estate trades, retail services, agriculture, government, utilities, and the manufacturing, transportation, tourism, healthcare, and educational **sectors**.

◀ Corporations, like J. B. Hunt Transport, Inc. headquartered in Lowell (Benton County), contribute to Arkansas's gross state product.

I Am an Arkansan

J. B. Hunt (1927–2006)

Johnnie Bryant "J. B." Hunt was reared in rural Cleburne County. After leaving school in the seventh grade to work at his uncle's sawmill, he moved on to picking cotton and selling lumber. He later served in the army and spent much of the 1950s driving a truck throughout the mid-south region.

In the early 1960s, he hit upon the idea to begin producing poultry litter (used for fertilizer, livestock feed, and poultry-house bedding) and selling it to the many poultry companies in Arkansas. He set up such a company in Stuttgart (Arkansas County) and lost money the first year. Eventually the company turned around, and Hunt was shipping poultry litter throughout the nation. By the late 1960s, Hunt was thinking of opening a trucking company—just a few tractor-trailers—as a sideline business to his poultry-feed company. A decade later, J. B. Hunt Transport, Inc. was shipping goods across the country, and the firm eventually became the largest trucking company in America. In the 1980s and 1990s, J. B. Hunt presided over a company that was earning over one billion dollars annually and employing thousands of people. Today, J. B. Hunt Transport, Inc. is headquartered in Lowell (Benton County), where Hunt made his home after retiring in 2004 until his death in late 2006.

J. B. Hunt was just one of Arkansas's many important business leaders. Sam Walton, the founder of Wal-Mart, is perhaps the best known—and certainly the wealthiest, but Arkansans have had considerable economic success in several different industries.

Among the state's many business leaders are Don and John Tyson of Springdale (Washington County), who have helped make Tyson Foods into the world's largest meat processor and supplier; Charles Murphy of El Dorado (Union County), who founded Murphy Oil after getting into the business at age sixteen and whose company operates retail gasoline outlets at Wal-Mart Supercenters throughout the country (in addition to the petroleum side of the business); William Dillard of Mineral Springs (Howard County), who in 1938 in Nashville, Arkansas, began the successful clothing store that bears his name and that has grown to become the sixth-largest department store in America and number thirty-seven of the top one hundred retailers in 2005 (according to the National Retail Federation) with 330 stores in eleven states; and brothers Jack and Witt Stephens of Prattsville (Grant County), who ran one of the largest, off–Wall Street investment banking firms in the Unites States, Stephens, Incorporated, of Little Rock (founded in 1933). Since 1986, Jack's son Warren has managed the firm. All of these business leaders have found international success while remaining close to their Arkansas roots.

Read more about Mr. Hunt in *J. B. Hunt: The Long Haul to Success*, by Marvin Schwartz (Fayetteville: University of Arkansas Press, 1992).

Log on to Learn More
http://www.encyclopediaofarkansas.net/

Section 2

Where We Learn

Guide to Reading

Terms

districts   economy

economy a system for exchange of goods and services whether through barter or buying and selling.

district a structural division used to organize and manage groups of schools.

Arkansas's Schools

The biggest factor to improving a state's economy, reputation, healthcare, image, and success is education. Without our public and private schools, universities, colleges, and museums, Arkansans would be unable to contribute to the progress of our state.

Arkansas has 310 kindergarten through twelfth grade (K–12) public-school districts, which around 420,000 students attend. There are 40 state-sponsored magnet, charter, and extended-year schools in Arkansas. There are over 33,000 public-school teachers in our state, working to provide Arkansas students with a well-rounded view of their state and a sense of pride in the possibilities it has to offer. Arkansas also has 181 private K–12 schools with approximately 31,000 students in attendance.

The largest public-school districts are the Little Rock School District (Pulaski County), Pulaski County Special School District, and Fort Smith School District. Once Arkansas students have completed their primary education, they have an opportunity to attend one of many challenging, interesting, and competitive colleges, universities, technical colleges, or junior colleges in our state as well as out-of-state schools.

Arkansas's Colleges and Universities

In 2004, there were over twenty-four thousand technical certificates and associate, bachelor's, master's, doctoral, and professional degrees (such as an MD or doctor of medicine degree) awarded from Arkansas's institutions of higher education. The most bachelor's and master's degrees in Arkansas were awarded for programs in the area of business studies,

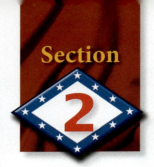

County Quest

St. Francis

Named after: St. Francis River

Chief Source of Income: Agriculture and manufacturing

Seat: Forrest City

St. Francis County was created in 1827. This area offers fertile agricultural lands and is also home to several factories. The Arkansas geographical region of Crowley's Ridge is a prominent land feature of the area. The St. Francis County Museum is located near the founding site of the town, and the federal government recently built the Forrest City Federal Correctional Complex, which provided many new jobs for area residents.

ARKANSAS COLLEGES & UNIVERSITIES

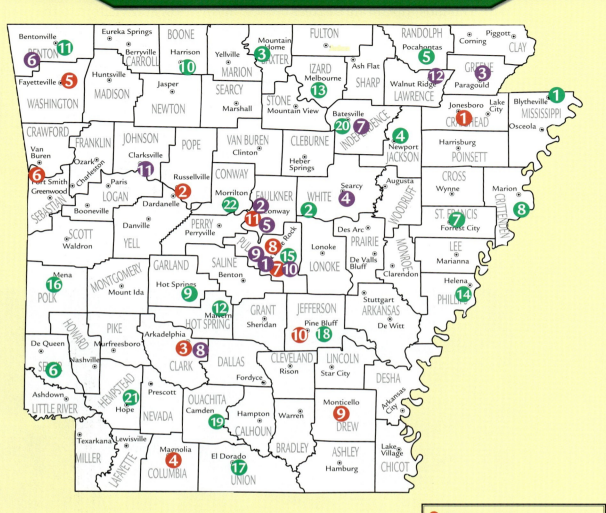

- Four-Year Public Universities
- Two-Year Public Colleges
- Private Colleges and Universities

1. Arkansas State University
2. Arkansas Tech University
3. Henderson State University
4. Southern Arkansas University
5. University of Arkansas – Fayetteville
6. University of Arkansas – Fort Smith
7. University of Arkansas – Little Rock
8. University of Arkansas for Medical Sciences
9. University of Arkansas – Monticello
10. University of Arkansas – Pine Bluff
11. University of Central Arkansas

1. Arkansas Northeastern College
2. Arkansas State University – Beebe
3. Arkansas State University – Mountain Home
4. Arkansas State University – Newport
5. Black River Technical College
6. Cossatot Community College of the University of Arkansas
7. East Arkansas Community College
8. Mid-South Community College
9. National Park Community College
10. North Arkansas Community College
11. NW Arkansas Community College
12. Ouachita Technical College
13. Ozarka College
14. Phillips County Community College of the University of Arkansas – Helena
15. Pulaski Technical College
16. Rich Mountain Community College
17. South Arkansas Community College
18. Southeast Arkansas College
19. Southern Arkansas University Tech
20. University of Arkansas Community College at Batesville
21. University of Arkansas Community College at Hope
22. University of Arkansas Community College at Morrilton

1. Arkansas Baptist College
2. Central Baptist College
3. Crowley's Ridge College
4. Harding University
5. Hendrix College
6. John Brown University
7. Lyon College
8. Ouachita Baptist University
9. Philander Smith College
10. Shorter College
11. University of the Ozarks
12. Williams Baptist College

© 2007 University of Arkansas Press

Economics and Tourism

followed by education and healthcare. The most doctorate degrees were awarded in physical therapy and education, and the most professional degrees were in law.

Four-year and two-year public, private, and technical colleges and museums are in all six geographic regions of our state. They provide not only wonderful opportunities for the students but also many jobs for citizens and often make a positive contribution to the culture, arts, and pride or sense of community in an area. Graduates of these Arkansas educational institutions often get jobs in the state's many businesses and industries, and visitors to the many museums in the state contribute to the economy.

Arkansas Museums

Arkansas is full of small, local, unique, and sometimes quirky museums, displays, and collections. This map highlights some of them around the state. Take time to do a little research and see what each has to offer. Have fun visiting the museums of Arkansas!

▶ Wal-Mart founder Sam Walton always drove a Ford pickup truck, which you can see at the Wal-Mart Visitors Center.

ARKANSAS MUSEUMS

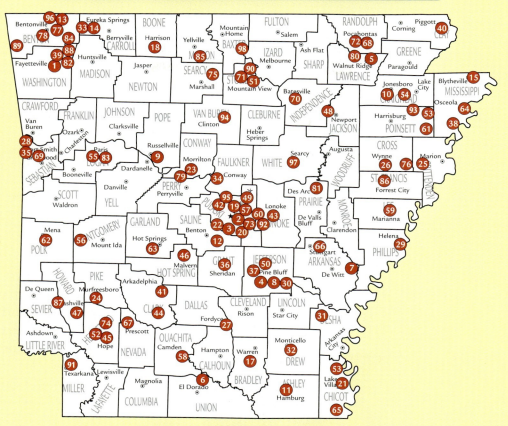

1. Arkansas Air Museum
2. Arkansas Arts Center
3. Arkansas Children's Museum
4. Arkansas Entertainers Hall of Fame
5. Arkansas Historic Wine Museum
6. Arkansas Museum of Natural Resources
7. Arkansas Post National Monument
8. Arkansas Railroad Museum
9. Arkansas River Visitor Center
10. Arkansas State Univ. at Jonesboro Museum
11. Ashley County Museum
12. Bauxite Museum
13. Bella Vista Historical Museum
14. Blue Spring Heritage Center
15. Blytheville Heritage Museum
16. Boone County Heritage Museum and Genealogy Library
17. Bradley County Historical Museum
18. Buffalo National River/Tyler Bend Visitor Center
19. Camp Robinson Entrance
20. Central High School Museum Visitor Center
21. Chicot County Museum
22. Clinton Presidential Center
23. Conway County Historical Museum
24. Crater of Diamonds State Park
25. Crittenden County Museum
26. Cross County Historical Society
27. Dallas County Museum
28. Darby House
29. Delta Cultural Center
30. Delta Rivers Nature Center
31. Desha County Museum
32. Drew County Museum
33. Eureka Springs Historical Museum
34. Faulkner County Museum
35. Fort Smith National Historic Site
36. Grant County Museum
37. Grider Field Memorial Museum
38. Hampson Museum State Park
39. Headquarters House Museum
40. Hemingway-Pfeiffer Museum
41. Henderson State University Museum
42. Historic Arkansas Museum
43. Hogan State Fish Hatchery
44. Hoo-Hoo Museum
45. Hope Visitor Center and Museum
46. Hot Spring County Museum (Boyle House)
47. Howard County Museum
48. Jacksonport State Park
49. Jacksonville Museum of Military History
50. Jefferson County Historical Museum
51. Jimmy Driftwood Barn and Folk Museum
52. Klipsch Museum
53. Lake Chicot State Park Museum
54. Lepanto Museum
55. Logan County Museum
56. Lum 'n Abner Museum and Jot 'em Down Store
57. MacArthur Birthplace
58. McCollum-Chidester House Museum
59. Marianna-Lee County Museum
60. Marisgate Plantation
61. Marked Tree Delta Area Museum
62. Mena Depot Center
63. Mid-America Science Museum
64. Mississippi County Historical Center
65. MOCCA (Museum of Chicot County Arkansas)
66. Museum of the Grand Prairie
67. Nevada County Depot and Museum
68. Old Davidsonville State Park Visitors' Center
69. Old Fort Museum
70. Old Independence Regional Museum
71. Old Mill
72. Old Randolph County Courthouse
73. Old State House
74. Old Washington State Park
75. Ozark Heritage Arts Center and Museum
76. Parkin Archaeological State Park
77. Pea Ridge National Military Park
78. Peel House Museum and Historical Garden
79. Petit Jean State Park Visitor's Center
80. Powhatan Courthouse
81. Prairie County Museum
82. Prairie Grove Battlefield State Park
83. Resettlement Village
84. Rogers Historical Museum
85. Rush Historic District
86. St. Francis County Museum
87. Sevier County Museum
88. Shiloh Museum of Ozark History
89. Siloam Springs Museum
90. Stone County Museum
91. Texarkana Historical Society and Museum
92. Toltec Mounds
93. Trumann Public Library and Museum
94. Van Buren County Hist. Society Museum
95. Villa Marre
96. Wal-Mart Visitors Center
97. White County Historical Museum
98. Wolf House

© 2007 University of Arkansas Press

Economics and Tourism

Section 3

Where We Work

Guide to Reading

Terms

annually   per capita

Big Business, Entrepreneurs, and Transport

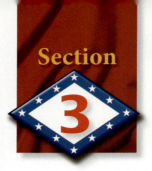

▼ The original Walton's 5 & 10 store, which was the start of the Wal-Mart chain, now houses the Wal-Mart Visitors Center in Bentonville (Benton County).

▲ The Wal-Mart Visitors Center in Bentonville (Benton County) teaches visitors about the start of what is now the largest company in the world.

Arkansas has produced many businesses and corporations that rank among the best in the nation. Five of the Fortune 500's firms in the United States were founded in Arkansas. Wal-Mart (retail), Dillard's (retail), Tyson Foods (food products), Alltel (wireless technology), and Murphy Oil (petroleum) are all headquartered in our state. To move goods provided by these companies, Arkansas has more than 1,600 freight carriers (truck lines). Four large rivers—the Mississippi, the Arkansas, the Ouachita, and the White—create a valuable waterway-transportation system for the state. Twenty-four railroad companies (three among the nation's largest) and many commercial airlines serve our state. J. B. Hunt, founded in Arkansas in 1969 and based in Lowell (Benton Country), is one of the nation's leading trucking companies.

Other Arkansas-based companies and organizations include Acxiom (technology), Allen Canning (food products), America's Car Mart (automotive), Arkansas Best Corporation (trucking), Arkansas Children's Hospital (healthcare), Aromatique (home décor), Arvest Bank Group (banking), Deltic Timber (lumber), George's (poultry), Heifer International (livestock and humanitarian development), Mountain Valley Spring Water (food products), PAM Transport (trucking), Petit Jean Meats

82 Chapter 4

ARKANSAS'S LARGEST EMPLOYERS

© 2007 University of Arkansas Press

MAJOR MUNICIPAL AIRPORTS

© 2007 University of Arkansas Press

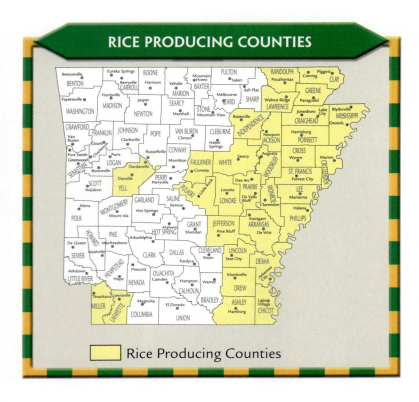

▼ Rice harvesting is completed with the help of a combine.

(food products), Producers Rice Mill (food products), Ranger Boats (recreational equipment), Riceland Foods (food products), Simmons First National (banking), Simmons Foods (food products), Sparks Health (healthcare), Stephens Group (finance), Winrock International (education and philanthropy), and Yarnell's Ice Cream (food products).

Agriculture

One of Arkansas's leading industries is agriculture. Much of the state's history is based in agriculture. In 2004, Arkansas was the number-one producer of rice in the United States, ninth in soybeans (which, among other things, are used to make cooking oil and ink), second in poultry, and fifth in cotton. Our state farmers

I Am an Arkansan

Mark Martin (1959–)

Mark Martin, born in Batesville (Independence County), is one of the top drivers competing in the National Association of Stock Car Auto Racing (NASCAR). He ranks tenth on the all-time win list. Martin's father built him a racecar in the fall of 1973. The following year, at the age of fifteen, Martin drove it in his first stock car race at a dirt track in Locust Grove (Independence County). He won on his third attempt and completed the season by winning the Arkansas State Championship held at the Benton Speedbowl (Saline County).

After succeeding in statewide races, Martin struggled to make the next step. He made his first leap into NASCAR Winston Cup competition in 1981, but it was not until 1988 that he became one of the leading drivers. He earned his first victory in October 1989 at North Carolina Motor Speedway. Since then, Martin has had thirty-five victories in the NASCAR Nextel Cup (formerly Winston Cup) division and finished second in the point standings four times.

He has finished in the top ten over 350 times in over 600 career starts. Martin has captured five championships (1994, 1996, 1997, 1998, and 2005) in the International Race of Champions series and is the series' all-time winner with thirteen victories. During much of his racing career, Martin has lived in North Carolina, but he and his wife Arlene and their five children have a home in Batesville and have opened a museum there to share his racing career and memorabilia with fans and friends.

THE ENCYCLOPEDIA OF ARKANSAS HISTORY & CULTURE

Log on to Learn More
http://www.encyclopediaofarkansas.net/

Economics and Tourism

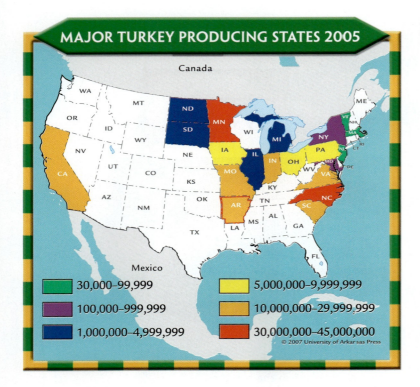

MAJOR TURKEY PRODUCING STATES 2005

- 30,000–99,999
- 100,000–999,999
- 1,000,000–4,999,999
- 5,000,000–9,999,999
- 10,000,000–29,999,999
- 30,000,000–45,000,000

© 2007 University of Arkansas Press

also raise milo (for livestock feed), wheat, corn, hay, cattle, and swine. Arkansas farmers grow grapes, strawberries, spinach, peaches, apples, tomatoes, pumpkins, and pecans. Arkansas's abundant natural resources also provide many jobs and contribute to the state's **annual** income. Those resources include bauxite, gravel, sand, oil, coal, timber (also used to make paper), natural gas, and novaculite.

The majority of Arkansans work in the trade (retail), transportation, and utility sectors. The state and federal government and manufacturing groups employ a large number of Arkansans as well. Arkansans spend the majority of their yearly income on healthcare, food, and transportation.

annual taking place yearly, once per year.

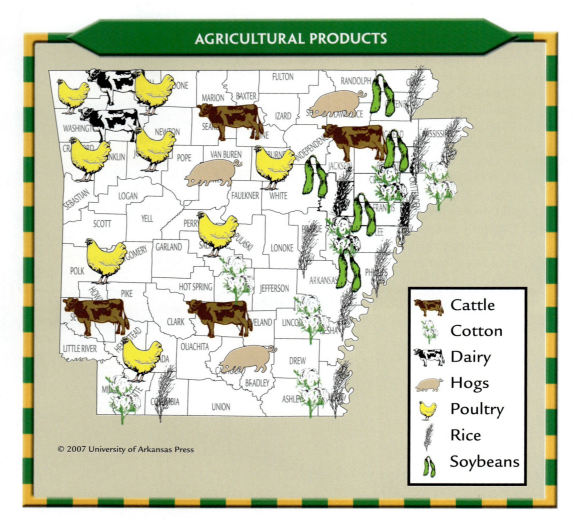

AGRICULTURAL PRODUCTS

- Cattle
- Cotton
- Dairy
- Hogs
- Poultry
- Rice
- Soybeans

© 2007 University of Arkansas Press

Arkansas's annual per capita income is $25,724. That is 22 percent less than the national **per capita** income (based on 2004 calculations). Arkansans work hard in many different jobs to provide for their families and enjoy a comfortable lifestyle. Their wages also allow them to build safe homes and care for their families and occasionally to spend some time experiencing Arkansas's natural beauty, parks, museums, and other fun activities—all of which add to our state's economic prosperity.

County Quest

Sevier

Named after: *Ambrose Sevier, former speaker of the Arkansas house of representatives and a U.S. senator.*

Chief Source of Income: *Manufacturing*

Seat: *DeQueen*

In 1828, Sevier County was created from neighboring Hempstead and Miller counties. The Cossatot (a Native American term which roughly translates to "skull crusher") River runs through the county and attracts many tourists who kayak, hike, and canoe in and around the river in the Cossatot River State Park–Natural Area. DeQueen is the childhood home of country music star Collin Raye.

per capita per unit of population, counted for each person or person by person.

I Am an Arkansan

Sonny Boy Williamson (1899–1965)

Sonny Boy Williamson became a famous blues harmonica player in 1941, appearing on the groundbreaking *King Biscuit Time* radio program on station KFFA in Helena (Phillips County). His real name was Aleck Miller, and he was born on December 5, most likely in 1899, in Glendora, Mississippi. As a child, he taught himself to play harmonica and by six or seven was performing at church events and local parties.

For more than thirty years, he was a traveling musician, performing alone and with many other famous bluesmen, such as Elmore James, Robert Johnson, and Howlin' Wolf Burnett.

For much of his career, he enjoyed the appreciation of European blues fans, touring in Denmark, Germany, and Poland, and he played several English concerts with the famous rock-and-roll bands such as the Animals and the Yardbirds. He considered moving to England permanently but eventually returned to Helena, where he regularly appeared on the *King Biscuit Time* show until his death in 1965. Williamson's life was chronicled in *Our Own Sweet Sounds* by Robert Cochran in 2005 (University of Arkansas Press).

THE ENCYCLOPEDIA OF ARKANSAS HISTORY & CULTURE

Log on to Learn More
http://www.encyclopediaofarkansas.net/

Economics and Tourism

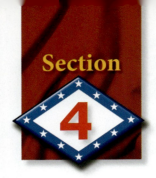

Section 4

Where We Live

Our Communities

Arkansas is made up of regions, counties, cities, towns, communities, farms, and rural areas. In 2005, there were approximately 2,800,000 people living in Arkansas. The majority of them were between eighteen and sixty-four years old. There were more females (51 percent) than males (49 percent), and 81 percent of the population was white, 15 percent black, 4 percent of Hispanic or Latino origin, 0.7 percent American Indian, 0.9 percent Asian, 0.1 percent Hawaiian or other Pacific Islander, and 1.2 percent mixed race. Almost 70 percent of Arkansans own their own home. Nearly 75 percent have graduated from high school and 16 percent from a four-year college.

▼ The Lonoke water tower in Lonoke County commemorates the lone oak for which the county was named. Lonoke is the only county seat to have the same name as the county. What is a *county seat*?

Population Trends

In 2005, Arkansas's largest cities were Little Rock (population 185,164), Fort Smith (82,481), Fayetteville (Washington County) (66,655), Springdale (Washington County) (60,096), Jonesboro (Craighead County) (59,358), North Little Rock (Pulaski County) (58,803), Pine Bluff (Jefferson County) (52,693), Rogers (Benton County) (48,353), Conway (Faulkner County) (51,999), and Hot Springs (Garland County) (37,847). Arkansas's population is ever changing, becoming more diverse, and growing rapidly.

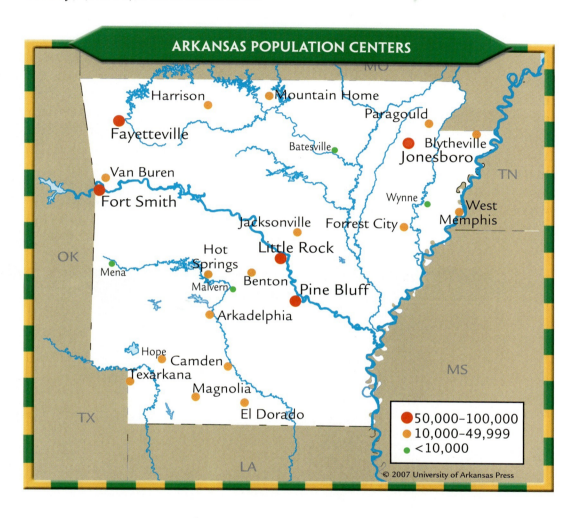

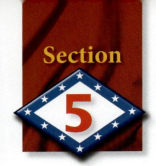

Section 5

Where We Play

Taking a Vacation Right in Your Own Backyard

There is more to do than just work and live in Arkansas. You can take a great vacation—right in your own home state! Arkansas is filled with lakes, rivers, campgrounds, shops, theaters, festivals, hotels, restaurants, hiking trails, bed and breakfasts, scenic roadways, music, and wonderful people and stories all waiting to enchant you.

The Ozarks

The Ozarks offer many natural wonders including Blanchard Springs Caverns, a system of limestone cavern and caves near Mountain View (Stone County) that you can tour; the Buffalo National River, the United States' first national river, which offers hiking, fishing, camping, swimming, and canoeing adventures; and Greer's Ferry Lake near Heber Springs in Cleburne County and Beaver Lake in

ARKANSAS FESTIVALS

1. Apple Festival–Lincoln
2. Arkansas Folk Festival–Mountain View
3. Arkansas Rice Festival–Weiner
4. Arkansas State Fair–Little Rock
5. Big Woods Birding Festival–Clarendon
6. Bikes, Blues and BBQ–Fayetteville
7. BluesFest–Eureka Springs
8. Brickfest–Malvern
9. Coon Supper–Gillett
10. Crawfish Festival–Dermott
11. Daffodil Festival–Camden
12. Diamond Festival–Murfreesboro
13. Documentary Film Festival and Institute–Hot Springs
14. Featherfest–Springdale
15. Frisco Festival–Rogers
16. Good Ole Days–Mount Ida
17. Grape Festival–Tontitown
18. Great Arkansas Pig Out–Morrilton
19. Greek Food Fest–Little Rock
20. International Butterfly Festival–Mount Magazine
21. Jump, Jive and JamFest–Texarkana
22. King Biscuit Blues Fest–Helena
23. MusicFest–El Dorado Stardaze
24. MusicFest–Hot Springs
25. Oil Town Festival–Smackover
26. Old Timers Days–Van Buren
27. On The Cotton Belt Festival–Fordyce
28. Peach Festival–Johnson Co.
29. PickleFest–Atkins
30. Pink Tomato Festival–Bradley Co.
31. Purple Hull Pea Festival–Emerson
32. Quartz Crystal Festival–Mount Ida
33. Riverfest–Little Rock
34. Riverfront Bluesfest–Fort Smith
35. Rollin' on the River–Newport
36. Scottish Festival–Batesville
37. Smoke on the Water BBQ Fest–Pine Bluff
38. Stardaze–Star City
39. Steamboat Festival–Des Arc
40. Toadsuck Daze–Conway
41. Turkey Trot–Yellville
42. War Eagle Craft Fair–Benton Co.
43. Watermelon Festival–Hope
44. Wiederkehr Wine Festival–Altus
45. Wild Duck Festival–Trumann
46. Wings over the Prairie (Duck Gumbo)–Stuttgart

© 2007 University of Arkansas Press

90 Chapter 4

Washington and Benton counties where Arkansans and tourists alike can ski, swim, fish, and camp. Visitors can fish for trout in the White and Little Red rivers in north-central Arkansas and swim and fish at Mammoth Spring State Park (Fulton County), named for a spring that flows at a rate of nine million gallons of fifty-eight-degree water per hour. If you are in the mood for music, head over to the Ozark Folk Center in Mountain View, the town that lays claim to being the Folk Music Capital of the World, where guests can watch pioneer demonstrations and listen to songs of Arkansas's past.

For another look into the past, visit Pea Ridge (Benton County) and Prairie Grove (Washington County) battlefield parks where visitors can relive Civil War history. You can walk in Sam Walton's shoes at the Wal-Mart Visitors Center and Museum in Bentonville (Benton County). Ready for shopping? Try the War Eagle Crafts Fair in Benton

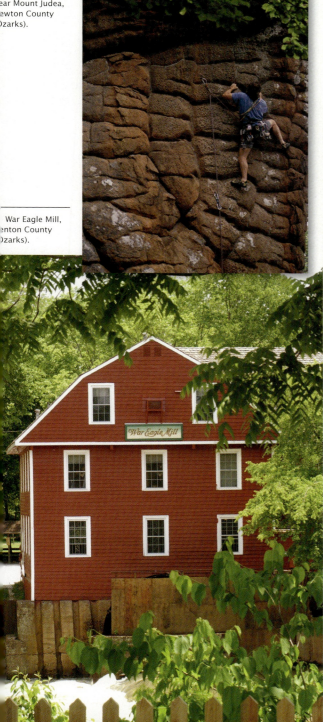

Rock climbing at Sam's Throne near Mount Judea, Newton County (Ozarks).

War Eagle Mill, Benton County (Ozarks).

County Quest

Washington

Named after: *George Washington*

Chief Source of Income: *University of Arkansas, tourism, agriculture, and manufacturing*

Seat: *Fayetteville*

In 1828, Washington County was created from Osage lands, and by the late 1820s, white settlers began to move to the area. Today, the county is one of the state's most economically prosperous and is home to a number of important businesses. Springdale is home to Tyson Foods headquarters. Fayetteville is the location of the University of Arkansas, home of the Razorbacks; the Walton Arts Center; and the annual Bikes, Blues and BBQ Festival, one of the fastest growing motorcycle rallies in the United States.

Springdale is also home to a growing Hispanic population and around five thousand Marshallese residents, the largest population outside of their native Marshall Islands. Terra Studios in Durham is home to craftsmen who created the original Bluebird of Happiness. The area is also a state leader in poultry production. The first residence of Bill and Hillary Clinton is in Fayetteville. Washington County is home to Devil's Den State Park, a major attraction for hikers, and portions of Beaver Lake.

Economics and Tourism

▲ Folk singers perform at the Ozark Folk Center, Mountain View, Stone County (Ozarks).

▶ Cotter Bridge over the White River in Baxter County (Ozarks).

▲ Fayetteville farmer's market, Washington County. (Ozarks).

County, the farmer's market on the downtown Fayetteville square, or historic Eureka Springs (Carroll County) for clothing and antiques. While in Eureka Springs, be sure to visit one of the great architectural works of our time, Thorncrown Chapel, which was designed by legendary Arkansan architect E. Fay Jones.

The Arkansas River Valley

When you have wrapped up your visit to the Ozarks, head south to the Arkansas River Valley, where you can relax in Arkansas's own wine country, with stops at the many wineries in Altus (Franklin County). If you want to get outdoors, venture to Mount Magazine State Park (Logan County), the highest point in Arkansas. While there, you can hang glide, rappel, rock climb, camp, hike, and ride horses. Mount Nebo State Park (Dardanelle in Yell County), Petit Jean State Park (near Morrilton in Conway County), and Lake Dardanelle State Park offer visitors exercise, amazing views, and plenty of outdoor fun.

History buffs can take a scenic ride on the restored Arkansas and Missouri Railroad from Springdale to Van Buren (Crawford County) and while in historic downtown Van Buren enjoy shopping, dining, and antiquing. Traveling west from Van Buren to Fort Smith, another glimpse of the past can be seen at the Fort Smith Historic Site, home to Judge Parker's hanging court. The River Valley will also lead you to the Scenic 7 Byway (which runs from near El Dorado to the Bull Shoals Lake area) and will take you on a journey through two beautiful mountain ranges—the Ozarks and Ouachitas. Once you arrive in the Ouachitas, there is even more of Arkansas to explore!

▲ Stomping grapes at the Altus Grape Festival, Franklin County (AR River Valley).

▲ Bridge over the Arkansas River at Ozark, Franklin County (AR River Valley).

◀ Altus, Franklin County (AR River Valley).

I Am an Arkansan

John Daly (1966–)

Born in California, John Daly moved with his family to Dardanelle (Yell County) when he was four years old, and he began playing golf. After attending the University of Arkansas, Fayetteville, he became a professional golfer in 1987. By 1991, he had joined the Professional Golf Association (PGA) tour. During his rookie season, he shocked the sports world by winning the prestigious PGA Championship. His long drives and unique personality won him many fans, and throughout his career he has been one of the most notorious players on tour. Even when not challenging for the lead, Daly often draws the largest crowds.

In 1995, he assured his status as one of golf's elite players when he won his second major championship, the British Open. He continued to hit the ball farther than almost every other player, averaging over three hundred yards per drive.

Throughout his career, Daly has openly struggled with smoking, alcohol, gambling, anger, and weight issues, at times damaging his game and reputation, but he has publicly acknowledged his problems and sought frequent treatment.

In 2004 and 2005, he had his most consistent years, finishing in the top ten several times and winning the Buick Invitational. A fan favorite, "Long" John Daly remains one of the most recognizable golfers in America. His autobiography, *My Life in and out of the Rough: The Truth Behind All That Bull**** You Think You Know about Me,* was published in 2006 by Harper Collins.

THE ENCYCLOPEDIA OF ARKANSAS HISTORY & CULTURE

Log on to Learn More
http://www.encyclopediaofarkansas.net/

The Ouachitas

One of Arkansas's most popular attractions, Crater of Diamonds State Park (Pike County), is found in the Ouachita region. It is the world's only diamond mine that allows treasure hunters to keep what they find! Other outdoor adventures in the Ouachitas include DeGray Lake, Lake Catherine, Lake Hamilton, Garvan Woodland Gardens, and Magic Springs and Crystal Falls Amusement and Water Park. Ready to step back in time? Hot Springs National Park, where guests can experience historic Bathhouse Row, once a retreat for gangsters, showcases the thermal springs of the area that gave the city the nicknames "America's First Resort" and the "American Spa." Hot Springs is also home to historic Oaklawn Park, one of the nation's premier thoroughbred horse-racing venues.

▼ Historic Bathhouse Row, Hot Springs, Garland County (Ouachitas).

▼ Garvan Woodland Gardens, Hot Springs, Garland County (Ouachitas).

▶ Lake Greeson, near Murfreesboro, Pike County (Ouachitas).

▼ Oaklawn racetrack, Hot Springs, Garland County (Ouachitas).

▲ The historic Arlington Hotel, Hot Springs, Garland County (Ouachitas).

The Gulf Coastal Plain

After cheering on your favorite horse, head south from Oaklawn into the Timberlands or Gulf Coastal Plain region of the state. There, you can visit Hope, the hometown of former president Bill Clinton and former governor Mike Huckabee. You can experience nineteenth-century life at the former Confederate capital of our state, Old Washington, near Hope (Hempstead County). You can continue your historic adventure by visiting the recently refurbished historic district in downtown El Dorado (Union County).

◀ The state line between Arkansas and Texas at the post office in Texarkana, Miller County (Gulf Coastal Plain).

I Am an Arkansan

Evanescence

Members of the alternative-rock group Evanescence, whose music is sometimes described as goth pop with a classical influence, are from Little Rock (Pulaski County) and they have performed around the world and sold millions of records.

After meeting in 1999 at an Arkansas summer camp, the group's founding members, Amy Lee and Ben Moody, decided to form a group. While still teenagers, they wrote and played music together and recorded several songs on their own at their families' homes. After trying out several band names, they settled on "Evanescence," which means dissipation or a disappearance, as in vapor or smoke.

The band's members include Lee as lead singer and pianist, guitarists John LeCompt and Terry Balsamo, and drummer Rocky Gray. Ben Moody left the band in the fall of 2003. Their unique blend of classically based strings with a hard-rock edge produced several top-ten hits, including "Call Me When You're Sober," "Bring Me to Life," and "My Immortal." Their songs are found on *Open Door* (2006), *Fallen* (2003), and the *Daredevil* movie soundtrack. *Fallen* rose to number three on the Billboard 200 charts in the summer of 2003 and stayed in the top ten for much of the year. Grammy Awards for best hard-rock performance and best new artist were awarded to the group in 2004. They continue to entertain music fans around the world and are among Arkansas's most successful musicians.

Log on to Learn More
http://www.encyclopediaofarkansas.net/

The area offers dining, shops, historic architecture, and theater and was recently listed on the National Register of Historic Places. The Arkansas Museum of Natural Resources in Smackover (Union County) has exhibits exploring the history of southwest Arkansas's boomtown oil days that created the diverse, dynamic atmosphere that is still in the air today.

The Mississippi Alluvial Plain

Arkansas's Delta, or the Mississippi Alluvial Plain, is east of the timberlands and runs from the northeastern corner of the state, at the Missouri border, to the southeastern reaches at the Louisiana border. In the Delta, you will find people and history as splendid and strong as the bountiful soil of the croplands. The Great River Road runs the length of the Delta, and travelers can stop and visit Lake Chicot State Park, Arkansas's largest natural lake and North America's largest oxbow lake. Arkansas Post, the state's first established European community and the state's first territorial capital, is in the southeastern area of the Delta and offers visitors a valuable museum experience, and the Louisiana Purchase Historic State Park marks the spot where all exploration and surveys of the land began. The Museum of the Grand Prairie in Stuttgart (Arkansas County) highlights Arkansas's success in the rice industry and shares Stuttgart's German heritage with visitors. Like the Ozark Folk Center in Mountain View, the Delta Cultural Center in Helena (Phillips County) focuses on the history of the Delta region and

▼ Ace of Clubs House, Texarkana, Miller County (Gulf Coastal Plain).

▲ Tourists enjoy a day of shopping in downtown El Dorado, Union County (Gulf Coastal Plain).

▶ Downtown El Dorado, Union County (Gulf Coastal Plain).

▲ Jacksonport State Park, Newport, Jackson County (Delta region).

▲ Duck hunting in Bayou Meto WMA, Arkansas County (Delta region).

▲ Cooks prepare food at the Smoke on the Water BBQ Festival, Pine Bluff, Jefferson County (Delta region).

I Am an Arkansan

Levon Helm (1940–)

Mark Lavon "Levon" Helm was a world famous drummer and singer for the rock group The Band, and his work is considered among the finest rock music ever made.

He was born near Elaine (Phillips County), the son of cotton farmers. When he was just seventeen, Helm got his first big musical break when he met Ronnie Hawkins, the rockabilly performer born in Huntsville (Madison County). Eventually Hawkins asked him to join his backing band, the Hawks, but only after Helm graduated high school.

With this group, Helm toured Canada and much of the United States. In 1965, the Hawks were asked to be the supporting band for Bob Dylan as he made his first worldwide tour. Music fans were not ready to hear Dylan's new electric sound, and the band was loudly booed at every concert. Helm left the band in the middle of the tour and returned to Helena.

By 1967, he had returned to play with the Hawks, who had settled in a large pink house in Woodstock, New York. There, with Dylan, the group recorded dozens of new songs and changed the name of the group to The Band. After releasing their first record in 1968, The Band, with Helm on drums, quickly became one of the most successful, influential groups in rock-and-roll history and was inducted into the Rock and Roll Hall of Fame in 1994. Their famous farewell concert, performed in San Francisco on Thanksgiving, 1976, was dubbed the "Last Waltz" and featured some of the most famous musicians in the country. Since the break-up of the original lineup of The Band, Helm has recorded several solo albums and has acted in several high-profile Hollywood films, including *The Right Stuff* (1983). Although he currently lives in upstate New York and survived throat cancer, he continues to make concert appearances in Arkansas and across the country with his band, the Barn Burners.

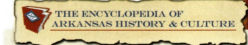

THE ENCYCLOPEDIA OF ARKANSAS HISTORY & CULTURE

Log on to Learn More
http://www.encyclopediaofarkansas.net/

Economics and Tourism

Arkansas's amazing and soulful musical roots. The stories of Delta life provided inspiration for many of the founding fathers of the blues, soul, and rock-and-roll music. Sonny Boy Williamson, Johnny Cash, Levon Helm, Charlie Rich, Chester "Howlin' Wolf" Burnett, and Jimmy Driftwood all shared in the musical ancestry of Arkansas. You can also listen to the sultry sounds of the blues at the King Biscuit Blues Festival held each year.

▲ A performer plays at the King Biscuit Blues Festival, Helena, Phillips County (Delta region).

▶ King Biscuit Blues Festival flier (Delta region).

▼ A musician plays on the street at the King Biscuit Blues Festival, Helena, Phillips County (Delta region).

▲ King Biscuit Blues Festival, Helena, Phillips County (Delta region).

Crowley's Ridge

As you travel toward the northeastern region of the Delta, visits to the White River National Wildlife Refuge near St. Charles (Arkansas County), the Parkin Archaeological State Park, Crowley's Ridge Parkway, and Forrest L. Wood Crowley's Ridge Nature Center will almost complete your trip. However, before heading to central Arkansas, you must see the Hemingway-Pfeiffer Home in Piggott (Clay County) where Ernest Hemingway wrote some of *A Farewell to Arms* while married to Arkansas native Pauline Pfeiffer. You can go to the raceway in Batesville, the town where NASCAR driver Mark Martin is from, and visit the museum built in his honor. As a last stop, head through Lepanto (Poinsett County) where scenes for the movie *A Painted House,* based on the novel by native Arkansan author, John Grisham, were filmed.

Economics and Tourism

Central Arkansas

Finally, head toward central Arkansas and the state capital and largest city, Little Rock. There, you can visit the Clinton Presidential Library and Museum, the state capitol building and grounds, the Old State House Museum, the Historic Arkansas Museum, the Little Rock Central High School National Historic Site, the MacArthur Military Museum, the River Market District, the Little Rock Zoo, and the USS *Razorback,* a 311-foot World War II submarine that was in Japan for the signing of Japan's surrender.

Arkansans have a wealth of opportunity at their doorstep—education, jobs, community, and travel. By doing well in school and working and

▶ The Old Mill, North Little Rock, Pulaski County (Central Arkansas).

traveling in our state, you too can contribute to our continued growth and prosperity. You have an opportunity to guarantee a rich and exciting future—a future that will fill history books with as much progress, drama, learning, culture, diversity, triumph, and failure as the history you are about to study. Be proud of your history, heritage, and state and enjoy learning about Arkansas.

▼ Arkansas State Fair, Little Rock, Pulaski County (Central Arkansas).

▲ Cedar Falls at Petit Jean State Park, Morrilton, Conway County (Central Arkansas).

▲ The MacArthur Museum of Military History, Little Rock, Pulaski County (Central Arkansas).

◄ The USS Razorback submarine, Little Rock, Pulaski County (Central Arkansas).

Economics and Tourism 101

Chapter Reflection

Reflective Questions

1. What are the main agricultural products (products grown or raised, not manufactured) in Arkansas?

2. What are some of the newer Arkansas crops? Why do you think our state's farmers have changed what they grow over the years?

3. What is a technology company headquartered in Arkansas? Financial? Retail?

4. For each region, list a product or tourist attraction most associated with that area:

    Ozarks

    Arkansas River Valley

    Ouachitas

    Timberlands or Gulf Coastal Plain

    Mississippi Alluvial Plain or Delta

    Crowley's Ridge

5. What do you think Arkansas's most important crop is and why? Be sure to support your answer with reasons, facts, and examples.

6. What do you think is Arkansas's most valuable natural resource and why? Be sure to support your answer with reasons, facts, and examples.

7. What roles do the rivers and lakes play in our state's economic structure?

8. Why do you think the personal annual per capita income in Arkansas is lower than that of much of the nation? What can people who want to live and work in our state and Arkansas companies do to change that?

9. If Arkansas's personal annual per capita income is $25,725 and the national average is 22 percent higher, what is the national annual per capita personal income?

10. In your opinion, how would a tourist who lives outside our state and who visits Arkansas for the first time describe what they saw (based on what you learned in this chapter and your own personal knowledge)?

Organization and Visualization

On your own paper, copy the chart below and write in the tourism attraction or feature that best matches each category. Remember, that when you compare something, you are looking for similarities. When you contrast something, you are looking for differences.

Compare and Contrast

	Ozarks	AR River Valley	Ouachitas	Timberlands	Delta	Crowley's Ridge
History or Landmarks						
Outdoor Recreation						
Shopping, Dining						
College/ Universities						
Businesses, Industries, Largest Employers						
Museums						
Airports						
State Parks						
Agricultural Products						

Economics and Tourism   103

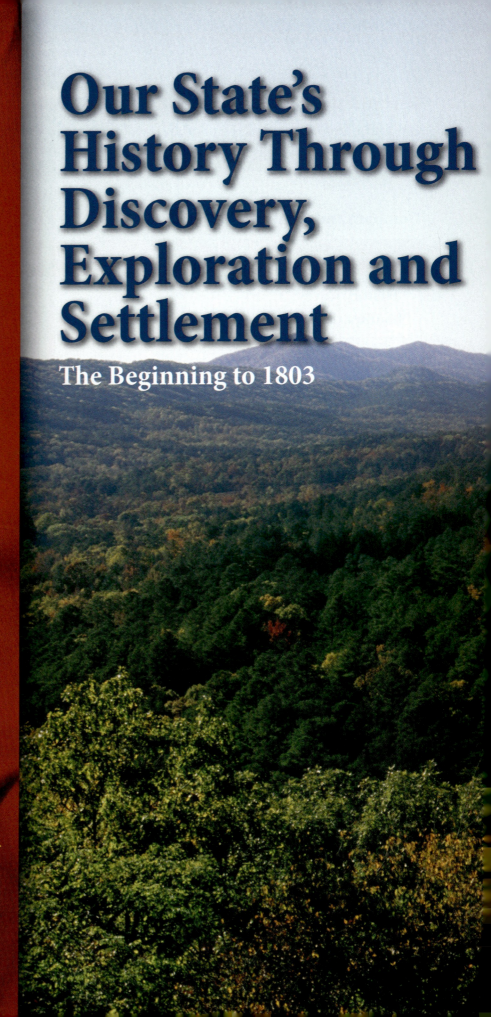

UNIT 2

Our State's History Through Discovery, Exploration and Settlement

The Beginning to 1803

Chapter 5
The First Arkansans, The Beginning to 1540

Chapter 6
Discovery, Exploration, and Settlement, 1541–1802

The lands of Arkansas ▶

Chapter 5

The First Arkansans
The Beginning to 1540

◀ The uninhabited lands of Arkansas.

Timeline

	12,500 BC	7500 BC		2500 BC	
Arkansas	**11,500 to 9500 BC** The Paleo-Indians inhabit what is now Arkansas.	**9500 to 1000 BC** The Archaic tradition begins. Indians dwell in bluff shelters, weave baskets and nets, make axes, and learn to bake.		**1000 BC to 950 AD** The Woodland tradition begins. People grow squash and learn to make pottery and a basic bow and arrow.	
United States					
World		**5000 to 4001 BC** The Egyptian calendar is developed. The earliest cities are founded in Mesopotamia (present-day Iraq).	**2500 to 1500 BC** The first libraries open in Egypt. First code of laws is written in Babylon. Potter's wheel, wheeled vehicle (cart), and weaving loom are first used.	**800 to 701 BC** Rome is founded. First Olympics are held in Greece.	

106 Chapter 5

Why Do We Study This?

Why must we study history? A rich nation deserves a rich culture, and our nation and state certainly have a complex and amazing past. Understanding concepts in history makes you a more well-rounded, complete person and teaches you how to react to various situations, based on established customs and traditions. It gives you a chance to walk in someone else's shoes and possibly better understand the struggles and victories of others.

The past is a usable, instructive tool. It teaches you how to be a thinking citizen; how to become a successful, capable businessperson; and how to analyze, interpret, and solve complex problems. It also improves reading, writing, and research skills.

History helps us as individuals and as a nation to establish an identity and to determine how best to navigate our future and not to repeat mistakes. History explains our progress and failures and is an exercise in investigation, adventure, and storytelling.

History is alive—embrace it and enjoy it. One day, your very own life experiences may be part of the records of our past.

> ### Big Picture Questions
> - In your own words, why must we as a people study history? What should it or can it teach us? Support your opinion with facts and examples.
> - What sort of evidence will historians have about us in one hundred, five hundred, or five thousand years? What will be the historical artifacts of our lives, and what will those pieces of evidence tell about our culture?
> - What are the major discoveries or advancements of our lifetime? Have they made our lives better? If so, how?
> - How do values, beliefs, and physical characteristics and attributes play a role in the development of societies? Give examples.

---

500 AD — **1000 AD** — **1500 AD**

950 to 1540 AD
The Mississippian tradition thrives. People live in large villages like small, modern-day cities, trade beautiful pottery, and conduct religious ceremonies.

800 AD
Maize (corn) is widely grown in what is now the United States.

1000 to 1100 AD
A Pueblo dwelling is built at modern-day Mesa Verde, Colorado. The city of Cahokia prospers in modern-day Illinois.

350 BC to 350 AD
Much of Greece and Asia are conquered and ruled by Alexander the Great. The Roman Empire emerges under leader Caesar Augustus. Christianity spreads after the death of Jesus.

600 to 700 AD
First books are printed in China. Mohammed dictates the Koran (central religious book of Islam).

1000 to 1100 AD
Leif Ericson, a Viking, discovers North America. *Beowulf* is written in Old English.

1250 to 1350 AD
Marco Polo journeys to China. Aztecs establish Mexico City.

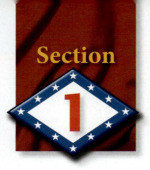

Section 1

What Is History?

Guide to Reading

Terms
AD, BC, bias, era, history, period, prehistory, tradition

People
anthropologists, archeologists, historians

history a written record of past events, people, and places.

historians students or scholars who study written records of a time or produce such records.

prehistory existing before written history.

archeologists (ARE-kee-AH-luh-jists) scientists who carefully uncover objects left behind by earlier people. Archeologists are able to judge how and when people lived by putting together the physical clues from artifacts found. Their field of study is called archaeology.

anthropologists those who study race, social relationships, culture, origin, and physical characteristics of human beings.

As defined by the *Merriam-Webster Dictionary*, **history** is "a tale or a story; a chronological, *written* record of significant events (for example, as affecting a nation or institution) often including an explanation of their causes; an established record (for example, a prisoner with a *history* of violence); a branch of knowledge that records and explains past events (for example, medieval *history*); events that form the subject matter of a history; events of the past; one that is finished or done for (for example, 'you're *history*')."

▲ A Mississippian tradition headpot from the Nodena site.

History: How Do We Know What We Know?

Learning about the past is based on gathering evidence and studying it. History usually means the study of the written records that were made by people in past times and that still exist. **Historians** are the people who think of questions about the past and then gather written evidence, judge its value, and draw conclusions from the evidence to answer their questions. The more records we have from different sources, the better we can understand the past.

The word **prehistory** usually means the time before people learned to write. Writing was invented at different times in different places, but the earliest writing dates from five to six thousand years ago. To gather evidence about the lives of people who did not write, **archeologists** and **anthropologists** look for any kind of physical evidence that might have survived, such as tools, weapons, bones, art, and parts of houses and other buildings. This kind of evidence is hard to interpret, and it cannot tell us all we want to know. A lot of what we know about the early Indians in America and Arkansas is based on such physical evidence.

108   Chapter 5

Sometimes, the written evidence we do have comes from one viewpoint, such as when the first European explorers met the American Indians (the only written records were those of the Europeans—we do not have an account from the Indians' point of view). This means we have to be careful studying prehistoric and historic evidence and be aware of possible **bias** that might reflect the opinions of the people who wrote it.

BC, AD, and the Passage of Time: What Does it Mean?

The world has many different calendars, or ways of marking the passage of years. In this book, we are using the Western calendar, which is based on the Christian tradition. In that calendar, all years are dated before and after the birth of Jesus.

For example, the year 1541 is when Hernando de Soto explored Arkansas, 1,541 years after the birth of Jesus. Sometimes that is written **AD** 1541. AD stands for *anno Domini*, Latin for "in the year of the Lord." The length of a year itself is measured by the Earth's passage around the sun (365 days).

The years before the birth of Jesus are marked **BC**, which stands for "before Christ," and are counted backwards. Thus the year 5,000 BC occurs before 3,000 BC.

In this chapter, the Western or Christian calendar is used to date events in the lives of the Indians, even though they did not use that method themselves. We do not know what kinds of calendars Indians used. They probably measured the passage of a year by observing the position of the sun at different times of the year. They most likely dated the years by great events in the history of their tribes. Many such groups of people selected a wise man to remember the group's history, repeat it to the people, and pass it on to the next generation.

The word *generation* has been used to describe the passage of time. It means the amount of time between the birth of parents and the birth of their children. For example, a grandchild would be the second generation after grandparents, and the third generation after great-grandparents. It is not a precise period of time, but a generation is usually considered to be twenty or twenty-five years.

The words **era**, **period**, and **tradition** are also used to designate the passing of an amount of time. When years are counted from a certain point in time to another, that is referred to as an era. A period is a lesser amount of time within an era. Traditions often occur in families or groups with shared or common cultures and beliefs. Traditions can include behaviors, rituals, holiday celebrations, religious beliefs, intimate language, and other customs that are passed down through storytelling and/or example. The period of time in which this type of information is shared or handed down is called a tradition.

bias (by-USS) tendency or slant toward one side of a story without considering alternative viewpoints. Unfairness, favoritism, or prejudice.

AD an abbreviation for the Latin term *anno Domini*, meaning "in the year of the Lord."

BC an abbreviation for "before Christ," used to describe the period of time before the birth of Christ.

era a certain point in time from which a number of years is determined.

period a division of time within an era.

tradition a period of time in which behavior, rituals, and/or customs are shared or passed down verbally or by example and are continuous.

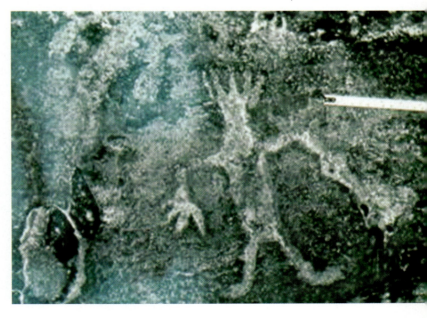

▼ Prehistoric Native American petroglyph from the Woodland period.

The First Arkansans

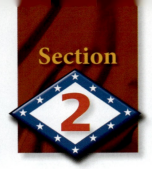

Section 2

The First People

Guide to Reading

Terms

adze, alluvial, atlatl, archeology, Delta, glaciers, goosefoot, marsh elder, sumpweed, gruel, hematite, mastodon, moats, novaculite, sloth, tapir, woolly mammoth

People

Archaic tradition, European, Mississippian tradition, Paleo, Woodland tradition

---

delta the land around the mouth of a river built up by the river as it deposits silt or soil as it empties into the sea. In Arkansas and Mississippi, the entire flatland region of alluvial soil on either side of the Mississippi River is called the "Delta."

glaciers (GLAY-shurs) sheets of snow and ice that never completely melt, even in the midst of summer.

archeology (ARE-kee-oll-O-gee) the use of historic objects and artifacts to study and/or determine the activities and lifestyles of humankind throughout history.

woolly mammoth a mammal similar to an elephant with shaggy, thick hair, and long, curved tusks.

mastodon (MASS-tuh-dahn) an ancestor of the modern elephant that lived in the Pleistocene era, or during the Ice Age.

The Paleo-Arkansans Arrive, 11,500 BC to 9,500 BC

Long before the arrival of the first Arkansans, about 600 million years ago, the land that would be called Arkansas was covered by water. Slowly, the movement of the Earth's land masses forced up mountains. About 230 million years ago, parts of the flat plain of the southwest and what would later become the **Delta** of the Mississippi gradually started to become dry land. At one time, dinosaurs roamed here, and they left their footprints in mud that would become rock.

The dinosaurs disappeared, however, and the once warm and swampy Earth turned cooler and entered a series of Ice Ages. Far to the north, glaciers formed, moved south, and then melted back to the north. The glaciers never quite reached Arkansas, but they did make the climate colder.

During the most recent advance of the **glaciers**, a bridge of land, called Beringia, connected what is now Russia with what is now Alaska. The first human beings probably came to North America over this land. Whole tribes of men, women, and children traveled together, perhaps with their dogs, following the herds of wild animals upon which they depended for food and clothing. As they spread through North America, some came to the land that would be called Arkansas. They must have had many different names for themselves, but we call them American Indians or Native Americans. The European explorer Christopher Columbus gave us our name for them much later when he came to America, because he thought he had reached the East Indies, some islands off the coast of Asia, thus the word *Indian*. Through research and scientific processes, the remains of tools, weapons, and burials can be dated to show that Indians reached Arkansas by about 10,000 BC. These early people could speak to each other but apparently did not have written languages. Evidence they left of their lives (pottery, drawings, pieces of clothing) must be reviewed to try to imagine the situation. The study of what they left behind is called **archeology**.

Indians lived by hunting animals and gathering wild plants. They shared the land with large animals such as the **woolly mammoth**, the **mastodon**, the

110 Chapter 5

▶ Fluted arrowhead points from the Paleo period.

sloth (SLAWTH) a mammal (a relative of the bear family) that lives in trees; hangs upside-down from branches, always keeping its back to the ground; eats fruit and leaves; and moves very slowly.

tapir (TAY-purr) a large, hoofed animal, weighing 350 to 900 pounds. A close relative to the primitive horse or rhinoceros. Hunted for its tough hide and meat.

Paleo early, primitive, or ancient.

alluvial (uh-LOO-vee-uhl) soils left behind by streams and rivers. The Mississippi Alluvial Plain covers much of eastern Arkansas and is referred to in Arkansas as "the Delta."

sloth, the musk ox, and the tapir. They also hunted smaller animals, birds, and fish. The people had to be strong and sturdy to live, and they must have known how to work with each other on the hunt.

They most likely lived in groups of about twenty men, women, and children. They moved frequently, following the animals, and they may have had dogs as pets. Although they did not have a lot of material things we have today, these early Indians did have important skills. They knew about fire, so they could keep warm and cook their food. They could make tools of stone, like their spear points and knives, and probably used wood and animal bones for tools, too.

By the time the Indians of the Paleo period arrived and settled, the land we now call Arkansas looked very much as it does today. One big difference was that it had a drier climate then, with less plant life and rainfall each year. Then as now, the land was divided into two major regions that differ greatly from each other, the Uplands (consisting of the Ozarks and Ouachitas [WASH-ih-tawz], and the Arkansas River Valley), and the Lowlands that include the Gulf Coastal Plain, the Mississippi Alluvial Plain and Crowley's (CROH-leez) Ridge.

The tough big-game hunters known as the Paleo-Arkansans were the first people in our state, living and working long ago. The hunters tracked game in small bands, and they depended on their intelligence as well as their pointed stones to catch their prey. One of the most impressive animals they hunted was the mastodon, a huge, shaggy ancestor of the modern elephant. Killing a mastodon would provide food for weeks and clothing for the cold winter months. We do not know very much about the people of

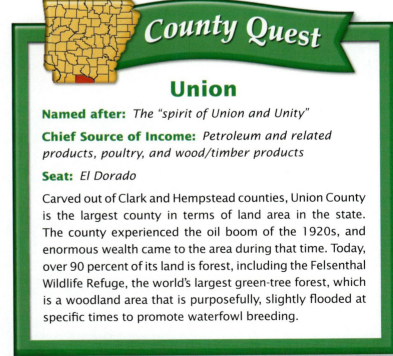

Union

Named after: The "spirit of Union and Unity"

Chief Source of Income: Petroleum and related products, poultry, and wood/timber products

Seat: El Dorado

Carved out of Clark and Hempstead counties, Union County is the largest county in terms of land area in the state. The county experienced the oil boom of the 1920s, and enormous wealth came to the area during that time. Today, over 90 percent of its land is forest, including the Felsenthal Wildlife Refuge, the world's largest green-tree forest, which is a woodland area that is purposefully, slightly flooded at specific times to promote waterfowl breeding.

The First Arkansans **111**

Archaic tradition native people of Arkansas who were less nomadic than their ancestors, baked primitive bread, and developed the atlatl and adze.

atlatl (AT-LAT-uhl or ott-lottle) a tool used by the early Indians for throwing spears.

adze (ads, like newspaper "ads") a tool similar to an ax, with the blade attached crosswise to the handle, that was used to carve a canoe out of a whole log.

the Paleo period, except that they were the ancestors of today's American Indians, and they were here as early as 12,500 years ago.

The Archaic Tradition Begins, 9500 BC to 1000 BC

Major changes in the climate made for changes in the lives of the Indians. As the glaciers retreated for the last time, the climate became warmer and drier. Large animals better suited for the colder weather, such as the mastodon, died out or moved far to the north, leaving Arkansas forests filled with smaller animals, such as bears, deer, elk, wolves, raccoons, rabbits, and squirrels.

Humans, among the most adaptable of animals, also prospered. Indians became more numerous and more widespread. Their tools and weapons were more efficient. Instead of traveling constantly on the trails of the animals, Indians could settle down part of the year. These new conditions are what archeologists call the **Archaic tradition**, beginning about 8,000 BC.

Frequently, the Archaic Indians selected ridges along the riverbanks or other kinds of high ground for their homes. The Indians dug pits in the ground for garbage dumps. To bake a kind of bread made from wild grains, they surrounded the dough with clay balls and then built a fire over them. The clay would heat up just like an oven and bake the bread without burning it. From the streams, the Indians collected mussels and crawfish to eat. Indians still traveled to the lowlands for big hunts or to areas where nuts and berries could be harvested in the fall. There, groups of Indians would meet each other and exchange ideas and ways of doing things. Thus, new tools spread quickly.

The tool called an **atlatl**, or throwing stick, made a spear go farther and faster. The **adze** allowed Indians to dig the wood out of a log to make a canoe. Some of their handmade objects, such as beads and little statues carved from stone, had decorative or religious purposes. The Indians of this time buried their dead with care, in

▼ The skeleton of a mastodon. Why was the mastodon so important to the native peoples?

112   Chapter 5

individual graves indicating the possibility of developing religious beliefs or some type of afterlife.

The Woodland Tradition Begins, 1000 BC to 950 AD

The most important change of the Woodland tradition was the widespread practice of agriculture. The Arkansas Indians either learned for themselves or borrowed from others the idea that seeds, planted in the ground and cared for, would grow and provide a secure source of food.

The first crops in Arkansas were varieties of squash and weedlike grains that we no longer eat, with names like goosefoot, marsh elder, and sumpweed. People continued to hunt, fish, and gather wild berries and nuts, but at times the crops they grew must have made the difference between hunger and comfort. Farming was responsible for many important changes. The tribe had to stay in one place to protect and cultivate the crops. A more secure food supply meant that the tribal government had to have more power, deciding when and what to plant.

In hundreds of places along the Arkansas River Valley and in the Ozark Mountains, Indian artists drew pictures on rocks. Using paint made of clay or powdered rock, or carving into the face of the rock, they drew stylized images of animals or fish. Many of these pictures can still be seen today. Some of the carvings are spiral designs, with circles inside of circles to a point in the middle. The sun or the moon probably shone on different parts of the design at different times of the year, so these drawings may have been a kind of calendar, which helped the Indians predict the seasons and the movements of animals.

In the Ozark Mountains, the Woodland Indians made their homes on the ledges and cliffs, where the rocky overhang of the cliff walls protected them from wind and rain. They built fires to warm themselves and cook the food they gathered or hunted. They also made moccasins from woven grass.

Some of their bluff shelters were so dry and protected that a few of the objects they made and stored in their shelters have lasted more than a thousand years for us to see. Some of the Indians of this period began to set aside one section of their settlement as a burial place for their dead. The graves were covered with earth, forming small hills or mounds.

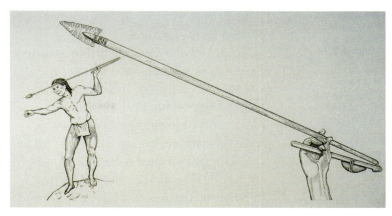

▲ An atlatl—a device to increase the speed and force of the spear.

Woodland tradition prehistoric Native Arkansans who made advances in agriculture and communication via rock art and lived in bluff shelters of the Ozark Mountains.

goosefoot, marsh elder, sumpweed plants grown during the Native periods that produced herblike leaves (goosefoot), berries (marsh elder), and oily seeds (sumpweed).

DID YOU KNOW?

Toltec Mounds State Park near Little Rock is one of the largest existing Woodland tradition sites, and visitors can see the remains of the burial mounds along with films and displays. The name "Toltec" is one example of how our knowledge of Arkansas Indians has changed and grown. When Europeans first discovered the mounds, they assumed that the Indians must have learned mound-building skills from more distant cultures, like the Toltec Indians of Mexico. We know now that the mound-building cultures in Arkansas and elsewhere in the Mississippi Valley developed out of the local Indians' own efforts. They were designed to be functional in nature, used for dwellings as well as for religious ceremonies and burials.

Log on to Learn More
http://www.encyclopediaofarkansas.net/

hematite (HEE-muh-tite) a stone native to Arkansas that is especially heavy because it contains iron.

novaculite (no-VAH-cyoo-lite) a stone native to southwestern Arkansas that is a natural sharpening tool and used to make arrowheads and other weapons or tools. Known and traded widely among the Indian tribes of the eastern United States, it is still very much in demand today.

Mississippian tradition great farmers who built plazas in the center of the village and developed sophisticated bows and arrows and pottery.

moats (motes) water-filled circular ditches surrounding a building or set of buildings, usually designed to protect the buildings from attack.

Important items were sometimes placed in the graves.

Trade among various Indian groups seems to have increased during the Woodland tradition. In some years, Indians may have had different or extra food to exchange. Arkansas Indians also had rocks, minerals, and salt sought by other tribes. **Hematite** could be used as weights for fishing nets; **novaculite** could be made into tools with a fine edge; and quartz crystal was always in demand. In return, Arkansas Indians might get seashells from the Gulf coast or copper from Indians from Missouri, Tennessee, or even from as far away as Wisconsin.

Another important addition to the Indian culture at this time was the making of pottery. At first, the clay pots had straight sides, like flower pots today. Later, the Indians began to decorate their pots with lines carved into the wet clay. The presence of pottery is important to our knowledge of Indians. Since well-made clay pots, or pieces of them, can last a long time, their remains give us a way of measuring the Indians' cultural stages and their contacts with other pottery-making Indians.

The Mississippian Tradition Begins, 950 AD to 1541 AD

The Arkansas Indian culture had grown into what we call the **Mississippian tradition** by about the year 700 AD. The population grew very large, living for the most part in villages or farmsteads. In the center of the villages would be a large open field or plaza, like a town square. At one end of the plaza would be a mound, or several mounds, built not for burials but as a place for public buildings. The buildings on the mounds were connected with religious practices, but they also housed something like government offices and served as home sites for the chiefs.

The plaza and the temple mounds were used for special occasions, when all the people from the surrounding village would gather for a meeting, a harvest festival, or a religious service. In some cases, the plaza and mounds were surrounded by wooden and earthen walls and by ditches like **moats**. The walls and ditches made the area look like a fort, and they

▲ ▶ King's Creek bowl (far right) from the Poverty Point site near the junction of the Arkansas and Mississippi rivers—the oldest example of graphic art found thus far in America.

were probably used for protection against other tribes. One of the largest temple mound cities in Arkansas was at Parkin, between present-day Wynne in Cross County and West Memphis in Crittenden County.

During the Mississippian tradition, the Indians' technical skills continued to increase. By about the eighth century, Arkansas Indians were using the bow and arrow, certainly for hunting and possibly for protection or warfare. Another great advance for Indian culture was the growing of corn, an extremely useful food and a crop originally grown only in the Americas that eventually spread throughout the world. An issue with corn was that it contains more starch (sugar) than the earlier diet of the Indians, and they began to suffer from tooth decay and other nutritional problems. However, babies could switch from milk at a much earlier stage and be fed a sort of corn **gruel** as baby food and this was positive. Children were big helpers in an agricultural society because they could help plant the seeds and care for the growing plants.

Pottery became sturdier when the Indians began mixing crushed and burned mussel shell, which contained lime, with the clay, making the pots lighter and stronger so they could be larger and more carefully shaped. Much of the pottery of this period is truly beautiful, with complex designs and intricate shapes. Some pieces are even shaped like animals.

Although we can piece together an account of the early Indians of Arkansas based on nothing more than the few objects that survive, there is still so much we do not know and probably never will. All the important questions about what these people thought about themselves, the other people they met, and the larger world will remain unknown.

This study of the Indians covers more than ten thousand years in the lives of Arkansas people over hundreds of generations. Our knowledge of these fascinating people expanded when **European** explorers and settlers begin to appear in their country, but as a consequence we generally see the Indians through the eyes of European culture.

gruel (grool) a weak or diluted cereal or porridge made with water.

European describing a person who is from the continent of Europe who is not of African or Indian (Native American) descent.

County Quest

Pope

Named after: *Gov. John Pope*

Chief Source of Income: *Trucking, agriculture, and timber*

Seat: *Russellville*

Pope County rests in the Arkansas River Valley, and its seat, Russellville, is the location of Arkansas Tech University. The Arkansas Nuclear 1 power plant is located just west of Russellville, and its six-story tower releases water vapor that can be seen for miles, particularly along Interstate 40.

The First Arkansans

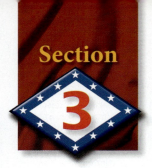

Section 3

The Historic Indians

Guide to Reading

People
Caddos
Osages
Quapaws

Places
Kappa

Caddos (ca-DOES) Native American people who lived in the southern and western parts of the state, known for family farms, mound building, personal tattooing, and the salt trade.

The first European explorers came to Arkansas around 1500. The Indians living in Arkansas during this time were organized in distinct tribes, for each of which the Europeans recorded a name. These groups of Native Arkansans are said to have lived in Arkansas during the historic period because we have these written records from the European travelers to supplement the physical remains Indians left behind. In the Red River and Ouachita valleys of the southwest lived the **Caddos**, who had productive farms. In the eastern

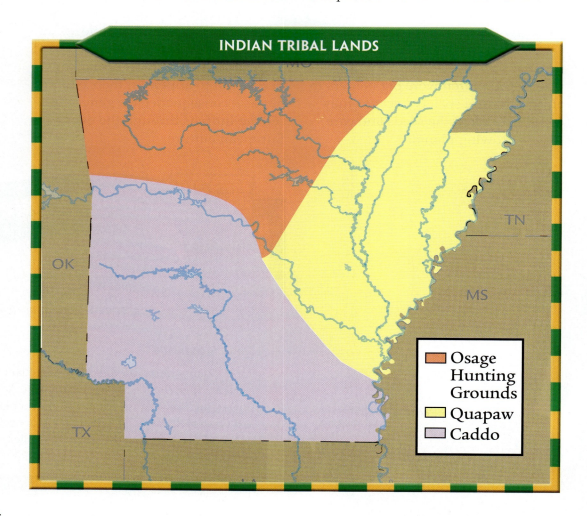

INDIAN TRIBAL LANDS

- Osage Hunting Grounds
- Quapaw
- Caddo

116 Chapter 5

part of Arkansas were the **Quapaws**, the inheritors of the temple mound traditions and the first Indians to be encountered by the Europeans. Sometime later, possibly after 1700, the **Osages** would come to dominate the northwest part of Arkansas.

The Caddos

The first records of the Caddos date back to the late Mississippian period in southwest Arkansas. One can recognize tools, pottery, and houses made by the ancestors of today's Caddo Indians. The Caddos' way of life was spread over a large region covering parts of what are now Oklahoma, Texas, Arkansas, and Louisiana.

The Caddos built mounds, too, where important leaders were buried and temples were built. The Caddos lived on small family farms rather than sharing their fields with the whole group. Each household had an outdoor fireplace for cooking with a garden nearby. The Caddos grew tobacco, which they smoked on special occasions.

▲ The clothing and headdresses pictured are typical of how the Caddo are thought to have dressed.

▲ ▶ Recreation of Caddo clothing, hairstyles, and a traditional drum.

There may have been as many as eight thousand Caddos, organized into tribes and larger groups. They had a large and complex farming culture and produced large crops of corn and beans, and they did some hunting, too.

Their houses were shaped like cones, made by setting long poles in the ground in a circle and tying them together at the top. The Caddos would cover the frame with a thick thatch made out of grass. Men wore tanned deerskins, sometimes decorated with fringes and small seeds. Women wore skirts made of woven grass or a kind of cloth made from plants. Caddo men and women thought that tattoos and body paint made them more attractive.

▲ A sketch of a Caddo mask that was used in ceremonies.

Quapaws (KWA-paws) descendants of the ancient Sioux (SOO) tribe, who moved down the Mississippi River to live in Arkansas. The name of our state comes from a translation of their name, meaning "downstream people."

Osages (OH-sajes) tribe of southwest Missouri that hunted in northern and northwestern Arkansas who sometimes had conflicts with the Quapaws and Caddos.

The First Arkansans 117

Kappa a Quapaw village.

The Caddos in Arkansas also had an important "industry," one of the first true, large-scale industries in Arkansas—making salt. The Indians poured water through sand to dissolve the salt out and then boiled the water to evaporate the moisture. When the water boiled off, little chunks of usable salt remained. The salt was widely traded, and the final product was often in the shape of a brick. Tiny bits were broken off and used for seasoning and preservation. In Clark County, one of the most important sites for the study of prehistoric salt making, the Hardman Site, has been analyzed and has provided archeologists with much of what we know today about Arkansas's first large-scale industry.

The Quapaws

Some researchers believe that the Quapaws may have begun as a branch of the large Sioux-language group of Indians of middle North America. They think that at least 350 years ago, and possibly earlier, part of this group moved south down the Ohio River valley, then down the Mississippi to the mouth of the Arkansas River.

Others believe the Quapaws were descendants of the great Mississippian tribes described by de Soto's expedition in 1542. In any case, they were the "downstream people," in their own language, the Quapaws. Others called them the "Arkansas."

The Quapaws lived in the river valleys of eastern Arkansas, along the lower Mississippi, the White, and especially near the mouth of the Arkansas River. They grew squash, beans, and corn and also fished and did some hunting. The Quapaws believed that the land should be respected and that parcels of land were not, and should not be, owned by individual people. They believed everyone should benefit from the land and have access to its bounties. Their houses, usually shared by several families, were long rectangles with curved roofs, made of wood and covered by bark. **Kappa**, the home of about four thousand Quapaws, was one of their largest villages and was located in present-day Arkansas County.

▲ Quapaw warrior painting by Charles Banks Wilson. This is the artist's idea of what warriors might have looked like around 1700.

County Quest

Monroe

Named after: President James Monroe

Chief Source of Income: Agriculture

Seat: Clarendon

The boundaries of Monroe County were drawn from neighboring Arkansas and Phillips counties. Its county seat, Clarendon, lies along the White River. Brinkley, the largest community in the county, features Low's Bridal, a well-known bridal gown design store that offers one-of-a-kind gowns and caters to clients from all over the country. The Louisiana Purchase State Park can be found along the borders of Lee, Monroe, and Phillips counties, and notes the point from which the land of the Louisiana Purchase was first surveyed in 1803.

◄ The Quapaws built long and narrow houses with curved walls and a roof covered in bark.

Because the Quapaws lived along the Mississippi and Arkansas rivers, they were usually the first Arkansas Indians seen by the European explorers. Almost always, the explorers described the Quapaws as a tall and handsome people, friendly and peaceful. Generally, they were kind to strangers and were willing to share shelter and food.

The Osages

The Osages were a hunting tribe. They did not actually live in Arkansas. Their home villages were in what is now southern Missouri. Although they did some farming in the home villages, they still relied on hunting for much of their food. They considered northern and northwestern Arkansas to be their hunting lands, and their hunting parties sometimes raided Quapaws' and Caddos' settlements.

The Osages dressed in animal skins: breechcloths and leggings for the men, shirts and dresses for the women. At home they lived in villages based on family ties. Their houses were shaped like rectangles and made of small tree trunks covered with animal skins or mats woven out of brush. Each house was home to several families. Hard work was part of the Osage way of life. Those who did not do their fair share of work, or who were considered lazy, often received less food or the leftover scraps.

It was in the lands of the Quapaws, however, that the first contact between the Indian and the European cultures began in the future state of Arkansas.

Jefferson

Named after: President Thomas Jefferson

Chief Source of Income: Manufacturing

Seat: Pine Bluff

Jefferson County was first created in 1829 and contains valuable and productive farmlands. Pine Bluff is home to International Paper Mill, as well as the University of Arkansas–Pine Bluff and the Arkansas Entertainers Hall of Fame. One of the county's largest employers, the Pine Bluff Arsenal, was established during World War II and supplied munitions to the American forces. Pine Bluff is also home to the University of Arkansas Aquaculture Extension (commonly referred to as the State Catfish Lab). Famous Arkansans Willie Hocker (the designer of the Arkansas state flag) and Geleve Grice (photographer) are natives of the county.

The First Arkansans

Chapter Reflection

Reflective Questions

1. Take a moment to think about what you have learned about the first people to live in what is now Arkansas. Discuss where they came from and their methods of survival (travel, food, shelter, family, and so on).

2. What are some of the plants, animals, and minerals that existed in prehistoric Arkansas? Discuss and describe at least two of each.

3. Building on what you have read and learned in this chapter, determine and discuss two ways of recording and remembering history (of people, places, events) *before* there was a written language.

4. List two inventions or discoveries of the Archaic Indians. Then, describe one in a paragraph or story using words and describe the other using illustrations.

5. What was the most important change in Indian life during the Woodland tradition?

6. What kinds of things did the various Indian tribes trade? Name at least two.

7. Create a diagram or a blueprint of a Mississippian tradition village. Discuss and describe the function and purpose of the mounds.

8. The introduction of corn had good and bad effects. What were they? What food products have a similar impact on our health today? Defend your choices with reasons, facts, and examples.

9. In which of the six geographic regions of our state did the Caddos primarily settle?

10. Salt was very important to the Caddos' way of life. Identify three specific reasons why it was valuable.

11. Discuss the reason why the Quapaws were known as the "downstream people."

12. List the ways in which the Quapaws obtained their food.

13. What was the relationship of the Osages to northwest Arkansas? Did they live in northwest Arkansas?

14. If you had to choose one group of the seven Native Arkansans with which to live, who would it be and why? Be sure to use reasons, facts, and examples to support and discuss your opinion.

Organization and Visualization

What were the four prehistoric periods or traditions of Arkansas and the three historic Indian tribes of Arkansas? How were they alike? How were they different? To respond to this question, copy and complete the graphic organizers below on your paper. Be sure to include as many facts as possible for each group. You may use your book and your notes. Consider things such as time period, food, shelter, movement, family structure, trade, religion, weapons, and death when organizing your information.

Prehistoric Native Arkansans

	Time Period	Food	Shelter	Movement	Towns/ Family	Trade	Religion	Death	Weapons/ Tools
Paleo									
Archaic									
Woodland									
Mississippian									

Historic Native Arkansans

	Time Period	Food	Shelter	Movement	Towns/ Family	Trade	Religion	Death	Weapons/ Tools
Caddo									
Quapaw									
Osage									

HisStory, HerStory, YourStory, OurStory...

1. Come up with your own definitions for the words *legend*, *myth*, *story*, and *fable*. These were ways in which history was passed down from generation to generation in prehistoric times. Is there a legend, myth, story, or fable that is specific or unique to your family? If so, please describe and share.

Telling an Arkansas Story— The Written Word

2. Write two or three sentences that correctly assign chronological order to each of the seven prehistoric and historic Native Arkansan groups. You must include at least one of the following words in each of your sentences: *first*, *then*, *before*, *next*, and *last*.

The First Arkansans

Chapter 6

Discovery, Exploration, and Settlement
1541–1802

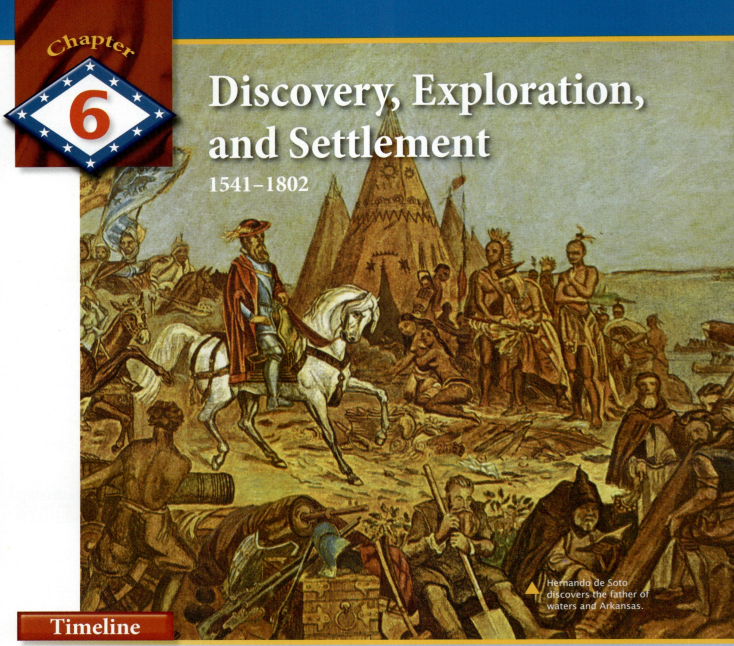

Hernando de Soto discovers the father of waters and Arkansas.

Timeline

	1540	1600	1650	1700
Arkansas	**1541** Hernando de Soto and his Spanish expedition cross the Mississippi River into Arkansas and explore for months.		**1673** A French priest and an explorer, Father Jacques Marquette and Louis Joliet, travel the Mississippi River as far south as the Quapaws' land in Arkansas.	**1682** René Robert de La Salle formally claims land that includes Arkansas as the property of the King of France.	**1686** Henri de Tonti establishes Arkansas Post as a French fort and trading post.
United States		**1603** Jamestown is founded by the English in the Virginia colony.	**1619** The first African slaves are introduced into English America.		
World		**1558–1603** Elizabeth I reigns as the Queen of England, and Shakespeare writes *Hamlet*.			

122 Chapter 6

Why Do We Study This?

The effect that European explorers and settlers had on Native Americans and on Arkansas from 1541 to 1803 is part of a very broad picture. All over the world, Spain, France, and England were competing with each other to dominate newly discovered lands and peoples. An area of major importance to these nations was North America, including the Mississippi River valley where Arkansas is located.

Through a revolution, a new nation was established as the English colonies in North America became the United States of America. The leaders of the new United States understood the value of the land that all those other nations had struggled over.

It is important that we reflect upon and analyze this time in our state's history to understand the bravery and drive of our ancestors to change and develop the wild frontier known as Arkansas. They faced struggles that are similar to many in the modern world, and they had to work to build relationships with the Native Arkansans, who were different and unknown to them, just as we have to peacefully coexist with people who have beliefs and customs that are different from ours.

BIG PICTURE QUESTIONS

- What is a legacy? Does everyone leave behind a legacy? Is a legacy positive, negative, both, or neither? Support your opinions with facts and examples.

- Identify a living person whom you believe will have a lasting legacy and discuss why you chose that person. What will the legacy be? Describe and explain.

- What types of current or modern-day exploration are seen in our state? For what reasons do we still explore today? What are the unexplored frontiers of the modern world? Will there come a point in the future when there is nothing left to be explored or discovered? Why or why not? Summarize your thoughts and reflections on these questions into a concise response.

1720 — **1750** — **1780** — **1800**

1717 Scotsman John Law unsuccessfully attempts to develop, sell, and colonize Arkansas Post without ever having traveled there.

1719 Bernard de la Harpe explores the Arkansas River and names it "Little Rock."

1783 The only battle in Arkansas connected with the Revolutionary War takes place near Arkansas Post.

1775 The American Revolutionary War begins.

1776 The Declaration of Independence is written and signed.

1787 The United States Constitution is written, and the Northwest Ordinance, which banned slavery in the areas north and west of the Ohio River, is passed.

1789 George Washington becomes the first president of the United States.

1793 Eli Whitney invents the cotton gin.

1800 Thomas Jefferson is elected president of the United States.

1756–1763 The French and Indian War, or Seven Years' War, is fought between France and Great Britain (England).

1796 The population of China reaches 275 million. The population of Europe is close to 185 million.

Discovery, Exploration, and Settlement

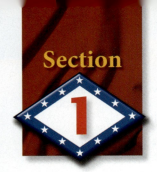

Section 1

The First Explorers

Guide to Reading

Terms
calumet
coat of arms
crude
Great Red River Raft
legacy
savages
trade

Events
Renaissance

People
Casqui

Places
Indies
Louisiana

Renaissance (REHN-uh-sahns) "rebirth"; a surge of creativity in Europe resulting in artistic, scientific, and literary achievement brought on in part by rediscovery of Greek and Roman cultures and accomplishments. It began around 1400 in Italy and continued through the Elizabethan era of the early 1600s in England.

trade the buying, selling, or bartering of goods for profit or benefit.

Indies lands and islands of southeastern Asia including India, Indochina, also called the East Indies.

Europeans in the Americas

Around 1500, European ideas, culture, and ways of life began to spread all around the world. These European influences would dramatically affect the Indian cultures in what is now North America, the United States, and Arkansas. Though they did not know it, the Indians were about to have a significant role in the struggle for control of the newly discovered continent.

The people of Europe were forming new ideas and new ways of doing things. The burst of creative activity called the Renaissance had made people curious about the world. Technology was changing rapidly: ship design and tools for navigation allowed for longer voyages, firearms made for easier conquests, and the printing press helped to spread news quickly. Spain, France, and England became powerful nation-states and had strong kings and queens. They were now able to organize and carry out large-scale plans to explore and colonize the New World.

These nations competed with each other for power and influence. Differences in religion in Roman Catholic and Protestant nations heightened the rivalry. Trade was growing more important as a way for individuals and their nations to become rich. Establishing a sea route to Asia was of vital importance to European countries because Asia provided sought-after goods like silk, tea, and spices.

This was the time of Christopher Columbus. He was a skilled Italian ship captain, explorer, and navigator. Columbus was convinced that he could open a new trade route to the Indies by sailing straight west from Europe. He thought he could sail around the world to the coasts of India and China, countries on the Asian continent.

The king and queen of Spain, Ferdinand and Isabella, backed his voyage, and in 1492, his three ships touched what we now know as the islands of the Caribbean. Columbus was convinced he had found the Indies (the reason he called the people he met "Indians"). He made several more voyages trying to find the mainland of Asia.

We now know that Columbus had made a more amazing discovery than he realized. He had found two entire continents never before known to

124 Chapter 6

Europeans. The European explorers wanted to extend the power of their nations, spread their religion, and find wealth for themselves and their rulers. Following the motto: "for glory for God, and for gold," explorers from the European nations began to move through the Americas.

Although the explorers were curious about the Indians they encountered, Europeans did not recognize or understand the achievements and success of the well-adjusted Indian cultures. Because the Indians lacked the technology of Europeans, were not Christians, and had a different economic system, the Europeans called them all **savages**. To the Europeans, that meant they could take the Indians' lands and goods, make slaves of them, or even kill them for no reason.

However, the Europeans' most significant impact on the Indians was the spread of diseases that often proved to be deadly. Smallpox, measles, and influenza (the "flu") had been common diseases in Europe for centuries, and the people there had some natural resistance to them. These diseases were unknown in the Americas, however, and the Indians had no defenses against them.

The Quapaws of Arkansas, for example, may have numbered in the tens of thousands when they first met Europeans. Two hundred years after that first contact, there were only about 1,500 Quapaws. When they left Arkansas for good, around one hundred years later, the tribe had approximately 500 members. Although many other things affected them, European diseases probably took the most lives.

De Soto Comes to Arkansas

The Spanish, traveling from the Caribbean Sea and Florida, were the first Europeans to set foot in Arkansas.

◀ Hernando de Soto, a Spanish explorer, is shown riding a horse.

In 1539, Hernando de Soto left Florida with six hundred men including some African slaves, two hundred horses, hogs, and a pack of fighting dogs. His main reason for the expedition was to gain riches—gold.

They had a long, hard journey. De Soto and his men often dealt with the Indians ruthlessly. They fought with some tribes and killed at least four

savages rude, unmannerly, brutal, uncivilized persons.

Hot Spring

Named after: *The natural thermal springs within its boundaries*

Chief Source of Income: *Manufacturing*

Seat: *Malvern*

The timber industry has played a large part in Hot Spring County history. Malvern is known as the "Brick Capital of the World" and is the home of Acme Brick. Tourists and outdoor enthusiasts are drawn to nearby Lake Catherine, the Ouachita River, and the Rockport Ledge whitewater area, known for its great kayaking.

Discovery, Exploration, and Settlement

thousand Indians in battle. They took captives whenever they needed laborers. Through warfare, disease, and accidents, de Soto's group grew smaller as the trip grew longer.

Two years after they started in 1541, de Soto and his men reached the banks of a huge river. In Spanish, de Soto called it the *Rio Grande,* or the "Great/Large River." Later, it would take on the Indian name that means the "father of waters," or the Mississippi River. De Soto stood on the east bank in what is now the state of Mississippi. Across the broad and swift river, he gazed upon what is now Arkansas.

▲ Hernando de Soto.

De Soto ordered his men to build rafts for the crossing. As the Spaniards were working, unfriendly Indians came from the other bank in a fleet of two hundred canoes and showered them with arrows, no doubt frightening the Spanish. But de Soto's men finished their four big rafts and, after a rough crossing on the fast-running river, made it to Arkansas. It was June 28, 1541.

There are four different accounts of de Soto's journey, three of them written during and immediately after the journey by men who actually traveled with him. The fourth was written many years later and was primarily based on interviews and memories. Each described land features and Indian towns. It has been determined that de Soto landed somewhere north of modern-day Helena, Arkansas (Phillips County), and south of modern-day Memphis, Tennessee.

Once on the west side of the river, thousands of Native Arkansans were waiting. It is still uncertain exactly which tribe or tribes they were. The Spanish records describe them in ways that make them seem much like the

DID YOU ? KNOW?

Did you know that according to legend, some of the wild pigs brought for food for de Soto and his men got loose during the expedition and became the ancestors of the wild razorback hog?

These "razorbacks" earned their name because they have a high backbone covered with hair, and they have a very aggressive temperament. This animal was viewed as having the potential to be hostile or vicious if challenged.

The original "wild boar" came to the Americas with Christopher Columbus. Eventually, they began to wander the countryside and towns, and residents would trap them for food or to sell. In modern Arkansas, wild hogs are considered wild-game animals to be hunted and can be found in over fifty Arkansas counties.

Wild boars are smart, quick, and highly aware of their surroundings and any possible danger. They are known to be ready to attack when cornered. They are most often in motion, even when eating, and can achieve speeds of thirty-five miles per hour.

Problems with wild hogs are numerous. They destroy agriculture and plant life, eat small animals, and can transmit diseases to other animals. There is even recorded evidence in Arkansas of wild hogs spreading disease to humans as well.

Despite the problems hogs cause, they provide great hunting opportunities for the expert hunter and have provided our state with a legendary "tale" of our Razorbacks. Go Hogs, Go!

Log on to Learn More
http://www.encyclopediaofarkansas.net/

I Am an Arkansan

Casqui (1491?–?)

In the 1500s, Casqui was a Native American chief who ruled a portion of northeast Arkansas. Casqui was the earliest Arkansan about whom we have historical records. In the journals of the de Soto expedition, his name was written as *Casqui, Casquin,* or *Icasqui.* The explorers used his name to refer to him, the town in which he resided, and the area over which he ruled.

In summer of 1541, de Soto's expedition crossed the Mississippi River into Arkansas, and as they traveled, they heard of two chiefs in what is now northeast Arkansas: Casqui and Pacaha. As the explorers moved north, they entered the land of Casqui. Residents of his outlying towns sent notice to Casqui that foreigners were approaching. After hearing of the approach of the Spanish, Casqui and his tribe embarked on a walk of great distance to meet them—bringing gifts of food, clothing, and animal hides to welcome de Soto.

According to writings from de Soto's crew, Casqui believed that de Soto had come from heaven. Casqui asked de Soto to end the drought and also brought two blind men to be healed by him. De Soto declined to heal the men. Some say de Soto did pray for rain for Casqui and that it actually rained in the following days.

Very little is known about Casqui himself. One account suggests that in 1541, he was about fifty years old. When the de Soto expedition moved westward after about a month in the area, Casqui's name was never mentioned again, and no other information exists about him, the remainder of his life, or his legacy.

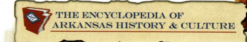

THE ENCYCLOPEDIA OF ARKANSAS HISTORY & CULTURE

Log on to Learn More
http://www.encyclopediaofarkansas.net/

◀ Many believe this is what the noble leader Casqui looked like when his village was visited by de Soto. Today, you can visit the Parkin Site, on the St. Francis River in Cross County.

Discovery, Exploration, and Settlement

Casqui (cass-KEE) a Native American chief who ruled over an area in northeast Arkansas in the 1500s.

temple mound builders of the Parkin site. If they were the Parkin mound builders, they must have moved or died from exposure to European diseases around one hundred or so years after the Spanish visit. The Indians who greeted de Soto and his men were friendlier than those who had attacked with arrows from canoes. De Soto and his men followed the Indians' directions to a large town hoping the gold they were looking for would be there. De Soto's group noted in their records that they moved north past large, established villages and fields of corn.

Eventually, he arrived at the Native American village that was the home of the chief **Casqui**. They were a group of Indians living around a temple mound settlement. De Soto stayed for three days in the chief's house, located high on one of the mounds. When the chief asked de Soto if his god could make it rain, de Soto built a Christian cross as tall as a tree on one of the mounds. The Catholic priests who traveled with him performed a religious service. De Soto's men wrote that fifteen thousand Indians watched. They also wrote that it did actually rain a few days later, making de Soto appear godlike and somewhat like a powerful "chief" to the Indians.

Still hunting for gold, de Soto explored eastern Arkansas, traveling some distance north up the White River, then west. Some modern historians and archaeologists have suggested that his route went deep into the Ouachita Mountains and then circled back to the Arkansas River. It was once thought that de Soto's expedition spent the winter somewhere near Camden, but it is more likely that de Soto and his men were closer to what is now Little Rock.

At winter's end, they followed the Arkansas downriver, with plans to reach the Gulf of Mexico. On May 21, 1542, de Soto died from a fever somewhere in

▶ Chief Casqui leads a greeting ceremony. Do you think the people behind him were arranged in a specific order? Why or why not? If so, how?

◀ The Great Red River Raft.

modern-day Chicot County. Afraid of what the Indians might do if they learned that their white "chief" was dead, his men hid his body and carried it with them until they reached the Mississippi River, probably at a location near present-day Helena. There, they secretly slipped de Soto's coffin into the great river he had discovered, and it floated away.

Over the course of the next year, de Soto's remaining men tried to reach Mexico. Traveling through Caddo Indian country, they had many battles with the fierce and crafty warriors. According to modern evidence, they followed the Red River southward. However, they were probably prevented from continuing by the **Great Red River Raft**, and so they headed west.

From there, they went deep into Texas, about as far as modern-day Dallas. But the land was bare, harsh, and empty, and they had trouble finding enough food to survive. Instead of going on to Mexico, they retraced their steps all the way back to the Mississippi around Helena. There, they built **crude** boats and escaped downriver to the Gulf of Mexico.

After three years of travel, which included a summer and winter in Arkansas, the men of the expedition were tired, sick, and frustrated. About three hundred men and twenty horses were left of the original expedition group of six hundred people and two hundred horses. They had recorded seeing towns of four hundred houses and thousands of Indians, piles of stored grain, and wonders

Great Red River Raft a huge tangle of logs, mud, and brush that accumulated over the centuries in the Red River that greatly impeded travel until its removal in the mid-nineteenth century.

crude primitive, basic, uncultivated simplicity; not sophisticated.

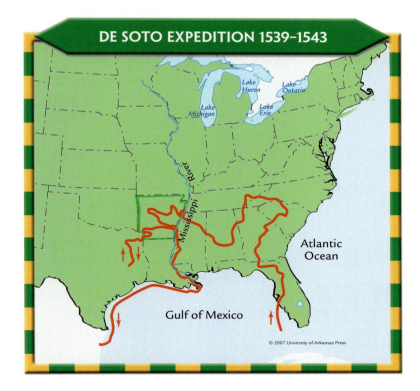

DE SOTO EXPEDITION 1539–1543

Discovery, Exploration, and Settlement

A Day in the Life

Should We Eat It? A Day of Discovery with de Soto and His Men

As the European explorers moved through the Americas, they were amazed to find many kinds of plants and animals that did not exist in Europe.

Here is the way a man traveling with Hernando de Soto described a fish that the Indians caught in the waters of Arkansas:

> "There was a fish which they called bagres; the third part of it was head, and it had on both sides the gills, and along the sides great pricks like very sharp awls. Those of the kind that were in the lakes were as big as pikes; and in the river there were some of a hundred and of a hundred and fifty pounds weight and many of them were taken with the hook."

Recognize it? De Soto and his followers had just met their first catfish.

Sarah M. Fountain, *Authentic Voices: Arkansas Culture, 1541–1860* (Conway: University of Central Arkansas Press, 1986), p. 9.

---

like natural hot springs, but they had not discovered gold.

The Spanish mission of de Soto was ultimately considered a failure. They left no permanent settlements in Arkansas or anywhere else in the Mississippi valley. It is believed they spread European diseases among the Indians, killing many, causing severe depopulation in the region, and never discovering treasures or riches. In the end, de Soto left a **legacy** of destruction, death, and disappointment.

The French in Arkansas

It would be another 130 years before Europeans again visited Arkansas. Meanwhile, Europeans continued to fight for control of the newly discovered American continent. The Spanish continued to rule Mexico, the southwestern part of the North American continent, Florida, and parts of the Gulf coast. The French expanded their control over Canada, founding Quebec in the early 1600s. Also competing in the race for North America, the English began creating colonies in Virginia in 1603 and in New England in 1620 along the eastern seaboard.

The French settlements usually included small bands of men who were soldiers, priests, traders, and trappers. Since they did not have enough manpower to actually conquer the Indians, the French tried to make friends with them. These friendships made the fur trade more successful.

In 1673, two Frenchmen in Canada planned a voyage down the Mississippi River. Father Jacques Marquette (ZHAHK mahr-KET) was a Roman Catholic priest, who hoped to convert the Indians to the Christian faith. Louis Joliet (LOO-ee ZHOL-yay) was a fur trapper and trader, interested in new ways to trade. Both hoped, like many of the early explorers, to also find gold or a water route through North America to the Indies.

In two big canoes, with five other men and a supply of food, Marquette and Joliet

legacy something passed down by an ancestor or someone or something from the past; the remembrance or impact left by a person, place, thing, or event.

MARQUETTE AND JOLIET EXPLORE THE MISSISSIPPI

◀ Marquette and Joliet (France) Explore the Upper and Middle Mississippi 1673.

set out down the river. The Illinois Indians had given the Frenchmen a long-stemmed pipe made of red stone, called a **calumet** or peace pipe, that would serve as a type of passport and a guarantee of safe travel. Marquette and Joliet showed it several times as they made their way downstream.

When they reached Arkansas, the Quapaws, possibly living in the same towns de Soto had visited much earlier, met them. The Quapaws were friendly, sharing their abundant food with the Frenchmen. By that time, the Quapaws had European hatchets, knives, and beads acquired in trade from other Indians, but they did not have guns. Marquette and Joliet learned that they were only about ten or twelve days from the mouth of the Mississippi. They realized that the Mississippi did not empty into the Pacific Ocean or the Gulf of California and that they were getting closer to Spanish lands, which they feared to be dangerous since the French and Spanish were competitors.

Marquette and Joliet decided to go back to Canada. After the long trip paddling upstream, they prepared a map

calumet (CAL-yoo-MET) an Indian pipe made of stone and signifying peaceful intentions.

▲ Jacques Marquette.

▲ Louis Joliet.

Discovery, Exploration, and Settlement

Louisiana the French name given to lands claimed by La Salle, chosen in honor of King Louis XIV.

coat of arms pictorial symbols forming a design that represents an individual or family, usually royalty. They are generally displayed on a shield or embroidered onto a flag or piece of clothing.

and wrote a report of their trip. It was written from memory because Marquette had lost his original notes when his canoe tipped over. Their report designated a name to the future state. They called the people they had met and their land "Arkansas" based on the French translation of the Illinois Indian word for "Quapaws," (meaning "downstream people").

Marquette and Joliet's journey inspired another Frenchman to explore as well. René Robert de La Salle (luh-SAL) had been born into a wealthy family in France, but he had gone to Canada as a young man to enter the fur trade. He had visions of a large expedition that could secure the entire Mississippi valley for France and even challenge Spain for control of the mouth of the river.

With fifty men, La Salle headed down the Mississippi in 1682, nine years after Marquette and Joliet. The group included La Salle's lieutenant, Henri de Tonti (OHN-ree day TOHN-tee). De Tonti was an Italian by birth, and sometimes his name is spelled "Henry de Tonty." La Salle also visited the same Arkansas towns de Soto, Marquette, and Joliet had and was met with a friendly reception. Near the Quapaws' village of Kappa (Arkansas County), La Salle informed the Indians that he claimed the entire Mississippi River valley in the name of the king of France, King Louis XIV, and called it **Louisiana**. La Salle first promised the Quapaws that France would protect them against their enemies, like the Osages. In return, he asked the Quapaws to allow him to place the seal of the king of France on their land. To La Salle, that meant the king of France would own the land.

To complete the bargain, La Salle arranged a ceremony. First he formed his fifty men into two companies, one headed by him and the other headed by his assistant Henri de Tonti. Then the two companies marched to the plaza, or central area, of the village, carrying with them a tall pole bearing a cross and the **coat of arms** of Louis XIV. They marched around the plaza three times, singing hymns and psalms. They stopped, fired their guns, shouted *"vive le roi"* ("long live the king"), and planted their pole in the ground.

Then La Salle, speaking in French, made the long formal announcement:

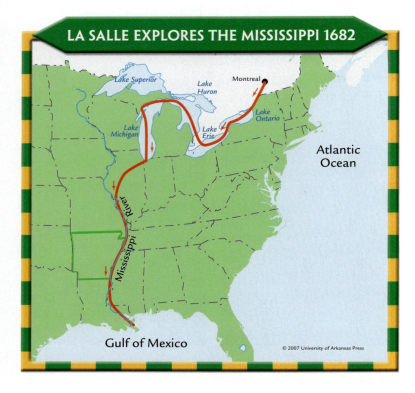

LA SALLE EXPLORES THE MISSISSIPPI 1682

> On behalf of the very high, very invincible, and victorious prince Louis the Great, by the grace of God, King of France and of Navarre, the fourteen of this name, today, the 13th of March, 1682, with the consent of the nation of the Arkansas assembled at the village of Kappa and present in this place, in the name of the king and his allies, I . . . have taken possession in the name of His Majesty . . . of the country of Louisiana and of all the nations, mines, minerals, ports, harbors, seas, straits, and roadsteads, and of everything contained within the same. . . .

Morris S. Arnold, *Unequal Laws Unto a Savage Race: European Legal Traditions in Arkansas, 1686–1836* (Fayetteville: University of Arkansas Press, 1985), 3.

The French shouted some more, fired their guns again, and it was done. By their standards, the French owned Arkansas and all of Louisiana. The Quapaws, who probably did not understand a word of La Salle's speech in French, must have thought it was all great fun and totally meaningless. The Indians most likely thought La Salle's action was a strange way to establish control or power—to leave behind only a tall painted pole with the king's coat of arms on it.

From Arkansas, with two Quapaw Indians as his guides, La Salle went all the way to the mouth of the Mississippi. There, La Salle repeated his claim on the entire river valley for his king. He had determined that the Mississippi did indeed empty into the Gulf of Mexico, ending the belief that the river would provide a water route to the Indies.

With grand plans for establishing a city at the mouth of the Mississippi to control the river, La Salle went back to France to prepare an even larger expedition for 1684. He planned to sail by ship to the mouth of the Mississippi and then head up the river. At the same time, he planned for his assistant de Tonti to sail down the river from Canada to meet him.

Unfortunately for La Salle and the country of France, he missed the mouth of the Mississippi. When his ship headed toward Texas, it got caught in a storm and ended up wrecked along the coast. La Salle went ashore with the goal of returning to the Mississippi River by land. But as his small expedition headed east, some of the men, tired, frightened, and fearful that La Salle had failed as their leader and guide, murdered him on March 19, 1687.

▲ La Salle taking possession of land at the mouth of the Arkansas River, 1682. Describe what you think La Salle's men were discussing as they disembarked and stood on the shore.

La Salle left a somewhat more positive legacy in Arkansas than did de Soto. He opened the waterways for exploration, was the first to attempt to establish a permanent European settlement in the area, claimed land for France, and built positive and trusting relationships with the Indians—especially the Quapaws of Arkansas—who made friends with the French to obtain firearms and support to face their enemies. The French also traded goods with the Quapaws and married them. It was a useful relationship for both the Quapaws and the French, all brought about by the contact made by La Salle.

▼ An artist's rendering of La Salle claiming land for France by planting a pole with the king's coat of arms upon it. He named the land "Louisiana" in honor of King Louis XIV of France. What would you imagine were the Indians' reactions to La Salle and his claims?

Discovery, Exploration, and Settlement **133**

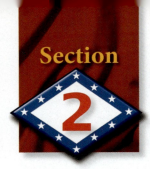

Section 2

Arkansas Post

Guide to Reading

Terms
buckskins
confluence
dogtrot
loo
reel

Events
French and Indian War
Revolutionary War

People
Chickasaws
John Law

Places
Arkansas Post
Oil Trough

Arkansas Post the first and most important European establishment in Arkansas. From 1686 to 1821, it served as the local governmental, military, and trade headquarters for the French, the Spanish, and finally the United States.

De Tonti

De Tonti, La Salle's lieutenant, waiting near the site that would later become St. Louis, was worried after hearing nothing from La Salle for two years. He feared La Salle would not arrive at their meeting place. De Tonti set out to find his commander. Traveling as far as the Quapaw towns where the Arkansas River meets the Mississippi River, de Tonti decided to settle down there until La Salle arrived. La Salle had given de Tonti the right to claim land for himself, so he decided to claim the land around the mouth of the Arkansas River.

In 1686, de Tonti established his fort and trading post at the mouth of the Arkansas and named it "Poste aux Arkansas," or **Arkansas Post**. Finally, de Tonti gave up on La Salle and headed back to Canada, and eventually he returned to France. But he left six of his men at Arkansas Post. That modest beginning in Arkansas was the first permanent European settlement on the western bank of the Mississippi River.

De Tonti did not find out what happened to La Salle until he got back to France. In the meantime, the few survivors of the La Salle group had made it overland from Texas to the Mississippi River, arriving by chance at Arkansas Post.

Because the country of France was focused on war in Europe and lacked another explorer who shared La Salle's vision and dreams, the nation did not continue to pursue its claim to the Mississippi valley or send over large numbers of settlers. The French did try to limit Spanish and English claims by forming some towns along the Gulf

▶ Henri de Tonti, who established Arkansas Post. De Tonti had one iron hand due to an injury.

134 Chapter 6

◀ French traders traveling along an inland river rest and eat on the bank.

coast, such as Mobile (Alabama) in 1702 and New Orleans (Louisiana) in 1718. The French founded St. Louis (Missouri), upstream from Arkansas, in 1764 as a trading post. The French, who tried to dominate Arkansas for almost one hundred years, did leave the sound of their language on our land.

For example, the L'Anguille (the French word for *eel*) River twists around like an eel. There is a place in south Arkansas that the French called *"sumac couvert,"* meaning covered with sumac trees. An English-speaking American, after hearing those French words, spelled out the name of what became the town Smackover.

For its first hundred years, Arkansas Post remained a remote outpost with few inhabitants. The main French settlements were far to the north in Canada. Only scattered trading posts existed in the Mississippi River valley otherwise known as French Louisiana. The Spanish continued to focus on maintaining their colonies in Mexico and what is now the Southwest, with posts in Florida and along the Gulf coast. Along the Atlantic or eastern coast, the British extended their settlements from New England to Georgia.

John Law

The French colony at Arkansas Post, hundreds of miles from the main settlements, never attracted many Europeans. But thanks to one man, **John Law**, it had a brief burst of popularity in Europe.

John Law a Scottish inventor and land speculator who convinced the King of France that he could sell and develop parts of New France (Louisiana) to French settlers. He advertised Arkansas Post and falsely claimed it had a great deal of gold to be mined. He then went bankrupt and abandoned the settlers. The colony failed.

The Naming of Tontitown

Did you know, although not established by Henri de Tonti, Tontitown in Washington County in northwest Arkansas was named after the French explorer who settled Arkansas Post? Father Pietro Bandini founded Tontitown in 1898 and named it after the explorer often referred to as the "Father of Arkansas" because he established the first European settlement in the state. Tontitown was created as an independent colony for immigrants from Italy. Today, the area is widely known for its annual Grape Festival and many wonderful Italian restaurants.

THE ENCYCLOPEDIA OF ARKANSAS HISTORY & CULTURE

Log on to Learn More
http://www.encyclopediaofarkansas.net/

Discovery, Exploration, and Settlement

Law, a Scottish man who was working with the French king, was a real-estate investor. Law convinced the French king to give him the right to sell land in Louisiana and tried to get settlers to go there and buy the land from him. He also hoped people in Europe would buy stock, or shares, in his business so he would make a large profit.

By only looking at a map, never having set foot in Arkansas, Law picked the site of Arkansas Post as one of the main areas to be colonized. Although he knew nothing about the land there, he thought prospective buyers and settlers would see the location as suitable for both trade and farming because of nearby rivers. Beginning in 1717, he recruited settlers by describing Arkansas as a beautiful land where no one would have to

▲ John Law.

work hard because gold and silver were easily mined there. Others, who had a more accurate knowledge of Arkansas and less interest in trying to sell land or stock, pointed out that gold and silver had not been discovered in Arkansas. However, many hopeful but uninformed people wanted to believe that Arkansas held the promise of instant wealth.

In 1721, about eighty of John Law's French colonists arrived at the site of de Tonti's Arkansas Post settlement. The Quapaws were friendly to the new arrivals as usual, but there were no white men to greet Law's settlers. De Tonti's original settlers had left long before, leaving behind only one log house. The colonists thought Law was going to help them get set up. But even before the settlers arrived in Arkansas, John Law had gone bankrupt, and his grand scheme had fallen apart. The colonists were left to take care of themselves.

Through much of the rest of the 1700s, the population at Arkansas Post was about thirty to fifty people—mostly traders, hunters, trappers, and their families. Usually a

County Quest

Jackson

Named after: President Andrew Jackson

Chief Source of Income: Service industry

Seat: Newport

Jackson County was created in 1829. Within its boundaries are the scenic White, Cache, and Black rivers. Newport was named the county seat when the Iron Mountain Railroad began conducting business in the county. The town is home to Jacksonport State Park, the annual Port Days Festival, and Arkansas State University at Newport.

From the late 1800s to the 1970s, freshwater pearl farming in the White and Black rivers thrived in Jackson County. English royalty once selected one of these Arkansas pearls to be mounted as a crown jewel. Pearls Unique of Newport sells these Arkansas treasures.

The King of Clubs in Swifton claims to be where the rockabilly movement started, and Elvis, Johnny Cash, Roy Orbison, Carl Perkins, Jerry Lee Lewis, Conway Twitty, and Sonny Burgess all played there.

small band of French soldiers was stationed at the Post. The population did not reach three hundred people until the late 1700s.

The settlement itself also was moved several times to try to find a location that would be free from floods yet still close enough to the Mississippi to serve traders. The original location, where the de Tonti and Law colonists lived, was up the Arkansas River about twenty-seven miles from its **confluence** with the Mississippi. In the mid-1700s, the settlers moved upstream to higher ground called the Red Bluffs. After a while, they moved downstream, closer to the Mississippi, then back up to the Red Bluffs (present-day Arkansas Post State Park is at the Red Bluffs site).

Arkansas Post remained the only French settlement in Arkansas. The French decided to focus on the area downriver, closer to the mouth of the Mississippi. They also blocked trade with the Spanish to the west, so the chances of Arkansas Post growing were limited.

However, French explorers continued to visit the region. In 1719, Bernard de La Harpe traveled the Arkansas River. Because he hoped to find

> **confluence** (kahn-FLU-unss) the point where two or more streams or rivers join and flow together.

I Am an Arkansan

Sarasin
Saracen, Sarrasin
(–1832)

Living in the villages along the Arkansas River below Pine Bluff, Sarasin was a Quapaw leader who became a legend among Arkansas settlers after rescuing white children captured by Indians raiding in the territory. Many versions of this story in Arkansas folklore indicate the high regard in which his white neighbors held Sarasin. During the era of Indian removal, Sarasin and other Quapaws attempted to prevent removal.

Sarasin's actions drew the attention of territorial leaders, and he was honored with a presidential medal from the first territorial governor, James Miller. Miller did not extend the same respect to the rest of the Quapaws, however. Settlers valued Quapaw land on the Arkansas River and began to call for the removal of the Quapaws in the 1820s.

The Quapaws moved to the Caddo region in 1826 and suffered through many disasters. Floods destroyed crops, and starvation killed sixty people, including Sarasin's wife and several family members. After six months, Sarasin led one-fourth of his people back to the land reserved for him along the Arkansas River.

After briefly moving to Louisiana, Sarasin eventually returned to Arkansas and lived in Jefferson County until he died. Although his gravestone states that he died in 1832, most scholars believe that he lived beyond that year. His gravestone reads: "Friend of the Missionaries. Rescuer of captive children."

THE ENCYCLOPEDIA OF ARKANSAS HISTORY & CULTURE

Log on to Learn More
http://www.encyclopediaofarkansas.net/

Discovery, Exploration, and Settlement **137**

dogtrot a roofed passage similar to a breezeway; especially one connecting two parts of a cabin.

reel a rhythmic tune for dancing, usually played on a fiddle; also used to refer to the dance itself.

loo short for *lanterloo*; an old card game involving money staked on the winning hand and involving the taking of card tricks (four cards of the same suit, such as hearts) as in the game of bridge.

gold or precious stones, he was extremely careful to look for large rock formations. He made a note in his journal about the site we know as Big Rock, calling it "French Rock." He stopped there and climbed to the top to admire the view, looking out over the area that would one day become Little Rock. Legend has it that La Harpe gave it the name Little Rock, but there is no proof of this.

Daily Life at Arkansas Post

On any Saturday night at the Arkansas Post settlement, a visitor to the typical **dogtrot** house might have found logs blazing in the two open fireplaces with neighbors all around speaking in their native French. The house had two square rooms, with an open porch (where the dogs would trot) in between them. Often, someone would play the fiddle and dancing would begin. With a line of men facing a line of women, they began a lively **reel**. Because it was a rugged, rural frontier town, there were always more men than women, so the men took turns dancing with each of the women. In the other room, people could be found drinking, eating, or playing cards. A favorite card game called **loo** resembled the modern-day game of bridge. If the children got sleepy, they made a bed wherever they could, but the party continued. The pioneers at Arkansas Post created entertainment for themselves because they were far away from larger settlements.

There was no school and no church, although a French priest sometimes visited. Some of the traders operated stores for the other settlers, as well as for the Indians. The people lived, for the most part, in the log-house village itself, staying close together for safety. The Quapaws living near the settlement were generally friendly and were also brave and effective warriors offering good protection. But they were becoming fewer in number each year, probably because of the white settlers' diseases. The pioneers feared raids from the Osages to the north and west and the

▶ The Wolf House, a bigger and grander version of a dogtrot. It is the oldest standing public structure in Arkansas, and can be found in Baxter County.

▼ What an evening at Arkansas Post might have looked like. The French danced to fiddle music while Indians observed.

138 Chapter 6

◀ A painting of a typical log dogtrot found in Cane Hill (Benton County). The smaller house to the left is the kitchen. Why was the kitchen separated from the rest of the house?

Chickasaws to the east across the Mississippi River. During one attack by 150 Chickasaws warriors, six men were killed and eight women and children were taken as slaves.

Most of the people at Arkansas Post owned small amounts of land, and they tried to raise food for themselves and their livestock. But hunting and fishing still provided much of their food. Their clothing came from hunting, too. Almost everyone wore **buckskins**, which were tanned, deerskin clothes.

Trading with the Indians was the major business of the settlers of Arkansas Post. Traveling by canoe up the Arkansas, White, and St. Francis rivers, the traders sought out the Indians in order to exchange goods. For the French, the most desired trade goods were animal furs and skins. They preferred deerskins but would also accept bear, buffalo, beaver, mink, and muskrat. The traders collected bear oil, too, to use in cooking and in lanterns. Bear oil came from melting a bear's fat, often in big troughs around the town. There is still a town in Arkansas named **Oil Trough** (Independence County).

In return for animal skins and furs, the Europeans gave the Indians knives, hatchets, hoes, plows, animal traps, cloth, glass, metal cooking pots, bells, and beads. The visiting British traders sold guns to the Indians, though the French traders, perhaps because they had to live among the Indians, did not

Chickasaws a Native American people of the United States related to the Choctaws. The Chickasaws were one of the Five Civilized Tribes who were forced to abandon their homelands and relocate to the Indian Territory during Indian removal.

buckskins clothing made from buckskin, the soft suedelike leather usually made of deer hide.

Oil Trough a community in northeast Arkansas named for the troughs settlers used to melt bear fat.

County Quest

Mississippi

Named after: Mississippi River

Chief Source of Income: Agriculture and manufacturing

Seat: Osceola, Blytheville

Created in 1833, Mississippi County is named after the Mississippi River, which borders the land. The county offers some of the most fertile land in the state and was home to the Wilson Plantation, once one of the largest plantations in the United States.

The New Deal Era Farm Colony Resettlement area of Dyess is also in Mississippi County and was the childhood home of Johnny Cash.

Discovery, Exploration, and Settlement **139**

approve of their having firearms. The government of France tried to stop the trading of whiskey to the Indians, but people did it anyway. Like many other diseases, alcoholism and its associated problems (for example, poor decision-making, violence, and poor physical health) were introduced to the Native Arkansans by the Europeans.

When enough furs had been collected, traders headed by canoe or raft down the Mississippi River to New Orleans, a trip that took ten or twelve days from Arkansas Post (a trip that today would take about six hours by car). From there, the furs and skins were shipped to Europe. Many fashionable people in Paris or London wore a fine beaver hat or coat made of fur that came from Arkansas.

The Arkansas trader collected fees in money or, more often, in goods. Needed items included salt, sugar, guns, gunpowder, and many other things not available in the undeveloped land of Arkansas. Many Europeans were reminded of home and thought it a better life for their families if they had a set of fine china dishes or a few bottles of wine from their native countries.

Less is known about the life of the slaves at Arkansas Post. Europeans discovered Africa about the same time they discovered the Americas, and enslaved black Africans were an important part of the process of settling the New World. De Soto had slaves on his expedition, and the settlers at Arkansas Post always had slaves, who sometimes made up as much as a third of the total population. Probably each slave-owning white man had just one or two slaves, or more rarely, an entire family of slaves. The slaves did the household chores and the hard labor.

There were interracial marriages between whites, blacks, and Indians. Many French and Quapaw intermarried, and this created a multilingual community. Sometimes a white father would free his children from an interracial marriage, so there were some free blacks at Arkansas Post. Free and enslaved blacks both faced uncertainty and sometimes cruelty in their lives. Free blacks were unsure of their status—they

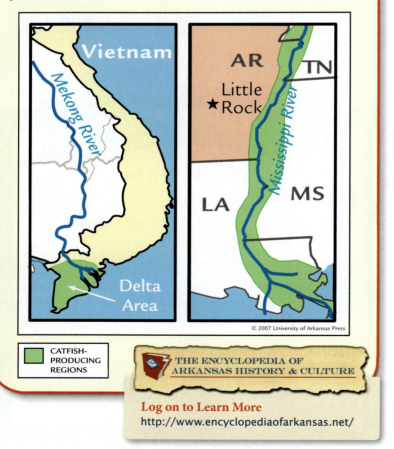

DID YOU ❓ KNOW?

Did you know commercial catfish farms were first seen in Arkansas in the 1950s, and the industry originated in the state? Arkansans consume more catfish per capita than any other state in the nation, followed by Mississippi and Alabama. Of all the seafood consumed in the United States each year, catfish is the fifth most popular. Over the past fifteen years, overall consumption has risen 57 percent.

In 2004, Arkansas experienced catfish sales of $62.8 million, and an overall economic impact of $576 million. Thirty-three thousand acres of Arkansas farmland are used in production of the fish. Arkansas is second in the catfish-production industry, behind Mississippi. Catfish farming and its related industries in Chicot County alone created 2,665 jobs and $117 million in additional economic income in 2001.

THE ENCYCLOPEDIA OF ARKANSAS HISTORY & CULTURE

Log on to Learn More
http://www.encyclopediaofarkansas.net/

could suddenly find themselves "slaves" and defenseless before the law. Cruelty could range from daily humiliations, to beatings, to the sale of black slaves away from their families.

Revolution

At this time, while Arkansas Post was struggling along, British colonists such as Col. George Washington of the Virginia Militia faced off against the French and their Indian allies in battle. The colonists called this war the **French and Indian War**. It is also referred to as the Seven Years' War. When it was over, the British had defeated the French and claimed many French lands. In 1763 in Paris, the peace treaty to end the war was signed, and leaders from both sides sat around a table, studied maps, and decided the future of North America, including Arkansas.

They decided to divide the continent at the Mississippi River. Great Britain got all the land east of the river, where the original thirteen colonies were, as well as Canada in the north. France gave Spain all the land west of the river, including Arkansas, to repay Spain for its assistance during the war. France lost all its land and claims in North America and had to abandon its settlers, including those at Arkansas Post.

For some time, the people of Arkansas Post probably did not know what had happened as a result of the French and Indian War. It was five years after the treaty when a Spanish army officer finally arrived at Arkansas Post to take command. In reality, he changed very few things. Major change would come later, after the American Revolution.

A conflict between England and its colonists in North America began over unfair taxes and a harsh colonial government and quickly got out of control. The colonists declared their independence in July 1776. The **Revolutionary War** or War for American Independence was underway. France and Spain, eager to get revenge on Britain, also declared war against the British. The residents of Arkansas Post, under Spanish rule, were against the British, but the people of the Post did not consider the settlement "American" in the sense of being one of the thirteen English colonies in North America.

Only one brief episode of the Revolutionary War occurred in Arkansas. A daring British supporter, John Colbert, began a series of raids against Spanish trade in the Mississippi River valley. In April of 1783, Colbert's raiders crossed the Mississippi south of Arkansas Post and surprised the settlers there with an early morning attack. The fight at Arkansas Post was not much of a battle, but it meant that later, as Americans began to move west, they would face weak Spanish outposts instead of British strongholds. Peace was declared in 1783, and America was free from British rule.

French and Indian War the nine-year North American conflict of the Seven Years' War. As a result of the war, Canada fell under British control, while Spain gained Louisiana in return for its loss of Florida to the British. The role of the French, their rule and presence in North America was virtually eliminated.

Revolutionary War the War for American Independence fought between the British and their American colonists from 1776 to 1783.

County Quest

Pike

Named after: Lt. Zebulon Pike, an explorer of the southwestern United States in the early 1800s

Chief Source of Income: Timber, agriculture, and tourism

Seat: Murfreesboro

Pike County was created in 1833. This county boasts Crater of Diamonds State Park, Arkansas's only diamond mine and the world's only diamond mine where the public can dig for gems and keep what they find. Because of the Ouachita Mountains and Ouachita River, the geology of the county is as diverse as anywhere else in the United States. Delight was home to country star Glen Campbell, whose hits include "Rhinestone Cowboy."

Discovery, Exploration, and Settlement

Chapter Reflection

Reflective Questions

1. Discuss the reasons the European explorers had a low opinion of the Native American population of the New World.

2. What was the single greatest cause of death among Native American populations after contact with Europeans? Why?

3. What were the goals of de Soto's expedition? Discuss its purpose and legacy using reasons, facts, and examples.

4. Did the voyage of Marquette and Joliet help or hurt La Salle? Why or why not? How?

5. Determine the reason for Arkansas Post's location. What were some good and bad points about the location of Arkansas Post? What challenges were faced, and what successes were achieved as a result of its location?

6. Was Arkansas Post significant? Valuable? Why or why not? List specific reasons.

7. Were the white American settlers at Arkansas Post heavily involved in the Revolutionary War? Why or why not? Whose side was Arkansas on during the American Revolution and why?

8. The land that became the state of Arkansas belonged to four different groups or nations at different times. Name these groups or nations.

9. Using your prior knowledge, identify and discuss how the unique and varied geography of our state presented benefits and challenges for the explorers.

10. If you were traveling with Bernard de La Harpe from Arkansas Post to the place where he named the "Big Rock" or the "French Rock," in which direction would you travel and on what river?

Picture It!

Invent a role or persona for yourself as an explorer in the 1500s and 1600s preparing to embark on a journey to the New World. You need to "advertise" for crew. Compile a list of plans, facts, and ideas based on these questions:

1. What are the qualities you will require of your men?

2. How will you promote or "advertise" the job to make it sound appealing to your future employees?

3. What benefits and wages will you offer?

4. How long will the journey last?

5. What will your planned route be?

6. What will your departure date and location be?

7. What size will your ship be, and what will the meal and sleeping arrangements be?

8. How will the crew protect themselves from natives?

Good Luck!

Now create an authentic-looking flier or poster about your hometown in Spain or France. Be sure to use color, words, and pictures to entice people to join your expedition.

Organization and Visualization

Who were the important European explorers who visited Arkansas from 1540 to 1800? How were they alike? How were they different? To respond to this question, copy and complete the graphic organizer below on your paper. Be sure to include as many facts as possible for each group.

You may use your book and your notes. Consider things such as time period, food, shelter, movement, crew, trade, religion, goals, attitudes, success, failure, weapons, death, and legacy when organizing your information.

Exploring!

	Country of Origin	Dates of Journey	Goals	Success or Failure	Legacy
de Soto					
Marquette and Joliet					
La Salle					
de Tonti					
de La Harpe					

HisStory, HerStory, YourStory, OurStory...

Write a one- or two-paragraph journal entry as if you were Henri de Tonti or one of his men, making your home at the newly established Arkansas Post. Consider describing some of the following factors in your report: housing, food, clothing, weather, location of the Post, daily chores, visitors, fears, entertainment, religion, challenges, weapons, successes, hopes, Indians, transportation, trade, leadership, and decision-making.

Telling an Arkansas Story— The Written Word

Discovery, Exploration, and Settlement

UNIT 3

Chapter 7
Jefferson's Louisiana and the Exploration of a Rugged New Land, 1803–1812

Chapter 8
Growing Pains: Territorial Power, Politics, and Compromise, 1803–1835

Chapter 9
Statehood and Slavery, 1836–1860

▶ An artist's interpretation of slaves picking cotton.

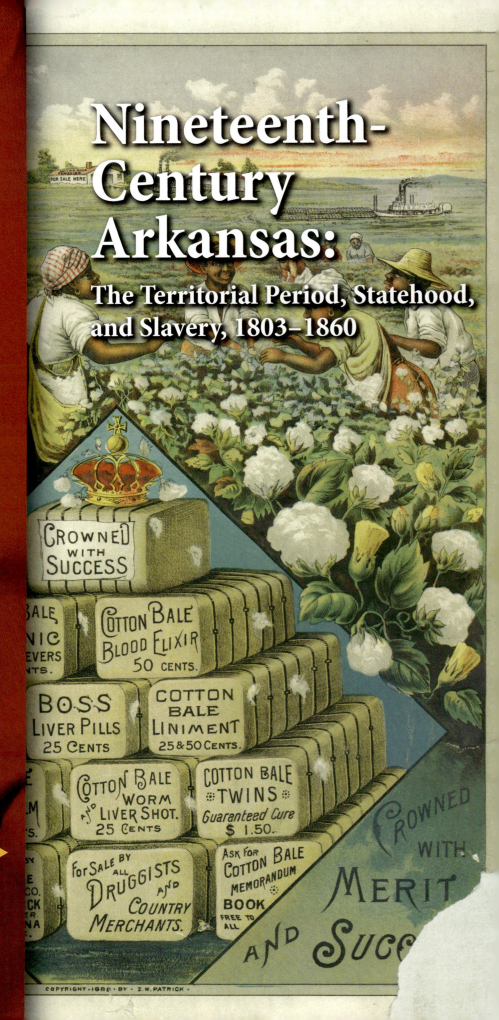

Nineteenth-Century Arkansas:
The Territorial Period, Statehood, and Slavery, 1803–1860

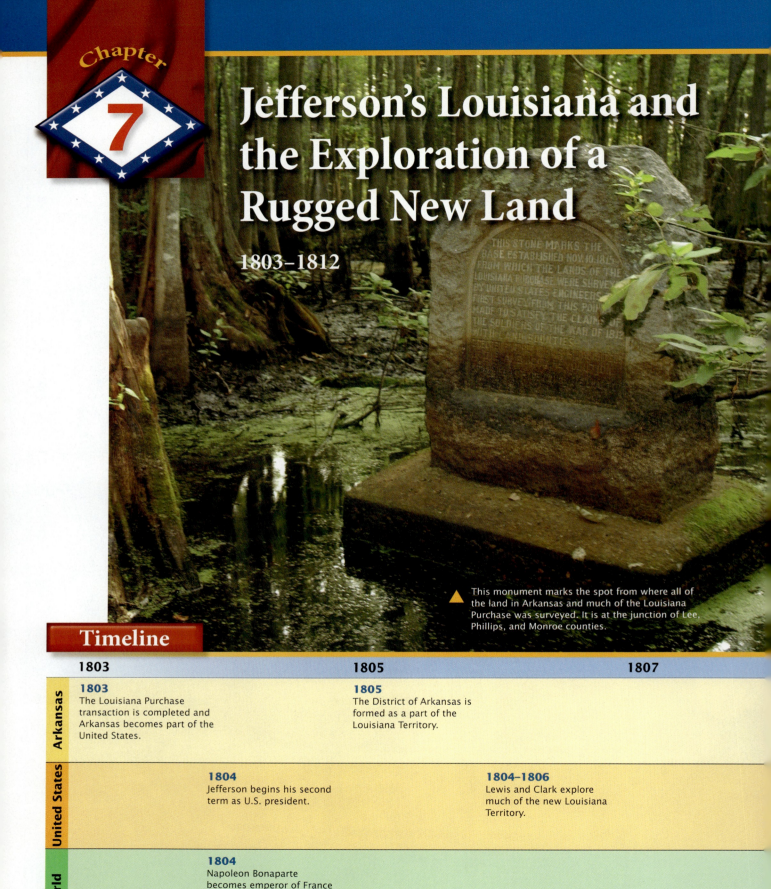

Chapter 7

Jefferson's Louisiana and the Exploration of a Rugged New Land

1803–1812

▲ This monument marks the spot from where all of the land in Arkansas and much of the Louisiana Purchase was surveyed. It is at the junction of Lee, Phillips, and Monroe counties.

Timeline

	1803	1805	1807
Arkansas	**1803** The Louisiana Purchase transaction is completed and Arkansas becomes part of the United States.	**1805** The District of Arkansas is formed as a part of the Louisiana Territory.	
United States		**1804** Jefferson begins his second term as U.S. president.	**1804–1806** Lewis and Clark explore much of the new Louisiana Territory.
World		**1804** Napoleon Bonaparte becomes emperor of France after war victories against other European powers.	

146 Chapter 7

BIG PICTURE QUESTIONS

- What was the long-term impact of the Louisiana Purchase on the nation as a whole, on the people living in the newly acquired lands, and in other lands adjoining the United States? Imagine what our nation would be like today if the transaction had not occurred and summarize your response.

- Put yourself in President Jefferson's position at the time of the Louisiana Purchase. Why did you make the decision to purchase the land and why did you then divide it?

- What would the results have been had Lewis and Clark been the explorers assigned to report on Arkansas, rather than Dunbar and Hunter? Predict what Arkansas's image and reputation might be today if Lewis and Clark had visited our state first. Why is the Dunbar and Hunter expedition referred to as the "Forgotten Expedition"?

- Examine the role of agriculture in the past, present, and future of Arkansas. How would Arkansas be different without it? Positives? Negatives? Use reasons, facts, and examples in your answer.

- Natural disasters have a long record of altering the shape, face, and population of lands they affect. How would Arkansas be different had the New Madrid earthquake not occurred? What recent significant changes have been witnessed in the modern United States because of natural disasters? Use specific examples to support your opinion.

Why Do We Study This?

This chapter covers the period from the Louisiana Purchase in 1803 through the devastating New Madrid earthquake in late 1811 and early 1812. Arkansas was first a county in the Territory of Missouri and then a territory itself. Early explorations, the development of transportation methods, and the beginning of farming took place in Arkansas during this time period.

For the first time, Arkansas was truly revealed and described, for better or worse, to other Americans and the rest of the world. The review of these years in history might tell us something about Arkansas's current image and reputation as well as the changes and struggles we had to experience and overcome to develop from a rural, wild territory ruled by a foreign land to a state of the United States.

1808

1811

1813

1811–1812
The New Madrid earthquake rocks southern Missouri and northeastern Arkansas.

1808
James Madison is elected the fourth president.

1808
The international slave trade is abolished.

Jefferson's Louisiana and the Exploration of a Rugged New Land

Section 1

The Journey Began In Arkansas

The Louisiana Purchase and President Jefferson

The new United States of America, freed from Great Britain, did not at first include Arkansas. The new country's western boundary was the Mississippi River, and Arkansas was still in Spanish territory. While most Americans still lived along the east coast, they created a new government under the Constitution that established a procedure for admitting new states into the Union.

When the Revolutionary War was over, more and more Americans began to move west into the land between the Appalachian Mountains and the Mississippi River. These settlers looked to the Mississippi River as their hope for future economic success. If they were to sell their crops to outside markets, they would have to be transported downriver. The major threat to this venture was Spain, with its outposts along the west bank of the Mississippi River, including Arkansas Post. Spain also governed New Orleans, which controlled the mouth of the river and access to ships sailing the oceans. The American government knew that it could not maintain the loyalty of these settlers unless it could guarantee them the use of the Mississippi River.

Once again, European issues would influence the future of Arkansas and the United States. Twenty years after the end of the Revolutionary War, Emperor Napoleon Bonaparte had taken over France. Very much like La Salle before him, he hoped to create a great French empire. An important part

▶ Visitors view the Louisiana Purchase historical monument at the Louisiana Purchase State Park.

of his plan was Louisiana as the French called the land between the Mississippi River and the Rocky Mountains, including Arkansas. On the European continent, Napoleon had conquered many other European nations, including Spain. He forced Spain to return control of Louisiana to his country.

Because of distance, money, and the ongoing war in Europe, Napoleon abandoned the Louisiana project before it really got started, even before the new French soldiers and governors had time to replace the Spanish there. Because of its focus on its matters in Europe, France also struggled to manage its other colonies in the Americas, and so Napoleon decided to cut his losses and sell Louisiana.

The United States was the most likely buyer. President Thomas Jefferson had already sent representatives to France to try to buy New Orleans at the mouth of the Mississippi River. When Napoleon asked if they would like to have all of Louisiana, they at first were not sure they had heard correctly, but the Americans did not hesitate about accepting the offer, and the deal was made. Louisiana became a part of America for about $15 million (around $250 million in modern U.S. dollars). No one was very clear about the exact boundaries, but most certainly they included both banks of the Mississippi River, from its source to its mouth, along with Arkansas.

Arkansas had at first been Indian land, then French, briefly Spanish, and then French again. Now it became part of the United States. American society would begin to transform the wilderness into a successful farming frontier.

President Thomas Jefferson moved quickly to find out more about the new lands of the Louisiana Purchase. Official exploring parties prepared maps and reports on the land, animal life, and natural resources. Explorers commented on the location and nature of the Indians and on the few white settlements that existed. For pioneers planning to move west, the new government reports paved the way.

THE LOUISIANA PURCHASE – 1803

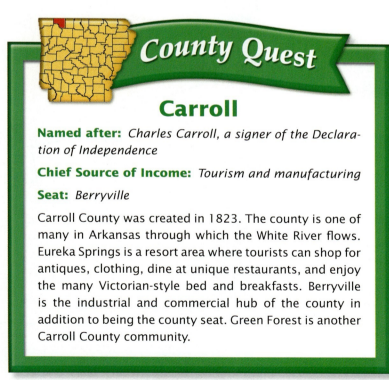

County Quest

Carroll

Named after: *Charles Carroll, a signer of the Declaration of Independence*

Chief Source of Income: *Tourism and manufacturing*

Seat: *Berryville*

Carroll County was created in 1823. The county is one of many in Arkansas through which the White River flows. Eureka Springs is a resort area where tourists can shop for antiques, clothing, dine at unique restaurants, and enjoy the many Victorian-style bed and breakfasts. Berryville is the industrial and commercial hub of the county in addition to being the county seat. Green Forest is another Carroll County community.

Jefferson's Louisiana and the Exploration of a Rugged New Land

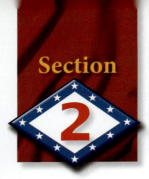

Section 2

Ready, Set, Explore!

Guide to Reading

Terms
diplomat   medicinal

Places
Mammoth Spring

Lewis and Clark

The most famous expedition Jefferson supported, led by Meriwether Lewis and William Clark, went to the sources of the Missouri River and beyond from 1803 to 1806. The pair and their crew of about thirty-three traveled around eight thousand miles in more than two years. By river, they explored what would become the states of Illinois, Missouri, Nebraska, Kansas, Iowa, South Dakota, North Dakota, Montana, Idaho, Washington,

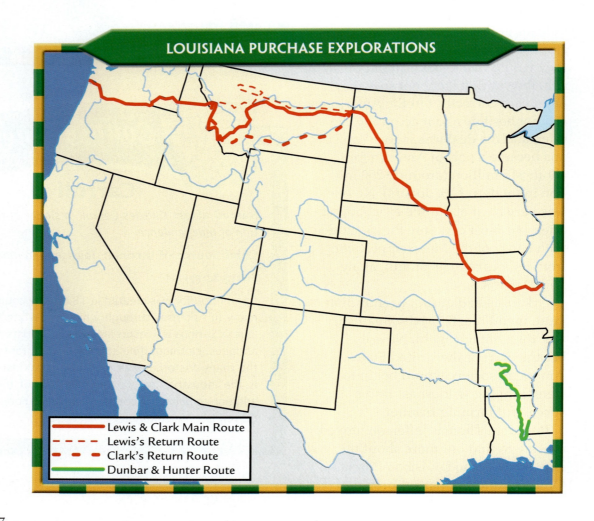

LOUISIANA PURCHASE EXPLORATIONS

— Lewis & Clark Main Route
--- Lewis's Return Route
--- Clark's Return Route
— Dunbar & Hunter Route

150   Chapter 7

A Day in the Life

"All the luxuries of life that a new country could afford."

Writing more than fifty years after he came to Arkansas, John Billingsley described what life was like for the early white settlers.

> My father, with two other families moved from Middle Tennessee... six in each family, made eighteen persons. That was in 1814. We came to the Post of Arkansas in a flatboat. There we found a French and Creole village. The Quapaw Indians lived on the south side of the river. There we exchanged our flatboat for a keelboat with an old Indian trader.... We made our way the best we could until we got to the Cadron; there we found one of my father's brothers that had moved from Kentucky in an early day. We stayed there one year.... Then we moved to Big Mulberry. In 1816 we made up about thirty families and lived there two years in all the luxuries of life that a new country could afford, such as buffalo, bear, deer, and elk and fish and honey; we had pound cake every day, for we beat all the [corn] meal we ate in a mortar, and the first year our corn gave out about six weeks before roasting ears came in. Our substitute for bread was venison dried by the fire and then pounded in the mortar and made up in small cakes and fried in bear's oil....
>
> Well, the way we clothed ourselves—that is, the men and boys—was by dressing bucksuits and wore full suits of the same. The French came up the river in large canoes and supplied us with domestic and checks and earthing ware [dishes] and calico.... This was all paid for in bear skins and deer skins and coon skins and bear oil, some beaver and otter skins and bees wax and that in abundance. For we had honey in any amount.

Note: This document serves as an example of some of the symbols used in writing history. This is a direct quotation from the original, taken from a book that reprints many documents from Arkansas history. The ellipsis points (...) mean that we left something out of the original, in this case to make the quotation shorter. The brackets mean we added something to make items within the quotation clearer.

C. Fred Williams, S. Charles Bolton, Carl H. Moneyhon, and LeRoy T. Williams, *A Documentary History of Arkansas* (Fayetteville: University of Arkansas Press, 1984), 18–19.

Jefferson's Louisiana and the Exploration of a Rugged New Land

▲ William Dunbar.

and Oregon. This journey provided new knowledge of the geography of the western portion of the country. The fur trade was expanded, relationships with the Native Americans were improved, and new maps of major rivers and mountain ranges were created. Lewis and Clark also noted over 150 types of plants and around 120 species of animals. The diaries of Lewis and Clark became, and still remain, important pieces of literature and research manuals.

Dunbar and Hunter and the Forgotten Expedition

At the same time as the Lewis and Clark expedition, Jefferson commissioned William Dunbar of Mississippi, a farmer, scientist, and **diplomat**, to explore the Ouachita River in Louisiana and Arkansas. With George Hunter, a medical doctor, Dunbar spent 1804 and 1805 traveling up the Ouachita, as far as the hot springs. The Ouachita River expedition was not as well publicized as the Lewis and Clark journey. However, the exploration of Dunbar and Hunter remains important to Arkansans for several reasons. For the first time, official studies were conducted and reports submitted on the features of the land, the animals, and the plants of south Arkansas. Hunter and Dunbar reported many meetings with European trappers, hunters, planters, and settlers along the riverbanks as well as fellow waterway travelers. Their records indicate that all the people—Indians and European settlers alike—truly lived off the land, using all of the many natural resources of the rivers and land efficiently and fully.

The journals of both explorers show that throughout their travels, they met many people who were traveling to and from the springs and the hot "baths." Word had spread, and many people throughout the country had heard of the hot springs as a place to go for healing and to relieve aches, pains, and sickness. Upon arrival at the springs, they discovered evidence that various people had actually come to live in the area for long periods of time to benefit from the waters' supposed **medicinal** properties.

The journals of Dunbar and Hunter were used to write the first reports to Jefferson about the new purchase. Theirs were the first words in English to describe the Ouachita River region, Arkansas, and a part of the southern lands of the Louisiana Purchase.

Schoolcraft and Nuttall

Later, Arkansas attracted the attention of two private explorers, Henry R. Schoolcraft and Thomas Nuttall. Schoolcraft, a writer and geologist, entered

diplomat one skilled in negotiations or building relationships with foreign leaders and nations.

medicinal referring to medicine; having an ability or quality to treat or heal.

County Quest

Greene

Named after: Revolutionary War general Nathaniel Greene

Chief Source of Income: Agriculture, transportation, and manufacturing

Seat: Paragould

In 1835, Gov. John Pope ordered the creation of Greene County. Today, large-scale agriculture and manufacturing provide the county its main sources of income. Crowley's Ridge State Park is located in the county, and the Cache River flows through the area.

Valuable research discoveries about Native Americans of the ice age have been made at the Dalton Period Cemetery at the well-known Sloan Site in the county. Tools from the site have provided important insight about the lives of these people. The cemetery is the oldest documented Native American burial site in the Western Hemisphere.

I Am an Arkansan

Albert Pike (1809–1891)

Albert Pike was a politician, editor, farmer, soldier, and writer. He was most proud of his extensive writings about the Masonic Order, but his most popular work was a poem he wrote in 1852 about the "Fine Arkansas Gentleman." The unnamed subject is almost certainly Elias Rector, who lived near the border with the Indian country. The first verse goes like this:

Now all good fellows, listen, and a story I will tell
Of a mighty clever gentleman who lives extremely well
In the western part of Arkansas, close to the Indian line,
Where he gets drunk once a week on whiskey, and
Immediately sobers himself completely on the very best of wine;
A fine Arkansas gentleman
Close to the Choctaw line!

Pike fought to free Texas from Mexican control in the Mexican War and commanded Cherokee troops during the Civil War as a Confederate general. His home in Little Rock now houses the Decorative Arts Museum.

Arkansas in 1818 at **Mammoth Spring** (Fulton County) in the northeast. He traveled through the valleys of the Spring, Black, and White rivers. He went as far as the settlements at Calico Rock and Poke Bayou (later Batesville, Independence County) on the White River.

> "Nothing can exceed the roughness and sterility of the country . . . and the endless succession of steep declivities, and broken, rocky precipices. . . ."
> —Henry R. Schoolcraft

THE ENCYCLOPEDIA OF ARKANSAS HISTORY & CULTURE
Log on to Learn More
http://www.encyclopediaofarkansas.net/

Schoolcraft was impressed with the hospitality of Arkansas hunters and families (Wells, M'Gary, Coker, Holt, and Fisher are some mentioned by name). They took him in and shared what they had. However, he commented negatively on their formal religious practices, which he called "witchcraft," and their lack of education. He recorded notes about the cabins that had floors of dirt, their stained clothing, untidy appearance, and the generally awful condition of the people in the rugged district.

Nuttall, an Englishman and a biologist, started at Arkansas Post in 1819 and went up the Arkansas River to Fort Smith. Both men were trained observers and skilled writers, and each published a book about his trip in 1821. Still enjoyable and informative reading today, their accounts helped publicize Arkansas to the rest of the United States. According to these accounts, Arkansas was a scenic land, rich in animal and plant life and natural resources, but thinly settled.

Mammoth Spring discovered in 1850 and made a state park in 1957, Mammoth Spring is Arkansas's largest spring. Nine million gallons of water flow from the spring on an hourly basis. The spring forms a ten-acre lake and then flows southward to become the Spring River, where residents and visitors alike enjoy floating and trout fishing.

Jefferson's Louisiana and the Exploration of a Rugged New Land

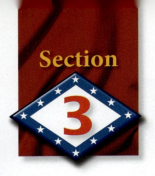

Section 3

Life in the Rugged New Land

Guide to Reading

Terms
ague
bilious fever
bison
census
epidemics
flatboat
fugitives
geologic fault
hemp
indigo
keel
keelboat
malaria
milled
passenger pigeons
Richter scale
tremors
yellow fever

Events
New Madrid earthquake

Places
New Madrid
Southwest Trail

---

flatboat a raftlike boat used for floating downstream.

keelboat a boat with a rounded bottom and a keel to help it move straight that could be pulled upstream by men or horses or pushed along with poles.

keel on the bottom of a boat, a ridge where the rounded sides of the vessel come together, used to stabilize the boat and keep it on a straight course.

Southwest Trail the main thoroughfare to Spanish settlements in the southwest, starting at Sainte Genevieve, Missouri, and traversing Arkansas into Texas and beyond.

In the early years of the nineteenth century (the 1800s), settlement was slow because Arkansas was hard to reach and not on the way to anywhere. Americans moving westward tended to move directly west, going to land that would grow the same crops as the land they had left behind. However, the swampy lowlands of eastern Arkansas presented a major challenge to the settlers coming from Tennessee or Mississippi.

In addition, Arkansas was not on any of the major paths for expansion to the far west. To the southwest of Arkansas was Spanish-owned Texas. Oklahoma, to the west, was not open to white settlement because it had been designated by the national government as Indian territory. So Arkansas was somewhat "off the beaten path" and sometimes viewed as undesirable or a wasteland.

Overland travel was very difficult for wagons carrying household goods, so the Arkansas River was the major avenue into Arkansas. In the southwestern part of Arkansas, the Red and Ouachita rivers also served as migration routes. However, the Great Red River Raft blocked the Red River for much of its length.

People traveled on the rivers by canoe, **flatboat**, or **keelboat**. The flatboat was usually nothing more than a crude raft, useful only for going downstream at the rate of the current. The keelboat, with a rounded bottom and a **keel** to help keep it going straight, could move upstream, but it was a slow process. The keelboat was either pushed along by poles against the bottom of the river or pulled by horses or men walking along the bank. Ten miles a day was a good speed for a keelboat.

On land, travelers either walked or rode horseback. The **Southwest Trail**, an old Indian path, ran from Sainte Genevieve in southeast Missouri, through central Arkansas, and on through to the Red River settlements to Texas. However, it was actually no more than a path through the forest. After the Arkansas territory became part of the United States in 1803, the Southwest Trail was the first "road" to be chosen by the national government for improvement. Another major trail followed the north bank of the Arkansas River from Arkansas Post to Crystal Hill (Pulaski County), just north of Little Rock.

The remote position of Arkansas helped it become known as a haven for people who wanted to become "lost." Stories spread that a lot of the early settlers in Arkansas were men who had gotten in trouble with the law "back in the states." They fled to Arkansas

154 Chapter 7

◀ A flatboat could go downstream with the current, guided by poles, while carrying an entire family and all of their belongings.

because they were fairly sure no sheriff was going to find them in its wilderness. There were most likely **fugitives** among the early Arkansas settlers, but there probably never were as many outlaws in Arkansas as some of the stories and legends claimed.

Early Settlements

By 1810, when a special **census** was taken, there were a little more than a thousand people in Arkansas, not counting the Indians. About three-fourths of them lived in the Arkansas River Valley, including villages at Arkansas Post, Pine Bluff, Little Rock, Crystal Hill, and Cadron (CAD-run) (Faulkner County). Most of the rest were scattered along the Mississippi River, especially at St. Francis (later Helena) and Hopefield (later West Memphis).

Other pioneers were in the valleys of the Red and Ouachita rivers in the southwest, in villages such as Blakely Town (later Arkadelphia) and Ecore á Fabri (eh-COHR-ah-fah-BREE) (later Camden). There were also people living in the White River valley in the north, where Poke Bayou was the main settlement.

In these early years, there were two different types of settlers, the hunters and the farmers. The hunters, many of them single men but some with families, lived in the more isolated areas. They hunted and trapped for animal skins and traded with the Indians. Although a hunter's family might sometimes have a garden to provide some vegetables or greens or berries in a diet of wild game, the hunters did not think of themselves as farmers.

For the hunters, Arkansas in those days was rich in animal life, very much the "natural state." There were herds of American **bison**, which the settlers called buffalos. However, mass hunting and the clearing of land for farming thinned out the bison. Deer, elk, beavers, bears, panthers, wildcats, and wolves were plentiful, and all were valued for their hides or furs. One hunters' trick learned from the Indians was to burn off the underbrush, scrub, or groundcover each year to make the hunting easier. Overhead, birds were in abundance, including

fugitives (FYOO-gih-tivs) outlaws on the run from justice.

census a complete and specific count of a population.

bison (BY-suhn) a wild creature known in America as the buffalo, a member of the bovine (cow) family.

County Quest

Scott

Named after: *Andrew Scott, an early settler and judge of Arkansas's superior court*

Chief Source of Income: *Manufacturing and poultry*

Seat: *Waldron*

Scott County was created in 1833 and is located in the western part of the state. The area has become well known for Lake Hinkle, the Turkey Track Bluegrass Festival, and the Ouachita National Forest.

Jefferson's Louisiana and the Exploration of a Rugged New Land

▲ "The Arkansas Traveller." This is a depiction of the popular Arkansas folk tale. A settler would not welcome a traveler until he proved he knew the tune "The Arkansas Traveller." Painting by artist Edward Washbourne.

passenger pigeons a once-plentiful breed of bird in North America that became extinct during the 1800s from excessive hunting.

milled ground by a large stone wheel rotated by animal or water power in order to turn wheat or other grains into flour.

hemp a type of fibrous herb that produces material suitable for making rope.

indigo (in-dih-goe) a plant that yields a dark blue dye.

huge flocks of **passenger pigeons**, which were soon made extinct.

Early Agriculture

For farmers, Arkansas had fertile land and a long growing season, around 230 days. Rainfall averaged about forty-five inches a year, which was plenty to water the crops. There were abundant trees to use for fuel, fences, and log cabins.

Most parts of Arkansas had soil and climate conditions that were suitable for growing cotton, corn, or wheat. Cotton was most common in the Arkansas River Valley and along the Mississippi River in the southeast, where the rivers allowed easy transport to the markets in New Orleans. Wheat, which was **milled** into flour, was generally grown and used locally, and corn provided food for the farm family and its horses, cows, and pigs.

Many small farms would also grow some vegetables and fruit trees for the family's use. Some early Arkansans also planted rice, tobacco, **hemp** (for rope), **indigo** (for a blue dye), and grapes (for wine). None of these, however, became important crops in the early years because each of them

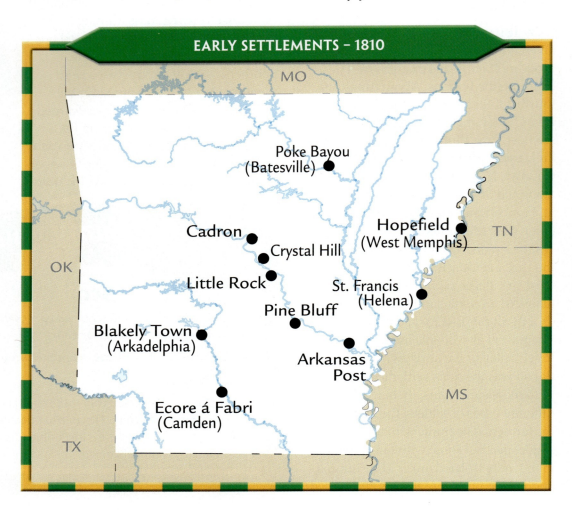

156 Chapter 7

required a skill or a market that had not yet been developed in Arkansas.

The weather could be harsh and unpredictable. Usually in the late winter or early spring, new crops were planted and heavy rains often flooded the rivers. Or a farmer could experience a drought in the hot summer, like the one that ruined the crops in 1818.

One of Arkansas's early problems was being known as an unhealthy place to live. Arkansans suspected some connection between the weather and disease. In those days, before knowledge of germs and insect-borne disease, they were unable to establish the connection. It is now known that heavy rainfall and frequent floods left large areas of standing water. The standing water became the breeding ground for the kinds of mosquitoes that carry **malaria** and **yellow fever**.

The settlers frequently complained about the **ague**, **bilious fever**, or the "chills and fever," all of them names for malaria. Mosquitoes flourished in the hot summer months, and chills, followed by fever and often frequent vomiting, were common. For many, the ague caused death. For others, attacks of the disease could come back year after year. Yellow fever, also carried by

malaria (MUH-lare-ee-uh) a mosquito-borne chronic illness characterized by chills and fever.

yellow fever a lethal mosquito-borne disease that swept through the South periodically during the 1800s.

ague (uh-GYOO) another name for malaria or flu.

bilious fever (BILL-yuss FEE-ver) another name for malaria.

A Day in the Life

From the Journals of William Dunbar and George Hunter, January 1805

. . . having made several stops to examine certain objects on our way down, we made a considerable delay at the camp of a M. Le Fevre [a prosperous landowner near Arkansas Post]. This was an intelligent man, a native of the Ill[i]nois, now residing at the Arcansas, he is come here with some Delaware and some other Indians whom he has fitted out with goods & receives the peltry, fur &c at a stipulated price, as it is brought in by the hunters. The gentleman informs us that a considerable party of the Osages from the Arcansas river have made an excursion round by the prairie towards the red river . . . and there meeting with a small party of Cherokees, are supposed to have killed four of their number and others are missing: Three Americans and ten Chickasaws went a hunting into that quarter, who may have also been in danger; those Osages being no respecter of persons.

Quoted in Trey Berry, Pam Beasley, and Jeanne Clements, eds., *The Forgotten Expedition, 1804–1805: The Louisiana Purchase Journals of Dunbar and Hunter* (Baton Rouge: Louisiana State University Press, 2006), 166–67.

epidemics (EPP-ih-demics) major outbreaks of contagious diseases.

geologic fault a place where the Earth's underlying plates come together.

New Madrid (noo MAD-rid) a town in southeast Missouri, near the Mississippi River and just north of the Arkansas border.

New Madrid earthquake the 1811–12 earthquake along the New Madrid fault in northeast Arkansas and southeast Missouri.

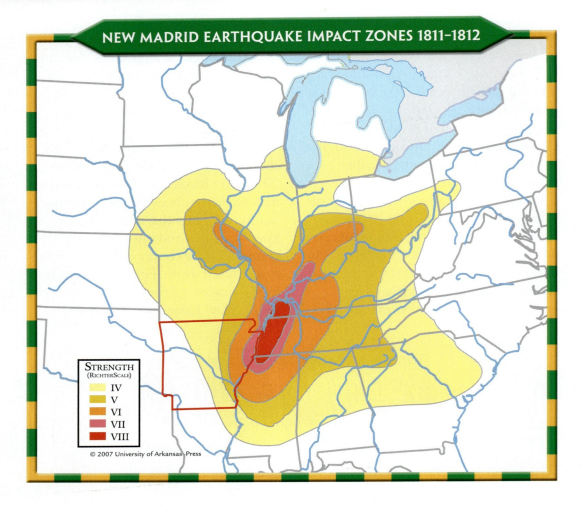

NEW MADRID EARTHQUAKE IMPACT ZONES 1811–1812

STRENGTH (Richter Scale)
- IV
- V
- VI
- VII
- VIII

© 2007 University of Arkansas Press

mosquitoes, had an even higher death rate than malaria. Yellow fever was not always present like malaria but swept through in **epidemics**. It tended to spread up the Mississippi River valley into Arkansas, as it did in 1818.

County Quest

Van Buren

Named after: President Martin Van Buren
Chief Source of Income: Tourism and agriculture
Seat: Clinton

The Little Red River runs through the county. A portion of popular tourist destination Greer's Ferry Lake is within the county, and the annual Labor Day Chuckwagon Racing Festival also draws many visitors.

The New Madrid Earthquake and the Sunken Lands

Arkansas had a major earthquake in 1811 and 1812—probably the most severe and longest lasting earthquake ever to take place in what is now the United States. Luckily, it occurred in a sparsely settled area and had little direct effect on people. A great **geologic fault** runs northeast to southwest, deep in the earth under **New Madrid** (MAD-rid). The New Madrid zone runs from around Marked Tree (Poinsett County) to the northeast. It goes through Blytheville (Mississippi County) and cuts across the Mississippi River in three places. When those plates slipped, the earth moved and shook in what was named the **New Madrid earthquake**.

The earthquake began in December of 1811, and shocks continued for almost

158   Chapter 7

four months until March of 1812. The most severe shocks were along a line from New Madrid to near where Parkin, Arkansas, is today. The tremors from the earthquake were felt as far away as Canada and Massachusetts. A man in Louisville, Kentucky, kept a careful record of almost two thousand separate tremors over the four-month period. On today's Richter scale, the quake would register somewhere around an 8.0 and cause over $15 billion in damage.

▲ "The sunken lands."

> One witness described the ground heaving up in swells "resembling waves, which increased in elevation as they advanced, and when they had attained a certain fearful height the earth would burst and vast columns of water and sand and pit coal were discharged, as high as the tops of trees, leaving large crevices or chasms where the ground had burst."

For miles, the Mississippi River looked like "a boiling cauldron," and some swore that it ran backward for several days. The earthquake totally altered much of the land, creating new lakes such as Reelfoot Lake in Tennessee. As a result, parts of northeast Arkansas may have been pushed even lower than they had been, making the swamps larger.

There was very little permanent settlement in that area then, perhaps a few hundred Indian and white hunters. Apparently no one was killed in Arkansas, but the earthquake severely frightened settlers. The traveling Methodist preachers in the region reported an increase in church membership of almost 50 percent that year.

The New Madrid earthquake also caused parts of Craighead, Mississippi, and Poinsett counties to move, sink, and be covered by standing floodwaters. New lakes and swamps emerged, and much of Arkansas's wildlife drowned. Snakes and mosquitoes were abundant. Settlers lost their land, arguments over ownership and property rights erupted, and many just moved away. This area came to be called the "sunken lands."

The environment, natural resources, and discovery are an important part of Arkansas's early territorial history, and much was learned during that time. However, there were also major changes in politics, government, and society during the early nineteenth century. True progress and development would be somewhat overshadowed by the issues associated with the government's and settlers' treatment of Indians and those of African descent. It would affect Arkansas's history for years to come.

tremors (TREH-merz) shaking of the ground that occurs during earthquakes.

Richter scale a numeric scale used to describe the intensity of an earthquake based on the amount of the energy it has.

County Quest

Johnson

Named after: Benjamin Johnson, a territorial judge in the 1820s and a member of a politically prominent family

Chief Source of Income: Manufacturing

Seat: Clarksville

Johnson County was established in 1833 and can be found in the western part of the state. The county is located in the Arkansas River Valley, and the Ozark Mountains form its northern borders. Outdoor activities in the area's many rivers and streams are enjoyed by tourists as well as the annual Johnson County Peach Festival.

Jefferson's Louisiana and the Exploration of a Rugged New Land

Chapter Reflection

Reflective Questions

1. What are two states besides Arkansas that were formed from land acquired in the Louisiana Purchase?
2. How would you describe the early efforts to explore Arkansas?
3. How would you describe the importance of transportation to the people of Arkansas, giving three specific examples?
4. Discuss what you think to be the best method of transportation during this time and why. Be sure to support your opinion.
5. Sketch the state of Arkansas. Plot or mark the approximate place where you live or go to school and label it correctly. Now, correctly plot two or three locations of the first Arkansas settlements.
6. List eight crops grown in Arkansas during this time.
7. Arkansas presented many challenges to settlers who moved to the area between 1803 and 1812. Discuss what three of these challenges were and how they affected Arkansas's population.

HisStory, HerStory, YourStory, OurStory...

Read each of the following prompts. Consider them journal entries or letters of a person living in early nineteenth-century Arkansas. Choose one to complete. You must write at least *four* accurate, appropriate sentences that use terms, examples, and knowledge you obtained while studying the chapter. Make sure that your final product has an introduction, body, and conclusion and is logical.

1. "I am a member of the territorial expedition of 1803 led by Dunbar and Hunter. Today we began floating the Ouachita River. Our destination is what the red man calls the 'hot spring.' . . . "

Telling an Arkansas Story—The Written Word

2. "I have lived at Arkansas Post for three years now. Our little village has grown from 30 trappers and families to over 250 townsfolk! My husband, who was once a trapper, and I now own our own dry-goods store! Even though it is a small store. . . ."
3. "Farming this season has been difficult. With the drought and having tried new crops. . . ."
4. "Our little dogtrot shook something fierce! The children ran screaming to their beds. . . ."

Vocab en Verse

Create an original poem using any four words from the "Guide to Reading" list. Your poem must be in verse form—that is, have stanzas and a rhythm—and the word must be used correctly. That means you must know and understand the meaning of the word to use it correctly in your poem. Your poem should have a title and can rhyme, but it is not required.

Read and Respond . . .

Read the following passage carefully. Then, complete the activities below on your own paper.

Children in Territorial Arkansas

Many of the settlers of early Arkansas were hunters and trappers who lived isolated lives in remote parts of the country. Henry Rowe Schoolcraft, a New Yorker who toured Arkansas in 1819, was disturbed by the effect of this kind of life on the hunters' children. This is the way he described them:

> Schools are . . . unknown, and no species of learning cultivated. Children are wholly ignorant of the knowledge of books, and have not learned even the rudiments of their own tongue. Thus situated, without moral restraint, brought up in the uncontrolled indulgence of every passion and without a regard of religion, the state of society among the rising generation in this region is truly deplorable. In their childish disputes, boys frequently stab each other with knives, two instances of which have occurred since our residence here. No correction was administered in either case, the act being rather looked upon as a promising trait of character. They begin to assert their independence as soon as they can walk, and by the time they have reached the age of fourteen, have completely learned the use of rifle, the arts of trapping beaver and otter, killing the bear, deer, and buffalo, and dressing skins and making mockasons [sic] and leather clothes.

Note: *Sic* is Latin for "thus" or "just so." Historians have to reproduce quotations exactly like the original source. If the source has a mistake in it or a word that appears to be misspelled, the historian uses the term *sic* to indicate that it was that way in the original.

Henry R. Schoolcraft, *Rude Pursuits and Rugged Peaks: Schoolcraft's Ozark Journal, 1818–1819*, ed. Milton D. Rafferty (Fayetteville: University of Arkansas Press, 1996), p. 74.

1. What is Henry Schoolcraft's opinion of children in Arkansas during the territorial period? (Use a dictionary to look up words you do not understand.)

2. What animals do the boys kill with their rifles?

3. Describe the clothing of children in territorial Arkansas.

4. What act did Schoolcraft describe as "a promising trait of character"? Did he agree with this practice (activity) or not?

5. What does he say most fourteen-year-old boys in Arkansas know how to do?

Chapter 8

Growing Pains
Territorial Power, Politics, and Compromise
1803–1835

$105 REWARD.
RAN AWAY from the subscriber, living on the Mississippi river, 15 miles above Columbia, Chicot county, Arkansas Territory, on Thursday night, 8th August (inst.),

A negro man named **Pleasant**, about five feet 7 or 8 inches high, some of his fore teeth out, a scar on the top of his head, and has some scars on his arm, from his shoulder to his hand, occasioned by a burn. He took with him a rifle gun, the property of James Russell. I will pay a reward of SEVENTY-FIVE DOLLARS for his apprehension and delivery to me, at my residence.

Also—A negro man named **Peter**; he is about five feet high, and about thirty years of age. I will give FIFTEEN DOLLARS reward for his apprehension and delivery to me at my house.

▶ Slaves often ran away to try to gain their freedom. Notices such as this ran in Arkansas newspapers.

Timeline

	1810	1815	1820	
Arkansas	**1813** Arkansas's status is upgraded from a district to a county.	**1818** The Quapaws surrender the majority of their Arkansas lands to white settlers.	**1819** The county of Arkansas is declared a territory on July 4, with a population of 14,000. The *Arkansas Gazette* is established at Arkansas Post.	**1821** Arkansas's territorial government moves from Arkansas Post to Little Rock.
United States	**1812** Britain and the United States battle each other in the War of 1812 over trade rights and shipping. There is no clear victor and no lands changed hands, but the United States gains respect for challenging Britain.		**1819** Florida is purchased by the United States from Spain.	**1820** The Missouri Compromise is passed in Congress to balance the number of free and slave states that enter the Union.
World	**1813** Jane Austen publishes *Pride and Prejudice*.	**1815** Napoleon is defeated at Waterloo.	**1818** Mary Shelley publishes *Frankenstein*.	**1821** Egyptian hieroglyphs are deciphered using the Rosetta Stone.

Why Do We Study This?

The time period 1803–35 offers us a great deal of understanding about the importance and value of a piece of land becoming a functioning part of a larger nation. The government provides necessary services and institutional structures for all its people, while development and growth provide opportunities and the possibility of a better life.

The issue of slavery first surfaced in Arkansas during these years. We will learn the background that will provide us with additional understanding of the later conflicts that arose because of this issue. Also during this period, the national government carried out a policy called Indian removal. The last of the American Indian tribes in Arkansas were forced to move west.

This period of time is an illustration of the mistreatment of minorities and sometimes unfair practices that take place when people do not treat others with respect and compassion, especially those with different skin color or belief systems. Understanding the reasons for these behaviors, determining whether they are from fear or lack of knowledge, and working to educate ourselves so as not to repeat mistakes of the past are the responsibility of citizenship.

Big Picture Questions

- Must a government sometimes allow for special circumstances or situations when writing policy or laws? Why do policies change over time? Why are rules modified or rewritten? Use examples to support your opinion.

- What is the responsibility and role of the media in a free or democratic nation such as the United States? Do you believe it contributes to the process of democracy or takes away from it, or both? Be specific in your discussion and be sure to clearly explain why and how.

- Does growth and progress leave some behind or exclude certain groups or people? If so, how? If no, why not?

- In government, is it more beneficial for those in power to be replaced frequently or to serve for a long period of time? Should those of a particular background, educational level, family, geographic location, race, sex, religion, or age be the only ones to serve? Why or why not?

1825

1824 Quapaws are forced to move to northwestern Louisiana.

1825 Choctaw Indians move from Arkansas to Oklahoma, establishing the western boundary of the Arkansas Territory at the "Choctaw Line."

1826 James Fenimore Cooper publishes *The Last of the Mohicans*.

1830

1827 Henry Conway is elected to U.S. Congress but is killed in a duel with Robert Crittenden.

1827 *Freedom's Journal*, the first black-owned and operated newspaper, is published in New York City.

1831 Nat Turner leads the slave rebellion in Virginia.

1835

1833 Construction begins on the Old State House.

1832 Samuel Morse invents the telegraph.

1835 Davy Crockett visits Little Rock.

Growing Pains

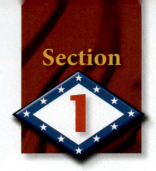

Section 1

Territorial Power

Guide to Reading

Terms
- abolished
- *Arkansas Gazette*
- cotton gin
- delegate
- militia
- sections
- slavery
- surveyed
- townships
- veteran's bonus

Events
- Missouri Compromise
- Northwest Ordinance

People
- ambassador
- William Woodruff

Places
- bootheel
- capital

---

delegate (DEL-uh-gut) one elected to represent others; for instance, a member of the U.S. Congress.

veteran's bonus a reward in the form of free land given to soldiers who fought on behalf of the U.S. government.

surveyed areas of land having been measured and divided into townships and sections.

townships measurements of land equal to thirty-six square miles.

sections measurements of land equal to one square mile; there are thirty-six sections per township.

The First Governments

Although the early settlers of Arkansas were self-sufficient in many ways, they did need a government structure to help in making laws, operating courts, building roads, and dealing with the Indians. The U.S. Constitution and national laws provided an orderly process for new lands to develop government by stages: new lands first became territories and then moved on to statehood.

When Arkansas and the rest of the Louisiana Purchase became part of the United States, the national government divided it into two big sections. In the north was the Territory of Louisiana, which included present-day Arkansas; in the south was the Territory of Orleans. In 1806, Arkansas was named a district within the Territory of Louisiana. When the southern Territory of Orleans became a state in 1812, it took the name "Louisiana," so the name of the northern territory was changed to Missouri. In 1814, the lands of Arkansas became a county of the Territory of Missouri.

As the number of settlers grew, Arkansas was split into more counties. In 1815, the Missouri legislature divided it into two counties—Arkansas County in the south and Lawrence County in the north. In 1818, three more counties were created out of Arkansas County—Clark, Hempstead, and Pulaski. Each county had its own sheriff and justices of the peace, and each sent a **delegate** to the Missouri legislature.

In 1815, Americans had a new sense of national pride, a growing population, and a prosperous economy. All of this encouraged people to move west. In addition, men who had served in the army during the War of 1812 (where the United States once again had battled Great Britain) were given a **veteran's bonus**. The government set aside two million acres of land in Arkansas to be given to veterans. A veteran could either settle the land himself or sell it to someone else. People who lost land in the New Madrid earthquake were also given replacement land in Arkansas.

Also during this time, the land in Arkansas was beginning to be **surveyed** into lots for sale. In 1815, the deputy surveyor of the Missouri Territory, William Rector, started the process of creating **townships** and **sections**. One team of surveyors marked a line north

164 Chapter 8

from the mouth of the Arkansas River, and another team marked a line west from the mouth of the St. Francis River. The place where the two lines met was the starting point for measuring all land in Arkansas and most of the Louisiana Purchase. (Today, that point, northwest of Helena, on the Lee and Phillips county lines, is the Louisiana Purchase Historical State Park.) Surveying is difficult work, and the process of measuring all the land moved very slowly, but starting the survey further encouraged settlement in Arkansas.

After 1815, the population of Arkansas began to increase rapidly. In 1818, there were around 3,000 white and black settlers in Arkansas. Only two years later, the U.S. census showed 14,273 white and black people. The increase in residents encouraged Arkansans to think about becoming a territory separate from Missouri.

Meanwhile, the people of Missouri Territory applied to Congress for statehood. They asked for a boundary that included the **bootheel** area around New Madrid but did not include the five counties of Arkansas. In Arkansas, the people responded by asking Congress for status as a stand-alone territory.

Slavery and the Missouri Compromise

Missouri's request to be a state and Arkansas's to be a territory created a serious debate in Congress over **slavery**. Many congressmen thought that slavery should be outlawed in both the proposed territory of Arkansas and the proposed state of Missouri.

Slavery had come to the Americas with the Europeans. Although there were attempts to enslave the Indians, American slavery almost always involved the enslavement of people of African descent. Slavery was a labor system, a way of ensuring a large supply of workers, but it also became a social system, or a common public practice—a way whites could keep the blacks under control. Most white people of the time believed that blacks were actually inferior to whites.

Throughout much of the world, people were rethinking the system of slavery, and it was slowly dying out. In 1776, slavery had existed in all parts of America, but as early as 1777, Vermont **abolished** slavery, and by 1800, all the northern states had done the same. In 1787, Congress passed the **Northwest Ordinance**, which permanently and completely outlawed slavery in the land north and west of the Ohio River. By 1808, the international (worldwide) slave trade had been outlawed. Even with these laws, illegal slave trade continued.

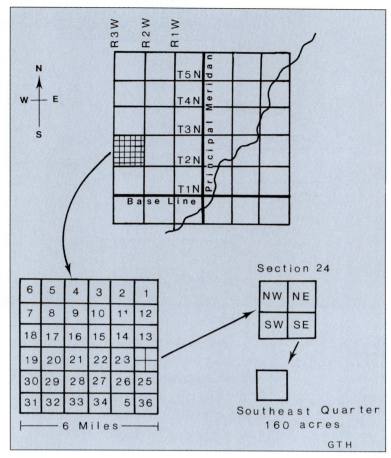

▲ Township and section divisions (160 acres).

bootheel (BOOT-heel) the name given—on the basis of its shape—to the land south of 36°30' (the Arkansas/Missouri border elsewhere) that belongs to Missouri.

slavery the practice of owning human beings as laborers.

abolished having been destroyed or ended totally, as in slavery.

Northwest Ordinance act of the U.S. Congress prohibiting the practice of slavery in the land north and west of the Ohio River (not including the Louisiana Purchase, which came later).

Growing Pains **165**

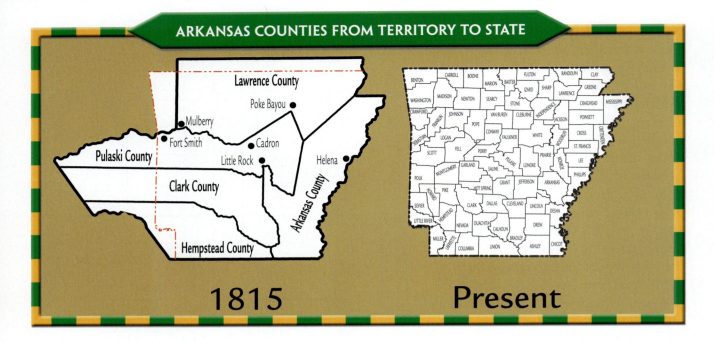

cotton gin (KAH-tuhn JIHN) a machine that removes seeds from cotton.

Missouri Compromise (MIHZ-oo-ree CAHM-pro-mize) the 1820–21 U.S. congressional prohibition of slavery north of 36°30' latitude except in Missouri, which was admitted as a slave state to balance Maine's admission as a free state.

▼ A drawing of the first cotton gin by William L. Sheppard.

However, the invention of the **cotton gin** (short for "engine") in 1793 delayed the end of slavery in the southern United States. The new machine made growing cotton extremely profitable, and cotton growing demanded large numbers of laborers. Cotton growing was well suited to the southern states. Before long, the South committed itself to cotton as its chief cash crop, and black slavery made mass production of the crop possible. Southern states adopted, promoted, and defended black slavery just when the northern states wanted to end it. For one thing, the North did not depend on large-scale farming, so slavery was not as important there.

The hope of gaining quick riches through cotton growing and slave owning was one of the things drawing settlers to Arkansas. At the time Arkansas applied to become a territory, about 12 percent of its people were of African descent, and all but a very few of them were slaves. Ten existing states were slave-holding southern states, and ten were northern states where slavery was banned. The question remained: would Missouri and Arkansas be "slave" or "free"?

The issue of slavery in Arkansas was settled in March of 1819 when Congress narrowly approved Arkansas as a territory in which slavery was allowed. In 1820, Congress approved statehood for Missouri as a slave state.

The **Missouri Compromise** had three parts:

1) Missouri would become a slave state.

2) At the same time, Maine, which had been a part of Massachusetts, would come into the Union as a free state. From this point forward, every slave state would

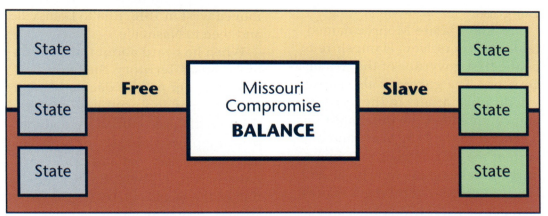

have to enter the union with a free state to maintain balance.

3) Except in Missouri itself, slavery would not be allowed in any territories or states created out of the rest of the Louisiana Purchase north of the 36°30′ line of latitude. This was the border between Arkansas and Missouri.

The debate over slavery remained a constant and critical issue, but sometimes leaders were forced to handle other issues of the developing territory and nation. State and national leaders knew that compromise on such an important moral and economic issue might not be possible.

Growing Pains   **167**

▲ Arkansas pilgrims. This sketch represents what settlers moving west might have looked like. What supplies do you think they carried in their wagon?

capital the city that is the seat of government in a country or state.

militia a part-time citizen army.

Arkansas Gazette newspaper founded by William Woodruff at Arkansas Post (Arkansas County) in 1819 before being moved to Little Rock in 1821 after relocation of the territorial capital. The current *Arkansas Democrat-Gazette* is the oldest, continuously published newspaper west of the Mississippi River.

William Woodruff the founder of the *Arkansas Gazette*.

ambassador (am-BASS-uh-dohr) one who is appointed to represent one nation to another.

The New Territory

Arkansas Territory came into existence on July 4, 1819, with its *capital* at Arkansas Post. It had its own government, with leaders who were appointed by the president of the United States. The people of the territory elected their own legislature as well as a delegate to the U.S. Congress.

President James Monroe named James Miller of New Hampshire to be the first governor of the Arkansas Territory. The governor also supervised Indian affairs in the territory and commanded the *militia*. Miller, a general in the U.S. Army and a hero of the War of 1812, was in no hurry to take up his new position. He did not leave for Arkansas until October of 1819. It was December, the day after Christmas, before his boat arrived at Arkansas Post.

In the meantime, Robert Crittenden (CRITT-tehn-dihn), the man appointed territorial secretary, had arrived in Arkansas and seized control. Just twenty-two years old, Crittenden was a veteran of the War of 1812, a lawyer, and a member of an important Kentucky family. He ordered an election in November of 1819 to create the first General Assembly (state legislature). It had a legislative council of five men, one from each county, and a house of representatives with nine men chosen from the counties based on population. The people also elected James Woodson Bates to be Arkansas's delegate to the U.S. Congress in Washington, D.C. Reluctantly, Miller accepted Crittenden's actions.

The leaders of the territory wanted a capital with a healthier climate (less dampness and without swamp-like conditions) and one that had a more central location than Arkansas Post's. The Cadron settlement on the Arkansas River was a possible site, but nearby Little Rock was chosen. When the government moved from Arkansas Post to Little Rock in 1821, so did the territory's first newspaper. This was the *Arkansas Gazette*, owned by *William Woodruff*. Woodruff was born in New York state, where he learned the printing trade. He had moved west in 1818, first to Louisville and then to Nashville.

When he heard about the creation of Arkansas Territory, the twenty-four-year-old printer decided to start a newspaper and printing business there. With a secondhand wooden printing press and cases of type, he traveled by keelboat and canoe to Arkansas Post. There, the first edition of the weekly *Arkansas Gazette* appeared on November 20, 1819. Woodruff became a major figure in Arkansas, and the newspaper he started lasted until 1991, when it was bought out by the *Arkansas Democrat*.

Secretary Crittenden was the most important man in politics in Arkansas for ten years. Governor Miller sometimes worked hard at his job, with special attention to Indian affairs, but he never adjusted to the frontier life. His wife and family never moved to Arkansas. He took longer and longer trips to visit them in New Hampshire,

▲ William Woodruff, October 1819.

and he finally resigned in 1824, claiming bad health.

President John Quincy Adams then appointed George Izard of South Carolina as the new governor of Arkansas. Izard, who really wanted to be an ambassador, was not pleased with his new post and was often absent. So Crittenden, who was very ambitious, worked hard and continued to dominate the new government.

▼ William Woodruff entering Arkansas. He came by boat and brought with him the newspaper press that he would use for the first issue of the *Arkansas Gazette*. Do you think a modern-day newspaper press would look like this? Why or why not?

DID YOU KNOW?

Honor on a Sandbar: Dueling

Did you know Arkansans did not invent the duel, but they became some of its most eager practitioners? A duel is a formal fight conducted with rules and the very real possibility of death. Dueling was a custom of men who considered themselves gentlemen, with a code of honor demanding that almost any sort of insult be met with a challenge to a duel.

Pistols were the usual weapons. Each duelist chose a "second," or a close friend, to accompany him. The seconds agreed on the rules and conducted the duel. Often a doctor and other witnesses were present. The two duelists faced each other across a specified distance—it could be anywhere from ten feet to ten yards—and fired on a signal. Even if both missed, the duelists could declare that their honor was satisfied. If one or both were hit, death was often the result.

Dueling was common in early America. In 1804, the vice-president of the United States, Aaron Burr, killed the first Secretary of the Treasury, Alexander Hamilton, in a duel. Andrew Jackson's many duels were campaign material in the presidential election of 1828, and the stories about his dueling probably helped him with the voters as much as they hurt him.

Many realized that dueling was both unwise, foolish, and harmful to public order. The first Arkansas legislature made dueling illegal, which is why Arkansans went just outside the territory to fight, to places like sandbars in the Mississippi River or to Indian country.

Perhaps more importantly, influential men realized that real honor and bravery consisted of not playing such a foolish game. William Woodruff, editor of the *Gazette*, for one, refused to give or accept a challenge.

However, there were many other duels in addition to the Conway-Crittenden duel mentioned in the text. For example, Andrew Scott and Joseph Selden, both judges of the Arkansas Superior Court, got into an argument during a game of cards in 1824. Feeling their honor was involved, they went across the Mississippi from Helena and fired away. Scott killed Selden with a bullet to the heart on the first shot. Scott and Selden, like Conway and Crittenden, were public officials charged with enforcing the laws, including the law against dueling.

Often, prominent men got into less formal fights. In 1828, the same Andrew Scott lost an election to Edmund Hogan, once a general in the Arkansas militia. The two quarreled. Scott called Hogan a liar; Hogan started a fistfight. The 250-pound Hogan knocked the 150-pound Scott to the ground. Scott pulled out his sword cane and stabbed Hogan four times, killing him. It was ruled self-defense.

Log on to Learn More
http://www.encyclopediaofarkansas.net/

Growing Pains **169**

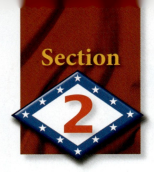

Section 2: Politics, People, and the Challenges of Progress

Guide to Reading

Terms
Democratic Party
dynasty
paddlewheels
political machine
sawyers
snag boats
treaty
Whigs

Events
duel
Trail of Tears

People
Sequoyah

Places
capitol
Dwight Mission
Fort Smith
Military Road

---

political machine a highly organized political group under the leadership of a boss or small elite group of chosen or privileged leaders; an unofficial system of political organization based on patronage (the power to make appointments to government jobs based on family relations or friendships, rather than qualifications; used to control or influence political policies).

dynasty another name for the Family, the Democratic power elite of territorial and early statehood days in Arkansas; in general, the term means a group of rulers related by birth or marriage.

Democratic Party the political party founded by Thomas Jefferson that became known as the Democratic Party under the leadership of Andrew Jackson.

The "Family"

The "Family" was a group of men finally formed to oppose Crittenden and his supporters. It is sometimes viewed as an early form or type of **political machine** or a **dynasty**. The Conways, Rectors, Seviers, Ashleys, and Johnsons were all related to each other by birth or marriage. (For example, Ambrose H. Sevier's mother's maiden name was Conway, his grandmother was a Rector before marriage, and his wife was a former Johnson.) In national politics, the Family was associated with the **Democratic Party**.

▶ Robert Crittenden, left.
▶ James Miller, right.

170 Chapter 8

Many had family ties to politicians in Tennessee and Missouri, just as Crittenden was related to an important Kentucky family.

A growing feud between Crittenden and members of the Family was made public in the election of 1827 for Arkansas's delegate to Congress. Crittenden supported one of his friends, Robert C. Oden. The Family backed Henry W. Conway. It was a mean and dirty campaign, with many personal charges on both sides. Conway won the election by a large margin, but that was not the end of it.

Crittenden believed that he had been insulted during and after the election, so he challenged Conway to a **duel**. The two met across the Mississippi from the mouth of the White River and exchanged pistol shots at a distance of thirty feet. Crittenden's shot wounded Conway, who died three days later.

Ambrose Sevier (suh-VEER) or (se-VERE), a member of the Family, won the special election for a new delegate to Congress. Although he tried for many years, Crittenden never regained the influence he once had in Arkansas and died at age thirty-seven. The cause of his death is uncertain and has been reported as a heart attack, stroke, or pleurisy (lung disease).

Soon, the political divisions in Arkansas began to reflect the divisions in national politics. The members of the Family were strong supporters of Andrew Jackson, who was elected president of the United States in 1828. When Jackson's supporters became part of the Democratic Party, the Family became the leaders of that party in Arkansas. The Crittenden group in Arkansas joined the party opposing Jackson, which came to be called the Whig Party.

With Jackson as president, the Family's control of Arkansas became even stronger. Izard died in 1828. The appointment of a new governor was delayed until Jackson took office in 1829. His choice for governor was John Pope of Kentucky. Pope had campaigned for Jackson in 1828 even though his opponent, John Quincy Adams, was Pope's brother-in-law.

◀ Albert Pike.

duel (DOOHL) a fight between two men in response to an insult, to settle a matter of honor.

County Quest

White

Named after: *Hugh L. White, a Whig candidate for president of the United States*

Chief Source of Income: *Agriculture and wildlife management*

Seat: *Searcy*

White County is the state's second largest county in land area and was created in 1835. During his explorations of the Mississippi River valley in 1541, de Soto encountered a large rock and named it "Bald Knob." Before the coming of European settlers, Native American tribes used it during their hunting trips up and down the White River valley as a marker. The area is home to Yarnell's Ice Cream and Harding University. Bald Knob National Wildlife Refuge, Henry Gray Hurricane Lake Wildlife Management Area, and Steven Wilson Raft Creek Bottoms Wildlife Management Area have been developed as premier wildlife management areas in the county and attract numerous outdoorsmen.

Growing Pains

Whigs the political party formed in opposition to Jackson's Democratic Party.

treaty an agreement between the U.S. government and an Indian tribe defining land ownership.

Sequoyah (SUH-koy-uh) Cherokees' leader, also known as George Gist, best known for his development of the written Cherokee language; he lived in Arkansas River valley around 1824.

Jackson dismissed Crittenden as secretary of the territory and replaced him with William S. Fulton. A native of Maryland who had moved to Tennessee, Fulton had been Jackson's military aide in one of the general's early campaigns, the Indian wars in the southeast. Then, in 1835, Jackson appointed him to replace Pope as governor.

In those days, newspapers frequently chose sides in political disputes, and each party hoped to have its own newspaper. Woodruff of the *Gazette* sided with the Family. The supporters of Crittenden, who would later become the **Whigs** in 1829, started a new newspaper in Little Rock, the *Arkansas Advocate*. In 1835, the *Advocate* was taken over by Albert Pike, a skilled writer who became a leader of the Whig Party in Arkansas.

Indian Removal

The increase in white settlement led to the removal of the Indians from Arkansas. The U.S. government's Indian policy was simple. Pressured by white settlers, the government, with a written **treaty**, would force a tribe of Indians to leave their homes to go to new land "reserved" for them. When settlement caught up with the new land, the Indians were moved again. For most, the final removal was to the Indian Territory of Oklahoma, west of Arkansas.

The removal of the Quapaws illustrates the process. These Indians, who had been the Europeans' first peaceful contact in Arkansas, were forced to leave their lands along the south bank of the Arkansas River. They were made to join the Caddos in the Red River valley. The arrangement was difficult for the Caddos and the Quapaws, but the Quapaws tried for a time to work hard and planted their fields. The Red River flooded and washed away their new crops not once, but twice in the first spring, and the displaced Quapaws nearly starved.

One group of Quapaws refused to stay, and they went back home to their Arkansas River land. Others followed, but they were not allowed to stay. In 1833, when only about five hundred Quapaws remained, the government moved them to a small reservation in northeast Oklahoma. The land they were moved to was only about 150 square miles. They were paid two thousand dollars each year for twenty years. Any other prior agreements for payment were void. The Caddos were moved two years later to a reservation in Texas.

In the meantime, northern Arkansas continued to be a hunting ground for the Osages and home for some newcomers, the Cherokees. In their homelands in the American southeast (Alabama, Georgia, North Carolina, and Tennessee), the Cherokees had been one of the "five civilized tribes" (Choctaws, Chickasaws, Creeks, Seminoles, and the Cherokees), tribes that were made up of skilled farmers. Shortly after the Ameri-

County Quest

Randolph

Named after: Believed to have been named after John Randolph, a settler of the Roanoke colony in Virginia

Chief Source of Income: Manufacturing and agriculture

Seat: Pocahontas

In 1835, Gov. William Fulton created Randolph County in northeast Arkansas. In the late 1700s, it had been a popular trading area on the Black River for the French and Native Arkansans. Visitors to the county can see one of Arkansas's two oldest standing structures, the Rice-Upshaw House, or visit Old Davidsonville State Park, which commemorates one of Arkansas's oldest settlements.

can Revolution, some Cherokees began moving to Arkansas on their own. By the 1820s, about 3,500 Cherokees, about a third of the whole tribe, had followed. They lived in the St. Francis River valley and around the site of present-day Russellville. For a time, **Sequoyah**, the inventor of the alphabet for the written Cherokee language, lived among them.

> "[Sequoyah] who in his own way was to be one of the most remarkable people either white man or Indian has ever seen. Inventor of the only alphabet achieved by an Indian for the transliteration of his own language . . . left his tribesmen . . . a literate people."
>
> —John Gould Fletcher, *Arkansas* (Fayetteville: University of Arkansas Press, 1989), 43.

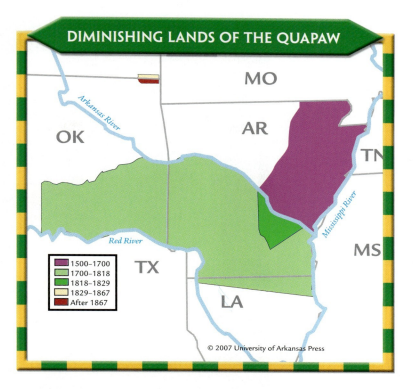

DIMINISHING LANDS OF THE QUAPAW

- 1500–1700
- 1700–1818
- 1818–1829
- 1829–1867
- After 1867

© 2007 University of Arkansas Press

▲ The Treaty of 1818 between the Quapaws and the U.S. government. The map is centered on the Arkansas River and shows the land the tribe was giving up to the U.S. government for white settlement. It was drawn by an Army officer.

▲ An artist's rendering of George Guess, the Cherokee leader better known as Sequoyah. He developed the written alphabet of his people, which is represented on the scroll in his left hand.

▶ *The Trail of Tears*—a painting by Robert Lindneux. How would you describe the emotions of these people?

Growing Pains **173**

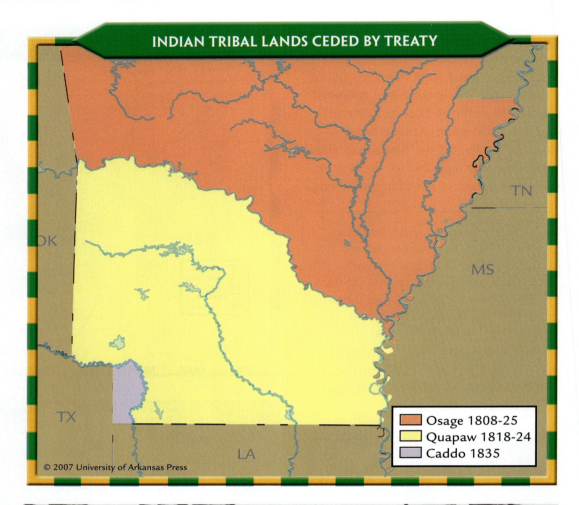

▶ Dwight Mission, in Cherokee Country near present-day Russellville, was illustrated as having a church and school building, cabins and farm buildings.

Quapaw Removal

1815

1817 War Against Cherokees
Cherokees who had been removed from homelands in the eastern United States conflict with Osages over sharing territory. The Quapaws offer to cede some of their land to ease these tensions if the U.S. government pays them, but the government does not agree to the terms.

1820

1818 Treaty of 1818
The government now needs the Quapaws' cooperation for further land exchange with the Cherokees, so they agree to the terms the Quapaws had set forth in 1817. Treaties are signed and monies promised, and the Quapaws retain only one million acres of tribal lands.

1825

1824 Treaty of 1824
Robert Crittenden drafts a document that forces Quapaws living in the Arkansas River Valley to the southwest to share the territory of the Caddos.

A Protestant group started **Dwight Mission** near Russellville in 1820 to bring the Christian faith to the Cherokees. Leaders of the mission ran a school, hospital, gardens, a general store, and a church. They stayed for the nine years that the Cherokees remained in Arkansas. The efforts of the mission were sometimes resisted by the Cherokees, as they believed it might take away from their heritage. Others thought it might help their children learn how to successfully live and work with whites.

The farming Cherokees and the hunting Osages often fought each other over their adjoining lands. In an effort to control them, the U.S. Army established **Fort Smith** in 1817 at the western edge of Arkansas. A small detachment of soldiers was supposed to keep Indians from fighting. They also tried to keep whites from trading in illegal goods with the Indians or settling on Indian land. It was a difficult job.

The government finally moved the Osages and the Arkansas Cherokees to Oklahoma. The Osages went by stages ending in 1825, and the Cherokees went in 1828. Arkansans witnessed one last sad scene in this story. In the 1830s, the national government decided to force all of the five civilized tribes to leave their homes in the southeast and go to Oklahoma.

Over a period of several years, the Choctaws, Chickasaws, Creeks, Seminoles, and the Cherokees East migrated to Oklahoma under the guidance of the U.S. Army. Some went by boat up the Arkansas River. Most walked over several different trails through Arkansas.

The Cherokees traveled the northwest Arkansas routes. The Arkansas portion of their journey began in Benton County, then headed west near Fayetteville in Washington County. In 1987, the Trail of Tears National Historic Trail memorialized this route by placing markers along the way to commemorate their struggle.

During this process, the Chickasaws, Choctaws, Creeks, and Seminoles also journeyed through Arkansas on their way to present-day Oklahoma but took a route through the Arkansas River Valley; only the Cherokees used the northern route.

This is one of the most painful times in our nation's history. The Native Americans were forced from their homelands, their dignity diminished, their heritage and culture compromised, and many deaths were brought on by starvation or disease while on the trail. Between sixteen

Dwight Mission Protestant organization to teach and promote the Christian faith to the Cherokees and to provide needed services.

Fort Smith town in the Arkansas River Valley that was originally established as a military outpost to monitor Indian Territory.

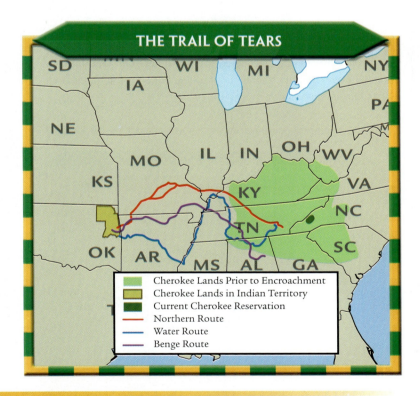

THE TRAIL OF TEARS
- Cherokee Lands Prior to Encroachment
- Cherokee Lands in Indian Territory
- Current Cherokee Reservation
- Northern Route
- Water Route
- Benge Route

1830

1826 Forced Removal to Red River
The tribe is relocated in 1826 as set forth by Crittenden's decree. The Quapaws eventually return to the River Valley (1830) because of floods, starvation, and a hostile environment created by the Caddos.

1835

1833 Treaty of 1833
The treaty renders all previous treaties void. It signs over only 150 square miles in present-day Oklahoma to the Quapaws.

1840

1836 Final Relocation to Indian Territory
The Quapaws finally settle in Indian Territory.

Growing Pains 175

Trail of Tears the immigration route of southeastern Indian tribes forcibly removed from their native land to Indian Territory.

Military Road a road built by the U.S. government to traverse Arkansas from Memphis to Fort Smith.

paddlewheels wheels made of horizontal blades powered by a steam engine that moved steamboats up and down America's rivers.

thousand and thirty thousand men, women, and children started on the journey. About four thousand died along the way. The Indians called it the **Trail of Tears**.

Progress toward Statehood

The same year Arkansas became a territory, 1819, the United States had a national economic crisis. Rapid growth of the nation encouraged many people to buy land and start businesses. Some borrowed too much money. When they could not pay back their loans, the Panic of 1819 hit the country as banks and businesses failed and people lost their money. The panic and its aftermath slowed westward movement for several years, but by the late 1820s, good times seemed to be returning.

Settlers continued to make their way to Arkansas. From 1820 to 1830, the non-Indian population more than doubled, from 14,273 to 30,388. About one-third of the people moving to Arkansas came from Tennessee. Most of the rest came from Missouri or from the southeastern states of Mississippi and Alabama.

Travel began to get easier. The national government paid to build a road from Memphis to Little Rock, and later on to Fort Smith. Called the **Military Road**, it was supposed to be twenty-four feet wide and cleared of trees, with sturdy bridges across the rivers and creeks. The first section, from Memphis to Little Rock, opened in 1828. However, tree stumps remained in the road until they rotted away, and floods often washed out the bridges. Sometimes a horse-drawn coach could go only about three miles an hour. The national government also began mail service. By the 1820s, most of the larger towns in Arkansas had mail every week or two, and connections could be made from Little Rock to Memphis, St. Louis, and Monroe, Louisiana.

The latest development in travel was the arrival of the steamboat. For western waterways, Americans had invented a unique new vessel. It was actually a big raft with a steam engine and one or two **paddlewheels**. On top of that was the cabin, one, two, or even three decks high, with fanciful wooden decorations. The steamboat could float in very shallow water.

The first steamboat went down the Mississippi River in 1811 and 1812 and then made the return trip back up the river. (It was on its way to New Orleans when the New Madrid earthquake occurred.) In 1820, the *Comet* became the first steamboat to call at Arkansas Post, and two years later, the *Eagle* made the first steamboat landing at Little Rock.

DID YOU KNOW?

Did you know modern roads and highways are anywhere from thirty-five to fifty feet wide for two lanes (one lane in each direction) and seventy to one hundred feet wide for four lanes (two lanes in each direction)?

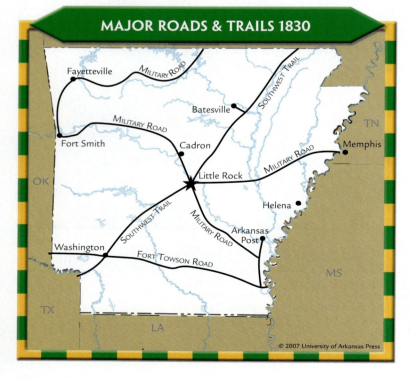

MAJOR ROADS & TRAILS 1830

▲ The Old State House, Arkansas's first capitol building, in Little Rock.

Little Rock was as far as steamboats could go up the Arkansas River, except during the high-water period in the spring when vessels could go all the way to Fort Smith and beyond. Fast and comfortable, steamboats could carry people and goods much more cheaply than any form of land transport. However, they were often dangerous, frequently exploding, catching fire, or running aground.

By the 1830s, steamboats were running scheduled routes on the Arkansas River. They were also beginning to run on the lower parts of the White, Black, St. Francis, Red, and Ouachita rivers. Steamboat pilots had to worry about the constantly changing river levels and about the snags and **sawyers**. Capt. Henry Shreve invented a boat to pull snags out of rivers. In the 1830s, he began to work for the government on clearing the Arkansas River. His **snag boats** also began to chew away at the Great Red River Raft.

By the mid-1830s, the nation and Arkansas experienced another boom period of expansion and growth. More people were coming to Arkansas all the time, and the territory was beginning to look civilized, too. In 1835, a Tennessee newspaper editor who had read a great deal of bad publicity about Arkansas visited Little Rock and was surprised. "Instead of a rude backwoods village," he said, "we found a handsome flourishing town, built up and refined. The citizens . . . were moral, polite, and hospitable, and the ladies pretty, accomplished and amiable."

As a symbol of progress, a new **capitol** building was under construction in Little Rock. With the profit from the sale of ten sections of public land donated by Congress, Governor Pope set out to build one big building to house all the functions of government.

The popular Greek Revival style was chosen for the building and the front was lined with tall, round columns. Americans in this period liked their public buildings to look like those of ancient Greece because Greece was the birthplace of democracy. As the new building began to take shape, it became the background for the next major step toward Arkansas's statehood.

sawyers (SOY-erz) entire trees caught on a river bottom that could "saw" a boat into pieces; similar to a snag.

snag boats boats designed to remove snags from river channels; used to remove the Red River Raft.

capitol the building that houses a state's legislature.

Saline

Named after: The salt works located within the county

Chief Source of Income: Retail trade, healthcare, manufacturing, and education services

Seat: Benton

Saline County was formed in 1835. The county's namesake salt mines were established in the 1820s, and William Woodruff, founder of the *Arkansas Gazette*, owned a productive salt mine there in the late 1820s. The county is the boyhood home of actor Billy Bob Thornton. The entire movie *Slingblade*, starring Thornton, was filmed in Saline County.

Bauxite, an aluminum ore, is found in Saline County. Miners who mined aluminum in the early 1900s were said to have "bauxite teeth," which were brown-stained teeth, with incredibly hard enamel created by the minerals in the local water. Today, the town hall in the community of Bauxite is now the Bauxite Museum.

Growing Pains **177**

Chapter Reflection

Reflective Questions

1. Elaborate on the Missouri Compromise, with emphasis on the sections that applied to Arkansas.

2. Discuss reasons why those in the Arkansas district wanted to become a territory.

3. Why was the territorial capital moved from Arkansas Post to Little Rock? Be sure to give detailed reasons in your explanation.

4. Explain the role of the Family in territorial politics.

5. Discuss who Robert Crittenden was and his immediate and long-term impact on Arkansas.

You Don't Say!

On your paper, number *1* through *10*. Clearly mark each phrase with a *T* for *True* or an *F* for *False*:

Information will be from both chapters on the territorial period, chapters 7 and 8.

1. The early, official U.S. exploring parties paved the way for U.S. expansion.

2. Arkansas was inviting to settlers because it bordered on Oklahoma and Texas.

3. Territorial Arkansas was a great hideout for outlaws.

4. The New Madrid earthquake caused tremendous loss of human life.

5. The Missouri Compromise admitted Missouri as a slave state and Minnesota as its partner free state.

6. Little Rock was chosen as the new state capital because of its beauty.

7. The *Arkansas Gazette* was established by William Woodruff and is still operating today as the only state newspaper in Arkansas.

8. Dwight Mission was established to spread Christianity to the Cherokees.

9. Cherokees from the southeastern United States traveled through Arkansas on the Trail of Tears.

10. The Military Road began in Missouri, crossed through Arkansas, and ended in Texas.

Prove It!

Now that you have completed the "You Don't Say!" exercise above, look at your answers and review the statements you said were false. Use your book and class discussion notes to find evidence to rewrite each of the false statements to be true.

Unlock the Meaning...

The *key* to new terms from the chapter...

Look at the "Guide to Reading" sections throughout the chapter. Choose five that are brand new to you. Write and number them *1* through *5* on your paper. Copy or trace the diagram below. Then...

1. In the section of the state where the majority of Indians on the Trail of Tears would have traveled, write two synonyms for the first term you chose.

2. In the section of the state where Arkansas Post was located, write a sentence that uses your second term correctly and conveys the meaning.

3. In the spot where the *new* capital was located, write the third term.

4. In the southwest corner, define the fourth term using *your own* words.

5. Finally, in the section of the state that was most directly affected by the New Madrid earthquake, quickly sketch an illustration of the fifth term.

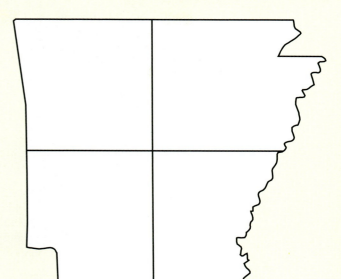

Make It Match!

On your own paper, match the letter with the appropriate phrase or definition...

1. The leading political party in Arkansas during the mid-1800s.

2. In early days of statehood, elections were held using a _____ vote.

3. Arkansas chartered two banks. The _____ was primarily for "regular" citizens. The _____ was primarily for planters.

4. The _____ was the newspaper established by William Woodruff that was affiliated with the _____ political party.

5. Albert Pike was most closely associated with the _____ political party.

A. Real Estate Bank
B. State Bank
C. Whig
D. Democrats/The "Family"
E. *Gazette*
F. secret ballot
G. voice
H. *Times*

Growing Pains 179

Chapter 9

Statehood and Slavery
1836–1860

Ballou's Pictorial—An antebellum-era newspaper article describing Arkansas. How does this Boston publication depict Arkansas?

Timeline

1836 – 1845

Arkansas

- **1836** Arkansas is admitted as the twenty-fifth state of the Union.
- **1837** The first state banks begin operating.
- **1842** State banks are forced to close.
- **1843** William Woodruff establishes the state's first library.

United States

- **1836** Under the leadership of Gen. Sam Houston, Texas wins independence from Mexico and becomes a republic. Sam Houston is president.
- **1837** Financial panic sweeps the United States.
- **1842** An American doctor is the first to use ether (early anesthesia) for surgery.
- **1845** Texas enters the Union as the twenty-eighth state.

World

- **1837** Victoria becomes queen of England; period referred to as the Victorian era.
- **1843** Charles Dickens publishes *A Christmas Carol*.

180 Chapter 9

Why Do We Study This?

After debating the issues of becoming a slave state, national politics, and local issues, the people of Arkansas wrote a state constitution and applied for statehood. Congress made Arkansas a state in 1836. Statehood meant Arkansas had to elect a new state government, with parties that followed the national Democratic and Whig parties. An attempt to create state banks failed, leaving a lot of bitterness.

The population grew in both number and prosperity. Religion and town life in Arkansas developed and became more sophisticated. While most white Arkansans were small farmers, a few became planters, owners of many slaves and large amounts of land. For the slaves, life was hard. Through these years, the issue of slavery also became more controversial. The argument over the expansion of slavery put Arkansas and the nation on the path toward civil war.

The consequences, both positive and negative, of this time period were significant to Arkansas's future.

> ### Big Picture Questions
>
> - Think about geography in our state. How did it divide Arkansas? What was geography's role in statehood and slavery? How does geography still divide our state today? Use reasons and examples to support your view.
>
> - Statehood was a tremendous change for many settlers in the territory. Classify reasons as to why some would believe statehood to be either necessary and positive or negative and foolish. What was the long-term impact of our statehood on the people and on our economy as the nation moved toward war? Which state was our "partner" state?
>
> - What was the role of the new state of Arkansas in the idea of Manifest Destiny? What is an idea or concept in practice in today's America that might be seen as similar to that of Manifest Destiny?

Geography, racism, and economy played a large part in determining the personality, reputation, image, and purpose of our state—all of which are still concerns today. Growth, progress, and change all have two sides—positive and negative—and we must carefully study and analyze every angle with open minds and understanding hearts to work to solve modern challenges and problems.

Timeline

1850
- **1851** Mt. St. Mary's Academy for Girls is established in Little Rock.
- **1846–1848** The United States battles Mexico; Archibald Yell is killed at the battle of Buena Vista.
- **1849** In California, gold is discovered and the "Gold Rush" begins.

1855
- **1857** Arkansans are murdered as they travel west in what would be called the Mountain Meadows Massacre.
- **1859** Edward Payson Washburn paints the famous, and sometimes controversial, "Arkansas Traveller."
- **1857** The Dred Scott Supreme Court decision denies citizenship to black people in the United States and allows slavery to exist in the territories.
- **1859** In England, Charles Darwin publishes *On the Origin of Species*.

1860
- **1860** Law requiring all free blacks to leave the state passes.
- **1860** Abraham Lincoln is elected sixteenth president of the United States. South Carolina is the first state to secede from the Union.

Statehood and Slavery

Section 1

The Decision for Statehood

Guide to Reading

Terms
bonds
capital
charter
Common School Law
credit
elite
free state
specie
Specie Circular

Events
Panic of 1837

People
assessor
planters

Places
arsenal
plantations
Real Estate Bank
State Bank

---

planters a small group of wealthy men who owned large amounts of land, many slaves, and typically focused on the production of cotton.

free state a state without slavery; where slavery was illegal.

By the spring of 1835, an air of excitement had spread through Arkansas. Talk among Arkansans was about the chance of becoming a full-fledged state in the Union, and almost everyone had an opinion. Statehood rallies took place all over the territory that spring and summer. In August of 1835, an unofficial, territory-wide vote resulted in 1,942 votes in favor of statehood and 908 against. Many of those in favor of statehood wanted a stronger voice in the nation's capital and more rights (states' rights) when dealing with the national government. Those against felt that statehood only benefited **planters** who could afford to pay the high taxes required of states and who would gain more political power because they generally dominated politics.

The twenty-four states in the Union were divided equally in half between free states, in which slavery was illegal, and slave states, in which it was allowed. With the Missouri Compromise of 1820 had come the idea that new states would come into the Union in pairs—one slave and one free—so balance would be maintained. This balance was critical to the slave states because an equal vote in the Senate gave them the strength to fight any proposed laws that they feared would be harmful to slavery. The Michigan Territory, which would be a **free state**, had applied for statehood. If Arkansas did not pair itself with Michigan, Florida Territory might. Then, it might be many years before another non-slave area would be ready for statehood to be Arkansas's "partner" state.

Arkansas had an acceptable number of people required for statehood—a

Searcy

Named after: Richard Searcy, the first clerk of and a judge in Lawrence County

Chief Source of Income: Timber, cattle, and tourism

Seat: Marshall

In 1838, Gov. James Conway created Searcy County in north central Arkansas. The county is home to the world-famous Buffalo National River and the Ozark National Forest. Searcy County is one of the most rural in the state, with a particularly rugged landscape.

182 Chapter 9

◄ What an Arkansas "plantation" house might have looked like in the 1830s and 1840s.

special census in 1835 showed a total population of 52,240. However, most Arkansans did not think of themselves as wealthy, and they lacked the cash required to pay the required taxes of a state and, as a territory, were used to receiving funds from the national government. On the other hand, a state could **charter** banks and in that way create a source of wealth.

Delegates met in January of 1836 to write a proposed state constitution to send to Congress for approval. The issue of slavery, or the influence of slave owners, divided the convention. Many of the eastern and southern counties of Arkansas were a part of the cotton belt and had large **plantations** dependent upon slave labor.

The upland counties to the northwest were made up of many farmers working small plots with just their family members and few or no slaves. The document they drew up arranged a compromise on how the parts of the state would be represented in the proposed General Assembly. The southern and eastern slave counties would have more representatives in the senate, but the northern and western free counties would have more in the house.

The delegates picked Charles Noland of Batesville to take the new constitution to Washington. He traveled across the South and then up the Atlantic coast, slowed by winter weather. Meanwhile, William Woodruff had sent a special edition of the *Gazette* that contained the

charter a guarantee of privilege granted by the power of a state or county.

plantation a very large farm devoted to production of one chief crop, such as cotton or sugar, associated with a slave labor force; a farm with at least a thousand acres and twenty slaves was considered a plantation.

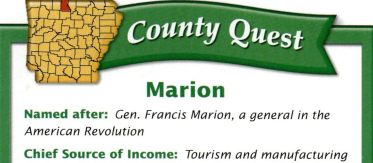

County Quest

Marion

Named after: *Gen. Francis Marion, a general in the American Revolution*

Chief Source of Income: *Tourism and manufacturing*

Seat: *Yellville*

Marion County was created in 1835 and the county seat, Yellville, was named in honor of Gov. Archibald Yell. Flippin is home to world-famous Ranger Boats and nearby Bull Shoals Lake, the White River, and the Buffalo National River, where enthusiasts enjoy fishing, floating, and hiking. The annual Turkey Trot Festival is held each year in Yellville.

Statehood and Slavery

elite a small, wealthy, and powerful group of individuals.

entire state constitution by way of the U.S. Postal Service. The post office beat Noland to Washington, and a congressional committee approved Arkansas statehood on the basis of the newspaper version of the proposed constitution.

Regardless of some people not feeling prepared, Arkansas became the twenty-fifth state of the Union on June 15, 1836, and Andrew Jackson signed the act into law. Michigan, delayed by a border dispute with a neighboring state, followed in January of 1837. In the fall of 1836, Arkansas's three electoral votes helped elect another Democrat, Jackson's vice-president, Martin Van Buren, as president.

The First State Constitution

The final version of the first state constitution of Arkansas was completed on January 30, 1836, after much discussion. It stated:

- that the governor, state legislators, and almost all local officials were to be elected by popular vote;
- that the governor had to be at least thirty years old, and have lived in Arkansas for ten years, and would serve four-year terms;
- that the legislature (ultimately the most powerful branch of state government because of these powers) would choose U.S. senators to represent Arkansas in Washington, state supreme court judges, the secretary of state, the state treasurer, and many other important state offices;
- that voting was limited to free white adult males, but that they did not have to own property to run for office or to vote; and
- that poll taxes were prohibited unless levied to raise money for county needs.

The New State Government

Although the leaders of the twenty-fifth state, who would be sworn to uphold the words of the constitution, were of two different political parties and almost all came from the wealthy **elite**, the voters who chose Democrats tended to be small farmers and from the poorer classes. Whig support tended to come from the planters and town merchants.

The Democrats won most elections for statewide offices and for president. But the Whigs held one-third of the seats in both the house and the senate. By Arkansas law, only white males over twenty-one who had lived in the state at least six months could vote. Voters were not required to be taxpayers, and there was no system to register voters. Voting was done by voice in public. On election day, the voter would go to the county seat and announce out loud his choices to the sheriff or county clerk, who would record the vote. Often a crowd of people, including those running for office, would be present. It was a popular form of entertainment for many settlers. For example, during one election, the Whig Party handed out free whiskey and played music during voting. The crowd would listen eagerly to the voting and applaud or boo the voters' choices. All of this may have contributed to the high voter turnout of the era. For a time in the 1840s, the state used secret paper ballots, but it soon went back to voice voting.

When the voters chose their new state government in 1836, the Family won all the offices. James Sevier Conway became governor, and Archibald Yell was sent to the U.S. House of Representatives. Conway was a younger brother of Henry Conway, the territorial delegate killed in the 1827 duel with Crittenden.

Arkansas Political Parties, 1818–1861

Party	Leaders	Political Views	Supporters
Democrat	"The Family": Johnson, Conway, Sevier, Rector	States' Rights Supported Pres. Andrew Jackson	planters yeoman
Whigs	Robert Crittenden David Walker Albert Pike	Federally-sponsored internal improvements: roads, canals, bridges, etc.	planters businessmen
American (Know-Nothing)	Solon Borland	Avoided slavery issue Anti-immigrant, Anti-Catholic	yeoman working poor

Archibald Yell was one of the most popular politicians in Arkansas history. At a very young age, the Tennessean had fought alongside Andrew Jackson at the Battle of New Orleans. He served again with Jackson in the Florida campaign against the Seminole Indians. Yell's ambition took him to the new state of Arkansas, to Fayetteville, where he became a judge. He was a friend to the common man and that made him a favorite among the people of his new home.

In those days, the state General Assembly, not the direct vote of the people, chose the members of the U.S. Senate. The winners were again Democrats. They were William S. Fulton, the most recent governor of the territory, and Ambrose H. Sevier, Conway's cousin and the former delegate from the territory to Congress.

The new state's economy was doing well in the boom years of the late 1830s. In 1837, the state government realized that it had a fifty-thousand-dollar surplus. Some members of the General Assembly wanted to use it to start a state university, but more of them chose to turn the money back to the people in the form of lower taxes. However, the government did authorize twenty thousand dollars, and another forty thousand in 1840, to build a prison on a hill west of Little Rock, at the current site of the state capitol building. The federal government began a major building project to create a military **arsenal** at Little Rock.

arsenal (AHR-suh-nuhl) storage or repair place for firearms or other weapons.

◀ Archibald Yell (left), James Sevier Conway (middle), Ambrose H. Sevier (right).

Statehood and Slavery

DID YOU KNOW?

Did you know the arsenal's central building is now the MacArthur Museum of Arkansas Military History in MacArthur Park?

capital money available for investment, construction, or expansion of business.

credit the provision of money, goods, or services with the expectation of future payment.

Real Estate Bank an Arkansas state bank created in the 1830s primarily for the use of the planters and the wealthy.

State Bank an Arkansas bank created in the 1830s to serve primarily merchants and the "common" man.

bonds interest-bearing certificates of public or private indebtedness; a method of borrowing money.

assessor (UH-sess-uhr) one who determines the value of land or other property.

The State Banks

A serious obstacle to growth in Arkansas was the lack of **capital**, in the form of either cash or **credit**. Under pressure from planters and businessmen, the legislature decided to establish two state banks. The 1830s were times of great economic hope all over the country. Almost any hardworking man thought he could get rich if only he could borrow some money to get started. That made it very tempting for banks to grant as many loans as possible. To complicate the issue, President Jackson strongly opposed a central national bank. He ordered the Bank of the United States to be closed, even though it had worked to limit bad loans given by state banks.

In Arkansas, the **Real Estate Bank** and the **State Bank** opened in 1837. From the beginning, the banks had problems. The state gave formal support and partly financed them through the sale of **bonds**. Even so, the state government had little control over the operation of the banks. For instance, 30 percent of the stockholders in the Real Estate Bank lived in Chicot County. As a result, the planters were in complete control of its funds.

The Real Estate Bank loaned large sums of money with only land as security for the loans. In one instance, Senator Sevier obtained a $15,000 loan secured on land the bank valued at $32,000. The tax **assessor** estimated the same land to

▶ The Nobe Dilbeck Home in Saltillo (Faulkner County), originally built around 1830, was a typical Arkansas frontier log cabin.

186 Chapter 9

be worth only $13,975. It was not long before the bank ran out of money and had to start borrowing from banks in other states like New York. The State Bank performed no better. Two years after it opened, it had debts of $2,000,000. Much of that was in loans that had little chance of being repaid.

The state banks issued their own bank notes. The value of this paper money was not supposed to be more than the value of actual gold and silver held by the banks. However, both banks issued far more paper money than their gold and silver reserves would allow. State banks all over the country were doing the same thing. President Jackson issued the **Specie Circular** that said that the federal government would accept only **specie**—gold and silver—as payment for public lands.

When the Specie Circular went into effect, it helped prompt a nationwide economic disaster, the **Panic of 1837**. That was the start of a severe economic depression, which also affected Arkansas. The panic spelled disaster for the state banks. Borrowers failed to pay their loans, and the banks tried issuing even more paper money to stay afloat. By 1842, both Arkansas banks were forced to close their doors. Many Arkansas bank managers left the state and moved west to Texas. The huge debts they left behind, which the state was legally obliged to pay, negatively affected state finances for decades to come. In frustration, the state outlawed the existence of banks and proceeded to default on the debts. It was a poor decision for a state short of capital. There were no state banks, and the state's credit was ruined with all the big banks in the East.

In 1840, in the middle of this unpleasant situation, the popular congressman, Archibald Yell, was elected governor. Despite remaining problems caused by the banking disaster, he looked to the future. In his first official speech as governor, he called for the development of a public-education system, internal improvements, and financial reform.

Putting the governor's program into action, the General Assembly in 1842 passed the **Common School Law**. It set aside sixteen sections of land in each township to generate money for schools. The lands were to be sold, and the income used by the local people to build and operate public schools. It was not yet a real public-school system, but it was a start. Most schools were still private schools, where parents had to pay tuition for their children.

Specie Circular an 1836 policy issued by President Jackson and implemented by President Van Buren that required payment for public lands be in gold and silver or "hard" money, as opposed to paper money that was "soft."

specie (SPEE-shee) or (SPEE-see) hard currency, namely gold or silver, as opposed to paper money.

Panic of 1837 a severe economic depression caused by falling cotton prices, failure of the wheat crop in the United States, and financial hardships in England.

Common School Law a law specifying that public lands be set aside and sold to raise cash to build schools.

County Quest

Benton

Named after: *Thomas Hart Benton, a prominent U.S. senator from Missouri*

Chief Source of Income: *Retail trade, agriculture, and trucking*

Seat: *Bentonville*

Established in 1836 from lands in Washington County, Benton County hosted the largest battle of the Civil War in Arkansas—the 1862 fight at Elkhorn Tavern at Pea Ridge.

Benton County was the home of the founder of Wal-Mart, Sam Walton, and is the location of Wal-Mart World Headquarters and J. B. Hunt Trucking. It is one of the fastest growing areas in Arkansas and the nation. Rogers is the largest city in the county, and students in the county can attend Northwest Arkansas Community College in Bentonville or John Brown University in Siloam Springs. The county is also home to the well-known War Eagle Crafts Fair and Beaver Lake.

Statehood and Slavery

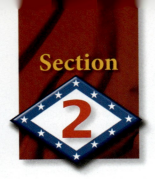

Section 2

Agricultural Life and Society

Guide to Reading

Terms
bolls
compress
hominy
privy

People
overseer
speculator
squatters
wheelwrights
Elisha Worthington
yeoman

yeoman (YOH-muhn) an independent, small, or family farmer.

squatters residents on land who do not hold legal title to the land.

speculator someone interested in the buying and selling of land for quick and/or large profit; real-estate investor.

hominy (HAH-mih-nee) hulled corn with the germ removed, from which grits are made.

The Yeoman Farmers

Most Arkansans were **yeoman** farmers. A good-sized farm might have 150 acres, a third of which was planted with crops and the rest occupied by woodlands or pasture. The typical family home was a log cabin. It was often built dogtrot style. Large families lived together in very close quarters.

Sometimes a family would simply assume ownership of a piece of land. They did not bother to buy it because it had not been surveyed or because there were no nearby land offices in operation to sell the property. Often, they did not have cash or credit to pay for it. People who simply took over land this way were called **squatters**. After several years, they might be forced to move to new land. Yet many of these families kept their property for generations without ever having legal title to the land. For those who did have money or credit, buying and selling land could be a source of wealth. A land **speculator** bought land at the government price, then sold it later at a higher price.

Arkansas settlers proved to be productive farmers. In 1840, Arkansas farmers raised enough corn to feed everyone in the state for a year, plus everyone in a second state of the same size. Arkansas had more cattle and hogs per person than any other southern state, and only Missouri had more horses per person. During this time, there were four hogs for every person. Corn and pork, sometimes called "**hominy** and hogs," were the basics of the Arkansan's diet. Extra hogs were driven to market to sell. Many families also raised a small crop of cotton or tobacco as a money crop to sell. The money they earned was used to buy flour, coffee, and other household goods that they could not raise or make themselves.

Family members worked together to make their own clothing. Many families had looms for weaving cloth and spinning wheels for making

▼ An Arkansas plantation house.

188   Chapter 9

thread and yarn. These machines were among the family's most valuable possessions. The pioneers dyed the cloth with colors from tree bark, flowers, and berries. Bear oil was still the chief fuel for lighting lamps. Taking a bath was considered a luxury, and did not often occur. Water had to be hauled in from a spring or well and heated over the fire. Chairs, beds, and tables had to be moved aside in an often-crowded room to make space for the washtub. Some distance from the well or creek that provided drinking water would be a **privy**.

Alongside the simple and nearly self-sufficient life of the yeoman farmer, the planter class was developing a different lifestyle. Far fewer in number than the yeoman farmers, the wealthy planters were known for owning large amounts of land, having many slaves, and producing large amounts of cotton.

privy (PRIH-vee) outdoor toilet or outhouse.

The Life of the Planters, Their Plantations, and Their Slaves

Most of the planters lived near the rivers. They lived in the Delta of the southeast, the Red River Valley of the southwest, and up the Arkansas River Valley as far as Fort Smith. This river bottomland was fertile, and the rivers were important for getting the cotton crop to market. Many planters had their own steamboat or flatboat landings, where they received goods and loaded up their cotton for the return journey. More than 90 percent of Arkansas cotton was grown in ten counties, nine of them in the lowlands

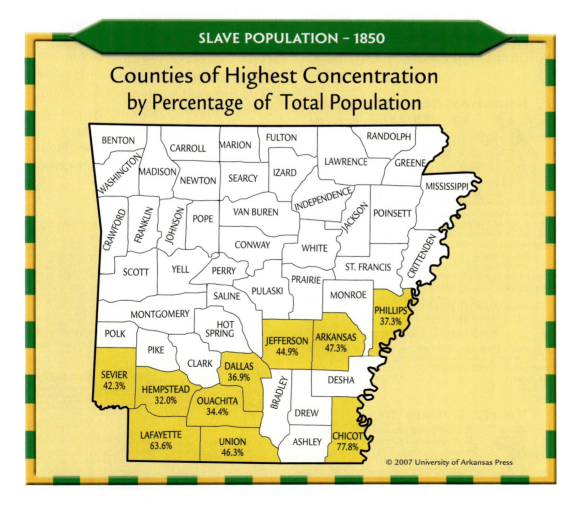

SLAVE POPULATION – 1850
Counties of Highest Concentration by Percentage of Total Population

© 2007 University of Arkansas Press

Elisha Worthington a Chicot County slave owner.

overseer boss of a group of slaves, usually a white man, hired to manage the plantation.

and one on the upper Arkansas River. Those same areas had 58 percent of the slaves and only 24 percent of the state's white people.

Unlike plantations in the older slave states, such as Virginia and South Carolina, these frontier plantations could be crude places. The planter and his family might hope to have a grand white house with columns in front, but for the time being, they were likely to be living in a house that began as a log cabin and grew with extra rooms added as the planter's wealth grew. But the planters and their families might also enjoy the luxuries of oysters, champagne, cigars, brandy, silk hose, cashmere, silver, glass, and china.

Black Arkansans and the Slave Codes

By 1860, only six people in Arkansas owned between two and three hundred slaves, and one man, **Elisha Worthington** of Chicot County, owned more than five hundred slaves. About half the slaves were owned in groups of four or fewer. Often the slave family worked side by side in the fields with the white family that owned them. They lived and worked closely with each other. Still, slaves could never forget that they were property, to be worked or sold as the owner saw fit.

Larger plantations most often grew cotton, the cash crop of Arkansas. Growing cotton required larger numbers of slaves and a plantation boss. He might have been the owner or a member of the owner's family. The boss may also have been an **overseer**. By 1860, there were about a thousand people in Arkansas who claimed a job as an overseer.

On a well-run plantation, the slave-labor force was closely managed to get the most out of each worker. The elderly and the children might have light tasks such as tending the livestock, but most slaves, men and women alike, worked the fields. Cotton growing required hard work all year-round, each day from dawn to dusk. Plowing and readying the fields began in January. Workers planted the crop in the spring. Field hands spent the long-summer grow-

▼ Poster advertising a slave auction in 1857.

▶ Typical newspaper advertisements of 1851 seeking to locate runaway slaves.

ing season chopping cotton, or working by hand up and down the long rows to keep weeds and grasses out of the valuable crop.

By early fall, the cotton was ready for the first picking. Slaves picked the cotton **bolls** by hand, bending over to reach inside the scratchy plants that scraped and tore at their hands, often causing cuts and bleeding. They plucked the soft, white boll from the prickly leaves and dropped it into a long sack slung over their shoulders. The slaves would pick over a single cotton field many times through the fall to be sure they got all the cotton. The picked cotton then went to a gin to have the seeds removed. From there, it went to a **compress**, then to market to be sold. Then, there was just barely time left in the year to repair the fences and tools before the cycle started again.

On plantations, some slaves had special roles based on their skills. They were blacksmiths, brick masons, **wheelwrights**, carpenters, and so on. These workers were valued by their owners and carried a high price. Some slaves might be house servants, cooks, and maids to the planter family, or nannies to their children.

In the towns, slaves were servants, coachmen, stable boys, laborers, and skilled craftsmen. Chester Ashley, a wealthy Little Rock lawyer and real-estate investor, and a relative of the Family, had a number of slaves to run his large house. The sons of Anne Warren, his cook, formed a music group that Ashley rented out for parties. They were the most sought-after band in Little Rock at the time.

The slave owner was the total master of his slaves, backed up by the customs and

bolls (bohlz) the pods and their white, billowy, puffy fiber that is picked and spun into cotton thread.

compress a device that pressed loose cotton into bales.

wheelwright a skilled craftsman who makes wheels.

PLANTATION COUNTIES – 1860

COUNTIES WITH LARGER PLANTATION ACREAGE

© 2007 University of Arkansas Press

Statehood and Slavery **191**

Black Arkansans and Slave Stats Chart (1860)

Slaves in Arkansas	Slave owners	Non-slave owners	Planters Class
111,115	11,481 (18% of the population)	82% of the population	1,363 total
About one-fourth of the population	More than half owned only one to four slaves	About 4 out of every 5 whites had no ties to slavery	Owned 20 or more slaves, 78% of the slaves and 63% of the land

By 1860, 111,115 slaves lived in Arkansas, forming about one-fourth of the population. Slave owners were few in number, and even fewer owned large numbers of slaves. In 1860, only 11,481 white Arkansans owned slaves. Assuming the average family was about five people, only about 18 percent of the whites were in a slave-owning family. That means 82 percent of whites (about four out of every five) did not have any ties to slavery. Among slave owners, more than half of them owned only one to four slaves. Only 1,363 white people owned twenty or more slaves, which placed them in the "planter class." They held 78 percent of the slaves and 63 percent of the land.

laws of society and the state. Slaves were not allowed to leave their owner's land without a pass. Whites ran patrols to catch slaves who did not have such a permit or who tried to run away. If a slave broke any of the rules or refused to work, he or she would be whipped with a lash.

Although slavery was too strict a system to allow much resistance, some slaves did fight back. Slave owners often complained that their slaves were lazy or purposefully broke tools. On one plantation, a slave refused to be whipped and was shot to death by the white overseer. When slaves ran away, the newspapers ran notices offering rewards for the return of the escapees.

Free blacks were rare in Arkansas, never reaching more than a few hundred. In many ways, their positions were unstable. One of the white arguments for slavery was that blacks were not capable

▶ Slaves pressing cotton into bales.

◀ Slaves picking cotton and dragging their cotton bags behind.

of living as free people. This argument assumed that black people were mentally and socially inferior to whites and that blacks had to depend on their white masters to survive—they had to turn to them for food, clothes, and shelter. The very existence of free blacks was seen as a threat to slavery. In Little Rock, the free black Nathan Warren became famous as a candymaker. Over time, he was able to buy the freedom of his wife, his brother, and some of his children. The debate over slavery intensified in the 1850s, and life became even more difficult for free blacks. Finally, in January of 1860, the Arkansas General Assembly passed a law that required all of them to leave the state, claiming they would be safer elsewhere.

Even under these conditions, blacks were still able to maintain home and family lives. Although the law did not recognize slave marriage, most slaves did marry and raise children. They kept some customs of their African heritage, largely passed down by storytelling. For many black people, religion provided comfort. Some slaves blended Christian faith with African traditions in music to produce the stirring songs we know as "spirituals." African traditions also enriched the eating habits of Arkansas. Gumbo, hushpuppies, and fried catfish are just a few of Arkansas's favorite foods that came to us from West Africa.

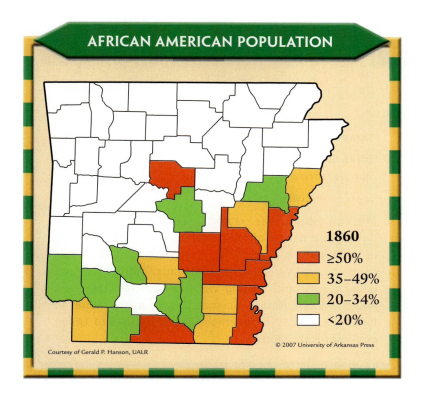

AFRICAN AMERICAN POPULATION

1860
- ≥50%
- 35–49%
- 20–34%
- <20%

Courtesy of Gerald P. Hanson, UALR
© 2007 University of Arkansas Press

Statehood and Slavery

Section 3
Daily Life in the Fledgling State

Guide to Reading

Terms
civil
courtship
excursion
lean-to
Lyceum

People
Daughters of Rebekah
Masons
Odd Fellows

Town Life

During the early statehood years, the population of Arkansas more than doubled every ten years. New people poured into the state, mostly from neighboring states such as Tennessee, Mississippi, and Missouri, with others coming from Alabama, Georgia, and North Carolina. Many of the newcomers were slaves, brought by their masters to establish new plantations.

It was becoming easier to travel to Arkansas. The major overland route was the road from Memphis to Little Rock, completed in 1836 after ten long, hard years of work. There was also the old Southwest Trail that slanted from the northeast corner to the southwest corner of the state. The rivers still carried much of the traffic. On the Arkansas River, steamboats began to run on regular schedules. In the southwest, Capt. Henry Shreve finally cleared the raft of piled-up logs in the Red River by 1838, although some clearing was necessary for many years after.

Like the rest of the nation, Arkansans knew transportation was critical to economic success, and they were eager to have railroads. The most discussed route was the Cairo and Fulton, which would run from St. Louis through Jacksonport (Jackson County) and Little Rock to Fulton (Hempstead County) on the Red River. Branch lines would go from Little Rock to Memphis and to Fort Smith (Sebastian County). Late in the 1850s, construction began on the Little Rock to Memphis link, but it was difficult. By 1860, only two short segments had been built, from Little Rock eastward to DeVall's Bluff (Prairie County) and from Hopefield (now West Memphis)

Madison

Named after: *President James Madison*

Chief Source of Income: *Agriculture, tourism, and manufacturing*

Seat: *Huntsville*

Madison County was created in 1836 from Washington County and named after President James Madison. Most of the county is used for agricultural purposes. People enjoy hiking, canoeing in the Kings, War Eagle, and White rivers, and visiting Withrow Springs State Park and the Ozark Natural Science Center. It was home to infamous Arkansas governor Orval Faubus and Union governor Isaac Murphy.

194 Chapter 9

A Day in the Life

Thirty-Nine Lashes "Well Laid On"

The institution of slavery was backed up by a set of state laws, the "slave code." Here are some excerpts from the Arkansas slave code:

> No slave shall go from the tenements of his master . . . without a pass, or some letter or token whereby it may appear that he is proceeding by authority from his master, employer or overseer; if he does, it shall be lawful for any person to apprehend and carry him before a justice of the peace, to be by his order punished with stripes or not at his discretion. No slave or mulatto whatsoever shall keep or carry a gun, powder, shot, club or other weapon whatsoever, offensive or defensive . . . every such offender shall have and receive . . . any number of lashes not exceeding thirty nine on his or her bare back well laid on for every such offense. Whereas many times slaves run away and lie hid and lurking in swamps woods and other obscure places, killing hogs and committing other injuries . . . any two justices of the peace . . . are empowered and required . . . to direct the sheriff . . . to take such power with him as he shall think fit and necessary for the effectual apprehending of such out lying slave or slaves and go in search of them, and upon their being apprehended commit them to jail . . . for further trial. If any negro or other slave shall at any time consult, advise or conspire to rebel or make insurrection, or shall plot or conspire the murder of any person or persons whatsoever . . . the slave or slaves convicted thereof shall suffer death and be utterly excluded all benefit of clergy.

westward to Madison (St. Francis County). The state's first locomotive, the *Little Rock,* ran **excursion** trips on the limited rail routes.

Those who left their old homes behind to make a new life on the Arkansas frontier were bold and hardy people. Many of them were young, single males who could easily take a chance on something new. Part of the violence on the Arkansas frontier was due to the high proportion of young, unmarried men in the state. However, a large number of the

excursion (ehks-ker-zhun) a short trip or voyage, usually for pleasure.

Statehood and Slavery

new settlers were young married couples with very small children. In the more settled parts of the United States, families of this time were having fewer children, and women were beginning to get involved in life outside of the home. However, in frontier Arkansas, the young women of the 1840s were having more children than those in any other state. The typical frontier woman married at the age of twenty-two and had a child every two years, for around six to eight children. In those days, infants and children had little protection against diseases like measles and mumps. Even complications from simple illnesses might result in death. Sometimes only four or five of the children born to a family would live to be adults.

Although most Arkansans were farmers living in rural areas, there was growth in the towns, as they were market and trade centers. Every town of any size had a hotel and boarding houses. Merchants sold food, cloth and dyes, kitchen goods, and liquor. Doctors, lawyers, and dentists set up offices throughout the state. A few women opened hat and dressmaking shops. Other craftsmen made and sold guns, furniture, and shoes and boots.

People in towns had the opportunity to develop a more sophisticated cultural life than people in rural areas. Reading groups, debate clubs, and history groups formed, such as the

▲ Most nineteenth-century rifles were handcrafted by artisans. This one, trimmed with silver from melted coins, was crafted in 1870 by W. O. Robertson of Pulaski County.

Population Growth in Arkansas 1830–2004

	1830	1840	1850	1860	2004
Total Population	30,388	97,574	209,897	435,450	2,675,872
White Population	25,671	77,174	162,189	324,143	2,124,002
Black Population	4,717	20,400	47,708	111,307	409,064
Black Population as a Percentage of Total Population	15.5	20.9	22.7	25.6	15.2

The United States census, taken every ten years, shows the rapid population growth in Arkansas. The total population more than doubled every ten years from 1830, in the Territorial Period, to 1860, the eve of secession. Note, too, that the black population, almost all slaves, increased at a slightly faster rate than the white population. In the same period, the total population of the United States went from about 12,900,000 in 1830 to about 31,500,000 in 1860. The population of the United States in July of 2006 was 299,182,966, and in October of that same year, went over 300,000,000.

Club of Forty and the **Lyceum** in Little Rock. Speakers traveled from town to town and charged an entrance fee for lectures on a number of subjects. People organized singing clubs, concerts, and dramas to entertain themselves. Men and women formed community groups like the **Odd Fellows**, **Daughters of Rebekah**, and the **Masons**.

A number of magazines were created like the *Christian Teacher, Memphis and Arkansas Christian Advocate, Southern Gem,* and *Arkansas Magazine.* Gambling and horse racing, however, were probably the most common, and popular, pastimes. Traveling artisans, architects, portrait painters, musicians, comics, and entertainers enhanced frontier town life. They traveled all over the South, and mainly visited the river towns in Arkansas. The circus was extremely popular, coming to towns of all sizes on a regular basis.

Holidays offered special times for festivities and fun. The Fourth of July was perhaps the most important. Parades, speeches, and fireworks marked the event. Christmas, on the other hand, was not such a big holiday. It was of special importance to plantation slaves because it brought the only days of rest they were allowed throughout the year.

Religion in Arkansas

Churches were important forces on the frontier because they promoted the idea of behaving in a **civil** manner. As early as 1825, Little Rock had a Baptist meetinghouse that served as a public gathering spot for all kinds of meetings. Presbyterianism came early to Arkansas, and Little Rock's First Presbyterian Church was organized in 1828. The Christian Church organized in 1832. There were soon many Methodist churches in the northwest. In 1845, a group of slaves formed the First Missionary Baptist Church of Little Rock.

The Roman Catholic Church had been brought to Arkansas with the first French and Spanish settlers, but a formal diocese was not formed until the 1840s. Its school in Little Rock, St. Mary's Academy for Girls, was founded in 1851 by the Sisters of Mercy. It is now the oldest continuing school in Arkansas.

For those living scattered throughout the countryside, the camp meeting was both a religious and a social event. Once a year, usually in late September, entire rural communities would turn out for ten days to three weeks of preaching. The preacher might be a local man or a visitor from another state. Some church campground sites were used over and over and had a building to house the pulpit and rows of benches. Many came to stay for the whole meeting, living in wooden log tents, sometimes called a **lean-to**, or in the backs of their wagons.

The camp meetings gave people a common bond and shared moral teachings. Besides hymn singing, preaching, and praying, camp meetings gave young farm men and women rare chances for meeting and **courtship**. The events also drew merchants selling their wares, sometimes even liquor. Politicians attended and tried to earn followers and votes. Despite wealth, gender, color, or age, all were free to express their fears, hopes, and feelings at these camp meetings.

◀ Mount Saint Mary's Academy for Girls, Little Rock.

Lyceum guest speakers, who were considered to be authorities on topics such as art, culture, or politics, who traveled throughout the countryside to give lectures or conduct discussions among the citizenry.

Odd Fellows a fraternal organization, founded in Baltimore, Maryland, in 1819; named as such because outsiders considered it "odd" to see people coming together to assist others less fortunate; with addition of Daughters of Rebekah in 1851, first national fraternity to include men and women.

Daughters of Rebekah see Odd Fellows.

Masons an organization, once a "secret society," of men who believe in one Supreme Being and work to better themselves through the building of character, giving to charity, and/or volunteering, and by strengthening moral values. Formally established in 1717.

civil as in behavior: polite, courteous, well-mannered, decent; of or having to do with the general public or citizenry. A war between the citizens of a nation, as in the Civil War.

lean-to a small shelter, shack, or shanty with a sloped roof held up by a pole.

courtship dating; attracting, engaging, or attempting to form a bond.

Statehood and Slavery

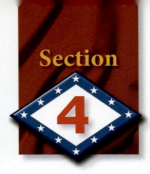

Section 4

Expansion

Guide to Reading

Terms
Manifest Destiny   receivership

People
forty-niners

Manifest Destiny
the belief, ideology, or doctrine that Americans had a right and responsibility to expand westward all the way to the Pacific coast.

Manifest Destiny

In 1836, Arkansas became a state, and it was also the year of the Texas Revolution. Arkansans had watched events to their southwest with interest. Many American settlers had moved through Arkansas to get to Texas, and quite a few Texas leaders had Arkansas connections.

Stephen F. Austin had been one of the land speculators who promoted the city of Little Rock as Arkansas Territory's capital city. Davy Crockett was honored with a dinner in Little Rock on his way to Texas. Jim Bowie's famous Bowie knife (BOO-ee nife) was crafted by James Black of the town of Washington (Hempstead County). Crockett and Bowie both later died at the Alamo.

By the mid-1840s, the urge of Americans to expand the size of their country was referred to as **Manifest Destiny**. That drive became all-powerful. The government and settlers felt that nothing should stop the push westward. Congress voted

▶ An artist's representation of Manifest Destiny. Describe and discuss the elements of the painting. Put yourself "inside" the painting: what do you hear, see, smell, taste, feel?

198 Chapter 9

to annex Texas in 1845. Arkansas was no longer the westernmost state in the Union. From the standpoint of Mexico, which had never given up its rights to Texas, the United States had just annexed a state of Mexico's. Talk of war became common. Americans also wanted control of Mexican lands in what would later become California and New Mexico. Because of this, an exchange of shots along the Rio Grande brought war in the spring of 1846. President James K. Polk asked Arkansas to provide a regiment of mounted infantry to fight in Mexico. He also asked for soldiers from Arkansas to relieve regular U.S. Army troops on the Indian frontier.

Arkansans quickly volunteered. By this time, Archibald Yell was back in Congress, and Thomas Drew, a Lawrence County planter who had come from Tennessee, was governor. Yell came home from Washington, D.C., to enlist as a private, and he was elected colonel of his volunteer unit. Yell was a Democrat. Albert Pike, a Whig, served as a captain of the unit and later had many bad things to say about Yell's lack of military skill. In fact, the Arkansas troops, like most volunteers in the Mexican War, were strong on spirit and weak on training. Some newspaper reporters called them "The Mounted Devils of Arkansas."

> Davy Crockett also said of Arkansas:
>
> *"If I could rest anywhere, it would be in Arkansaw, where men are of the real half-horse, half-alligator breed such as grows nowhere else on the universal earth."*
>
> Allen C. Paulson, *Roadside History of Arkansas* (Missoula, MT: Mountain Press Publishing Company, 1998), 92.

The Arkansas soldiers' major battle was at Buena Vista, deep in northern Mexico, on February 22 and 23, 1847.

DID YOU KNOW?

Did you know Davy Crockett visited Arkansas on his way to Texas and the Alamo? Little Rock citizens honored him with a banquet. In his speech after dinner, the former Tennessee congressman offered some general advice on running for office:

"When the day of election approaches, visit your constituents far and wide. Treat liberally, and drink freely. . . . Do all you can to appear to advantage in the eyes of the women. That's easily done—you have but to kiss and slobber their children, wipe their noses, and pat them on the head; this cannot fail to please their mothers. . . . Get up on all occasions, and sometimes on no occasion at all, and make long-winded speeches . . . talk of your devotion to your country, your modesty and disinterestedness, or any such fanciful subject. Rail against taxes of all kinds, office holders, and bad harvest weather; and wind up with a flourish about the heroes who fought and bled for our liberties in the times that tried men's souls."

James R. Masterson, *Arkansas Folklore: The Arkansas Traveler, Davey Crockett, and Other Legends.* (Little Rock: Rose Publishing, 1974), 23–24.

Under Mexican attack, the Arkansans began to break ranks, and some men ran away. Trying to rally the men, Colonel Yell was killed when a Mexican lance pierced his head. The war secured Texas for the United States, but claimed the life of one of Arkansas's favorite sons.

As soon as the war with Mexico was over, Arkansans heard great news from California. Gold had been found and the gold rush began. The first groups of Arkansas "**forty-niners**," 128 men in fifty wagons, left Fort Smith for the gold fields of California in April of 1849. Arkansas served as the starting point for one of the major trails to California. Beginning in Fort Smith, Van Buren, or Fayetteville, this southern route went through Santa Fe and on to the gold fields. Thousands of men, including many Arkansans, made the long journey to California. A few got rich, but most failed to find wealth.

forty-niners gold hunters who traveled to California in the Gold Rush of 1849.

Statehood and Slavery **199**

The Prosperous 1850s

	1850	1860	2005
Number of farms	17,785	39,004	47,500
Acres in farms	2,598,214	9,573,706	14.5 mil
Improved farm acres	781,530	1,983,313	n/a
Average acreage per farm	146	245	306
Average value of farms	$860	$2,350	n/a
Total value of farm livestock	$6,647,969	$22,096,977	$9,508,746
Average livestock value per farm	$374	$567	n/a
Bales of cotton	65,344	367,393	1.8 mil
Bushels of corn	8,893,939	17,823,588	35 mil
Pounds of tobacco	218,936	989,980	n/a
Pounds of rice	63,179	16,831	10,779,600,000

The decade of the 1850s, the last ten years before the Civil War, was a very prosperous period for Arkansans, most of whom were farmers. Statistics from the United States census show large increases in almost every farm measurement.

County Quest

Franklin

Named after: Benjamin Franklin

Chief Source of Income: Manufacturing and tourism

Seat: Ozark, Charleston

Franklin County was established in the northwestern part of the state in 1837. The first settlers to the area were from Tennessee, and they settled on Mulberry Creek. The reality show *The Simple Life* with Paris Hilton and Nicole Richie was filmed in Altus and Ozark. Charleston is known for being one of the first school districts in Arkansas to desegregate successfully in the late 1950s. Altus is home to the Arkansas Winemaking Industry, which includes several family vineyards. Near the community of Mulberry, the Mulberry River is a popular destination for kayakers and canoeists.

Mountain Meadows Massacre

On September 11, 1857, Mormon settlers in southwest Utah massacred 121 men, women, and children on a wagon train bound for California. The wagon train was made up of families from Benton, Carroll, Johnson, and Marion counties of Arkansas. In honor of their leaders, this wagon train became known in history as the Fancher-Baker train. Capt. Alexander Fancher was responsible for the wagons and families, while Capt. John Twitty Baker was in charge of the livestock. Prior to the Oklahoma City bombing, the Mountain Meadows Massacre was the largest act of domestic terrorism to ever occur on American soil. The massacre continues to be an unsettled issue with thousands of direct descendants of the victims and survivors of the Mountain Meadows Massacre. There have been many books and documentary films on the massacre.

Although the early 1850s was a prosperous time in Arkansas, the Panic of 1857 brought hardships to many Ozark families. They thought California offered them a better future for their growing families. Others were looking for the adventure of moving west.

Mormons had lived in several states before moving to Utah in 1847. After being driven out of Missouri, the Latter Day Saints Church settled in Nauvoo, Illinois, where their leaders, including Joseph Smith and his brother Hyrum, were jailed and killed. Joseph Smith's followers felt persecuted in Missouri and Illinois. Brigham Young assumed leadership of the Mormons and moved the group to Utah. Utah was unsettled when the Mormons arrived there.

On July 24, 1857, Brigham Young and his followers were holding a celebratory picnic in Cottonwood Canyon near Salt Lake City, when he received word that the U.S. Army was moving toward Utah. He was to be replaced as governor of Utah Territory. The picnic occurred one week before the Fancher-Baker wagon train reached Salt Lake City.

Some historians cite robbery as a motive for attacking the wagon train. Others believe that the Mormons were avenging the death of Prophet Joseph Smith and Apostle Parley Pratt. Pratt had been murdered in Alma, Arkansas, a short time before the wagon train reached Utah.

Most accounts state that the massacre was disguised as a Paiute Indian massacre. However, recent forensic evidence confirmed that the Paiutes had very little involvement in the massacre. In all, seventeen children

DID YOU KNOW?

Bowie Knives to the Death in the House of Representatives

Did you know in the first session of the Arkansas General Assembly, the speaker of the house of representatives murdered another legislator on the floor of the house?

It started with a debate in the house on a bill to offer bounties for wolf hides. Maj. Joseph J. Anthony of Randolph County was bitterly opposed to the Real Estate Bank, which the legislature had created earlier in the session, and he thought he would try to make his point again.

Anthony offered an amendment to the wolf-scalp bill, requiring the president of the Real Estate Bank to sign each bounty certificate. Anthony knew that the president of the Real Estate Bank was John Wilson of Clark County, speaker of the house of representatives.

Wilson, from his chair as presiding officer, demanded to know if Anthony intended a personal slur. As Anthony tried to explain himself, Wilson ordered him to sit down. When Anthony remained standing, Wilson drew his Bowie knife, shouted, "Sit down or I'll make you!" He then moved toward Anthony.

Anthony drew his Bowie knife, too, and moved to meet Wilson. Wilson seized a chair to use as a shield, and the two fought. Anthony lost his knife and grabbed another chair to defend himself.

Wilson pushed aside Anthony's chair and thrust his knife into Anthony's chest up to the hilt. Anthony died instantly, without a word or a cry. Watching all this were the members of the Arkansas house of representatives, none of whom had even tried to stop the fight.

Wilson wiped the blood from his knife with his thumb and finger and resumed the speaker's seat.

When Wilson was finally brought before a court at the insistence of Anthony's relatives, the jury acquitted him of murder.

One account says that Wilson then treated all the jurors to drinks, and he later led a parade with noisemakers through town to the lodgings of Anthony's relatives "to shout and scream and yell, as in triumph over them and over the law."

▶ A Bowie knife.

Statehood and Slavery

under the age of seven survived the massacre.

Accounts state that victims were stripped of clothing and left unburied for the next eighteen months. Other wagon trains, when they passed through Mountain Meadows after the massacre, reported that wolves were dragging the exposed bodies about the meadows.

In May of 1859, army officers and soldiers came from California to Mountain Meadows. They collected the remains of the massacre victims and buried them in several mass graves. Soldiers erected a twenty-four-foot cross over the graves, and they also carved on a large rock the words "Here 120 men, women, and children were murdered in Cold Blood in early September 1857. They were from Arkansas." This memorial to the massacre victims was destroyed, possibly by Brigham Young's orders, in 1861.

Eighteen months after the massacre, Dr. Jacob Forney and Capt. James Lynch came to the area and searched for the children. The Mormons claimed the Indians had the children. After an intense search, seventeen orphans were taken into the custody of Dr. Forney. The children claimed the Indians never kept them. The survivors were then taken to Salt Lake City. From there, they were returned to Arkansas. Their relatives met them at Carrollton, Arkansas, on September 25, 1859, and took them into their homes.

Arrest warrants were sworn out for over a hundred people including Brigham Young by Judge John Cradlebaugh. The judge's military escort was pulled from him, leaving it unsafe for him to continue his investigation of the massacre. After the Civil War, newspapers started asking questions. To satisfy that renewed call for justice, John D. Lee was brought to trial in 1875. A jury of citizens of various faiths did not convict Lee. He was brought to trial a second time with an all-Mormon jury. Lee was sentenced to death. In May of 1877, twenty years after the massacre, John D. Lee was taken to Mountain Meadows and executed by firing squad. He was the only one to be brought to justice for the massacre.

Today, memorials stand in Harrison, Arkansas, and at Mountain Meadows to honor those who perished.

Looking Back at Pre–Civil War Arkansas

Despite its many ups and downs, the state was growing swiftly in population and wealth as it emerged from the frontier era. The cotton trade was prospering, and railroad construction had begun at last.

Elias Nelson Conway, the governor from 1852 to 1860, did much to put the state on a sound financial path. Conway was yet another member of the Family. He managed to obtain an accurate account of the Real Estate Bank's assets and put the bank into

County Quest

Poinsett

Named after: *Joel R. Poinsett of South Carolina, U.S. secretary of war*

Chief Source of Income: *Manufacturing*

Seat: *Harrisburg*

Poinsett County was established by Gov. James Conway in 1838. It was the location of much of the Southern Tenant Farmers Union's activities during the 1930s. Lepanto was the setting for filming of the movie *A Painted House*, based on the novel by native Arkansan author John Grisham. The St. Francis Sunken Lands, created by the New Madrid earthquake in 1811–12, are also located in parts of the county.

I Am an Arkansan

Peter Caulder (1795?–1861?)

Peter Caulder was an African American born in South Carolina. His time in Arkansas represents the success and freedom some blacks could enjoy before 1859 when the state government banned free blacks from Arkansas. Caulder served in the U.S. Army during the War of 1812—he helped defend the U.S. capitol from British attack—and within a decade had settled in Arkansas along the White River in what is today Marion County.

He and his wife Eliza raised seven children, and for thirty-five years, his family lived self-sufficiently and prosperously, with little conflict with their white neighbors.

Caulder's life demonstrates a high degree of success and independence, especially for a free African American family living in a slave society. This changed abruptly in 1859, when the Arkansas state legislature passed an exclusion law. This measure aimed to drive free blacks from the state. Along with the other 160 free black people in Marion County, Peter Caulder and his family left Arkansas, banished from the state they had called home for over thirty years.

THE ENCYCLOPEDIA OF ARKANSAS HISTORY & CULTURE

Log on to Learn More
http://www.encyclopediaofarkansas.net/

---

receivership. Economic growth increased the state's tax base by $100 million. Conway left more than three hundred thousand dollars in gold and silver in the state treasury and vetoed a bill to reduce taxes that the General Assembly had passed.

But looming over all was the growing argument between the North and South, between free and slave states. Starting with a dispute over the status of slavery in the new lands obtained from Mexico, the fight grew harsher and more intense throughout the decade. Border states such as Arkansas, as much western as southern, were being pushed closer to the point where they would have to choose sides.

receivership (ruh-SEEV-er-ship) placing a bankrupt institution into the hands of new management, often appointed by a court.

Chapter Reflection

Reflective Questions

1. Considering two points of view, discuss the arguments for Arkansas's statehood. Divide your paper in half with a vertical line and have one column with the heading *For* and the other *Against*.

2. Using colored pencils or markers, accurately illustrate the dramatic incident in the first session of the Arkansas legislature that left one representative dead.

3. From where did the new settlers in Arkansas come and why?

4. Describe the differences between a yeoman farmer and a planter.

Make It Match!

1. ruling Arkansas Democrats
2. appointed to represent one nation to another
3. a white plantation manager
4. fruit of the cotton plant spun into thread
5. pressed loose cotton into bales

A. bolls
B. compress
C. dynasty
D. Whig
E. overseer
F. ambassador

1. large-scale farmers in south and southeast Arkansas
2. smaller family farmers in north and northwest Arkansas
3. outhouse
4. living on land that is not owned by the resident
5. interest-bearing certificates—raise money for state

A. privy
B. squatter
C. dogtrot
D. bonds
E. planters
F. yeoman

204   Chapter 9

THE OL' FILLIN' STATION

Fill in the blank—choose the letter that represents the word that best fills in the blank.

1. Many believed Arkansas was not ready for statehood because _____.
   A. it would benefit planters who could pay high taxes and who would have a larger marketplace to sell goods more than small farmers
   B. they desperately needed and wanted federal government control
   C. the population was too small
   D. there was not a state newspaper

2. Arkansas became a state on _____.
   A. January 30, 1836
   B. June 5, 1835
   C. July 4, 1776
   D. June 15, 1836

3. Arkansas was the _____ state.
   A. thirty-fifth
   B. twenty-sixth
   C. twenty-fifth
   D. twenty-seventh

4. The oldest Arkansas school still in existence was established by the _____ _____ in the 1830s.
   A. "Family" Dynasty
   B. Catholic Church
   C. state government
   D. territorial restoration

5. A _____ was a person who lived on land he or she did not own.
   A. poacher
   B. renegade
   C. specie
   D. squatter

6. People who left for the gold rush in California were called _____.
   A. miners
   B. gold-diggers
   C. forty-niners
   D. hard-liners

HisStory, HerStory, YourStory, OurStory... Telling an Arkansas Story— The Written Word

1. Pretend you are a news reporter at the *Arkansas Gazette* in 1836. Write an unbiased, exciting article describing your first experience as a voter. You are choosing the leaders of the new Arkansas state government. Be sure to describe yourself and include the five *W*s and one *H*: who, what, when, where, why, and how. Use specific and accurate facts from the chapter to convey what you have learned.

2. Does your family have wonderful recipes that are served at holidays and special occasions, that have passed down from generation to generation, or that use special or secret ingredients? Create a recipe card or page from an Arkansas cookbook so that the recipe can be shared. Be sure to include all ingredients, instructions, the history of the recipe, and an illustration.

Then and Now

Based on what you studied in chapters 8 and 9, compare and contrast the typical Arkansas way of life in early statehood days with current times. Divide your paper into five columns and nine rows. The first column will be labeled with the category name. The second category will be labeled *Then* and the third will be labeled *Now* and so on. A sample has been designed for you below.

Category Names	Then	Now	Then	Now
personal hygiene				
food				
clothing				
home furnishings and comfort				
entertainment				
education				
health				
church				
dating, marriage, and family size				

Statehood and Slavery

UNIT 4

The Civil War, Reconstruction, and the New South, 1861–1899

Chapter 10
Secession and Civil War, 1861–1865

Chapter 11
The Politics of Rebuilding, 1866–1899

Chapter 12
Something Old, Something New—Society, the Economy, and Race in Reconstruction-Era Arkansas, 1866–1899

A Civil War reenactment takes place at Pea Ridge (Benton County).

Pea Ridge Battlefield as it is seen today.

Chapter 10

Secession and Civil War
1861–1865

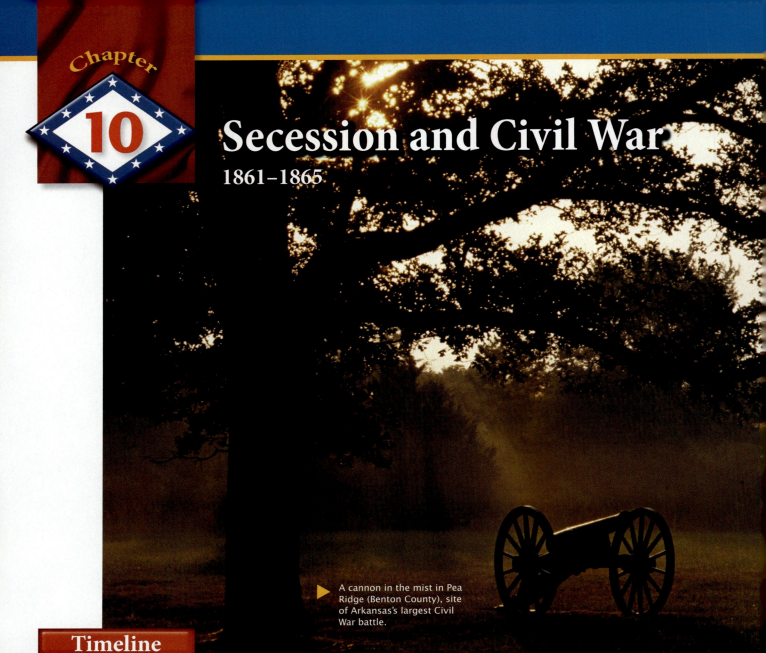

▶ A cannon in the mist in Pea Ridge (Benton County), site of Arkansas's largest Civil War battle.

Timeline

	1860	1861	1862
Arkansas		**1861** Telegraph lines link Little Rock and Memphis. Arkansas secedes from the Union on May 6. The Battle of Wilson's Creek takes place in August.	**1862** The Battle of Pea Ridge is fought in March. Union troops occupy Batesville and Helena from May to July. The Battle of Prairie Grove takes place in December.
United States	**1860** Abraham Lincoln is elected president. South Carolina is the first state to secede from the Union.	**1861** Mississippi, Florida, Alabama, Georgia, Louisiana, Texas, Virginia, Tennessee, and North Carolina secede from the Union. The Confederate States of America is established. Paper money becomes the national currency.	**1862** The Homestead Act declares that American citizens can have 160 acres of western land free of charge, provided they live on the land for five years and develop it.
World			

Why Do We Study This?

Studying, analyzing, and understanding the Civil War and its causes to the best of our ability is one of our most critical responsibilities as Americans. United States citizens taking up arms against fellow citizens was an unprecedented act with far-reaching consequences.

We must examine the motivation of soldiers on both sides to fight for what they believed to be right and to proudly and bravely answer the call of service from their country. Over sixty thousand lives were sacrificed in the conflict.

The impact on race relations, the economy, society, industry, the government, and the American citizenry as a whole was, and still is, tremendous. Laws that resulted from the conflict determined the power of the states to govern themselves and also affected the state of Arkansas.

This is one of the most difficult periods in our nation's and state's history. Today, we see the beliefs held by many in our state as senseless or cruel. As young historians and scholars, we must understand that the only way we can become stronger, better, more successful citizens is through awareness, intelligent, respectful discussion, and education.

Big Picture Questions

- How do you explain the concept of loyalty? What are its characteristics? Is being loyal important? Why or why not? Give modern-day examples of how family members, friends, employees, or teammates display loyalty.

- What is conflict? How can conflicts be resolved? Are the results of conflict always negative? Why or why not? Can results be positive? If yes, give examples. Recall a time you were involved in a conflict—how was it resolved? Would you choose a different way in which to manage that situation now? Why or why not? If yes, how?

- What would you choose as the three most important qualities of a good or effective leader? List three qualities of a poor leader. Choose someone (living or dead) whom you believe represents a strong leader and a weak leader and support your choices with reasons, facts, and examples. Remember to consider leaders from all walks of life: politics, military, community, school, friends, church, family, sports, celebrities, famous, unknown, living, dead, historic, modern-day, children, adults, new leaders, experienced leaders, and so on.

- Determine the role or significance of geography in the Civil War in Arkansas. Did it impact battles and victories? If so, how? If not, why not? Consider the state's economy, military strategy and maneuvers, weather, transportation, supply lines, and so on in your discussion. Be sure to include accurate and specific details and examples in your explanation.

1863	1864	1865
1863 Union forces capture Arkansas Post in January. The Battle of Helena is fought in July. Union forces capture Fort Smith and Little Rock in September.	**1864** The Union establishes a government in Arkansas under Gov. Isaac Murphy. The battles of Poison Spring, Mark's Mill, and Jenkin's Ferry take place in April.	
1863 The Emancipation Proclamation is issued in January. Some of the bloodiest fighting of the war takes place at Gettysburg, Pennsylvania, and Vicksburg, Mississippi, in July. President Lincoln establishes the first national Thanksgiving Day.	**1864** Under the command of General Sherman, Atlanta, Georgia, a Southern stronghold, falls to the Union in September. Lincoln is reelected president in November.	**1865** The Thirteenth Amendment abolishes slavery. Gen. Robert E. Lee, Confederate commander, surrenders to Union general Ulysses S. Grant at Appomattox Courthouse, Virginia, in April. Lincoln is assassinated by John Wilkes Booth on April 14.
1863 The French capture Mexico City.	**1864** The Geneva Convention, a document pledging that nations will respect humanitarian rules of war, is signed by twenty-six nations.	**1865** The Salvation Army is founded in London. After studying the genetic composition of peas, Gregor Mendel, an Austrian botanist, first describes the laws of heredity. In honor of his friend Alice Liddell, mathematician Lewis Carroll writes *Alice's Adventures in Wonderland*.

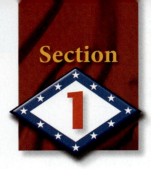

Section 1

War Looms

Guide to Reading

Terms
abolish
abolition
Electoral College
Federal
Homestead Act
insurrection
moderate
patronage
secede
Southern consciousness
states' rights
unanimous

People
Conditionalists
Cooperationists
Jefferson Davis
Isaac Murphy
Mrs. Frederick Trapnall
Judge David Walker

Places
Confederate States of America

Southern consciousness (CON-SHUSS-nuss) the belief that the Southern way of life was distinct from and incompatible with the Northern "Yankee" way of life.

secede (se-SEED or suh-SEED) to withdraw from an organization or a government.

abolish to end totally and completely; to end immediately, as in slavery.

The Union Trembles

In 1860, many Arkansans, particularly those in the northwestern counties where there were very few slaves, faced difficult choices. They did not wish to cut off ties to the Union they had so proudly joined less than twenty-five years before. But the planters, mostly in the southeastern region of the state, worked hard to create a **Southern consciousness**. They made people feel they were not loyal if they bought goods from northern states or sent their children east to school.

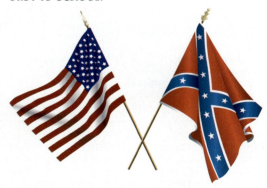

There were old divisions between northwest and southeast and between yeoman farmers and planters in the state. Hard feelings grew stronger as people became involved in the issues and emotions of the time. Arkansas had to face the critical presidential election of 1860 and the need to choose whether to stay with the Union or **secede**.

The Election of 1860

After more than a decade of national debate over slavery and other issues that tended to separate North and South, Arkansans were deeply divided as they approached 1860. Some Southerners were talking about leaving the Union if those in the North who wished to limit or **abolish** slavery succeeded in electing a president of their choice. Secession might lead to conflict, but many believed it would be a brief war and a clear victory for Southern fighters.

In Arkansas, times were unstable. This was due in part to the state's long-standing division between slave and non-slave areas. Banking failures of the 1830s and 1840s, combined with political changes, also contributed to the problems. The Whig Party had broken apart over the slavery question and vanished, leaving Arkansas Whigs without an official organization. Also,

212 Chapter 10

the Democratic "Family," strong for so long in Arkansas politics, was weaker than it had been in years.

A newcomer to Arkansas, Thomas C. Hindman, challenged the Family's control of the state. Hindman was born in Tennessee, grew up in Mississippi, and moved to Helena in the 1850s. At first, he was an ally of the Family. He broke away from them in the late 1850s, probably over **patronage** disputes. In the governor's race of 1860, he backed Henry Rector against the Family's Richard H. Johnson. Rector won.

Meanwhile, focus turned to the presidential race. In the spring of 1860, the Democratic Party split and nominated two candidates for president. Stephen A. Douglas of Illinois was the candidate of the traditional Democrats. That party still voiced a **moderate** position on the slavery issue. They supported the idea of leaving slavery in place where it already existed, but not allowing it to spread west. John C. Breckinridge of Kentucky was the candidate for the **states' rights** Democrats. They maintained the time had come for the Southern states to insist on their rights, especially against the growing strength of the Republican Party. A group of former Whigs nominated John Bell of Tennessee for president. His platform asked only that everyone follow the Constitution and maintain the Union.

The Republican Party faced the election with definite hopes of victory. The party was formed in the 1850s out of several political parties in the Northern states. The Republican Party stood for some policies that Southerners opposed, such as federal aid to railroads and the **Homestead Act** to give free land to settlers. Its platform was also against extending slavery into the western lands. However, most members of the Republican Party did not support **abolition**. The difference between the two positions was unclear and unimportant to many white Southerners.

The 1860 Republican candidate for president was Abraham Lincoln of Illinois. Very little was known about him at the time. Many people assumed he would be a frontman for the more radical elements of his party, who tended to favor abolition. The Republicans were convinced Lincoln could be elected on the vote of Northern states alone. This was because the Northern states had a larger population and more eligible voters than the Southern states. Lincoln did not intend to campaign in the South and was not even on the ballot in most Southern states.

In Arkansas, the race went along strict party lines, or at least along what was left of old party lines. Hindman, along with the leaders of the Family, viewed Breckinridge as the true Democratic candidate. The old Whigs thought of Bell as a revival of their party. The vote in Arkansas was Breckinridge, 28,783 votes; Bell, 20,094; and

patronage (PAT-ruh-nej) to make appointments to government jobs based on grounds other than merit.

moderate a reasonable viewpoint that is not considered extreme; in the middle.

states' rights the belief that if a law passed by the federal government was deemed unfair or unconstitutional, the states had a right to accept, deny, or evaluate the policy.

Homestead Act (HOHM-sted act) to encourage western settlement, the U.S. Congress in 1862 passed a law granting 160 acres free to any man who would occupy and cultivate the land.

abolition (AB-uh-LISH-shun) the immediate and total end to slavery.

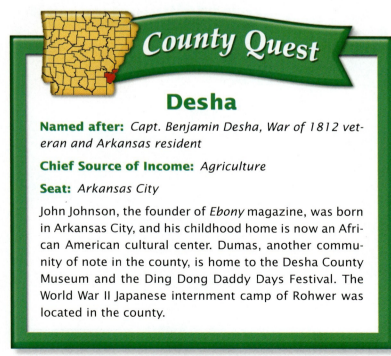

County Quest

Desha

Named after: Capt. Benjamin Desha, War of 1812 veteran and Arkansas resident

Chief Source of Income: Agriculture

Seat: Arkansas City

John Johnson, the founder of *Ebony* magazine, was born in Arkansas City, and his childhood home is now an African American cultural center. Dumas, another community of note in the county, is home to the Desha County Museum and the Ding Dong Daddy Days Festival. The World War II Japanese internment camp of Rohwer was located in the county.

Secession and Civil War **213**

Electoral College (ee-LEK-toh-ruhl KAH-lej) a group representing all states that casts the final vote in presidential elections, based upon the majority vote in each state. A candidate may win only 51 percent of the popular votes in a state but win all the state's electoral votes. The number of electoral votes assigned each state is based upon population; the electoral vote of each state is equal to the number of its members of the House of Representatives plus its two senators.

Confederate States of America the nation formed by Southern states that seceded from the Union because of fears of the elimination of slavery and the threat to states' rights.

Jefferson Davis the president of the Confederate States of America.

Douglas, 5,227. There were no votes cast for Lincoln in the state. Lincoln won the national election. He got more votes than any of the other three men, and he carried eighteen free states to win a clear victory with 180 votes in the **Electoral College**. Breckinridge carried Arkansas and ten other slave states. In the end, the North had elected the president.

A Nation Breaks Apart—Secession

The slave states faced a new question: did the election of Lincoln, his party, and his platform mean that the South would have to secede from the Union? Some said it did. Others said the South should wait until the new president took action against the wishes of the South before taking its own action. Few argued about the actual right to secede. The Southern policy of states' rights had long been viewed as enough reason for secession.

At first, most Arkansans took a "wait-and-see" attitude. Some, including Johnson and Hindman, urged immediate action. When Governor Rector spoke to the General Assembly soon after the election, he took a fairly mild tone. However, he did warn Arkansans that they might soon have to choose between "the Union without slavery, or slavery without the Union." South Carolina was the first to make that choice. It seceded in late December of 1860. Mississippi, Florida, and Alabama joined South Carolina early in January of 1861.

Arkansans were still reluctant to act. Demands for quick action from southern and eastern counties were matched by appeals for careful and patient decision-making from the northern and western counties. The General Assembly's answer, on January 15, 1861, was to call for a vote of the people in February. Citizens would vote on whether to hold a secession convention, and at the same time they would select delegates to that convention.

Meanwhile, Georgia, Louisiana, and Texas also left the Union. The first seven states that had seceded met in Montgomery, Alabama, early in February. They formed a government, called the new nation, the **Confederate States of America**, and elected a president, **Jefferson Davis** of Mississippi.

While Arkansans debated their coming election, some took matters into their own hands. A group of armed men who supported secession assembled in Little Rock to take over the U.S. Army arsenal there. When threatened, the **Federal** commander, Capt. James Totten, surrendered to prevent bloodshed. He was allowed to get away with his sixty-five men, but they had to leave their weapons behind.

On February 18, Arkansans voted 27,412 to 15,826 to call a convention to discuss secession. At the same time, they chose mostly moderate delegates. Those who wanted immediate secession

SECESSION OF THE SOUTHERN STATES

- Free States and Territories
- Border States That Stayed in the Union
- Slave States That Seceded before the Attack on Fort Sumter
- Slave States That Seceded after the Attack on Fort Sumter

© 2007 University of Arkansas Press

▲ Gov. Henry M. Rector.

▲ Judge David Walker.

received 17,927 votes. Those who wanted to await further events (they called themselves **Cooperationists** or **Conditionalists**) earned 23,626 votes.

The secession convention met March 4, the same day Lincoln was sworn in as president. The moderates were in control by a slim margin. **Judge David Walker**, a Unionist from Fayetteville, was chosen to preside. After two weeks of debate, the group turned down secession by a vote of thirty-nine to thirty-five. They also called for a new vote of the people on the question of secession, to be held in August. That vote never took place.

In the harbor at Charleston, South Carolina, Fort Sumter stood as a Federal stronghold. South Carolina demanded the American forces surrender control of the fort to the state. Lincoln refused to give it up. When a U.S. Navy ship tried to supply the fort with food in April of 1861, the South Carolinians fired upon it. It was the first fight of the Civil War. As a result, Lincoln declared that an **insurrection** was taking place and requested seventy-five thousand volunteer soldiers. His demands were met and exceeded. The North would fight to preserve the Union at all costs. In Arkansas, Governor Rector refused Lincoln's request for volunteers. As Virginia, Tennessee, and North Carolina acted to secede, the Arkansas convention met once again.

David Walker, now on the side of the Confederacy because of the attack on Fort Sumter, called the group back into session at the statehouse on May 6, 1861. After a few hours of talk, all but five men voted to secede. Walker called for a second ballot to make the vote **unanimous**. Only one man, **Isaac Murphy**, refused and voted to stay with the Union. The other members were angry with him. But **Mrs. Frederick Trapnall** of Little Rock threw him a bouquet of flowers from the upstairs gallery to honor the courage he showed in sticking with his beliefs. Secession would create a long and difficult path for Arkansas, which would be revealed in the brutal years to come.

The new Confederate state constitution, written in 1861, called for an election for governor in 1862. Rector was defeated for a second term as Arkansas's governor by Harris Flanagin of Arkadelphia.

Federal a large or central government under which states are governed. In this context, the United States government in Washington, D.C., the Union government.

Cooperationists those in the South who were willing to wait and see what Lincoln might do as president rather than secede merely on the basis of his election.

Conditionalists (kuhn-DISH-shun-uh-lists) those in the South who wanted to secede from the Union only under certain conditions, namely, if President Lincoln took actions harmful to the South.

Judge David Walker Unionist from Fayetteville who lead secession conventions. At the second convention, he voted for secession.

insurrection (IN-sir-EK-shun) revolt, uprising.

unanimous (yoo-NAN-ih-muss) in total; one hundred percent agreement.

Isaac Murphy from Madison County, the only person to vote against Arkansas secession. Later, he served as the Union governor in Little Rock.

Mrs. Frederick Trapnall a wealthy Little Rock resident who threw flowers from the balcony of the statehouse to Isaac Murphy when he voted against secession.

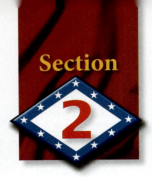

Section 2

War Arrives

Guide to Reading

Terms
artillery batteries
casualties
cavalry
contraband
dysentery
emancipation
Freedmen's Bureau
guerilla
infantry
martial law
morphine
quinine

Events
draft
Emancipation Proclamation

People
bushwhackers
jayhawkers

Places
Arkansas Post

Pride and Glory

In those first thrilling days of the war, young men in Arkansas, like young men all over the country, scrambled to get into the action. Many feared the war would be over before they could get their share of the glory. It was common to hear Southerners talk about "one big battle" that would whip the Yankees once and for all. The first volunteers signed up for three months because that was as long as the conflict was predicted to last.

In almost all Arkansas towns, military companies formed, chose their officers, and selected fancy names. Arkansas had the "Hempstead Hornets," the "Tyronza

▶ Uniforms of the Union army during the Civil War, according to rank or home state.

216 Chapter 10

Union Generals

Name	Role in the War	Notable Battles
Ulysses S. Grant	General-in-Chief, Union forces	Shiloh, TN; Vicksburg, MS; Richmond, VA; Lee's surrender at Appomattox Courthouse, VA
James G. Blunt	Union General	Prairie Grove, AR
Samuel R. Curtis	Union General	Pea Ridge, Batesville, Helena, Cotton Plant, AR
Nathaniel Lyon	Union General	Wilson's Creek, MO
William T. Sherman	Union General	Shiloh, TN; Atlanta, GA; Savannah, GA
Frederick Steele	Union General	Little Rock, Fort Smith, Camden, Poison Springs, Mark's Mill, Jenkin's Ferry, AR

Confederate Generals

Name	Role in the War	Notable Battles
Robert E. Lee	General-in-Chief, Confederate forces	Antietam, MD; Gettysburg, PA; Richmond, VA; surrendered at Appomattox Courthouse, VA
Patrick Cleburne	Confederate General Arkansas war hero	Shiloh, Chattanooga, Franklin, TN
Thomas C. Hindman	Confederate General "Total war" guerilla fighters	Prairie Grove, AR
Ben McCulloch	Confederate General	Wilson's Creek, MO; Pea Ridge, AR
N. B. Pearce	Confederate General	Wilson's Creek, MO
Albert Pike	Confederate General; Leader of Cherokees Regiment	Pea Ridge, AR
Sterling Price	Confederate General	Wilson's Creek, MO; Pea Ridge, AR
Earl Van Dorn	Confederate General	Pea Ridge, AR

Rebels," the "Polk County Invincibles," the "Camden Knights," the "Montgomery Hunters," and the "Muddy Bayou Heroes." Some units had uniforms with fancy militia costumes. Some just showed up in their everyday homespun clothes. Men brought their own weapons: a mixture of rifles, muskets, shotguns, and Bowie knives. Women created bright flags, made uniforms, and encouraged the men.

By the end of the war, about sixty thousand Arkansas men had served in the Confederate army. That was more than one-third of the adult white male population of Arkansas in 1860. Some joined army units from other states, but most served in Arkansas units. The state raised thirty-six **infantry** regiments, fifteen **cavalry** regiments, and thirteen **artillery batteries**. Most Arkansas soldiers actually served outside the state, many in battles in Virginia and Tennessee.

As the war dragged on, the enthusiasm for volunteering lessened. The Confederacy started a **draft** in the spring of 1862. Every healthy white male from the ages of eighteen to thirty-five was required to serve. The

infantry (IN-fun-tree) foot soldiers carrying rifles; the largest group in an army.

cavalry soldiers mounted on horseback.

artillery batteries heavy guns and cannons and the soldiers who operate them.

draft the selection of a person or persons for required military service. A requirement or order to join.

Secession and Civil War

▶ Confederate uniforms during the Civil War varied based on where the soldier was from or his rank.

draft law did excuse some, such as managers of plantations with more than twenty slaves. These larger plantations were expected to grow crops to provide food for troops and for trade, which contributed to the economy of the Confederacy. The draft encouraged volunteering, because men who volunteered got to choose the units with which they would serve.

A Confederate infantry private, when he was paid at all, received only eleven dollars a month (approximately $212 in 2005 dollars). Gen. Patrick Cleburne, an Arkansas war hero, offered a unique plan in 1863. He suggested that the Confederacy ought to arm slaves as soldiers, giving freedom to any black men who would fight for the South. Cleburne's troops repelled Gen. William T. Sherman for an entire day at Chattanooga's Missionary Ridge. Cleburne was killed in November of 1864 in a battle in Franklin, Tennessee. This battle cost the Confederacy five of its generals in one day.

In keeping with the prewar social and political factions in the state, 8,289 white Arkansans served in the Union army. That was more than any other Confederate state except Tennessee. One of these, 1st Sgt. William Ellis of the Third Wisconsin Cavalry, was the

▲ Gen. Patrick Cleburne of Helena (Phillips County), Army of the Confederate States of America.

first Arkansan to win the Medal of Honor. In a skirmish at Dardanelle, he held his position even after being wounded three times. More than 5,500 black Arkansans also joined the Union forces in infantry, cavalry, and artillery units. The army put the former slaves into all-black units with white officers. Black soldiers were proud members of regiments such as the U.S. First Arkansas, African Descent.

As it turned out, Missouri would set the stage for the first major battle for Arkansans. The people of Missouri were seriously divided over the war. Unionists managed to stay in control of Missouri, but there were enough Confederate supporters to create their own civil war within the state. The future of Missouri was important. It could be a major addition to either side.

The pro-Southern forces in Missouri called for help, and Arkansas and the Confederacy responded. In the late summer of 1861, three groups gathered to invade Missouri: the Arkansas army under Gen. N. B. Pearce, a Confederate force under the former Texas Ranger Gen. Ben McCulloch; and the Missouri soldiers under Gen. Sterling Price. In total, there were about 12,000 men—2,200 of them Arkansans.

These were still amateur armies, poorly equipped, poorly trained, and poorly organized. The three generals disliked each other and could not agree on a battle plan. They stumbled toward a place called Wilson's Creek in southwest Missouri near Springfield, forty miles north of the Arkansas border. Gen. Nathaniel Lyon was close by with a force of about 5,400 Union soldiers.

In the end, the total **casualties** from the battle were about 1,300 on the Northern side and about 1,200 on the Southern side. The ratio of injuries and deaths, compared to the total number of men who fought, was high in comparison to later battles—it was one of the bloodiest days of the war. Wilson's Creek was also an early example of an indecisive battle. In one sense, the Confederates won. The Union army left, giving Confederates control of the field. But the Confederates were too weak and disorganized to follow up on their victory. Missouri was still controlled by Unionists.

casualties (KAZH-OO-ehl-teez) in war, not only the dead, it also includes the number of wounded and missing.

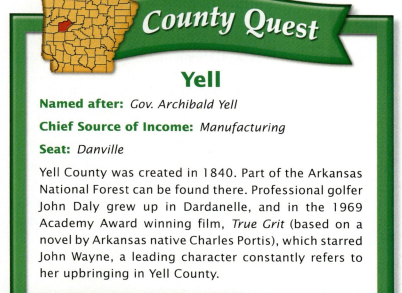

County Quest

Yell

Named after: Gov. Archibald Yell

Chief Source of Income: Manufacturing

Seat: Danville

Yell County was created in 1840. Part of the Arkansas National Forest can be found there. Professional golfer John Daly grew up in Dardanelle, and in the 1969 Academy Award winning film, *True Grit* (based on a novel by Arkansas native Charles Portis), which starred John Wayne, a leading character constantly refers to her upbringing in Yell County.

Secession and Civil War **219**

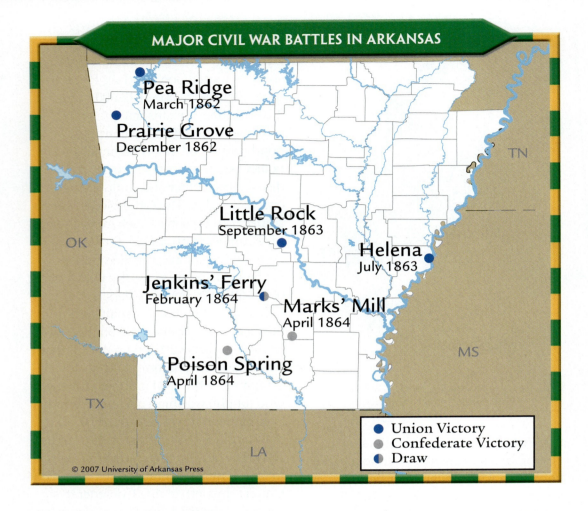

The Battle of Pea Ridge

Early in 1862, events in Missouri again called Arkansans to action. Federal forces led by Gen. Samuel R. Curtis pushed Gen. Sterling Price's Missouri Confederates out of the state and into northwest Arkansas. Curtis followed them, moving into Arkansas. At that point, the Confederacy sent Gen. Earl Van Dorn, a West Point graduate with a good record in previous wars, to take charge of Arkansas.

Under Van Dorn's command, Price and McCulloch began to work together. They chose to attack Curtis, who had about 10,500 soldiers. The Confederate forces in northwest Arkansas had about 15,000 men on hand to fight. Within this group was one of the war's most unusual units, the Confederate Indian brigade. Arkansas's Albert Pike was now General Pike. He had convinced some of the Indians to fight with the South, and led two regiments of Cherokees.

The Union army was just inside the Arkansas border, on the main road to Missouri. The road ran past the Elkhorn Tavern stage stop, along a long, low hill called Pea Ridge. The Confederate army moved into place in front of Union troops, so close they could see each other's campfires.

Van Dorn had a daring plan. The night of March 6, he ordered the soldiers to leave their campfires burning to fool the enemy. Then he moved his army out on a night march, around Curtis's forces, to come up behind the Union army and attack from the north. During the night, the Confederate army split apart. When morning came on March 7, Van Dorn and Price were

A Day in the Life

Campaigning in Arkansas

For most soldiers with the Confederate forces in Arkansas, the war involved a lot of waiting broken by small skirmishes and raids. This is part of a letter from William Wakefield Garner of Quitman (Cleburne County), who was a lieutenant in a "Home Guard" mounted infantry company. His company served mostly in central Arkansas, but in 1863, it was part of a raid into Union-occupied Missouri. The letter was written after the raiders were back in Arkansas.

> Greene County, Ark.
>
> 30 miles East [of] Powhatan
>
> May 6th, 1863
>
> The enemy followed us from Cape Girardeau [Missouri] to [the] St. Francis River, over 100 miles. We fought them every day for 7 days. When we could make a stand they would not attack us, but made their attack while [we were] on march. They surprised us once by calvalry [sic] raid, run into our lines while we stopped to cook.... If I should always feel as I did then I will never suffer from fear. We killed many a Blue Coat and think got but 5 killed....
>
> We took a decided stand at Bloomfield, stayed on the battlefield 24 hours: lay on our arms all night without fire. Suffice to say we made a speedy and successful retreat: but the trip or raid I look on as a complete failure, done but little less than rob and steal from friend and foe alike. In some instances took the last horse, bushel of corn, lb. of bacon from women and their husbands in our army. Took all the horses on the way. Took mares from young colts. I think the Federals do not do worse than we have done....
>
> I have stood this trip very well. I had sore eyes a few days very badly caused for want of sleep and exposure. I did without sleep, only what I got on my horse for 60 hours. We did without anything to eat except some corn burnt on the cob and 2 small slices of bacon.... We bake bread on a board and broil our meat and think we are doing well.

D. D. McBrien, ed., "Documents: . . . Letters of an Arkansas Confederate Soldier," *Arkansas Historical Quarterly* 2 (March 1943), 69–70.

▲ Members of Albert Pike's Cherokee regiment scalped victims to celebrate their victory.

▲ Elkhorn Tavern witnessed some of the most brutal fighting of the Battle of Pea Ridge. This picture was taken several years after the war.

north of Curtis with half the army, and McCulloch and Pike were about two miles away to the west with the other half. This type of troop movement was unusual because traditional European warfare, on which most battle strategies of the time were based, did not use nighttime maneuvers.

The Battle of Pea Ridge (or Elkhorn Tavern) opened in the middle of the morning. Van Dorn attacked Curtis from the north, and McCulloch attacked from the west. The attack in the west collapsed when McCulloch was killed. Unable to effectively control his forces, Pike watched in horror as the Confederate Indians scalped eight Federals and murdered others after they were wounded. On the other part of the battlefield, Van Dorn and Price's troops fought hard all day, but could not break the Federal lines.

Both armies slept that night around Elkhorn Tavern. The next morning, the Federals attacked and forced the Confederates to retreat. The Union army lost 1,384 men, counting those killed, wounded, and missing. The Confederates lost nearly 2,000 men. The Federal army still controlled the road to Missouri, and the Confederate army in Arkansas was in disarray.

Pea Ridge was the largest battle fought west of the Mississippi River. The Federal victory there meant that the Confederacy had to give up any hope of winning Missouri. Now Arkansas was open to Federal attack.

Things also were not going well for the Confederacy in the Mississippi River Valley. The Union army captured forts to open the Kentucky and Tennessee rivers to attack. In April, the Federals defeated a Confederate army at Shiloh, Tennessee, and captured New Orleans. Union troops then captured Memphis in June. Only Vicksburg, Mississippi, held out as a major Confederate stronghold on the Mississippi River.

War Marches through Arkansas

General Curtis led his army from Pea Ridge across northern Arkansas to Batesville. In the summer of 1862, he moved south to Helena. The Union soldiers stripped the land bare of food, horses, and firewood as they went. At the Cache

▲ An artist's rendering of the Battle of Pea Ridge. What was the other battle name given to Pea Ridge? Why did many Civil War battles have two names?

◀ Thomas Hindman.

(cash) River, near Cotton Plant (Woodruff County), a small battle took place on July 7. The Federals easily defeated a small force of Confederate cavalry who tried to block the road to Helena.

It appeared the rest of the Confederacy had abandoned Arkansas. Some people were so upset there was talk of Arkansas seceding from the Confederacy to become a freestanding state. Because of this, the Confederacy sent Thomas C. Hindman, by now a general, to take control of events in Arkansas.

Hindman took a "total war" approach that shocked even the most loyal Confederates in Arkansas. He took money, weapons, medical supplies, and men wherever he could find them. He encouraged the cruel, uncontrolled **guerilla** fighters in the mountains. Hindman put the state under **martial law**, placing army officers, instead of elected public officials, in charge of affairs. He shot suspected deserters without trial. He brought in all the cotton he could find so that it could be burned instead of letting it fall into the hands of the enemy. Hindman strengthened Arkansas for the Confederacy, but his methods lost him the support of the Arkansas people. Albert Pike was a vocal critic of Hindman, who was eventually arrested for crimes associated with his "total war" methods.

The Battle of Prairie Grove

The Union renewed its attack on Arkansas, again from the northwest, with a small army led by Gen. James G. Blunt. Hindman responded by marching across the Boston Mountains to meet the Federal troops at Prairie

guerilla (guh-RILL-uh) individuals and independent bands taking part in irregular warfare, or special forces engaged in harassment and sabotage.

martial law (MARSH-uhl law) military rule that may take over the civil government in times of crisis or war.

Secession and Civil War   223

Arkansas Post established by Henri de Tonti in 1686, Arkansas Post was the first permanent European settlement in Arkansas. The area was near the confluence of the Arkansas and Mississippi rivers.

Grove, southwest of Fayetteville, on December 7, 1862. Each side had about ten thousand men, but the Confederates had the advantage of fighting from a defensive position on top of a hill.

The battle was intense and losses were heavy. The Federals lost 1,251 men, counting those killed, wounded, and missing. The Confederates suffered the loss of over 1,300 men, and probably more who were never counted. Once again, as at Pea Ridge, the Federals won a hard-fought victory. Hindman's army retreated all the way to Little Rock. Union soldiers pursued his troops, raiding Van Buren and destroying supplies.

On January 10 and 11, 1863, a force of 33,000 Union troops routed a defending force of 4,500 Confederate troops at **Arkansas Post**. This opened the way to Little Rock. In July, in an effort to draw Union forces away from Vicksburg, a Confederate force tried to retake Helena (Phillips County). They failed and suffered heavy losses. The attack on Helena came the same day that Vicksburg fell, July 4.

The capital city of Little Rock was exposed to capture. The Confederate government of Arkansas fled the city and moved to Washington, in the southwest part of the state, where Flanagin would run the state government for the rest of the war. Meeting little resistance,

▲ Newspaper article from New York about the capture of Arkansas Post.

Gen. Frederick Steele led Federal troops into Little Rock in September of 1863. Fort Smith fell to a Union army coming out of Indian Territory the same month, and the entire Arkansas River Valley fell into Union hands.

After Little Rock fell in September of 1863, Union loyalists elected a governor in 1864. Twelve thousand voters chose Isaac Murphy of Madison County, the only man to have voted against secession for Arkansas, as governor.

Steele's Southern Campaign

In the spring of 1864, the Union army planned the Red River Campaign to take Shreveport, Louisiana, a center of the cotton trade and headquarters of the Confederate forces west of the Mississippi River. In Arkansas, General Steele was ordered to meet the other approaching Federal troops at Shreveport. Steele moved

▼ An illustration of the bombardment and capture of Fort Hindman, Arkansas Post, 1863.

I Am an Arkansan

David O. Dodd
The "Boy Hero" of Arkansas

David O. Dodd was seventeen years old in 1863. He had spent the early war years traveling with his father, who had business dealings in several Southern states. They eventually went to Camden, which was in Confederate hands. Dodd decided, late in 1863, to visit friends in Little Rock, which was then occupied by Union troops under the command of Gen. Frederick Steele.

As Dodd was leaving Little Rock to return to Camden, a Union patrol stopped him, searched his clothes, and discovered a paper with mysterious markings. The marks turned out to be Morse code, which Dodd had learned when he worked in a telegraph office. The code was interpreted as a list of the numbers and locations of Union forces in Little Rock.

Dodd was arrested and charged with spying, specifically with carrying military information for the Confederate forces in Camden. A court martial—a Union army court—found him guilty and sentenced him to death by hanging.

Although many Little Rock residents pleaded with General Steele for mercy on the grounds of Dodd's age, Steele said Dodd had been found guilty and would have to pay the penalty. One version of the story says that Steele offered Dodd his freedom if he would name the person who gave him the military information, but Dodd refused to tell. Dodd was executed January 8, 1864.

Thus, Arkansas acquired a Civil War martyr (someone who sacrifices for a cause). David O. Dodd became the "boy hero" of the Confederacy, although many "boys" of seventeen were serving in the armies on both sides. Today, a monument to Dodd stands near Little Rock's MacArthur Park.

▲ David O. Dodd.

THE ENCYCLOPEDIA OF ARKANSAS HISTORY & CULTURE

Log on to Learn More
http://www.encyclopediaofarkansas.net/

▲ Letter from a resident of DeValls Bluff (Prairie County) to President Lincoln. How does the letter describe conditions of the time?

DID YOU KNOW?

Did you know the infamous outlaw Jesse James is reported to have spent time in Arkansas? Along with his brother Frank, Cole Younger, and other outlaws, known as the James–Younger Gang, and later the James Gang, James was said to have left his mark on our state.

Reportedly, the gang spent the night with a couple in Russellville where, upon leaving, Jesse James fired bullets into a tree on the property and left the mark of "J." Later, members of the gang were named as robbers of a stage coach near Malvern (Hot Spring County).

Frank and Jesse James were the two men identified to be involved in a shootout with local authorities in Gaddy's Corner (modern-day Burlington in northern Boone County). They had been accused of robbing a mail pouch and stealing $150.

---

south from Little Rock with a small army of five thousand men. They took over Camden (Ouachita County), a trade center and manufacturing town. Meanwhile, a major Union advance in the Red River Valley had been turned back, leaving the Confederates free to focus on Steele. At Camden, Steele was short of supplies.

He sent seven hundred men, including five hundred from the First Kansas Colored Infantry, to find food for his soldiers. A Confederate force of Arkansan, Texan, and Indian troops met them at Poison Spring (Ouachita County). The Confederates almost wiped out the Union force, and they were accused of shooting wounded black soldiers.

Steele now had to depend on supplies from Pine Bluff (Jefferson County), but at the Battle of Marks's Mill (Cleveland County), the Confederates captured his supply train. That meant Steele had to leave Camden and return to Little Rock. On the way, Steele's men slowed down trying to cross the Saline River at Jenkins's Ferry (Grant County). A force of ten thousand Confederates attacked them there, but the Federals managed to fight them off and escaped to Little Rock.

That was the last organized fighting in Arkansas. Again in spring of 1864, Gen. Ulysses S. Grant in Virginia and Gen. William T. Sherman in Tennessee began to move south against the remaining Confederate armies. These were the final campaigns of the war.

In addition to the terror of the official battles, most of Arkansas was at the mercy of ruthless guerilla fighters, deserters, and outlaws. They were known as **jayhawkers** or **bushwhackers**. Some of these claimed to belong to one of the armies, but most were just plain outlaws. The lack of law and order attracted bandits from Texas, Missouri, and Kansas. Among the outlaws who got their start in wartime Arkansas were the

◀ Union troops burn the Confederate Rebel Ram "Arkansas" on the Mississippi River, 1862. Why do you think the Union gunboat destroyed the Confederate vessel?

James brothers and the Younger brothers. They kept up their reign of terror long after the war was over.

Many times, bushwhackers raided their own neighbors. In the mountain counties of north Arkansas, many places were split in their loyalties: some families were loyal to the Union side and some supported the Confederacy. Great bitterness and hatred arose between some of these families. Many Union supporters were forced to flee to the North or to Texas, leaving their Arkansas homes behind. Others kept up family feuds for years.

Nearly every family north of the Arkansas River had a bushwhacker story to tell. In one case, Nancy Morton Staples of Washington County watched as robbers burned her father's feet. She threw water on the hot shovels the bushwhackers were using to burn her father. One stuck a pistol in her face, and she was beaten until she was black and blue. But when the men tried to put hot coals on her father's body, she was ready again and threw water on the fire, putting it out. When the bushwhackers choked her mother and threatened to hang her father, the family finally revealed where their money was hidden to save their lives.

Women and Blacks in the War and at Home

The impact of the war was very different in the North than in the South. In the North, where there was more industry, the war demands on factories of all kinds increased production and fed a growing economy. In the South, however, there had always been limited industry because of the agricultural-based economy. The few supplies the South could provide to its armies were captured Federal goods or came directly from people's homes. The women of Arkansas took on the kind of work that was being done by factories in the North. They spun, wove, and dyed cloth at amazing production levels. They produced uniforms, blankets, and bandages for an entire army. There were some sewing machines at that time, but most of the work was done by hand. Keeping the armies supplied with boots was another challenge. The few shoe factories that existed faced a shortage of

Jayhawkers outlaws who terrorized civilians during and after the Civil War; so called because they were believed to have come from Kansas, the Jayhawk State.

bushwhackers (BUSH-hwak-erz) guerilla fighters and outlaws who terrorized civilians during and after the Civil War.

Secession and Civil War

morphine (MORE-feen) a powerful narcotic derived from opium used to deaden pain.

quinine (KWI-nine) a drug derived from cinchona (Peruvian) bark used to treat the symptoms of malaria.

dysentery (DISS-uhn-tair-ee) a disease characterized by severe cramps and diarrhea resulting in dehydration and sometimes death. It is usually caused by a bacterial infection from unclean water or food.

leather, and Arkansas soldiers sometimes continued to fight despite bare and bleeding feet.

With the men off to war, the women had to maintain their typical roles while also taking over the men's jobs. They managed businesses and farms, harvested the crops, and, in some areas, tried to manage slaves. Some slaves stayed to serve their owners, but many ran away. Due in part to deserters and thieves, women sometimes smuggled food and medicine to the soldiers, hiding the goods under their clothes. They cared for the sick and wounded, buried the dead, and raised their children.

Women had to defend their homes and fields as well. Both Union and Confederate armies, often in short supply of food, took it wherever they could find it, even if the citizens were starving. The women in many northern Arkansas counties drew together from the country into villages where they could find greater safety in numbers. Wives of Union and Confederate soldiers frequently sounded the alarm for one another when strangers approached. If the strangers were Confederate, a Confederate wife asked the soldiers to leave them alone. If the troops were Union, the wife of a Union soldier would do the same.

Almost as soon as the war began, Southerners suffered a severe shortage of salt and coffee. Salt was needed to preserve meat, vital for the armies' nutrition. Civilians in Arkansas opened salt works that had been shut down for many years. In the northern counties, families retrieved what salt they could from the floors of their smokehouses. To replace coffee, people tried all kinds of substitutes, such as acorn coffee.

Other food was also in short supply. Efforts were made to convert cotton plantations to fields of grain to feed those at home and in the army. Even when food was grown, the breakdown of transportation often kept it from getting where it was needed.

The most difficult challenge soldiers faced was disease. A trip to an army hospital during the Civil War was often followed by a trip to the grave. Many more soldiers died of disease than died in battle. The extreme shortage of food greatly increased the men's chances of getting sick.

In Arkansas, there was added danger because of the shortage of medicines. **Morphine** was used to kill pain. Without it, a man might have to have his arm or leg amputated while fully awake. Another important medicine in the South was **quinine**, or Peruvian bark. This was needed to fight the fevers of malaria so common in the region. Quinine had to be brought in from South America, and supplies were used quickly.

Measles, mumps, **dysentery** from bad water supplies, smallpox, malaria, and flu were greater enemies than the Yankees. Caring for the wounded and burying the dead were tasks that local women helped the armies perform.

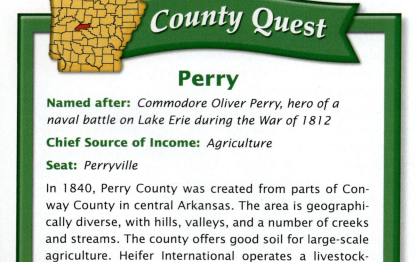

County Quest

Perry

Named after: Commodore Oliver Perry, hero of a naval battle on Lake Erie during the War of 1812

Chief Source of Income: Agriculture

Seat: Perryville

In 1840, Perry County was created from parts of Conway County in central Arkansas. The area is geographically diverse, with hills, valleys, and a number of creeks and streams. The county offers good soil for large-scale agriculture. Heifer International operates a livestock-holding facility in the county.

After the battle of Prairie Grove, for instance, the city of Fayetteville became one big hospital.

Black Arkansans were at the center of the war from its start to its finish. As the war began, slave owners hoped their slaves would remain loyal, but feared revolt. Some slaves did stay through the troubled times, but many ran away. Sometimes, a young Southern soldier volunteered not only himself for service in the Confederate army, but also his servants. A number of slaves made the trek from Arkansas to northern Virginia with their masters to tend the horses and cook meals. They did heavy labor for the army when needed. They faced danger, illness, and hardship like the soldiers.

Food shortages often caused starvation on the home front. This was especially hard on slaves. Although they had worked to grow crops and tend livestock, black families always received second best or leftovers. They had always kept small gardens around their cabins, and the men hunted small game to add to their diets. But during wartime, available guns and spare bullets for hunting were not to be found.

With the movement of Union armies into Arkansas, slaves began to experience their first tastes of freedom. This began as Union soldiers took control of parts of Arkansas, starting with General Curtis's march from Pea Ridge to Batesville and then to Helena. Black men, women, and children swarmed to the Federal army camps for safety. The Union army referred to them as **contraband**. At these Union army camps, former slaves lived a harsh life. The Union troops had difficulty keeping themselves supplied, much less caring for the freed slaves. Finding food, clothing, and shelter so deep in Confederate lands was often beyond their ability. Many black people, often children, became sick and died in the Union army camps. But slavery in Arkansas was also beginning to fail because of blacks taking matters into their own hands and running away from farms and plantations.

contraband (KAHN-truh-band) the Union army term for slaves from the Confederacy who fled their homes into the Union army camps.

◄ The color guard for one of Arkansas's African American Union army units, with its fife and drum corps.

Secession and Civil War

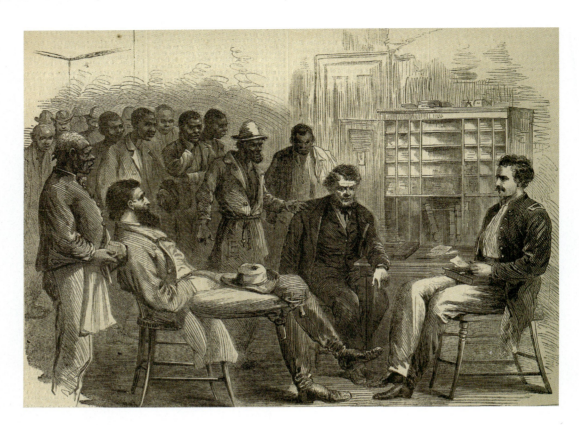

► An illustration of the office of the Freedmen's Bureau in Memphis, Tennessee.

Freedmen's Bureau an agency set up by the U.S. government to provide food, clothing, shelter, and education to blacks after they were freed from slavery.

emancipation to end restrictions or limitations; to free, as from slavery.

Emancipation Proclamation issued by Abraham Lincoln on January 1, 1863, it freed slaves who lived in states that were fighting against the Union.

For some Arkansas slaves, the war meant forced separations. To keep their slaves of greatest value from running away or being taken by the enemy, some planters sent their young male slaves to Texas. Entire slave communities were broken up, and countless families were torn apart. The years after the war were lonely, painful years of searching for lost family members, most of whom were never found. Moses Mitchell, born near Arkansas Post, was moved to Texas and sold at age twelve.

> "When they took us to Texas they left my mother and baby sister here in Arkansas . . . I never saw her [my mother] again and when I came back to Arkansas, they said she had been dead twenty-eight years," he said. "Never did hear of my father again."

Many black people who lived as freedmen in Arkansas after the war were not natives of Arkansas. They were ex-slaves who had been moved by their masters from Mississippi, Tennessee, and Alabama as Union troops moved into those states.

The federal government answered the crisis of displaced black people by forming the Freedmen's Bureau. Funded and run by the government, the bureau relied heavily on volunteers from religious groups. The bureau started schools in eastern Arkansas counties and opened refugee camps, called "home farms," near Pine Bluff (Jefferson County), DeVall's Bluff (Prairie County), Little Rock (Pulaski County), and Helena (Phillips County).

The Emancipation Proclamation: "Then, Thenceforward, and Forever Free"

When the Civil War began, President Abraham Lincoln made preservation of the Union the major goal of the United

States. Bringing an end to slavery would be a challenge. Several slave states (Delaware, Kentucky, Maryland, Missouri, and West Virginia) were still a part of the United States. Lincoln feared some of them might join the Confederacy if the Union announced that slavery was ended everywhere. As the war continued, however, more and more Northern people wanted the **emancipation** of the slaves to be a clear goal of the Union.

Lincoln first issued a preliminary **Emancipation Proclamation** after the battle of Antietam in September of 1862. He then issued the permanent Emancipation Proclamation on January 1, 1863. The Emancipation Proclamation did not free all the slaves immediately. It freed the slaves in those Southern states that were fighting against the Union. If the Union won the war, slaves would be, in the words of the proclamation, "then, thenceforward, and forever free." As Union armies advanced, Union commanders began treating slaves as free. In Arkansas, the Union army housed and fed former slaves, accepted them as soldiers, and in some cases helped them get farmland. Federal officials in Texas declared the end of slavery in that state as of June 19, 1865. Blacks in Texas made "Juneteenth" a holiday celebration, an idea that spread to other states.

▲ The Emancipation Proclamation.

Thirteenth Amendment—1865

"Neither slavery or involuntary servitude . . . shall exist within the United States or any place subject to their jurisdiction."

Slavery ended everywhere in the United States eight months after the end of the war. The Thirteenth Amendment to the Constitution was approved by the states in December of 1865.

DID YOU KNOW?

Did you know that the *Sultana* steamboat disaster in 1865 killed more people than the *Titanic*? In 1865, the *Sultana* was taking Union soldiers home from Southern Civil War prisoner of war camps. The *Sultana* sank after a boiler exploded. The remains of the vessel are believed to be buried under soybean crops planted in the alluvial fields of Arkansas. Although reports vary, estimates said 1,800 bodies were floating among the debris in the murky river water when Memphians awoke on the morning of April 27, 1865, to discover that a tragedy had occurred. Today, a memorial stands in Marion, Arkansas (Crittenden County), to honor those who perished on the *Sultana*.

Log on to Learn More
http://www.encyclopediaofarkansas.net/

Secession and Civil War   231

War Ends

The long and tragic war finally ended in the spring of 1865. Cut off by Gen. Ulysses S. Grant's forces, Confederate general Robert E. Lee surrendered in the town of Appomattox Courthouse, Virginia, in April of 1865. Just days later, President Lincoln was assassinated at Ford's Theatre in Washington, D.C. The battered remnants of the Army of Tennessee, in which so many Arkansans had served, surrendered a few days later. Then, in June, the Confederate forces in the Trans-Mississippi theater gave up. It was over. More than six hundred thousand men on both sides were dead. Another four hundred thousand were wounded, many of them missing arms or legs. More people died in the Civil War than have died in all other American wars combined.

The war settled two major issues: first, that the United States of America was one nation that could not be divided; and second, slavery would not exist in this nation. However, Arkansas and the rest of the country paid a terrible price to recognize these truths. Nothing in the history of America compares to the sufferings of the Civil War. It remains central to the American experience. Its causes and its consequences (KAHN-suh-kwen-sez) haunt the nation nearly 150 years after the last battle was fought.

DID YOU KNOW?

A Guide to Some Civil War Terms

Many Civil War battles have two names, one favored by the Union forces and the other used by Confederate forces. For instance, the first and second Battles of Manassas (the name of a town) are also known as the first and second Battles of Bull Run (a creek). In Arkansas, the Battle of Pea Ridge is sometimes referred to as the Battle of Elkhorn Tavern, named after a nearby building.

The name of the entire war has also been debated. The Civil War is the most common one. But the national government used the term the War of the Rebellion. Southerners have used several names, including the War Between the States and the War for States' Rights.

During the war, people came to be familiar with the "theaters," or major regions, of war. The Eastern theater was the area east of the Appalachian Mountains, and most of the battles were fought in Virginia. The Western theater was the area between the Appalachians and the Mississippi River. Arkansas, along with Louisiana and Texas, was in the Trans-Mississippi theater, the area west of the Mississippi River.

Civil War military units varied a great deal in their size. Roughly, an infantry company was fifty or a hundred men. A unit of the same size in the cavalry was called a company or a troop, and a unit of the same size in the artillery was called a battery. Officers at this level were lieutenants and captains.

Several companies together made up a regiment, which was supposed to be about a thousand men, but in the Civil War was usually much smaller. Officers at the regimental level, or field-grade officers, were majors, lieutenant colonels, and colonels.

Several infantry regiments, along with supporting cavalry and artillery units, could be organized into a brigade. A general officer (brigadier general) commanded at this level.

Finally, both sides organized brigades into corps (pronounced CORES) and corps into armies, commanded by major generals and lieutenant generals. Neither side had one single military commander of all its armies until the very end of the war. Grant (Union) and Lee (Confederacy) were then given those positions.

Chapter Reflection

Reflective Questions

1. Organize the following events into chronological order on your own paper:

   The Battle of Pea Ridge

   The slaves are freed in Arkansas

   Arkansas secedes from the Union

   The Arkansas convention votes against secession

   Lincoln is elected president for the first time

   Fort Sumter is attacked

2. At the time of secession, did some people feel more loyalty to their state rather than their country? Why or why not? Were Union or Confederate supporters more loyal? Why? How? Was loyalty more important in Civil War times or now? Why?

3. At first, the Confederates predicted the war would last _____.

   a. three years
   b. three months
   c. six months
   d. one year

4. The Confederate draft laws excused plantation managers if the plantation had more than twenty slaves because _____.

   a. the rich planters paid off the government
   b. women could not be left alone
   c. cotton production was critical to success in the war

5. Arkansas considers _____ _____ one of its greatest war heroes.

   a. Ulysses S. Grant
   b. Patrick Cleburne
   c. Robert E. Lee
   d. Isaac Murphy

6. The Battle of Pea Ridge _____.

   a. was the largest battle fought west of the Mississippi
   b. was a huge and clear victory for the Confederate Army
   c. helped secure Arkansas and Missouri for Mexico
   d. opened Arkansas to attack from American Indians from Indian Territory

7. The leading cause of death of soldiers in the Civil War was _____.

   a. hangings
   b. disease
   c. gangrene
   d. rifle fire

8. Bushwhackers were _____.

   a. outlaws
   b. bandits
   c. mostly from Kansas
   d. a and b

9. Once the Union troops occupied Arkansas, black Arkansans _____.

   a. were given their freedom
   b. were shot
   c. were transported by railroad to the North for high-paying factory jobs

10. The six hundred thousand American lives that were lost during the Civil War were second in number only to the number lost in _____.

    a. World War II
    b. Vietnam
    c. none of the choices
    d. The Korean War

Secession and Civil War

Picture It!

1. Carefully review all of the "Guide to Reading" sections from the chapter.
2. Choose four terms that were brand new to you or that you felt had the most interesting definitions.
3. Take a clean sheet of paper and draw one horizontal line all the way across the page and one vertical line from top to bottom, to divide the paper into four equal parts.
4. In the first box, neatly print the first word you chose in the upper left-hand corner.
5. Use markers or colored pencils to illustrate the word.

Continue the process until you have labeled and illustrated all four words. Be sure to include plenty of accurate detail in your drawing. Your illustration should result in a creative explanation of the meaning (definition) of the term.

Who Says?

Distinguishing Between Fact and Opinion

On your paper, number 1 through 10. Carefully read each statement below and based on your studies, determine if it is a *fact* or an *opinion*. Write an *F* or *O* beside the corresponding number to indicate your choice.

1. The delegates at the second Arkansas secession convention were correct when they voted in favor of secession.
2. Only one man voted against secession in the second convention.
3. The Confederate governor of Arkansas was Harris Flanagin.
4. Ulysses S. Grant was the general-in-chief of the Union military forces.
5. It is obvious that Ulysses S. Grant was a far stronger, more effective leader than Robert E. Lee because Grant was later elected president.
6. Nothing positive has ever resulted from a war.
7. Blue was a better choice for a uniform color than gray.
8. The Union was in control of Little Rock in late 1863.
9. Sneak attacks, nighttime battles, and guerilla warfare are more effective than traditional military warfare.
10. Lincoln's assassination had an impact on both the North and the South.

Read and Respond . . .

Read the following passage carefully. Then, complete the activities below on your own paper.

Letters to Home from Arkansas Soldiers in Virginia

Most of the soldiers from Arkansas were ordinary men who believed in what they were doing and did the best job they could. The conditions of their lives in camp were hard, and they missed their families. Here are letters to home from two of the four Butler brothers of Tulip, Arkansas (Dallas County), to their sister Emma Butler. The Butler boys were with the Confederate army in Virginia. Lewis Butler wrote Emma three weeks after the first Battle of Bull Run (Manassas):

**Camp Alleghany, Va.
August 12, 1861**

Last night was Sunday night, a night always commemorated by you all by singing the sacred melodies which have been hymned in our house since childhood. Billy Paisley, Dunkan Durham, Mr. Jones and myself gathered around one of our camp fires and made the camp ring with some of the same good old songs which we have learned to love for their very age, and which I doubt not you were singing in that same hour. I remembered you all then, and imagination showed me the lighted parlor, and my ear caught the sound of my mother's voice as she sang the treble to some of those time honored songs, and my heart ran out in sighs that I might be permitted once again to be with you all at home, dear home....

It is now growing late at night, it has been raining hard upon our tents for hours and many a sick soldier is now suffering and moaning as the rain borne on the wind beat[s] upon the thin covering above him and sends the damp to his weakened and languishing frame....

Tomorrow we leave here to go in the neighborhood of our enemies, and in a short time we expect to meet and conquer them. How pleasant it would be to be with you all this Summer enjoying the luxuries of the season, but we willingly yield up this when a more important work calls us away, and if we can be instrumental in speedily establishing our government in peace and prosperity we shall be content.

George Butler's letter to Emma was written just after the terrible series of battles called the Wilderness, Spotsylvania, and Cold Harbor, Virginia. Gen. Ulysses S. Grant's Army of the Potomac was battering Gen. Robert E. Lee's Army of Northern Virginia:

**near Richmond
June 9, 1864**

We have been fighting in Va. more or less every day for one entire month, and still the fighting continues. Cannon are now booming in the distance. Bro. Henry is still safe. He had one horse killed under him. You just ought to be thankful to God that none of your brothers have been killed in so many battles. I have heard (indirectly) from brother Charlie. He is certainly in Ft. Delaware [a Union prison in Maryland], and is well....

Our soldiers have fought well since the commencement of these fights. Gen. Lee, by the blessing of God, has not been driven from any position he has taken.... Our loss has been very small in comparison with that of the enemy. They have lost four or five times as many men as we have. Thousands of them were left unburied on the field of battle. The inhumanity of Gen. Grant to his own men, well, wounded, and killed is beyond question. Our men are in good spirits and never more confident of success.

Elizabeth Paisley Huckaby and Ethel C. Simpson, eds., *Tulip Evermore: Emma Butler and William Paisley: Their Lives in Letters, 1857–1887* (Fayetteville: University of Arkansas Press, 1985), 26, 43.

1. Which statement in George's letter is an opinion?

2. Which statement shows the writer's point of view and best explains his experience?

3. From the letters, determine the number of Butler brothers that are fighting in the war.

4. In your opinion, based on what you read in the passage, is the Butler family a family of faith? Why or why not? Give examples.

5. Rewrite the phrases below in your own words. Assume that you are a present-day soldier writing to your own family at home.

"I remembered you all then, and imagination showed me the lighted parlor, and my ear caught the sound of my mother's voice as she sang the treble to some of those time honored songs, and my heart ran out in sighs that I might be permitted once again to be with you all at home, dear home."

"Many a sick soldier is now suffering and moaning as the rain borne on the wind beat upon the thin covering above him and sends the damp to his weakened and languishing frame."

Secession and Civil War

Chapter 11

The Politics of Rebuilding
1866–1899

The Fifteenth Amendment.

Although the Civil War helped bring an end to slavery, the Thirteenth, Fourteenth, and Fifteenth Amendments caused bitter divisions between Americans. Why? What other laws have stirred people's passions and why?

Timeline

	1865	1870	1875	1880
Arkansas	**1868** A state Reconstruction government is created. A new state constitution is adopted, which assures political rights to newly freed slaves.	**1871** A railroad line is completed between Little Rock and Memphis.	**1874** The Brooks-Baxter War takes place. Conservative Democrats gain power in the state. Cotton prices fall to eleven cents per pound from around seventeen cents a pound.	**1875** Judge Isaac Parker assumes position in Federal District Court for western Arkansas.
United States	**1865** President Lincoln is assassinated at Ford's Theatre in Washington, D.C. **1868** The Fourteenth Amendment is ratified. **1869** The Trans-Continental Railroad is completed from Omaha, Nebraska, to Sacramento, California.	**1870** The Fifteenth Amendment gives African Americans the right to vote. **1873** Financial panic hits New York City.	**1876** Sitting Bull and Crazy Horse defeat General Custer at the Battle of Little Big Horn, Montana.	**1881** President Garfield is assassinated by Charles Giteau.
World		**1873** Severe financial panic hits Vienna, Austria, and spreads through Europe and North America. Famine ravages Bengal (India).		

Why Do We Study This?

Understanding the political, legal, and economic aspects of the Reconstruction era is critical because in an amazing effort, we, as a nation, worked to put our Union back together in a period of only about thirty-five years. Americans tried to put aside the hate and violence we had inflicted upon each other and worked to overcome the consequences of a brutal internal clash. This effort still continues today.

Unlike many nations that suffer the harm and losses of a civil war, our nation was able to rebound without having to spend decades placing blame or conducting investigations and trials at great expense. The 1860s, 1870s, and 1880s were volatile, but regional tensions eventually calmed. In a remarkably brief period, we cobbled together some form of national unity. The majority of countries that experience civil wars never put themselves back together at all—or if they do, it is often with the help or insistence of other countries.

In some ways, Reconstruction can be seen as having taught the nation to function as a society in which the members of diverse ethnic, racial, religious, and social groups were able to achieve individual goals and live by their personal belief systems. The intent of a free, democratic nation is to allow the development of all people's traditional cultures or special interests within the confines of a common civilization with rules, guidelines, and laws for the protection of all. This is called pluralism.

Reconstruction was a sort of revolution, in which a group of people made a difficult transition toward free labor, a new and diverse economy, and all people being treated as equal citizens. With all of the enormous change that took place in less than a century, it is amazing that it was not more violent than it was.

BIG PICTURE QUESTIONS

- What were the conflicts and changes Arkansas experienced during Reconstruction? Discuss and give specific examples.

- The Reconstruction economy was complex—analyze the successes, failures, and overall impact of sharecropping, new businesses, a manufacturing society, and taxes in Arkansas.

- How did Reconstruction affect Arkansans? Discuss various citizens' groups and the direct impacts on their lives. Does it still impact Arkansas today? If so, how? If no, why not?

1885	1890	1895	1900
1882 The farmers' political organization, the Agricultural Wheel, is formed in Des Arc (Prairie County).	**1885** The state capitol undergoes extensive renovations.	**1892** Poll taxes are established as voting requirements.	
1883 The National Convention of Colored Men is held in Louisville, Kentucky. Railroads in the United States and Canada introduce four standard time zones.	**1889** The territory of Oklahoma is opened to white settlement.	**1890** The Battle of Wounded Knee takes place in South Dakota.	**1896** The *Plessy v. Ferguson* decision is handed down by the U.S. Supreme Court, calling for "separate but equal" facilities for blacks and whites.
1883 The Mt. Krakatoa volcano erupts, killing thirty-four thousand Indonesians.	**1892** Rudolf Diesel patents the internal-combustion engine in Germany.	**1894** German scientist Wilhelm Roentgen discovers X-rays.	**1898** Marie Curie discovers radium. The Spanish-American war is fought in the Caribbean. The United States gains control of Spain's Caribbean and Pacific islands.

The Politics of Rebuilding

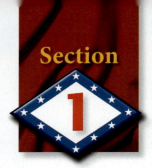

Section 1

Lincoln, Johnson, and Their Impacts on Arkansas

Guide to Reading

Terms
Fourteenth Amendment
inaugural
morale

Events
Reconstruction

People
George Atzerodt
John Wilkes Booth
Dr. Samuel Mudd
Louis Powell
Maj. Henry Rathbone
Mary Surratt

Places
Ford's Theatre

---

morale positive attitude or spirit.

inaugural first, beginning, or opening, as in the first speech of a newly-elected official.

John Wilkes Booth the assassin of President Abraham Lincoln.

Ford's Theatre the Washington, D.C., location of President Lincoln's assassination.

"Charity for All": Lincoln's "Soft" Reconstruction Plan

President Lincoln had hoped for a quick and diplomatic end to the war. He wanted the South to rejoin the Union as quickly and painlessly as possible and for all people to move forward so the nation would prosper and not falter. Many in the North believed that the South should be punished or suffer consequences for the act of secession. Lincoln disagreed. He believed forgiveness was best for the morale of the nation and the economy, and all should move forward. In his second inaugural address, after the 1864 presidential election, he said, "With malice towards none; with charity for all; . . . let us strive to finish the work we are in; to bind up the nation's wounds; to . . . achieve and cherish a just, and lasting peace." After his death, his hopes would struggle to survive. Fear and unrest would take hold of many Arkansans and Americans.

Lincoln's Assassination

Less than a week after the war ended—after Gen. Robert E. Lee surrendered to Gen. Ulysses S. Grant at Appomattox Courthouse, Virginia—the bullet of a Confederate sympathizer, John Wilkes Booth, took the life of President Lincoln. Lincoln was not able to carry out his Reconstruction plan.

Sequence of Events

Morning, April 14, 1865

- President and Mrs. Lincoln plan to go to Ford's Theatre in Washington, D.C., to see the play *Our American Cousin* that evening.
- General Grant and his wife are supposed to attend, but change plans at the last minute.
- Staff members beg Lincoln not to go because they have a "bad feeling."
- Mrs. Lincoln does not feel well, but decides to go anyway.

Evening, April 14, 1865

- The Lincolns and Maj. and Mrs. Henry Rathbone enter their box at Ford's Theatre.

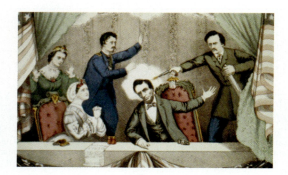

▶ An artist's rendering of the assassination of President Abraham Lincoln.

238 Chapter 11

- Police guard John Parker leaves his guard post outside the box.
- Booth steps in, points his Derringer pistol, and shoots Lincoln in the back of the head.
- Dagger in hand, Booth yells, "Sic semper tyrranis!" ("Thus always to tyrants!").
- Booth slashes Rathbone's arm and leaps from the balcony box to the level below.
- He becomes tangled in some fabric as he falls and breaks his leg.
- Booth drags himself out the back door of the theater.

Night, April 14, 1865

- A plan for Booth coconspirator George Atzerodt to kill Vice President Andrew Johnson was not attempted, and Lewis Powell, who planned to kill Secretary of State William H. Seward, fails.
- Booth flees Washington on horseback and meets an accomplice, David Herold, on a country road.
- They stop at an inn owned by Mary Surratt for supplies they had hidden earlier.

Early Morning, April 15, 1865

- Booth and friend ride to the home of Dr. Samuel Mudd because of the pain in Booth's leg.
- After offering some aid, Mudd becomes frightened of what they did and orders them away from his home.
- President Lincoln, shot through the left side of his brain, dies.

Evening, April 25, 1865

- After riding around the countryside for days, Booth and Herold arrive at a farm and are allowed to hide in the barn.

Early Morning, April 26, 1865

- The New York Cavalry finds Booth and Herold and orders them to give up. Herold runs out of the barn, while Booth does not.
- The cavalry burns the barn.
- A sergeant guns Booth down as he hobbles around inside the burning barn. He dies.

In the aftermath, conspirators Atzerodt, Powell, and Surratt were convicted and sentenced to death by hanging. A sentence of life in prison was given to Mudd. In 1869, President Johnson pardoned the surviving conspirators.

President Andrew Johnson

Upon the news of Lincoln's death, Vice President Andrew Johnson assumed the office of president. A Tennessean who had opposed secession, Johnson shared Lincoln's basic ideas about Reconstruction. The aim was to get the southern states back in the Union as quickly as possible.

Under this plan, Union Gov. Isaac Murphy continued to serve in Arkansas. The General Assembly was made up of mostly Democrats and ex-Confederates. Murphy upheld the principles of civil rights, but the state legislature refused to honor the rights of African Americans. They were kept from voting, serving on juries, going to school with whites, and marrying outside their race.

By a vote of 72–2, the state General Assembly refused to accept the Fourteenth Amendment to the U.S. Constitution. The U.S. Congress required acceptance of the amendment in order for a state to rejoin the Union.

> "No State shall make or enforce any law which shall abridge the privileges or immunities of citizens of the United States; nor shall any state deprive a person of life, liberty, or property, without due process of law; nor deny to any person within its jurisdiction the equal protection of the laws."

The Fourteenth Amendment to the U.S. Constitution, 1868

▲ Reward poster for the capture of John Wilkes Booth and his accomplices.

Maj. Henry Rathbone a guest of the Lincolns in their box at Ford's Theatre the evening of Lincoln's assassination.

George Atzerodt a coconspirator of John Wilkes Booth who had been assigned to kill Vice President Johnson, but did not follow through.

Lewis Powell a Booth accomplice who stabbed Secretary of State Seward as part of the Lincoln assassination plot, but failed to kill him.

Mary Surratt an accomplice of Booth, she kept supplies for him in her inn.

Dr. Samuel Mudd doctor who tended to the injured leg of Booth.

Reconstruction the U.S. government's plans to rebuild the South following the Civil War.

Fourteenth Amendment made blacks citizens of the United States and prevented states from denying the rights of any citizen.

Section 2

Government Muscle

Guide to Reading

Terms
carpetbaggers
factions
impeach
iron-clad oath
levee
scalawags
sharecropper
skirmishes

Events
Brooks-Baxter War
Radical Reconstruction

People
Elisha Baxter
Joseph Brooks
Powell Clayton
Conservatives
Democrat-Conservatives
Augustus Garland
Ku Klux Klan
Redeemers

Places
Coal Hill

Radical Reconstruction harsh measures imposed by the U.S. Congress upon the South following President Lincoln's and Johnson's unsuccessful "soft" approaches.

impeach to accuse a person of improper conduct in office. In the United States, the president can only be impeached for "high crimes and misdemeanors."

Things Get Radical

Former Confederate states that rejected the Fourteenth Amendment forced the U.S. Congress to take a tougher stand on Reconstruction. After the congressional elections of 1866, most members of Congress favored harsh treatment of the South. Congress's new stand became known as **Radical Reconstruction**. The Radicals had a desire to punish the South for the war. They also wished to continue the power of the Republican Party and to protect newly freed African Americans.

Angered by Johnson's forgiving approach, the Republican Congress took control of Reconstruction policy. Congress then **impeached** him. After a close vote, he was not convicted because the impeachment was based primarily on disagreements about legislative issues, not proven criminal activities. In the spring of 1867, Congress passed several

▶ Reunion of Confederate soldiers, 1890.

240 Chapter 11

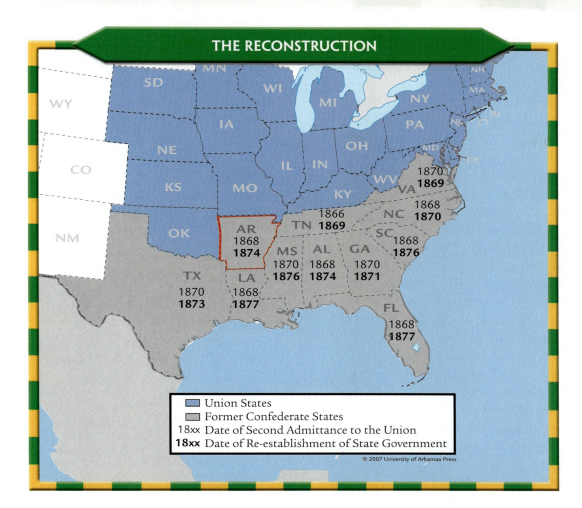

iron-clad oath sworn loyalty to the United States both prior to the Civil War and following the war; effectively excluded all ex-Confederates from voting during Reconstruction.

Powell Clayton a Union army general from Pennsylvania who moved to Arkansas, became governor, and was effective in limiting the success of the Ku Klux Klan in Arkansas after the war.

Reconstruction acts that laid down the rules for new state governments in the South. Under the Radical Reconstruction plan (Congress's plan), officers of the U.S. Army would register the voters in each of the Confederate states. All adult black males could vote. White males could vote if they took the **iron-clad oath**. In Arkansas, roughly twenty percent of possible white voters were not able to pass this test or live up to the words of this oath.

By 1868, Arkansas had a new state constitution and a new state government, with Radical Republicans in control. The new governor was **Powell Clayton**. Born in Pennsylvania, he had moved to Kansas in the 1850s and came to Arkansas in 1863 with the Union army. He became a general and a well-known cavalry commander. He bought a cotton plantation near Pine Bluff, married a local woman, and decided to stay in Arkansas.

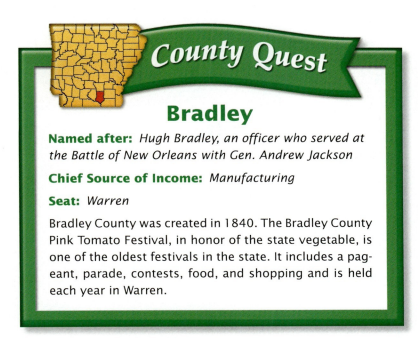

County Quest

Bradley

Named after: Hugh Bradley, an officer who served at the Battle of New Orleans with Gen. Andrew Jackson

Chief Source of Income: Manufacturing

Seat: Warren

Bradley County was created in 1840. The Bradley County Pink Tomato Festival, in honor of the state vegetable, is one of the oldest festivals in the state. It includes a pageant, parade, contests, food, and shopping and is held each year in Warren.

The Politics of Rebuilding **241**

scalawags (SKAL-ih-WAGZ) native southerners who supported the Republican government.

carpetbaggers northerners who moved south after the Civil War, presumably to get rich. However, some were teachers or agents of the Freedmen's Bureau.

Ku Klux Klan (KOO KLUKS KLAN) a secret group organized to harass and harm black citizens and to obstruct their participation in society.

In June of 1868, Congress approved Arkansas's political decisions and allowed its elected members into Congress. The Radical Reconstruction period in Arkansas had begun. Times were confusing, and many people were bitter about the war and Reconstruction. Some Americans would later see this as a time when the southern states were unfairly and badly governed. Those who held political power during Reconstruction were often made out to be a combination of African Americans, scalawags, and carpetbaggers. The stereotypical description of a carpetbagger was a Yankee, who sometimes used a suitcase made of carpet fabric, whose goal was to go to the South, take advantage of the bad times, and quickly make lots of money.

The political situation in Arkansas and the other southern states was much more complex. Although the Republicans strongly promoted black voting, many African Americans did not vote, and most people who held major offices were white. Many scalawags who served as Reconstruction-era leaders in Arkansas had been Whigs before the war. They often shared the Republicans' economic ideas.

Some carpetbaggers may have been out to get rich. But many first visited Arkansas during service with the Union army, liked the state and its people, and chose it for their new home. People had been moving into the state from all over the country for decades before the war began. Some of these new people brought with them cash that was good for the state's economy. Many northerners, like the teachers in Freedmen's Bureau schools, came to help the African Americans.

> *"The right of citizens of the United States to vote shall not be abridged or denied by the United States or any State on account of race, color or previous condition of servitude. The Congress shall have the power to enforce this article by appropriate legislation."*
>
> The Fifteenth Amendment to the U.S. Constitution, 1870

The Republicans

The first job of the new Republican government was to bring law and order to the state. Brutal assaults, robbery, and murder were still common. Arkansans and other southerners opposed to African American rights formed an extremist group called the **Ku Klux Klan**, based on a movement founded in Tennessee. Hiding behind masks and robes, Klansmen tried to terrify African Americans. Sometimes, Klansmen murdered them. The names of members were kept secret, but they seemed to have the support of many of the state's prewar leaders. Determined to stop violence in the state, Governor Clayton took advantage of the strong powers afforded to him under the constitution of 1868 and approached the problem based on his military training. He called out the militia and declared martial law in a number of counties. Despite widespread citizen reports about abuse of power by the militia, the violence was eventually

County Quest

Fulton

Named after: William S. Fulton, last territorial governor of Arkansas

Chief Source of Income: Agriculture

Seat: Salem

Fulton County was created in 1842. Mammoth Spring, home of Frisco Depot and Mammoth Spring State Park, where the headwaters of the Spring River are located, can be found there.

brought under control. Many whites deeply resented Clayton's methods.

As order was being restored, the Republicans began to carry out their plans for the state. Economic progress and public education were two major goals. In many ways, the Republicans hoped to bring to Arkansas the kind of active state government that was common in the North.

A real education system was desperately needed. In the 1860s, about 30 percent of whites and 95 percent of African Americans were unable to read and write. The Republicans began the first statewide public-school system. It featured trained leaders, a standard curriculum, and requirements that teachers had to meet to get a license. It was, however, a segregated system, with separate schools for black and white children. The number of teachers almost doubled. The new government also started the state's first public college, the Arkansas Industrial University in Fayetteville (Washington County). Later, this would become the University of Arkansas.

Economic progress focused first and foremost on railroad building. To aid private railroad companies, the state borrowed money by selling bonds and gave the almost $10 million collected to the railroads. During the Reconstruction period, more than six hundred miles of track were built. The Memphis to Little Rock railroad project proved to be very beneficial to the state, but the state was still too poor for many of the railroads to make a profit. Unfortunately, some of the state bond money was wasted on unsound projects.

The Reconstruction government also established several new state programs. It opened the School for the Deaf and moved the School for the Blind from Arkadelphia (Clark County) to Little Rock (Pulaski County). It formed a Bureau of Immigration and State Lands to recruit people to move to Arkansas. In eastern Arkansas, the state also funded **levee** building and swamp drainage to make more farmland.

All of these programs cost a great deal of money, far more than the state had spent before the Civil War. Even though the Republicans raised taxes, the cost of government and the state bonds meant that the state was accumulating a large debt. There were also some corrupt Republican leaders who achieved personal gain from their connections with state government. As the state sank more deeply into debt, many began to worry about the cost of Reconstruction programs. The state's revenues declined as prices for the

levee an earthen wall extending a river's natural banks upward to contain high water in order to avoid floods.

▼ An artist captured this scene in front of the capitol in Little Rock as volunteers chose sides in the Brooks-Baxter War.

The Politics of Rebuilding **243**

factions small groups or segments of the population, often with a special cause.

Conservatives (kun-SIR-vuh-tivz) name adopted by the Democrats to distinguish themselves from the "radical" Republicans during and after Reconstruction.

Brooks-Baxter War armed conflict after 1872 governor's election when results were thought to be unfair.

Elisha Baxter an Arkansas Unionist who was a Powell Clayton follower in the group called the "regular Republicans" who ran for governor in 1872.

Joseph Brooks a Methodist preacher who formed a Republican faction opposing Powell Clayton and his followers, which included Elisha Baxter, in the Arkansas governor's race of 1872.

skirmish (SKUR-mish) a small, armed battle.

cash crop of the state, cotton, fell from seventeen or eighteen cents a pound in 1868 to eleven cents a pound in 1874.

Political Chaos

Despite some progress with state programs, Republicans had political and policy troubles within their own party. The party began to split into two separate groups or **factions**. Democrats—or **Conservatives**, as they called themselves—made the most of these problems. They were able to play one Republican faction against the other. Most whites who had been kept from voting because of their Confederate ties earned the vote again in 1872 and most often favored the Democrats.

The most well-known example of Republican infighting was the **Brooks-Baxter War**—an armed conflict that broke out in 1874 between supporters of Gov. **Elisha Baxter** and those of **Joseph Brooks**, who claimed to be the rightful governor but said he was a victim of voting fraud during the election. Both were Republicans. Each side organized militia units. While this complex political situation was not really a full-scale war, there were a few bloody **skirmishes**. These took place in Little Rock, Pine Bluff, and along the Arkansas River. Perhaps as many as two hundred people were killed between April 15 and May 15, 1874. U.S. Army troops from the Little Rock Arsenal, stationed along Main Street between the two armed camps in Little Rock, helped prevent a major clash. Ultimately, President Ulysses S. Grant, and later a Congressional committee, ruled in favor of Baxter.

> Lee County Sheriff W. H. Furbush, who was African American, expressed the feelings of most Arkansas voters in his telegram to President Ulysses S. Grant:
>
> *"We do not care . . . who is governor; all we want is peace. The people will obey."*

▶ Another view of the scene during the Brooks-Baxter War. How does a political battle like this escalate into physical violence? Can you describe a modern-day political "battle"? How would a conflict like this be solved today?

A Day in the Life

Life on a Small Farm

John Quincy Wolf grew up in the 1870s and 1880s in the "Leatherwoods" near Calico Rock (Izard County). His parents died when he was twelve years old, and he and his sister went to live with an uncle and aunt, Mr. and Mrs. William T. Swan. The Swans, childless themselves, raised at least thirteen orphans, children of their relatives and neighbors. In his autobiography, Wolf described growing up on Uncle Will's nearly self-sufficient eighty-acre farm.

> *Unlike almost all the other houses in the Leatherwoods, which were one-room log cabins, the Swan home had two good-sized rooms and a porch in the front the entire width of the house. There were no windows in either room, but each had two doors and a fireplace. The kitchen and the smoke-house were twenty-five feet removed from the cabin. Three hundred yards away a fine cold spring poured out of a limestone cave. . . . We were a hundred miles from a railroad, and the so-called roads through the hills were very bad. Reaching our cabin by buggy was out of the question, and by wagon, difficult.*

> *Mail came to the post office a few miles away once a week, on Saturdays. . . . We got up at 4 A.M., and in the warm months we planted, plowed, hoed, chopped cotton, picked cotton. In the winter we cut wood, made fires, cleaned out fence corners, cleared land, shucked corn, fed the horses, often nubbined [fed] stunted ears of corn to some thirty head of cattle, and gave corn to the hogs. We went to bed not long after dark. . . .*

> *We never had to look for entertainment. If we were not eating or working or pampering the animals or teasing them, we might be trying to follow a bee-line or playing games with the large green glade-lizards—very handsome creatures—that sunned themselves on sandrocks all over the hills. Hunting bee-trees was an interesting pastime, and sometimes we were rewarded with rich finds. . . .*

John Quincy Wolf, Life in the Leatherwoods (1974; reprint, Fayetteville: University of Arkansas Press, 2000) 31–39.

Democratic-Conservatives a group of Democrats who called themselves "Redeemers" because they had freed the state from the Radical Republicans. They wanted to promote industry in Arkansas, but kept taxes too low to help schools.

Redeemers (ree-DEE-merz) name taken by the Democrats who came to power following the Brooks-Baxter War and who ended Reconstruction.

Augustus Hill Garland Arkansas's governor in 1874, he was also a U.S. senator, U.S. attorney general, and had a distinguished record of service to his state.

sharecropper a farmer who rents or does not own land, who is loaned necessary supplies such as shelter, tools, and equipment to work the land, and receives a portion (or share) of the profit from the crop after paying fees to the landowner.

The Brooks-Baxter War was over and internal bickering had weakened the party, contributing to the end of Republican-led Reconstruction in Arkansas. The real winners were the **Democratic-Conservatives**. They liked to call themselves the **Redeemers** because they had ousted the Radical Republicans, redeeming the state. Democrats controlled the legislature, and soon called for a constitutional convention in the summer of 1874.

The Constitution of 1874

The new state constitution was a direct response to the difficulties of Radical Reconstruction. It retained some features of the Reconstruction constitution of 1868, such as support for public schools, but the new document made it very hard to raise taxes. In addition, it cut the power of the governor by changing the term from four years to two years (which was not modified until 1986 when governors again began to serve four-year terms). The two-year term took away much of the governor's power to appoint people to office. Major state offices, such as secretary of state, attorney general, treasurer, auditor, and land commissioner, would be elected, not appointed. The constitution of 1874 is still the basic law that governs the state today. It has been amended often, and, over the years, attempts have been made to replace it entirely.

The new constitution called for a prompt election for a new governor. The Redeemers considered Baxter, but he declined. Their second choice was **Augustus Hill Garland**. He served in the governor's office from 1874 to 1877. He was a former Whig, then a Democrat, who had served in the congress of the Confederate States of America. Garland was a man of learning, an expert on constitutional law, and a kind man. He went on to enjoy a long and distinguished career as a U.S. senator and as attorney general of the United States under President Grover Cleveland.

The Democrats

After 1874, the Democratic Party was firmly in control of the state with no major threats to its power. The leaders of the party were a close-knit group of planters and businessmen, many of whom were former Confederates. For a time, and because it was federal law, they tolerated African Americans voting. They felt certain that they could control this situation because of their economic power over the black **sharecroppers**. A small Republican Party remained, but it was too weak to elect people to statewide office.

The Democratic leaders were very concerned with cutting the cost of state government. The state debt, almost $18 million in 1877 (more than $333 million in modern money), had to be addressed. The state had to

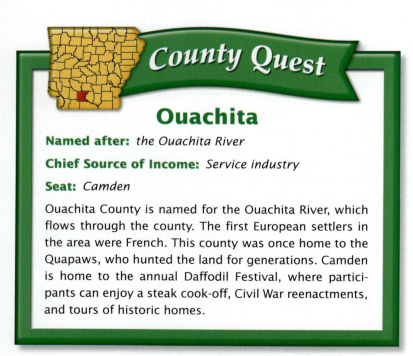

County Quest

Ouachita

Named after: the Ouachita River

Chief Source of Income: Service industry

Seat: Camden

Ouachita County is named for the Ouachita River, which flows through the county. The first European settlers in the area were French. This county was once home to the Quapaws, who hunted the land for generations. Camden is home to the annual Daffodil Festival, where participants can enjoy a steak cook-off, Civil War reenactments, and tours of historic homes.

pay a large amount of interest each year on the debt. Some wanted simply to cancel the debt. They said they should not be made to pay for the actions of the Reconstruction Republicans who had spent a great deal on state programs. Yet others pointed out that canceling the debt would destroy the state's credit rating. That would make it almost certain that the state could never borrow money again.

In the end, the debt was canceled. In 1877, the state supreme court declared part of the debt invalid. In 1885, the legislature proposed, and the voters approved, a constitutional amendment that wiped out most of the rest of it. Therefore, the people who had loaned money to Arkansas by buying state bonds, mostly eastern banks and businessmen, lost their money. As a result, many refused to invest in Arkansas for years to come.

The Democrats kept taxes very low. That meant several state-funded programs were cut back or dropped. Democrats wanted to keep the costs of running the state prison down. To help the prison pay for itself, they leased the inmates out to work for private businesses and industries. The practice had been going on since the 1840s. This caused a string of scandals because the inmates were overworked, poorly fed, and lived in overcrowded, run-down facilities. Many of them died while working on lease. Conditions were so bad in the mines at **Coal Hill** (Johnson County) that the prisoners leased to the mines went on strike. Still, there were no changes in the system.

The Democrats' low taxes also hurt education in Arkansas. The public-school system from the Reconstruction era was still in place, but it suffered from a lack of funding. The school term was short, sometimes only a few weeks long. Rural schools closed down so children could help with the spring planting and the fall harvest on the family farm. There was no law that required children to attend school. Books and other supplies were hard to obtain or to afford. Few teachers themselves had gone past the eighth grade. By 1900, only about one-half of the children in Arkansas were going to school. The literacy rate had improved, but nearly 20 percent of whites could not read and write.

Despite the problems of Reconstruction Democrats and their policies, the constitution of 1874 and the weak and crumbling Republican Party allowed these Conservative-Democrats to maintain control of Arkansas state politics until the mid-1900s, when there was a shift in fundamental party beliefs.

Coal Hill the location of mines in Johnson County with horrible working conditions where prisoners, who were used for labor, had a strike.

County Quest

Montgomery

Named after: Richard Montgomery, a general in the American Revolution who was killed in Quebec in 1775

Chief Source of Income: Agriculture

Seat: Mount Ida

In 1842, Montgomery County was created from part of Hot Spring County in southeast Arkansas. James H. "Mo" Alley Jr., a World War II veteran and member of the "Easy Company" paratroopers, an elite military unit that fought at D-Day and the Battle of the Bulge, grew up in Mount Ida. The unit's experiences were portrayed in the 2001 HBO series *Band of Brothers*. Mount Ida is known as the Quartz Crystal Capital of the World. Dortha Scott, designer of the Arkansas state quarter, is also from Mount Ida.

The Politics of Rebuilding

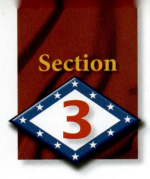

Section 3

Power to the People

Guide to Reading

Terms
glut
Jim Crow Laws

People
Agricultural Wheel
Grangers
Greenback Party
Patrons of Husbandry
Populist Party
Union Labor Party

---

glut an economic situation or strategy to lower prices by supplying the market with more of a product than is in demand.

Patrons of Husbandry (PAY-trunz uhv HUZ-bun-dree) a farmers' self-help and improvement organization. (Husbandry is the raising of crops and animals.)

Grangers (GRAYNJ-erz) another name for the Patrons of Husbandry; each chapter was known as a "grange." (The word is an old-fashioned word for granary or barn.)

Greenback Party the political party formed by farmers to support an increased paper money supply.

Farmers' Political Organizations

At the end of the 1800s, most Arkansans still lived and worked on farms or in farm-related industries. Modern farming methods suggested that farmers should plant diverse crops, but almost all Arkansas farmers, large and small, still grew cotton as their cash crop. By 1880, Arkansas was growing more cotton than it had before the Civil War. The well-being, sometimes even the survival, of Arkansas farmers was tied up in that one crop. But the price kept going down.

Cotton was selling for eleven cents a pound in 1874, and the price declined to five cents a pound by the mid-1890s. At that price, it cost more to produce cotton than the farmer would get paid for the harvested crop. Few farmers knew it, but they were the victims of a worldwide market **glut**. Egypt and India were growing cotton, too. The more cotton the world's farmers produced, the lower the price went.

The farmers also had other troubles. The U.S. government kept the supply of money tight, which meant that loans were hard to get. Moreover, the farmers had to move their crops to market by the railroads, which charged high rates. The middlemen, or those who processed and sold the crops, also took a share of the profit. They often made more than the farmers. Under these conditions, more and more small farmers, white and black, went broke. They had to give up their land to the banker or merchant and become sharecroppers.

These stark conditions moved the farmers to organize in hopes of solving their problems. Generally they blamed bankers, middlemen, railroads, and politicians. The farmers' protest movement spread all over the country, with Arkansans playing a key role.

The first effort to organize produced the **Patrons of Husbandry**, or **Grangers**. The organization began in the 1870s with self-help improvement clubs for rural men and women. The Grangers pushed for better homes, growing varied crops, and more. The master of the Arkansas state Grange was John T. Jones of Helena. He was chosen master of the national Grange in 1875, and his wife was elected to the top national office for women.

As times grew tougher, some farmers began to think about political action as a way to solve their problems. In 1880, some Arkansas farmers worked for the small **Greenback Party**. This group called for the U.S. government to print paper money in order to make cash easier to obtain. They did not have much success.

248 Chapter 11

▲ The members of Enola Farmer's Union assembled in 1900. What common features do you see throughout this photograph?

Agricultural Wheel a national farmers' political organization.

Union Labor Party a political party formed by joining the Agricultural Wheel with Republicans.

Populist Party (POP-yoo-list PAR-tee) a political party formed by joining many farmers' and working men's organizations nationwide to fight big business on behalf of the common man.

The next stage in the farmers' protest movement was the founding of the **Agricultural Wheel** in 1882. Some farmers were aware that their problems were the same, regardless of their different races. White members of the Agricultural Wheel urged blacks to form similar groups. The Wheel wanted fairer taxes, easier credit, better public schools, regulation of the railroads, and a political process more open to the common man.

> The rallying song of the Agricultural Wheel began, "Come all ye sunburnt sons of toil, Arise from thine oppression."

In Arkansas, as in many southern states, the major question was whether the farmers should work within the Democratic Party or form a new party. The leaders of the Democratic Party did not show very much concern about the farmers' demands. Farmers were so desperate that many of them broke with the Democratic Party. In 1888, white and black members of the Agricultural Wheel, joined by those who used to be Republicans, formed a new political party, the **Union Labor Party**. They supported Charles M. Norwood of Prescott (Nevada County), a disabled Confederate veteran, for governor. The Democrats nominated a party regular, James P. Eagle of Lonoke (Lonoke County), a Baptist minister who was also a Confederate veteran. Despite the best efforts of the farmers, the Democratic election officials declared Eagle the winner with 56 percent of the vote.

Although the peak of the farmers' protest in Arkansas was in 1888, the movement continued into the next decade. Its support went to the **Populist Party** in 1892 and to William Jennings Bryan as the Democratic candidate for president in 1896. Although the Populists did not carry the vote, the movement

The Politics of Rebuilding **249**

▲ A black fraternal group in Helena, 1880, which includes A. H. Miller, a state representative, and J. T. White, a state senator.

Jim Crow laws the name given to the system of laws and social practices that intimidated, disenfranchised, and oppressed black citizens in America for close to ninety years. The name comes from a leading role in minstrel song-and-dance shows.

forced the Democrats to pass some laws that imposed basic regulations on railroads and simple limits on the power of big businesses. These measures were actually an effort to lessen the effectiveness of the farmers' protests, not meaningful reforms.

One major effect of the farmers' protest in Arkansas and in other southern states was to remove African Americans from voting and, therefore, from any political power. The farmers' protest movement threatened to divide the white vote, which in turn meant that black voters might hold the balance of power.

The Democratic leaders played upon that fear and urged the common people to take out their frustrations on African Americans. The state legislature in the early 1890s passed a series of measures that served to keep African Americans from being involved in politics. These laws became known as **Jim Crow laws**.

One act put control of the voting process fully in the hands of the Democratic Party, with no role for other parties or groups. A second law made it harder for those who could not read or write to vote. This law said only the election judge could help such a person mark his ballot. The third and perhaps toughest measure required a dollar poll tax for voting at a time when many Arkansans did not see twenty-five dollars cash in an entire year. The law further required that the poll tax be paid well in advance of an election. In a fourth act, the Democratic Party proclaimed that its primary elections, which selected the party nominees, were for whites only. Since the primary was the only real election in a one-party state like Arkansas, the whites-only primary finished the process of ousting blacks from politics.

Some African Americans would keep voting, but none held any high office after the 1890s. The voting laws also hurt many poor whites. From 1890 to 1900, the voter turnout in Arkansas elections declined by 30 percent because of fear and hassles at the polls. This was a barrier to what was supposed to be a free and democratic society.

Arkansas approached the new century with tremendous disadvantages. The Reconstruction period and the threat of change in general had prompted a backlash from political conservatives—the Democrats/Redeemers. The restrictive new state constitution, with its limits on taxation and the executive branch, and efforts to limit the rights of newly freed blacks with measures like the Jim Crow laws, would hinder long-term progress in the state.

I Am an Arkansan

William Grant Still (1895–1978)

William Grant Still was born in 1895 in Woodville, Mississippi. Still and his mother moved to Little Rock (Pulaski County) after the death of his father in 1895. Still grew up in Little Rock and went on to become an internationally-acclaimed composer of symphonies and popular music. As an African American, he was particularly interested in promoting fellow African American musicians and composers.

Still attended high school in Little Rock and graduated in 1911 as class valedictorian. Later that year, he enrolled at Wilberforce University in Ohio. In 1915, though, he left the college without a degree in order to pursue a musical career.

In 1916, Still met Memphis blues musician W. C. Handy, who asked Still to perform with his band and arrange some of the music. The following year, he entered the Oberlin Conservatory of Music in Ohio to study music, but was interrupted by World War I, when he served in the U.S. Navy. After the war, and throughout the 1920s, Still became a highly successful composer, with contacts and fans around the world. Most notably, he wrote the theme music for the 1939–40 World's Fair, along with dozens of highly, acclaimed works.

In 1940, he debuted *And They Lynched Him on a Tree*, performed by the New York Philharmonic. Orchestras throughout the United States soon began performing his work, and he went on to write over two hundred symphonies, ballets, operas, and other pieces of music. He won numerous awards, including a Guggenheim Fellowship. By the time of his death in 1978, he had also been awarded several honorary degrees—further evidence of his enormous contribution to American music.

THE ENCYCLOPEDIA OF ARKANSAS HISTORY & CULTURE

Log on to Learn More
http://www.encyclopediaofarkansas.net/

Chapter Reflection

Reflective Questions

1. In your own words, explain Reconstruction.
2. What were Lincoln's goals or ideas for a Reconstruction plan?
3. How did Lincoln's plan differ from Congress's Reconstruction plan?
4. In your own words, discuss what you would assume to be the impact of President Lincoln's assassination on Arkansas and Arkansans and support your opinion.
5. Divide your paper into two columns and list facts that will help you compare and contrast the Arkansas constitution of 1868 and the constitution of 1874.
6. What were three of Arkansas's difficulties in developing industry?
7. When the farmers entered politics, what were their major goals? Were they successful? If so, how? If no, why not?
8. If you had served as a Confederate officer in the Civil War and were a vocal supporter of the South, would you have been able to vote in the election of 1874? If yes, how? If no, why not?
9. By the mid-1890s, the price of cotton had fallen to five cents a pound from a previously higher price. Re-read to determine the higher price and then calculate the percentage price change per pound.

THE OL' FILLIN' STATION

Fill in the Blank: Copy the phrase on your own paper and fill in the blank with the correct word or phrase from the chapter:

1. General _____ (C) surrendered to General _____ (U), April, 1865, in Appomattox Courthouse, Virginia. The _____ _____ was over.
2. Southerners and Arkansans felt _____ when Lincoln was assassinated.
3. The _____ (amendment number) Amendment abolished slavery in the United States.
4. "Malice for none and charity for all," was said by _____ and means _____ _____.

You Don't Say!

On your own paper, number 1–5, copy each phrase, and clearly mark each with a T for *True* or an F for *False*:

_____ 1. Lincoln had a "soft" plan for the post-war transition period.

_____ 2. Andrew Johnson did the best he could to carry out Lincoln's Reconstruction plan, but Congress fought him.

_____ 3. The Brooks-Baxter War was basically about accusations of election fraud.

_____ 4. Carpetbaggers came to Arkansas and other southern states to work the crop fields on the plantations.

_____ 5. Booth lived to tell of his assassination conspiracy, and the United States has his signed confession.

Prove It!

Now that you have completed the *You Don't Say!* exercise above, look at your answers and review the statements you said to be false. Use your book and class discussion notes to find evidence to rewrite each of the false statements to be true. Do this on your own paper.

Organization and Visualization

Lincoln Assassination

On a blank sheet of paper, use colors and markers to create an illustrated timeline of the events of the Lincoln assassination. Place the events in correct chronological order. Give an accurate written description of each event that took place by writing above or below the date marker on your timeline. Then, choose four of the events to illustrate. Create your illustration above or below its corresponding point on the timeline.

Brooks-Baxter War

Copy the chart below on your paper. In the columns after each name, write one descriptive characteristic or fact about that person that you learned while studying the chapter. When you finish, you will have an organized, understandable comparison and contrast chart about the Brooks-Baxter War. Consider political beliefs, results, consequences, actions, and so on when completing your chart.

Log on to Learn More
http://www.encyclopediaofarkansas.net/

Brooks				
Baxter				

The Politics of Rebuilding

Chapter 12

Something Old, Something New

Society, the Economy, and Race in Reconstruction-Era Arkansas, 1866–1899

▶ A black aristocratic family.

Timeline

	1866	1870	1875	1880
Arkansas		**1871** Arkansas Industrial University, later called the University of Arkansas, is established in Fayetteville (Washington County).	**1873** Branch Normal College is founded in Pine Bluff (Jefferson County).	**1879** The first telephone exchange opens in Little Rock (Pulaski County).	**1881** The first Colored State Fair is held in Pine Bluff.
United States	**1866** Ku Klux Klan is organized in Tennessee. **1868** Louisa May Alcott publishes *Little Women*.	**1871** The Great Fire destroys more than four miles of buildings in Chicago.	**1874** The first American zoo opens in Philadelphia. **1875** Tchaikovsky debuts his Concerto No. 1 in Boston.	**1876** Alexander Graham Bell patents the telephone.	**1879** Thomas Edison invents the light bulb.
World	**1867** Karl Marx writes *Das Kapital*.	**1871** *Aida* by Giuseppe Verdi debuts in Cairo, Egypt.	**1874** The first impressionist art exhibit is held in Paris.		

254 Chapter 12

Why Do We Study This?

The social and racial issues of the Reconstruction era in the United States are some of the most important pieces of our nation's history. The already present cycle of conflict and change in our nation took on new importance and consequence during these years. Its impact would be seen into the twenty-first century.

After the Civil War, from 1866 to 1868, the Arkansas government was in the hands of the people who had run the government before the war—those who believed in an obsolete society where one group was considered superior to another. They acted as if nothing had changed, continuing to discriminate against the former slaves.

The Reconstruction era, and the laws, people, progresses, and failures of the day reflect our nation's struggle to overcome the incredibly negative effects of slavery. Most countries never have and never will attempt the level of reform that the United States undertook during this period. That is, we recognized grave weaknesses in our system and society and took steps to change them. Even though victories for equality and progress were sometimes few and far between, the inspiration and drive for justice had emerged and would not be abandoned.

BIG PICTURE QUESTIONS

- Was a freedman's life truly free? Why or why not?
- Segregation was and is a social, political, economic, and legal injustice. Evaluate the reasons why.
- What other groups of people, besides African Americans, were still not equal after the war? Why? In what ways?
- Identify a segment of today's population that is underrepresented in the voting process or feels excluded from participating. Justify your choice with examples.

1885 | **1890** | **1895** | **1900**

1884 Arkansas Baptist College is established in Little Rock.

1891 Segregation is introduced on railroads.

1894 The University of Arkansas fields its first football team, then known as the Cardinals.

1884 Mark Twain publishes *Huckleberry Finn*. The first national baseball championship is held in New York City between the Providence Grays and the New York Metropolitans.

1885 American Telephone and Telegraph, later known as AT&T, is organized.

1888 *National Geographic* publishes its first issue. George Eastman perfects the inexpensive, easy-to-use, hand-held camera.

1889 Belle Starr, the "Bandit Queen of the West," is shot to death near her ranch in Indian Territory (now Oklahoma), an area under Judge Parker's jurisdiction.

1895 The first U.S. Open golf championship is played in Rhode Island.

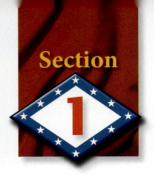

Section 1

Picking Up the Pieces

Guide to Reading

Terms

New South   regulation   shrapnel   tainted

Physical Damage and Human Agony

As the war ended in 1865, Arkansans faced the problems of settling back into daily life and rebuilding. The wounds of war, both physical and mental, would last for a long time. The violence of the war years would also linger.

Across the state, but especially in northwestern Arkansas, farms and homes had been abandoned, burglarized, burned, or completely demolished. In a few areas, entire small communities had been ravaged and dissolved into ruins. Many plantations were inactive because there were no slaves to work the fields. Livestock had been lost or stolen—horse, mule, and cattle numbers dropped by around 50 percent compared to before the war. Trampled bushes and snapped trees

▶ A sawmill in Jefferson County, 1888.

256   Chapter 12

▲ When a railroad completed part of its line, it was considered a celebration and a ceremony was held. This is a "spike" ceremony in the late 1860s on the Iron Mountain Railroad in Arkansas.

dotted the battlefield landscapes of Arkansas. The soil was sometimes **tainted** with **shrapnel**, bodies, trash, and blood. The cost of property damage and loss in the state was in the millions of dollars.

Black, white, Confederate, and Union Arkansans gave their lives to the war—more than ten thousand in all. Thousands of others were wounded, contracted illnesses, or ended up separated from their families. Wives had lost husbands, fathers lost sons, and brothers lost brothers. Many people wandered the countryside looking for missing family members. Starvation drove many to beg for food from neighbors.

Suffering from interruption more than total ruin, the economic structure of the state would have to be rebuilt. Above all, there were new roles for African Americans, now legally free, but socially and financially limited. Under the ideology of the **New South**, the state tried to bring itself into the modern age. The years of Reconstruction, from 1866 to 1874, and rebuilding that would continue through the end of the century, were a bridge from the well-known and established past into the unknown and sometimes frightening world of the future.

Too poor to develop industry, the state continued to be mostly agricultural. Black Arkansans, without the money to buy land, became workers on white men's land, marking the beginning of sharecropping. The brightest spot in the economy was the introduction of railroads.

The New South

Although Arkansas was and would remain dependent on agriculture as its main economic resource, the Democratic-Conservative leaders of the state wanted to promote industry. All over the South, people were talking about a New South that would have its own factories. However, Arkansas lacked much of what was needed for such progress: money to invest, a skilled labor force, people wealthy enough to buy goods that such plants might produce, and good transportation.

The move to develop industry went forward slowly. In 1900, the U.S. Census counted 4,794 manufacturing-type businesses in the state, made up generally of small businesses with five or six people in their work force. Only about 26,500 Arkansans, or 2 percent of the total, were listed as wage earners in industry/manufacturing. Today, about 8 percent, or around 213,000 Arkansans, work at these types of jobs.

The state did see some success in railroad building. The state no longer

tainted not pure; stained, infected, polluted, or spoiled.

shrapnel splinters, chips, or pieces of a cannon ball or mortar round that are scattered upon explosion.

New South a model for the future of the South that included factories and less dependence on agriculture; a South with a diverse economy.

Something Old, Something New   **257**

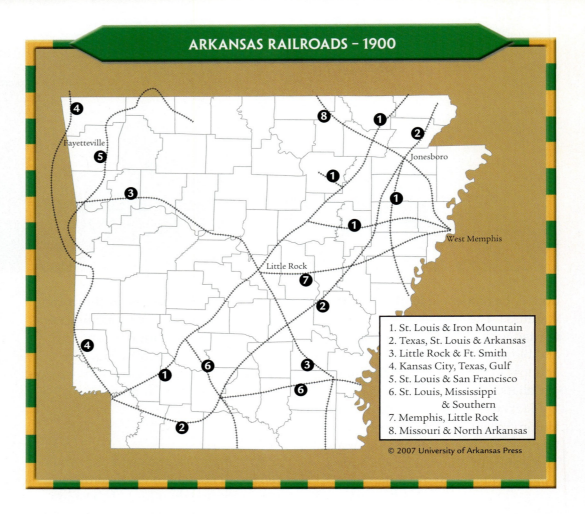

ARKANSAS RAILROADS – 1900

1. St. Louis & Iron Mountain
2. Texas, St. Louis & Arkansas
3. Little Rock & Ft. Smith
4. Kansas City, Texas, Gulf
5. St. Louis & San Francisco
6. St. Louis, Mississippi & Southern
7. Memphis, Little Rock
8. Missouri & North Arkansas

© 2007 University of Arkansas Press

regulation a rule, law, or procedure saying what can and cannot be done.

offered bond money to railroad companies, but it did promise low or no taxes and little **regulation**. The U.S. government aided the building program by giving the railroads huge grants of public lands along their routes. By 1900, Arkansas had more than three thousand miles of track. Large areas in the Ozarks and Ouachitas were still out of reach, but railroads covered much of eastern, central, and southern Arkansas. They also opened routes to Arkansas's neighboring states and the rest of the nation. There were four lines crisscrossing the state: the Rock Island Line from Memphis into Oklahoma; the Missouri Pacific from Memphis to Fort Smith; the St. Louis Southwestern, or "Cotton Belt," which crossed the southern part of the state through Pine Bluff and Texarkana and on to Texas; and the Frisco from Memphis up the Mississippi and into Missouri.

The railroads held a great deal of power over Arkansas towns. A town

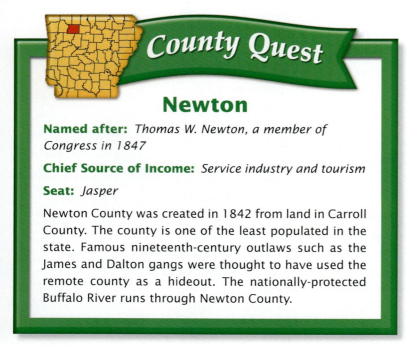

County Quest

Newton

Named after: Thomas W. Newton, a member of Congress in 1847

Chief Source of Income: Service industry and tourism

Seat: Jasper

Newton County was created in 1842 from land in Carroll County. The county is one of the least populated in the state. Famous nineteenth-century outlaws such as the James and Dalton gangs were thought to have used the remote county as a hideout. The nationally-protected Buffalo River runs through Newton County.

I Am an Arkansan

Charlotte Stephens (1854–1951)

A teacher for more than seventy years, Charlotte Stephens was the first African American to teach in the Little Rock (Pulaski County) school district.

She was born in Little Rock in 1854 as a slave. At the age of fifteen, she became a teacher after substituting for her own teacher who had fallen ill. In 1869, Stephens was hired to teach, making her the first black teacher in the district. A year later, she took a leave to attend Oberlin College in Ohio. Three years later, she returned to Little Rock and resumed her teaching career. In 1910, the Little Rock School District recognized her achievements and named Stephens Elementary School in her honor. Stephens retired in 1939. (See photo on page 262.)

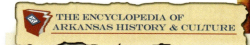

THE ENCYCLOPEDIA OF ARKANSAS HISTORY & CULTURE

Log on to Learn More
http://www.encyclopediaofarkansas.net/

---

that was bypassed by the railroad might vanish, while new towns developed quickly along the routes. Most areas were served by only one railroad, so the people in those places had to pay any price the railroad wanted to charge to move goods. Five large companies based in the northern United States owned almost all of the railroad tracks in Arkansas.

The railroads, eager to sell their land grants, joined the state in trying to attract new settlers. Glowing advertisements and stories raved about Arkansas as a lush garden. In 1875, the railroads brought in newswriters from the North and West to tour the state.

Some effort was made to attract European settlers. There were quite a few Germans in Arkansas, and more moved to Little Rock, Fort Smith (Sebastian County), and Stuttgart (Arkansas County). A Polish group settled in Marche, near Little Rock. A group of Italians tried delta farming in Chicot County. Some of them then moved to establish Tontitown (Washington County) north of Fayetteville. In spite of these efforts, by 1900, just a little over one percent of Arkansas's people were foreign-born.

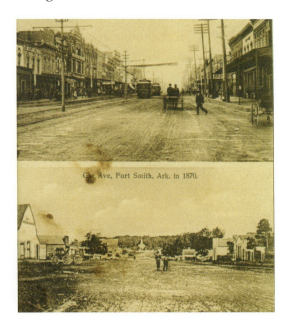

◀ The streets of Fort Smith (Sebastian County) in 1870.

Something Old, Something New

Section 2

Opportunity Knocks

Guide to Reading

Terms
Arkansas Federation of Women's Clubs
commencement
elocution
enlightenment
Mosaic Templars of America
Sisters Union Society
temperance

People
Joseph Carter Corbin

Places
Arkansas Baptist College
Branch Normal College
Philander Smith
Shorter College
Southland Institute
University of Arkansas

---

enlightenment to achieve freedom from ignorance or unawareness. To have something made clear.

Arkansas Federation of Women's Clubs a group of social, arts, and betterment clubs for women in the Reconstruction era that joined together to promote positive causes and change.

temperance (TEM-per-uns) the effort to reduce, restrict, or outlaw the use of alcohol.

New Responsibilities for Women

These were also changing times for women. Some of the laws that restricted the rights of women were removed. The constitution of 1874 honored a woman's right to own property in her own name. In rural areas, however, life was still very hard. For the most part, rural women lived out days of harsh, routine chores with only the company of their many children. In a rural setting, the poorly-paid schoolteacher might be the only woman for miles around with any money of her own.

The growing cities in Arkansas offered new freedom and greater opportunities for wealth to many women. Urban women often had fewer children than rural women, and the possibility of greater wealth and the increased convenience of town services helped create a new upper-middle class of city women. These women had the time, opportunity, and skills to improve their status and that of their towns.

By the 1880s, women were forming clubs to channel their efforts. Some groups were for the cultural **enlightenment** of their members, focusing on the study of art, music, or books. Other clubs had civic reform goals, such as better schools. In 1897, forty-eight clubs joined into the **Arkansas Federation of Women's Clubs**. Much of this reform urge focused on the **temperance** movement. Alcohol abuse was a serious problem

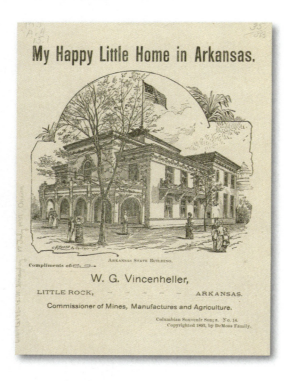

▶ A sheet music cover depicting a "happy home" in Arkansas, 1893.

260   Chapter 12

for many men, women, and families, as well as society at large. The efforts of women's groups helped to enact a series of laws from 1881 to 1897 that tightened local control over alcohol. By 1900, forty-two of Arkansas's seventy-five counties had fully banned the sale of liquor. These women, their clubs, and their organized political efforts gave them real, yet behind-the-scenes power, even though they did not have the right to vote.

The Establishment of the University of Arkansas–Fayetteville

Another positive Reconstruction-era legacy is the **University of Arkansas**. Congress passed the Morrill Land Grant Act in 1862, allowing thirty thousand acres of public lands to be sold in each state to supply funds for a university. This would provide support for each state's college of agriculture and the mechanical arts (engineering).

The Union-governed legislature of Arkansas accepted the terms of the Morrill Act in 1864, but the end of the Civil War and Reconstruction delayed action. In the spring of 1871, the legislature authorized the board of trustees to seek a location for the school. Arkansas Industrial University was created in 1871. This was Arkansas's first state-supported college, which was officially renamed the University of Arkansas in 1899.

The legislature asked communities to bid for the location of the college by offering local financial support. In Little Rock, voters turned down both city and county bond issues for the university. Batesville and Independence counties offered $69,000, but Fayetteville and Washington counties offered $150,000 in bond issues and gifts. The legislators on the committee who were to review possible sites

▲ Sheet music for an 1893 song, "My Happy Little Home in Arkansas."

reported that Fayetteville had every requirement for the university, although they had some questions about its remote location. To get to Fayetteville, the committee went by train from Little Rock to the end of the line in Morrilton (Conway County), up the Arkansas River on a steamboat

University of Arkansas the state university located in Fayetteville, which offers almost two hundred programs of study. It is considered the "flagship" state institution and is the major land-grant university in Arkansas.

▼ Old Main, at the University of Arkansas, Fayetteville (Washington County).

Something Old, Something New

commencement graduation day or ceremony.

Joseph Carter Corbin Reconstruction-era state superintendent of education who authorized the start of construction on the University of Arkansas and served as president of Branch Normal College.

to Van Buren (Crawford County), and by stagecoach to Fayetteville. To return, the committee took a stage to the railhead in southwest Missouri, and then traveled by train through St. Louis and back to Little Rock.

The site for the college ended up being the 160-acre McIlroy farm, then about a mile northwest of Fayetteville. Classes started in January of 1872. None of the first eight students were high-school graduates, because Arkansas had few public high schools at that time. Anna Putman of Washington County was the only woman in the class.

The first real **commencement** ceremony was held in 1876 for eight graduates. Total enrollment in the 1870s was usually 250 or 300 students. Total enrollment in 2005 was almost 17,000 students. The Main Building (now known as Old Main) was modeled on the Main Building at the University of Illinois, which was also completed in the 1870s. In 1873, the construction contract was signed by **Joseph Carter Corbin** and construction began.

In 1873, the *Little Rock Daily Republican* published an article that said an African American student from Woodruff County, James McGahee, who was studying to become a minister, was receiving private instruction from university president Noah Gates, but that McGahee was not formally enrolled as a student. This progressive and forward-thinking action most likely laid the groundwork for the UA Law School to officially enroll its first African American student in 1948. This made the University of Arkansas the first major Southern public university to do so without a lawsuit. This man was Silas Hunt.

Today, the University of Arkansas is most often recognized by its Razorback mascot. However, that was not always the case. In 1895, the official mascot and school colors were voted on by the student body. They chose cardinal red and white for the colors and the cardinal (a red bird) as the mascot. But in 1909, Arkansas football coach Hugo Bezdek would forever change the school's history.

Bezdek spoke in a frenzied and emotional manner to an energized crowd of fans in Fayetteville about the Cardinal football team that had scored a major victory on the road, defeating favored Louisiana State University. The coach exclaimed that the team had performed "like a wild band of Razorback hogs." The crowd went wild, and in 1910, the students of the university officially adopted the Razorback as the school's mascot.

Only in Arkansas!

Chi Omega founded at the University of Arkansas

The Chi Omega women's fraternity (sorority) that was founded at the University of Arkansas in 1895 established a lasting legacy on the University of Arkansas campus with a special gift: the Chi Omega Greek Theater. It was built in 1930 and is a reproduction of an ancient amphitheater located in Athens, Greece. The theater is located on Dickson Street in Fayetteville and is used for pep rallies, commencements, concerts, guest speakers, plays, as a student study and social area, and for many other events. The university erected a Chi Omega historical marker on Dickson Street near the theater to commemorate the gift.

With more than three hundred thousand current members and alumnae in 170 chapters, Chi Omega is the world's largest fraternal organization for women. Arkansas Senator Blanche Lincoln was a member of Chi Omega when she attended Randolph-Macon Women's College.

◀ "Mustered out" black volunteers in Little Rock, May 19, 1866. What does it mean when a soldier is "mustered out"?

Opportunities for African Americans

Meanwhile, ex-slaves were intent on building new lives in freedom. As early as 1865, a group of African American leaders gathered in Little Rock to define their goals. Their wishes were simple: they wanted to own land on which to farm, good schools for their children, and legal protection so they could go about their lives in peace.

Many were not focused on getting even with former slave owners. They only wished to be equal citizens.

> William H. Grey, a Helena grocer, put it this way: *"Our future is sure— God has marked it out with his own finger; here we lived, suffered, fought, bled, and many have died. We will not leave the graves of our fathers, but here we will rear our children; here we will educate them to a higher destiny; here, where we have been degraded, will we be exalted."*

Some African Americans did get ahead by moving to the towns, where they had the chance to create good careers as barbers, bakers, plasterers, brick masons, blacksmiths, and carpenters. Little Rock's African American population increased from 23 percent (3,500 in number) in 1860 to 43 percent (13,708) in 1870. The estimated 2000 African American population in Little Rock was 40.4 percent, or approximately 73,600.

County Quest

Polk

Named after: President James K. Polk

Chief Source of Income: Manufacturing

Seat: Mena

In 1844, Gov. Thomas Drew created Polk County and named it for the sitting president. The county offers a number of beautiful geographical features, including the Ouachita National Forest, the Cossatot and Ouachita rivers, Queen Wilhemenia State Park, and the Talimena National Scenic Byway. These attractions draw visitors from throughout the state. Hiking, fishing, hunting, and rafting are among the many outdoor adventures that can be had here.

Something Old, Something New

▲ Charlotte Stephens

▲ Mifflin W. Gibbs.

For some black women, careers as teachers offered a way to make a solid living. Charlotte Stephens, a former slave who had gone to Oberlin College in Ohio, was Little Rock's first African American teacher. She worked in the city's schools for seventy years, from 1869 to 1939. African American women also found work as laundresses, cooks, and maids. Stephens later called them "homespun heroines who kept their own homes neat, made their children's clothes, cooked and washed for them and sent them to school, while working from daylight to dark in a white woman's kitchen."

Republican Reconstruction meant many African Americans could hold public office. Blacks never held office in equal proportion to their numbers in the state, though many served in the state legislature. During the Reconstruction period, there were also many African American local officials, including 160 justices of the peace and ninety-five constables, sheriffs, county clerks, assessors, and militia officers. William A. Rector served as Little Rock city collector and as city marshal for six years. Mifflin W. Gibbs of Little Rock was the first African American municipal judge in the United States and later served as the United States consul to Madagascar.

Most Arkansas African Americans were still farmers, and most of them were sharecroppers. To own land was their major goal. By 1900, about 25 percent of African American farmers in Arkansas had achieved that dream. Among the most successful was Scott

County Quest

Dallas

Named after: George Dallas, American vice president

Chief Source of Income: Manufacturing

Seat: Fordyce

Dallas County was established in 1845. Fordyce was the hometown of legendary football coach Paul "Bear" Bryant, who coached the University of Alabama to several national championships. The Klappenbach Bakery in Fordyce has been featured in *Southern Living* magazine.

Bond, who started out as a sharecropper near Forrest City. He saved enough money to buy land and in time, owned twenty-one farms with about twelve thousand acres of land, five cotton gins, and a large general store.

Black businesses began to flourish. At the end of the nineteenth century, African American people had developed their own banks, insurance companies, hospitals, and care facilities for the elderly. By 1900, the state had 680 African American preachers, 400 teachers, 91 physicians, 27 lawyers, and 101 others in professional positions. An example of one of the true African American success stories of the day was Wiley Jones of Pine Bluff. He began his career as a barber. He then bought real estate, built Pine Bluff's first streetcar line, and ran a fifty-acre park and racetrack south of the city. His park was the site of the yearly Colored State Fair, which featured music and art as well as farm produce and livestock.

The center of the black community was the church, which was more than just a religious institution. The church was the social gathering place for African Americans and often the hub of politics. Preachers were seen as leaders in the black community, and whites often saw them as the spokesmen for their race. When African Americans needed a place to organize and produce leaders, the church structure provided that venue.

Black Arkansans kept their faith in education as a road to a better future. In many ways, black schools were often kept below the standards of white schools, yet they still stood as symbols of hope. In 1875, the state created the **Branch Normal College** to train teachers. There were also private and church-sponsored colleges, such as **Philander Smith**. **Arkansas Baptist College** was begun in 1884 to prepare preachers. **Shorter College** opened in North Little Rock in 1887, and **Southland Institute** at Helena also became a college.

Secret fraternal societies provided another outlet for community social activity. Besides recreation, the clubs offered business services, such as insurance, that African Americans could not get elsewhere. One of the first of these organizations was the **Sisters Union Society**, designed to improve "**elocution**, composition, and debate and for enlarging our fund of general intelligence." The **Mosaic Templars of America** started in Arkansas in 1883; it had chapters in twenty-six states.

Branch Normal College originally headed by J. C. Corbin, it later became Arkansas Agricultural, Mechanical, and Normal College, and is now the University of Arkansas at Pine Bluff.

Philander Smith College a Methodist college established in Little Rock in 1877.

Arkansas Baptist College a school opened in 1884 in Little Rock to train teachers.

Shorter College an African Methodist Episcopal school.

Southland Institute originally founded by Quakers in 1863 as a home for African American orphans, it also became a college.

Sisters Union Society founded by thirty-eight African American women of Pulaski County in 1877, it was a self-help group.

elocution speaking using formal, correct word pronunciation; skill in public speaking.

Mosaic Templars of America an organization established in Little Rock during Reconstruction to provide insurance for newly freed black citizens. It was a social center during the segregation years and would eventually offer a nursing school, a hospital, a business college, and a publishing company.

◀ Wiley Jones began his career as a barber and later became very wealthy. Here, he holds his racehorse, "Executor," near a Pine Bluff racetrack.

Something Old, Something New **265**

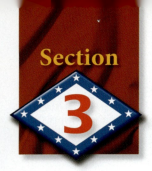

Section 3: The Challenge of Change

Guide to Reading

Terms
Arkansas Separate Coach Law of 1891
fiscal
gallows
mortgage
segregation
suffrage
urban

Events
lynching
Plessy v. Ferguson

People
Judge Isaac C. Parker
Bass Reeves

---

mortgage an agreement made when money is borrowed and something such as property, livestock, or a business is put against the loan as collateral so if it is unpaid at the end of the agreement term, the lender receives the product or property.

Sharecropping

Newly freed African Americans had little or nothing in the way of personal possessions, clothes, tools, livestock, or land. They had to work themselves up from the bottom of society. Farming was their major skill, but most of the good farmland was still owned by whites. In the 1870s, perhaps only one in twenty black farmers owned land.

African Americans heard rumors that the U.S. government was going to give every black family forty acres and a mule. For the most part, even the Radical Republican Congress would not think of taking land from whites to give to blacks. On the other hand, white landowners were concerned about getting a steady supply of labor for their fields. As a result, the sharecropping system developed.

Black farmers needed land to work and a harvest, and white landowners needed someone to work their fields and bring in the crops. A white landowner would allow a group of black families to farm part of his land in return for a share of the crop. The landowner would provide land, a house, and perhaps mules and tools. The landowner would also allow the sharecropper to buy food and clothing at his store on credit. The debt was to be paid when the crop came in. The sharecropper and his family would provide the labor. To make sure he got paid, the landowner held a **mortgage** on the sharecropper's harvest.

It was a flawed system. It was virtually impossible for sharecroppers to get ahead. Each year the crop would barely pay off the debt to the

▶ A family near Pine Bluff (Jefferson County) and their collard patch, around 1897. What are collards?

266 Chapter 12

landowner. Sometimes, the sharecropper could not pay off his debt, and more would be owed the next year. The system continued to promote cotton as the main crop, since people thought it was the easiest crop to sell. Many blacks, and even some whites, would be trapped in the sharecropping system for decades to come.

The Beginning of Jim Crow in Society and the Rise of the Ku Klux Klan (KKK)

Besides the severe limits on political participation, as discussed in the previous chapter, there was social **segregation**, which completed the Jim Crow system. In all aspects of public and private life, blacks and whites were kept apart. The Jim Crow laws slowed the progress of Arkansas during Reconstruction and made it even more difficult for blacks to integrate into the structure of an already established white society.

Many whites continued to treat blacks as if they were property. They spoke harshly to them, would not allow them to shop in their stores, and expected them to always "take a back seat" to whites. White-owned businesses and public places either did not serve African Americans or had a special entrance or separate section for them. State laws, such as **Arkansas's Separate Coach Law of 1891**, combined with social custom to enforce separation.

> M. M. Murray of Lafayette County sized up the challenge to blacks by saying, "the salvation of our race lies entirely with us."

The U.S. government went along with these customs of racial discrimination. Federal buildings in the South, such as courthouses and post offices, were fully segregated. In the 1896 *Plessy v. Ferguson* case, the U.S. Supreme Court allowed the practice, using the phrase "separate but equal." The case applied to railroads, but the practice of segregation was soon applied to all other aspects of life,

segregation keeping ethnic, racial, religious, or gender groups separate, especially by enforcing the use of separate schools, transportation, housing, and other facilities. Often, discrimination against a minority group.

Arkansas's Separate Coach Law of 1891 a law stating that, on public transport, including railroads and streetcars, blacks could ride only in their own cars or in the back of the cars.

Plessy v. Ferguson (PLESS-ee vuhr-suss FURG-uh-sun) the U.S. Supreme Court decision in 1896 that defined the principle of "separate but equal," the legal foundation for all the laws and practices of segregation.

▲ On a small farm, everyone did chores, even the youngest children. Lawrence County, 1890.

▼ A black farming family works in the cotton fields while their children sit in a basket.

Something Old, Something New **267**

fiscal (FISS-kull) of or relating to money or economic matters.

lynching (LINCH-ing) an act of mob violence in which whites tortured or killed a black person without a trial for a presumed crime.

suffrage the right to vote.

particularly public schooling. Segregation and the idea of two, or dual, societies—one white and one black—would consume huge amounts of human and **fiscal** resources, both of which were always in short supply in Arkansas. The unfairness, hardship, and sheer awkwardness of keeping this dual society would hurt Arkansas into the twenty-first century.

Legally, publicly, and socially, blacks were abused and forced into the role of second-class citizens. This allowed white Arkansans to unleash pent-up anger over the outcome of the Civil War. Many times, this was demonstrated as violence against African Americans, which sometimes resulted in **lynching**. In 1892 alone, mobs killed twenty African Americans in Arkansas.

Just as African American Arkansans began to exercise their newly-granted voting rights, a group of white extremists began to organize their members and attempt to establish a presence in Arkansas. This group was the Ku Klux Klan. In April of 1868, the Klan took action to display their dislike for the new **suffrage** rights that had been granted to African Americans. They posted frightening fliers in plain sight throughout Little Rock in an attempt to recruit new Klan members. The Klan was popular and quickly spread throughout the state.

The Klan used many violent tactics to threaten and harm blacks when they attempted to vote. They interfered in their spiritual services and physically attacked them, most often without reason. They often stole weapons the African Americans owned in an attempt to make them feel insecure and powerless. Any people or agencies that offered assistance and protection for African Americans (such as the Freedmen's Bureau) were also threatened and harmed. During this time, more than two hundred murders were reported. Many people assumed the deaths were a warning for African Americans planning to vote in the upcoming 1868 general election.

Governor Clayton was reported as saying the Klan held the state in a "reign of terror." For the safety of citizens in several counties, martial law was declared. The governor had established

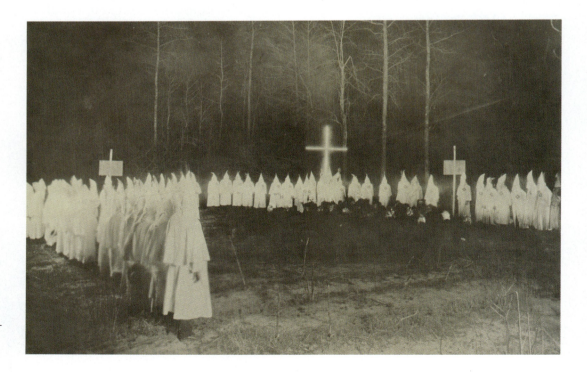

▶ A Ku Klux Klan rally in Union County.

a militia, which frequently battled the Klan. After three months, the militia was mostly successful in minimizing the efforts of the Klan by arresting and even killing some its members.

The next year, a state law was passed that made Klan activity illegal in the state. Many of the group's members had moved to Tennessee and other southern states after Clayton's militia attacks and, for the most part, the Klan was not seen in Arkansas again until the 1920s. In early 1869, Conway, Craighead, Fulton, Greene, Mississippi, and Woodruff counties were at peace again as the militia and the KKK left their communities and calm settled in.

Arkansas at the End of the Century

In these final years of the nineteenth century, rapid progress was being made all over America in spreading culture and making life more convenient. The number of newspapers and magazines in Arkansas more than quadrupled from fifty-six in 1870 to 257 in 1900, and Arkansas's population was slowly becoming more concentrated in cities. By the late 1800s, there were fifteen communities in the state considered to be **urban**. Those places had 8.5 percent of the state's population in 1900. Still, only three cities had populations greater than 10,000 people: Pine Bluff, 11,496; Fort Smith, 11,587; and Little Rock, 38,307.

The technical advances that were making life easier for Americans showed up first in Arkansas's cities. The streetcar arrived in Little Rock in 1876. Ice plants opened in Batesville (Independence County), Little Rock, and other towns around 1877. Electric street lamps came in 1888. In 1892, Little Rock started a full-time professional fire department. Little Rock, Fort Smith (Crawford County), Fayetteville (Washington County), and a few other cities had opera houses.

> "I have ever had the single aim of justice in view. . . . 'Do equal and exact justice,' is my motto, and I have often said to the grand jury, 'Permit no innocent man to be punished, but let no guilty man escape.'"
>
> —Judge Isaac C. Parker, 1896
>
> Glenn Shirley, *Law West of Fort Smith* (Lincoln: University of Nebraska Press, 1968), 203.

Fortunately, much of the frontier violence of northern and western Arkansas that took place in the post–Civil War period vanished and the area worked toward a more civilized future. One reason much of the violence subsided was because of **Judge Isaac Parker**, who was often

urban an area that was defined in the 1870s as having a population of more than 2,500.

Judge Isaac C. Parker a judge on the U.S. Federal District Court in Fort Smith.

◀ Judge Isaac Parker.

Something Old, Something New

Bass Reeves an African American who was the first to be commissioned as a U.S. deputy marshal west of the Mississippi River and worked in Judge Parker's court.

gallows a structure with two vertical posts and one horizontal beam across the top designed for hanging a person with a noose (rope).

▼ The gallows at Judge Parker's court, as seen today at the National Historic Site in Fort Smith.

referred to as the "Hanging Judge." At the time, the offenses of rape and murder were punishable by death. In reality, Parker had no authority to make the decision to hang a person—that was up to a jury. His responsibility was to read the decision of the jury.

Until Parker's court cleaned up the area, outlaws could live outside the state in the Indian Territory without fear of arrest. From there, they could raid towns in western Arkansas. To maintain order in the area, Parker had to swear in a United States marshal and two hundred deputies. Outlaws ruthlessly terrorized the Indian tribes, and white men were feared and unwelcome in the territory. **Bass Reeves** was recruited as Parker's deputy marshal because he knew the tribal languages and country well. He was born a slave in 1824 in Texas. He escaped to Indian Territory to hide out after brutally attacking his young master over a card game. He lived there until 1863. After the Emancipation Proclamation, he left Indian Territory, bought land in the Van Buren area (Crawford County), and successfully farmed. He married twice and had many children. He could not read or write, but was well-respected for always following the law and was known to be reliable and trustworthy. He obeyed the law so carefully and worked so hard to uphold the duties of his badge, that he even arrested his son for murder (his son later received a full pardon).

With Reeves's help, notorious outlaws like Cherokee Bill, Colorado Bill, and the Rufus Buck Gang were brought to justice, sentenced to death, and executed in Parker's court. Parker served twenty-one years as a judge, and in his court, 160 people were sentenced to death. Reports say anywhere from 79 to 88 died by hanging on the **gallows**.

I Am an Arkansan

Frank Coffin (1870–1951)

Born in Mississippi, Frank Coffin was an African American pharmacist who established one of the earliest drugstores for blacks in Little Rock (Pulaski County). He studied at Fisk University in Nashville, among other schools, earning his pharmaceutical degree from Meharry Medical College in Nashville in 1893. Though he was not the first African American to open a pharmacy in the city, he became a fixture in the community, serving his neighbors' needs well into the twentieth century.

Though his work is often overlooked today, he was also an accomplished poet who wrote two collections of poems. In 1897, Coffin published his first collection of poems, *Coffin's Poems and AJAX Ordeal*. He wrote about children, family life, love, and racism, and wrote poems saluting famous Americans such as Harriet Beecher Stowe, Fredrick Douglass, and Abraham Lincoln. An active member of the Little Rock African American community, he worked in support of Little Rock's Philander Smith College, and was an active member of his local Methodist church.

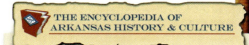

Log on to Learn More
http://www.encyclopediaofarkansas.net/

▲ Bass Reeves was one of the U.S. deputy marshals who served under Judge Parker. He tracked outlaws in Indian Territory (Oklahoma) and brought them to justice in Parker's court. Why did outlaws hide in Indian Territory? Why was it easier for Bass Reeves to travel in Indian Territory?

The wild, open lands of the American frontier were gone, as the last of the publicly-owned farmland came into the hands of private owners. In Arkansas, many of the frontier ways of life began to fade. Arkansans and other Americans looked to the new century with a sense that life was starting to change rapidly. Arkansas shared in those changes, but in many ways still retained its unique traits, culture, and heritage while having to fight to defeat the demons of racism and limited economic and social progress.

Chapter Reflection

Reflective Questions

1. Describe the social and political discrimination against African Americans at the end of the 1800s.

2. Discuss why and how the practice of sharecropping helped or hurt our state and its legacy. Be sure to consider lifestyle, economy, race, inequality, and opportunity in your answer.

3. Identify and describe women's roles, hardships, achievements, and new ways of life during Reconstruction.

4. List the advances in technology, convenience, and the arts in our state at the end of the century.

5. In a general way, describe the goal or goals of the Ku Klux Klan. What can you infer from the reading that would explain their motivation?

Make it Match!

On your own paper, number 1 through 7 and write the correct letter beside the corresponding number. Information and answers will come from both chapters 11 and 12.

_____ 1. "separate but equal" ruling

_____ 2. the movement to rid society of alcohol

_____ 3. the organization that assaulted and terrorized blacks

_____ 4. set of laws designed to suppress rights of blacks

_____ 5. Northerners who came south to make money, sometimes taking advantage of poor, suffering southerners

_____ 6. constitution that is still our state's ruling document today

_____ 7. a political "war"

A. 1868
B. lynching
C. 1874
D. carpetbaggers
E. jayhawker
F. temperance
G. segregation
H. *Plessy v. Ferguson*
I. Brooks-Baxter War
J. 14th Amendment
K. Jim Crow laws
L. martial law
M. Ku Klux Klan

HisStory, HerStory, YourStory, OurStory... Telling an Arkansas Story—The Written Word

1. Pretend that you are a newspaper writer in the Reconstruction era and you have been assigned to write the obituary of Judge Isaac Parker. Remember to be sensitive and to use facts in your piece. Be sure to include the when, where, who, and what of the funeral services. Be accurate and descriptive. You might consider reviewing an actual obituary from a current newspaper as a guide.

2. Newspaper reporters often use two types of basic question formats when interviewing someone:

Closed-ended: can be answered with yes, no, or a basic simple fact. No discussion.

Open-ended: encourages discussion and storytelling. Gives the reporter ideas for other questions.

Continue in your role as a newspaper reporter, but this time, pretend you are interviewing Charlotte Stephens, Mifflin Gibbs, or Wiley Jones. On your paper, write one closed-ended question that you would ask during the course of the interview and one open-ended question to learn more about the challenges they faced as free African Americans in the changing reconstruction society.

Who, What, When, Where, Why, and How?

Identify the six terms below by establishing the who, what, when, where, why, and how of each. Copy the term on your paper, then below the term, write the five Ws and one H. An example has been done for you.

Example:

University of Arkansas

- **who** — the U.S. government
- **what** — established a university
- **when** — 1862–71
- **where** — Fayetteville
- **why** — to help Arkansas's citizens by providing better educational opportunities
- **how** — the Morrill Land Grant Act

1. lynching
2. *Plessy v. Ferguson*
3. segregation
4. temperance
5. New South

Something Old, Something New

UNIT 5

Chapter 13
Progressing into the New Century, 1900–1920s

Chapter 14
Wars and Wonderment, 1914–1928

Chapter 15
Hard Times—The Great Depression, 1927–1939

Students registering for classes at the University of Arkansas, 1920s.

Early Twentieth-Century Arkansas
A New South—Progression, War, and Depression, 1900–1939

Chapter 13
Progressing into the New Century
1900s–1920s

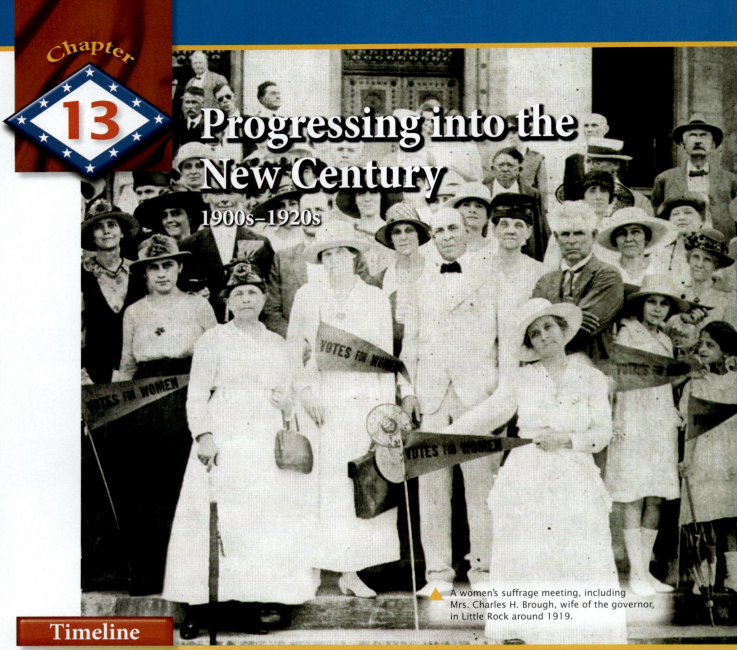

▲ A women's suffrage meeting, including Mrs. Charles H. Brough, wife of the governor, in Little Rock around 1919.

Timeline

	1900	1903	1906	1909
Arkansas	**1901** Monte Ne resort near Rogers (Benton County) opens. A rice experiment station is established at Lonoke; large-scale rice growing begins in Arkansas.	**1905** Fire devastates downtown Hot Springs (Garland County). President Theodore Roosevelt visits Arkansas.	**1905** The movie *The Great Train Robbery* starred famous Arkansan Broncho Billy Anderson.	**1906** Diamonds are discovered in Pike City (Pike County).	**1911** For the first time, the Arkansas state legislature meets in the new capitol building. Booker T. Washington speaks to a crowd of two thousand in Little Rock.
United States	**1901** President William McKinley is assassinated and Theodore Roosevelt succeeds him. Oil is discovered in Texas in the Spindletop Gusher south of Beaumont in southeast Texas.	**1903** The Wright brothers launch their first airplane.	**1905** Madame C. J. Walker from Louisiana becomes the first black female millionaire by developing and selling her own hair tonic and cosmetics.	**1906** Seven hundred people are killed in the San Francisco, California, earthquake.	**1909** The National Association for the Advancement of Colored People is formed in New York City.
World	**1901** In England, Queen Victoria dies.	**1902** Beatrix Potter publishes *Peter Rabbit*. **1903** Construction begins on the Panama Canal.			

276 Chapter 13

Why Do We Study This?

Studying historical progress helps us understand the power and strength of the human spirit. We would not be as advanced as we are today if we did not have citizens who challenged and questioned our systems and proposed daring changes, as people did during the Progressive movement, an attempt to adjust society to modern needs.

We must understand our political process and work to include and educate all citizens in the process and let everyone know they have an equal voice. The government of a diverse and complex nation must be responsive to change while offering guidance. The government must create public systems and management structures to ensure safety, equality, and progress.

Big Picture Questions

- In your opinion, what is the responsibility of government in helping citizens make desired or necessary changes that lead to progress? Discuss using reasons, facts, and examples to support your opinion.
- Is progress always positive? Why or why not? If so, how?
- Why are people and societies resistant to change? Explain your answer with specific examples.
- During the course of progress, is someone always left behind? If so, who and why? If no, what roles do different groups have in progress?
- Why must individuals, a people, a society, a nation, a world make continual progress? Use three valid pieces of historical evidence in your discussion.

	1912	1915		1920		1925
	1912 Governor Donaghey pardons 360 inmates as a result of the convict-lease system. The number of school districts in Arkansas reaches 5,143.	**1915** The first convention of Arkansas Women's Suffrage Association meets in Little Rock.	**1916** Arkansas prohibits alcoholic beverages.	**1917** "Arkansas," by Eva Ware Barnett, becomes the official state song.	**1920** The Arkansas legislature ratifies the Nineteenth Amendment.	**1925** Arkansas Children's Hospital is founded in Little Rock.
	1912 American Indian Jim Thorpe wins the decathlon and pentathlon at the Olympic games in Sweden.	**1913** Notre Dame uses the forward pass in football for the first time. Robert Frost publishes his first book of poetry, *A Boy's Will*.		**1919** The Eighteenth Amendment to the U.S. Constitution prohibits the sale and use of alcohol. Jack Dempsey becomes the heavyweight-boxing champion of the world.	**1920** The Nineteenth Amendment gives women the right to vote.	
	1912 The *Titanic* sinks in the North Atlantic and 1,500 passengers die.					

Progressing into the New Century

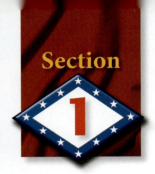

Section 1

Progressing with Spirit

Guide to Reading

Terms
antitrust law
civic
Corporation
  Commission
dominion
illiteracy
monopoly
poet laureate
primary
progressive
reform
wool hat boys

Events
initiative
Progressive
  movement
referendum

Places
Cummins farm
Tucker plantation

People
Booker T.
  Washington

Progressive movement the social reform movement of the early twentieth century aimed at improving healthcare, education, working conditions (especially concerning child labor), prisons, and other social institutions.

reform to restructure, improve, or make better.

The Progressive Era

Americans' interest in a more modern way of life emerged in a new form at the beginning of the twentieth century: the **Progressive movement**. One of the first of the great **reform** movements, the farmers' Populist movement of the late nineteenth century, had lost its force. Discouraged by their lack of success and temporarily soothed by an increase in crop prices, the farmers were quiet. The urban middle class saw a need for changes and that widespread feeling that was called "Progressive."

Much of this progress was seen in urban areas, and Americans moved to the cities in huge numbers. In the American North and far West, waves of immigrants from Europe and Asia brought labor, the richness of foreign cultures, and often conflict. Few such immigrants made their way to Arkansas, where Caucasians and African Americans remained the major ethnic groups.

▶ Among other Progressive-Era inventions was the biplane.

278 Chapter 13

Large, productive factories and new types of manufacturing and commerce shaped the economy and lifestyles of Americans. Arkansas also saw the development of its first major industries, chiefly in timber and mining. By the early 1900s, America produced the tools and technology that would change people's lives. Automobiles and airplanes, electric lights, and motion pictures all had an impact. Science and medicine had perhaps the greatest impact, bringing major improvements in public health.

Some of the **Progressive** reforms were carried out by private action. People worked through churches or other groups to deal with a wide range of issues like drinking, **illiteracy**, poor health, and the need to improve personal hygiene. Many people seemed to have extra money and extra time to give to **civic** work in the twentieth century. The results across the nation and in Arkansas were far-reaching.

Politics, Policy, and State Government in Progressive-Era Arkansas

Many problems of the day seemed too large for anything but governmental action. These problems included the overwhelming power of huge businesses, low wages and bad working conditions in the factories, and the need for better schools. Many Progressives believed that state governments could better meet the needs of the people. Some also called for a more active federal government.

Some of Arkansas's farmers felt they were being left out of the progress and that no one in power cared about them. The city dwellers were "rich folks" to the common farmer. Farmers had been given some hope by the Populist movement. The anger they felt at being left out of the new social structure found an outlet in

▲ A baby sits in an early twentieth-century airplane.

◀ A "wool hat boy," which was a nickname for the hill people and small farmers who supported Gov. Jeff Davis.

progressive forward-thinking.

illiteracy (ih-LIT-er-uh-see) the inability to read and write.

civic having to do with the responsibilities and duties of a citizen.

primary system a system that allows voters to choose the candidate who will run for office as a representative of a particular political party.

wool hat boys term Jeff Davis used to describe the hill folks and farmers who supported him; they wore wool hats instead of stylish and expensive silk or felt hats.

Jeff Davis, a man of great force and energy. Thanks to the Populist movement, there was now a **primary system**. Davis carried seventy-four of the seventy-five counties in the Democratic primary. In the general election, Davis won two-to-one over his opponent.

Even though Davis was a lawyer raised in the city, he had a gift for reaching the small farmers and hill-country folks. They were his **wool hat boys**, as opposed to the silk-hat crowd in the cities. Davis dominated Arkansas politics for ten years by posing as the hero of the poor whites, speaking out against the rich.

Progressing into the New Century **279**

antitrust law a law passed to limit the power of business monopolies, to protect trade and small business owners from unfair business practices.

monopoly (muh-NAH-pull-ee) a company that controls all the business in its industry, operating without any competition; also known as a "trust."

Cummins farm a prison farm that can now house more than 1,700 inmates in Grady (Lincoln County). It was established in 1902.

Tucker plantation a 4,400-acre farm in Jefferson County purchased by the state to be used as a prison farm.

Davis began his public career in 1898 as the state's attorney general, winning when his opponent died during the race. Davis dug up the state **antitrust law**, passed years before during the farmers' revolt but never enforced. A trust is also known as a **monopoly**.

Although Davis's speeches expressed ideas from both the older Populist movement and the new Progressive movement, he was not really a reformer. His main goal was to be elected to and keep public office, and his achievements were few. Davis showed a mean and bitter streak of racism. He portrayed himself as the "white man's man," determined to keep blacks "in their place." Davis was very successful at using fear as a tactic. He knew that some whites worried about the new rights of black people and he used a message that would secure their votes.

The one area in which Davis made some headway was with the state's disgraceful prison system. For years, the state had leased or rented convicts to businesses such as railroads and coal mines. Some of the business owners worked the inmates like slaves, whipping them and keeping them in poor living quarters with little food.

By leasing out convicts, the state had no direct control over their lives. In some years, the annual death rate among convicts was 25 percent. Six out of every one hundred inmates were children under the age of sixteen, some as young as nine years of age. Two out of every three convicts were African American. Many of them were serving lengthy terms for "crimes" such as moving during the summer, selling cotton after dark, or buying whiskey. Some people were aware of the brutalities of the system, but for the most part, it was kept behind closed doors. However, the convict-lease system earned the state twenty-five thousand dollars a year. No public official had the courage to raise taxes to pay for a better system.

A report on prisoner-labor conditions at the Coal Hill (Johnson County) mines released in 1887 caused such a large scandal that the state was forced to adopt a prison farm system. The state prison west of downtown Little Rock was torn down in 1899 to make room for a new state capitol. Then the state bought the eleven-thousand-acre **Cummins farm**, in Lincoln County, southeast of Pine Bluff. Later, the state added a second prison farm by buying the nearby **Tucker plantation**.

The state began to take control of the lives of the inmates, but the prison system still leased out some of them. Davis raised his voice against the horrors of the convict-lease system, even though he did not like having to pay for the Cummins farm. He also started a reform school for boys so that children in trouble with the law did not have to serve in prison with grown men.

Davis pardoned hundreds of African American convicts and worked to reform a prison system whose inmates were mostly black. At the same time, he became more and more racist in his speeches and his actions. In the 1904 campaign, for example, he said, "I stand for the Cauca-

County Quest

Drew

Named after: Arkansas's third governor, Thomas Drew

Chief Source of Income: Manufacturing and agriculture

Seat: Monticello

Drew County was created in 1846. The city of Monticello is home to the University of Arkansas at Monticello. Lake Monticello, the Drew County Historical Museum, and the UAM Fine Arts Gallery are popular attractions.

sian race in government, and I say that [Negro] **dominion** will never prevail in this beautiful Southland of ours, as long as shotguns and rifles lie around loose, and we are able to pull the trigger."

He took the lead in making the vote in the Democratic primary for whites only. This removed what little remained of black participation in voting. When President Theodore Roosevelt came to Arkansas in 1905, Davis used his formal welcome speech to defend lynching. Roosevelt, who had shocked southern whites by having **Booker T. Washington** to lunch, ignored his planned remarks and condemned Davis's lawless and disrespectful ideas.

> "I will let no man drag me down so low as to make me hate him."
>
> —Booker T. Washington, African American Activist and Educator

In 1906, Davis was elected to the U.S. Senate, but his methods did not work well in Washington. He won a second term in 1912 by the smallest margin of his career. Distraught and out of his element, Davis died of a heart attack at his home in Little Rock on New Year's Day, 1913. His funeral was the largest Little Rock had ever seen. A more true Progressive movement did come to Arkansas after Davis, mostly with governors George W. Donaghey and Charles Hillman Brough.

Progressive Politicians

George W. Donaghey left his Louisiana home at age fifteen and worked as a cowboy and farmer in Texas. He then moved to Conway (Faulkner County), where he worked as a carpenter and eventually became a major builder. He was named to the state capitol building commission, which sparked his interest in government. He became governor in 1909, serving until 1913.

▲ Prisoners working at Cummins Farm.

▲ Booker T. Washington (center) was a national leader in education for African Americans. He founded the Tuskegee Institute in Alabama in 1881, which led the way in technical training for blacks. Here he is shown visiting Scott Bond and his family in 1911.

Donaghey lost his bid for a third term to Joseph T. Robinson, a well-liked member of Congress from Arkansas. But Senator Jeff Davis died just three days before Robinson was to take office, and the legislature chose Robinson to become senator. He was to serve a long and distinguished career in the senate. In a space of just two weeks, he was a congressman, governor, and senator.

George W. Hays, a lawyer and former county judge, became governor in 1913, but he did little to bring about change in the state. Charles Hillman

dominion zone or area of influence or dominance.

Booker T. Washington One of the first African American rights activists and political leaders, he was sometimes criticized for working too closely with whites on policy and compromise. He worked to raise money for black schools across the country.

Progressing into the New Century **281**

Brough, who had been a professor at the University of Arkansas, was the next true reform governor. He was born in Mississippi in 1876. In 1898, he earned a doctoral degree in history, economics, and law from Johns Hopkins University in Maryland. He went to the University of Arkansas in 1903 to teach law, economics, sociology, and history. Brough was well known as a speaker for Progressive Democratic candidates. He ran for governor in 1916 on a reform platform. Serving as governor until 1921, he strongly opposed lynching and worked hard to pass antilynching legislation.

Nationwide, the reform movement was well underway. Nearly half of the states had some form of reform government during this time. In Washington, Republican president Theodore Roosevelt, who served from 1901 to 1909, and Democrat president Woodrow Wilson, who served from 1913 to 1921, both showed how government action could improve the lives of people. Progressives believed that businessmen, like Donaghey, and scholars, like Brough, could bring special skills to government. Arkansas began to make real progress in improving schools, roads, and health, reforming the prison system, and providing many state services. Donaghey, Robinson, and Brough were responsible for many of the reforms of the Progressive Era.

Prohibition and Suffrage

The campaign to end the manufacture and sale of alcohol was successful in the early 1900s. Active in this movement were many groups, including the Woman's Christian Temperance Union and the Anti-Saloon League. One of the temperance movement's most famous figures, Carry Nation, moved to Eureka Springs (Carroll County) near the end of her life. She called her Steele Street home "Hatchet Hall." "Hatchet Carry" continued the temperance cause by chopping up bars and taverns with a hand ax.

By 1913, a state local-option law required a yes vote of all adult, white,

▼ Carry Nation, a Prohibition activist, also known as "Hatchet Carry," retired to Arkansas.

▶ Rosa Marinoni, a leader in the women's suffrage movement.

male residents before a liquor license could be issued in a town. On its own, that law made most of the state "dry" (without alcohol) by 1915, when the General Assembly passed a total prohibition law. The Eighteenth Amendment, passed in 1919, was the national law that banned the production and sale of alcoholic beverages.

The Progressive movement also gave new life to the effort to allow women to vote. After the all-male legislature failed to approve voting for women in both 1911 and 1913, the Arkansas Woman Suffrage (SUFF-ruj) Association formed to press for such a measure. National leaders, such as Carrie Chapman Catt, president of the National American Woman Suffrage Association, came to the state. Local leaders included women like Bernie Babcock, whose 1900 reform novel The Daughter of a Republican sold one hundred thousand copies. Dr. Ida Jo Brooks, a professor at the University of Arkansas Medical School, was also involved. Rosa Marinoni of Fayetteville, who would become Arkansas's **poet laureate** in 1953, was also a leader in the suffrage movement.

The women's suffrage movement sponsored rallies and parades with women and children (and even a few men) dressed in white marching to show support for the movement. In 1917, the General Assembly finally allowed women to vote in the crucial primary election. Under Governor Brough, Arkansas became the only southern state to allow women to vote before the Nineteenth Amendment. Two years later, in 1919, Arkansas passed the Nineteenth Amendment to the Constitution, which allowed women to vote in all elections. Arkansas was the twelfth state in the nation, and the second in the South, to ratify the amendment. Shortly after the passage of the Nineteenth Amendment,

the town of Winslow (Washington County) won national fame by choosing an all-female town government. The town government worked so well that all the women were elected to a second term.

A More Active State Government

The Progressives also called for more active oversight of the business world. For example, during Governor Brough's term, Arkansas formed a **Corporation Commission**. The Railroad Commission that already existed was given more power over railroad business practices. The state also made it against the law to employ children under sixteen in most kinds of work.

Governor Donaghey brought an end to the shameful convict-lease system with a single act. He studied the records of all the state's prison inmates, learning that many were serving long terms for minor crimes. In December of 1912, he pardoned and released 360 men from prison. Those 360 men made

poet laureate a poet appointed or chosen to advocate poetry in a state or country.

Corporation Commission a state government entity that had the power to control prices charged by electric power and gas companies.

▶ Capitol Avenue in Little Rock, 1910.

initiative (ih-NISH-uh-tiv) the power of citizens to create a new law by obtaining enough signatures on a petition to place the proposed law on the ballot for a popular vote.

referendum (REFF-er-END-um) the ability of the legislature to place proposed laws on the ballot for a popular vote.

up about half the total male prison population in Arkansas at the time. Donaghey's actions reduced the value of a leased convict and focused the public eye on the prison system. The next year, the state General Assembly ended the convict-lease system altogether. All convicts would be kept on prison farms and could no longer be abused by private leaseholders. The elimination of the convict-lease system was an improvement, but some prison farms would become almost as bad.

Progressives also thought the state government should respond more to the will of the people. The formation of the primary system had been a step in this direction. Arkansas also put into effect the **initiative**, which allowed voters to write their own laws or amendments. They also adopted the **referendum**, which allowed the General Assembly to refer a law to a vote of the people.

The state had outgrown the 1836 capitol building on Markham Street in Little Rock, and in 1899, work started on a new one. The site was on a low hill in western Little Rock where the old state prison had been. Gov. Jeff Davis had delayed work on the building, claiming that rich people were getting richer by building it. But Governor Donaghey pushed to complete the work. The new building, which looked similar to the U.S. Capitol in Washington, D.C., was first used by the Arkansas General Assembly in 1911.

Prairie

Named after: The prairie, another name for the grasslands in the area

Chief Source of Income: Agriculture

Seat: DeVall's Bluff, Des Arc

Established in 1846, Prairie County is located in central Arkansas. Agriculture is a key part of the area's economy. In DeVall's Bluff, there are large minnow farm operations and regionally famous restaurants known for barbecue and pies, Craig's Bar-B-Q and Mary's Family Pies. Hunting, fishing, and boating on the White River and nearby lakes are enjoyed by many in the region.

I Am an Arkansan

William "Coin" Harvey (1851–1936)

William Hope "Coin" Harvey, a writer, lecturer, politician, and activist, founded the resort of Monte Ne (Benton County) as well as the Ozark Trails Association, and was an early promoter of Arkansas tourism. As a 1932 presidential candidate, he was the first Arkansan to run for the office.

Coin Harvey was born August 16, 1851, in West Virginia. After teaching school and studying law, he became a writer on economic issues, favoring silver-based currency. His best-selling 1894 novel, *Coin's Financial School,* made him a nationally-known figure and gave him his nickname. During the 1896 presidential election, he campaigned on behalf of candidate William Jennings Bryan. He lived in several places in the United States—Ohio, Illinois, Colorado, and Utah—before settling in northwest Arkansas in 1900. By the spring of 1901, he had constructed a resort, the Hotel Monte Ne. Within a few years, he added two more hotels, a tennis court, and the state's first indoor swimming pool.

After his failed run as the Liberty Party presidential candidate in 1932, Harvey attempted to build a 130-foot pyramid, as well as a large amphitheater. The amphitheater was completed, but the pyramid was never built.

Throughout his time in Arkansas, he wrote books on politics and economics, and his formation of the Ozark Trails Association brought much-needed funding for improvement of Arkansas's rugged road system. In the 1960s, the state dammed part of the White River, submerging Harvey's amphitheater and resort beneath the newly-created Beaver Lake. In 2005 and 2006, parts of the resort, long covered by the lake water, could be seen as drought conditions caused the lake water level to drop.

▼ William "Coin" Harvey.

▶ Books published by William "Coin" Harvey.

THE ENCYCLOPEDIA OF ARKANSAS HISTORY & CULTURE

Log on to Learn More
http://www.encyclopediaofarkansas.net/

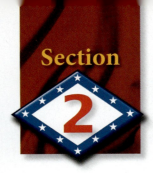

Section 2
A Poor State Continues the Struggle for Progress

Guide to Reading

Terms
diphtheria
hookworm
lobby
Martineau Road Plan
pellagra
smallpox
tuberculosis
typhoid

People
midwives

Places
sanatorium

Improvements in Education

Education in Arkansas suffered the problems of a poor, rural, racially-divided state. The Arkansas superintendent of public instruction said in 1904 that "in the cause of education we stand at the bottom, or dangerously near, no matter how the states are grouped or classified in respect to the length of school terms, the amount expended per pupil, average daily attendance, in salaries paid, and in providing the means of training teachers."

About half the public schools in the state were one-room schoolhouses, in which one teacher taught all grades and all subjects. Of the 10,000 teachers, only about 800 were college graduates, and more than 1,600 had not gone beyond the eighth grade. Arkansas teachers were paid $34.46 per month

► Children in a one-room schoolhouse in the 1920s. What would the advantages of attending school in a one-room schoolhouse have been? Disadvantages? Why?

286 Chapter 13

◄ After learning about the state of education in Arkansas during this time, why would you think this student had his head down on the desk?

($759.42 in modern-day money), compared to $59.80 ($1,317.86 in modern-day money) in other states. There were only about four hundred high schools in the state. The school term was arranged around the farm schedule. School started in July, dismissed for the harvest in the fall, resumed in December, and ended in time for spring planting.

During this time, about 45 percent of black children went to school, compared to 54 percent of whites. African American schools were separate, and far from equal. By all measures—including state and local funding, teachers' wages, and buildings—black schools received less than white schools. The state spent about twice as much on white schools as it did on black schools. Only nine counties had high schools for blacks. Fewer than 2 percent of African American youths were able to get as far as high school. Some black Arkansans built their own schools. Floyd Brown, a minister and supporter of education for the black community who had studied under Booker T. Washington, borrowed money and supplies to open a school for African Americans in Fargo (Monroe County).

A rural state with poor roads had to have many school districts because people could not travel far to get to schools. Despite some efforts toward mergers, there were 5,143 school districts in the state in 1912. Some of them had as few as forty students in the entire district. In Washington County alone, there were 161 school districts (today there are 7). Around this same time, the state began an effort to provide

Progressing into the New Century

school bus service. The first "buses" were old flatbed trucks with a bumpy ride. Students rode atop the flatbed on benches that were fastened to the back.

A major part of the problem was money. In the early 1920s, Arkansas spent about twenty-three dollars per pupil per year. The amount in Missouri was about fifty-four dollars, and in Oklahoma about sixty-four dollars. The rural nature of the state and the hardships of travel posed other problems. In fact, Gov. John Martineau's road campaign was pushed forward in part because of its effect on education. Martineau's slogan was "Better Roads to Better Schools."

The state began to address some of these problems, and education did improve somewhat, with the best results in the towns and cities. People, particularly women, trained at state teachers' colleges, then called Normal Schools, and pursued professional careers in teaching. In 1907, the state opened the Arkansas State Normal School in Conway to prepare teachers. (It later became the University of Central Arkansas.) The state teachers formed a group during this period and had 1,500 members by 1915. In 1927, African American teachers were allowed to take courses by mail from the University of Arkansas and the state teachers' college. Around two thousand teachers enrolled in these courses.

A new State Literacy Council kept track of the number of people who could not read or write. The council reported that about 20 percent of the people could not read or write in 1900. By 1920, the figure was down to about 9.4 percent. New laws required all children between seven and fifteen years of age to attend school and called for standard textbooks in the grade schools. The number of high schools more than doubled between 1909 and 1919. In 1911, the state formed a State Board of Education and offered aid to high schools. By 1920, over half of school children regularly attended school.

Little Rock High School (later Central High) moved into its new building in 1927. The National Association of Architects labeled it "America's Most Beautiful High School." It was America's largest high school until the 1940s.

As sports like football and basketball gained popularity in the 1920s, schools started having their own bands instead of using the city bands as they had done in the past. Each town took great pride in its local teams. The University of Arkansas in Fayetteville became a member of the Southwest Conference—in which it remained until 1991 when it joined the Southeastern Conference—but still played other Arkansas schools such as Hendrix in Conway (Faulkner County). Arkansas Agricultural, Mining, and Normal College in Pine Bluff (Jefferson County), now known as the University of Arkansas, Pine Bluff, fielded its first football team in 1929.

Through the efforts of the Arkansas Farmers' Union, four technical high

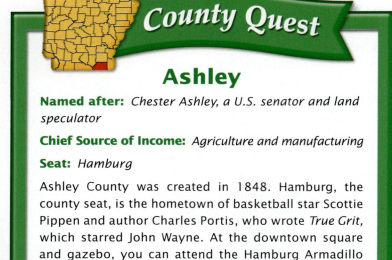

County Quest

Ashley

Named after: Chester Ashley, a U.S. senator and land speculator

Chief Source of Income: Agriculture and manufacturing

Seat: Hamburg

Ashley County was created in 1848. Hamburg, the county seat, is the hometown of basketball star Scottie Pippen and author Charles Portis, who wrote *True Grit*, which starred John Wayne. At the downtown square and gazebo, you can attend the Hamburg Armadillo Festival, held the first weekend in May.

◀ The Brady School, near Little Rock, July 1909. Why would students have attended school in July?

schools opened in 1909 at Russellville (Pope County), Jonesboro (Craighead County), Magnolia (Columbia County), and Monticello (Drew County). They taught farming and textile-making. All of these schools eventually became four-year colleges. The state acquired Henderson-Brown College in Arkadelphia (Clark County) in 1929 from the Methodist Church. In Little Rock, the school board started a junior college in 1927, using extra space in Little Rock High School. The number of students at the university in Fayetteville rose steadily.

Arkansas Takes to the Road

The arrival of the automobile in the early years of the century, people having the desire and money to get out and see and do more, and the need for efficient travel to school and work brought the start of a road system in Arkansas. In 1903, there were only fifty cars in the state. The owners formed the Arkansas Good Roads Association. They started to **lobby** for new laws to promote road building.

The legislature responded in 1909 with a law that allowed local improvement districts to charge local taxes to pay for roads. That replaced the old system under which the county could require able-bodied males to work a certain number of days per year building roads.

In 1913, the State Department of Lands, Highways, and Improvements was begun, funded by a ten-dollar tax on motor vehicles. By 1914, there were 4,800 cars in Arkansas, and the state required drivers to have a license. William Hope "Coin" Harvey founded the Ozark Trails Association in 1913. The association marked roads clearly and painted white rings around trees along roadsides.

The Federal Road Act of 1916, which called for the U.S. government to pay half the cost of road building, further encouraged road building. Through a series of steps, Arkansas built a state-highway system. One example in this process was the legislature shifting the burden of taxes for roads from local property owners to

lobby to use money, power, persuasion, intellect, debate, or manipulation to influence, change opinions, or gain votes or favors.

Progressing into the New Century

▶ A typical, muddy Arkansas road.

▼ A common sight with the arrival of the automobile in the 1920s—a filling station in Fort Smith.

▲ An Arkansas dirt road lined with houses is filled with ruts.

Martineau Road Plan (MAR-tin-oh ROHD PLAN) the ambitious highway-building program Governor Martineau began in 1927.

road users. The legislature did this by charging a fee to obtain a car license and by putting taxes on gas and oil. The state began a system of numbered highways in 1917.

The state government took over the road-building debts of the local districts. The state began to issue bonds to pay for roads. In the late 1920s, the nation was still seeing good times, and raising bond money for roads did not seem too risky. However, the state was piling up a large debt that would become a big problem in just a few years.

In 1920, there were sixty thousand cars in the state and, in 1921, about seven thousand miles of roads. Even though building roads was very expensive, an improved Arkansas road was basically still a gravel road. Less than two hundred miles of the state's highways were all-weather, hard-surfaced roads.

By 1926, there were 210,000 cars on Arkansas's roads. The next step in developing roads took place during the term of Governor Martineau, who served only briefly, from 1927 until 1928 when he became a federal judge. His Martineau Road Plan linked improved roads to better education and further committed the state to road building. By 1928, Arkansas had 8,716 miles of roads, about a fourth of them paved. There were no paved roads in forty-six of Arkansas's seventy-five counties. Two counties had no roads of any kind.

A Healthier State

Few things improved life in Arkansas more than new knowledge and action related to the prevention and treatment of diseases. Progress in science inspired private groups and the government to work to control diseases that had given Arkansas a reputation as an unhealthy place to live. The Progressive spirit promoted the cause of improved public health in the 1920s for all Arkansans and Americans.

The state joined the nationwide public-health movement by forming the state Board of Health in 1913. The next year, a Bureau of Vital Statistics opened to record births, deaths, and marriages. Laws authorized a system to license doctors of all types, as well as dentists, nurses, and embalmers. Prenatal healthcare workers received aid from a 1920 federal program that offered instruction to rural pregnant women and midwives. The University of Arkansas School of Medicine (founded in 1918) earned increased funding from the General Assembly in 1922 and again in 1925.

Members of the Arkansas Federation of Women's Clubs campaigned to promote physical therapy, sponsored "healthy baby" contests to promote and reward health in the home, and worked to prevent crime. They gave support to programs for children in trouble with the law. They set standards of child healthcare that required every child to have "normal vision or properly fitted glasses, normal hearing . . . good teeth and gums, correct posture." The new standards also called for each child to be well nourished and vaccinated against typhoid, diphtheria, and smallpox.

Before the practice of vaccination became common, the state had nearly ten thousand cases of smallpox a year, many of them fatal. Arkansas was the first state to pass a law that required all children to have a smallpox vaccination. The concern over proper nutrition led to milk and hot lunch programs in

midwives women who assist other women in delivering their babies.

typhoid (TIE-foyd) a contagious disease caused by bacteria, with symptoms resembling the flu with very high fever.

diphtheria (dif-THEER-ee-uh) a bacteria-caused contagious disease resulting in inflammation of the heart and nervous system.

smallpox (SMAHL-pahks) an acute viral disease characterized by skin eruptions with pustules and scar formation.

DID YOU KNOW?

Did you know Arkansas got an official state flower in 1901 and a state flag in 1913?

The designation of a state flower came after a fierce battle between proponents of the passion flower and the apple blossom. The Arkansas Federation of Women's Clubs wanted the passion flower and the Floral Emblem Society wanted the apple blossom. The 1901 legislature, heavily lobbied by both sides, picked the apple blossom.

The state flag originated when the Pine Bluff chapter of the Daughters of the American Revolution wanted to present a state flag to the newly commissioned U.S. Navy battleship *Arkansas*. They discovered there was not a state flag, so the group sponsored a statewide contest to design a flag. The winner, picked from sixty-five entries by a committee headed by Arkansas secretary of state Earle W. Hodges, was Miss Willie Kavanaugh Hocker of Wabbaseka (Jefferson County). The state legislature made it official in 1913. The design has a white diamond bordered by a starred blue band on a field of bright red. The committee added the word *Arkansas* in the diamond.

THE ENCYCLOPEDIA OF ARKANSAS HISTORY & CULTURE

Log on to Learn More
http://www.encyclopediaofarkansas.net/

▶ The children's building at the Arkansas Tuberculosis Sanatorium at Alexander (Pulaski County) around 1935.

tuberculosis (too-BERR-kyoo-LOH-sis) a bacteria-caused lung disease that is highly contagious.

sanatorium (SAN-ih-TOR-ee-um) a hospital created for the long-term treatment of one particular ailment.

hookworm a parasite that lives in its victim's intestines and that can enter the body through bare feet.

pellagra (pull-LAY-gruh) a chronic disease of the skin and digestive tract caused by deficiencies of protein and niacin (vitamin B3).

the schools. Child-care classes for parents of preschool children and infants were also offered.

Mainly because of the civic involvement of these women, private groups such as the Red Cross, the Arkansas Tuberculosis Association, and the Arkansas Society for Crippled Children also joined the effort to promote better health education and care statewide. The Reverend Orlando P. Christian raised one hundred thousand dollars to build the first free children's hospital in the state in 1925, which became known as Arkansas Children's Hospital in Little Rock. Gov. Thomas McRae started a **tuberculosis sanatorium** for African Americans in Alexander (Pulaski County), and the state built a tuberculosis hospital in Booneville (Logan County).

Progress in medical research and awareness also led to a reduction in cases of **hookworm** and **pellagra**. Both are chronic illnesses that make a victim tired all the time.

Hookworm came from animal waste and entered the body through bare feet. A parasite that lives in the host's intestines and drains nutrition from the body, hookworm leaves the victim very weak. Controlling it was as simple as cleaning up the barnyard and wearing shoes. Pellagra, a deficiency of niacin that results in chronic fatigue and a skin disease, was caused by poor diet, such as the statewide standard meal of "hogs and hominy." Learning better eating habits and enjoying more varied foods could control it. Additional vitamins could also limit its effects. Private groups, such as the Rockefeller Foundation, were helpful in the attack on this disease.

Malaria had also weakened Arkansans through the years. Medical research discovered that a parasite carried by a certain kind of mosquito caused malaria. That knowledge meant malaria could be controlled. Draining swamps destroyed the breeding areas for mosquitoes and made more land available for farming. Spraying areas of standing water could also prevent breeding. Simple devices like window screens could keep mosquitoes and other insects out of homes. To help alleviate standing or polluted, unhealthy water that mosquitoes used to breed, towns began to build pure-water systems and sewer systems. As a result, many Arkansans would have the modern convenience of indoor plumbing with safer, cleaner water for drinking and cooking.

A Day in the Life

Growing Up in the Country

Bethel May Stockburger Jones, born in 1903, grew up in Washington County on farms near West Fork and Winslow. Years later, this is how she remembered her childhood:

Mama had us three girls and house to keep and laundry to do. Laundry? What a job that was! She'd haul her big black iron kettle down to the cave-spring. Rubbin' clothes on a washboard and punchin' 'em with a stick is a far cry from washing machines today. Next day she kept a fire going all day to heat the little sad irons. . . . One of my jobs was churnin' the sour milk into butter. When I first started doin' this chore, I'd stand on a box 'cause I was too short to reach the dasher otherwise. I'd pump that dasher up and down for about thirty minutes, but o' course, it seemed a lot longer than it was when I wanted to be out playin'. . . .

Papa's work day was almost as full as Mama's. There was wood to chop, or things to fix, or fields to work. Papa'd be growin' corn or winter wheat or oats to feed to stock, nothin' to sell or help make a living. . . .

Our house was up on one hill and we had to go down through town and up to the schoolhouse on the other side. On cold wintery days we wrapped up in everything we had, but we still got so cold it was pitiful. We always wore long underwear. . . .

When we first started school I couldn't separate multiplication and division; those two words just didn't make any sense to me. . . . I loved English, we'd diagram sentences and I was pretty good at it. I could not remember geography, though, and I couldn't remember dates. Another special time was Christmas—goin' to the Christmas tree. People didn't have Christmas trees at home, they'd put the tree up at the church. The young people gathered to decorate the tree, then waited for everyone else to come for the program. We could hardly wait in the crowded church for the program to be over and Santa Claus to come.

Elizabeth Jacoway, ed. *Behold, Our Works Were Good: A Handbook of Arkansas Women's History* (Little Rock: Arkansas Women's History Institute, in association with August House, 1988), 63–75.

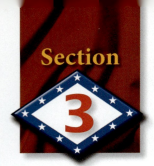

Section 3

New Developments in Industry

Guide to Reading

Terms
bauxite
furnish
manganese
sorghum
staves
sustained yield forestry

Events
Great Depression

People
tenant farmers

Lumber and Mining

Timber companies that had left the northern states during the 1880s and 1890s turned their eyes to Arkansas's vast acres of untouched timber around 1900. Two-thirds of the state was still forest, much of it highly-valued pinewoods. The timber industry employed more than 36,000 workers in Arkansas by 1909. This was about three-fourths of all the state's nonfarm employees.

The untouched Ouachita Mountains region held the greatest appeal for timber companies. Bigelow Brothers and Walker Company was a Chicago-based firm that moved into the area along the Fourche LaFave River in 1904. Using the name Fourche River Lumber Company, they built Arkansas's first large, modern two-band sawmill (a

▶ A timber camp somewhere along the Missouri Pacific Railroad line.

294 Chapter 13

◀ A firefighter with the U.S. Forest Service demonstrates his equipment during the heavy logging days in the Ouachitas.

mill that cuts a log with two saw blades at once). The town of Bigelow grew up at the mill site. At least a dozen more big mills in the Ouachitas were to follow.

The logging industry had no trouble finding workers to cut the trees and run the sawmills. Farmers in the Ouachitas were tilling land that could produce barely enough crops to feed a family, let alone provide a cash sale. The wage offered by the lumber companies was low by national standards but was more money than most of the workers had ever seen.

A logging job often came with room and board, sometimes in temporary, movable towns created by the logging company. When the company cleared out a section of forest, it laid new railroad tracks into the next section of timber. Then it took apart its houses, churches, stores, and schools, loaded them onto railroad cars, and moved down the line to be rebuilt, making a new town.

A good-sized mill town had a hotel for single men and a store where families did their shopping. The towns offered baseball teams, motion pictures, races, picnics, and other ways to entertain the workers. The companies employed black and white workers, but the mill town living areas were segregated. Often, the white workers' houses were painted and the black workers' homes were not.

Not all of the mills were run by northern companies. James Thomas Rosborough of Texarkana (Miller County) owned the Bowie Lumber Company. His son Thomas Whitaker Rosborough became owner of the giant Caddo River Lumber Company. The Bemis family of Prescott (Nevada County) were relatives of Rosborough and owned the Ozan Lumber Company. The Dierks Lumber and Coal Company was the largest and longest-lived of its kind in the state.

The mills produced mostly plain lumber, as well as some barrel **staves** and railroad crossties. Businesses such as

staves narrow pieces of wood used to make the sides of barrels.

Progressing into the New Century **295**

sustained yield forestry a method to manage forests for economic uses by planting new trees as others are cut.

bauxite (BOX-ite) the raw ore from which aluminum is derived.

manganese (MANG-guh-neez) a hard metal used to strengthen steel.

furniture-making plants opened in Fort Smith and Little Rock and used the wood produced at the mills. In 1909, at the peak of the timber industry in Arkansas, the state was the fourth-largest producer of lumber in the nation. Unfortunately, the clear cutting techniques of the time soon used up the forests. Logging began to fade as a major industry, to be revived later with newer methods, such as **sustained yield forestry**.

Another source of jobs was the mining industry, chiefly coal, **bauxite**, and **manganese** mining. Coal was found in Sebastian, Johnson, and Franklin counties in western Arkansas. The high-quality coal produced in Arkansas was used to power railroad engines.

Bauxite was a key mineral resource in Arkansas. Bauxite is found in only a few places in the United States, and at the time, the deposits in Arkansas were the nation's largest. The Aluminum Company of America, based in Pennsylvania, began large-scale bauxite mining in Saline and Pulaski counties during the early 1900s. The bauxite ore was mined in Arkansas and shipped elsewhere to be made into metal. Arkansas produced 70 percent of the nation's supply of bauxite in 1923. Manganese, which was used to strengthen steel, was mined around Cushman (Independence County). Zinc and lead were also mined in small, remote areas of the Ozarks, such as the town of Rush (Marion County) on the Buffalo River.

Some of the workers in the new timber and mining industries tried to form labor unions, uniting in groups to bargain with owners or managers about wages and working conditions. Arkansas and the United States were generally not very friendly to labor unions. The Brotherhood of Timber Workers tried to recruit blacks and whites in the lumber industry in Arkansas, Texas, and Louisiana, but owners broke the union. There were always more people needing jobs and willing to work for low wages than there were jobs, so the owners could fire anyone who supported the union.

For the most part, Arkansas industry extracted raw resources from the mines and the forests. The raw products were shipped to other places to be processed.

▶ United Mine Workers district officers, around 1916.

◀ Newberry Farm, Van Buren (Crawford County).

There were never many factories in Arkansas that produced finished goods, as there were in the states of the Northeast. Wages paid to workers were very low, close to the lowest in the nation. As logger Bill McBride put it, "the wages were cheap; the work was hard. But actually it was about the only thing there was in this country to do." Many children left school some time after the third grade to work for $2.50 a week (approximately $48.26 in today's money) in Little Rock factories.

Attempts to organize the coal miners had a little more success than the timber industry efforts. When a 1914 United Mine Workers' strike in Sebastian County turned violent, President Woodrow Wilson sent in U.S. Army troops to stop the strike. Workers in skilled trades, such as printing, were able to maintain unions. The skilled-trade unions usually belonged to the American Federation of Labor, which formed its first Arkansas chapters in 1904.

Tenant Farming

Arkansas was still a very rural state. In the early twentieth century, almost eight out of every ten Arkansans were tied to farming for their living. Even though there was a growing level of well-being in Arkansas in the 1920s, it had little effect on the farmers. Most farmers still relied upon cotton as their cash crop, and cotton prices were at rock bottom in the late 1920s.

During World War I, cotton prices were good, reaching thirty-five cents a pound. Right after the war, the price began to drop as cotton farmers produced more cotton than the world markets could absorb. The price was twenty cents a pound by 1920, and it declined throughout the decade. In a way, the **Great Depression** began for Arkansas farmers in 1920. Most farmers could not pay for land of their own

Great Depression the name given to the global economic collapse that took place from 1929 through 1942, during which business came to a virtual standstill, resulting in high unemployment.

▼ Entire sharecropping families worked long days in the fields to plant, hoe, chop, and pick cotton, which left little time for the children to attend school. The sharecropper had a difficult time working his way out of debt.

Progressing into the New Century   297

tenant farmers (TEN-uhnt FAR-merz) people who rent someone else's fields, plant and grow crops, and pay a fee to the landowner after the crops are sold.

furnish the means of a sharecropper's survival, including seed, tools, draft animals, and food.

and remained sharecroppers (SHAIR-krahp-erz) or **tenant farmers** on someone else's land. This system trapped many poor white farmers, as well as blacks.

The tenant promised the owner a share of his crop in return for the use of the land and, if needed, a house, mules, tools, and seed. Each tenant's contract varied a little, but in almost all cases, the system was an economic trap. The owner charged the costs of growing the crop, plus food and other living costs, called **furnish**, against the proposed profits. The tenant family was always in debt to the landowner.

Most sharecropping plots were small and required intense farming even to hope to meet the debt to the landowner. In most cases, the cotton fields came right up to the front door of the house. Everyone worked in the fields: men, women, and children. School was often ignored because the tenant needed his children working to help support the family. Many tenant farms were without roads, and most lacked electric power and running water. It was always the landowner who sold the cotton crop. The tenants never knew how much the profit was or the exact amount of debt that would be deducted from the profit.

In the early 1900s, sharecropping had been a labor system that primarily involved African Americans. In the 1920s, more white farmers were becoming sharecroppers. In 1900, about a third of the white farmers in Arkansas had been sharecroppers at one point or another. After the decline in crop prices of the 1920s and the Great Depression, more than half of white farmers were tenants. Of the total number among blacks and whites, nearly two-thirds of Arkansas farmers were tenants.

New Developments in Agriculture

Even though cotton was still the major crop of the early 1900s, corn, hay, oats,

▶ Fruit farming was very successful in northwest Arkansas, but also prospered in other areas of the state. These peaches were harvested in Nashville (Howard County).

wheat, rice, sorghum, and peanuts were also important. Those eight crops used 95 percent of the farmland in the state. Farmers also produced some fruit, dairy products, eggs and chickens, and hogs.

Rice was a promising new crop. The prairie lands around Hazen (Prairie County) and Lonoke (Lonoke County) were best suited to rice growing, which used a great deal of water. Although the crop required expensive machines to pump water and prepare soil, the payoff could be very large. These were also good years for growing fruit. Apples were a common fruit crop in northwest Arkansas. The University of Arkansas opened a School of Agriculture in 1906.

Despite considerable improvements and cultural changes, Arkansas remained quite poor and rural. It was hard to make a living on the farm. Arkansas's major industries, such as timber and mining, paid low wages. Arkansas produced the raw resources, but other states did the high-paying, skilled work needed to process the goods. In 1919, the per-capita income of Arkansans was $379 a year. That may have been more money than many Arkansans had ever seen, but the national per-capita income was $627.

The early twentieth century was time of enormous contrasts. Significant progress was made in the areas of road building, economic diversification, education, and healthcare. However, race relations and social acceptance still struggled to advance. The cycle of conflict and change raged on.

sorghum (SOAR-guhm) a cane-like grass that produces sweet sap that is made into syrup.

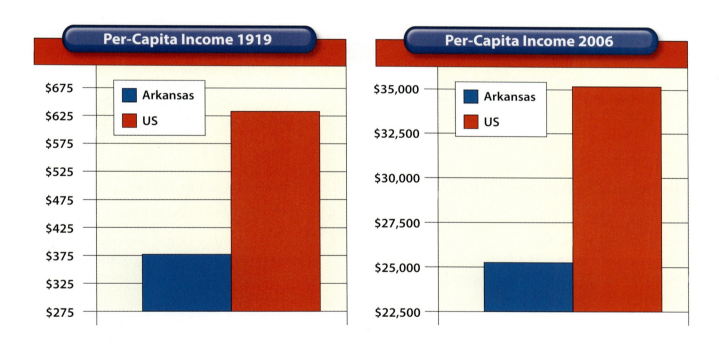

▲ Use your math and graph interpretation skills to fill in the blanks in the following statements. In 1919, Arkansans' per-capita income of $379 a year was _____ % of the national per-capita income of $627 a year. In 2006, Arkansas's per-capita income of approximately _____ per year is _____% of the national per-capita income of _____ a year.

Progressing into the New Century **299**

Chapter Reflection

Reflective Questions

1. Describe the group of voters Gov. Jeff Davis appealed to the most. How and why?
2. What were the structure and conditions in Arkansas prisons during this period?
3. What made it necessary to build better roads in Arkansas?
4. Describe the improvements in public health in Arkansas during the Progressive years. Why do state and national governments have an interest in the public health of citizens? Why is public health of importance? Use specifics in your discussion.
5. Create two columns on your paper—one labeled *Positive* and one labeled *Negative.* Then fill in the chart with positive and negative points about the lumber and mining industries. Be sure to consider long-term benefits and consequences.
6. Discuss two areas in which the Progressive movement in Arkansas failed. Are we still facing these issues today? Why or why not? If not, how did we correct the problems? If so, what are we doing now to better the situation?
7. How did women's roles change during this period?
8. Discuss the reasoning for and importance of a state having a symbolic or representative state flag and state flower. Use your prior knowledge from Chapter 1, as well as what you learned in this chapter.

Who Says?

Distinguishing Between Fact and Opinion

On your paper, number *1* through *5.* Carefully read each statement below and, based on your studies, determine if it is a fact or an opinion. Write an *F* or *O* beside the corresponding number to indicate your choice.

1. The design of the Arkansas state flag is one of the most symbolic in the nation.
2. Jeff Davis was an outstanding governor.
3. In 1903, there were only fifty cars in the state.
4. Many of Arkansas's rural farm people felt that they were being left out of the new progress and that no one in power cared about them.
5. Rosa Marinoni of Fayetteville was Arkansas's poet laureate in 1953.

Picture It!

Carefully review all of the "Guide to Reading" terms from the chapter. Choose four that were brand new to you or that you felt had the most interesting definitions. Take a clean sheet of paper and draw one horizontal line all the way across the page and one vertical line, from top to bottom, to divide it into four equal parts. In the first box, neatly print the first word you chose in the upper left-hand corner.

Use markers or colored pencils to illustrate the word. Continue the process until you have labeled and illustrated all four words. Be sure to include plenty of accurate details in your drawing. Your illustration should result in a creative explanation of the meaning (definition) of the term.

Then and Now

Based on what you studied in Chapter 13, compare and contrast roads, education, and healthcare in Arkansas during the Progressive Era with current times. Additionally, be sure to mention things that are still the same. Divide your paper into five columns and three rows. The first column will be labeled with the category name. The second column will be labeled *Then* and the third will be labeled *Now*, and so on. A sample has been designed for you below.

Category Names	Then	Now	Then	Now
Roads				
Education				
Healthcare				

Read and Respond

Carefully read the "A Day in the Life" passage on page 293. Then complete the activities below on your own paper.

1. Using emotional or descriptive words or phrases, tell how you think Bethel May Stockburger Jones would complete the following statement.

    "My childhood was _____ ."

2. Describe Bethel's journey to school.

3. How many sisters did Bethel have?
4. What was Bethel's favorite subject in school?
5. In the passage, Bethel compares and contrasts an "appliance." What was the "appliance" and what was her description?

Chapter 14
Wars and Wonderment
1914–1928

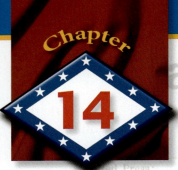
A newspaper article about the Elaine race riot from the *Arkansas Gazette*.

Timeline

	1914	1916	1919
Arkansas	**1914** Electric lines connect Malvern (Hot Spring County) and Arkadelphia (Clark County).		**1919** More than one hundred people are killed in the Elaine race riot (Phillips County).
United States	**1914** W. C. Handy, a son of freed slaves, composes "St. Louis Blues." He will become a famous resident of Memphis and be called the "Father of the Blues." Edgar Rice Burroughs publishes *Tarzan of the Apes*.	**1915** The Ku Klux Klan reorganizes. **1916** The National Park Service is established. Gen. John Thompson invents the submachine gun or "Tommy Gun."	**1917** The U.S. enters World War I. The "bobbed" hair fashion for women sweeps the country.
World	**1914** World War I begins after the assassination of Austrian Archduke Franz Ferdinand in Sarajevo.		**1919** The Treaty of Versailles ends World War I.

302 Chapter 14

Why Do We Study This?

We study this time in Arkansas history because it is important to understand the long-lasting impact that conflict and change have had on our society, culture, and economy. We continue to learn that people sometimes hate or act violently toward others who they see as different from themselves.

This period saw many contrasts. Arkansans suffered through another tragic war, felt the rush of wealth of the oil boom, enjoyed the modern convenience of electricity, debated our origins, explored a modern lifestyle filled with unique and sometimes controversial art, music, literature, and clothing, and began to promote the state as a place of abundant natural resources and opportunities for prosperity. However, some were left behind—some on purpose and some by circumstance. Racism continued to resurface and would further damage our state's reputation and limit potential progress throughout the century.

Big Picture Questions

- Analyze and discuss events and circumstances that led to a revival of Ku Klux Klan activity in the 1920s.
- Do rapid changes in technology force people to change their lifestyles? Is this positive or negative? Why?
- What are some cultural or social issues in modern-day society that spark change or controversy?
- Why is change or controversy necessary? Why or why not?

1922			1925		1928
1921 Oil is discovered in El Dorado (Union County).	**1923** The Arlington Hotel in Hot Springs (Garland County) burns.	**1924** Former Democratic Party presidential candidate William Jennings Bryan gives a speech on evolution in Little Rock.			
		1924 Led by Coach Knute Rockne, Notre Dame has an undefeated football season.	**1925** The Scopes "monkey trial" about teaching evolution is held in Dayton, Tennessee.		**1927** The Harlem Globetrotters African American professional basketball team is founded. Babe Ruth of the New York Yankees hits sixty home runs.

Wars and Wonderment

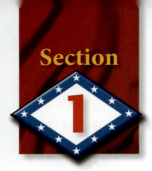

Section 1

Wars with the World

Guide to Reading

Terms
catalyst
draft

Events
Meatless Tuesdays
Wheatless Mondays

People
Herman Davis
John Grider
Oscar Miller

catalyst some person, event, or issue that brings about change, and often, controversy or debate.

draft government selection of individual young men for service in the nation's armed forces without their having any choice in the matter.

Wheatless Mondays days when American citizens gave up eating wheat and wheat products during World War I so there would be more for the servicemen.

Arkansas and the First Great War: World War I

In August of 1914, Europe found itself in the largest international conflict ever seen up to that time. For more than a generation, national rivalries over economics, colonies, and weapons had made Europe volatile and vulnerable. The **catalyst** for conflict was the assassination of a member of the Austrian royal family. Although no nation intended to start a full-scale war, fear, suspicion, and a complicated alliance system quickly brought all the major nations of Europe to war. At first, England, France, and Russia joined forces against Germany and Austria. But the war soon involved many other nations and became a world war, fought on the battlefields of Europe.

Most Americans strongly disapproved of the war and hoped the United States would stay out of it. With German submarines on the attack against U.S. and British ships, and after diplomatic negotiations failed, Americans began to favor entering the war on the side of the Allies: England, France, and Russia.

In the spring of 1917, the United States officially entered the war. The nation quickly mobilized and sent soldiers to the trenches in Europe. The war ended in November of 1918, and the American presence had helped strengthen the British and French efforts. The war was a complicated, difficult experience; nevertheless, the Allies declared victory.

In Arkansas, Gov. George Donaghey formed a Council of State Defense in May of 1917. Its task was to register young men to serve in the war. It was an involuntary **draft**, and it met with resistance at first because the war still seemed remote to many Arkansans.

For the most part, Arkansans were patriots who supported the war effort.

Cross

Named after: Edward Cross, a territorial judge and a founder of the Cairo and Fulton Railroad

Chief Source of Income: Agriculture and manufacturing

Seat: Wynne

Cross County was established in 1862 in east central Arkansas. The lands of Cross County are alluvial farmland. Communities in the county include Cherry Valley, Hickory Ridge, and Parkin. The archaeological site at Parkin showcases the remains of a seventeen-acre American Indian village near the St. Francis River.

▲ Field E. Kindley, a native of Gravette (Benton County) and a World War I flying ace, earned the British Distinguished Flying Cross and the American Distinguished Service Cross with an oak leaf cluster. Only two people in the war shot down more aircraft for the United States Army Air Service during World War I.

At war's end, the top one hundred heroes of the war were named. The list included Maj. **Oscar Franklin Miller** of Franklin County and Pvt. **Herman Davis** of Manila in Mississippi County. Ace fighter pilots also came from Arkansas. Among them were Capt. Field E. Kindley of Gravette (Benton County) and Lt. **John McGavock Grider** from the east Arkansas Delta region, who was killed in action.

Just as the war was nearing its end, a fierce killer—an epidemic of a severe form of the flu—struck Arkansas and the rest of the world. Through the fall of 1917, the disease overran the nation and its healthcare units. In Arkansas, seven thousand men, women, and children died from the flu, far more than the wartime death toll.

Meatless Tuesdays days when American citizens gave up eating meat during World War I so there would be more products for the servicemen.

Oscar Franklin Miller an Arkansas soldier killed in action during World War I who received the Congressional Medal of Honor.

Herman Davis an accomplished marksman in the U.S. Army during World War I, he was awarded the Distinguished Service Cross.

John Grider a soldier who served two months in World War I before his plane was shot down. Later, his diary was assembled into *War Birds: The Diary of an Unknown Aviator* and published. It recorded the memories and horrors of World War I fighter pilots. The Pine Bluff airport is named Grider Field.

They engaged in **Wheatless Mondays** and **Meatless Tuesdays** and bought nearly $2 million in war bonds, which helped finance the war effort. They served in the American Red Cross and grew cotton and mined bauxite that were processed for wartime supplies. Counting draftees, volunteers, and three regiments of the Arkansas National Guard, all of which included whites and African Americans, about seventy-two thousand Arkansans served in the armed forces. Women also contributed to the war effort as nurses and factory workers. About two thousand Arkansas soldiers died—five hundred in combat and the rest from diseases and accidents.

County Quest

Woodruff

Named after: William Woodruff, founder of the first newspaper published in Arkansas, the *Arkansas Gazette*

Chief Source of Income: Agriculture

Seat: Augusta

Created in 1862, Woodruff County offers land highly suited for agriculture. McCrory hosts MosquitoFest and the Cache River/Bayou Deview Duck Gumbo Cook-off. Hunters bring a great deal of income to the county, and the Cache River Natural Area and the Rex Hancock Black Swamp Wildlife Management area are in the county.

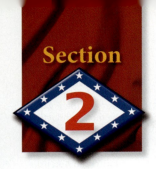

Section 2

Wars with Weapons and Words

Guide to Reading

Terms
communist
posse
Progressive Farmers and Household Union of America
verdicts

Events
Elaine race riot
Red Scare

People
Bolshevik
whiskey runner

Places
Elaine

Bolshevik (BOWL-shuh-vik) a member of the political party in Russia responsible for the Russian Revolution of 1917; commonly used to mean the same thing as communist.

Red Scare a widespread fear of a communist takeover in the United States. Because of the red and gold colors on the communist hammer and sickle flag, a slang term sometimes used to refer to communists was "reds."

communist a person who participates in or is governed by a political structure designed to establish a society without social and financial classes, based on common ownership of production (factories, for example) and the absence of private property. Associated with the former Union of Soviet Socialist Republics.

Elaine a farming community in Phillips County and site of Arkansas's largest race riot.

The Elaine Race Riot

The speed of change and the tensions of the war years produced a new unease in the years after the war. The **Bolshevik** Revolution in Russia in 1917 sparked a great **Red Scare** in the United States that would resurface in the 1950s and 1980s. U.S. citizens would long fear a communist takeover, or eventually even the frightening possibility of nuclear war, from Russia, which was then a dominant **communist** state. Some saw the possibility of revolt at home, mainly in labor unions and among immigrants.

There was also fear of social change, which was reflected most clearly in the concern over the status of African Americans. Many African American soldiers had served in the armed forces during World War I and moved north to work in defense plants after the war. A sense that things were changing gave hope to blacks, but provoked fear in some whites.

One result of these fears was an outbreak of race riots, in which groups of blacks and whites clashed, fought, and sometimes killed each other. In 1917, there was a significant racial conflict in Houston, Texas, when rumors circulated that a police officer had murdered a black soldier. In 1919, there were twenty-five race riots all over the nation. There were major riots in Longview, Texas; Washington, D.C.; and Chicago, Illinois. In Tulsa, Oklahoma, in 1921, the Ku Klux Klan was gaining strength and popularity, and a race riot occurred on Memorial Day weekend. Reports said anywhere from thirty-nine to three hundred people were killed, while eight hundred were injured, more than thirty city blocks burned, and there was a reported $1.8 million (about $17 million by current standards) in damage. One of the worst of the riots, in terms of numbers of deaths, was in the Arkansas Delta town of **Elaine** in Phillips County.

While the war had brought high cotton prices and some new wealth to Delta planters, African American sharecroppers felt they had not received their fair share. Many wished to belong to a

> Governor Brough once said,
>
> "[T]he Negro is entitled to life, liberty, and the pursuit of happiness and the equal protection of our laws for the safe-guarding of these inalienable rights."

306 Chapter 14

◀ Governor Brough tries to ease tensions with residents of Elaine (Phillips County) at the Elaine Mercantile during the riots of 1919.

Progressive Farmers and Household Union of America an organization designed to unite black sharecroppers to fight for fair wages, which was established by Winchester (Drew County) resident Robert Hill.

whiskey runner a bootlegger.

posse (PAH-see) a band of citizens authorized by law enforcement officers to assist in the search for and arrest of suspected criminals.

new union, the **Progressive Farmers and Household Union of America**.

Although many have thoroughly studied the events that took place in Elaine, the complete story may never be known. African Americans said the main purpose of the union was to help blacks get a better deal from the planters. They planned to file lawsuits against whites who had cheated them. Whites believed that the union, a secret society, was giving members guns and encouraging violence.

In late September of 1919, union members were at an evening meeting three miles north of Elaine, at a church in Hoop Spur. Because of many rumors circulating in the community, African American armed guards patrolled outside the building. A car arrived, carrying two armed men—a deputy sheriff and a railroad agent—along with a black trusty from the local jail. The lawmen later said they were hunting for a **whiskey runner**. They said showing up at the union meeting was an accident. It is not known who fired first, but shots broke out. The railroad agent was killed, and the deputy was wounded.

The sheriff formed a **posse** to hunt down the African Americans involved in the incident. For the most part, there was cooperation on the part of the African

▼ The defendants in the Elaine race riot trial.

Wars and Wonderment **307**

Elaine race riot a 1919 conflict that occurred in the days after a shooting during a meeting of a black farmers' group at Hoop Spur Church near Elaine.

Americans during the investigation, but fears and rumors circulated and the violence escalated into mob scenes. More than 500 white people from many other Arkansas counties, and even from Mississippi, came to help control the supposed uprising of the blacks, who outnumbered the whites in Phillips County by almost ten to one. Finally, Gov. Charles Hillman Brough called in five hundred U.S. Army soldiers to restore order.

The official reports stated blacks were herded into stockades for questioning. There were other reports that the military and white residents tortured black suspects being held, but they were never proven. On the two days and one night of the Elaine race riot, accounts said five whites and twenty-five blacks were killed. Other reports put the number of African Americans killed at closer to one hundred or more. The highest estimate is 856.

I Am an Arkansan

Scipio Jones (1863–1942)

Born a slave in 1863 near Tulip (Dallas County), Scipio Africanus Jones was an African American attorney, judge, and Republican politician for many years. He was most well known for his legal counsel in the appeals process of the twelve men sentenced to death following the Elaine race riots.

As was the practice of the day, Jones attended segregated, all-black schools. He moved to Little Rock (Pulaski County) in the 1880s to study at Philander Smith College. He received a bachelor's degree from Little Rock's Shorter College in 1887.

Jones worked as a schoolteacher and law apprentice until he was accepted into the Arkansas Bar Association in 1889. He soon became a prominent black Republican in the state and was a delegate to the Republican National Convention several times.

Typically, African American attorneys were not allowed to argue cases and were only permitted to assist white attorneys. During the Elaine race riot trial, Jones was assigned to assist George W. Murphy with the defense and did much of the research for the case. When Murphy died suddenly, Jones took the lead in guiding the appeals process and successfully saw the case to the Supreme Court of the United States. During the trials, Jones is said to have slept in a different home each night in order to protect his safety.

For the remainder of his career until his death in 1942, Jones was active in supporting the war effort during World War II, as well as providing legal defense for African American Arkansans. His last case involved a lawsuit that aimed at gaining equal pay for black teachers in Little Rock. Though he did not live to see the outcome, Jones won the case.

THE ENCYCLOPEDIA OF ARKANSAS HISTORY & CULTURE

Log on to Learn More
http://www.encyclopediaofarkansas.net/

▲ Scipio Jones.

After the riot, sixty-five African Americans were tried on various charges. The trials were brief: all-white juries reached **verdicts** in as little as two minutes in some of the cases. Twelve African Americans were sentenced to death for murder. They quickly appealed to higher courts. The key defense lawyer in the process was Scipio Jones, Little Rock's leading African American lawyer. The new National Association for the Advancement of Colored People (NAACP) helped finance the appeals. In the end, the higher courts freed all of the men who had been condemned to death.

After the Elaine riot, Governor Brough convened a group to discuss the problems between the races and to search for ways to work together. But he could not control the larger social forces at work. In 2000, another conference was held to discuss the still strained race relations in Phillips County. Feelings were still raw and sadly, resolution could not be achieved.

verdicts in trials, the juries' judgments about the guilt or innocence of the accused parties.

▲ Those charged with violence in the Elaine race riots.

▲ Scipio Jones walking with an officer during the Elaine race riots.

TO THE NEGROES
OF PHILLIPS COUNTY
Helena, Ark., Oct. 7, 1919

The trouble at Hoop Spur and Elaine has been settled.

Soldiers now here to preserve order will return to Little Rock within a short time.

No innocent negro has been arrested, and those of you who are at home and at work have no occasion to worry.

All you have to do is to remain at work just as if nothing had happened.

Phillips County has always been a peaceful, lawabiding community, and normal conditions must be restored right away.

STOP TALKING!
Stay at home---Go to work---Don't worry!

F. F. KITCHENS, Sheriff   COMMITTEE
Edward Bevens J. C. Meyers S. Straub E. M. Allen
T. W. Keesee D. A. Keeshan Amos Jarman
H. D. Moore J. G. Knight Jno. L. Moore E. C. Hornor

Nicholls Print, Helena, Ark.

▲ A flier urges citizens to "stop talking" about the riots and the "trouble at Hoop Spur." Why do you think a poster like this was printed and displayed around the community?

Wars and Wonderment

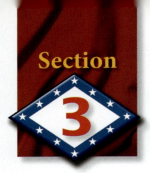

Section 3

Wonderment

Guide to Reading

Terms
Arkansas Power and Light
art deco
Bear State
Climber Company
expressionism
gusher
surrealism
WOK
Wonder State

Events
oil boom
Roaring Twenties

People
Harvey Couch
flapper

Places
Cotton Club
El Dorado
Lake Catherine
Lake Hamilton
Smackover
speakeasies

The Prosperity of a Nation and the Beginning of a Modern Arkansas

Roaring Twenties a term for the 1920s, a period of influential changes in lifestyles, the arts, and technology.

For most Americans and Arkansans, the decade of the 1920s marked the start of modern times. Industry produced a wide variety and large number of new consumer goods. There were cars, electric lights, refrigerators, and washing machines. There were telephones, radios, and motion pictures. These new technologies had the power to reshape the lives of Americans. Going where the factory jobs were, Americans began to move away from the farms. By 1920, more than half the people of the United States lived in cities.

City life meant a new, fast-paced cultural lifestyle in what was called the **Roaring Twenties**. The decade was filled with not only significant advances in technology and inventions, but also considerable cultural changes. Women's roles, fashion, music, cinema, dance, art, architecture, and literature, as well as shifts in political beliefs and race relations, were all seen during the twenties.

Prohibition, women's suffrage, and the return of soldiers who fought in the war all had tremendous influence on the culture of the twenties. Women felt freer and more empowered than ever before and began to cut their hair off into a bob style, wear a great deal of makeup, drink liquor, dance provocatively, and smoke cigarettes. They were mimicking European trends and rebelling against traditional behavioral expectations. They also began to wear

Calhoun

Named after: South Carolina statesman John C. Calhoun

Chief Source of Income: Manufacturing

Seat: Hampton

Visitors to Calhoun County, established in 1850, will see beautiful rivers and lakes, historic main street squares, and untouched outdoor settings. Visitors can enjoy the Hogskin Holidays celebration, which recounts the area's colorful history.

310   Chapter 14

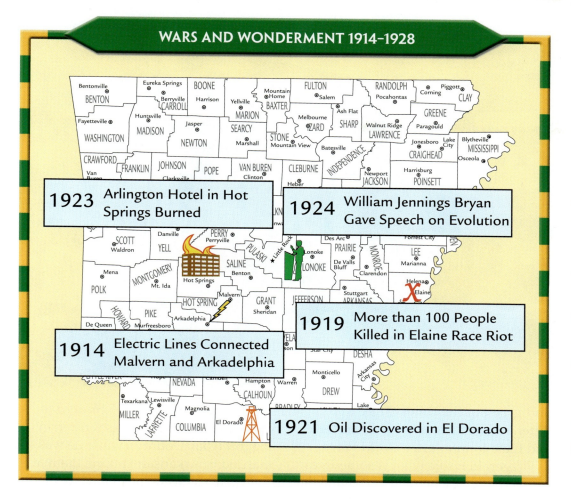

WARS AND WONDERMENT 1914–1928

- **1923** Arlington Hotel in Hot Springs Burned
- **1924** William Jennings Bryan Gave Speech on Evolution
- **1919** More than 100 People Killed in Elaine Race Riot
- **1914** Electric Lines Connected Malvern and Arkadelphia
- **1921** Oil Discovered in El Dorado

flapper a woman, influenced by European trends, who dressed and acted in a way that was considered rebellious for the time.

speakeasies hidden establishments where alcohol was sold illegally during Prohibition.

Cotton Club a jazz speakeasy or club in Harlem, New York, which featured some of the greatest black entertainers of the day, but only served white customers.

expressionism an artistic style that seeks to convey the personal emotional reactions, opinions, or perspectives of an artist brought about by seeing, hearing, or feeling objects and events.

surrealism art that portrayed the subconscious mind with incredible, strange imagery.

art deco a popular style of architectural design in the late 1920s and 1930s that used geometric designs and often bold splashes of pinks, greens, blues, and silver.

new fashions known as the **flapper** style, influenced by French fashion trends. Women would wear these spirited, sometimes shocking outfits to the underground drinking and music clubs of the day known as **speakeasies**. One of the most well-known was the **Cotton Club** in Harlem, run by gangster Owney Madden, who later retired to Hot Springs (Garland County).

In these secret, glamorous clubs, African American vocalists and bands played the music we now call jazz, with its roots in a combination of native African rhythms and refined European instruments; the streets of Harlem, Chicago, and New Orleans; and the plantation fields of the South. Louis Armstrong and Duke Ellington were famous bandleaders in what was also called the Jazz Age. Dances like the "Charleston" and "Lindy Hop" were popular throughout the twenties. These dance styles would eventually evolve into the swing style of the forties.

In the world of visual arts, the painting styles of **expressionism** and **surrealism** became popular. Architecture of the era was dominated by what is known as the **art deco** style. Shapes in nature influenced its geometric designs. One of the most famous art deco buildings of the era was New York City's Chrysler Building, constructed in 1928.

Some of the greatest artistic achievements of the 1920s were in literature. Authors Sinclair Lewis, F. Scott Fitzgerald, Willa Cather, and Ernest Hemingway published works that would influence generations to come. Many of these writers felt disenchanted by the rapid changes

Wars and Wonderment

▶ Downtown of an oil boomtown of Union County.

Harvey Couch the founder of Arkansas Light and Power and WOK radio. He also built dams that created lakes Catherine and Hamilton in Garland County.

Arkansas Power and Light a company formed by Harvey Couch to bring electricity to the state. It eventually became known as Entergy.

Lake Catherine a lake named after Harvey Couch's daughter, one of two lakes he created in Garland County by building dams that were necessary to generate power for his electric companies.

Lake Hamilton one of two lakes created by Harvey Couch in Garland County.

and greed of the times. They were bitter and had lost hope for themselves and their country after World War I.

Fitzgerald wrote what is sometimes referred to as the novel that defined the Jazz Age, *The Great Gatsby*. In 1929, Hemingway published *A Farewell to Arms*, much of which was written in Piggott (Clay County), while he was married to Arkansan Pauline Pfeiffer.

Arkansans were mostly aware of all these phenomenal cultural developments, but to a lesser degree than places with larger urban populations. Arkansans were still poor by the standards of the rest of the nation. Most people remained on farms and in rural areas. Because of this, modernization and change came somewhat slowly to Arkansas.

Electrification

Arkansas joined the electric age largely through the efforts of **Harvey Couch**. A farmer's son from Calhoun in Columbia County, Couch saw the potential of the telephone. He built telephone lines to serve parts of Arkansas, Mississippi, and Louisiana. When he sold his phone systems to American Telephone and Telegraph, he became a millionaire at the age of thirty-four.

DID YOU KNOW?

WOK

Did you know that the call letters of the first Arkansas radio station, WOK, located in Pine Bluff, stood for "Workers of Kilowatts," because the electricity company paid for the station and there were no commercials?

WOK was the first radio station in Arkansas to broadcast a sports event, a live music concert, and a sermon. Brother Bogard of Little Rock, an opponent of Darwinism and evolution, was the first Arkansas preacher to effectively use radio to communicate his message. His radio show helped promote the legislation that would ban the teaching of evolution in Arkansas public schools.

Log on to Learn More
http://www.encyclopediaofarkansas.net/

Next, Couch started the statewide power system that came to be known as Arkansas Power and Light Company. By the early 1920s, Couch was selling electric power to nearly fifty towns in Arkansas. His plan was to connect many small city electric systems into a large network. He was also able to convince northern bankers to invest money in him and his plans. To produce even more power, he built dams on the Ouachita River. The first dam formed Lake Catherine, and the second formed Lake Hamilton. But it would take several decades before most of the rural areas of Arkansas would be wired for electricity.

Radio was one of the new users of electric power. In 1921, Couch started the state's first radio station, WOK, in Pine Bluff. That first station broadcast programs only on Tuesday and Friday nights.

The decade also brought motion pictures. At first, they were silent films with subtitles on the screen. In some movie houses, there was organ music to go along with the film. By 1928, motion pictures with sound had been developed. Audiences were excited by the new technology and flocked to theatres.

Modern businessmen of the early 1900s hoped to attract more industry and tourists to the state. They combined efforts to create the Arkansas Advancement Association, which promoted the good points of the state to out-of-state investors. They brought news and magazine writers to tour the state. They hired former governor Brough to make speeches all over the nation about the glory of Arkansas. In 1923, inspired by this group and their ideas, the General Assembly felt that the Arkansas state nickname, the Bear State, was no longer fitting. They renamed Arkansas the Wonder State.

The Oil Boom

Modern changes were abundant in 1920s Arkansas. The southwestern part of the state shared the thrill and hope of prosperous times when the cry of "It's a gusher!" rang out in El Dorado

WOK Arkansas's first radio station, established by Harvey Couch in 1921 in Pine Bluff.

Bear State the unofficial state nickname that described Arkansas as an outdoorsman's playground with abundant bear hunting. This image promoted the untamed and rugged aspects of the state.

Wonder State the state's official nickname, adopted in the 1920s, that promoted the state's resources and investment opportunities. The wonders were considered to be minerals, rich alluvial soil, and vast timber forests. Governor Brough was the main advocate of the Wonder State idea and said Arkansas was completely self-sufficient because of these resources. Arkansas had previously been known as the "Bear State," and in more recent years has been called the "Land of Opportunity" and the "Natural State."

gusher an oil well that spurts oil as it is struck by drilling equipment and pressure is released.

El Dorado Arkansas's original oil boomtown and county seat of Union County in southwest Arkansas.

▲ A hoedown. At what time of year do you think this occurred? Why?

◀ A "boomtown" street of El Dorado during the days of oil discovery.

oil boom rapid population and economic growth following the discovery of oil in an area.

Smackover a town in Union County. After oil was discovered there in the 1920s, it became, for a time, one of the largest oil producing areas in the country.

Climber Company established in 1919, the Climber Motor Company was Arkansas's only car company and produced cars that claimed to be tough enough to travel Arkansas's rugged roads.

(Union County) in 1921. Arkansas's **oil boom** was under way. The town's size quickly swelled to three times its normal population. Nearby **Smackover**, where there was an oil strike the next year, soon was home to twenty thousand people. Strangers flooded into town each day to seek their fortunes. Like the California gold rush of 1849, the oil boom of the 1920s spawned wild, frontier-style towns, and, in a few cases, instant wealth.

With production peaking at more than seventy-seven million barrels a year, Arkansas produced the fourth-largest amount of oil among all the states by 1924. Hopes of even larger oil strikes eventually faded, and the oil boom was confined to a small part of south Arkansas. The oil producers learned that the natural gas from the wells, at first burned off as waste, was also a valuable resource.

The timber industry and related work such as furniture making remained the state's largest money-maker. Its products equaled four times the value of any other products made in Arkansas. Railroads still employed many Arkansans. For a short time, Arkansas had its own in-state automobile manufacturer. The **Climber Company** of Little Rock produced around three hundred cars and trucks in the early 1920s.

County Quest

Sebastian

Named after: *William K. Sebastian, a judge for the U.S. Circuit Court*

Chief Source of Income: *Service industry*

Seat: *Fort Smith, Greenwood*

Sebastian County was created in 1851. Fort Smith, originally called Belle Point, was a U.S. military base established along the Arkansas River. The notorious "hanging judge," Isaac Parker, lived there in the late 1800s. Today, Fort Smith is one of the largest cities in the state and is home to the University of Arkansas, Fort Smith, and the Fort Smith National Historic Site.

▲ A gusher near El Dorado (Union County).

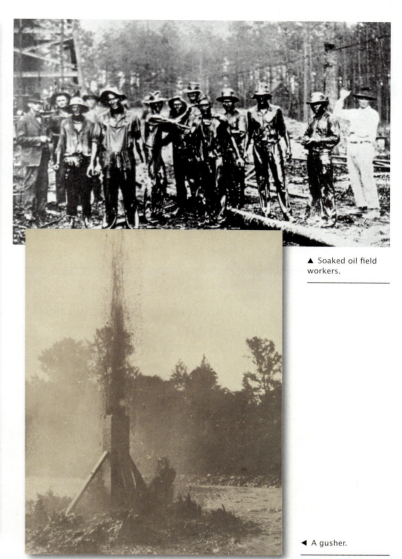

▲ Soaked oil field workers.

◀ A gusher.

◀ An oil boomtown.

Wars and Wonderment **315**

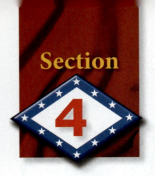

Section 4

War Against Change

Guide to Reading

Terms
agnostic
evolution
fundamentalism
natural selection
oppressed
racist
species
survival of the fittest

Events
monkey trial

People
bootleggers
Charles Darwin
John T. Scopes

---

evolution (EV-oh-LOO-shun) the gradual change of a species over time to better adapt to environmental conditions.

racist (RAY-sist) the belief that one race is superior to another, or a person who holds this belief.

Although many Americans had enjoyed new economic success in the 1920s, Arkansas remained a poor state with slow progress. Disagreements over traditional values were revealed in the revival of the Ku Klux Klan and an attack on Charles Darwin's theory of *evolution*.

Resurgence of the Ku Klux Klan—Weapons and Words of War

Progress and change did not suit everyone. Some were deeply uncomfortable with the fast pace of motorcars and telephones. They could not adjust to the shock of different cultures they learned about on the radio and in the movies. To them, the new ideas that seemed to be coming from the big cities spelled disaster. Many people went to extreme lengths to turn back the clock to what they believed were "the good old days" of traditional American values and patriotism.

One of their outlets was a revived Ku Klux Klan. Starting in Georgia in 1915, the new Klan spread quickly through the small towns of the United States. It had its greatest strength in the Midwest and the South. The Klan started to gain power in Arkansas in 1921, and within a few years claimed to have forty thousand members.

Unlike the Klan of old, the new Klan did not focus its *racist* acts solely on African Americans. The new Klan members also attacked and punished those who seemed to differ in any way

◄ A poster recruiting members for the Ku Klux Klan, representative of those posted on Little Rock street corners.

316 Chapter 14

◀ The lynching of John Carter in Little Rock. Why were lynchings public during this time?

from the customs and morals of white Protestant Americans, such as those of Jewish faith, or people who were considered abnormal such as Gypsies and the disabled. The Klan's victims included **bootleggers**, wife-beaters, gamblers, Catholics, union members, and foreigners of all types. Because of the wide variety of newcomers who moved to boomtowns to seek riches, the Klan was very active in southwest Arkansas.

The Klan flourished in Arkansas from 1921 to 1924 and controlled the politics of many counties and towns. They were a major factor in the governor's election of 1924. The Klan declined after 1924, partly because members learned that its national leaders were corrupt and using members to make money for themselves.

A War of Words Over Evolution

The debate between change and tradition had a forceful impact on religion as well as race issues. Church attendance, then as now, was a key part in the lives of many Arkansans. Some church groups argued that change was part of God's plan. Others saw any change as tearing down moral values. The debate split churches and families.

Many of those who hoped to maintain the old ways believed in the concept of **fundamentalism**. This belief held that the Bible was the sole guide to life and morals. Those who believed in this concept were strongly opposed to some new concepts in science.

In the late 1800s, British scientist Charles Darwin theorized that all life forms changed over time by the process of **natural selection**. When a certain **species** could adapt itself to conditions in the struggle for life, that species survived. Those that did not change died out. Thus, by **survival of the fittest**, life forms changed over a long period of time. He called the process evolution.

Applied to humans, evolutionary theory argued that the rise of the human species was a slow process, taking place over many millions of years. Darwin's theory was widely studied and approved of by many scientists, and word of it spread across

bootleggers people who sold, smuggled, and, in some cases, made liquor illegally, particularly during Prohibition.

fundamentalism (FUN-duh-MENT-uhl-izm) the literal interpretation of the Bible.

natural selection the gradual improvement of a species through a process known as survival of the fittest.

species (SPEE-seez) a group of animals similar enough to one another to reproduce with each other, such as *Homo sapiens*, or humans.

survival of the fittest the theory that the best and strongest examples of a species live and reproduce themselves. This was a key component of Darwin's theory of evolution.

Wars and Wonderment

John T. Scopes a high-school science teacher in Dayton, Tennessee, whose teaching of evolution brought about the trial that would become known as the Scopes monkey trial.

monkey trial newspapers' name for the trial of John T. Scopes, which involved the teaching of biological evolution in the public schools.

oppressed those who are restricted, restrained, limited, or denied rights and opportunities by a larger entity or controlling person or force.

agnostic (ag-NOSS-tik) a person who holds the view that any ultimate reality (or the existence of God) is unknown and probably unknowable.

the world, eventually affecting Americans and Arkansans.

The theory of evolution became a key symbol in the clash of values in the 1920s. Some church leaders believed evolution went against accounts of creation in the Bible's book of Genesis. This belief led to attempts to limit or stop the teaching of evolution in public schools. In the 1920s, the Arkansas General Assembly discussed and voted against such a law twice. However, neighboring state Tennessee completely outlawed the teaching of evolution. That set the stage for a great showdown between the two sides in 1925.

John T. Scopes deliberately broke the law by teaching the theory of evolution in his classes with the intent to test the law in court. The Scopes trial, often referred to as the **monkey trial**, became a national focus of the debate between change and tradition. Scopes's lawyer was Clarence Darrow, famous for his defense of the **oppressed**, and was the most well-known lawyer of the day.

Darrow was **agnostic**. The state's key witness, and the prosecuting attorney for the state, was none other than the great speaker and former Populist Party presidential candidate, William Jennings Bryan. He was now an advocate for traditional moral values. The state found Scopes guilty. The trial was so stressful that Bryan died in Dayton at its conclusion.

The people of Arkansas then put into effect their own anti-evolution law. Passed in 1928 by 63 percent of the public who voted, the act outlawed teaching that "mankind ascended or descended from a lower order of animals." The law stayed on the books for forty years, though it was not actively enforced.

In the 1968 case of *Epperson v. Arkansas*, the Supreme Court struck down the law that had banned teaching evolution in Arkansas schools because it violated the First Amendment. In January of 1982, Judge William Overton struck down a law requiring creationism be taught, and the court case of *McLean v. Arkansas* came to an end when the Arkansas attorney general decided not to appeal the ruling.

The first twenty-five years of the twentieth century were exciting, confusing, positive, painful, and amazing for Arkansas. Arkansans continued to bear the burden of racial conflicts and unease. Many different kinds of wars were fought on the home front and abroad, and precious lives were lost in World War I, the Elaine race riots, and to the Ku Klux Klan. It was a struggle to modernize both the technologies and the thoughts of Arkansans. Equality and progress were still important goals for the majority of people in the state. Tourists and businesses were encouraged to come and share in the "wonder" of our state. Progress had been made, but unfortunately, devastation and setbacks would lie ahead.

Only in Arkansas!

Climber Motor Company

Climber Motor Company, Arkansas's only automobile manufacturer, was founded in 1919 in Little Rock. Climber produced rugged cars and trucks that could manage Arkansas's poor roads better than other models. Its vehicles were far more expensive than the more popular Ford Model T. Today, only two Climbers are known to still exist. The Climber can be viewed at the Museum of Automobiles near Morrilton (Conway County).

THE ENCYCLOPEDIA OF ARKANSAS HISTORY & CULTURE

Log on to Learn More
http://www.encyclopediaofarkansas.net/

I Am an Arkansan

John H. Johnson (1918–2005)

John H. Johnson was born in Arkansas City (Desha County), the grandson of slaves. His father was killed in a sawmill accident. He later recalled that while growing up, race relations were generally peaceful. "The only problem, dim at first but constantly growing clearer," he said, "was a feeling that we were not in control of our own destiny, that a word or a frown from a white person could change our plans and lives."

His mother saw another problem: the black school only went up to the eighth grade; there was no high school for blacks. So, during the Great Depression, when John was fifteen years old, she moved with him to Chicago, where he could get an education.

Johnson made the best of it. In 1942, he founded his first magazine, *Negro Digest,* with five hundred dollars borrowed by using his mother's furniture as collateral. He went on to create *Ebony* and *Jet* magazines, Fashion Fair Cosmetics, and Supreme Beauty Products. He also bought Supreme Life Insurance Company, where he had once worked. By the 1980s, he was one of the wealthiest men in America.

In his autobiography, Johnson gave much of the credit for his success to his mother and to the African American community:

I was born into a strong family and reared in a strong community where every Black adult was charged with the responsibility of monitoring and supervising every Black child. I was reared in a community where every Black adult was authorized to whip me, if I needed whipping, and to send me home for second whipping from my mother, whether I needed it or not.

Sixty years later, I attended a meeting . . . with among others, Sam Moore Walton, the richest man in America. We discovered with surprise and delight that we had six things in common. We were nonsmokers and nondrinkers who were born into poverty. We grew up in small southern towns and were reared by strong and loving parents who spared neither hugs or rods. . . .

I didn't have a lot of clothes. But I had a lot of love. . . .

[My mother] had known pain and discouragement and fear. Out of all this came a special kind of dignity. The dignity of a person who'd seen a lot and survived and wasn't afraid of the future.

After his death in 2005, the city of Chicago named a portion of one of its most prominent streets, Michigan Avenue, after John H. Johnson.

John H. Johnson, with Lerone Bennett, Jr., *Succeeding Against the Odds* (New York: Warner Books, 1989), 41, 37–39.

Log on to Learn More
http://www.encyclopediaofarkansas.net/

Chapter Reflection

Reflective Questions

1. List five ways in which Arkansans contributed to the war effort.

2. Based on what you have studied, what industrial or agricultural products from Arkansas might be beneficial or useful in wartime? Be sure to explain which products and how they would be useful in your answer.

3. Pinpoint one element or aspect of the Elaine race riot that fits into each of the following categories or that has a relationship to the topics/categories listed:

    a. society, community, or groups

    b. the military

    c. religion, beliefs, or faith

    d. technology or industry

    e. politics or government

    f. ideas, plans, or strategies

    g. economy, money, or jobs

4. Compare and contrast the way of life in Arkansas during the time of Arkansas Post and the 1920s. Consider housing, clothes, daily life, and entertainment when crafting your answer.

5. What were three modern advances or discoveries available in Arkansas during the 1920s? In what ways did these benefit Arkansans or make life easier?

6. List two of Harvey Couch's accomplishments.

7. What is the purpose of states having nicknames? If you were contacted by the governor's office to choose the new nickname for the state of Arkansas, what would you select and why? Be sure to validate your choice with reasons.

8. What is Arkansas's current state nickname and why?

9. What were the goals of the Ku Klux Klan?

10. What issue is similar to evolution that schools, families, churches, and politicians debate today? Describe and give examples in your answer.

Unlock the Meaning . . .

The *Key* to new *Terms* from the chapter . . .

Look at the list of terms in all the "Guide to Reading" sections in the chapter. Choose four that are brand new to you. Write and number them *a, b, c,* and *d* on your paper. Then, copy or trace the diagram below. Then . . .

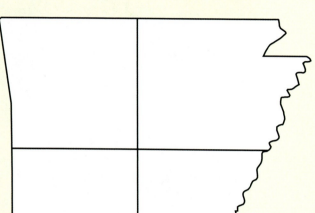

a. In the section of the state where Herman Davis was from, write two synonyms for the first term you chose.

b. In the section of the state where oil was discovered, write a sentence that uses your second term correctly and conveys the meaning of the term.

c. In the section of the state where the hometown of Field E. Kindley is located, define the third term in your own words.

d. Finally, in the remaining section, where the Elaine race riot took place, quickly sketch an illustration of the fourth term.

You Don't Say!

On your own paper, number *1* through *5* and clearly mark each phrase with a *T* for *True* or an *F* for *False*.

1. An agnostic is one who wholeheartedly believes in God.
2. Today, the "Wonder State" is the most common nickname for Arkansas.
3. Arkansas allows its public schools to choose and freely teach either creationism or evolution theory.
4. Music had no significance in the 1920s.
5. Electricity brought important, modern changes to Arkansas.

Prove It!

Now that you have completed the "You Don't Say!" exercise above, look at your answers and review the statements you said were false. Use your book and class discussion notes to find evidence to rewrite each of the false statements to be true.

Wars and Wonderment

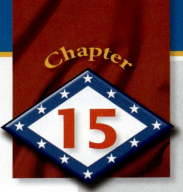

Chapter 15
Hard Times
The Great Depression
1927–1939

▲ The Missouri Pacific Railroad bridge in Little Rock during the 1927 flood.
▶ Dermott Grocery, Chicot County, during the floods of 1927.

Timeline

	1927	1928	1930	1932	1933
Arkansas	**1927** A flood kills 127 people and leaves half the state under water.	**1929** Arkansas Agricultural, Mining, and Normal College fields its first football team. Female pilot Louise Thaden beats fellow aviator Amelia Earhart in the National Women's Air Derby, the first transcontinental air race for women.	**1930** The largest recorded meteorite to that date, and the third largest ever found on Earth, lands in Paragould, weighing in at 816 pounds.	**1932** Cotton prices drop to five cents per pound.	**1933** Hattie Caraway becomes the first elected female U.S. senator.
United States		**1928** Amelia Earhart becomes the first woman to fly across the Atlantic Ocean solo.	**1930** William Faulkner publishes *As I Lay Dying*.	**1932** Franklin Delano Roosevelt is elected president and promises citizens a "New Deal."	**1933** The first U.S. aircraft carrier is launched. Roosevelt appoints the first female cabinet member, Frances Perkins, who becomes his Secretary of Labor.
World					**1933** Hitler becomes chancellor of Germany.

322 Chapter 15

Why Do We Study This?

As with the Progressive Era, the government continued to take a role in the order, organization, and regulation of businesses and society during the 1930s. The liberal-minded leaders of the time wanted to make the most of what they saw as the good aspects of the government. They believed in the effectiveness, capability, and promise of the nation's leaders and legislators.

After surviving much catastrophe, Arkansans and Americans alike continued to realize the importance of receiving aid, and, in turn, lending a helping hand to others when times were hard.

Big Picture Questions

- In some ways, it seems more difficult to recover from natural disasters today, in modern times, than in the past. Do you agree or disagree? Why or why not? Support your opinion.

- What challenges do Arkansans and Americans face in protecting their lands, homes, personal safety, and families? What measures should we as citizens be taking to ensure success and prosperity?

- Why is it important to elect both males and females of all races, religions, and backgrounds to our state and local government offices? In your opinion, what is the next political "first" Americans will encounter?

From this point forward, Americans would have daily interactions with the national government, unlike ever before. This was a new mentality that would play a role in events through the next eighty years and beyond.

1934	1936	1938	1940
1934 The Southern Tenant Farmers Union is formed in Tyronza (Poinsett County) by black and white sharecroppers.		**1938** John Gould Fletcher wins the Pulitzer Prize for his *Selected Poems*. Wilbur D. Mills is elected to the U.S. House of Representatives.	**1939** J. William Fulbright becomes president of the University of Arkansas, making him the youngest college head in the United States at age 34.
1934 Members of the Federal Bureau of Investigation shoot and kill John Dillinger, known as "public enemy number one."		**1937** Joe Louis wins the world heavyweight boxing title.	
1934 Hitler names himself *Führer* of Germany.		**1937** Japan invades China.	**1939** Germany invades Poland. Britain and France declare war against Germany.	**1940** The Germans conquer France.

Hard Times—The Great Depression

Section 1

Nature's Wrath

Guide to Reading

Terms
boll weevil
catastrophic
livestock
refugee

Events
Dust Bowl
flood of 1927

People
Arkies
Okies

boll weevil (BOHL WEE-vuhl) a destructive beetle that infested southern cotton crops, causing great damage. Aggressive programs to keep them at bay are still in place today.

flood of 1927 often described as the most destructive river flood in U.S. history, especially in Arkansas, which was the hardest hit of the eight states flooded.

The 1927 Flood

Nature was hard on Arkansas farmers, bringing troubles ranging from the **boll weevil** to the **flood of 1927**. After a cold, hard, wet winter, excessive rains fell through April and into May. It rained 20 inches in Yell County in the month of April alone—almost half the yearly total of around 42 inches. In Little Rock, 8.3 inches of rain fell in two days—typically, around 48 inches fall in an entire year. A large section of the Baring Cross Bridge across the Arkansas River washed away.

The floods began in mid-April all along the Mississippi River. Heavy snows in Canada melted, filling the northern reaches of the river. This, combined with excessive rains, forced the raging waters of the Mississippi to fill the Arkansas, White, and St. Francis rivers to capacity. Eventually, all three overflowed their banks and flooded thousands of acres of land. Arkansas was more dramatically affected than any of the other Mississippi River valley states that were flooded (including Illinois, Kentucky, Louisiana, Mississippi, Missouri, Oklahoma, and Tennessee), with about two million acres of the state's croplands under water. Over fifty thousand homes were altered by the floodwaters. In some places, the muddy

▶ Flooding in Fort Smith (Sebastian County), April 1927.

324 Chapter 15

▲ A flooded street in Dermott (Chicot County).

FLOOD OF 1927

waters were thirty feet deep. Some people who lived through the flood called it the "Great Flood" because of the extent of the damage and the way it affected their lives.

Throughout the early 1900s, farmers had plowed many new acres of cropland and felt shielded by new levees and drainage systems. However, those systems could not contain the massive volume of water that flowed through the rivers in the spring of 1927. *National Geographic* noted in its September 1927 issue that the streets of Arkansas City (Desha County) were dry and dusty at noon, but by two in the afternoon, "mules were drowning on Main Street faster than people could unhitch them from wagons."

The floods caused more waste, wreckage, and ruin than Arkansas has suffered from any other natural disaster. The human and financial loss was **catastrophic**. There were more than a hundred deaths in the state and the loss of an estimated fifty thousand head of **livestock**. Thousands of Arkansans were homeless for weeks, camping out on levees and in other high spots. Near Pine Bluff, about five hundred people were stranded for days on a bridge where they had taken refuge. Many were without clean drinking water and food, and the threat of waterborne disease was severe.

James Fieser, vice chairman of domestic disaster relief for the American Red Cross, compared the damage he saw caused by the Mississippi flood in 1927 to other disasters he had seen, including "the Galveston flood, the San Francisco earthquake, the great mid-western tornado of 1925," and other calamities:

"But I say unqualifiedly that this flood of the Mississippi and its tributaries by comparison has been far more devastating than any of these disasters."

Pete Daniel, *Deep'n as It Come: The 1927 Mississippi River Flood* (Fayetteville: University of Arkansas Press, 1996), 78.

catastrophic causing mass devastation or disaster.

livestock farm animals, especially cattle, sheep, horses, and hogs.

◀ Looking for shelter during the flood in Marianna (Lee County).

Hard Times—The Great Depression   **325**

▶ The flood overtook whole towns, including McGehee (Desha County).

refugee someone who is seeking safety or shelter.

The American Red Cross and other private groups helped flood victims with food, clothing, and shelter. They constructed around fifty temporary **refugee** camps for the victims. The camps were segregated and crude and could not manage all those who poured in. Sickness and mosquitoes spread in the camps. Pellagra resurfaced as the waters receded, and people faced starvation, unemployment, and homelessness. Farmers were unable to plant crops on the ravaged land that was covered with stale, impure water—some of which stood in areas of the state until September.

Arkansans looked to their state and federal government leaders for help and guidance. President Calvin Coolidge, a Republican, named Herbert Hoover to arrange private relief efforts. However, due to government "red tape" and restructuring efforts, none of the relief funds went directly to the victims.

Roads, bridges, and levees had to be rebuilt, homes had to be cleaned and restored, and farmlands reestablished. The Red Cross continued to provide the majority of assistance as entire communities worked to rebuild. This changed the way many people viewed charitable organizations, and support, respect, and donations seemed to increase. Many people lost some faith in the government as their guardian and protector in a time of need. The lack of immediate, large-scale response and money during and after the flood raised many political questions from the citizens.

DID YOU KNOW?

Baring Cross Bridge

Did you know the Baring Cross Bridge in downtown Little Rock (Pulaski County) is one of six bridges in the city that spans the Arkansas River? The Baring Cross Bridge is the westernmost of the six. It opened in 1873 and was constructed with iron and wood. A large part of it was washed away during the 1927 flood and had to be rebuilt. The current bridge is made of steel and is owned by Union Pacific Railroad, among the country's most active railroad companies.

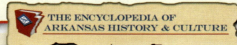

THE ENCYCLOPEDIA OF ARKANSAS HISTORY & CULTURE

Log on to Learn More
http://www.encyclopediaofarkansas.net/

The flood brought national attention to Arkansas. The coverage of the event exposed the sharecropping system and racism that still existed in Arkansas. People began to question the sharecropping system. Many African Americans moved to cities like Chicago to look for work away from the farms. Others shifted their political support from the Republicans to the Democrats. A substantial change in political beliefs had taken place in Arkansas that would hold true for years to come.

The farmers were not alone in their struggles. The fruit growers of northwest Arkansas came upon hard times, too. Disease attacked many types of fruit trees and ruined the orchards within a few years. Fruit growers also faced growing competition from new and well-organized growers in states of the Pacific Northwest. New trade in the Northwest also had its effect on the lumber industry. Timber output in Arkansas in 1925 was half of what it had been in the peak year of 1909.

However, one firm tried a new approach. In 1925, the Dierks Lumber Company began the practice of sustained-yield forestry. This meant they kept their land and planted new seedlings where trees had been cut. They managed the forest's new growth with the intent of growing and cutting trees on the same land for years to come.

The Drought and the Dustbowl

After surviving the record floods, nature hit the South and Southwest during the 1930 growing season with the worst drought on record. Arkansas received only 35 percent of its average rainfall. The central part of the state went without a drop of rain for seventy-one days in the summer of 1930. The temperature was around one hundred degrees for days on end, burning up home gardens along with the state's cotton crop.

Throughout the heartland of America, farmers were hopeless and helpless as they watched their fields turn to dust and blow away in the wind. Farms stood empty as farmers loaded their goods into cars and trucks and headed west to California, looking for food and work. Out in California, they called the displaced farmers **Arkies** and **Okies**.

In the late 1920s, agricultural technology made great advances. Farmers aggressively tilled millions of acres of southern farmland in hope of greater crop yield and profits. Farmers were anxious to plant wheat and became somewhat greedy in their efforts. This would cause irreversible damage to the land and ecosystem of the Great Plains. When combined with previous floods and the drought, it would contribute to what we now know as the **Dust Bowl**. People would forever write and talk about the Dust Bowl that hit the Great Plains in the mid-1930s. The combined forces of flood, drought, and ultimately the Great Depression hit Arkansas harder than any other section of the nation.

Arkies (ARK-eez) the name given to 1930s refugees from Arkansas who traveled primarily to California seeking work.

Okies (OH-keez) the name given to refugees from Oklahoma during the Depression who traveled primarily to California seeking work.

Dust Bowl the ruinous condition of drought during the 1930s that caused horrible dust storms.

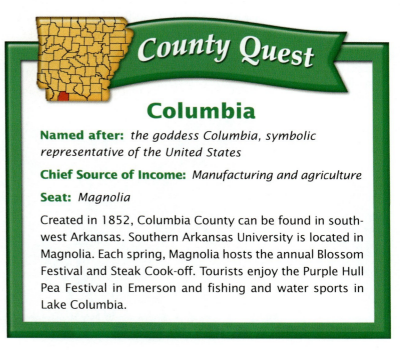

County Quest

Columbia

Named after: the goddess Columbia, symbolic representative of the United States

Chief Source of Income: Manufacturing and agriculture

Seat: Magnolia

Created in 1852, Columbia County can be found in southwest Arkansas. Southern Arkansas University is located in Magnolia. Each spring, Magnolia hosts the annual Blossom Festival and Steak Cook-off. Tourists enjoy the Purple Hull Pea Festival in Emerson and fishing and water sports in Lake Columbia.

THE DUST BOWL, EARLY 1930s

Impact by County
- Seriously Affected
- Moderately Affected
- Relatively Unaffected

© 2007 University of Arkansas Press

▼ A family seeks to escape hardship by traveling west.

During the winter of 1930–31, many people in Arkansas faced not just hunger, but real, true starvation. Neither the state nor the U.S. government had any means for giving relief. One-third of Arkansas's people relied solely upon private relief efforts. They were mostly living on the one meal a day offered by the American Red Cross. In Chicot County, 21,912 people out of a total population of 22,646 received Red Cross aid each day. Many others made do with wild game, turnips, roots, herbs, and nuts.

Starvation drove people to be angry and irrational. Some lost their patience and were frightened about not being able to provide for their families. Their frustrations began to rise to the surface. England (Lonoke County) almost had a food riot in January of 1931. The town's merchants had run out of the Red Cross forms they needed in order to be paid back for the food they gave to hungry farmers and their families. The farmers threatened to take the food by force. The merchants' response was to give them the food and hope the Red Cross would pay them back. The entire nation heard about this event, and before long, thirty-two states sent hundreds of train cars filled with food to Arkansas.

I Am an Arkansan

John Gould Fletcher (1886–1950)

An important voice from Arkansas in the 1920s and 1930s was that of poet John Gould Fletcher. Fletcher, the son of a wealthy banker, cotton merchant, and frequent candidate for governor, grew up in a house in Little Rock built by Albert Pike in 1844. (Today it is open to the public as the Arkansas Decorative Arts Museum.) It was a privileged and often lonely life for a little boy.

After a few years at Harvard University, Fletcher visited Italy and France and then settled in London. There, Ezra Pound and other poets influenced him. As Fletcher developed his own poetic style, he was closely associated with the imagist poets, emphasizing a simple, lyrical, and musical style of poetry. He published many books of poetry. In 1939, after the publication of his *Selected Poems,* he was awarded the Pulitzer Prize.

Although Arkansas and the South were not often the subjects of his poetry, Fletcher increasingly came to believe that the Old South of the years before the Civil War represented something gracious and fine that was lacking in the modern world. Like many who were offended by the emphasis on materialism in the 1920s and shocked by the collapse of the economy in the 1930s, Fletcher liked to recall (or invent) a time when life was simpler. He was associated with a group of writers at Vanderbilt University called the Agrarians or the Fugitives, who shared Fletcher's longing for a pre–Civil War past. Fletcher

contributed an essay on education to a collection of the Agrarians' essays, *I'll Take My Stand* (1930).

Fletcher was also a leader in reviving interest in Arkansas folklore and folk songs. His major prose work, *Arkansas,* is a history of the state that was published in 1947 and is still good reading.

Fletcher's second wife was Charlie May Simon, an author of books for children. They built a house they called Johnswood in the hills west of Little Rock. As he grew older, Fletcher suffered severe attacks of depression. In 1950, in the pond near Johnswood, he drowned himself.

Log on to Learn More
http://www.encyclopediaofarkansas.net/

Hard Times—The Great Depression

Section 2

The Great Depression

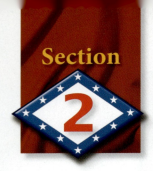

Guide to Reading

Terms
default
speculate

Events
Black Tuesday

People
Hattie Wyatt Caraway
socialist

Places
Commonwealth College

speculate (SPEK-yoo-layt) to assume a business risk in the hope of profit, especially by buying and selling stocks.

Black Tuesday October 29, 1929, the date of one of the largest percentage losses in U.S. stock market history.

Black Tuesday

During the 1920s, high profits had been used to build new and improved factories, but goods were often being produced much faster than people were able to buy them. Overall product output was increased. Wages for workers increased, but not enough to buy all the goods that were being produced. Also, many rural parts of the country, like Arkansas, had not been a part of the boom of the 1920s. There were signs of business troubles as early as 1926 and 1927, but people refused to believe that the good times could end.

Many began to **speculate** on the stock market. After several days of massive up-and-down buying and selling in the stock market, the eventual collapse on October 29, 1929, was the signal that the economy was failing and marked the start of the Depression. This was known as **Black Tuesday**.

The Plight of Arkansans

First, the banks were forced to close. People who had borrowed money could not repay their loans. Many who had placed their savings in the banks stormed the banks' doors to withdraw their money. The government did not back the banks then, as they do now, so funds were not insured. Soon, factories shortened their work hours or even closed their doors. Hundreds of thousands of men and women were without jobs, which meant they had no money to buy cars or houses, not to mention clothing and food. Therefore, even more firms, including small retail shops, had to close or cut back. By the early 1930s, about 25 percent of the American labor force was out of work and without any steady income.

Craighead

Named after: State senator Thomas Craighead

Chief Source of Income: Service industry and agriculture

Seat: Jonesboro

Created in 1859, Craighead County is the commercial and agricultural center of northeast Arkansas. Crowley's Ridge runs through the county and the Forrest L. Wood Crowley's Ridge Nature Center is in Jonesboro. Arkansas State University's main campus is located in Jonesboro. Jonesboro was in the national spotlight in March of 1998 for the fatal Westside Middle School shooting, in which four students and a teacher were killed. Jonesboro is one of the five largest cities in Arkansas.

330 Chapter 15

▲ Desperation sets in for many Arkansans.

Through the early 1930s, the Depression spread throughout the United States and eventually, the entire world.

In Arkansas during 1930 and 1931, 192 banks failed. Total bank holdings dropped from $137.6 million in 1929 to $41.8 million in 1934. The biggest bank in the state, the American Exchange and Trust Bank, shut down in 1930, taking with it many other banks. Many people who had checking or savings accounts at the banks lost all their money.

Nearly half of the businesses in Arkansas had closed by 1931. Between 1929 and 1933, construction of all types dropped by two-thirds, and the number of workers in Arkansas lumber mills was reduced by about 60 percent. In all, about 245,000 people lost their jobs, more than a third of the state's wage-earning workforce. Those who still had jobs took wage cuts. People worked for fifty cents a day and were grateful for the chance to work and earn any money at all. The annual income of Arkansans fell from $705 in 1929 to $152 in 1933, with only Mississippi falling further behind.

The State Government in Turmoil

Local and county governments were without funds, and public schools faced disaster. By 1933, lack of money had forced 725 schools to close and another 1,200 to shorten their terms. Arkansas already had the lowest-paid teachers in the nation, and during the Depression, some worked without wages.

On the farms, what was already bad quickly became worse. Cotton that sold for twenty cents a pound in 1927 was at seventeen cents a pound in 1929, and five cents a pound by 1932. That was less than it cost to actually grow the crop. Nearly 80 percent of the people in Arkansas were farmers, and low crop prices limited their earnings and their ability to buy goods, which hurt every business in the state.

The state government seemed neither willing nor able to give relief. Harvey Parnell, a merchant and owner of a large farm in Chicot County, was governor from 1928 to 1933. Parnell increased highway building and the state debt. As the Depression hit and deepened in Arkansas, Parnell claimed that things would get better soon, perhaps by cutting expenses. He reduced the wages of state workers by 10 percent. The General Assembly met in special session in 1931 to talk about the crisis, but did nothing to help.

Junius Marion Futrell, a lawyer and judge from Paragould (Greene County), was elected governor in

▼ A young girl looks out the window of a sharecropper's cabin. There is a chopping block, an ax, and a washtub on the porch.

Hard Times—The Great Depression **331**

default (dee-FAWLT) to fail to make payments on a loan.

Commonwealth College a college in Mena, Arkansas, operated on socialist belief systems.

socialist (SOH-shull-ist) a person who believes the government, as an agent of all people, should own the majority of businesses and industries like utilities and healthcare facilities, rather than private, individual ownership.

Hattie Wyatt Caraway the first elected female U.S. senator.

1932 and won again in 1934. At first, Futrell saw no active role for state government during the Depression. Eager to reduce state expenses, he proposed that the state not fund public schools beyond the eighth grade.

The state's chief problem was the huge burden of debt acquired during the 1920s, mostly from building roads. By 1934, Arkansas's total debt stood at $174,633,000. Over half of each year's state income was used to pay interest on the loans. As the Depression dried up tax income, the state borrowed even more to meet its costs. In 1934, Arkansas was forced to **default** on its payments and extend the due date on its bonds. It was the third time in one hundred years of statehood that Arkansas defaulted on its state debt.

Social Unrest

The failure of the economic system during the Great Depression led people to consider other systems. People were jobless, desperate, hungry, and angry, and many voices called out for major changes in American society and the economy.

County Quest

Little River

Named after: The Little River

Chief Source of Income: Manufacturing

Seat: Ashdown

In the extreme southwest corner of the state is Little River County. It was created in 1867 from portions of Hempstead and Sevier counties. This area is largely agricultural and is also home to many poultry farms. Cossatot Community College, a part of the University of Arkansas system, is in Ashdown, and residents and tourists alike enjoy outdoor recreation and fishing at Millwood Lake.

One of those ideas took shape in the form of **Commonwealth College** in Mena (Polk County)—a **socialist** institution. Formed in California and briefly located in Louisiana, Commonwealth College moved to Mena in 1925. It only had about fifty-five students, and no degrees were offered. The goal of the group was for members to produce all they needed to survive by constructing their own buildings, growing their own food, and sharing in all labor equally. The college, at its best, was about 70 percent self-sufficient.

It was viewed with suspicion by the local people because of the students' unusual clothes and rumors of their practice of "free love." The American flag was not flown on campus; instead, the hammer and sickle of communist Russia was displayed frequently. Residents of Polk County filed a lawsuit against the college on these grounds in 1940. The college was found guilty, and its members could not pay the fines the court imposed. Appeals failed and all of the college's property was sold to pay the fine. By the end of 1940, Commonwealth College was gone.

Hattie Wyatt Caraway had been named to fill the Senate seat of her husband, Thad Caraway, upon his death in November of 1931. She won a special election to confirm her appointment in January of 1932. To the surprise of all, in 1932, she sought her own full term. She opposed six male party regulars, among them former Governor Brough.

Huey Long, an influential Louisiana senator who was popular with poor southern voters, endorsed Caraway, and his support was instrumental in her victory. She gave thirty-nine speeches in seven days while traveling the state with Long. Caraway seemed to draw poor and

332   Chapter 15

hungry Arkansans into a kind of social protest. She won by a large margin. Arkansas had elected the nation's first female United States senator. She would continue to break barriers in her career by also being the first female to preside over the Senate, to chair a Senate committee, and to supervise a Senate hearing. She was a loyal supporter of President Franklin Delano Roosevelt and his New Deal economic plans.

I Am an Arkansan

Hattie Caraway (1878–1950)

Born in Tennessee, Hattie Caraway settled in Jonesboro after marrying her husband, Thaddeus, in 1902. While he developed a law practice and began his political career, Hattie Caraway tended to the family farm and raised the couple's three sons. After Mr. Caraway was elected to the U.S. House of Representatives in 1912, the Caraways moved to Maryland. In 1920, Thaddeus Caraway was elected to the U.S. Senate, serving until his death in 1931. In November of that year, Arkansas governor Harvey Parnell appointed Hattie Caraway to take her husband's senate seat. With this, she became the first woman to serve in the Senate, and the people of Arkansas voiced their approval in 1932 when she was elected to continue serving as senator.

Caraway spoke on the Senate floor so rarely that she became known as "Silent Hattie." However, she was an outspoken supporter of President Franklin Roosevelt's New

Deal programs. She also served on the Senate Agriculture Committee, and helped bring much-needed funds to Arkansas to deal with the 1927 flood that wrecked much of the state. In 1943, she became the first person to sponsor an equal rights amendment.

After leaving the Senate in 1945, she spoke out in favor of more rights for employees, and continued to live in Washington, D.C., in order to help further this cause. She died of a stroke in 1950, and was buried in Jonesboro, alongside her husband.

Log on to Learn More
http://www.encyclopediaofarkansas.net/

Section 3
A Hero With a Plan

Guide to Reading

Terms
commodity
conservation
domestic workers
erosion
liberals
New Deal
parity
Social Security

Events
bank holiday
Hundred Days
inaugural

People
Civilian Conservation Corps
Franklin Delano Roosevelt

Places
co-op

Franklin Delano Roosevelt elected in 1932, the thirty-second president of the United States. A Democrat, he was well known for his New Deal programs during the Great Depression.

inaugural (in-OGG-yoo-ruhl) upon taking office, the first address given by a new governor or president.

New Deal President Roosevelt's programs aimed at alleviating the effects of the Great Depression and preventing another economic depression.

Hundred Days the first one hundred days of Roosevelt's administration, when many relief and recovery bills were enacted.

bank holiday the forced closing of all banks by President Roosevelt to stem the nationwide run on banks.

The New Deal and Franklin D. Roosevelt

Real help for Arkansans would eventually come from the U.S. government. When Republican Herbert Hoover was president, the government gave no aid to individuals and only some aid to businesses. In the 1932 election, the Democrat **Franklin Delano Roosevelt** defeated Hoover.

Roosevelt was a distant cousin of former president Theodore Roosevelt and a former governor of New York. He was deeply concerned about people's distress and was willing to try a number of new federal programs. He had a gift for reassuring the people and rebuilding their confidence. Arkansans elected Roosevelt by a huge margin. Hopeful, they listened to his **inaugural** address over the radio. Roosevelt said: "Let me assert my firm belief that the only thing we have to fear is fear itself."

Roosevelt promised the American people a **New Deal**. The Democrats had also won most of the seats in the U.S. Senate and House of Representatives. The people were clearly ready for new ideas. At the very beginning of Roosevelt's term, Congress produced a

▲ President Franklin Delano Roosevelt.

flurry of new programs in what became known as the **Hundred Days** of the 1933 session. Through the mid- and late 1930s, the New Deal offered relief for the needy, recovery for business and industry, and reform for the economic system. Sometimes these New Deal programs were referred to as "alphabet soup" because of the three- and four-letter acronyms used as agency nicknames.

One of the first measures was a **bank holiday** that closed all the banks in the country. Those that were financially

334 Chapter 15

strong were later allowed to reopen, but those that were not closed for good. The Federal Deposit Insurance Corporation (FDIC) was formed to back savings accounts from that point forward. The Home Owners' Loan Corporation (HOLC) backed thousands of home loans. The Farm Credit Administration (FCA) did the same for farm loans.

One of the most pressing needs was food and shelter for people without jobs. The Federal Emergency Relief Administration (FERA) gave $9 million to needy Arkansans within a few months of its start. Soon, 15 percent of all people in the state were getting relief—one of the highest rates in the nation. The program ran in Arkansas under the forceful guidance of W. R. Dyess of Osceola (Mississippi County).

The federal relief programs moved from direct relief, in the form of handouts, to work programs, in which the government paid people to work on useful projects. The Public Works Administration (PWA) hired skilled workers to build major public buildings, such as Robinson Auditorium in Little Rock.

A very popular work program was the **Civilian Conservation Corps** (CCC). The CCC hired mostly young men, gave them a military form of life, and put them to work on outdoor projects. In Arkansas, the CCC built the state park system. Although the state had approved state parks before, little had been done to implement the projects. The CCC crews built the cabins, lodges, and trails at Petit Jean Mountain, Mount Nebo, the Buffalo River, Lake Catherine, Crowley's Ridge State Park, and Devil's Den. They also constructed buildings on university campuses. All were built well, and the majority of their projects contributed to the economy, tourism, and architectural heritage of our state.

By 1935, the work relief concept had grown into the Works Progress Administration (WPA). Because its goal was to hire as many people as it could, and to end their need for government aid, thus putting money into the economy,

Civilian Conservation Corps a New Deal work relief program for young men involving heavy construction work. It was one of the more popular New Deal programs.

◄ The Works Progress Administration was one of the New Deal agencies that provided many jobs for Arkansans during the Great Depression and recovery in the 1930s.

Hard Times—The Great Depression

Social Security a government organization that collects taxes set aside to pay pensions (PEN-shunz) for retired people, the unemployed, and disabled people.

domestic workers maids, housekeepers, and others who perform labor in the home of someone else for pay.

parity (PAIR-it-ee) as used in New Deal agricultural programs, the goal of setting prices for farm products to give the farmer a fair share of the national income.

almost no project was out of the question for the WPA. Through the 1930s, WPA workers in Arkansas built thousands of miles of roads and more than seven hundred new buildings, including hospitals, airports, fire stations, almost three hundred schools, and even houses for the animals at the zoo in Little Rock.

The WPA also ran reading programs for thirty thousand people and served hot lunches in the schools. The WPA hired out-of-work actors, painters, and writers. The WPA Writers' Project produced *Arkansas: A Guide to the State*, first published in 1941, which still serves as a fine account of Arkansas's history and folklore. At its peak, the WPA was spending $2 million a month on wages in Arkansas. As late as 1941, the WPA was the largest single source of jobs in Arkansas, with thirty-three thousand people on its payrolls.

The New Deal also aided American workers with a law that set a minimum wage for most urban workers. In what Roosevelt saw as the greatest economic policy of his four terms as president, the United States created the **Social Security** system.

The New Deal was not designed to address racial issues, but it did, in fact, affect the lives of blacks. New Deal programs such as the WPA were segregated, and most relief payments were not equal, with blacks getting less than whites. Even the first minimum-wage law did not apply either to farm laborers or **domestic workers**, two major sources of jobs for African Americans in Arkansas. But most major New Deal programs, such as Social Security, did apply to African Americans. The New Deal helped the poor, and, in Arkansas, African Americans were among the poorest.

The New Deal's Impact on Agriculture

For Arkansas farmers, an important New Deal program with long-range impact was the Agricultural Adjustment Administration (AAA). During the 1920s, it had become clear that the root of the nation's farm problem was putting too much of a product on the market. This was most clearly evident with major crops such as cotton.

American farmers produced more crops than the American and world markets could absorb. The result was low prices that plagued farmers through the 1920s. Neither local nor state action could deal with the problem. Arkansas and other southern states tried to reduce the cotton crop in the early 1930s but had no success.

The answer was a national program that required farmers in the major crop areas to take land out of production. The goal was a crop that would meet demand at a fair price to the farmers, called **parity**. The AAA was designed to achieve parity by paying farmers to

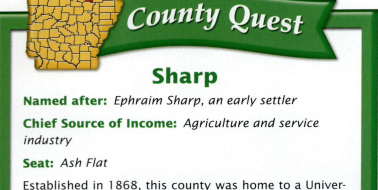

County Quest

Sharp

Named after: Ephraim Sharp, an early settler

Chief Source of Income: Agriculture and service industry

Seat: Ash Flat

Established in 1868, this county was home to a University of Arkansas president, David W. Mullins. A native of Ash Flat, Mullins was president of the university from 1960 to 1974, and the library on campus in Fayetteville is named for him. The towns of Hardy and Evening Shade are also located in Sharp County. Old Hardy Town is the revitalized downtown district of Hardy, which features motorcycle rallies, craft fairs, shopping, and dining. Cherokee Village is a popular resort and retirement community with golf, tennis, and fishing.

336 Chapter 15

take as much as a third of their land out of production. Some farmers were eager to try the new program and rushed to sign up, but others were confused about the reasons for the program and felt it went against their natural instinct to work and plant the land.

When the AAA was first passed in the spring of 1933, there was a problem. Planting time had passed, and crops were in the ground. For that year only, farmers plowed up a quarter of their crop—a shocking and uncomfortable sight. Farmers shared stories about how hard it was to get a mule to plow through the cotton plants instead of around them as they had been trained to do. In the years after that, farmers in the AAA planted only part of their land. The AAA reached its goal of reducing the crop and raising the price the farmer was paid, and it became a long-term program.

The Southern Tenant Farmers' Union

In the end, the program to reduce crops made life worse for tenant farmers and sharecroppers. The government payments for farmers went to the landowners, not the tenants who really farmed the land. The landowners were supposed to share the money with their tenants, but few did. Also, because less land was being used to grow crops, the owners needed fewer people to sharecrop. Landowners with large tracts of cropland also used part of their payments to buy tractors and other machines, which further reduced their need for human labor. Many tenants were forced to leave the land and faced an economy with few available jobs. In Arkansas, one out of every five tenant families left the land between 1933 and 1940.

Two young white men in Tyronza, in northeast Arkansas, thought the times of

DID YOU KNOW?

The *Southerner* Crash

Did you know W. R. Dyess, FERA (Federal Emergency Relief Administration) director in Arkansas during the Roosevelt administration and designer of the Dyess Colony, died in an airplane crash near Goodwin (St. Francis County) that is considered the worst plane crash in Arkansas history?

The American Airlines DC-2 flight from Washington, D.C., to Los Angeles crashed January 14, 1936. The airplane was called the *Southerner*. Farmers in the area claim to have seen the plane fly over and then disappear into the fog-filled woods. Eventually, they heard the deadly crash.

Upon discovery, the scene was reported as being gruesome, with a great deal of wreckage tossed about. There was never any proven cause for the crash. Many believe a passenger attempted to hijack the plane, which would make it the first recorded hijacking of an American aircraft. No evidence was ever found to validate these claims, and the true cause remains unknown.

▲ H. L. Mitchell.

crisis called for bold action. H. L. Mitchell was a former sharecropper who owned a dry-cleaning shop, and H. Clay East ran a service station. They had read socialist literature and also knew about the work of labor unions. With their help,

I Am an Arkansan

Louise Thaden (1905–1979)

Louise Thaden was an Arkansas-born pilot who established several flight records during the late 1920s and 1930s. Along with Amelia Earhart, she was one of the most famous female aviators in the country.

She was born Louise McPhetridge in Bentonville (Benton County) on November 12, 1905. Raised on a farm, she became interested in aviation after riding in a barnstorming plane. She briefly studied at the University of Arkansas, but left school in 1925 to take a job in Wichita, Kansas, selling oil, fuel, and lumber. Through her sales work, she traveled around Wichita and ended up spending much of her time around the local airplane factory. Soon she had a job as a salesperson with an airplane dealership in Oakland, California. In addition to her salary, free pilot's lessons were included.

In 1928, she earned her pilot's license, signed by Orville Wright of the Wright Brothers. She eventually became the first and only pilot to hold the women's altitude, solo endurance, and speed records simultaneously. Thaden retired from competition in 1938 to spend more time with her two children and to write her memoir, *High, Wide and Frightened*, detailing her successful aviation records. She also wrote

numerous newspaper and magazine articles dealing with various aviation issues, and continued to be active in several aviation organizations. She also helped establish the Arkansas Aviation Hall of Fame in Little Rock.

The airfield in Bentonville bears her name, and in 1976, Gov. David Pryor proclaimed August 22 of that year to be "Louise Thaden Day." She died in North Carolina in 1979.

THE ENCYCLOPEDIA OF ARKANSAS HISTORY & CULTURE

Log on to Learn More
http://www.encyclopediaofarkansas.net/

a small group of sharecroppers, black and white alike, formed a union in 1934. They called it the Southern Tenant Farmers' Union (STFU). Their goals included: 1) getting a fair share of the government payments, 2) higher wages for hired hands, and 3) a better deal for tenants. Within three years, the union had more than eleven thousand members, mostly in the five counties of the northeast Arkansas Delta.

The union was despised, harassed, and accused of being led by communists from outside the state. Those who feared or opposed the union fired rifles into their meeting halls. But the union's actions caused the nation to focus on the plight of the sharecropper. The very idea of a mixed black and white union caused a great uproar. Writers came to visit the state, and filmmakers produced a movie about the union.

The STFU inspired President Roosevelt to create the Farm Security Administration (FSA). This agency aimed at moving displaced farmers onto new lands. One model the FSA used was a program that had been tried in Arkansas. W. R. Dyess, the state's FERA chief and a plantation owner in Mississippi County, had used FERA funds to create an ideal farm community for Arkansas's relief clients. Called the Dyess Colony, it was west of Wilson (Mississippi County).

The Dyess Colony divided sixteen thousand acres into five hundred farmsteads for three thousand white Arkansans. The colony was a new town with a post office, cafe, stores, school, barbershop, furniture store, icehouse, printer, hospital, co-op, and cotton gin. The town was designed in the shape of a wagon wheel, and 1,300 unemployed laborers were brought in to build it.

White farmers who were already receiving aid from government agencies could apply to live in one of the five-room clapboard houses with two porches and a chicken coop. Applicants

▲ An active member of the Southern Tenant Farmers Union, this Arkansas sharecropper and his family were evicted from their homes.

▲ Dyess Colony house.

were interviewed and had to demonstrate good moral character. The colony was communal, meaning seed was bought and shared and all profits from the sale of crops and from the businesses were shared. The planned community interested the national media, and First Lady Eleanor Roosevelt visited the area and spoke to residents in 1936.

The FSA formed additional farm colonies, some of which included Lake Dick (Jefferson County), Trumann (Poinsett County), and Clover Bend (Lawrence County). Fifty thousand Arkansas farmers received loans to acquire farms and homes. The FSA program helped many move from being tenants to owning their own land.

cooperative or **co-op** (koh-AHP-er-uh-tiv, KOH-ahp) a business that is owned cooperatively by producers (such as farmers who collectively sell their produce) or consumers (homeowners who collectively buy their electricity).

Hard Times—The Great Depression

I Am an Arkansan

Maya Angelou (1928–)

An internationally famous poet, Maya Angelou was born in St. Louis, Missouri, but grew up in Stamps, Arkansas. As a child, she also spent time in San Francisco, California. She became a writer and poet as a young girl, and in her twenties, she performed as a nightclub singer at a club called the Purple Onion in California. After moving to New York City in 1960, she married a civil-rights activist, and the couple eventually moved to Cairo, Egypt. There, Angelou became an editor and writer. She also learned several African languages and developed a friendship with civil-rights leader Malcolm X.

Encouraged by the writer James Baldwin, Angelou began to compose her autobiography, *I Know Why the Caged Bird Sings.* Published in 1970, it became an international bestseller. In 1972, her movie script *Georgia, Georgia* was the first screenplay written by an African American to be made into a major motion picture. She was nominated for an Emmy award for her performance in the popular television miniseries *Roots.* Since 1981, she

has been a professor of literature at Wake Forest University in North Carolina. She has appeared on programs such as the *Oprah Winfrey Show*, and has continued to be an activist for better race relations in America. Her poems were featured in the 1993 Janet Jackson movie *Poetic Justice*, and she also read her poem, "On the Pulse of Morning," at President Bill Clinton's 1993 presidential inauguration.

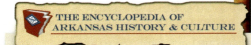

THE ENCYCLOPEDIA OF ARKANSAS HISTORY & CULTURE

Log on to Learn More
http://www.encyclopediaofarkansas.net/

---

commodity (kum-MAHD-it-ee) a product of value that can be bought, sold, or traded, like oranges, televisions, tractors, or clothing.

conservation (KAHN-ser-VAY-shun) saving something, such as farm soil through contour plowing, windbreaks, and rotating crops.

erosion (ee-ROH-zhun) the wearing away of soil through the action of wind and water.

In the late 1930s, still more federal programs helped reshape Arkansas. Loan programs like the **Commodity** Credit Corporation became the basic source of funds for farmers. A Soil **Conservation** Service taught farmers ways to protect the land against soil **erosion**. The Rural Electrification Administration (REA) gave low-interest loans to local groups to bring electric lines, and later phone lines, to even the most remote rural areas. Before the REA, fewer than 10 percent of Arkansas farms had electric power. The federal government was instrumental in bringing modern changes to Arkansas's rural landscape.

The State Government and the New Deal

While the U.S. government was putting massive amounts of money into Arkansas, the state itself was giving very little. When Arkansas teachers were added to the FERA relief rolls, the state's response was to cut back its share of school spending. Then, the U.S. government threatened to withdraw federal relief funds if the state did not share at least part of the costs.

In the end, Governor Futrell asked the General Assembly to create a Department of Public Welfare and to raise new taxes. In 1935, Arkansas once again made the sale of liquor legal and put a tax on it. The government also legalized betting on dog races in West Memphis and horse races in Hot Springs, and taxed the money gambled. The state imposed its first sales tax, a 2 percent tax on most consumer goods except for food and medicine.

By the late 1930s, the New Deal was having an impact on state politics. Some felt the New Deal had gone too far. Local political leaders feared the power of the national government. White racists feared the power that government programs might be giving blacks. But other whites became **liberals** who gave support to the New Deal programs and the concepts behind them. During the New Deal, much like during the aftermath of the 1927 flood, there was a continued political shift of African Americans from the Republican Party of Abraham Lincoln to the Democratic Party of Franklin D. Roosevelt, because of the aid and recognition the programs provided them. This pattern would continue and establish itself as the standard throughout the twentieth and twenty-first centuries.

By 1939, $474,986,972 had been spent on New Deal programs in Arkansas. The government had also loaned $244,767,279 to Arkansans. Arkansas had not fully emerged from the Great Depression, nor was the state close to national standards in most areas. But the relief programs had allowed many Arkansans to survive a time of grave crisis. They were better off than they had been in 1928, before the Depression. The long-term reforms, from the farm programs to Social Security, promised a better future for all.

The relationship of the people of Arkansas to the U.S. government would never be the same. Also, Arkansas's state government had taken steps to respond to the needs of all the people in a way it never had before. Against this background, Arkansans would face another crisis: the world was once again headed toward war.

liberals people who subscribe to a political ideology promoting more even distribution of wealth and resources and protection of personal liberties.

DID YOU KNOW?

Hot Springs Gangsters and Gambling

Did you know that in addition to betting on horse racing becoming legal in the 1930s, Hot Springs was a popular hangout for gangsters?

Of the many gaming houses in the resort town, some of the most popular were the Indiana Club, the Arkansas Club, and the Southern Club. Visitors placed bets, played cards, and drank in an upscale environment. During this time, gangster boss Alphonse "Al" Capone was frequently seen at the Southern Club playing poker or staying at the nearby Arlington Hotel.

Owney Madden was a well-known character of the "underworld" who permanently relocated to Hot Springs in the 1930s after having to leave New York City under questionable circumstances. It is rumored that he ran a "bookie" operation in Hot Springs and provided betting information to his many mafia contacts. Some, such as Charles "Lucky" Luciano and Meyer Lansky, visited him and his wife from time to time in Hot Springs.

THE ENCYCLOPEDIA OF ARKANSAS HISTORY & CULTURE

Log on to Learn More
http://www.encyclopediaofarkansas.net/

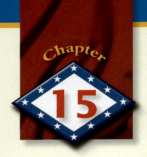

Chapter Reflection

Reflective Questions

1. Determine two specific causes and two results or consequences of the flood of 1927.

2. Discuss three specific reasons why the flood was considered the largest natural disaster to impact Arkansas.

3. Compare and contrast the flood to the New Madrid earthquake (chapter 7). Consider population, time period, economy, causes, and geography when constructing your answer.

4. Compare and contrast the flood to Hurricane Katrina or the terrorist attacks of September 11, 2001. Consider population, time period, economy, causes, and geography when constructing your answer.

5. What were the issues of concern for Arkansans during the Progressive Era that continued to be of concern in the 1920s and 1930s? Why?

6. Nationally, about 25 percent of Americans were out of work during the Depression. Re-read the "Plight of Arkansas" section in this chapter to figure the percentage in Arkansas. Why might there be a difference in the national and state rates of unemployment?

7. What was the effect of the Depression on Arkansas's schools?

8. In your opinion, what are the two New Deal relief agencies that most benefited Arkansas? Why?

9. Identify two facts about Louise Thaden.

Vocab en Verse

Create an original poem using any four words from the "Guides to Reading." Your poem must be in verse form, or have stanzas, or a rhythm, and the term must be used correctly. That means you must know and understand the meaning of the word to use it correctly in your poem. Your poem should have a title and can rhyme, but it is not required.

Organization and Visualization

Beginning with the flood of 1927, put the following events in correct chronological order and write the year in which they occurred on a mini-timeline. There will be seven events.

a. Hattie Caraway is the first elected female senator
b. the drought
c. Britain and France declare war on Germany
d. the election of Franklin Delano Roosevelt
e. the Dust Bowl
f. the 1929 stock market crash
g. Louise Thaden received her pilot's license

Who, What, When, Where, Why, and How?

Identify the five terms below by establishing the who, what, when, where, why, and how of each. Copy the term on your paper, then below the term, write the five Ws and one H. An example has been done for you.

Example:

University of Arkansas

- **who** — the U.S. government
- **what** — established a university
- **when** — 1862–71
- **where** — Fayetteville
- **why** — to help Arkansas's citizens by providing better educational opportunities
- **how** — the Morrill Land Grant Act

1. Arkies
2. Hundred Days
3. New Deal
4. parity
5. socialist

Make it Match!

On your own paper, number 1 through 5 and write the correct letter beside the corresponding number.

1. What factors combined to create hardship and financial depression for Arkansans in the 1930s?
   a. an earthquake, the stock market crash, and the Civil War
   b. New Deal programs, taxes, and poor roads
   c. flood, drought, and the stock market crash
   d. the building of the Dyess Colony, the election of Hattie Caraway, and the stock market crash

2. Commonwealth College _____.
   a. was owned by gypsies
   b. is still enrolling students today
   c. burned to the ground
   d. was in Mena

3. The Dyess Colony was begun by _____.
   a. Franklin Delano Roosevelt
   b. J. R. Cash
   c. W. R. Dyess
   d. John Fitzgerald Kennedy

4. The purpose of the Dyess Colony was to provide new opportunities for _____.
   a. African Americans
   b. farmers
   c. women
   d. American Indians

5. The overall goal of the Southern Tenant Farmers' Union was _____.
   a. better conditions for tenant farmers
   b. to be super, terrific, fun undertakers
   c. ending prohibition
   d. women's suffrage

UNIT 6

Chapter 16
World War II and the Postwar World, 1940–1954

Chapter 17
From Fulbright to Faubus—Representation and Circumstance, 1942–1966

Mid-Twentieth–Century Arkansas: The Great War, Recovery, and Prosperity
1940–1966

▶ The newsroom of the *Arkansas Democrat*, Little Rock, 1940s.

Chapter 16

World War II and the Postwar World
1940–1954

▶ Women who worked in factories during World War II, often called "Rosie the Riveters," hold the American flag.

▼ African American soldiers returning from war.

Timeline

	1940	1942	1945
Arkansas	**1940** At this time, only 8.7 percent of Arkansans are graduating high school.	**1942** Internment camps for Japanese Americans are set up in Rohwer and Jerome.	
United States		**1941** The Japanese attack Pearl Harbor, Hawaii, on December 7, and the United States enters World War II. **1941** Orson Welles directs the Academy Award–winning film Citizen Kane.	**1944** *Smith v. Allwright* strikes down the all-white primary. **1944** Franklin Delano Roosevelt wins a fourth consecutive term. **1944** Anne Frank and her family are captured by Nazis and sent to concentration camps.
World		**1944** Two crucial World War II battles, the Battle of the Bulge (Belgium) and D-Day (Normandy, France), are fought, both of which were Allied victories.	**1945** Germany surrenders. America drops atomic bombs on Hiroshima and Nagasaki, Japan, causing Japan to surrender.

Why Do We Study This?

The period 1940 to 1954 began with another war, World War II. The war started in Asia in 1937 and in Europe in 1939, but the United States did not join until the Japanese attacked Pearl Harbor in 1941. The United States—along with Great Britain, the Soviet Union, and others—was at war against Germany, Italy, and Japan.

Arkansans—black and white, men and women—served in the armed forces, many with distinction. The war to defend democracy abroad focused attention on some of America's own inequalities. African Americans in Arkansas and in the United States made some gains in civil rights, but the long fight ahead would be filled with heartbreak and violence.

It was a time of contradictions. People feared the war, possible death, and communism, but lived in a time of new industry, changing roles for women, and a booming economy. They were hoping for happy returns from war and began to enjoy new suburban development, automobiles, new music styles, and opportunity. These experiences would stay in people's minds and dramatically affect their behaviors and decisions about the challenging issues of the future.

Big Picture Questions

- Could we ever, or do we now, have another Hitler-type leader in our world? If so, whom? If no, why not? Give examples of what might cause someone to behave in a similar manner today.

- The Jewish people were a primary "target group" of Hitler. What are other "targeted groups" in modern times? Why are the targeted groups the ones who are selected to be mistreated? What are ways in which situations like these could be changed?

- Historically, women and African Americans have been subjected to exclusion and unfair treatment in a variety of American settings and situations. Why? Is this still true today? Why or why not? If so, how? If no, what progress has been made?

- In your opinion, is it the responsibility of the United States to participate in wars abroad even if they do not directly involve our nation or people? Why or why not? Does our nation's role in foreign conflicts have an impact on resources and efforts typically used to correct our internal problems? If so, how? If no, why not?

1950

1952

1954

1953 The first Arkansas television station, KRTV, a low-frequency station in Little Rock, is established.

1954 Fayetteville High School (Washington County) enrolls nine black students; Charleston schools (Franklin County) are desegregated. High-frequency television station KARK in Little Rock is established. It is still the NBC affiliate today.

1948 President Truman issues an executive order banning segregation in the armed forces.

1949 William Faulkner wins the Nobel Prize for literature.

1954 The U.S. Supreme Court declares school segregation unconstitutional in *Brown v. the Board of Education of Topeka.*

1954 Jonas Salk introduces the polio vaccine.

1953 Queen Elizabeth II is crowned in England.

World War II and the Postwar World

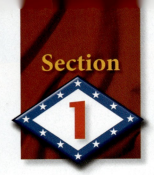

Section 1

War and Peace

Guide to Reading

Terms

Allied powers or Allies
Axis Powers
Blitzkrieg
Congressional Medal of Honor
fascism
Four Freedoms
heinous
infamy
National Socialist Party
Ranger battalions
rationed
Selective Service Act
victory gardens
war bonds

People

Aryans
Maurice "Footsie" Britt
William Darby
Führer
gypsies
Adolf Hitler
Samuel H. Marett
Pierce McKennon

Places

concentration camps

---

fascism (FASH-izm) political belief in one's nation and race as superior to all others and upholding highly-centralized government under an all-powerful dictator; extreme national pride with strong central control.

Adolf Hitler leader of Germany (1933–45) who started the National Socialist Party. He committed heinous acts against Jews and others during the Holocaust.

National Socialist Party Hitler's fascist party, also known as the Nazi Party.

Aryans (AIR-ee-unz) blond, blue-eyed Germans who, according to Hitler, were a superior "race" of people destined to rule the world.

Führer (FYUR-er) the title assumed by Hitler as all-powerful ruler of Nazi Germany, meaning "the Leader."

As the 1940s began, events in Europe and Asia were moving toward global war. For the second time in the twentieth century, warfare would change the face of the world. Arkansas would change along with it.

Germany and Italy had turned to **fascism**. Although Italy first came under the control of Benito Mussolini's Fascist Party early in the 1920s, Germany would become a more deadly threat. There, **Adolf Hitler** played an important role in the formation of the **National Socialist Party**. Part of Hitler's message to the German people was that they had been tricked into signing the World War I peace treaty and denied their rightful place as rulers of the world. He blamed Germany's economic troubles and other problems on the Jewish people. Because the Germans were the pure master race of **Aryans**, Hitler said, they could do as they wished with the Jews.

In 1933, the year Franklin D. Roosevelt became president of the United States, German leaders named Hitler chancellor. In 1934, Hitler declared himself supreme ruler for life, the *Führer*, of what he called the German Empire. Hitler began building for war. He built a huge and modern German military with guns, tanks, and airplanes as well as soldiers.

Within Germany, the Nazis, as the National Socialists were known, began to severely mistreat the Jews and

▲ The swastika was a symbol of Hitler's National Socialist Party.

348 Chapter 16

I Am an Arkansan

Douglas MacArthur (1880–1964)

Douglas MacArthur was an American general who led U.S. forces in the Pacific theater during World War II. During his long career, he served in three wars: World War I, World War II, and the Korean War. He also led the occupation of Japan from 1945 to 1951 after World War II, drawing praise and criticism for his work there. During the Korean War, he was relieved of duty by President Harry S. Truman in 1951 for disobeying the president's orders.

MacArthur was born on a military base in Little Rock (Pulaski County) in 1880, the son of a U.S. Army lieutenant general. His father, Gen. Arthur MacArthur, had received the Medal of Honor for his service in the Union army during the Civil War. Douglas MacArthur later denied his Arkansas roots, instead claiming Virginia as his home state. Indeed, his time in Arkansas was brief, as his father was transferred out of state when Douglas was just a year old.

MacArthur remains one of the most controversial figures in American history. After being harshly criticized by many after his disobedience to President Truman, MacArthur made a famous farewell speech before Congress, in which he remarked, "old soldiers never die, they just fade away."

---

stripped them of their legal rights. Hitler allied Germany with Mussolini's Italy. The two rulers planned to aid each other in conquest and to share the rewards. The rest of the world, preoccupied with a global economic depression and memories of World War I, watched as if in a daze as Hitler moved closer to war.

Meanwhile, in Asia, the leaders of Japan were on the same course toward war. Japan was the only major nation in Asia to achieve modern levels of industrial development, and it intended to rule the entire Pacific area. By the 1930s, Japan, under its emperor, had been taken over by military leaders. They intended to use force if needed to take what they wanted.

The Axis Powers

Germany, Italy, and Japan joined forces as the **Axis powers**. They had little in common except the desire to dominate at all costs. In 1935, Italy attacked Ethiopia in Africa, and Japan took over nearby nations, including Korea and Manchuria. In 1937, Japan attacked China.

Axis powers (AKS-iss POW-erz) the combined forces of Nazi Germany, fascist Italy, and imperial Japan during World War II.

World War II and the Postwar World **349**

Blitzkrieg (BLITS-kreeg) the German army's "lightning war" that quickly crushed European defenses at the beginning of World War II using infantry and tanks supported by airplanes and artillery.

heinous (HAY-nuss) hatefully, shockingly evil.

concentration camps places where people were gathered for slave labor, containment, or to be killed.

gypsies (JIP-seez) nomadic people, originally from India, who live all over the world.

Selective Service Act the law that reestablished the draft, requiring young men to serve in the armed forces.

Four Freedoms according to President Roosevelt, the freedoms of speech and worship, and freedoms from want and fear.

In 1938, Hitler issued a demand for part of Czechoslovakia. The leaders of Britain and France met with Hitler in Munich, Germany. They took Hitler at his word when he promised that he wanted only a small part of Czechoslovakia. Instead, Hitler took over the whole country. Next, he wanted Poland. This would be the threat that would drive Britain and France to fight.

World War II in Europe began in September of 1939 as German forces drove into Poland. Britain and France declared war against Germany and Italy, but there was little fighting until the spring of 1940. Hitler struck quickly in Denmark and Norway, then in Belgium, the Netherlands, and France. All of these nations fell before the *Blitzkrieg* of the new German army.

By June of 1940, France fell to Germany, leaving Britain alone in the fight against Hitler and Mussolini. Hitler attacked the Soviet Union in June of 1941, which broke a peace agreement between Russia and Germany. The Russians would now fight in the war on the side of Britain.

Hitler's army was only part of the threat he posed to the world. His mad belief in the supreme rule of Aryans led to **heinous** crimes. Hitler threw Jewish men, women, and children into **concentration camps**. Also, people with mental or physical disabilities, **gypsies**, and any leaders who opposed the Nazis were herded into the camps. Millions were killed during the war, worked to death, or murdered outright in gas chambers or by firing squads.

Even after war started abroad, most Americans did not want to get involved. Many had convinced themselves that the United States fighting in World War I had been a mistake. However, the rise of the Axis Powers did convince President Roosevelt and Congress to strengthen American armed forces. In 1940, Congress passed (for one year only) the **Selective Service Act** to draft young men into the armed forces. President Roosevelt said the war against Germany was an important and critical struggle to defend the **Four Freedoms**.

As happened during World War I, some Americans came to hate anything that had a German influence. At least one German immigrant, Frank Lewis of Danville (Yell County), was killed for trying to defend himself as a German, not a Nazi. As much as they disliked the Germans and the Japanese, most people in Arkansas still opposed American entry into the war, but this would soon change.

The United States Enters the War

America's sense of distance from world events was shattered on December 7, 1941. Early that Sunday morning (it was mid-afternoon in Arkansas), Japanese airplanes

Boone

Named after: Kentuckian explorer Daniel Boone

Chief Source of Income: Manufacturing

Seat: Harrison

Boone County was formed in 1869, and for many years was the center of zinc, lead, and other mineral mining operations in the state. Its rugged terrain prevented the establishment of plantation agriculture. Today, most money in the county comes from manufacturing. Harrison is home to North Arkansas College and the headquarters for the Buffalo National River. In the 1980s and 1990s, Harrison became known to people across the U.S. because the Grand Wizard of the Ku Klux Klan lived there.

bombed the American fleet at Pearl Harbor in the Hawaiian Islands. The surprise attack was a direct blow against American ships and men on American soil. The attack resulted in tremendous losses. Nearly one-third of the Pacific Fleet was destroyed or badly damaged. President Roosevelt asked Congress to declare war against Japan.

The next day, Arkansas schoolchildren listened to radios in their classrooms as President Roosevelt spoke. He described the attack as "a day that will live in **infamy**." A few days later, Germany and Italy declared war on the United States. Americans were once again at war. The United States joined the **Allied powers** with Britain. World War II would last until 1945 and would take fifty million lives worldwide.

Arkansans Serving in World War II

Young men in Arkansas rushed to sign up for the war effort. In Lepanto (Poinsett County), the entire high-school football team volunteered for the Navy. Before the war was over, two hundred thousand Arkansans—more than 10 percent of the state's people—served in the nation's armed forces. Thirty-five percent of would-be Arkansan recruits had severe health problems ranging from chronic malaria to malnutrition. Others could not read and write well enough to meet the Army's standards. Black Arkansans joined in large numbers, although the armed forces still put them in all-black units with white officers. Women also served in all branches of the armed forces.

Arkansas troops battled in both the European and the Pacific theaters. Some individuals who saw action

DID YOU KNOW?

Bravery "Above and Beyond the Call of Duty": Footsie Britt and the Medal of Honor.

Did you know one of our lieutenant governors was a war hero?

Maurice L. Britt was born in Carlisle, but he grew up in Lonoke (both in Lonoke County), where his family moved when he was very young. When he was a boy, he was delighted to win a pair of shoes in a contest, then dismayed to discover they were baby shoes. His friends called him "Footsie" from then on.

At the University of Arkansas, Britt majored in journalism and lettered in basketball and football. After graduation, he briefly played professional football for the Detroit Lions. But the United States was at war by then, so Britt went into the army as a lieutenant.

From bases in North Africa, Britt's unit went with the American and British forces that invaded the island of Sicily and mainland Italy in 1943. The Italian government surrendered almost immediately, but German forces dug in.

Britt was in tough fighting to take Naples. There he earned the Silver Star for bravery and the Purple Heart for being wounded.

Then, at Mount Rotundo, about one hundred German soldiers moved into the area. With eight men, Britt attacked the Germans. With rifles and hand grenades, Britt and his men killed thirty-five Germans. Britt was wounded again, but he held ground until other American forces moved in and he was ordered to get medical aid.

For that action, the British awarded him the Military Cross and the Americans awarded him the Congressional Medal of Honor, our nation's highest decoration for bravery in combat "above and beyond the call of duty."

Britt went on to do more fighting, including one engagement in which he lost his arm. He later became lieutenant governor of Arkansas in the administration of Gov. Winthrop Rockefeller.

infamy (IN-fuhm-ee) a reputation brought about by grossly criminal, shocking, or brutal acts.

Allied Powers Great Britain, the U.S., France, China, Russia, and others allied against the Axis powers in World War II.

World War II and the Postwar World 351

Samuel H. Marett the leader of a squadron of fighter-bombers against the Japanese. He died when he flew his airplane into a Japanese ship.

Pierce McKennon a famous flying ace from Arkansas who shot down more than twenty enemy airplanes in World War II.

William Darby a captain in World War II whose Rangers used tactics such as "hit and run" and night raids to conquer enemies. He died in 1945 in combat and was awarded the rank of brigadier general after his death. A movie was made about his military service.

Ranger battalions special forces formed during World War II by Col. William Darby, also known as "Darby's Rangers."

Maurice L. "Footsie" Britt an Arkansas World War II hero who later would become Arkansas's lieutenant governor.

Congressional Medal of Honor the highest award given in the United States for military valor.

war bonds a kind of citizen loan to the United States government to help pay for the war effort.

victory gardens home vegetable gardens promoted to boost American agricultural output for the war effort.

rationed (RASH-uhned) distributed on a limited basis as a way to share limited supplies fairly among the people. During the war, people could buy only a small amount of things that were rationed each month.

▲ Winthrop Rockefeller (far left, future governor of Arkansas) and other World War II soldiers waiting at the railroad station to depart for the war.

included Lt. **Samuel H. Marett**, a pilot from Little Rock, who fought in defense of the Philippine Islands. Maj. **Pierce McKennon** of Clarksville (Johnson County) was a flying ace who shot down more than twenty enemy planes. Col. **William Darby** of Fort Smith helped create the Army **Ranger battalions**. Capt. **Maurice L. "Footsie" Britt** of Carlisle (Lonoke County) earned the **Congressional Medal of Honor** for his brave deeds.

Families who sent sons and husbands to war put a white banner with a single star on it in their windows. A gold star meant the loved one had been killed. During the four years of war, 4,611 Arkansans died. Of those, 3,814 were in the Army or the Army Air Corps (then a part of the Army) and 797 were in the Navy or Marine Corps.

At home, Arkansans joined in the war effort any way they could. One way was to buy **war bonds**. Schoolchildren bought bonds at the rate of twenty-five cents a stamp until they had enough for a twenty-five-dollar bond. Children also helped collect scrap metal and rubber to be made into weapons. Women, like the all-black MacArthur Knitting Club of Pulaski County, went home from ten- to twelve-hour days at work to knit sweaters for soldiers.

Families planted **victory gardens** to help raise enough food to see the country through the war. Coffee, tea, sugar, meat, gas, and tires were in short supply and were **rationed**.

Question

How many stamps would it take to buy a twenty-five-dollar bond?

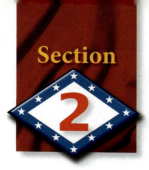

Section 2

Economy and Equality

Guide to Reading

Terms
boosters
Executive Order 8802
fuses
graven
interned
munitions
primer
rivet
tractorette

Events
Holocaust
Smith v. Allwright

People
Jehovah's Witnesses
Thurgood Marshall
Susie Morris
Nisei
Rosie the Riveter

Places
internment camps
Jerome
relocation centers
Rohwer

Wartime Economy and Education

The all-out war effort required new factories and new army bases. Arkansas's share of war industries was less than 2 percent of the national total, but that was enough to have a major effect on the state.

Arkansas had been a major source of bauxite, the raw ore for aluminum, for decades. The lightweight metal was used for the outer skin of many airplanes. During the war years, bauxite mining increased substantially. The government built new plants in Jones Mills (Hot Spring County) and Hurricane Creek (Franklin County) and leased them to the Aluminum Company of America (ALCOA) to run.

Producing aluminum requires huge amounts of electric power. Arkansas's own energy sources could not keep up with the new plants. The government helped build dams to produce more power at Blue Mountain (Logan County), Lake Catherine (Hot Spring County), and Norfork Lake (Baxter County). Even then, almost 70 percent of the electric power had to be imported from other states. Major defense plants were built in Camden (Ouachita County), Jacksonville (Pulaski County), Maumelle (Pulaski County), and Pine Bluff (Jefferson County). These all made some form of arms, bombs, or chemicals for the war effort. At Hope, the army carved a huge testing range out of the farmland. It even had its own airport.

Camp Robinson in North Little Rock became a training camp for soldiers, as it had been in World War I. The United States had begun building

County Quest

Grant

Named after: *President Ulysses S. Grant*

Chief Source of Income: *Manufacturing*

Seat: *Sheridan*

Grant County was established in 1869. The county has lush territory for hunting and trapping, and has drawn visitors since the 1840s. Jenkins's Ferry Civil War Battlefield State Park is in the county and there is an annual Timberfest held each year that includes a widely-attended lumberjack competition.

World War II and the Postwar World **353**

I Am an Arkansan

Hazel Walker (1914–1990)

Hazel Walker was a female basketball player born in Arkansas and is considered to be one of the greatest female players of all time. She grew up in the small community of Oak Hill (Little River County) near Ashdown.

She played for several seasons on the popular women's barnstorming team, the All-American Red Heads (barnstormers were generally baseball and basketball teams that traveled around playing local teams).

On the Red Heads, Walker quickly displayed her talents, but after three seasons, went out on her own to form the barnstorming basketball team Hazel Walker's Arkansas Travelers. The team played most nights of the week and won the majority of its games, even defeating teams that were all-male.

For sixteen seasons, Hazel Walker acted as player-coach until her retirement in 1965. In 2001, she was elected to the Women's Basketball Hall of Fame.

Camp Chaffee, near Fort Smith (Sebastian County), just before Pearl Harbor. After the United States entered the war, it was enlarged to train soldiers by the thousands. Other army bases were in Blytheville (Mississippi County), Newport (Jackson County), Stuttgart (Arkansas County), and Walnut Ridge (Lawrence County). Defense plants in Arkansas hired almost 28,000 people, 6 percent of the state's population. Cities near the defense plants and bases quickly increased in size. Little Rock grew by 25,000 people in six months during 1940. Hope grew from 7,475 in 1940 to 15,475 by the end of 1941. There were not enough houses to go around, and sometimes people had to live in tents, garages, or warehouses.

Every public-service unit, from school systems to fire departments, had to do more work with fewer people. Workers were leaving in droves to take jobs with the better-paying defense plants. This problem was particularly difficult for southern schools to deal with. Half of the prewar teaching staff left the schools by 1945. More students flocked to city school districts. At one point during the war, almost 60 percent of Arkansas's teens

County Quest

Logan

Named after: James Logan, an early settler

Chief Source of Income: Manufacturing

Seat: Booneville, Paris

Logan County was created in 1871 and, until 1875, was called Sarber County. The county boasts Arkansas's tallest mountain, Mount Magazine. Major League baseball players Jay Hanna "Dizzy" Dean and Paul Dean were from the area and Elizabeth Ward Gracen, Miss America 1982, is also a native of the county, hailing from Booneville.

354 Chapter 16

Selected Census Data for Arkansas 1940 to 1950

	1940	1950
Total population	1,949,511	1,909,511
White population	1,466,084	1,481,507
Black population	482,578	426,639
Total urban population	431,910	630,591
Percent urban population	22.2	33
Number of farms	216,674	182,429
Average acres per farm	83.3	103.4
Value of farms	$456,848,156	$1,135,671,000
Cotton bales produced	1,351,209	1,584,307
Bushels of corn produced	33,762,323	21,626,026
Bushels of rice produced	7,651,231	19,889,614
		1954
Manufacturing establishments	1,178	2,428
Wage earners	36,256	79,052

Notes: The figures for black and white population for each year will not add up to the exact figure for the total population. The difference is the small number of other races in the population.

had dropped out of school because of the lack of teachers.

Congress proposed special help for the schools, but southern congressmen refused federal aid. They feared accepting federal money might threaten what they saw as the right to have segregated schools. The Arkansas General Assembly also considered a bill designed to raise the sales tax to give the schools more money, but the measure failed. Schools in Arkansas struggled, suffered, and changed during this period, as did farming and agriculture in our state.

The Changing Agricultural Economy

The Depression, New Deal, and World War II, along with new farm machines and techniques, made

▶ Many women worked in factories during World War II.

▶ Members of the Women's Army Corps, or WACs, arrive in Arkansas for training.

sweeping changes in the way Arkansans farmed.

The number of farmers all over the state, and across the country, dropped sharply during the war. There were 1,113,000 Arkansans living on farms in 1940, but only 595,000 by 1954. The New Deal farming programs were still in effect. They favored large land holdings and gave the large landowners enough money to buy new machines such as cotton pickers. The use of machines allowed fewer farmers to work more land. Most of the

I Am an Arkansan

Jay Hanna "Dizzy" Dean (1910–1974)

Born in Lucas (Logan County), "Dizzy" Dean was a major league baseball player and radio and television baseball broadcaster. He is a member of both the National Baseball Hall of Fame and the Arkansas Sports Hall of Fame. During the 1930s, he and his younger brother, Paul, pitched as part of the famous "Gas House Gang" of the St. Louis Cardinals. During the 1930s, "Dizzy" Dean was among the game's most popular players.

Dean became a star for St. Louis during the 1933 season. He won twenty games that year and, in one game, struck out seventeen batters. The next season, Dean won thirty games, making him the last National League pitcher to win thirty in a season. He went on to win two games for the Cardinals in the 1934 World Series, guiding the team to the championship. He also won the National League's most valuable player award, and was voted onto the all-star team.

After his baseball career ended in 1941, Dean became a radio and television broadcaster. His colorful, often grammatically-challenged speech made him a popular sports personality. His baseball stories became legendary among fans. In 1953, he was elected to the Baseball Hall of Fame, and he is remembered as one of baseball's best-loved players.

Along with Dean, many Arkansans have been famous baseball players, including George Kell, the Hall of Fame infielder for the Detroit Tigers; Lou Brock, the base-stealing star of the St. Louis Cardinals; and Brooks Robinson, the defensive whiz of the Baltimore Orioles. In recent years, Arkansans such as Torii Hunter (from Pine Bluff, Jefferson County) have become stars on the baseball diamond.

Log on to Learn More
http://www.encyclopediaofarkansas.net/

people who left the farm and the state were those who had been sharecroppers or tenants. Arkansas lost 10.9 percent of its population when people left to seek work. Arkansas lost one of its six seats in the U.S. Congress after the 1950 census, due to the population decrease.

With the trend of larger farms using modern machines came changes in the types of farming in the state. In the northern and western mountain regions of the state, small farms switched to raising cattle or poultry. In the Delta, soybeans began to replace cotton as the chief cash crop. Rice growing also increased greatly during the war years and after.

Women in Wartime

Another tremendous change brought by the war was the presence of women in the workforce; they replaced men who had joined the armed forces.

munitions (myoo-NISH-unz) weapons, ammunition.

fuses detonating devices used to set off bombs or torpedoes.

boosters devices that increase force, power, or pressure.

primer (PRY-mer) a percussion cap used to ignite an explosive charge.

rivet (RIH-vet) to join two pieces of metal together with a bolt; or the bolt so used.

▼ John Watson (left) of Little Rock served in the U.S. Army in Germany during World War II.

Women at work outside the home increased from 13.9 percent of American workers in 1940 (the same level as in 1910) to 31 percent. In Arkansas, where there were fewer defense plants, the number of women workers was only 20 percent of the total number of workers, but that was still a major increase.

The **munitions** plants sought wome as line workers making **fuses**, **boosters**, and **primers** for weapons. Women worked in machine shops. They were also called upon to operate radios, **rivet** aircraft, and do sheet-metal work, woodworking, and drafting.

Across the United States, **Rosie the Riveter** became the symbol of women in defense work. Arkansas women trained as aircraft riveters had to leave the state because there were no airplane plants here. Women also managed farms. The International Harvester Company sponsored a national "**tractorette**" training program for them.

Defense plants were not alone in hirng women for the workforce. Private businesses also had a labor shortage. Women for the first time became bank tellers, cab and bus drivers, and mechanics in auto repair shops.

Many women had gone through relocations, rapid changes in social roles, dress, and expectations, and war-forced separations from their families. Many achieved financial independence, public recognition, and new levels of self-esteem. All this changed their lives and changed the American family. When the war ended in 1945, most wartime women workers returned to their roles as housewives. But many had acquired a taste for wider options. Another minority group of American citizens continued to face tremendous change during wartime as well.

African Americans in Wartime

In the armed services, African Americans were very aware that they were fighting a war to secure freedoms for others that they did not enjoy at home. In the defense plants, they got the worst jobs and the lowest pay. African Americans began to demand their full rights as citizens. Leaders of the black community began to insist that President Roosevelt order tax-financed defense plants to hire and pay blacks on an equal basis with whites.

When Roosevelt hesitated, a great march on Washington was planned to display support for equal employment

◀ African American soldiers ride in a parade after returning from the war.

Rosie the Riveter the artistic rendering and nickname for women in the workplace, primarily munitions factories, during World War II. She empowered women to enter the workforce as part of their patriotic duty.

tractorette (TRACK-tor-ETT) a term coined by International Harvester to refer to farming women whom the corporation trained to use heavy machinery when able-bodied men were away at war.

Executive Order 8802 an order issued by President Roosevelt during World War II to ban discrimination in hiring by federal contractors.

and pay. It was promised that one hundred thousand people would go to Washington. The president, with the help of First Lady Eleanor Roosevelt, negotiated with black leaders and got the march canceled. In exchange, the president ordered a halt to unfair job practices in public programs throughout the nation.

President Roosevelt issued **Executive Order 8802**, which outlawed hiring on a racial basis in public job-training programs and in private industries that received government contracts. Roosevelt also formed a Fair Employment Practices Commission to make sure business firms followed the new rules.

Job options for African Americans began to improve dramatically. The wartime labor shortage helped to speed the hiring of African American workers. But Roosevelt's rules on hiring practices for private businesses set the pace for future civil rights laws. Ultimately, the plans for a civil rights march did not go to waste. The basic plan was revived in 1963 at the height of the civil rights movement when the Reverend Martin Luther King Jr. took part in a famous march on Washington, D.C.

County Quest

Nevada

Named after: The state of Nevada

Chief Source of Income: Manufacturing

Seat: Prescott

Established in 1871, Nevada County was named for the state of Nevada because of the somewhat similar shapes of the county and the state. Visitors can explore the Nevada County Depot Museum, learn about the Prairie DeAnn Battlefield, or attend the Annual Chicken and Egg Festival.

World War II and the Postwar World

While businesses began to integrate, the armed forces did not. All-black units assigned to Arkansas for training were made to follow the legally- sanctioned racial rules of the South, both on and off the army bases. For many African American soldiers from the North, it was their first taste of legal segregation.

In March of 1942, Sgt. Thomas B. Foster, a black soldier stationed at Camp Robinson, was shot and killed by a white police officer on Little Rock's Ninth Street. After this incident, Daisy and L. C. Bates's *Arkansas State Press,* Arkansas's only African American newspaper at the time, led a campaign for the hiring of African American police officers. Under pressure from the Press and the Negro Citizens Committee of Little Rock, the Little Rock City Council agreed to hire eight black patrolmen.

These first African American police officers could work only in the black areas of the city. They could not arrest whites without the help of a white officer, and they did not get the pensions other officers received. Still, their hiring was a major step forward, and it helped reduce tension between black soldiers and white police in the city.

African American leaders also made some gains in seeking equal pay for public schoolteachers. In 1941, white teachers in Arkansas earned $625 a year, compared to $367 for black teachers. After the U.S. Supreme Court ruled in favor of an African American teacher in Virginia, Arkansas lawyer Scipio A.

Jones filed a lawsuit in 1942 on behalf of Little Rock Dunbar High School's teacher **Susie Morris** to obtain equal pay. **Thurgood Marshall**, a lawyer with the National Association for the Advancement of Colored People, who would later become a U.S. Supreme Court justice, also helped in the case. This was at a time when 22 percent of white teachers in Arkansas had less than one year of college training. Morris had a degree from Talladega College in Alabama and excellent grades in master's level English courses from the University of Chicago. She had been teaching for seven years. The school board's defense in court was that "regardless of college degrees and teaching experience no white teacher in Little Rock is inferior to the best Negro teacher."

Shockingly, this shameful racist statement influenced Judge T. C. Trimble. He ruled in favor of the school board. But the U.S. Court of Appeals struck down his finding in 1945. Susie Morris won a major victory, but was immediately fired from her job. In the end, she was hired back, but not until 1952.

The "separate but equal" policy from the 1896 *Plessy v. Ferguson* Supreme Court decision was weakened in 1937 in a Supreme Court finding on rail travel. Arthur W. Mitchell was an African American Democratic member of the U.S. House of Representatives from Illinois. He was thrown off a Pullman rail car in Arkansas on the way from Chicago to Hot Springs. The court ruled in Mitchell's favor, despite many filings in defense of segregation from most southern states.

A major part of the struggle for racial justice involved the right to vote. In Arkansas, the main issue was the right to vote in the Democratic Party's all-white primary. The Democrat's candidate always won the election, because the Republican Party was still weak. A

Susie Morris a black teacher who sued the Little Rock School District for equal pay compared to white teachers and won in the U.S. Court of Appeals.

Thurgood Marshall a lawyer for the National Association for the Advancement of Colored People, he argued many significant cases including *Smith v. Allwright* and *Brown v. the Board of Education of Topeka*. He was also the first black U.S. Supreme Court justice.

▼ A group of Nisei perform a school musical at the Rohwer Camp. Explain why there are stars and an American flag hanging behind the children.

World War II and the Postwar World **361**

Smith v. Allwright a U.S. Supreme Court case that originated in Texas and ultimately outlawed the all-white Democratic primary.

Nisei (nee-SAY) second-generation Japanese Americans, who were U.S. citizens by birth.

interned imprisoned, detained, or held in custody.

relocation centers (ree-LOH-kay-shun SENN-terz) the term used to describe internment camps for Japanese Americans during World War II who were relocated by force from their homes into prison-like settings.

Texas case, *Smith v. Allwright*, challenged the all-white primary. In 1944, the Supreme Court ruled that the all-white primary vote was illegal. Arkansas's African Americans were able to vote in the primary in the summer of 1944. They also voted in the runoff and in the general elections.

The white-controlled Democratic Party of Arkansas rallied and imposed new rules for joining the party. Once again, African Americans were kept out because poll taxes were too expensive since blacks were typically paid lower wages than whites. The new rules called for holding two sets of elections, one for national races and one for state offices. That meant taxpayers had to pay poll taxes in four elections, two primaries and two general elections. The path to peace at the polls proved to be a long one for black Arkansans.

The Internment Camps and New Wartime Prejudices

The Japanese attack on Pearl Harbor shocked and surprised the people of the United States. Many Americans took out their anger on the Japanese people living in America. In 1941, thousands of Japanese Americans lived on the West Coast, many of them in California. They had begun moving to that area early in the 1900s. Most of those first to arrive were now U.S. citizens. Their children, called *Nisei*, were U.S. citizens by birth.

Through hard work and skill, many Japanese people in America had achieved success. But after Pearl Harbor, many of their neighbors turned against them. Many Americans feared a Japanese landing on the West Coast. Many also hated the Japanese Americans for racial reasons.

The fear and hatred of Japanese Americans grew so strong that President Roosevelt agreed to round up 117,000 of these citizens as a military measure. They were removed from the West Coast and transferred into the interior of the country. In the process, the Japanese Americans lost their homes, their businesses, and most of their possessions.

The majority of Japanese Americans had not committed any crimes or acts of disloyalty to their country. Yet they were herded onto trains and moved thousands of miles away from home. They were locked up and *interned* in quickly-built *relocation centers* or *internment camps*.

▼ A monument at Rohwer (Desha County) commemorates the internment of Japanese Americans there during World War II.

A Day in the Life

A Young Girl Arrives at the Rohwer Internment Camp

Many of the Japanese Americans who came to the camps in Arkansas were young. At Rohwer, for example, 40 percent of the Japanese Americans were under nineteen years old; 30 percent were school-aged children.

One young girl wrote in her diary about her arrival at the Rohwer camp by train from the West Coast. Her first memory was "seeing the points of the barbed wire fences with droplets of rain stuck on them." Then she wrote:

> It must have been after 1:30 A.M. when they finally decided to let us off the train—we wanted to sleep in the car—most of the children were asleep or grouchy for the need of it. We were herded off the cars—MP's [military policemen] grabbed our arms as we slipped into the soft mud....
>
> "Our home"—38-1-e. Fujinos to the right and the block office to the left. Ought to be quiet—unit looks good—and empty, also. An ugly black stove and a suggestion of clothes closet—shelves and rod very low. They must think we are midgets.
>
> Well, we were led into our quarters wading through mud.... We struggled with cots only to discover that one was torn and terribly underslung. Sneaked into the next unit and did a quick exchange job. Had to wait for blankets.

Quoted in Russell Bearden, "Life Inside Arkansas's Japanese-American Relocation Centers," Arkansas Historical Quarterly 48 (Summer 1989): 177.

The young people managed to act like American young people everywhere. At Rohwer, the teenage students had school officers, honor societies, clubs, a newspaper, and a yearbook. Athletic teams were organized for games between classes or between the two schools at the camp. In Rohwer and Jerome together, there were 256 weddings.

◀ Japanese American children (known as Nisei) arrive at the Rohwer Internment Camp.

internment camps (in-TURN-munt KAMPS) compounds established to confine enemies during wartime.

World War II and the Postwar World

▲ A group of German prisoners of war were held at Camp Chaffee (Sebastian County) during World War II. This picture was taken at the funeral of one of the prisoners.

Rohwer site of a relocation camp that housed sixteen thousand Japanese Americans during World War II. The cemetery there is now a national historic landmark (Desha County).

Jerome site of one of two Arkansas Japanese relocation centers during World War II, located about eight miles south of Dermott (Chicot County).

Two of the Japanese American centers were in southeast Arkansas. One was in **Rohwer** (Desha County) and the other was in **Jerome** (Chicot and Drew counties). Some Arkansans were not pleased to host the Japanese Americans and were hostile to them. However, a few churches, particularly the Methodist churches, offered a hand of welcome. Beginning in the summer of 1942, about eight thousand people lived in each center. Families were able to stay intact but were crowded into poorly constructed wooden buildings. The government supplied housing, food, schools, and medical care. The Japanese Americans worked hard at clearing land for farming. They raised much of their own food and ran small factories within the camps.

Japanese Americans were not allowed to leave the camps for any reason, partly for their own safety.

A United States soldier of Japanese descent from Camp Robinson, in uniform, was shot and badly wounded in a Dermott (Chicot County) cafe. He had been on his way to visit relatives at Rohwer. The United States Army recruited soldiers from the camps in Arkansas and other camps around the country. These Japanese American soldiers served with honor in the war in Europe.

Toward the war's end, Arkansas also housed German prisoners of war. About twenty-three thousand Germans and a few Italians were shipped to Arkansas. To make a place for them, the Japanese Americans were moved from the Jerome camp to Rohwer and to other states. Captured German and Italian soldiers were also housed at Camp Robinson (Pulaski County), Camp Chaffee (Sebastian County), and Dermott. There were smaller "branch camps" in the Delta and the Grand Prairie. During these days of farm labor shortages, Arkansas farmers used many of these men for extra labor.

When the war was over, the soldiers were sent back to Germany and Italy, and the Japanese Americans were freed. Almost all the Japanese Americans left Arkansas, never to return. Only a few remained to make their homes in Arkansas.

Forty years after the war, the United States offered a small payment and a formal apology to the Japanese Americans whose civil rights had been so abused during the war. But there was no way to truly make up the losses to those Japanese Americans, especially those who had spent their childhood or teenage years penned up in the camps.

Other Americans were denied their civil rights during the war years, among them **Jehovah's Witnesses**. This church group believed in the literal interpretation of the Bible's commands against killing and making "**graven**" images. As a result, they would not salute the flag or join the armed forces. This was viewed as being unpatriotic. As a result, they were abused all across the country and became the objects of vicious mob attacks.

The Jehovah's Witnesses of Arkansas attempted to meet in Little Rock in 1942. As they gathered, seven Witnesses were shot and others were beaten with lead pipes while a crowd stood by and cheered. When the police arrived, they arrested the Jehovah's Witnesses. The police even arrested those who were badly wounded, instead of those who had attacked them. A sixty-five-year-old lawyer, Oscar Winn, was badly beaten after he agreed to defend the Witnesses in court. It took direct action by President Roosevelt and two U.S. Supreme Court rulings to protect the Witnesses throughout the country and create some sense of peace.

The war ended in Europe in May of 1945 and in Japan that August. The end of the war revealed its true horrors. As American and Allied forces moved through Europe, they found the few who had survived the **Holocaust** of the Nazi death camps. They learned that around six million Jews had been killed in the name of the German master race. The war against Japan ended with the cities of Hiroshima and Nagasaki demolished by the world's first atomic bombs dropped by the United States. It is estimated that more than two hundred thousand Japanese died as a result of these attacks.

Jehovah's Witnesses (jeh-HOH-vuhz WIT-ness-ez) a fundamentalist religious group that was persecuted during World War II for its pacifist beliefs.

graven an idol or image of false worship.

Holocaust (HALL-uh-kawst) name later given to Hitler's "final solution" for the "Jewish problem," the execution of at least six million Jews and other "undesirables" in the Nazi extermination camps.

World War II and the Postwar World **365**

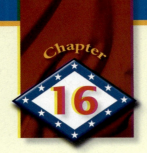

Chapter Reflection

Reflective Questions

1. Hitler blamed most of Germany's problems on _____.
   a. fascists
   b. Jewish people
   c. Aryans
   d. terrorists

2. The Axis powers consisted of _____, _____, and _____.
   a. Germany, Italy, and Britain
   b. Germany, Italy, and France
   c. Britain, the United States, and France
   d. Germany, Japan, and Italy

3. The Holocaust _____.
   a. led to the deaths of six million Jews and others
   b. did not occur
   c. was done without Hitler's knowledge
   d. occurred in Asia

4. The major effect of the war on women was _____.
   a. to have more children
   b. to picket and protest
   c. to move to Canada
   d. more opportunities and independence

5. Japanese Americans _____.
   a. had no relationship to Arkansas
   b. were treated the same as any other American-born citizens
   c. were interned in retention work camps
   d. were poverty-stricken

6. The introduction of new types of machinery to Arkansas farms _____.
   a. encouraged new agricultural products like poultry and cattle
   b. encouraged new farmers to move to Arkansas
   c. made indigo the new cash crop
   d. caused more injuries

7. List two civil rights accomplishments that happened during the war years.

8. Compare and contrast the trials and tribulations of the aftermath of December 7, 1941, and September 11, 2001.

9. In your opinion, what is the worst occurrence on American soil: the Revolutionary War, the Civil War, Pearl Harbor, or September 11, 2001? Explain why and support your choice with examples.

10. Considering the percentage of students who dropped out of Arkansas schools during the war, what can you infer (draw conclusions about) happened to many rural schools?

11. In your opinion, why was it dangerous for Japanese Americans to remain on the West Coast? Why were they moved to the interior of the country?

12. Was the American apology and payment forty years after the war enough for the Japanese Americans who were in the camps? Why or why not? What other suggestion would you make to the government to help it apologize?

Then and Now

Based on what you studied in this chapter, compare and contrast the typical Arkansas way of life in the World War II era with current times. Divide your paper into five columns and four rows. The first column will be labeled with the category name. The second category will be labeled *Then* and the third will be labeled *Now* and so on. A sample has been designed for you below.

Category Names	Then	Now	Then	Now
women's roles				
racism				
war and homefront support for war				
schools				

Who Says?

Distinguishing Between Fact and Opinion

On your paper, number 1–3. Carefully read each statement below and based on your studies, determine if it is a fact or an opinion. Write an *F* or *O* beside the corresponding number to indicate your choice.

1. ALCOA ran a bauxite processing plant in Jones Mills.
2. Arkansans on the homefront did nothing to help the war efforts.
3. Arkansas's "war heroes" were insignificant.

Picture It!

1. Carefully review all of the terms in the "Guide to Reading" from the chapter.
2. Choose four that were brand new to you or that you felt had the most interesting definitions.
3. Take a clean sheet of paper and draw one horizontal line all the way across the page and one vertical line, from top to bottom, to divide your paper into four equal parts.
4. In the first box, neatly print the first word you chose in the upper left-hand corner.
5. Use markers or colored pencils to illustrate the word.
6. Continue the process until you have labeled and illustrated all four words.

Be sure to include plenty of accurate detail in your drawing. Your illustration should result in a creative explanation of the meaning (definition) of the term.

World War II and the Postwar World

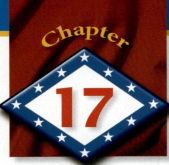

Chapter 17

From Fulbright to Faubus—Representation and Circumstance

1942–1966

▶ Sid McMath (center) smiles after winning the 1948 Arkansas governor's race.

Timeline

	1942		1945		1950
Arkansas	**1942** J. William Fulbright of Fayetteville is elected to the U.S. House of Representatives.	**1944** J. William Fulbright is elected to the U.S. Senate.	**1945** Native Arkansan John H. Johnson's first copy of African American magazine *Ebony* sells out of its first 25,000 issues.	**1948** Silas H. Hunt is admitted as the first black student at the University of Arkansas Law School. Edith Mae Irby enters the University of Arkansas School of Medicine as its first black student.	**1950** Democrat Sid McMath is elected to his second term as governor.
United States		**1943** Doctors begin to use the pap test to detect cervical cancer and it will no longer be the leading killer of women.		**1947** The Brooklyn Dodgers is the first Major League Baseball team to have an African American baseball player– Jackie Robinson.	**1950** Senator Joseph McCarthy begins to randomly accuse American citizens of being communist.	**1951** *Catcher in the Rye* is published by J.D. Salinger.
World				**1948** Racial apartheid begins in South Africa.		**1950** Korean conflict begins.

368   Chapter 17

Why Do We Study This?

Politics and politicians in Arkansas continued to make history during this time period. Although Arkansas is a small state, the far-reaching impact and legacies of some of its most well-known leaders shaped the state's image, reputation, and future. Analyzing and understanding their actions, successes, failures, and what they left behind is critical to solving some of Arkansas's modern challenges.

Big Picture Questions

- What are the responsibilities of a politician? Does power corrupt? Why or why not? If so, how? Whose responsibility is it to monitor politicians?

- In what ways does a politician's legacy affect a state or nation? What does it take to repair damage done by the politician? What must later politicians do to maintain and carry on the success of other leaders?

1954 — **1960** — **1966**

1955 Orval Faubus begins the first of six terms as governor.

1960 Due to population decline, Arkansas loses a seat in the U.S. House of Representatives.

1962 State Treasurer Nancy Hall is the first woman elected to a state office.

1954 Congress holds hearings to censure Senator Joseph McCarthy after his accusations that many Americans are communists.

1955 Disneyland opens in California. The first McDonald's and Kentucky Fried Chicken restaurants open.

1957 *Cat in the Hat* is published by Dr. Seuss.

1962 American sex symbol Marilyn Monroe dies.

1956 American film actress Grace Kelly marries Prince Rainier of Monaco.

1959 In Cuba, Fidel Castro comes into power.

1964 Nelson Mandela is imprisoned in South Africa.

1965 The mini-skirt debuts at London fashion shows and is a hit.

From Fulbright to Faubus—Representation and Circumstance

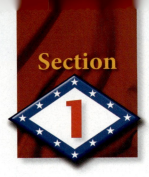

Section 1

The Election of 1944

Guide to Reading

Terms
censured
G.I. Bill
nepotism
police action
political machine

People
G.I.
Silas Hunt
Edith Irby

Events
baby boom
cold war
G.I. Revolt
million-dollar race

million-dollar race the 1944 Arkansas senatorial race, which was investigated for the massive amount of money spent.

G.I. Revolt the movement against corruption in government spearheaded by veterans returning to Arkansas from service in World War II.

During World War II, in the midst of a great deal of turmoil, Arkansas chose two U.S. senators who would serve the state for many years. When Sen. John E. Miller resigned to become a federal judge, John L. McClellan won his Senate seat in 1942. When Sen. Hattie Caraway's term expired in 1944, a number of men entered what would be called the **million-dollar race**.

Among those in the race was Gov. Homer Adkins, who had once given support to Hattie Caraway. Others were T. H. Barton, head of Lion Oil Company, and Congressman J. William Fulbright. Fulbright was a former president of the University of Arkansas. So much money was spent on the campaign that a special committee of the U.S. Senate was set up to look into campaign records.

The field narrowed to a runoff election between Fulbright and Adkins. Fulbright beat Adkins with 58 percent of the vote. So began a thirty-year career in the Senate for Fulbright. There, he gained worldwide respect for his knowledge of foreign affairs and his efforts for world peace. McClellan and Fulbright would be strong voices for Arkansas in Congress for decades to come. A third important leader from Arkansas was Rep. Wilbur Mills, who had been elected to Congress in 1937.

The G.I. Revolt

As Arkansans returned home from battle, many of them believed that things would have to change at home. They had been exposed to the wide world and had risked their lives on the battlefield in the name of the Four Freedoms. They wanted Arkansas to have those Four Freedoms, too. In what became known as the **G.I. Revolt**, these young former soldiers took on those who held the political power. They started at the local level and later moved onto the statewide scene.

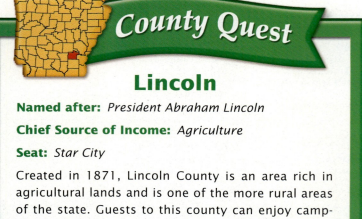

Lincoln

Named after: President Abraham Lincoln

Chief Source of Income: Agriculture

Seat: Star City

Created in 1871, Lincoln County is an area rich in agricultural lands and is one of the more rural areas of the state. Guests to this county can enjoy camping, kayaking, birding tours, and biking at Cane Creek State Park east of Star City.

370   Chapter 17

I Am an Arkansan

John L. McClellan (1896–1977)

John McClellan served longer in the U.S. Senate than any other Arkansas legislator, from 1942 to 1977. In the Senate, he was in charge of several important investigations, including a long probe into organized crime. His most lasting legacy, the McClellan-Kerr Arkansas River Navigation System, is one of many federal projects he helped bring to the state.

Born in 1896 on a farm outside of Sheridan (Grant County), McClellan studied law as a teenager, becoming an attorney at age seventeen. He was the youngest person ever admitted to the American Bar Association. From 1920 through the early 1940s, he served as a city attorney, then a prosecuting attorney, until being elected to the U.S. House of Representatives in 1934. After losing a Senate race against Hattie Caraway, he ran again in 1942, this time with success. As a senator, he brought millions of dollars in federal funding for improvements to Arkansas. Numerous dams, lakes, wildlife habitats, forest preserves, and recreational facilities bear his name as a result of his tireless work on behalf of the state.

For decades, McClellan, Sen. J. William Fulbright, and Rep. Wilbur D. Mills gave Arkansas one of the nation's most influential congressional delegations. Like many other southern politicians, McClellan voted against most civil-rights legislation. He was best known for his many investigations into corruption, the conduct of Wisconsin Senator Joseph McCarthy, organized crime, and labor issues.

Log on to Learn More
http://www.encyclopediaofarkansas.net/

In Hot Springs, Mayor Leo P. McLaughlin had been running a corrupt **political machine** for nearly thirty years. He allowed the town to be a national center for gambling, in open disregard for state laws. Young men who were set on reform challenged McLaughlin's power. Sidney S. McMath, a former marine and war hero, ran for prosecuting attorney of Garland County and led the group of political reformers.

Movements like this also occurred in Crittenden and Yell counties. The G.I.s joined forces to make those who monitored the elections obey the laws, to challenge poll tax fraud, and to expose **nepotism**. The G.I.s offered the voters honest candidates in place of those who were corrupt. McMath won his race. His efforts in Hot Springs did not end gambling there, but he did become known statewide. That made him a leader in the 1948 governor's race, which he won in a runoff.

McMath Takes a Stand

As governor, McMath, who served from 1949 to 1953, placed black Arkansans on state boards for the first time

---

political machine a tightly-controlled organization headed by a political boss that determines the outcome of elections and the distribution of political jobs and favors and often operates outside the law.

nepotism (NEH-poh-tizm) using the power of public office to offer government jobs to relatives.

From Fulbright to Faubus—Representation and Circumstance

▲ Senator John L. McClellan.

G.I. Bill a law enacted following World War II that provided a free college education to veterans.

baby boom a population explosion in the United States in the years following World War II.

cold war tension and confrontation short of total war between two nations or groups of nations. For example, Russia and the communist nations and America and democratic nations, beginning after World War II.

since Reconstruction. African Americans also made gains in local races, earning seats on city councils in Malvern (Hot Spring County) and Hot Springs (Garland County). McMath sponsored bills to end lynching and the poll tax, but the members of the General Assembly refused to pass many of his reforms.

The General Assembly did support McMath's highway program. Much work was needed after neglect during the hard times and heavy use of the war years. Arkansas was known throughout the nation for its bad roads. One carmaker touted its cars as having "passed the Arkansas mud test." In 1949, the state borrowed money through a bond issue to pay for repairs and new highways. Nearly $80 million in state and federal funds were spent to improve roads.

The public schools faced a new problem of crowding on top of the old funding problems. Thousands of veterans enrolled in colleges. The United States paid their tuition with the **G.I. Bill**, a thank you from a grateful nation. Also, an increase in the birthrate, known as the **baby boom**, began after the war. Those children arrived at public schools in the early 1950s, flooding the classrooms grade by grade.

Because of low tax collections and state money needed for other programs, Arkansas's teacher pay and spending per pupil were at the bottom of the country's scales, as in the past. One reform that did meet with success was an effort to consolidate school districts in 1948. In 1921, there had been 5,112 school districts. In 1948, there were 1,598. With the passage of the new law, these were further reduced to 424. School reform and consolidation are still major issues debated in today's state legislature.

Korea

Amid all the social change and baby boom growth, the United States went to war again in 1950, this time in the eastern Asian nation of Korea. Even before the end of World War II, it had become clear that the aims of the United States and its World War II ally, the Soviet Union, were at odds. The Soviet Union seemed intent on gaining control of people and lands all over Europe and the rest of the world. This led to a **cold war** between the two nations. In the United States, an intense fear of communism arose.

In 1950, North Korea, an ally of the Soviet Union, attacked South Korea, an ally of the United States. President Harry S. Truman ordered American armed forces to protect South Korea. Because war was not officially declared, it was called a **police action** by Truman. The purpose was to prevent the communists from taking over South Korea. The United Nations called on its members to help stop the communist aggression.

Many Arkansas veterans of World War II who had joined the Army Reserve or the National Guard were called up to fight again. Eighteen-year-olds learned that the cold war had led the United States to start the draft again. The fighting stopped in 1953, with the border between North Korea and South Korea remaining where it had been when the fighting started. In this undeclared and mostly unpopular war, 461 Arkansans died.

McCarthyism

From 1950 to 1954, a phenomenon took place in the U.S. Senate and across the country. It stemmed from the "red scare" of the 1940s and the cold war of the 1950s. It was based on the suspicions that many U.S. citizens, particularly in politics and the entertainment industry, were communists. Republican senator Joseph McCarthy of Wisconsin initiated accusations and government investigations that became known as "McCarthyism." It was a sort of "witch hunt" where many innocent people were accused and harassed based on rumor and suggestion, not proof. Many lost their jobs, and reputations were ruined. Many Hollywood actors, producers, and writers were accused because of their lavish or unusual (to the mainstream of America) lifestyles. Many who worked for the government were accused of being spies for the Communist Party. The United States government spent a good deal of time and tax dollars on committees for Senator McCarthy's investigations. In the end, only a few people were actually convicted of espionage.

Two Arkansas senators played a role in this event. Senator Fulbright gained recognition by challenging and eventually helping to punish McCarthy. Fulbright was the only senator to vote against funding McCarthy's Senate Permanent Investigative Subcommittee, and he helped establish the congressional committee that eventually disciplined McCarthy in 1954.

In a very public, televised moment in April of 1954, with around twenty million Americans watching, Sen. John L. McClellan led the other Democrats of the Republican-led Senate committee to walk out of hearings in protest of Sen. McCarthy's brash and aggressive behavior. This contributed to growing

◄ A cartoon portraying Senator McClellan as a fighter of corruption.

police action a term for the use of military action without a formal war being declared, such as in the Korean War, which was never officially declared by Congress.

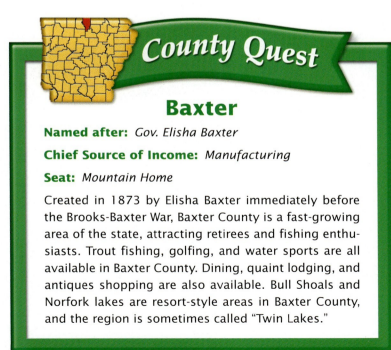

Baxter

Named after: Gov. Elisha Baxter

Chief Source of Income: Manufacturing

Seat: Mountain Home

Created in 1873 by Elisha Baxter immediately before the Brooks-Baxter War, Baxter County is a fast-growing area of the state, attracting retirees and fishing enthusiasts. Trout fishing, golfing, and water sports are all available in Baxter County. Dining, quaint lodging, and antiques shopping are also available. Bull Shoals and Norfork lakes are resort-style areas in Baxter County, and the region is sometimes called "Twin Lakes."

From Fulbright to Faubus—Representation and Circumstance

DID YOU KNOW?

Did you know that the movie *Good Night and Good Luck*, starring George Clooney (2005), is the story of Edward R. Murrow's reporting of the McCarthy story?

censured to be limited, condemned, or restricted from contribution and expression; a punishment for a legislator that shows disapproval.

Silas Hunt the first African American student to be admitted to any southern university for professional or graduate coursework.

Edith Irby the first black female to be admitted to UAMS in Little Rock in 1948. She inspired Jocelyn Elders (who later became Surgeon General of the United States during the Clinton administration) to become a physician.

public dislike and distrust of McCarthy and showed McClellan as a forthright, honest representative of the people.

CBS news reporter Edward R. Murrow broadcast an intensive series of investigative reports that severely weakened McCarthy's credibility and highlighted his lack of proof for his accusations. McCarthy later appeared on Murrow's program, supposedly to tell his side of the story, but ended up making harsh accusations against Murrow and lost even more public favor. Eventually, the Senate **censured** McCarthy. He quietly served in the Senate for two and a half more years, was periodically hospitalized for complications related to alcoholism, and died when he was only forty-eight years old.

County Quest

Cleveland

Named after: President Grover Cleveland

Chief Source of Income: Agriculture

Seat: Rison

Cleveland County was formed in 1873 and was originally named Dorsey County for a U.S. senator from Arkansas, Stephen Dorsey. It was changed to Cleveland County in 1885. Visitors can go to Pioneer Village and explore an 1800s blacksmith shop, a doctor's home, and a country mercantile or attend the Pioneer Village Craft Festival in March.

The Recovery Process

The war and postwar recovery years brought major changes to Arkansas's way of life. People shifted from rural to urban settings, and many displaced farm workers left for other states. Women continued to make advances in the workplace and earn higher wages. African Americans made slow but large strides in both jobs and civil rights.

African Americans made some gains at the college level after the war. For years, the state had paid to send African American students to other states to become doctors and lawyers because they had not been admitted to segregated Arkansas schools. This practice changed, partly because of the expense of this custom and partly under threat from the Supreme Court. **Silas Hunt** entered the University of Arkansas Law School in 1948 and **Edith Irby** enrolled at the University of Arkansas School of Medicine in Little Rock in 1948. For the first time in thirty years, most people were experiencing some aspects of prosperity and peace.

The corrupt politics that had so often been a part of Arkansas life began to change under public review and demands for reform. Farming continued the transition from small family farms to huge businesses. Food processing became a major industry in the state. Because of these industrial and economic advances and accomplishments, Arkansas would finally be released from the economic depression that had begun before the Great Depression.

A remarkable political team represented Arkansas in the House and Senate, and bright young leaders held public offices throughout the state. Arkansas still lagged far behind other parts of the country in education and many other sectors, but the state was well on its way to joining the mainstream of American life in the postwar era.

Through another turbulent and extraordinary time, Arkansas and Arkansans played critical roles in war, politics, international relations, the struggle for civil rights, and the ever-changing modern society. Nothing, however, would quite prepare our state or its people for the coming crisis that would focus world attention on the heart of our state.

I Am an Arkansan

Silas Hunt (1922–1949)

Born in Ashdown (Little River County) in 1922, Silas Hunt served in World War II and was a pioneer in the integration of higher education in Arkansas and the South. In 1948, he was admitted to the University of Arkansas Law School, thus becoming the first African American student allowed to attend the university since Reconstruction. He spent most of his childhood in Texarkana (Miller County) and attended college at the Agricultural, Mechanical, and Normal College in Pine Bluff (Jefferson County). World War II interrupted his studies and those of many Americans.

During the war, Hunt was seriously wounded in the brutal 1944 Battle of the Bulge. Returning to Arkansas, Hunt went to the University of Arkansas to meet with the dean of the law school, Robert Leflar. Leflar was impressed by Hunt's background and accepted him for admission to the law school. Hunt's admission to the school drew national attention.

His discipline and humble nature were traits friends and admirers often cited as important in order to thrive under such a spotlight. Hunt did not graduate from law school before illness cut his life short. He died of tuberculosis and complications from his war injuries in Springfield, Missouri, in 1949. In 2003, the University of Arkansas began awarding the Silas Hunt Distinguished Scholar Awards to deserving black students to celebrate Hunt's contributions to civil rights.

From Fulbright to Faubus—Representation and Circumstance

Section 2

The Rise and Demise of Orval Faubus

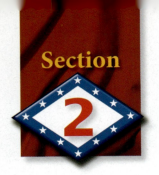

Guide to Reading

Terms
Arkansas Industrial Development Commission

People
Francis Cherry
Orval E. Faubus
Winthrop Rockefeller

Events
Little Red School House

Francis Cherry a candidate for governor who successfully used a radio campaign to win election over Sid McMath but served only one term and was defeated by Orval Faubus.

Orval Faubus infamous governor who served during the Little Rock Central High School crisis.

Little Red School House a nickname for Commonwealth College, referring to its communist, or "red," leanings. The Little Red School House was briefly attended by Orval Fabus.

Governor McMath served a respected and noteworthy four years in office, but got into a dispute with the director of Arkansas Power and Light (AP&L). At issue was a rural electrical cooperative, or co-op, in northwest Arkansas. AP&L thought that the co-op, which could get government loans, could compete on an unfair basis. McMath was in favor of the co-op. When McMath ran for a third term in 1952, AP&L and others in business opposed him.

Accusations were made that highway contracts had been given to friends of McMath, and this caused a scandal that hurt his G.I. reform image. The somewhat unknown **Francis Cherry** ran a clever, non-stop "radio talkathon" campaign that won over enough voters to defeat McMath. Cherry only served one term as governor. His administration oversaw a hefty rate increase by AP&L and caused a decrease in welfare coverage. He proved to be an easy target for the eager **Orval E. Faubus**.

Born in Huntsville (Madison County) in the Ozarks, Faubus was the son of a poor man with populist and socialist ideas. After high school, Faubus briefly went to Commonwealth College in Mena, also known as The **Little Red School House**. A schoolteacher for a time, Faubus joined the Army as a private soon after Pearl Harbor. He rose to the rank of major during the war. Upon coming home, he was named postmaster and bought the local newspaper, the *Madison County Record*. In the gubernatorial election of 1955, Faubus faced respectable opposition from the Republicans, but was able to secure a victory with 208,000 votes.

During his first term, Governor Faubus proved to be a strong advocate for the common man. He managed to keep a dog racing track from starting in West Memphis (Crittenden County) that would have led to gambling. He rolled back the AP&L rate increase, refunding $9 million to taxpayers. He stopped an ArkLa Gas rate increase. He also had success in luring new industry to the state.

Many people had left the state to find jobs, at a rate of about forty thousand a year. Arkansas lost 6.5 percent of its people between 1950 and 1960. The population loss, among other things, meant that Arkansas lost another congressional seat, leaving the state with only four members in the U.S. House of Representatives. In addition, Arkansans were poor by the country's standards. The average income per person in the state was $1,142 in 1955, or 60 percent of the United States average.

376 Chapter 17

Factory jobs tended to pay more than most farm work. By the mid-1950s, business leaders were ready for the state government to take a major role in attracting new industry to Arkansas. When Orval Faubus took office, he endorsed the idea of state action. The result, in 1955, was the start of the **Arkansas Industrial Development Commission** (AIDC).

To head the new agency, Faubus chose **Winthrop Rockefeller**. A grandson of John D. Rockefeller, founder of the Standard Oil Company, Rockefeller had just moved to Arkansas. An Army friend from Arkansas had told him that he could find a good home for himself in Arkansas and many opportunities to do good things for the state. An enormously wealthy man, Rockefeller started a large

Arkansas Industrial Development Commission a state agency established by the legislature in the administration of Orval Faubus to encourage industry to locate in Arkansas.

Winthrop Rockefeller the first Republican governor elected in Arkansas since Reconstruction; he replaced Orval Faubus. He was also a well-known philanthropist and business leader.

I Am an Arkansan

Wilbur D. Mills (1909–1992)

Wilbur Mills, born in Kensett (White County), served in the U.S. House of Representatives from 1939 to 1977, making him one of the longest-serving politicians in Arkansas history. As longtime chairman of the House Ways and Means Committee, Mills was also one of the most powerful lawmakers in the nation. The name "Mr. Chairman" was known throughout Washington to refer to Mills.

In 1930, he graduated from Hendrix College in Conway (Faulkner County) and he attended law school at Harvard University. After working at a bank in Kensett for several years, Mills became the youngest judge in Arkansas history and, by the age of twenty-nine, he had become the youngest U.S. congressman to that time.

By the late 1950s, he had risen to become chairman of the Ways and Means Committee, which decides how the government should spend money. During the 1960s, he was one of the creators of the Medicare program and also helped revamp Social Security. During his long tenure, he was only opposed in an election three times and never lost.

By the 1970s, however, Mills had developed a severe alcohol problem, and in 1974 was stopped by Washington, D.C., police for driving without headlights. He was found to be drunk, and a stripper ran out of his car and jumped into a nearby fountain. Though he won another reelection campaign, he soon admitted that his alcoholism had to be dealt with.

He retired from Congress in 1977 and devoted the rest of his life to practicing law in Washington, D.C. He also helped establish an alcohol recovery center in Searcy (White County), and spoke openly about his struggle to overcome his own drinking problems. A giant in Arkansas politics, Mills has had many buildings and roads named for him, including Mills High School in Little Rock, the Mills Center at Hendrix College, and the Wilbur D. Mills Expressway (Interstate 630) in Little Rock.

Log on to Learn More
http://www.encyclopediaofarkansas.net/

From Fulbright to Faubus—Representation and Circumstance

I Am an Arkansan

Sidney "Sid" McMath (1912–2003)

Sidney McMath, a U.S. Marine Corps veteran who served in World War II, was a progressive Democratic reformer and governor of Arkansas from 1949 to 1953. He was born in a log cabin near Magnolia (Columbia County). The family moved to Hot Springs (Garland County) when McMath was young, and he attended nearby Henderson University in Arkadelphia (Clark County).

During World War II, he fought in some of the deadliest battles in the Pacific theater and led jungle assaults against Japanese forces. He earned the Silver Star for valor.

McMath upset the balance of politics by fighting for more electric power, extensive highway and school construction projects, repeal of the poll tax, fair and honest elections, and greater opportunity for black Arkansans. After his defeat in the 1952 election, McMath was an outspoken critic of Gov. Orval Faubus. McMath staunchly opposed segregation of schools and was vocal in support of integrating Little Rock Central High. After leaving political life, McMath embarked on a long, successful career as a lawyer. He specialized in defending injured persons, and was involved in several high-profile cases.

THE ENCYCLOPEDIA OF ARKANSAS HISTORY & CULTURE

Log on to Learn More
http://www.encyclopediaofarkansas.net/

---

ranch on top of Petit Jean Mountain (Conway County) and became active in civic and cultural affairs.

Under Rockefeller, the AIDC hired a staff and began to seek businesses to locate in Arkansas. The state could offer its central location, its rich resource base, and its willing labor force. There were plenty of workers so badly in need of jobs that they were willing to work for about thirty percent less than the nation's average wage.

Combined with successes in industry, and his role in the state's racial issues, Faubus would gain widespread public support. He won six elections to the governorship. His twelve years in office increased power in the Arkansas governor's office as never before.

Faubus's control of the Democratic Party kept any serious threats to his power from forming within that party. A challenge finally appeared in the form of Republican Winthrop Rockefeller, who had fallen out with Faubus over the Central High crisis.

As head of the AIDC, Rockefeller knew how much the Little Rock crisis had hurt the drive to bring industry to the state. Eight new plants opened in Little Rock in 1957, before the crisis. For the next two years, not one new firm moved to Little Rock. Rockefeller also believed competition between two political parties produced healthier politics and government than did domination by one party.

Rockefeller's family had always been Republican. One brother, Nelson, would later become vice president of the United States under Republican president Gerald Ford. The Arkansas Republican Party was weak, but Rockefeller thought he could do something about that. His name and wealth carried great power. Also, many Democrats could be counted on to oppose Faubus.

Rockefeller ran for governor against Faubus in 1964, getting 254,561 votes to Faubus's 337,489. Rockefeller promised to run again in 1966. Faubus chose not to run again that year, and Rockefeller won the election.

Many saw Faubus as a racist and a segregationist, but others merely viewed him as a typical politician, willing to "flip-flop" in order to keep the money, power, and the vote. He did have many successes during his long service, but will always be remembered for the dark days of the Little Rock Central High School crisis.

I Am an Arkansan

Jimmy Driftwood (1907–1998)

Born near Mountain Home (Stone County) in 1907, Jimmy Driftwood was a pioneer folk singer–songwriter who wrote more than six thousand songs, the most famous of which was "The Battle of New Orleans," which was a hit for Johnny Horton in 1959. When he was still a small child, his grandfather made him his first guitar. After briefly attending John Brown University in Siloam Springs (Benton County), Driftwood traveled to Arizona, where he won a local talent show.

Eventually he made his way back to Stone County, where he worked as a teacher. He used his songs to describe the history of the area, and by the 1950s, he had written thousands of songs that tackled all kinds of topics, from the Civil War to more modern issues. He recorded his first album of folk songs in 1957, under the guidance of country music star Chet Atkins. During the next few years, Driftwood received a Grammy

nomination and performed at Carnegie Hall, the Grand Ole Opry, and at folk festivals across the country. He was instrumental in securing the funds necessary to establish the Ozark Folk Center in Mountain View (Stone County). Upon his death in 1998, he was considered one of the most important folk singer–songwriters in music history.

THE ENCYCLOPEDIA OF ARKANSAS HISTORY & CULTURE

Log on to Learn More
http://www.encyclopediaofarkansas.net/

Chapter Reflection

Reflective Questions

1. The G.I. Revolt was aimed against _____.
   a. Truman bombing Nagasaki and Hiroshima
   b. McLaughlin's political machine in Hot Springs, election fraud, and nepotism
   c. the draft
   d. wearing uniforms in the military

2. After the war, schools became overcrowded because of _____.
   a. the baby boom
   b. lack of supplies and furniture
   c. consolidation
   d. floods

3. Silas Hunt and Edith Irby were _____.
   a. athletes
   b. soldiers
   c. Nisei
   d. African American students

4. Senator McCarthy accused Americans of being _____.
   a. Nazis
   b. guerillas
   c. rebels
   d. communists

5. Senator McCarthy was _____ by the Senate.
   a. shot
   b. rewarded
   c. censured
   d. promoted

6. Discuss the purpose or goal of the Arkansas Industrial Development Commission.

7. What were some of Orval Faubus's strategies to improve the economy?

8. How was Republican Winthrop Rockefeller able to win the 1966 election for governor?

Who Says?

Distinguishing Between Fact and Opinion

On your paper, number 1 through 5. Carefully read each statement below and based on your studies, determine if it is a fact or an opinion. Write an F or O beside the corresponding number to indicate your choice.

1. Senator McCarthy should have been jailed.
2. Sid McMath continued his public service after he returned from the war.
3. Rockefeller was too rich for his own good.
4. Orval Faubus was evil.
5. Soldiers returning from war were given financial assistance for college and to buy homes.

Read and Respond

Carefully read the passage below. Then, on your own paper, respond to the following thoughts.

Governor McMath Speaks Up for Arkansas

Governor Sidney McMath worked at being a good ambassador for Arkansas. He was active in national Democratic politics, as a close associate of President Harry S Truman. He also spoke frequently to audiences all over the country, describing the progress he saw in Arkansas and the South. This is part of a speech he made to a northern audience in 1949, soon after he became governor:

We are not spending all our time on white-columned verandas sipping mint juleps, and plotting to keep our people in economic slavery. In fact, there is abroad in all the southland a vigorous progressive movement—a growing demand for the development of the human and economic resources of our region.

Jim Lester, *A Man for Arkansas: Sid McMath and the Southern Reform Tradition* (Little Rock: Rose Publishing Company, 1976), 129.

1. In your opinion, what is Governor McMath trying to tell outsiders about Arkansas and the "southland"?
2. What type of "movement" does Governor McMath describe?
3. What do you think he is referring to when he mentions "human and economic resources"?
4. From what book is this quote taken?
5. In what city was this book published?

UNIT 7

The Cycle of Conflict and Change
1955–1991

Chapter 18
Separate and Unequal, 1955–1965

Chapter 19
Defining Ourselves, 1966–1991

Segregationists rally at the state capitol in Little Rock.

Chapter 18

Separate and Unequal
1955–1965

An activist with the Student Nonviolent Coordinating Committee marches with a poster reading, "Black and White Together," in the 1960s.

Timeline

	1955	1957	1959	1960
Arkansas	**1955** Hoxie schools are integrated.	**1957** The Central High integration crisis draws national and international attention.		
United States	**1955** The U.S. Air Force Academy opens in Colorado Springs. Albert Einstein dies. "Rock Around the Clock" is the most popular song. President Dwight D. Eisenhower sends a military advisory group to Vietnam to train South Vietnamese soldiers.			**1960** Wilma Rudolph, a black woman, wins three Olympic gold medals in track at the summer Olympics in Rome. Democrat John F. Kennedy is elected president.
World				

Why Do We Study This?

The years from the mid-1950s to the late 1960s were one of the most monumental times in our state's and nation's histories. The events of this period would forever change Arkansans, Americans, and our place in the world. Politics, culture, lifestyles, race relations, and society would all experience revolutions. The roles and contributions of black Arkansans would slowly begin to be recognized and people would start to work together toward a common goal of equality. This time is a study of character, personal conviction, integrity, intelligence, and morality. Our reactions to moments such as these truly define us.

Big Picture Questions

- What causes hate? What is the motivation for violence?
- Can people's opinion of others be changed? Why or why not? If so, how? If no, why not?
- How does education prevent violence? Promote tolerance? Eliminate fear? Use specific examples in your discussion.
- What are modern-day examples of discrimination? Segregation? Who or what groups are judged, treated differently, or denied rights or services because they look different or have a different belief system? Use specific examples in your discussion.
- What is a mob mentality? Why is it powerful? Use examples in your discussion.

1961	1962	1963		1965
		1963 Donna Axum of El Dorado becomes Miss America. Black Arkansans are jailed for protests in Helena.	**1964** Voters end poll taxes, and gambling in Hot Springs is limited.	
1961 American-backed forces attempt to invade Cuba at the Bay of Pigs. Kennedy sends Green Beret "special advisors" to train soldiers in South Vietnam.	**1962** The Cuban missile crisis brings America close to nuclear war with Russia.	**1963** Kennedy sends 16,000 troops to Vietnam. Kennedy is assassinated in Dallas on November 22. Vice President Lyndon B. Johnson is sworn in as president aboard Air Force One.	**1964** The National Civil Rights Act is passed. Johnson is elected president.	**1965** Johnson begins his Great Society program to promote equality, fight poverty, and end voting fraud.
				1965 Former prime minister of Great Britain Winston Churchill dies. Doctors perform the first successful heart transplant in Capetown, South Africa.

Separate and Unequal

The National Civil Rights Movement and the Central High Crisis

May 1954
The U.S. Supreme Court in *Brown v. the Board of Education of Topeka* (Kansas) rules that racial segregation in public schools is unconstitutional.

1955

May 1955
The Little Rock School Board votes unanimously to implement the "Blossom Plan," put forth by superintendent Virgil Blossom, which would gradually integrate Little Rock schools, beginning at the high school level.

Summer 1955
Fourteen-year-old Emmett Till of Chicago is brutally murdered in Money, Mississippi, for allegedly whistling at a married white woman.

December 1955
In Montgomery, Alabama, Rosa Parks is arrested for refusing to give up her bus seat to a white person. This triggers a bus boycott that lasts for more than a year.

▼ Elizabeth Eckford, Melba Pattillo, Minnijean Brown, and Gloria Ray are escorted from Central High by Guard troops.

1956

January 1956
Black students attempt to register in Little Rock schools, but are denied and encouraged to attend all-black schools, like the new all-black high school, Horace Mann.

Fall 1956
Little Rock city buses are integrated without significant incident.

September 2, 1957
Arkansas's Gov. Faubus orders the Arkansas National Guard to bar nine black students from entering Central High School.

September 3, 1957
Two segregationist groups, the Mother's League of Central High School and the Capital Citizens Council, hold a sunrise service at the school, sing "Dixie," fly the Confederate flag, and support Faubus's actions.

September 3, 1957
A federal judge orders desegregation to continue, and Faubus orders the Guard to stay.

September 4, 1957
Nine black students attempt to enter Central High School, but are denied by the Guard.
• Due to a miscommunication, Elizabeth Eckford arrives at Central alone and attempts to enter through the front doors. An angry mob follows; racial slurs are yelled; photographers capture every moment; the world watches.

September 5, 1957
None of the nine attempt to go to Central, and desegregation is temporarily slowed.

September 23, 1957
After many days of media coverage and Governor Faubus meeting with President Eisenhower, the students again attempt to enter the school. Amid a thousand or so white protestors, they are successful.
• Some white students jump out of windows in protest, but most go about their day without incident.
• A small riot ensues in the street, and black and white reporters who support

1957

Spring 1957
African American students interested in attending Central High decide if they would attend Central or remain at Horace Mann.

August 1957
Gov. Marvin Griffin of Georgia visits Arkansas to encourage and praise those who favor segregation in schools.

1957–58 School Year

integration are harassed and beaten.
• Eisenhower sends in federal troops to control the scene and Daisy and L. C. Bates, publishers of the *Arkansas State Press*, an African American newspaper, continue their involvement as coordinators of media relations, advocates for the students, and advisors to their parents.
• The nine are escorted out of the school through a side door for their own protection.

September 25, 1957
The nine students are escorted into school by the federal troops. White students are told they have nothing to fear from the soldiers and should continue their normal, daily routines.

1957–58 school year
Several bomb threats are called in to Central High.
• School discipline records and National Guard accounts report that some white students verbally and physically harass black students throughout the school year, particularly in the hallways and cafeteria, where they are out of sight of faculty and administrators.
• Minnijean Brown, one of the nine, is suspended in December after being accused of dumping chili on a white student. She is expelled in February after an altercation with a white, female student. Minnijean transfers to a high school in New York City.
• White students secretly pass out cards that read, "One down, eight to go." Several are suspended, but not expelled.
• White students who are supportive of the nine are also harassed.

1958

Spring 1958
The only senior among the nine, Ernest Green, graduates without significant incident. Little Rock police and federal troops attend graduation ceremonies. Dr. Martin Luther King Jr., whose attendance was not made public or announced beforehand, also attends to honor Green.

June 1958
A federal judge grants a delay of integration in Little Rock until January of 1961, stating "the time has not come for them [black students] to enjoy that right [to attend white schools]." The NAACP appeals the decision.

August 1958
The U.S. Supreme Court announces a special session to discuss Little Rock's integration issues.

August 1958
Governor Faubus calls a special legislative session to pass a law allowing him to close public schools in Little Rock to avoid integration. More than 3,500 high school students have to find alternative school options.

September 1958
The U.S. Supreme Court orders that integration continue. Faubus closes all four Little Rock high schools, pending a public vote either for or against integration of the schools. Voters cast 129,470 ballots against integration and 7,561 ballots for integration. The result of this vote meant that the high schools would remain closed. This year would come to be known as "the lost year."

November 1958
All but one of the Little Rock School Board members resign because of confusion and frustration about integration.

Citizens of Little Rock protest in front of the state capitol.

1959

May 1959
Segregationist school board members vote to deny renewal of contracts for forty-four teachers and administrators who are viewed as supporters of integration.
- The Women's Emergency Committee and Stop This Outrageous Purge (STOP) are successful in an effort to recall segregationist board members.

June 1959
Federal District Court declares the state's school-closing law unconstitutional. High schools must reopen in the fall.

August 1959
Little Rock schools open early. Five black students successfully enter Hall High without confrontation. Two of the original Little Rock Nine return to Central for their senior year, along with sophomore Sybil Jordan.

1960

February 1960
Four black students sit at an all-white lunch counter at Woolworth in Greensboro, North Carolina, and passively continue to sit when asked to leave. This sparks a trend of sit-ins as a means of peaceful protest.

Cards passed out by white students after the expulsion of Minnijean Brown.

The National Civil Rights Movement and the Central High Crisis **387**

1961

May 1961
Among protests, and even fire bombings, white activists ride the buses of the South in attempts to integrate public transportation. They were known as "Freedom Riders."

1962

September 1962
James Meredith takes two classes at the University of Mississippi, "Ole Miss," in Oxford, Mississippi. Two are killed and 188 injured in the protests that ensue. Federal troops are sent in to ensure Meredith's safety.

1963

June 1963
Gov. George Wallace of Alabama tries to stop integration at the University of Alabama. President Kennedy sends in federal troops. Two black students are enrolled.

June 1963
The day after two black students enroll at the University of Alabama, Medgar Evers, an African American civil rights activist, is murdered in Jackson, Mississippi. The accused killer is a white supremacist.

August 1963
Two hundred and fifty thousand march on Washington, D.C., as Martin Luther King Jr. gives his famous "I Have a Dream" speech.

September 1963
Four young girls are murdered in a bombing at a church in Birmingham, Alabama, where civil rights activities were coordinated.

◄ Arkansas citizen demonstrating in favor of integration.

▼ Posters displayed by the Women's Emergency Committee to open our schools.

◄ Federal troops escort the Nine into Central High School.

388 The National Civil Rights Movement and the Central High Crisis

1964

1964
President Lyndon Johnson signs the Civil Rights Act, which outlaws employment discrimination and segregation or discrimination in public places.

June 1964
During drives to register African American voters, three young civil rights workers disappear in Mississippi. Their bodies are later discovered buried in a dirt dam outside Philadelphia, Mississippi.

1965

February 1965
Malcolm X is murdered in New York City.

March 1965
In a march to support equal voting rights, activists walking from Selma to Montgomery, Alabama, are gassed and beaten by law enforcement while thousands watch on television. This is called "Bloody Sunday."

August 1965
Lyndon Johnson signs the Voting Rights Act, which requires that all citizens be allowed to vote equally and freely. It is extended when re-signed by President George W. Bush in 2006.

1966

Summer 1966
The phrase "black power" is uttered for the first time and there is a trend to move away from the method of nonviolent protests of Gandhi and King.

October 1966
Black Panthers form in California.

April 1968

Dr. Martin Luther King Jr. is shot in the throat at the Lorraine Motel in Memphis, Tennessee. Upon news of his death, the nation mourns and riots.

Who's Who...

The Little Rock High School Crisis

- **President Dwight D. Eisenhower**
  U.S. president during the crisis
- **Orval Faubus**
  Governor of Arkansas
- **Marvin Griffin**
  Governor of Georgia
- **Woodrow Mann**
  Mayor of Little Rock
- **Virgil Blossom**
  Superintendent of Little Rock schools
- **Jess Matthews**
  Central High School principal
- **Elizabeth Huckaby**
  Central High School vice principal
- **J. O. Powell**
  Central High School vice principal
- **The Little Rock Nine**
  The nine black students who were the first to attend all-white Central High School

Fall 1972

All Little Rock schools are fully integrated.

The National Civil Rights Movement and the Central High Crisis

Section 1

Crisis in the Schools: The End of Segregation

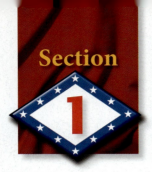

Guide to Reading

Terms
Blossom Plan
integration
purge
Southern Manifesto

Events
Aaron v. Cooper
Brown v. the Board of Education of Topeka

People
The Arkansas Council on Human Relations
The Little Rock Nine
segregationists
STOP
Urban League
White Citizens' Councils
Women's Emergency Committee to Open Our Schools

Places
Central High School
Dunbar High School
Negro School for Industrial Arts

Separate and Unequal No More

Although blacks and whites were still kept apart in almost all aspects of life, there were hints that change might come. In the early 1950s, after repeated demands from black community and political leaders, the major stores in Little Rock removed the "white" and "colored" signs on their drinking fountains. The Rock Island Railroad stopped seating people by race on its trains. Silas Hunt had been enrolled as the first African American student at the University of Arkansas law school in Fayetteville. Whites as well as blacks were starting to discuss the wrongs in the system and plans for solving them. The black and white public-school systems were still separate but not equal. In 1952, the Little Rock Council on Education, which contained members of both races, pointed out that the black schools were worse than the white schools in every way.

Brown v. the Board of Education, 1954

With a genuine faith in learning, African American leaders throughout the United States believed that equal education was the answer to achieving equal economic opportunities for blacks and whites. With the help of the National Association for the Advancement of Colored People (NAACP), African Americans began to bring

County Quest

Clay

Named after: State Senator John Clayton

Chief Source of Income: Agriculture and manufacturing

Seat: Corning, Piggott

Created in 1873, Clay County was originally named "Clayton," in honor of John Clayton, a member of the state senate. The name was changed to Clay in 1875. It is located in the northeastern corner of the state, near the northern end of Crowley's Ridge. Ernest Hemingway wrote a portion of his novel, *A Farewell to Arms*, while he lived in Piggott and was married to a local woman, Pauline Pfeiffer. Piggot is also home to "Aerial Bouquets," a locally owned enterprise that manufactures floral and mylar balloon arrangements that are sold in supermarkets nationwide.

390 Chapter 18

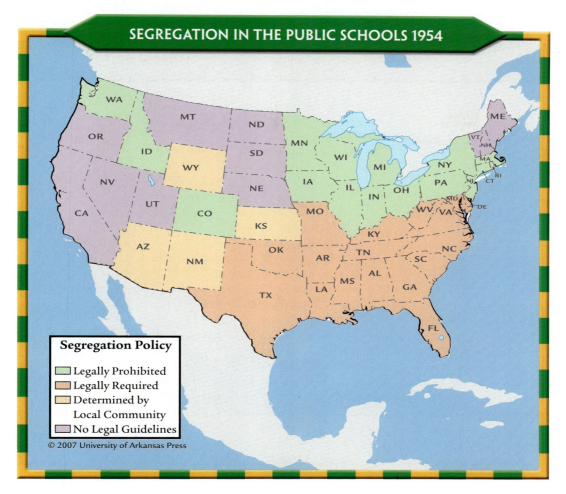

lawsuits to challenge the separate school systems. A number of these cases, combined as *Brown v. the Board of Education of Topeka*, reached the U.S. Supreme Court.

In 1954, the Supreme Court heard the *Brown* case and ruled that because separate education was not and could not be equal, it was not in keeping with the U.S. Constitution. In a second *Brown* decision the next year, the court said that school districts must integrate "with all deliberate speed."

Across the South, the response to this decision was mixed. In some places, people moved quickly to change their schools. In other regions, white leaders in public office said openly that they would never allow blacks and whites to go to the same schools.

As time went on, those opposed to change grew more vocal, with public leaders saying the Supreme Court could be ignored. In the U.S. Congress, almost all the members from the South signed a **Southern Manifesto** against school **integration**. All of Arkansas's members of Congress signed it, including Senators Fulbright and McClellan and Congressman Mills.

In Arkansas, a small number of interracial groups actively supported integration. **The Arkansas Council on Human Relations** was headed by Ozell Sutton and Ruth Arnold. Then came the **Urban League**, which had the support of Winthrop Rockefeller and Congressman Brooks Hays. In Little Rock, church leaders formed the Interracial Ministerial Alliance.

Brown v. the Board of Education of Topeka a 1954 U.S. Supreme Court ruling that stated the policy of "separate but equal" in public education was unconstitutional.

Southern Manifesto (SUTH-ern man-if-EST-oh) a written protest from southern members of Congress in response to the *Brown v. the Board of Education* decision to integrate schools.

integration combination, intermixing, or mingling of two or more groups.

The Arkansas Council on Human Relations a group of Arkansans who supported integration, headed by Ozell Sutton and Ruth Arnold.

Urban League a group of Little Rock integrationists who were supported by Winthrop Rockefeller and Congressman Brooks Hays.

Separate and Unequal **391**

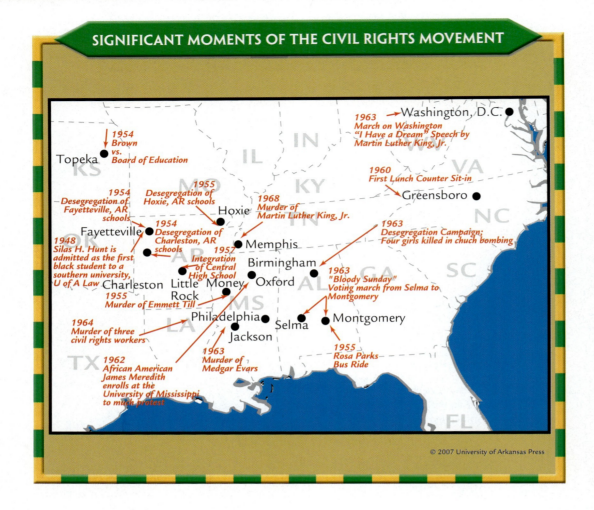

SIGNIFICANT MOMENTS OF THE CIVIL RIGHTS MOVEMENT

© 2007 University of Arkansas Press

September 1954: Charleston and Fayetteville

A few school districts complied with the *Brown* decision quickly and without trouble, particularly in sections of the state with few African American students. Charleston (Franklin County) successfully integrated all twelve grades and was the first district in the "Old South" to do so. When school opened in the fall of 1954, eleven African American students began attending formerly all-white public schools in Charleston. This news was kept secret until the day Fayetteville integrated, about three weeks later. During that school year, other schools refused to play Charleston in football or allow them in band competitions because of the black students. During the Central High crisis, two **segregationists** tried to run for school board in Charleston, but were defeated. The school is now a National Commemorative Site, due to legislation from Senator Dale Bumpers.

Fayetteville High School (Washington County) was integrated by six African American high-school students who began attending school with white students in the fall of 1954. Before integration, Fayetteville had sent them sixty-three miles by bus to a high school in Fort Smith. In 1955, the state colleges started to admit African American students as undergraduates.

September 1955: Hoxie

The first signs of trouble were in Hoxie (Lawrence County) in northeastern Arkansas. In 1955, the school board, in an attempt to be law-abiding and just— and following the lead of successful

segregationists (SEG-gruh-GAY-shun-ists) those driven by racial prejudice to keep the races separated at all costs.

392 Chapter 18

◀ "Justice" Jim Johnson.

integrations in Fayetteville and Charleston—moved the twenty-one black students living there into the white public schools. After the school term started with no problems, segregationists from Hoxie and outside of the community formed a group to begin a protest. The leaders were James D. "Justice Jim" Johnson of Crossett (Ashley County) and Amis Guthridge of Little Rock. The integration was photographed and pictures were published in *Life* magazine, and other segregationists from outside Arkansas arrived ready for a fight. Some people were so strongly against integration, they drove many miles to fight it.

An anti-integration farmer from Hoxie took the role of local leader when the out-of-state segregationist groups arrived. His remarks further resolved the school board to stand behind its decision to integrate. The school board requested help from the state government, but Faubus refused. The school board then obtained a court injunction preventing segregationists from interfering with school integration.

However, the segregationists had some small victories. The farmer was elected to the school board and some black students dropped out of school, but overall, integrationists were victorious in showing that the Hoxie school board would not be bullied. Segregationists turned their attentions to pressuring politicians by threatening to change their votes on Election Day.

Little Rock Central High School

Meanwhile, the Little Rock school board drew up a plan to desegregate. Named the **Blossom Plan**, after Superintendent Virgil Blossom, it was approved only ten days after the *Brown* decision. It was designed to desegregate the schools slowly, starting at the high-school level, specifically with **Little Rock Central High School**.

Central High School was opened in 1927 as Little Rock Senior High School. Its design used art deco and collegiate gothic architectural principles to inspire learning. It was modeled after such

Blossom Plan the Little Rock School District's original desegregation plan, proposed by the superintendent, Virgil Blossom.

Little Rock Central High School the location of the first attempts of public school integration in Little Rock in the 1950s. The conflicts between segregationists, law enforcement, the public, and civil rights activists drew international attention to the situation.

Separate and Unequal **393**

► The halls of Central High School.

Dunbar High School the "premier" African American high school in Little Rock until 1955, when its last class graduated.

Negro School for Industrial Arts opened in 1929, a black high school, only blocks from Central High; it was later renamed Dunbar High School.

institutions as New Jersey's Princeton University and the University of Oxford in England. It was later named "America's most beautiful high school." Roosevelt's New Deal Works Progress Administration built the football stadium. It was the largest and most modern stadium in the state and hosted University of Arkansas football games prior to the construction of War Memorial Stadium.

Under the Blossom Plan, Little Rock Central High School would accept a few African American students in the fall of 1957, many of whom attended the well-respected black high school, **Dunbar High School**, just blocks from Central. The first African American teacher in Little Rock, Charlotte Stephens, taught at Dunbar for many years. Dunbar is also where Sue Cowan Williams Morris was teaching when she successfully sued the Little Rock School District for equal pay for black and white teachers.

In 1929, Dunbar was originally built as the **Negro School for Industrial Arts** and later named for the poet Paul Laurence Dunbar. Parents objected to the school's initial emphasis on technical and art skills and wanted college preparatory courses as well. After many changes during the years of segregation, Dunbar's last high-school classes graduated in 1955. Despite its excellent academic record, Dunbar received less funding for its courses and was not able to offer as much course variety as white schools. It also had fewer classrooms and limited athletic facilities.

Horace Mann, a new high school, had opened in 1956, and would remain all black, according to the plan. Hall High School, to be finished in 1957, would be all white. The second phase of the Blossom Plan would open white junior high schools to a few blacks in 1960. The third phase would open white grade schools to a few blacks at some unspecified date in the future.

The Blossom Plan had major flaws. For example, putting off any action until 1957 allowed time for opponents of integration to organize. Instead of spreading the changes throughout the

◀ A young black boy watches as white protestors gather near Central High School in Little Rock.

◀ Daisy and L. C. Bates.

entire city, the plan focused on Central High. This was in a lower-income, working-class section of the city. The plan would allow richer whites living in the western part of the city to send their children to all-white Hall High.

From the standpoint of many African Americans, the Blossom Plan was both too little and too slow. In 1956, the parents of more than thirty African American schoolchildren filed suit against the school board. They said their children had been denied entry into their neighborhood all-white schools.

The NAACP worked on the lawsuit. The lawyer for the African American parents was Wiley Austin Branton of Pine Bluff, accompanied by the well-respected Thurgood Marshall. Branton was one of the first African American graduates of the University of Arkansas Law School, and he went on to a long career as a nationally respected civil rights lawyer. Media relations and communications between state and national NAACP offices were coordinated by the state NAACP president, Daisy Bates. In the case *Aaron v. Cooper*, federal judge John Miller ruled that the Blossom Plan should be carried out. The judge also said the court would supervise the plan, meaning that any opponents to the plan in Little Rock would be opposing the U.S. courts.

The forces against change were growing. In Little Rock and other towns, **White Citizens' Councils** were formed to oppose integration. Jim Johnson, who had opposed integration at Hoxie, proposed to amend the state

Aaron v. Cooper the lawsuit brought against the Little Rock School Board by the NAACP to integrate the schools.

White Citizens' Councils segregationist groups organized in Arkansas to fight school integration, which were mostly comprised of white, middle-, and upper-class people.

Separate and Unequal **395**

constitution. His aim was to defy the Supreme Court's *Brown v. the Board of Education* ruling. Johnson also ran against Faubus for governor in 1956.

Although Johnson was soundly beaten in the governor's race, his proposed amendment won by a vote of 185,374 to 146,064. The amendment required the General Assembly to take action against the *Brown* ruling.

Governor Faubus began to be concerned about the growing strength of segregationists. Up to this point, his position on race matters had been moderate to liberal. Soon after the *Brown* ruling, Faubus had declared himself neutral on the question. He said it was a matter for local school districts to handle. But during the campaign of 1956, Faubus began to feel the political pressure of the segregationists. He thought he needed their financial support to get his programs passed and their votes to win the next race for governor.

In the next session of the General Assembly in the spring of 1957, Faubus proposed a tax increase. Much of the new money would go to schools and would provide equal pay for African American teachers. In return for support of the tax increase, Faubus agreed to support Arkansas segregationists in the passage of their laws.

These laws ended required school attendance—so the children of segregationists would not be forced to go to school with black children—and gave state aid to districts threatened with court suits. Segregationists also wanted to require the NAACP to publish its list of members and to create a commission they thought would protect Arkansas from federal court rulings regarding integration. But once Faubus's tax increase was passed, the governor seemed to ignore the demands of the segregationists.

The Crisis

In Little Rock, the school board went forward with its plans to desegregate Central High in the fall of 1957. Superintendent Blossom asked African American students to apply for entry into Central. Blossom chose several African American students to be the first to attend Central based on administration standards. Of those chosen, only nine would show up on the first day of school. Still, the school officials and the city's white leaders assumed all was going well.

But throughout the summer of 1957, whites who opposed integration had been gaining strength. The White Citizens' Councils of Little Rock brought Marvin Griffin, the governor of Georgia, to Little Rock. He urged the group to defy the *Brown* ruling, then stayed with Faubus in the governor's mansion.

County Quest

Garland

Named after: Augustus Garland, governor and U.S. attorney general

Chief Source of Income: Tourism, service industries, and manufacturing

Seat: Hot Springs

Garland County was established in 1873. This scenic area is among the state's leading tourist centers, and visitors and residents alike enjoy digging in the quartz crystal mines, playing at Magic Springs Amusement Park, and experiencing the Mid-America Science Museum. Every racing season, Oaklawn Park in Hot Springs is filled with cheering spectators watching the thoroughbreds run, and guests also enjoy reliving the heyday of the bathhouses on Bathhouse Row in Hot Springs National Park. Garland County offers swimming and fishing in the county's many lakes, and hiking in the surrounding forests and mountain areas.

396 Chapter 18

A Day in the Life

Faubus and Little Rock: An Editor's View of the Governor's Motives

After Governor Orval Faubus defied the federal government to prevent the integration of Central High School, many people tried to understand his motives.

Harry Ashmore was editor of the *Arkansas Gazette* in 1957. The *Gazette's* reporting of and support for integration at Central High won it two Pulitzer Prizes, the highest honor for newspapers. One was for the *Gazette's* general coverage, and the other was for Ashmore's editorials.

Later, in a history of Arkansas, Ashmore wrote about Faubus's reasons for defying integration:

> Many of Faubus's supporters accepted him as a racist ideologue, and he was usually so portrayed in the national media, but few of his antagonists in Arkansas ever did. The Gazette contended from the outset that he had no real concern with racial matters, one way or the other, but was exploiting the highly charged school desegregation issue to maintain himself in power....
>
> The man who knew Orval Faubus longest was convinced that he was untouched by simple race prejudice. Old Sam Faubus [Orval's father] the self-educated hill farmer ... never abandoned the populist faith....
>
> Orval, Sam Faubus recalled, had never even seen a black until he was grown ... and he knew of nothing that had happened since to cause him to reject his father's teaching that racial equality was essential to progress as well as justice. His son went off the track, Sam Faubus thought, because he could never stand to be looked down on, and Orval believed that the leading citizens of Little Rock had done just that.... This personal resentment reinforced his suspicion that the Little Rock school desegregation plan was deliberately designed to discriminate against poor whites, requiring those in the downtown area to mingle their children with blacks, while the schools in the upper-income precincts ... would remain segregated.

Harry Ashmore, *Arkansas: A Bicentennial History* (New York: W. W. Norton; and Nashville: American Association for State and Local History, 1978),153–55.

I Am an Arkansan

Eldridge Cleaver (1935–1998)

Eldridge Cleaver was born August 31, 1935, in Wabbaseka (Jefferson County). He was one of the leaders of the African American black power movement in the 1960s and one of the early members of the Black Panther Party. In 1943, his family left Arkansas, moving west. By 1946, they had settled in the gritty Los Angeles Watts neighborhood. There, Cleaver found himself in trouble with the law and was convicted for selling drugs. Upon his release, he worked as a newspaper reporter and joined the Black Panther Party in 1967, serving as its minister of information. As a member of this group, Cleaver was involved in a 1968 shootout with Oakland police, and as a result, his parole was revoked. He became a fugitive from justice, living in Europe and Africa to avoid arrest.

In 1975, he returned to the United States, served a brief amount of jail time, and became an active Christian and supporter of the Republican Party. He wrote several books, most notably *Soul on Ice*, his controversial memoir of his experiences in prison. He died in 1998 in California and is buried there.

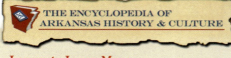

THE ENCYCLOPEDIA OF ARKANSAS HISTORY & CULTURE

Log on to Learn More
http://www.encyclopediaofarkansas.net/

Mothers' League of Central High a segregationist group that attempted to get a court order to stop Central High School from opening for the 1957 fall semester.

Little Rock Nine the nine black students admitted to Central High School in 1957.

The **Mothers' League of Central High**, a segregationist group, filed suit in an attempt to prevent the school from opening. Governor Faubus was the group's only witness. He said that he knew that black and white students had guns. He had learned that gangs were forming to threaten students at the high school. No one, then or since, has been able to find any proof to support the governor's claims. A local court agreed to delay the opening of school, but the federal court insisted that the plan proceed.

School was scheduled to start September 4. The day before, Faubus ordered units of the Arkansas National Guard to surround Central High. He told the guard to prevent the nine African American students from going into Central High. Drawn by the guard and urged on by the governor's actions, a crowd of whites gathered at the school. A mob mentality took hold of the crowd and many shouted at, pushed, and threw things at reporters, law enforcement officers, and the students. Reporters from all over the nation rushed to Little Rock.

The **Little Rock Nine**, as they would come to be known, included sixteen-year-old Minnijean Brown; fifteen-year-old Elizabeth Eckford; the only senior, Ernest Green, who was almost seventeen; Thelma Mothershed, seventeen; Melba Pattillo, sixteen; Gloria Ray, fifteen; sixteen-year-old Terrence Roberts; Jefferson Thomas, fifteen; and the youngest member of the group, Carlotta Walls, who was fourteen.

◄ Gov. Orval Faubus gives a press conference during the crisis.

▲ Elizabeth Eckford, one of the Little Rock Nine, tried to enter Central High School while followed by an angry, screaming mob.

On September 4, the African American students went to school. The guard turned them away at a side door. One of the students, Elizabeth Eckford, arrived at the north end of campus and was not able to join the others. When she tried to enter through the front door, she was told by a guardsman to leave. She then had to walk alone from the school to the bus stop at the south end of the campus.

All by herself, with her books clutched in her arms and fighting back tears, the fifteen-year-old girl walked a long block past the mob of whites. There were now around a thousand people lining the street. They screamed and shouted at her, but she kept her head held high. Pictures and stories of her ordeal were broadcast worldwide within hours.

It was a painful moment, and Little Rock and Arkansas would pay dearly for the shame of it. But it was a sort of beginning, a moment in which the effects of racism became embodied in the fear and courage of one teenaged girl. Americans were shocked at the sight, and they began to question tradition, themselves, and their world. In a very real sense, this was a major step forward in the civil rights movement.

The African American students waited. Meanwhile, the courts, the school board, the governor, and even the president of the United States wrestled with the problem. Arkansas congressman Brooks

Separate and Unequal **399**

Women's Emergency Committee to Open Our Schools a group of women, headed by Adolphine Fletcher Terry, who fought to reopen Little Rock schools in the 1958–59 school year with their STOP campaign. They were also instrumental in cutting segregationists from the school board by petitioning for a special election for their removal.

STOP the acronym for a group of Little Rock women organized to "Stop This Outrageous Purge"; the name of an organization that worked to return schools to normal operation.

Purge (PURJ) to remove in a drastic fashion, even by force.

Hays arranged a meeting between Governor Faubus and President Dwight D. Eisenhower. It failed to produce results. In the end, the federal court ordered Faubus to end the state's involvement at Central. Governor Faubus withdrew the National Guard.

On September 23, the nine African American students tried again to enter Central High. By this time, the white mob at the school was very large and unruly. The Little Rock police said they could not protect the students if they remained in school. The African American students left under police escort after only a few hours. Mayor Woodrow Mann called upon President Eisenhower for help.

Eisenhower had to uphold the authority of the federal court system. The president removed the Arkansas National Guard from the governor's command and put it under the command of the U.S. Army. Then the president ordered units from the U.S. Army's 101st Airborne Division into Little Rock. The combat troops swiftly set up guard posts around the high school and a command post on the field behind it.

Then, an army station wagon escorted by jeeps full of armed troops picked up the nine African American students. The army took them to Central High, and the nine students walked up the steps to the front door with an armed escort. Little Rock Central High was now an integrated school, and it was clear to all that the United States would enforce the *Brown* ruling.

During the 1957–58 school year, most of the white students ignored the Little Rock Nine. Some students and many teachers were helpful. But a small number of white students set out to make school days brutal for the black students. They tried to provoke them with words and sometimes physical abuse. One of the black students hit back and was suspended, along with the white student who had started the fight.

The army units were withdrawn after a few weeks. The National Guardsmen remained to patrol the halls. At the end of the school year, Ernest Green became the first African American graduate of the integrated Little Rock school. There to see him graduate was the Reverend Martin Luther King Jr., who had been in Pine Bluff to speak at Arkansas Agricultural, Mechanical, and Normal College (now the University of Arkansas at Pine Bluff).

"The Lost Year"

Conditions in Little Rock declined before they improved. Acting under a law passed in a special session of the General Assembly, Faubus closed the public high schools in Little Rock for the 1958–59 school year. Although the football teams played their schedules, black and white students alike either had to give up school, go live with family members or friends to attend schools in other communities, delay their graduations and college plans, or go to new, all-white private schools. Black students and whites too poor to pay had no choices. This is often referred to as "the lost year." Half the members of the new Little Rock school board were now segregationists.

The turning point came when the segregationists on the school board tried to refuse to renew contracts for forty-four teachers and officials whom they felt supported integration. In response, the **Women's Emergency Committee to Open Our Schools**, headed by Aldolphine Fletcher Terry, encouraged businessmen to form **STOP** (Stop This Outrageous **Purge**) and campaigned for a special recall election in the spring of 1959. The vote removed the segregationists from the school board.

The Little Rock high schools opened again in the fall of 1959, and some African American students attended Central High, while others attended

I Am an Arkansan

Daisy Lee Gaston Bates (1914–1999)

Daisy Bates was an important player in the state's struggle to achieve integration of public schools. Her efforts in this crisis brought her international fame.

Since 1941, Bates, along with her husband L. C. Bates, had published the *Arkansas State Press,* a weekly newspaper that focused on civil rights issues. In 1952, she was elected to lead the Arkansas branch of the National Association for the Advancement of Colored People (NAACP), one of the leading civil rights organizations in the United States. After her work in supporting the efforts of the Little Rock Nine in 1957, she was named by the Associated Press as the Woman of the Year in Education. She moved to New York City in 1960 in order to write what would become her widely praised memoir, *The Long Shadow of Little Rock.* For the rest of her career, she worked to provide better education for poor Arkansans, working primarily in Desha County. Two years after her death in 1999, the Arkansas legislature proclaimed "Daisy Gaston Bates Day" as a way of honoring her enormous contribution to the cause of civil rights in Arkansas. The street in front of Central High School now bears her name.

THE ENCYCLOPEDIA OF ARKANSAS HISTORY & CULTURE

Log on to Learn More
http://www.encyclopediaofarkansas.net/

Separate and Unequal

▶ During the "lost year" in Little Rock, students stayed at home, went to private schools, or were forced to move.

▲ Daisy Bates and Orval Faubus shake hands. What is the writer's opinion of Bates as reflected in the paragraph on the left? Describe the "tone" of the paragraph.

▲ Seen here with Arkansas environmentalist Lily Peter, Adolphine Fletcher Terry (left) led the movement that restored local control of the schools in Little Rock in 1958–59.

Hall High. Complete integration of the Little Rock schools at all grade levels did not come until the early 1970s, with court-ordered busing.

Those who study the crisis in Little Rock must attempt to recognize the emotional investment, sacrifices, and character this situation demanded of those involved. The level of commitment and caliber of character of the Little Rock Nine were remarkable for teenagers thrust into an unwanted spotlight.

Arkansans must also remember that every story has more than one side. We often see events from only one angle,

402   Chapter 18

based on our race, gender, background, experiences, age, religion, political beliefs, or personal bias. There are many facets to every moment in history, many perspectives, and many opinions. We must exhibit empathy for those involved. We should try as best we can to live each other's stories. To do so, the facts must be recalled, studied, and analyzed, even those that caused deep bruises on our state's past.

Where Are They Now?

The Little Rock Nine have gone on to live productive, successful lives. After earning degrees in journalism and social work, Minnijean Brown Trickey lived in Canada and worked for peace, environmental, and youth causes. She served as deputy assistant secretary for workforce diversity for the Department of the Interior in the Clinton administration and has taught at the community-college level. She has won numerous awards that recognize her work in race relations and social justice. Trickey has six children, one of whom is a ranger at the Central High School National Park Site.

Elizabeth Eckford served in the U.S. Army after earning her general equivalency diploma and attended college in Ohio. After college, she was the first African American in St. Louis to work in a bank. She has worked, among other things, as a military reporter, teacher, welfare counselor, and probation officer. She has two sons.

Ernest Green attended Michigan State University and earned bachelor's and master's degrees. He served as the assistant secretary of Housing and Urban Development under President Carter and now works at Lehman Brothers financial investment firm in Washington, D.C. He has served on the boards of the NAACP and the Winthrop Rockefeller Foundation. Green is married and has three children.

Thelma Mothershed Wair attended college in Illinois and taught home economics for twenty-eight years. She and her late husband have one son.

Melba Pattillo Beals earned a bachelor's degree from San Francisco State University and a master's from Columbia University. She worked as a journalist for an NBC station. Beals has a daughter and two twin sons. She wrote the book *Warriors Don't Cry* about her Central High experience.

Gloria Ray Karlmark transferred to an integrated high school in Kansas City after her mother was fired by the Faubus administration from her state government job. Karlmark earned degrees in chemistry and mathematics, worked as a teacher, and married while living in Chicago. She then

▼ Minnijean Brown Trickey speaks to a group of teachers in the auditorium of Central High School in 2005.

Separate and Unequal **403**

A Day in the Life

Elizabeth Eckford's First Day at Central High: "It was the longest block I ever walked in my whole life."

For many, the most dramatic moment of the integration crisis at Central High School in 1957 was fifteen-year-old Elizabeth Eckford's lonely walk in front of an angry mob after she had been turned away from entering the school by the Arkansas National Guard.

Soon after, Elizabeth described her day to Daisy Bates, the head of the NAACP in Arkansas, who was an advisor to the "Little Rock Nine" during the ordeal. Here are some of Elizabeth's recollections:

> You remember the day before we were to go in, we met Superintendent Blossom at the school board office. He told us what the mob might say and do but he never told us we wouldn't have any protection. He told our parents not to come because he wouldn't be able to protect the children if they did.
>
> That night I was so excited I couldn't sleep.... Before I left home Mother called us into the living room. She said we should have a word of prayer. Then I caught a bus and got off a block from the school. I saw a large crowd of people standing across the street from the [National Guard] soldiers guarding Central. As I walked on, the crowd suddenly got very quiet....
>
> The crowd moved in closer and then began to follow me, calling me names. I still wasn't afraid. Just a little bit nervous. Then my knees started to shake all of a sudden and I wondered whether I could make it to the center entrance a block away. It was the longest block I ever walked in my whole life.
>
> Even so, I still wasn't too scared because all the time I kept thinking that the guards would protect me.... So I walked until I was right in front of the path to the front door.
>
> I stood looking at the school—it looked so big! Just then the guards let some white students go through.... When I was able to steady my knees, I walked up to the guard who had let the

white students in. He . . . didn't move. When I tried to squeeze past him, he raised his bayonet and then the other guards closed in and they raised their bayonets.

They glared at me with a mean look and I was very frightened and didn't know what to do. I turned around and the crowd came toward me.

They moved closer and closer. Somebody started yelling, "Lynch her! Lynch her!"

I tried to see a friendly face somewhere in the mob—someone who maybe would help. I looked into the face of an old woman and it seemed a kind face, but when I looked at her again, she spat on me. . . .

I turned back to the guards but their faces told me I wouldn't get help from them. Then I looked down the block and saw a bench at the bus stop. I thought, "If I can only get there I will be safe." I don't know why the bench seemed a safe place to me, but I started walking toward it. I tried to close my mind to what they were shouting. . . .

When I finally got there, I don't think I could have gone another step. . . . Then, a white lady—she was very nice—she came over to me on the bench. . . . She put me on the bus and sat next to me. . . . I can't remember much about the bus ride. . . .

[Elizabeth rode to the Arkansas School for the Blind, where her mother was a teacher.] Mother was standing at the window with her head bowed, but she must have sensed I was there because she turned around. She looked as if she had been crying and I wanted to tell her I was all right. But I couldn't speak. She put her arms around me and I cried.

Quoted in Daisy Bates, *The Long Shadow of Little Rock* (1962; reprinted, Fayetteville: University of Arkansas Press, 1987), 72–76.

worked for McDonnell-Douglas and NASA on robotics projects. She moved to Europe, became an attorney, and now works and lives in the Netherlands. She and her husband have two children.

Terrence Roberts earned bachelor's and master's degrees from universities in California, and earned his doctorate in psychology from Southern Illinois University. He served as the director of a mental-health hospital and the assistant dean of the School of Social Welfare at UCLA. He then became chairman of the Department of Psychology at Antioch University, also in Los Angeles. He serves on boards of several organizations, including the Little Rock Nine Foundation, and he and his wife have two daughters and a grandson.

Jefferson Thomas is now retired, but served many years as an accountant for the U.S. Department of Defense. He is married with three children and two step-children.

Carlotta Walls Lanier, the youngest of the Little Rock Nine, graduated

▲ In September 1997, the fortieth anniversary of the integration of Central High School was marked. The Little Rock Nine are pictured here with President Clinton and former Governor Mike Huckabee.

from Central and then attended Michigan State University. After moving to Colorado, she earned her bachelor's degree and eventually went into real estate, forming her own firm. She is the president of the Little Rock Nine Foundation, and she and her husband have two grown children.

Central High Today

In 1999, President Clinton presented the Little Rock Nine with Congressional Gold Medals, the nation's highest honor for nonmilitary citizens. Previously, the Little Rock Central High School National Historic Site Visitor Center was housed in the old Magnolia Mobil gas station across the street from the school, where many reporters camped during the crisis. In 2007, a new visitor's center opened, which offered expanded exhibit space, more historical and archival storage, space for educational programs, and administrative offices. The opening of the new visitor's center was in conjunction with the fiftieth anniversary of the desegregation of Central High School.

County Quest

Faulkner

Named after: *Sandford C. Faulkner, writer of a state anthem, "The Arkansas Traveler"*

Chief Source of Income: *Service industry*

Seat: *Conway*

Faulkner County was formed in 1873. Today, the county is the home of the University of Central Arkansas, Hendrix College, and Central Baptist College, all located in Conway. Arkansas Educational Television Network is also based in Conway. It is home to the IC Company (formerly Ward Bus Company), one of the nation's largest school bus manufacturers. Toad Suck Daze is a well-known festival in the county.

Central High School is frequently recognized for its large number of National Merit Scholars and presidential and AP scholars. Central also produces the largest number of participants in Governor's School and the largest number of delegates to Boys State and Girls State. It has one of the oldest school newspapers in the country, the *Tiger,* and has a strong athletics program. In 2006, Central was named one of the twenty best high schools in the nation by *Newsweek* magazine. Central High School is on the National Register of Historic Places and is a national historic landmark, as well as a national historic site.

◀ The National Historic Site in 2006.

Separate and Unequal

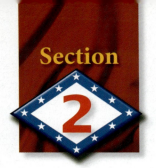

Section 2
The National Civil Rights Movement in Arkansas

Guide to Reading

Terms
sit-ins
Student Nonviolent Coordinating Committee

People
Martin Luther King Jr.

sit-ins forms of protest involving taking a seat in and refusing to leave an establishment from which one is excluded in order to protest the exclusion.

Student Nonviolent Coordinating Committee also known by its acronym SNCC (SNICK), a civil rights group made up of college students and other young people, formed to publicize and coordinate sit-ins and other protests.

Local Power

The civil rights movement in Arkansas moved faster than some whites would have believed could be true. It was also slower than blacks would have liked. In Little Rock, Philander Smith College students staged **sit-ins** and marched on the state capitol. In 1962, some African American leaders, among them Dr. William Townsend and Dr. Jerry Jewell, filed a lawsuit to integrate city-owned buildings and programs in Little Rock.

▲ Bobby Brown, a student at Philander Smith College in Little Rock, organized "sit-ins" to protest segregation. Why do you think this form of protest would be effective? Ineffective?

In Pine Bluff, the local **Student Nonviolent Coordinating Committee** staged protests to achieve equal hiring practices. By 1964, the city's major stores agreed to hire blacks on the same basis as whites. Even after the passage of the 1964 civil rights laws, Ozell Sutton of the Arkansas Council on Human Relations was thrown out of the state capitol dining room. Sutton filed a complaint that opened the dining room to African Americans.

African Americans had begun to gain voting rights in Arkansas before the Civil Rights Act of 1965. The state gave up the poll tax and began a fair system to register voters. The use of voting

County Quest

Lonoke

Named after: the "lone" oak tree

Chief Source of Income: Agriculture and service industries

Seat: Lonoke

Lonoke County was created in 1873, and is the only county in Arkansas whose county seat bears the same name as the county. A lush, largely agricultural area, several creeks and bayous can be found there. Terri Utley, who was Miss USA in 1982, was from Cabot, a prosperous city in this county. Ammunitions divisions of Remington Arms are also located in the county.

Martin Luther King Jr. a central figure in the United States civil rights movement. An African American leader, spiritual advisor, and non-violent activist. An inspiration to many people of all races.

▲ Students at the University of Arkansas mourn the death of Martin Luther King Jr.

machines in many places improved the chances for honest vote counting. In 1940, around 3 percent of black adults in Arkansas were registered to vote. By the 1970s, the number had risen to 72 percent, about the same as for white voters. Still, in the 1980s, there were only six African American members of the Arkansas General Assembly.

Governor Rockefeller named several African Americans to state offices, including the pardons and parole board, county boards of welfare, and state college boards. Rockefeller also formed a Governor's Council on Human Resources to foster hiring African American workers in public and private business. He named Ozell Sutton to head it.

In April of 1968, the Reverend **Martin Luther King Jr.** was shot and killed by a white man in Memphis, Tennessee. All over the nation, cities erupted in riots and burned in flames. In Arkansas, there was property destroyed in some cities. But most people, black and white, paid peaceful tribute to the great civil rights leader. Thousands gathered at the steps of the state capitol. Governor and Mrs. Rockefeller led them as everyone joined hands and sang the anthem of the civil rights movement, "We Shall Overcome."

DID YOU KNOW?

Kennedy in Arkansas

Did you know President John F. Kennedy visited Arkansas to dedicate the Greers Ferry Dam and Reservoir in 1963? He flew into Little Rock Air Force Base, then went to the dam site by helicopter. In his brief talk, he praised the Arkansas congressional delegation and defended federal projects such as the dam. After the speech, Kennedy talked to people who had gathered at a barbecue lunch and shook hands with schoolchildren.

Arkansas voted for Kennedy in the 1960 presidential election, but many whites had since become displeased with his support for civil rights activities. There were, however, no demonstrations at his speech. Kennedy visited Arkansas on October 3, 1963. On November 22, on a visit to Dallas, he was assassinated.

Separate and Unequal

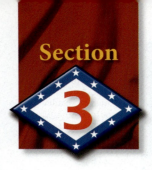

Section 3
Life in the 1960s

Guide to Reading

Terms
dropped out
Great Society
protest movement
War on Poverty

People
hippies

---

hippies (HIP-eez) young people who wore their hair long and dressed unconventionally to distance themselves from a mainstream culture they considered violent and destructive.

dropped out having foregone the typical middle-class life, creating a "counterculture" among young people during the sixties; often associated with drug use.

▼ Clarence Young of Little Rock served in Vietnam in 1966.

Counterculture and Music

Amid the civil rights revolutions of the late fifties and early sixties and the death and chaos of the Vietnam War, culture, personal freedoms, and lifestyles underwent noticeable change. Many young people rebelled against the ways of their parents, some styling themselves as **hippies** who **dropped out** of the American middle class. The hippie culture became a national phenomenon during what is called the "summer of love" which began in San Francisco in 1967. Many young Americans went to the West Coast to experience new things, and while there, adopted the way of life of a "flower child."

They showed their social freedom with long hair, casual clothing, and their support of rock and folk music. The Beatles, the Doors, Bob Dylan, Jimi Hendrix, and Janis Joplin were popular acts of the day. The Woodstock music festival held in 1969 in Bethel, New York, has been called the greatest music festival ever. The theme was "three days of peace and music," and in addition to Hendrix, Joplin, and the Doors, featured musical groups Credence Clearwater Revival, the Grateful Dead, and the Who, among others.

New sexual attitudes and a new drug culture also emerged in the sixties. Free love was a common theme, and old rules of behavior were challenged. Politics also seemed to take a more young and liberal turn with the election of John F. Kennedy as president, and later his brother Robert was a presidential candidate. For the most part, Arkansans were not very enthusiastic about hippies, although the lifestyle was common on college campuses throughout the country, including the University of Arkansas in Fayetteville.

410 Chapter 18

◀ Arkansas's Vietnam veteran's memorial lists the names of all Arkansans who died in the conflict.

▼ Vietnam veterans protesting the war in Fayetteville (Washington County).

Vietnam and Antiwar Protests

The Cold War emphasis on stopping the spread of communism caused the United States to commit itself to the defense of South Vietnam. That country was fighting a civil war against Communist North Vietnam.

At first, American military advisors worked to train the military of South Vietnam. But starting in 1965, the United States sent large numbers of American armed forces to fight the war. Arkansans again went to war in a far-off place. The U.S. armed forces did not call up guard and reserve units in large numbers. That meant that most of the fighting was done by eighteen- or nineteen-year-olds who were either drafted or volunteered. As the war dragged on, more and more Americans came to feel that the costly struggle in Vietnam was none of America's business.

Another aspect of the hippie or counterculture movement was the antiwar protests regarding the conflict in Vietnam and the draft. Many followed the lead of civil rights protesters and used sit-ins as a form of protest and made their presence known at political events. Rallies and marches were held and the peace symbol and two-fingered peace sign could be seen in many places.

All over the country, open protests of the war were staged on a steady basis, week after week. Voices within the government began to object as well, especially the voice of Arkansas's senator and chairman of the Foreign Relations Committee, J. William Fulbright. Arkansas saw very little of the **protest movement** until the last years of the war.

Arkansans, slow to experience the hippie counterculture and war protests, continued the business of trying to improve the state. Major federal aid programs helped to do that. One project was the interstate highway system, which built four-lane highways

protest movement a nationwide call to end the war in Vietnam.

Separate and Unequal **411**

Great Society the programs of Lyndon Johnson aimed at bringing African Americans and poor citizens into the mainstream of American life.

War on Poverty Lyndon Johnson's programs aimed at raising the standard of living among America's poorest citizens.

to connect Arkansas to other parts of the region and nation. The state road-building program, also with aid from the federal government, replaced dirt roads with paved roads.

The federal government, through the Army Corp of Engineers, built many lakes in Arkansas, including Norfork, Table Rock, Bull Shoals, Beaver, and Greers Ferry. The lakes offered Arkansans great fishing, boating, and other forms of water sports. They also enhanced the tourist business. The Corps of Engineers built the Greers Ferry dam at the Little Red River to provide flood control, hydroelectricity, and recreation. It cost more than $46 million.

Lyndon B. Johnson

After the assassination of John F. Kennedy, President Lyndon B. Johnson worked to carry on many programs of the Kennedy administration. One of his own policies, the **Great Society**, increased aid to improve social problems. His **War on Poverty** offered help with education, housing, healthcare, social services, job training, and solving the problems of cities. In 1956, 9.3 percent of state and local revenues came from the federal government. By 1966, that figure reached 18.1 percent and continued to rise with the help of this plan.

Arkansas in the 1960s

Politics, protests, and progress aside, Arkansans were able to enjoy some fun and build some state pride during the 1960s. One of the major developments of the decade was Arkansas's growing fascination with the football team of the University of Arkansas, the Razorbacks.

Under Frank Broyles, the head coach from 1958 to 1976, the team began to win regularly, not just in its own Southwest Conference, but also big games against nationally ranked opponents. During those years, Arkansas won the Southwest Conference championship seven times, went to ten bowl games, and once, in 1964, was national champion.

Ken Hatfield, a future Razorback head coach, played on the 1964 team, as well as Jerry Jones, future owner of the Dallas Cowboys, and Jimmy Johnson, future coach of the Dallas Cowboys. Lance Alworth, who would later play for the San Diego Chargers and Dallas Cowboys, and who would later be inducted into the National Football League Hall of Fame, was also a member of the 1964 team. Barry Switzer, future coach of the Oklahoma Sooners and Dallas Cowboys, and one of only two coaches to win both a collegiate national championship and a Super Bowl (the other was Johnson), was an assistant under Broyles during this winning season.

Arkansas still had many obstacles to overcome on its way to becoming a more urban, equal, industrial society with opportunities for all its citizens. The sixties were both frightening and incredible. Very little remained the same in Arkansas or the nation. Arkansans and Americans had to take a long, hard look at themselves, and sometimes they did not like what they saw. To determine the most productive and secure path for the future and to honor the sacrifices that had been made during the decade were their most important responsibilities.

I Am an Arkansan

Joycelyn Elders (1933–)

Joycelyn Elders was director of the Arkansas Department of Health and the U.S. surgeon general in the administration of President Bill Clinton. Her controversial opinions led to her resignation after just over a year as surgeon general.

Elders was born in Schaal (Howard County). Born Minnie Lee Jones, she took the name Joycelyn while attending college. After attending a lecture by Edith Irby Jones, the first woman to attend the University of Arkansas Medical School, Elders decided to become a physician. In 1956, she entered the University of Arkansas Medical School on the G.I. Bill. In 1961, after briefly working at the University of Minnesota, Elders returned to Little Rock for her residency and was soon appointed chief pediatric resident. For the next two decades, she devoted her time to improving the health of Arkansas's children. By the 1980s, 20 percent of children were born to teenage mothers, a problem that then-governor Bill Clinton considered a social and fiscal crisis. In 1987, he named Elders director of the Arkansas Department of Health.

In January of 1993, president-elect Clinton nominated Elders to the post of U.S. surgeon general, tapping her as the second African American ever named to a cabinet-level position. As surgeon general, Elders focused on several big health issues: tobacco-related disease, AIDS, and alcohol and drug abuse. She also continued her support for sex education. In 1994, she resigned after remarks she made concerning sexual education drew intense criticism. After retiring from medicine in 1999, Elders returned to Little Rock, where she continues to speak about public-health education and on issues such as AIDS, adolescent sexuality, and national healthcare.

THE ENCYCLOPEDIA OF ARKANSAS HISTORY & CULTURE

Log on to Learn More
http://www.encyclopediaofarkansas.net/

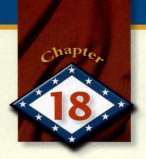

Chapter Reflection

Reflective Questions

1. What was the name of the landmark Supreme Court case that said separate was not equal, and in what year did it occur?

2. What does discrimination mean to you? Integration? Define both in your own words.

3. Think back through all that you have studied in your Arkansas history class this school year. Does Arkansas have history of discrimination or is the Central High School situation the first such case? Use the previous chapters of this book to help you craft your answer.

4. What was the first Arkansas public-school district to integrate? Second? Identify the years for each.

5. Did the Little Rock Nine have any protection at school? If so, from whom? If no, why not?

6. Why was Minnijean Brown finally expelled from Central? What did she do afterward?

7. During the "lost year," what school choices did Little Rock high-school students have?

8. Historically speaking, was "separate but equal" fair? If so, how? If no, why not?

9. In your opinion, what were Governor Faubus's reasons for closing the schools in 1958–59?

10. What do you believe were reasons people participated in the hippie or counterculture movement?

11. When and where was President Kennedy assassinated? Where in Arkansas did he visit only a few weeks before his death?

12. What were two of Lyndon Johnson's accomplishments related to equality?

13. When and where was Martin Luther King Jr. assassinated?

HisStory, HerStory, YourStory, OurStory...

1. Pretend that you are an out-of-state newspaper writer in Little Rock during the crisis and you have been assigned to cover the integration of Central High School. Remember to be sensitive and to use facts in your piece. Be sure to include the when, where, who, and what of the events. Be accurate and descriptive. You might consider reviewing the timeline of civil rights events in the chapter to use as your guide.

Telling an Arkansas Story— The Written Word

Newspaper reporters often use basic types of question formats when interviewing someone:

Close-ended: can be answered with yes, no, or a basic fact. No discussion.

Open-ended: encourages discussion and storytelling. Gives the reporter ideas for other questions.

2. Continue in your role as a newspaper reporter, but this time, assume that you are

counties of the northwest. Johnson secured much of the white vote, but Rockefeller received 90 percent of the black vote, assuring his victory. The voters also chose a Republican lieutenant governor, World War II hero Maurice "Footsie" Britt. Most voters either supported Rockefeller and his successful track record in business and **philanthropy**, or were just voting against Johnson. Some were turning their backs on the Faubus years, and thus voting Republican. In any case, it was not a lasting win for the Republican Party, as there would not be another Republican governor in the state until Mike Huckabee was appointed in the 1990s.

Rockefeller found out just how little had changed in Arkansas politics during the radical 1960s when he began working with the General Assembly. With 132 Democrats and just three Republicans, the legislature was in no mood to put up with a Republican governor. In the elections of 1968, Arkansas voters showed just how independent—or how strong-willed and unpredictable—they could be. That year, Arkansans reelected Rockefeller to a second term as governor, reelected Democrat J. William Fulbright to the U.S. Senate, and gave their electoral votes to George Wallace for president. Wallace, running as the **American Independent Party** candidate, was against integration, for the war in Vietnam, and expressed disgust with hippies. Fulbright, long a leader in America's international involvement, had begun to oppose the war in Vietnam.

Even after Rockefeller's second win in 1968, the General Assembly blocked most of his proposed laws. His terms did see passage of a **sunshine law** that opened government records to public view. The state also got its first minimum-wage law. Rockefeller started the Division of Mental Retardation Services, which was the state's first program to offer housing and training options to people with developmental disabilities.

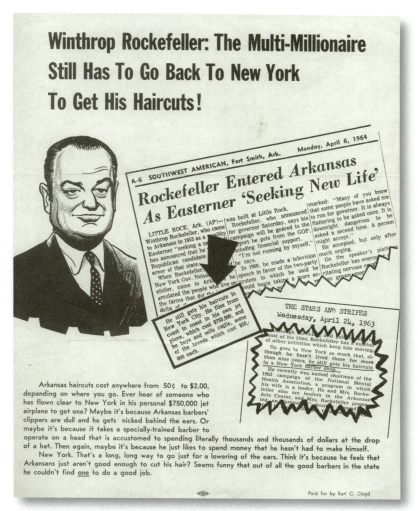

▲ What is this cartoon saying about Rockefeller?

Most of what Rockefeller achieved came from enforcement of existing laws. He enforced the laws against gambling in Hot Springs, finally closing the gambling houses there. Soon after taking office, Rockefeller received a report from the state police about the brutal treatment of inmates in the state prison system. The report revealed grim living conditions and outright torture of inmates. Long-term and often-armed inmates really ran the prisons. Known as **trustys**, they held all the important jobs and sold favors to others.

Rockefeller brought in a professional prison director, Tom Murton. Murton attracted national attention by digging up

philanthropy charitable contributions; to distribute or donate funds or goods.

American Independent Party a political party formed in 1968 by Alabama senator George Wallace; its members opposed welfare programs and the 1964 Civil Rights Act.

sunshine law also known as the Freedom of Information law, it opened government records to public review.

trustys (TRUSS-tees) long-term prison inmates entrusted with the oversight of other prisoners.

Defining Ourselves **419**

DID YOU KNOW?

Did you know we have a governor to thank for the arts center in Little Rock? In an effort to bring a broader cultural experience to the state, Gov. Winthrop Rockefeller and his wife, Jeanette, took the lead in establishing the Arkansas Arts Center in Little Rock. Public and private funds from all over the state contributed to the arts center. Under director Townsend Wolfe, the arts center housed and displayed its own permanent collection as well as national exhibits, offered a wide range of classes in visual and dance arts, and sponsored a children's theater. In 2001, the arts center opened a major new addition, and achieved national recognition for its collection of drawings. The arts center also took its traveling arts exhibitions all over the state. Examples of permanent exhibitions include pieces from the late-nineteenth-century impressionist movement, with drawings and paintings by Edgar Degas, Claude Monet, and Camille Pissarro. Twentieth-century pieces include those of artists Diego Rivera, Odilon Redon, the sculptor Auguste Rodin, Henry Moore, Pablo Picasso, and Andrew Wyeth.

THE ENCYCLOPEDIA OF ARKANSAS HISTORY & CULTURE

Log on to Learn More
http://www.encyclopediaofarkansas.net/

commuted a changed or lessened prison sentence or penalty.

Dale Bumpers a successful Arkansas governor and U.S. senator in the 1970s, '80s and '90s.

special interests powerful business, lobbyists or other activists who give money to a political candidate in an attempt to influence him or her on a specific issue.

what he said were the bodies of murdered inmates. It was later learned that he was digging in the site of an old graveyard, but he also discovered widespread torture—often administered by prison doctors. Robert Sarver, who worked to improve the prisons in a more discreet fashion, replaced Murton. Neither the public nor the General Assembly had much interest in prison reform.

At last, in the 1970s, a U.S. court declared the entire Arkansas prison system unconstitutional. The judge called it a "dark and evil world." The courts supervised the prisons for thirteen years. Just before he left office, Rockefeller **commuted** the sentences of all fifteen people then on death row to life in prison.

Bumpers and Pryor

The election for governor in 1970 brought a new face to Arkansas politics. **Dale Bumpers** of Charleston (Franklin County) first beat Orval Faubus in the Democratic primary run-off, then defeated Winthrop Rockefeller in the general election. Progressive and considered to be free of ties to **special interests**, Bumpers presided over the state's continued economic development.

Bumpers enacted a state government reorganization plan that Rockefeller had initially proposed, combining more than one hundred agencies into thirteen major departments. He also persuaded the legislature to enact tax reform that established a more progressive tax scale, increasing taxes on higher incomes while reducing the rates on lower incomes. The resulting increase in tax revenue allowed state support for kindergartens, free textbooks in the public schools, and the creation of community colleges. First Lady Betty Bumpers created a statewide immunization program to help children suffering from preventable diseases.

Bumpers was a popular governor, and easily won a second term in 1972. In 1974, he defeated the popular, long-

▼ Dale Bumpers.

420 Chapter 19

serving J. William Fulbright for his U.S. Senate seat. Replacing Bumpers as governor was former congressman **David Pryor** of Camden who, in the Democratic Party primary, fought off yet another comeback attempt by Orval Faubus.

By the late 1970s, there seemed to be a changing of the guard among the state's political leadership, as the older generation (Orval Faubus and Jim Johnson) gave way to younger leaders like Bumpers, Pryor, and, ultimately, Bill Clinton. Another older political force in the state, Wilbur Mills—who had once been considered the most powerful man in Washington—left the

◀ David Pryor.

David Pryor popular Arkansas politician who served as a state legislator, as governor, a U.S. senator, and in the U.S. House of Representatives.

I Am an Arkansan

Dale Bumpers (1925–)

Born in Charleston (Franklin County) in 1925, Dale Leon Bumpers was one of Arkansas's most prominent politicians in the twentieth century. As governor, Bumpers restructured the tax system and reorganized state government. As a U.S. senator (1975–99), he was fiscally conservative in matters of economics, yet socially liberal. He was widely respected by his fellow senators for his skills as a speaker. Many observers have said his 1999 speech during Clinton's impeachment trial was crucial in helping Clinton avoid a conviction.

After earning a bachelor's degree at the University of Arkansas, he graduated from Northwestern University Law School in Illinois. Returning to Arkansas, he practiced law for twenty years in Charleston, losing only three cases during that time.

In 1970, he ran for governor, although he was virtually unknown at the time. His surprise victory marked the end of Orval Faubus's domination of state politics. He won reelection in 1972. According to longtime political reporter Doug Smith, during Bumpers's administration, "there was more substantial progressive legislation enacted than in any other four-year period in Arkansas history."

In 1974, he ran for U.S. Senate, and was victorious against J. William Fulbright—whom Bumpers had admired for years. As a senator, Bumpers emerged as one of the most respected members of Congress. After retiring from the Senate in 1999, he has worked in Washington, D.C., as an attorney and consultant.

THE ENCYCLOPEDIA OF ARKANSAS HISTORY & CULTURE

Log on to Learn More
http://www.encyclopediaofarkansas.net/

Defining Ourselves

DID YOU KNOW?

Did you know *Brubaker*, a 1980 film starring Robert Redford, told the story of the grisly discovery of bodies buried at Cummins Prison, and the attempts to reform the state's brutal prison system?

Fannie Foxe an adult entertainer who was in the car with Congressman Wilbur Mills when he was pulled over by Washington, D.C., police in 1974.

U.S. House of Representatives in 1977 after enduring an embarrassing public scandal involving an exotic dancer named **Fannie Foxe**. Admitting his mistakes, and overcoming a serious problem with alcoholism, Mills went on to become an outspoken leader in the fight against alcohol and drug abuse. Long-time senator John McClellan died in 1977 and left behind a legacy as, among other things, a fierce opponent of organized crime. To fill out McClellan's term, Governor Pryor appointed Kaneaster Hodges. Pryor then won the Senate seat himself in 1978.

Although the Democrats were still the dominant party at the state and local level, Arkansans increasingly voted Republican in presidential elections. From Richard Nixon in 1972 until the election of Bill Clinton in 1992, only one Democratic candidate for president got Arkansas's electoral votes—Jimmy Carter of Georgia in 1976. Arkansans apparently liked the idea of a southerner in the White House.

Other Major Events of the Late 1960s and Early 1970s in Arkansas

In 1969, riding on the wave of popularity from the 1964 NCAA football championship, the Razorbacks played what was hyped as "the Game of the Century" or "the big shootout." The University of Texas Longhorns, ranked number one in the nation, traveled to Fayetteville to meet Arkansas, ranked number two. The game attracted national attention. President

▶ "The Game of the Century" was played between the Arkansas Razorbacks and the Texas Longhorns in 1969. President Richard Nixon (center, smiling) and George H. W. Bush (far right, light jacket, looking at Nixon) were in attendance.

I Am an Arkansan

Donald Roller Wilson (1938–)

Born in Houston, Texas, and a longtime resident of Fayetteville, Donald Roller Wilson is one of the most celebrated painters of his time. His work has graced the walls of famous performers such as Steve Martin, Jack Nicholson, and Robin Williams, and he designed album covers for Frank Zappa.

His unmistakable style and unmatched technique make him one of the most recognizable artists working today. While his art is widely collected by celebrities, he has also shown his paintings in galleries across the globe. His paintings are often filled with odd characters in mysterious settings—intricately crafted chimpanzees, dogs, and cats dressed in regal clothes are among his subjects.

His art, which has appeared in the Smithsonian in Washington, D.C., and the Brooklyn Museum in New York, among other places, has been described as divinely silly and has stirred the imagination of art lovers. After teaching at the University of Arkansas during the late 1960s, he has remained in Fayetteville as one of its most famous residents.

THE ENCYCLOPEDIA OF ARKANSAS HISTORY & CULTURE

Log on to Learn More
http://www.encyclopediaofarkansas.net/

Richard M. Nixon even flew in by helicopter to attend the game.

Texas won 15–14, scoring the winning touchdown in the final moments of the game. The game went on to achieve legendary status in the minds of Razorback fans everywhere, and helped cement a long-running rivalry with Texas.

In 1970, a true sign of progress was completed when the McClellan-Kerr Arkansas River Navigation System project was finished and named after Arkansas Senator John McClellan. The project was a series of locks and dams that created a system of navigable bodies of water. Boats and barges could go 445 miles from the mouth of the Arkansas River to Catoosa, Oklahoma, near Tulsa. At a cost of $1.2 billion, it was the largest project to that date undertaken by the U.S. Army Corps of Engineers.

The conflict in Vietnam continued from the 1960s into the 1970s. Before American forces finally withdrew in 1973, more than 580 Arkansans died in the war. The men and women who came home from Vietnam received little of the thanks and praise that had greeted their fathers' returns from World War II. Their service was not fully honored until the 1980s, when the Vietnam Veterans Memorial was built in Little Rock on the state capitol grounds. The memorial displays the names of Arkansans who died in the war.

Defining Ourselves

I Am an Arkansan

Miller Williams (1930–)

Miller Williams is an internationally known poet, one of the most important since World War II. He taught English for many years at the University of Arkansas, where he also helped form one of the country's best creative-writing programs. He is an accomplished editor and critic, and was one of the founders of the University of Arkansas Press. He is known among music fans as the father of Grammy-winning singer-songwriter and Fayetteville (Washington County) native Lucinda Williams.

The son of a Methodist minister, Williams studied biology at several Arkansas colleges and eventually earned a master's degree in zoology from the University of Arkansas. He published his first book of poems, *Et Cetera*, in 1952, when he was twenty-two years old. After teaching biology and English at LSU and Loyola in New Orleans through the 1950s and 1960s, Williams settled in Fayetteville in 1970. He then wrote several books of poetry, criticism, and fiction, and won a number of awards. In 1993, he received wide acclaim for the poem, "Of History and Hope," which he read at the second inauguration of President Bill Clinton. Among his many books are *Living on the Surface* (1989) and *Some Jazz a While* (1999).

Elsijane T. Roy in 1975 became the first woman appointed to the Arkansas Supreme Court.

Log on to Learn More
http://www.encyclopediaofarkansas.net/

County Quest

Lee

Named after: Confederate general Robert E. Lee
Chief Source of Income: Agriculture
Seat: Marianna

Lee County's eastern border is the Mississippi River, and the L'Anguille River skirts the northeast corner of Marianna, the county seat. The county was established in 1873. As with many counties in the Delta, Lee has had noticeable population shifts because of racial tension and the sometimes-unpredictable farm economy. The state prison at Brickeys helped create jobs in the area. Bear Creek Lake is a popular fishing spot in the county. Crowley's Ridge and the St. Francis National Forest are prominent geographical features in the area and provide many recreational and hunting opportunities for residents and visitors.

The late 1960s and early 1970s also saw the advance of the modern wave of the feminist movement in Arkansas and across the country. Women continued to work to improve their lives as they had in the late nineteenth century and the early years of the twentieth century, pursuing more and better-paying jobs. Many more women became doctors and lawyers, and they filled more top jobs in private business and public agencies they had never held before. In 1975, **Elsijane T. Roy** became the first woman on the Arkansas Supreme Court. When she moved up to a federal judgeship, African American civil rights lawyer George Howard took her place (he, too, later became a federal judge).

Not everyone approved of women gaining their share of political and social

TOGETHER WE CAN MAKE A DIFFERENCE

**PEACE DAY
SUNDAY, OCT. 2, 1983
STATE CAPITOL
LITTLE ROCK
1:00–4:00 P.M.**

power. Arkansas had passed the Nineteenth Amendment that granted women the right to vote in 1920, and the state had been progressive by electing Hattie Caraway, the first female member of the U.S. Senate. However, during the 1980s, the Arkansas General Assembly refused to ratify the proposed **Equal Rights Amendment** to the U.S. Constitution, which would have officially granted equal rights to women.

◀ A poster inviting the women of Little Rock and surrounding areas to participate in a "Peace Day."

Equal Rights Amendment a proposed constitutional amendment that would guarantee equality for women.

I Am an Arkansan

Ellen Gilchrist (1935–)

A successful novelist and a short story writer, Ellen Gilchrist won the 1984 National Book Award for her collection of stories, *Victory Over Japan.* She has won many other awards for her work, including a National Endowment for the Arts grant. A native of Mississippi, for many years she has lived in Fayetteville (Washington County), and has taught creative writing in the prestigious writing program at the University of Arkansas. As a college student at Millsaps College in Tennessee, she studied under author Eudora Welty. In 1976, she moved to New Orleans, where she worked as a journalist. During this time, she published her first book, a collection of poems, *The Land Surveyor's Daughter.*

Her first book of short stories, *In the Land of Dreamy Dreams,* was published in 1981. It sold over ten thousand copies in its first ten months of release. Critics from around the country praised her work. Since the 1980s, Gilchrist has been a contributor to National Public Radio. Her books have continued to receive wide acclaim from both critics and readers. She has also written a historical novel about ancient Greece, as well as several short-story collections such as *I, Rhoda Manning, Go Hunting with My Daddy: and Other Stories.*

Log on to Learn More
http://www.encyclopediaofarkansas.net/

Defining Ourselves

Section 2

The Arrival of Clinton

Guide to Reading

Terms

Alltel
Arkansas Gazette
Dillard's
J. B. Hunt Transport
Riceland Foods
Stephens, Incorporated
Tyson Foods
Wal-Mart

Places

The Arkansas School for Mathematics, Sciences, and the Arts

In 1978, Bill Clinton, a former Rhodes Scholar and state attorney general, won the Arkansas governorship. At thirty-two, he was the youngest governor in the nation. He started an ambitious program of education reform, highway construction, and economic development.

▼ Governor Clinton speaks at a rally.

Car Tags and Cubans

The voters became unhappy, however, when he increased car license fees and when Fort Chaffee near Fort Smith became home to thousands of refugees from Communist Cuba.

Cuba was a communist country that restricted the rights of its citizens to move from place to place. In the late 1970s, however, Cuba briefly allowed its citizens to move and travel out of the country. During this period, 120,000 Cubans traveled to the United States. Fort Chaffee, near Fort Smith, became a temporary home to eighteen thousand of the refugees. During their stay, around three hundred of the Cubans broke away from the Fort Chaffee grounds and charged up and down local roads, disrupting the peace and creating unease among locals. During the chaos, more than sixty people were injured and three buildings at Fort Chaffee were ruined. Frank White, a former banker and state official, later used a video of the incident against Clinton in his 1980 gubernatorial campaign advertisements. White also encouraged voters to remember that Clinton had raised their vehicle license fees (to pay for highway construction programs). This became known as the "car tags and Cubans"

426 Chapter 19

◀ Bill Clinton campaigns from a "paddy wagon" float during a parade. Why do politicians participate in these types of activities?

campaign and would ultimately help White defeat Clinton.

The White administration was marked by the passage of a state law that would have required schools teaching biological evolution (Darwinism) to also teach the creationist view of the origin of mankind. A federal judge declared the law unconstitutional, seeing it as an attempt by the government to dictate a specific religious concept in the public-school curriculum. The conservative mood of the state was also reflected in the rejection of a proposed new state constitution, the second time this had occurred in a decade.

Being Governor Is Better the Second Time Around

Clinton was reelected governor in 1982. With reelection and a change in the governor's term from two to four years, he would continue as governor until the early 1990s. During these years, Arkansans faced the same challenges as always: improving education, highways, and economic development. Clinton was especially interested in education. He appointed a special committee, headed by his wife, Hillary Rodham Clinton, to suggest changes to the public-school system. The legislature then enacted significant reforms aimed at improving teaching, student performance, course offerings, and teacher training. Although some claimed the reforms quickly began to show positive effects, getting the legislature to increase funding became a problem.

Clinton's emphasis on education was related to his strong push for

Defining Ourselves **427**

Dillard's a department store chain founded in Nashville, AR. Today, its world headquarters are located in Little Rock.

Wal-Mart headquartered in Bentonville and founded by Sam Walton in 1962, the company grew from one store in Rogers (Benton County) to almost seven thousand stores with almost two million employees, and it is the world's largest company.

Tyson Foods headquartered in Springdale and founded in 1935, it is the world's largest processor and marketer of beef, chicken, and pork.

Alltel a wireless technology and communications service provider founded in Little Rock in 1943.

economic development in the state. International corporations and investments made the Arkansas economy a genuinely global economy. Arkansans needed quality educations, to learn foreign languages, and to increase their understanding of the world beyond their borders if they were to make a living in a competitive, rapidly changing global marketplace. By the early 1990s, Arkansas led the nation in per-capita economic growth.

The Economy and Developing Big Business

The General Assembly and local cities and towns continued to offer enticements to new industry in Arkansas. In some cases, they allowed new businesses to be exempt from taxes. To help train job seekers, the state started the Vocational Technical Educational Program.

County Quest

Stone

Named after: The geology of the area

Chief Source of Income: Manufacturing

Seat: Mountain View

Stone County was created in 1873 from parts of Independence, Izard, Searcy, and Van Buren counties. Part of the Ozark National Forest is located within its borders. The Ozark Folk Center is a major tourist attraction, drawing folk music fans from around the nation. Jimmy Driftwood, a famous musician from the area, was instrumental in bringing attention to the region's folk traditions. Mountain View is home to one of the largest producers of handmade dulcimers in the world and is known as the "Folk Music Capital of the World." The area is also well known for horseback riding and trout fishing.

Through the 1970s and 1980s, hundreds of factories with thousands of jobs moved into the state. Jobs increased by 57 percent, and income increased by 65 percent, yet incomes in the state were still just 68 percent of the U.S. average. Many of the new jobs were in small towns and rural areas where they were most needed. The drive for industry continues in twenty-first century Arkansas.

By the 1980s, tourism developed into a major industry. In a typical year, more than fifteen million visitors came to Arkansas, spending almost $2 billion. Partly in tribute to the state's increasing tourist appeal, in the 1980s, the "Natural State" became Arkansas's new official nickname (it had already been the Bear State, the Wonder State, and the Land of Opportunity officially and unofficially).

Several Arkansas businessmen created major national corporations and kept their headquarters in Arkansas. William Dillard started with one country store and built **Dillard's**, a major department store chain with locations across the nation, based in Little Rock (Pulaski County). Sam Walton of Bentonville (Benton County) created the company that would become **Wal-Mart**. For several years, Walton was the richest man in the United States, and by the end of the twentieth century, Wal-Mart had become one of the most successful companies in American history and is now the world's largest retailer and the largest private employer in the United States.

Tyson Foods, based in Springdale, started as a chicken-processing company and is now the largest provider of protein (chicken, beef, and pork) in the country and provides thousands of jobs to farmers and processing plant workers. Little Rock's **Alltel** is a major nationwide operator of regular and wireless telephone systems. Alltel also acquired Systematics, which produced computer systems on an international scale. Arkansas is also home to several major trucking companies, such as **J. B. Hunt Transport** of Lowell. **Stephens, Incorporated**, based in Little Rock, is the largest bond trading business outside of New York. Even with all of this success, Arkansas still lagged behind the rest of the nation in some important areas, such as high-tech jobs involving computers and communication.

The median annual income per person in Arkansas, by the end of the twentieth century, was $32,714, or 78 percent of the national median. That was a considerable improvement over previous decades, when Arkansas's median income had been less than 70 percent of the national median. Arkansas's growth rate in areas such as investment in manufacturing, new jobs, and personal income was higher than the national average growth rate because the state started from such a low base. Arkansas still ranked near the bottom of the states in per-capita income.

By the beginning of the twenty-first century, Arkansas had finally achieved the goal of diversity in its economic enterprises. About one-fourth of the workers in the state were in service jobs. That included teaching, working at banks, restaurant work, and other activities that provided some sort of service to people, rather than making something to sell. The other leading areas of employment were manufacturing, at about 21 percent; retail sales, about 18 percent; and state and federal government, 16 percent.

DID YOU KNOW?

Did you know the KATV television tower in Jefferson County was the second largest man-made structure in the world until the mid-1970s?

The Rise of the Poultry and Agricultural Industries

The most important manufacturing area in the 1980s, in terms of value, was food processing. Most of that involved poultry, also the state's number one agricultural product. Food processing converted chickens into grocery store products, including frozen and fresh chicken and prepared meals. Second in manufacturing was electric and electronic products, such as

J. B. Hunt Transport one of the country's leading transport (trucking) and logistics (organized movement of goods) companies, founded in 1969; its headquarters are located in Lowell (Benton County).

Stephens, Incorporated an investment-banking firm (one of the largest outside of Wall Street in New York) founded in 1933 in Little Rock by W. R. "Witt" Stephens. Its headquarters remain in Little Rock.

◀ A crop duster in eastern Arkansas.

Defining Ourselves

Riceland Foods founded in 1921, a cooperative that sells and mills rice, soybeans, and wheat. It is one of the world's leading millers of rice, and is based in Stuttgart.

motors, transformers, lamps, television sets, microwave ovens, and missiles for the U.S. government. Other manufacturing areas included paper products, rubber and plastics, chemicals, cosmetics, and lumber and wood products.

The leading agricultural product, poultry, had a yearly value about three times as high as the next leading agricultural product—rice. The poultry industry involved thousands of small producers, raising chickens for the big processors like Tyson and George's (Springdale, Washington County). Arkansas was the leading rice grower in the nation, producing almost half the country's rice. **Riceland Foods**, a cooperative marketing association based in Stuttgart, was one of the state's largest agricultural businesses.

Other important agricultural products were soybeans, cotton, and cattle. In 1970,

I Am an Arkansan

John Franklin "Frank" Broyles (1924–)

Frank Broyles, born in Decatur, Georgia, is a former college football player, coach of the Arkansas Razorbacks from 1958 to 1976, and, since 1973, athletic director for the University of Arkansas. He graduated from Georgia Tech University in Atlanta with a degree in industrial management. He was the team's starting quarterback for four years, and his success as a player led him to a career in coaching.

After coaching jobs at Baylor University, Georgia Tech, and the University of Missouri, Broyles took the post of head coach of the Arkansas Razorbacks in 1958. He led the team to a share of the national championship in 1964. He also coached the team in its celebrated 1969 game against Texas. Though the Razorbacks lost the game 15–14, it was attended by then-president Richard Nixon, and was one of the biggest college football games of the decade.

As athletic director, Broyles has presided over the development of nationally ranked football and basketball teams, as well as the top

track and field program in the nation. His legacy as an Arkansas coaching legend secure, Broyles has seen more than thirty of his former players become college or professional football coaches. The prestigious Broyles Award, the annual award for best assistant coach, is named after him. He retired from his position as athletic director in late 2007.

Log on to Learn More
http://www.encyclopediaofarkansas.net/

Arkansas had about 72,000 farms, with an average size of 244 acres. At the end of the twentieth century, there were about 49,500 farms, with an average size of almost 300 acres.

A new enterprise was fish farming—raising catfish for grocery stores and restaurants, and minnows for bait. Much of this activity was centered in the area around Lonoke. Arkansas eventually became the second-largest producer of catfish in the U.S., trailing Mississippi.

Achievements in Public Education

All those who had worked to improve education through the years would have been proud of the improvement in areas such as test scores, high-school graduation rate, college-attendance rate, and teachers' salaries. Special programs like gifted and talented education became commonplace, and the state created **The Arkansas School for Mathematics, Sciences, and the Arts** in Hot Springs, a residential high school for gifted students. The legislature merged the community colleges and the vocational-technical schools, leading to more efficient management, a wider variety of programs, and increased enrollment. For many, this offered a meaningful and affordable path for education beyond high school.

In many areas, Arkansas made significant improvement but still lagged behind national averages. For example, by the end of the twentieth century, the high-school graduation rate increased to around 84 percent, close to the national average of about 86 percent. The number of Arkansans with a college degree increased by almost one-fourth in the last decade of the twentieth century, to about 16 percent of everyone over twenty-five-years old. But Arkansas was still far behind the national average of 24 percent of the population being college graduates. From 1970 to 2000, average public schoolteachers' salaries in Arkansas increased by about 16 percent, while the national average increase was 6 percent. As the new century began, Arkansas teacher salaries were still only about three-fourths of the national average.

Unequal funding among school districts was a continuing problem. School funding relied on local property taxes, with additional money from the state. Some districts, with a major industry or a large population within their boundaries, had reasonable funding. Other districts, especially in poor rural areas, had far less money. In May of 2001, a state court judge declared the funding of the school system unconstitutional, because of considerable differences in facilities, curriculum, and teacher pay among the 310 school districts. That was the third time in eighteen years such a ruling had been made. Arkansas continued to struggle with adequate tax collection because of the economy's continued dependence on agriculture. The governor and the legislature began searching for additional revenue or different ways of paying for the schools.

The Newspaper War

By the 1990s, there was a sense that some old institutions were passing. Former governor Orval Faubus died in 1994 at the age of eighty-four; former senator J. William Fulbright died in 1995 at the age of eighty-nine. Each of them, in different ways, had brought Arkansas national, and even world, attention.

For some Arkansans, the passing of the *Arkansas Gazette*—once the oldest newspaper west of the Mississippi River—was almost like a death in the family. In the late 1970s, Walter E. Hussman Jr.'s WEHCO company bought the *Arkansas Democrat,* which for years had been the second-place daily newspaper published in Little Rock. The *Democrat* and the *Gazette* began a fierce

The Arkansas School for Mathematics, Sciences, and the Arts a high school in Hot Springs (Garland County), which provides opportunities for academically talented high school juniors and seniors, with a focus on mathematics, sciences, and the arts.

Arkansas Gazette the statewide newspaper founded in 1819 by William Woodruff, which was bought by the owner of the *Arkansas Democrat* in 1991.

Defining Ourselves **431**

newspaper war, competing for readers and advertisers. In 1986, the Hugh Patterson family (related to longtime owner J. N. Heiskell) sold the *Gazette* to the Gannett Company, publisher of *USA Today* and many other newspapers throughout the nation.

The newspaper rivalry continued until, without warning, Gannett announced on October 18, 1991, that the *Gazette* had published its last edition. Within days, Hussman's company bought the remains of the *Gazette*. He changed the name of his newspaper to the *Arkansas Democrat-Gazette*, now the only statewide daily newspaper. It was a lesson in the modern economics of newspapers: few cities, or states, could support two major, independent daily newspapers.

As Arkansas moved through the early 1990s, rumors swirled that Governor Clinton would run for president, which, of course, he did. His 1992 election to the White House brought the state more attention than it had ever received. Critics of Clinton pointed out Arkansas's more negative aspects, while supporters noted the state's rapid social and economic development since the 1950s. The rise of Bill Clinton, as well as the staggering success of companies like Wal-Mart and Tyson Foods, clearly signaled that Arkansas had come a long way in a short period of time.

I Am an Arkansan

Euine Fay Jones (1921–2004)

The American Institute of Architects has awarded its gold medal for lifetime achievement to only about sixty people. One of them is E. Fay Jones of Arkansas. Jones was born in Pine Bluff (Jefferson County) in 1921 and grew up in El Dorado (Union County). He liked to say that his first important building was a good tree house. While he was in high school, he became fascinated with the work of one of America's greatest architects, Frank Lloyd Wright. Wright's buildings were filled with light, and many of them were designed to fit in a natural setting.

Jones graduated from the University of Arkansas's first class of architecture students. After graduate study at Rice University in Houston, he went to Wisconsin to join Wright as a student in his workshop.

Jones eventually returned to Arkansas, where he lived for the rest of his life, settling in Fayetteville. He joined the faculty at the University of Arkansas school of architecture, and served for a time as dean. He eventually left the faculty and pursued a private architecture practice.

He built mostly houses and chapels, using natural stone, wood, and glass to make structures that are nestled into the ground but soar above it. His best-known work is Thorncrown Chapel, west of Eureka Springs (Carroll County), completed in 1980. A wooden framework supports the glass walls. To avoid damaging the trees and plants on the site, Jones used standard lumber in sizes that could be carried onto the site by hand. In 1990, Jones received the American Institute of Architects Gold Medal Honor Award, and in 2006, the institute selected his Thorncrown Chapel to receive the "twenty-five year" award for a design that has withstood the test of time.

I Am an Arkansan

Johnny Cash (1932–2003)

Johnny Cash was a world-famous singer who scored many hits during his long career. His deep, unforgettable voice helped make him a music legend, and he continues to attract new fans even after his death.

John R. Cash was born in Kingsland (Cleveland County). His father was a farmer, and he had six brothers and sisters. In 1935, his family moved to Dyess (Mississippi County). Johnny was devastated at the loss of his brother Jack, who died in a sawmill accident, and his mother encouraged his interest in music as a way to heal the pain.

After briefly serving in the Army, Cash was honorably discharged in 1954. He eventually settled in Memphis, where he began his long career in music. Cash quickly formed a band and began to perform once a week on a Memphis radio station. In 1954, Cash and his band auditioned for legendary music producer Sam Phillips at Sun Records in Memphis. After several sessions, the trio recorded its first record, "Hey Porter" and "Cry, Cry, Cry" in 1955. With his third release, "I Walk the Line" and "Get Rhythm" (1956), Cash established himself as a rising star. The recording peaked at number 2 on the country charts and number 19 on the pop charts.

In 1957, Cash signed a recording contract with Columbia Records. By the end of the year, he was the third-largest-selling country artist in America and began appearing on national television programs. Known as "the man in black," Cash became a legendary figure in music, respected among country and rock-and-roll fans. He recorded with Bob Dylan and many other stars. In the last decade of his life, he produced some of his most critically-acclaimed music. During the course of his life, he overcame years of drug and alcohol abuse, but suffered from Parkinson's disease in his later years. He is a member of both the Rock and Roll and Country Music halls of fame, and his early career was chronicled in the 2005 hit film, *Walk the Line*.

THE ENCYCLOPEDIA OF ARKANSAS HISTORY & CULTURE

Log on to Learn More
http://www.encyclopediaofarkansas.net/

Defining Ourselves

Chapter 19

Chapter Reflection

Reflective Questions

1. Identify the three most positive aspects or accomplishments of the Rockefeller administration. Explain why you chose each.

2. Compare and contrast agriculture in modern Arkansas (today) with that of 150 years ago (1850s). Consider machinery, crops, labor, and profit in your answer.

3. What are two of the newest crops or agricultural products grown or processed in Arkansas?

4. In what ways is rice important to Arkansas's economy?

5. Describe three aspects of the relationship between Arkansas and rice.

6. Who was the first woman on the Arkansas Supreme Court?

7. In which elections during the 1970s did Arkansans vote for Democrats? Republicans?

8. In a few sentences, describe the McClellan-Kerr Arkansas River Navigation System.

9. What was the feminist movement?

10. What was the residential high school established in Hot Springs in the early 1990s?

Who, What, When, Where, Why, and How?

Identify the five key terms below by establishing the who, what, when, where, why, and how of each. Copy the term on your paper, then below the term, write the five *W*s and one *H*. An example has been done for you.

Example:

University of Arkansas

who — the U.S. government
what — established a university
when — 1862–71
where — Fayetteville
why — to help Arkansas's citizens by providing better educational opportunities
how — the Morrill Land Grant Act

1. Alltel
2. commuted
3. philanthropy
4. Riceland
5. sunshine law

Make It Match!

On your own paper, number *1* through *7* and write the letter that best matches or defines each phrase.

1. Statewide newspaper founded in 1819 by William Woodruff and bought by the *Arkansas Democrat* in 1991.

2. Arkansas war hero and lieutenant governor.

3. To change a prison sentence or penalty to a lesser one.

4. A Democrat and segregationist who was a state Supreme Court justice and ran for governor against Rockefeller in 1966.

5. Popular Arkansas politician who served in the state legislature, as governor, as a U.S. Senator, and in the U.S. House of Representatives.

6. The first female justice on the Arkansas Supreme Court.

7. A long-term prison inmate entrusted with the oversight of other prisoners.

A. Elsijane T. Roy
B. "Justice John"
C. trusty
D. warden
E. Bill Clinton
F. "Justice Jim"
G. Hattie Caraway
H. the *Chronicle*
I. commute
J. Dale Bumpers
K. The *Gazette*
L. Daisy Bates
M. David Pryor
N. Maurice "Footsie" Britt

UNIT 8

Chapter 20
The White House, Arkansas on the National Stage, and the Future, 1992–

A Global, Modern Arkansas,
1992–

An Arkansas pennant.

Chapter 20

The White House, Arkansas on the National Stage, and the Future

1992–

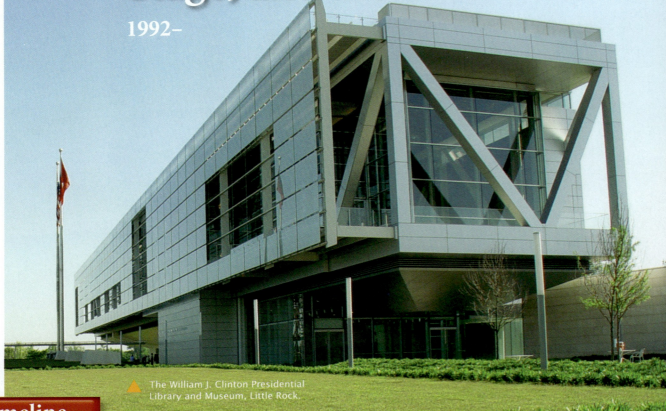

The William J. Clinton Presidential Library and Museum, Little Rock.

Timeline

1992 — 1995 — 1998

Arkansas

1992 Arkansas's native son, William Jefferson Clinton, is elected the forty-second president of the United States.

1993 Clinton names Dr. Jocelyn Elders, an African American woman and director of the Arkansas State Department of Health, surgeon general of the United States.

1994 The University of Arkansas Razorbacks men's basketball team, under coach Nolan Richardson, wins the national championship.

1997 Information uncovered from the Whitewater scandal, an investigation of the Clintons and their business partners' real estate dealings, leads to the resignation of Clinton's gubernatorial successor, Jim Guy Tucker. He is replaced by Mike Huckabee.

United States

1993 A terrorist bombing at the World Trade Center occurs in an attached, underground parking garage. Six people are killed. The Holocaust Memorial Museum is dedicated in Washington, D.C. Federal agents engage in a fifty-one-day standoff in Waco, Texas, with members of the Branch Davidian religious sect.

1995 Timothy McVeigh, a former U.S. army soldier, and others bomb the federal building in Oklahoma City. In the worst recorded act of domestic terrorism in U.S. history to that date, 168 people die.

1999 President Clinton is acquitted of impeachment charges related to the Lewinsky affair. Fifteen students are killed and twenty-three wounded in a shooting carried out by two Columbine High School students (CO).

World

1992 The first McDonald's opens in Beijing, China.

1996 Prince Charles, heir to the British throne, and his wife of fifteen years, the very popular Princess Diana, divorce.

1997 Princess Diana is killed in France in a car accident. Mother Teresa, a nun, activist, humanitarian, and Nobel Peace Prize winner, dies.

438 Chapter 20

Why Do We Study This?

As you near the end of your exploration of Arkansas and Arkansas history, know that *you* are the beginning of the next chapter—a new chapter. Your responsibility as an Arkansan is to seize the opportunities that lie before you, to learn from the mistakes of the past, and to cherish the successes that have moved our state forward.

The modern era of our state has been one of pride and promise, national attention, and continued growth and change. Arkansas and Arkansans were thrust on to the national stage as never before and would forever know the legacy of this time.

1998	2001	2004	2007
1998 At Westside Middle School in Jonesboro, two boys shoot and kill four classmates and one teacher, injuring 10 others.	**2003** Country music pioneer and Arkansan Johnny Cash dies.	**2004** The William J. Clinton Presidential Museum and Library is dedicated in Little Rock.	**2006** Mike Beebe, a Democrat, is elected Arkansas's forty-fifth governor.	**2007** Former governor Mike Huckabee announces his bid in the 2008 presidential election. Frank Broyles, who served as a football coach and athletic director at the University of Arkansas for fifty years, announces his retirement.
2001 Terrorists hijack four U.S. commercial jets, crashing two into the World Trade Center in New York City, one into the Pentagon in Washington, D.C., and the fourth into a field in Pennsylvania. In all, nearly 3,000 people are killed. Oklahoma City bomber Timothy McVeigh is executed.			**2005** Hurricane Katrina, the costliest natural disaster in U.S. history, demolishes the city of New Orleans, and destroys much of the Louisiana and Mississippi coasts.	**2007** The first female Speaker of the House of Representatives is sworn in. Former First Lady Sen. Hillary Clinton announces her bid for the presidency. Windows Vista operating system is released. Apple announces the iPhone.
2001 U.S. military involvement begins in Afghanistan.	**2004** More than three hundred thousand people in Indonesia, Thailand, and India die as a result of an earthquake-related tsunami in the Indian Ocean.	**2005** The deadly "bird flu" spreads from Asia to Europe. After more than twenty-six years as head of the Catholic Church, Pope John Paul II dies. His successor is Pope Benedict XVI.	**2006** The United States continues military action in Iraq and Afghanistan. Saddam Hussein is convicted of war crimes, sentenced to death, and hanged. Pluto is no longer considered a planet and is given an asteroid number.

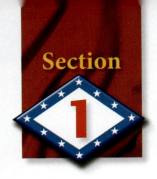

Section 1

The Presidency

In 1992, William Jefferson Clinton became the first native Arkansan to be elected president of the United States. In the presidential election of 1992, Democrat Clinton faced Republican challenger and President George H. W. Bush, and a candidate from the Independent party, Ross Perot, from Texarkana, Texas. Many considered both of Clinton's opponents to be "millionaire" candidates. Clinton's youth, enthusiasm, and relatively new "political face" appealed to many voters. They also felt he was from a background similar to theirs and that he could relate to their problems. Voters were concerned about the economy, jobs, and social security—things many felt Bush and Perot could not relate to.

Clinton reached citizens with his charisma and warmth and played on his Arkansas hometown roots by using the slogan, "I still believe in a place called Hope."

Clinton's campaign headquarters were in what many considered to be a small town—Little Rock—near friends and family. Clinton and his vice-presidential candidate Al Gore of Tennessee campaigned through the country by bus and held town meetings with ordinary people. Clinton also made an appearance on MTV, answered viewers' questions, and later played his saxophone on a late-night talk show.

On election night, Little Rock was transformed into an international media circus. Camera trucks and news crews from around the world watched as celebrities, musicians, politicians, and Arkansans shared in the celebration and joy while the Clinton and Gore families stood on the steps of the Old State House and sang the campaign theme song, "Don't Stop" by Fleetwood Mac. Clinton resigned as governor in 1993, and Lt. Gov. Jim Guy Tucker assumed office.

On January 20, 1993, about thirty-five thousand Arkansans, including Clinton's wife, Hillary Rodham Clinton, and their daughter, Chelsea, were in Washington, D.C., to celebrate the inauguration of Clinton as forty-second president. Famous Arkansan Maya Angelou read her poem "On the Pulse of Morning" at the inauguration to honor the new first family.

Howard

Named after: *James Howard, a state representative*

Chief Source of Income: *Timber and manufacturing*

Seat: *Nashville*

Howard County was created in 1873, and its original county seat was Center Point. The seat was moved to Nashville in 1884. Nashville is home to many peach orchards and was once an industry leader in peach harvesting. Nashville was the location of the first Dillard's department store opened by William T. Dillard. The area is rich in farmland and timber, and also has many poultry farms. The county is home to the Southwest Arkansas Super Speedway and Dierks Lake.

> "I challenge a new generation of young Americans to a season of service."
>
> "In serving, we recognize a simple but powerful truth—we need each other. And we must care for one another. Today, we do more than celebrate America; we rededicate ourselves to the very idea of America."
>
> William Jefferson Clinton, at his first inaugural address, January 20, 1993, in Washington, D.C.

Question

What does Clinton mean when he speaks of "service"?

Accomplishments of the Clinton Presidency

Clinton chose many to serve in his administration who were friends and colleagues from Arkansas, as well as some who had served under former Democratic President Jimmy Carter.

Thomas F. "Mack" McLarty, who was a childhood friend of the president, served as chief of staff, and Arkansan James Lee Witt received much praise for his service as head of the Federal Emergency Management Agency. African Americans from Arkansas also served in the administration. Rodney Slater was secretary of transportation, and Bob Nash worked as director of White House personnel. Clinton would appoint the first female secretary of state, Madeline Albright. Clinton worked hard to make his administration a true representation of America by appointing African Americans, women, and people with disabilities.

The Clinton administration worked to control the costs of healthcare and improve education. The administration encouraged those on welfare to go back to work and provided programs and training to help them do just that.

▲ Bill Clinton.

During Clinton's service, the United States benefited from the longest period of sustained economic growth in history. His administration managed to create four federal budget surpluses, the first in more than fifty years, through government spending reductions and tax increases. The Clintons were strong supporters of the rights of women and children and provided tax credits for college costs.

On the world front, Clinton's negotiations came closer to brokering a peace agreement than ever before between Israel and the Palestine Liberation Organization, as well as an agreement ending a long-term war between Israel and Jordan. He earned the friendship and respect of numerous world leaders. Clinton worked with the Irish and the English to help end violence in Northern Ireland. Clinton took action against

Iraq after the first Gulf War when the country refused to honor an established "no-fly" zone. He also ordered U.S. troops into Kosovo to fight genocide, the deliberate slaughter of minority populations of the country. Arkansan Gen. Wesley Clark, who would later run for president, commanded troops during this conflict.

Controversies

With all the successes of the Clinton administration, there were also many scandals. "Travelgate" was an investigation into alleged stealing of money from the staff administrator of the White House travel office. Hillary Clinton's extensive involvement with health-care policy and reform while in Washington, D.C., created some resentment among those who had actually been elected to office. Many felt her plans were too radical and she overstepped her bounds as First Lady. Congress failed to adopt this, the first major Clinton administration proposal.

"Whitewater" was a real estate investment deal on which the Clintons had lost money. A group, including the Clintons, had purchased land in Marion County and had a difficult time developing and selling the lots. Accusations were that the group had benefited from a Little Rock savings and loan association in the 1980s, which eventually went bankrupt. The Clintons' partners in the Whitewater real estate venture were Jim and Susan McDougal, who were also investigated. The investigations were headed by independent counsel Kenneth Starr. The Clintons were not charged as a result of the investigation. Many Arkansas associates of the Clintons, including Gov. Jim Guy Tucker, were investigated in the matter. Ultimately, Jim and Susan McDougal and Jim Guy Tucker were convicted of various charges related to Whitewater, and Susan McDougal spent 18 months in prison for civil contempt of court for refusing to answer questions related to the deal.

The greatest source of scandal and mistrust for President Clinton resulted from his involvement with a White House intern, Monica Lewinsky, and his initial dishonesty about the relationship. After much speculation and rumor, the president appeared on national television and addressed the nation, admitting the relationship and his lies about it, and offering an apology to the people. The House of Representatives impeached the president for this misconduct, but the Senate did not convict him.

The End of an Era

Clinton's term of service ended, but his legacy would carry on. In 2000, Clinton's vice president, Al Gore, ran unsuccessfully for president in an extremely controversial election. A ruling by the Supreme Court ultimately declared George W. Bush, a Republican and the son of former president George H. W. Bush, the winner. First Lady Hillary Clinton was elected to the U.S. Senate in 2000, representing the state of New York, where she and President Clinton had bought a home. Clinton began his "retirement" by establishing an office in Harlem in New York City. He then wrote his autobiography, titled

DID YOU KNOW?

The Clinton administration is considered to be the first e-mail administration?

My Life, which was published in 2004 and became a national bestseller.

The William J. Clinton Presidential Library and Museum was dedicated on a rainy day in November of 2004, and many heads of state, celebrities, friends, former staff members, and fellow Arkansans attended the event. That day, the Little Rock riverfront played host to three of the four living former presidents (Jimmy Carter, George H.W. Bush, and Clinton) and their wives, as well as the current president. Actors Kevin Spacey and Robin Williams joined singer Barbra Streisand and her husband, actor James Brolin, along with native Arkansan actress Mary Steenburgen and her husband, actor Ted Danson, in the celebration. Bono and The Edge from the group U2 performed as well.

I Am an Arkansan

George Fisher (1923–2003)

Born on April 8, 1923, near Searcy (White County), George Fisher was a political cartoonist whose work influenced Arkansas politics for decades. At his father's encouragement, the teenage Fisher published his first cartoon, a sketch that made fun of then-governor Homer Adkins.

While serving in the Army Reserves, Fisher attended college for only one year at Beebe College. In 1943, he was called to active duty in World War II. While stationed in England, he began attending drawing classes at a local college, and also contributed cartoons to an Army newspaper. After the war ended in 1945, he married and then returned to Arkansas, settling in West Memphis (Crittenden County). There he worked as a reporter and cartoonist for the controversial *West Memphis News*. In 1949, he moved to Little Rock, taking a position as a commercial artist while submitting cartoons to local newspapers. At first he drew cartoons for free, but gradually papers such as the *Arkansas Gazette* began to regularly publish—and pay for—his cartoons.

By 1976, when the *Gazette* hired him full-time, his cartoons had become one of the most recognizable parts of the paper. His lampooning of politicians made him an important voice in state politics. His memorable images include his portrayal of Gov. Bill Clinton (then the youngest governor in American history) as a little boy riding a tricycle. Fisher also hid the nickname of his wife, Snooky, in each of his cartoons. Finding "Snooky" became a popular game for readers, and inspired a contest to see who could find the most. After the *Arkansas Gazette* closed in 1991, he drew for the *Arkansas Times*. At the time of his death in 2003, he was considered by many to be among the best in the nation at his craft.

THE ENCYCLOPEDIA OF ARKANSAS HISTORY & CULTURE

Log on to Learn More
http://www.encyclopediaofarkansas.net/

The National Archives and Presidential Libraries

What is the National Archives and Records Administration?

The National Archives and Records Administration (NARA) is an independent federal agency that helps preserve our nation's history and defines us as a people by overseeing the management of all federal records. NARA ensures timely access to vital documents, information, and evidence from the federal government.

Prior to the official establishment of NARA, records were randomly stored in basements, garages, and warehouses, and many were lost to flood, fire, theft, and neglect.

In 1935, NARA was created to organize and maintain our nation's historical records, most notably the Declaration of Independence, the Bill of Rights, the Constitution, and the Emancipation Proclamation.

Now the agency is responsible for the management of thirty-three facilities and is in charge of over four billion original text materials (documents and letters) from all three branches of government. In addition to managing paper documents, NARA is responsible for the cataloging and preservation of three hundred thousand reels of motion picture film; five million maps, charts, and architectural renderings; more than nine million aerial (above ground) photos; almost fourteen million still photographs, and more than seven thousand pieces of computer data, which include e-mail and electronic documents.

What is a Presidential Library?

NARA is also responsible for the management of the Presidential Library system. A Presidential Library is not a typical library where one checks out books, but a place for the collection, organization, and housing of documents, objects, and other information related to or generated by the Office of the President during each term of service.

The first Presidential Library was the Franklin Delano Roosevelt Library dedicated in Hyde Park, New York in 1941. Roosevelt pledged land from his personal estate for the construction of the facility. Prior to the Roosevelt Library, many records had been, destroyed, sold for profit, or ruined by poor storage conditions. In 1955, legislation was passed to encourage other presidents to donate their materials to the country as President Roosevelt had, and then in 1978, further legislation stated that all presidential records that document constitutional, legal, legislative, or ceremonial duties of the president are property of the U.S. government.

Presidential Libraries are not established with tax dollars. After the president leaves office, they are built with private donations and then federally maintained as institutions of historical records and artifacts. The Presidential Libraries Act of 1986 allowed for increased private endowments to libraries to continue to maintain them.

All of the documents and records within a Presidential Library are cataloged and maintained by NARA archivists. With some exceptions related to classified information, the public is allowed access to those presidential records recommended by the archivist under the Freedom of Information Act, five years after the conclusion of the president's service.

However, any of six restrictions may be enacted to limit public access to records for up to twelve years. If review of any information could restrict, harm, compromise, or threaten anyone or any process related to any of the following, access is limited.

1) national defense
2) foreign policy
3) appointment to federal office
4) trade secrets and financial information
5) confidential communications or advice
6) personnel files or medical records

Museum curators create exhibits from presidential family heirlooms, campaign artifacts, awards, homemade gifts from citizens, cherished and priceless pieces of art from global leaders, and so on. Permanent exhibits use holdings from the Presidential Library to describe significant policy decisions made during the president's term, or to showcase national and world events that occurred during the president's service. Temporary exhibits explore other subjects related to the presidency.

▲ A replica of Clinton's White House Oval office can be seen by visitors of the museum in Little Rock.

Where You'll Find Them

Presidential libraries located across the country allow visitors to experience history:

- **Herbert Hoover Library,** West Branch, Iowa
- **Franklin D. Roosevelt,** Hyde Park, New York
- **Harry S. Truman,** Independence, Missouri
- **Dwight D. Eisenhower,** Abilene, Kansas
- **John F. Kennedy Library,** Boston, Massachusetts
- **Lyndon Baines Johnson Library,** Austin, Texas
- **Nixon Presidential Materials Staff,** College Park, Maryland
- **Nixon Library and Birthplace Museum,** Yorba Linda, California
- **Gerald R. Ford Museum,** Grand Rapids, Michigan
- **Gerald R. Ford Library,** Ann Arbor, Michigan
- **Jimmy Carter Library,** Atlanta, Georgia
- **Ronald Reagan Library,** Simi Valley, California
- **George Bush Library,** College Station, Texas
- **William J. Clinton Library,** Little Rock, Arkansas

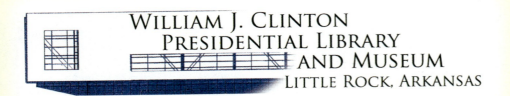

William J. Clinton Presidential Library and Museum
Little Rock, Arkansas

Welcome to the Clinton Library

Arkansas is the proud home of the William J. Clinton Presidential Library, located in our capital city. The $165 million library building was funded with private endowments, not taxpayer dollars. The Clinton library is comprised of two adjacent buildings—the museum and the archives. Also located on the grounds of the twenty-seven-acre city park are the offices of the Clinton Foundation and the Clinton School of Public Service, both housed in a preserved historic railroad station known as Sturgis Hall.

The main building of the Clinton Library is elevated to allow visitors to interact with the river and the surrounding natural landscape. Its bridge-like shape and presence refers to the six bridges that cross the river, connecting Little Rock and North Little Rock, and reflects upon the symbolic phrase used during much of Clinton's campaign and service, "a bridge to the twenty-first century." The dedication of the facilities and grounds took place November 17, 2004. In attendance were first lady, and now senator, Hillary Rodham Clinton, the Clintons' daughter Chelsea Clinton, former presidents

Jimmy Carter and George H. W. Bush, and President George W. Bush, as well as many senators, members of Congress, judges, dignitaries, heads of state, and foreign leaders. The audience of thirty thousand endured cold rain to witness this historic event.

Museum pieces in the Clinton library include a bicycle given to the president by Tour de France champion Lance Armstrong; a White House dining table set with place settings from the Clintons' White House china; some of the First Lady's dresses; President Clinton's baby shoes and high-school yearbook; and many documents, letters, and e-mails from the presidency. Those interested in learning more about the Clintons can visit homes where Clinton lived in Hope, Hot Springs, and Fayetteville, as well as the governor's mansion in Little Rock.

Log on to Learn More

National Archives and Records Administration
http://www.archives.gov

NARA Presidential Libraries Homepage
www.archives.gov/presidential-libraries

William J. Clinton Presidential Library and Museum
www.clintonlibrary.gov

The William J. Clinton Foundation
www.clintonfoundation.org/index.htm

▶ One of President Clinton's saxophones.

▼ One of Lance Armstrong's race bikes and a Tour de France leader jersey. These were a gift to President Clinton from Armstrong.

▶ An assortment of some of the many campaign buttons worn by supporters in Clinton's bid for reelection in 1996, now found in the Clinton Library.

The Clinton Presidential Library

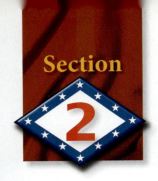

Section 2

Following in the Footsteps

In 1994, Jim Guy Tucker, a Democrat, was reelected governor. However, in 1996, he resigned his governorship due to his convictions for illegal business dealings related to the Whitewater scandal.

Mike Huckabee

Mike Huckabee assumed the role of governor upon Tucker's resignation. Huckabee had served as lieutenant governor since 1993. Huckabee was the third Republican governor in the 1900s. Huckabee, like Clinton, was from Hope (Hempstead County). He was an ordained Baptist minister.

Huckabee oversaw many important changes during his terms as governor. A constitutional amendment setting out term limits for legislators was enacted after a public vote. Members of the state house of representatives were limited to no more than three two-year terms. Members of the state senate were limited to no more than four two-year terms. The governor and other elected executive officers were limited to two four-year terms. These limits applied to all those elected after January of 1993.

Additionally, Huckabee established new college scholarships for students to attend state universities, reduced the number of Arkansans on welfare, increased funding for highway improvements, proposed and received the approval of the legislature for a three-thousand-dollar annual raise for teachers, created a state holiday to honor Daisy Bates, and made the process for registering vehicles in Arkansas simpler. Huckabee, diagnosed with diabetes and overweight himself before losing more than one hundred pounds, spearheaded a campaign that resulted in reforms to school lunch programs and children's health initiatives throughout the state, such as ARKids First, which provides healthcare for children. He also signed the Arkansas Clean Indoor Air Act of 2006—legislation that outlawed smoking in most workplaces in Arkansas (it is still allowed outdoors, in private homes, and at some establishments where people under the age of 21 are not allowed).

Arkansas experienced a balance of Republican and Democratic leaders through the 1990s and into the new millennium. Republican senator Tim Hutchinson of Springdale was elected in 1996 and his brother, Asa, also a Republican, served in the U.S.

DID YOU KNOW?

Did you know Andrew Johnson, Abraham Lincoln's vice president who succeeded him after his assassination, was the only president other than Clinton to have been impeached? Johnson was not convicted by the Senate. President Nixon resigned office before his likely impeachment and trial.

House of Representatives and was later appointed by George W. Bush as head of the Drug Enforcement Agency in Washington, D.C. Senator Blanche Lambert Lincoln, a child of Helena-area farmers, was the most visible Democrat in state politics. She first served in the U.S. House of Representatives and then stayed at home for two years after giving birth to twin boys. In 1998, Lincoln was the youngest woman ever elected to the Senate and Arkansas's second female senator.

Diversity and the Changing Face of Arkansas

The 1990s and 2000s saw diversity continue in Arkansas. The Hispanic population in Arkansas increased dramatically. Latinos from Mexico, Central America, South America, California, and Texas moved to Arkansas in increasing numbers for employment and family reasons. Arkansas had one of the fastest-growing Hispanic populations in the country, with an increase of 337 percent between 1990 and 2000. The populations from Asia and the Marshall Islands continued to grow as well.

Diversity and new residents contribute to the economy, heritage, culture, and opportunity in the state, and help make the future chapters of Arkansas as rich and important as those of the past.

Mike Beebe

In November of 2006, Arkansas voters elected Democrat Mike Beebe as the forty-second governor of Arkansas. He spent twenty years serving Arkansas as a state senator and as attorney general. Beebe was born in Amagon (Jackson County) and attended Arkansas State University and the University of Arkansas School of Law in Fayetteville. He was also a member of the U.S. Army Reserves.

Beebe pledged to work to improve education in Arkansas, create new jobs, and further enhance the state's economy. Governor Beebe and Arkansas First Lady Ginger Beebe have three grown children and five grandchildren.

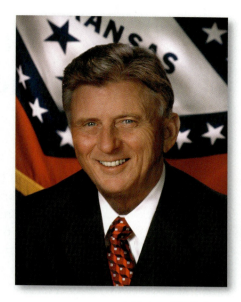

▲ Governor Mike Beebe.

Cleburne

Named after: Civil War general Patrick R. Cleburne of Helena

Chief Source of Income: Tourism and manufacturing

Seat: Heber Springs

Cleburne County was the last of the state's seventy-five counties to be formed, and was created in 1883. The county has an abundance of fishing and farming, and Greers Ferry Lake and the Little Red River annually attract tourists who engage in water sports including swimming, fishing, and boating. The famous Cardboard Boat Race is held in July on the lake. The county is home to Aromatique, a well-known home décor, candle, and home fragrance manufacturer. There is also a national fish hatchery in Heber Springs, and the Greers Ferry Dam visitor's center and campground, named in honor of John F. Kennedy, who dedicated the dam in 1963, is also in the county.

Section 3

You Are Arkansas's Future—The Crystal Ball

As you have completed your exploration of amazing Arkansas, you should have a true sense of the wonderful places and stories of your state and its people. You are lucky enough to live in a state with a rich and diverse cultural heritage, powerful history, and unique characters.

You explored everything from how our state got its name and what it means to be an Arkansan, to the big businesses of Arkansas, the fun outdoor adventures in our state, and sports. You traveled through time to better understand the experiences of the American Indians who were the first native Arkansans. You journeyed with explorers and walked in the shoes of powerful politicians and in those of women finding their place and making their mark. You found your way through the darkness of slavery to emerge in a fast-paced, modern society.

Your Arkansas journey took you through the development of flavorful foods and music that tells stories. You felt what it was like to be both poor and rich as our state struggled to find new economic opportunities. Together, we survived wars and mourned those who were lost, who proudly fought for our land and homes. We saw the

▶ Young Arkansans: Mrs. Hopper's 2006–2007 eighth grade students (left to right) Julia Allen, Jay Im, Banah Ghadbian, Vincent Chu, Ian Pace, and Tommye Jones at Woodland Junior High School in Fayetteville.

dreams of our ancestors washed away in raging floodwaters and crumble into dust. We conquered fear and hate with the Little Rock Nine and helped to build the largest corporation in the world. We shared in the spotlight of a native son's presidency. Challenge after challenge, victory after victory, we saw Arkansas and Arkansans continue with pride and dignity.

The future is yours to define. You will make the history. Be responsible and proud as you remember your state. Arkansas and Arkansans are unique—our history, our people, our land, our failures, and our successes make us that way. Continue the traditions and honor those who came before you.

DID YOU KNOW?

Did you know Joey Lauren Adams of North Little Rock (Pulaski County), star of films such as *Chasing Amy* and *The Break-Up*, is just one of many successful actors from Arkansas? Little Rock's "Broncho Billy" Anderson was one of the first movie stars. He appeared in silent movies as one of the early stars of westerns, most notably in the 1903 picture, *The Great Train Robbery*. Frank Bonner starred in *WKRP in Cincinnati*, a popular television show in the early 1980s. In most episodes, a Razorback coffee mug was prominently displayed on his character's desk. Other Arkansas-born actors include Lisa Blount, Tess Harper, and Josh Lucas. Lucas starred in *Sweet Home Alabama* with Reese Witherspoon and the 2006 remake of *Poseidon*.

I Am an Arkansan

Harry Thomason (1940–)

Harry Z. Thomason is a movie and television producer and director, best known for his television shows *Designing Women* and *Evening Shade*, which was set in Arkansas and starred Burt Reynolds. He and his wife Linda Bloodworth-Thomason created both of these shows and have a production company called Mozark, which is a combination of the names of their two home states, Missouri and Arkansas. They also became famous during the 1990s for their close friendship with President Bill Clinton. Thomason was born in Hampton (Calhoun County) and was a high-school speech teacher and football coach. *Evening Shade* was the first show to be set in the state, and portions of it were filmed in Arkansas. It also represented the state in a consistently positive light.

Linda is involved with the charitable organization she began in her hometown, Poplar Bluff, Missouri, called The Claudia Foundation. It strives to help young women, especially those in the Ozarks, reach and recognize their full potential and earn college scholarships. She released her first novel, *Liberating Paris*, in 2004. The Thomasons helped Clinton during his campaigns for office, and were frequent guests at the White House during Clinton's presidency. They produced campaign films for Clinton. They remain friends with the Clintons, and they continue to produce films and television programs.

THE ENCYCLOPEDIA OF ARKANSAS HISTORY & CULTURE

Log on to Learn More
http://www.encyclopediaofarkansas.net/

Chapter 20

Chapter Reflection

Reflective Questions

1. Arkansas was the twenty-fifth state admitted to the Union. Create your own personal "top twenty-five list" of the twenty-five most important events, people, or places in Arkansas and Arkansas history. Be sure to explain why you chose each.

2. What do you see happening in Arkansas's future? Why? How will this take place? Consider economics, population, tourism, environment, politics, education, and the citizens of Arkansas in your response

I Am an Arkansan

Billy Bob Thornton (1955–)

Billy Bob Thornton is an Academy Award–winning actor, writer, and director. He is also a successful playwright and a musician. He was born in Hot Springs (Garland County), and moved to Los Angeles, California, to try to break into the movies. While working several odd jobs, he began to write a screenplay. As he wrote the script that would eventually bring him fame, he also began to appear in small roles in several films and television shows.

In 1996, he found financing to produce *Slingblade*. This film, which he wrote, directed, and starred in, gained him worldwide attention and an Academy Award. It was filmed entirely in Benton (Saline County). Country music star Dwight Yoakam played a major supporting role. Thornton won the Academy Award for best adapted screenplay, and was also nominated for best actor. The success of this movie made him a celebrity, and he has continued to work as a director, writer, and actor.

He also toured the United States and Europe as a musician, performing songs from his three albums. Some of his films include *The Alamo*, *The Man Who Wasn't There*, *A Simple Plan*, *All the Pretty Horses*, and *The Bad News Bears*.

Log on to Learn More
http://www.encyclopediaofarkansas.net/

Appendix

Dorris Alexander "Dee" Brown 454

Helen Gurley Brown 455

Paul "Bear" Bryant. 456

Glen Campbell 457

Wesley Clark 458

Al Green 459

John Grisham 460

E. Lynn Harris 461

Louis Jordan 462

Susan Hampton Newton Pryor 463

Vance Randolph 464

Mary Steenburgen & Conway Twitty. 465

I Am an Arkansan

Dorris Alexander "Dee" Brown (1908–2002)

Dee Brown, from Stephens (Ouachita County), is the author of *Bury My Heart at Wounded Knee*, which the New York Public Library proclaimed one of the "most significant" books of the twentieth century. It tells the story of the mistreatment and displacement of American Indians in the West. Brown identified with American Indians. An instant success, *Bury My Heart at Wounded Knee* has sold over five million copies worldwide, and has been translated into several languages.

Brown was a trained librarian, having earned degrees in library sciences at prestigious universities after studying history at what is today the University of Central Arkansas. He credited his training as a librarian for his success as a writer. His knowledge of sources and historic documents helped him write other best-selling books such as a history of Union-Pacific Railroad and several other novels.

His love of Arkansas shone through with books such as *American Spas*, his lively look at Hot Springs tourism. He wrote his last book—his eleventh work of fiction—when he was ninety years old. He died in Little Rock in 2002.

THE ENCYCLOPEDIA OF ARKANSAS HISTORY & CULTURE

Log on to Learn More
http://www.encyclopediaofarkansas.net/

I Am an Arkansan

Helen Gurley Brown (1922–)

Helen Gurley Brown, born in Green Forest (Carroll County), is one of the leaders of the women's liberation movement of the twentieth century, as well as a pioneer in magazine publishing. Her career also includes important achievements in advertising. Her book *Sex and the Single Girl* (1962) propelled her into the limelight, and she went on to become editor-in-chief of *Cosmopolitan* magazine.

After graduating high school in 1939, she attended Texas State College for Women in Denton and later Woodbury Business College in Los Angeles. Brown had grown up in poverty in Arkansas, and so her reflections on her home state were never very positive.

In 1948, she took a job as a secretary in an advertising firm, but quickly rose through the ranks to become one of the top copywriters in the industry. After marrying famed Hollywood producer David Brown in 1959, she soon decided to write a memoir of her experiences as a single woman living in a big city. The resulting book made her famous, and she became a leading spokesperson for women's issues. In 1965, she was named as editor-in-chief of *Cosmopolitan* magazine, and she transformed it into one of the most popular publications in the United States. She ran *Cosmopolitan* until 1996. Since then, she has spoken out on many topics. Today, she lives with her husband in New York City.

THE ENCYCLOPEDIA OF ARKANSAS HISTORY & CULTURE

Log on to Learn More
http://www.encyclopediaofarkansas.net/

I Am an Arkansan

Paul "Bear" Bryant (1913–1983)

Paul "Bear" Bryant was one of the most successful college football coaches in American sports. He was born in 1913 near Kingsland (Cleveland County), one of nine children. His parents were poor and his father was often ill, so Bryant was sent as a child to live with his grandfather in Fordyce (Dallas County). There he learned how to play football and became a member of the Fordyce Redbugs high-school team. In 1927, he acquired his nickname after taking a challenge to wrestle a bear for money.

After considering an offer to take a football scholarship at the University of Arkansas, Bryant decided instead to play football for the University of Alabama. As a player, he quickly gained the respect of his teammates, most notably after a 1925 game in which, playing on the offensive line, he endured an entire game with a broken leg. He helped his team to victory in the 1936 Rose Bowl, giving them the national championship. When his playing days were finished, Bryant began a long, successful coaching career. After coaching at Union College and Vanderbilt University (both in Tennessee), he joined the Navy and served in World War II.

After the war, he coached at several major universities, including Maryland and Kentucky. In 1968, he took a job as head coach at Alabama and over the next twenty-five years became one of the most important

coaches in America. His Crimson Tide teams won the national championship in 1961, 1964 (shared with Arkansas), 1965, 1978, and 1979.

Bryant won this last championship with an undefeated season, which included a thrilling defeat of the Arkansas Razorbacks in the Sugar Bowl. He retired in 1982 with a career record of 232 wins, 46 losses, and 9 ties, with his teams appearing in twenty-four consecutive post-season bowl games. He was named Coach of the Year four times.

Less than a month after retiring, Paul "Bear" Bryant died, but his legacy as America's greatest football coach was intact. In 1983, President Ronald Reagan awarded him the Presidential Medal of Freedom.

THE ENCYCLOPEDIA OF ARKANSAS HISTORY & CULTURE

Log on to Learn More
http://www.encyclopediaofarkansas.net/

I Am an Arkansan

Glen Campbell (1936–)

Glen Campbell was born in Delight (Pike County) and learned to play guitar as a teen. By the time he was eighteen, Campbell was performing throughout the south as a member of the Western Wranglers. In 1958, he moved to Los Angeles to become a recording session musician. Campbell achieved much success as a session player and worked with Merle Haggard, the Monkees, Elvis Presley, and Frank Sinatra, among many others. He toured with the Beach Boys in 1964 and 1965 while lead singer Brian Wilson was ill.

His first successful solo record appeared with his Grammy-winning 1967 single "Gentle on My Mind," which propelled Campbell to stardom. He followed this with a number of other hit songs and in 1969 began hosting *The Glen Campbell Goodtime Hour*. That same year he starred opposite John Wayne in *True Grit* (which was based on a book by Arkansas native Charles Portis). The song from the movie *True Grit* received an Oscar nomination. Campbell performed at the awards show. He has continued to perform live and record albums. In the mid-1970s, Campbell had his biggest hit song, "Rhinestone Cowboy," which was also the name of his 1994 autobiography.

Glen Campbell struggled with substance abuse during his lifetime and had periods without a hit, but has achieved recent success by being inducted into the Country Music Hall of Fame and working on new musical material.

I Am an Arkansan

Wesley Clark (1944–)

A native of Little Rock, Wesley Clark is a retired four-star general in the U.S. Army and has been a candidate for president of the United States. The former supreme allied commander for Europe of the North Atlantic Treaty Organization, Clark was responsible for the defense of both Europe and the United States. From 1997 to 2000, he led the military forces involved in war in the eastern European nation of Kosovo, where his leadership brought him widespread attention and praise.

In 2004, Clark ran for president on the Democratic ticket. Many voters viewed his vast military experience as a highly desirable trait, but his lack of political experience (he had never run for office before) was viewed by many as a liability. He was not successful in his campaign.

He has a degree in economics and is a graduate of the prestigious West Point military academy. He was a Rhodes Scholar. He served in the Vietnam War, where he was cited for bravery and courage in battle. He is also a veteran of the Persian Gulf War. In addition to his military decorations, he has been named an honorary knight by both Great Britain and the Netherlands, has received the Presidential Medal of Freedom, and was given a National Audubon Society award for helping to save an endangered species of desert turtle. Today, he travels the country raising funds for the Democratic Party and is a popular speaker on the lecture circuit.

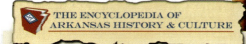

Log on to Learn More
http://www.encyclopediaofarkansas.net/

I Am an Arkansan

Al Green (1946–)

Al Green, born in Forrest City (St. Francis County) in 1946, is one of the most renowned gospel and rhythm and blues singers in American music history. His parents were sharecroppers, but instilled in Green a lifelong love for music. By the age of nine, he was performing in local groups, and throughout the 1950s, he and his brothers toured the South as the Greene Brothers. Eventually, famed music producer Willie Mitchell discovered him. By the early 1970s, Green had scored several major hits, including his most popular song, "Let's Stay Together" (1972), off the album of the same name.

Tragedy struck in 1974 when his girlfriend—angered when Green rejected her proposal of marriage—poured scalding hot grits on him while he showered. He suffered serious burns over much of his body, and his girlfriend took her own life. Intensely traumatized by the incident, he embraced Christianity, and ultimately became a Baptist pastor in Memphis, Tennessee, where he continues to hold regular church services.

Since becoming a born-again Christian, Green has recorded a number of popular gospel albums, and in the early twenty-first century, he returned to performing secular music, including many of his old hits from the 1970s. He remains a popular preacher and performer, tours the world extensively, and continues to gain new fans.

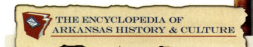

THE ENCYCLOPEDIA OF ARKANSAS HISTORY & CULTURE

Log on to Learn More
http://www.encyclopediaofarkansas.net/

I Am an Arkansan

John Grisham (1955–)

Born in Jonesboro (Craighead County), John Grisham is a former politician and attorney who began writing novels in his spare time. He eventually became one of the most successful writers in American history. His many legal thrillers have sold millions of books worldwide and have been translated into several languages.

His first book, *A Time to Kill,* was made into a Hollywood film, and many of his novels have been turned into movies. *The Firm,* another of his many bestsellers, tells the story of a young lawyer discovering a dangerous conspiracy where he works. The bestselling book was adapted into a popular movie starring Tom Cruise.

During the 1980s, he worked as a small-town lawyer in Southaven, Mississippi. He also served as a Mississippi state senator from 1983 to 1990. Grisham's novel, *A Painted House,* which reflects stories of his childhood in northeastern Arkansas, was made into a Hallmark Hall of Fame movie in 2001 and much of the movie was filmed in Poinsett County, near Lepanto. The movie premiered at Arkansas State University in Jonesboro in 2003.

Over the course of his career as a novelist, Grisham has sold over sixty million copies of his books. Some of his other titles include *The Client, The Chamber, The Runaway Jury,* and *Skipping Christmas.* He has continued to release roughly one book per year, and in 2006, released his first nonfiction work, about a murder case in Oklahoma. Today, he lives near Oxford, Mississippi, but is a frequent visitor to eastern Arkansas.

THE ENCYCLOPEDIA OF ARKANSAS HISTORY & CULTURE

Log on to Learn More
http://www.encyclopediaofarkansas.net/

I Am an Arkansan

E. Lynn Harris (1955–)

E. Lynn Harris was born in Flint, Michigan, and raised in Little Rock, Arkansas. He attended the University of Arkansas, where he was the school's first black yearbook editor, the first black male cheerleader, and the president of his fraternity. He graduated with honors with a degree in journalism.

Harris sold computers for IBM, Hewlett-Packard, and AT&T before quitting to write his first novel, *Invisible Life*, and, failing to find a publisher, published it himself in 1991. He sold it mostly at black-owned bookstores, beauty salons, and book clubs before he was "discovered" by Anchor Books. Anchor published *Invisible Life* in 1994 and thus his career as an author was "officially" launched.

Invisible Life was followed by *Just As I Am* (1994), *And This Too Shall Pass* (1996), *If This World Were Mine* (1997), *Abide With Me* (2000), all published by Doubleday. Currently, there are more than three million copies of Harris's novels in print, all of which have been bestsellers. His 2006 work *I Say A Little Prayer* debuted at number three in the *New York Times*.

Harris's writing has also appeared in *Sports Illustrated*, *Essence*, the *Washington Post Sunday Magazine*, the *New York Times Book Review*, *Atlanta Journal Constitution*, and many other publications.

An avid University of Arkansas Razorbacks fan, Harris is a part-time cheer coach for the Razorback cheerleaders. He divides his time between Fayetteville, Arkansas; Atlanta, Georgia; and Houston, Texas.

http://www.elynnharris.com

Log on to Learn More
http://www.encyclopediaofarkansas.net/

I Am an Arkansan

Louis Jordan (1908–1975)

In the 1940s, Louis Thomas Jordan soared to fame as a wildly innovative singer, bandleader, and saxophone player. He performed concerts across the nation, appeared in movies, and hit the top of the music charts. Along the way, he influenced the music of the 1950s and 1960s: rhythm and blues, rock-and-roll, and electric blues.

Born in Brinkley (Monroe County), Louis's father was a bandleader, and Louis studied under him, showing talent on the clarinet and the saxophone. Louis's mother died when he was young, and young Louis grew up on the road, in his father's band, performing in Arkansas, Tennessee, and Missouri.

By the 1930s, Louis Jordan was playing with legendary jazz stars like drummer Chick Webb and vocalist Ella Fitzgerald. He became known in New York City and Philadelphia as a top bandleader. But he reached his peak of commercial success in the 1940s and 1950s, when he recorded dozens of hits, including "Choo Choo Ch'Boogie," which stayed at number one for eighteen weeks. His sense of humor and good nature also became well known.

Fans loved his tough, yet fun, urban style of music that was perfected with hours of rehearsing. Among the first to join electric guitar and bass with horns, Jordan set the framework for decades of future rhythm and blues and rock combos. In 1987, he was inducted into the Rock and Roll Hall of Fame, and many music stars claim his influence, including Ray Charles and B. B. King. The Arkansas Entertainers Hall of Fame and the Arkansas Black Hall of Fame have also honored him as an inductee.

THE ENCYCLOPEDIA OF ARKANSAS HISTORY & CULTURE

Log on to Learn More
http://www.encyclopediaofarkansas.net/

I Am an Arkansan

Susan Hampton Newton Pryor (1900–1984)

The first woman in Arkansas to run for political office, Susan Pryor played a significant role in the state's politics for over a generation. She was the mother of former governor and U.S. senator David Pryor, and was the grandmother of Mark Pryor, who is currently representing Arkansas in the U.S. Senate.

She was born in Camden (Ouachita County) in 1900, the daughter of the sheriff of Ouachita County. After briefly attending the University of Arkansas, she returned to Camden where she worked in several businesses until 1924, when she was appointed deputy clerk of Ouachita County. In 1926, she ran in the Democratic Party primary for the post of circuit clerk. Losing by just two hundred votes, she devoted her attention to helping people in her county. She set up a fund to provide interest-free loans to the needy, and also founded Camden Community House, a program that offered aid and instruction to local children.

Her son, David, began his political career in 1960. She played an active, often outspoken, role in his ambitions. Though she did not live to see her grandson Mark become a U.S. senator, Susan Pryor's legacy as a community leader and activist is secure, and the Pryor family continues to help lead Arkansas into the twenty-first century.

Log on to Learn More
http://www.encyclopediaofarkansas.net/

I Am an Arkansan

Vance Randolph (1892–1980)

Vance Randolph was a folklorist who chronicled Ozark culture and traditions for over half a century, thus preserving the unique customs of the region. Born in Pittsburg, Kansas, he was drawn to the history of the Ozarks and moved to the area in 1920, making his first home in Pineville, Missouri.

Instead of completing his doctorate, he decided to devote his life and career to the study of Ozark folklore—the stories, songs, and cultural traditions of the region. He also studied the peculiar Ozark speech patterns, as well as jokes and other examples of the area's culture. For much of his life, most scholars did not consider such topics worthy of study. As such, scholars largely ignored his books, with compelling titles such as *Ozark Superstitions* and *Ozark Magic and Folklore*.

By the 1970s, however, many people began to realize that the rich tradition of Ozark life was a fascinating, often overlooked area of study. An avid collector of all things Ozark, Randolph made an important contribution to our understanding of the region by preserving the stories, music, and lessons of the land.

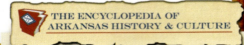
THE ENCYCLOPEDIA OF ARKANSAS HISTORY & CULTURE

Log on to Learn More
http://www.encyclopediaofarkansas.net/

I Am an Arkansan

Mary Steenburgen (1953–)

Mary Steenburgen was born in Newport (Jackson County), attended Hendrix College in Conway (Faulkner County), and moved to New York City in 1972 to study acting. She first rose to prominence in 1980, when she won an Academy Award for her performance in the movie *Melvin and Howard*. Since then, she has appeared in several successful films, including *Parenthood* with Steve Martin and *Back to the Future III* with Michael J. Fox. She is married to actor and former star of *Cheers*, Ted Danson.

I Am an Arkansan

Conway Twitty (1933–1993)

Conway Twitty was one of the most popular performers in country music history. He was born in Mississippi with the name Harold Jenkins, but moved to Helena (Phillips County) at the age of ten. Within two years, he had formed a band and was appearing on his own weekly radio program. He also became a successful baseball player, and received an offer to play in the Philadelphia Phillies organization. Instead, he served in the U.S. Army, and after his service, he began a long musical career that would gain him enormous fame.

In the early 1950s, he settled in Memphis and recorded for the famous record label Sun Records, whose other artists included Elvis Presley and Jerry Lee Lewis. In 1957, he changed his name, taking his first name from Conway, Arkansas (Faulkner County), and his last name from the town of Twitty, Texas. By the mid-1960s, he had become a country music artist, which would bring him greater success. In 1970, he released his most well-known song, "Hello Darlin'." Over the course of his long career, he scored over fifty-five number one hits—more than Elvis Presley, the Beatles, or Garth Brooks—and in 1999 was inducted into the Country Music Hall of Fame.

Index

A

Aaron v. Cooper, 390, 395
abolish/abolished, 164, 165, 212
abolition, 212, 213
absolute, 18, 19
Ace of Clubs House; *photo, 96*
AD, 106–9, 113–14
Adams, President John Quincy, 169, 171
adapt, 18, 19
Adkins, Gov. Homer, 370, 443
adze, 110, 112
Afghanistan, 439
Africa World War II, 349
African Americans (blacks), 164, 165, 193, 212, 213, 252, 261–69, 306–9, 316–17, 384–409; *photos, 254, 261, 265*
    boycott of businesses, 416
    businesses, 265
    civil rights, 239, 374, 384–409
    Civil War, 227, 229, 230–32
    Clinton Administration, 441
    convict-lease system, 280
    education, 265, 368
    farmers' groups, 249; *photo, 250*
    free blacks, 140, 181, 192, 193, 203, 240, 250, 251
    impact of New Deal, 336
    impacted by flood, 327
    in Arkansas politics, 262, 263
    in society, 263–69
    jobs/wages, 360, 361, 416, 424
    "Juneteenth," 231
    Ku Klux Klan (KKK), 242–43, 316–17
    music, 311
    newspaper. *See* Arkansas State Press
    political/politics, 250, 251, 264, 265, 416
    political shift, 341
    population, 263; *map, 193*
    Progressive Era, 278
    religion, 260, 261, 266
    segregation in schools, 286, 287, 374, 378, 379, 386–406
    slave codes (laws, restrictions), 190, 192
    spirituals, 193
    Union army units, 219; *photo, 229*
    voting issues during Reconstruction, 243, 250–51
    women, 438, 440
    World War II, 351, 358–62; *photos, 346, 358, 359*
agnostic, 316, 318
Agricultural Adjustment Administration (AAA), 336–37
agricultural/agriculture, 11, 27–28, 84–86, 113–19, 147, 156–58, 188–93, 248–51, 266, 284, 287–89, 429–31; *photos, 266, 267*
    aid to farmers, 335
    cotton, 429
    dairy farming, 299
    farm colonies, 339; *photo, 339*
    farmers' in politics, 248–51; *photo, 249*
    farmers' protests, 248–51
    fruit farming, 299; *photo, 298*
    impact of New Deal, 336–37
    impacted by flood, 327
    impacted by Great Depression, 331
    poultry, 299, 428–29, 430
    prices, 322, 331, 336
    products, map, 86
    prosperity, *chart, 200*
    soybeans, 429
    technology, 327
    union, 337
    way of life, 188–93
    World War II, 355–57
Agricultural, Mechanical, and Normal College, Pine Bluff (AM and N). *See* University of Arkansas–Pine Bluff
Agricultural Wheel, 237, 248, 249
ague, 154, 157
airplanes, 337, 338, 350, 352, 353, 358, 416; *photos, 278, 279*
airports, *map, 83*
Alabama, 140
    civil rights, 388
Alamo, The, 198
Alaska, 110
Albright, Secretary of State Madeline, 441
ALCOA, 296, 353
alcohol/alcoholism, 140, 260, 261, 377, 422
    prohibition, 277, 279, 282–83
Alexander, AR, 292
Alexander the Great, 107
All American Redheads, 354
Allied Forces
    World War II, 348, 351
Allies
    World War I, 304
Alma, AR, 25
"alphabet soup," 335–37. *See also* New Deal
Alltel, 426, 428
alluvial, 110, 111
Altus, AR, 92; *photos, 93*
aluminum, 25
Amagon, AR, 449
ambassador, 164, 169
American Independent Party, 418, 419
American (Know-Nothing) Party, 185; *chart, 185*
American Red Cross, 305
    drought and dustbowl, 327–28
    during flood, 325, 326
Angelou, Maya, 57, 440
    I Am an Arkansan, 340

Anno Domini. *See* AD
annually, 82, 86
antitrust law, 278, 280
appeals, 54, 57
apple blossom, 9, 291
apples, 84, 299
Appomattox Courthouse, VA, 232
Archaic Indians, 112
Archaic Tradition, 106, 110, 112
archeologist, 108
archeology, 108, 110
Arkadelphia, AR, 9, 155, 289, 302, 378; *map, 311*
    Civil War, 215
Arkansan, 7
Arkansas
    actors and actresses, 451
    border states, 22
    District of, 146
    first library, 180
    geography, 16–28
    governors, chart, 58
    land size, 27
    mineral resources, map, 26
    naming of, 8, 9, 132; *illustration, 8*
    population, 269
    precipitation, maps, 24
    roads, 372, 374, 426, 428; *map, 176*
    six geographical regions, 17, 18, 21, 22; *maps, 23*
    state capitol building, 57, 284; *photos, 52, 55, 56, 285*
    state creed, 11, 12
    state motto, 11
    state quarter, 14, 247, 439; *photo, 14*
    state songs, 11–13
    state symbols, 9–14; *map, 10*
    state seal, 11, 57
    state vegetable, 241
    state debt after the Civil War, 247
    state debt during Great Depression, 332
    state fair, photo, 2
    state flag, 13–14, 291; *photo, 4, 14*
    state flower, 9, 291
    state government, 52–53, 55–57, 279–81, 283, 299
        flood, drought, dustbowl, Great Depression, 331–32
    state government and New Deal, 341
    state government in turmoil, 331
    statehood days, 176–77, 180–203
    statehood politics, chart, 185
    temperatures, maps, 25
    territory, 164–72, 176–77; *map, 166*
    tornadoes, *map, 26*
    unique geographical features, 26
    US Congressional districts, *map, 57*
    World War II, 351–65
Arkansas (Fletcher book), 329
Arkansas (state song), 11, 13, 277
Arkansas Advancement Association, 313
Arkansas Advocate, 172
Arkansas Agricultural, Mechanical and Normal College (AM & N), 288, 322, 400. *See also* University of Arkansas–Pine Bluff
Arkansas: A Guide to the State, 336

Arkansas Arts Center, 420
Arkansas Baptist College, 255, 260, 265
Arkansas Bar Association, 308
Arkansas Children's Hospital, 82, 83, 277, 292
Arkansas City, AR, 213
    flood, 325
Arkansas colleges and universities, *map, 79*
Arkansas Council on Human Relations, 384, 390, 391, 408
Arkansas County, AR, 4, 77, 96, 97, 98, 118, 132, 164, 259; *photo, 97*
    County Quest, 5
Arkansas Decorative Arts Museum, 329
Arkansas Democrat, 431–32
Arkansas Education Television Network (AETN), 406
Arkansas Entertainers Hall of Fame, 119
Arkansas federal lands, *map, 100*
Arkansas Federation of Women's Clubs, 260
Arkansas Gazette, 5, 9, 162, 164, 168–69, 172, 302, 305, 397, 417, 426, 431–32, 443; *illustration, 169*
    state constitution, 183
Arkansas General Assembly, 54, 56, 168, 183, 185, 187, 201, 203, 214, 239, 283, 313, 318, 331, 341, 372, 409, 419, 425, 428
Arkansas Industrial Development Commission (AIDC), 376, 377–78
Arkansas Industrial University. *See* University of Arkansas–Fayetteville
Arkansas Museum of Natural Resources, 96
Arkansas National Guard, 305, 373
    Central High School, 392, 398, 404
Arkansas Population Centers, *map, 89*
Arkansas Post, 5, 96, 122, 134–41, 148, 153, 154, 155, 168; *photo, 138*
    children, 137, 138
    Civil War, 216, 230; *illustration, 224*
    daily life, 138–41
    education, 138
    French, 138
    music, 138
    Quapaw, 136–38
    Revolutionary War battle, 141
    slaves, 140–41
    State Park, 137
    trade, 134–39
Arkansas Power and Light (AP & L), 310, 312–13, 376
Arkansas River, 5, 9, 23, 24, 82, 118, 119, 128, 134, 137, 139, 165, 172, 175, 177, 190, 194, 261, 314, 446; *photos, 28, 93, 133*
    flood, 324–27
Arkansas River Valley, 18, 20, 21–22, 92–93, 111, 113, 155, 156, 159, 189; *photo, 93*
Arkansas School for the Mathematics, Sciences, and the Arts, 426, 431
Arkansas Separate Coach Law of 1891, 266, 267
Arkansas State Fair, *photo, 101*
Arkansas State Normal School, 288
Arkansas State Parks, *map, 99*
Arkansas State Press, 360, 401, 417
Arkansas State Tuberculosis Sanatorium, *photo, 292*
Arkansas State University, 449
Arkansas State University at Newport, 136
Arkansas Tech University, 115

Arkansas Traveller, The (painting), 181; *photo, 156*
Arkansas Traveller, The (song), 11, 406
Arkansas's largest employers, *map, 83*
Arkansas (You Run Deep In Me), 11, 12
Arkies, 324, 327; *photo, 328*
ArkLa Gas, 376
Arlington Hotel, 303, 341; *photo, 94; map, 311*
Armstrong, Lance, 447
    bike, jersey; *photo, 447*
Armstrong, Louis, 311
Armstrong, Neil 416
Army, US, 175, 241, 244, 308, 373
Army Reserves, US, 449
Aromatique, 449
arrowheads, *photo, 111*
arsenal, 182, 185, 186, 244
art/artists, 9, 156, 197, 198, 423; *photo, 156*
art deco, 310, 311
artillery, 217, 232
    batteries, 216, 232
Aryans, 348
Ash Flat, AR, 336
Ashdown, AR, 332, 375
Ashley, Chester, 191
Ashley County, AR, 393
    County Quest, 288
Ashmore, Harry, 397
Asia/Asians, 88, 110, 124, 449
    World War II, 348–49
assessor, 182, 186
Atlanta, GA, 211
atlatl, 110, 112; *photo, 113*
atomic bomb, 346, 365
Atzerodt, George, 238, 239
Augusta, AR, 305
Austin, Stephen F., 198
Austria/Austrian, 302, 304
automobiles, 279, 289, 310, 314, 318; *photo, 314*
Axis Powers, 348, 349
Axum, Donna, 385

B

Babcock, Bernie, 283
baby boom, 370, 372
Babylon, 106
Bald Knob, AR, 171
Bald Knob National Wildlife Refuge, 171
Bandini, Father Pietro, 135
banks, 186–87
    failures, 330–32, 334
    holiday, 334
Baptist, 448
Baring Cross Bridge, 324, 326
Barnett, Eva Ware, 8, 11, 13, 277
basketball, 288, 354, 438
Bates, Daisy, 360, 386, 395, 404, 405, 417, 448; *photos, 395, 401, 402*
    I Am an Arkansan, 401
Batesville, AR, 28, 85, 98, 153, 155, 183, 269; *map, 156*
    Civil War, 222, 229
Bathhouse Row, 94; *photo, 94*

Battle of the Bulge, 375
bauxite, 11, 25, 86, 177, 294, 296, 353
    Pulaski and Saline counties, 296
Baxter, Gov. Elisha, 240, 244, 246, 373
Baxter County, AR, 138; *photo, 92*
    County Quest, 373
Bayou Meto, *photo, 97*
BC, 106, 108–10, 112–13
Beals, Melba Pattillo, 398, 403
Bear Creek Lake, 424
bear oil, 189
"Bear State," 310, 313, 428
Beaver Lake, 90, 91, 187, 285, 412
Beebe, Gov. Mike, 65, 449; *photos, 65, 449*
    election, 439, 449
    letter from, 67
beehive, 11
"before Christ." *See* BC
Bell, Alexander Graham, 254
Bell, John, 213
bench, 54, 55
Benton, AR, 177, 452
Benton County, AR, 26, 77, 82, 89, 139, 175, 187, 200, 276, 285, 305, 338, 428; *photos, 80, 91*
    Civil War, *photo, 210*
    County Quest, 187
Bentonville, AR, 91, 187, 338, 428; *photo, 80*
Beringia, 110
Berryville, AR, 149
Bezdek, Hugo, 262
bias, 108–9
Bible, The, 317–18
"Big Arkie," 14, 75; *photo, 75*
bilious fever, 154, 157
Bill of Rights, 444
bills, 54
    how a bill becomes a law, 56
Birmingham, AL, 388
"bird flu," 439
bison, 154, 155
Black Panther Party, 389, 392, 398
"black power," 389, 398
Black River, AR, 6, 28, 136, 153, 172, 177
Black Rock, AR, 6
Black Tuesday, 330
Blakely Town, AR. *See* Arkadelphia, AR
Blanchard Springs Caverns, 27, 90; *photo, 27*
Blitzkrieg, 348, 350
"Bloody Sunday," 389
Blossom, Superintendent Virgil, 389, 396, 404
Blossom Plan, 386, 390, 394, 395
bluff shelters, 113
Blunt, Gen. James G., 217, 223
Blytheville, AR, 139, 158
boll weevil, 324
bolls, 188, 191
Bolshevik, 306
Bonaparte, Napoleon. *See* Napoleon
Bond, Scott, 265; *photo, 281*
bonds, 182, 186, 243
boomtown, 314; *photos, 314, 315*
Boone County, AR

Civil War, 226
County Quest, 350
Booneville, AR, 354
    tuberculosis sanatorium, 292
boosters, 353, 358
Booth, John Wilkes, 211, 238
    reward for capture; *illustration*, 239
bootheel, 164, 165
bootleggers, 316, 317
Borland, Solon, 185
bow and arrow, 106, 115
Bowie, Jim, 198
    knife, 198, 201; *photo, 201*
Bowie Lumber Company, 295
Bradley County, AR, 11
    County Quest, 241
Bradley County Pink Tomato Festival, 241
Branch Normal College, 254, 260, 264, 265
bread (baking), 112
Breckinridge, John C., 213, 214
"Brick Capital of the World," 125
Brickeys, AR (prison), 424
bridges, 446
brigade, 232
Brinkley, AR, 118, 357
Britt, Maurice "Footsie," 348, 351, 352
    lieutenant governor, 351, 419
bromine, 22, 25
"Broncho Billy" Anderson, 276
Brooks-Baxter War, 236, 240, 244, 246, 373; *illustrations*, 243, 244
    quote about, 244
Brooks, Dr. Ida Jo, 283
Brooks, Joseph, 240, 244
Brough, Gov. Charles Hillman, 281–82, 283, 308–9, 332; *photo, 307*
Brown, Dorris Alexander "Dee"
    I Am an Arkansan, 454
Brown, Helen Gurley
    I Am an Arkansan, 455
Brown Trickey, Minnijean, 386, 398, 403; *photos, 386, 403*
Brown v. the Board of Education of Topeka, 347, 386, 390, 391, 392, 393, 396, 400
Broyles, John Franklin "Frank," 412, 422; *photo, 430*
    "Game of the Century" (1969), 422, 430
    1964 championship, 422, 430
    retirement after fifty years of service to the University of Arkansas, 439
    I Am an Arkansan, 430
Brubaker, 422
Bryan, William Jennings, 250, 303, 318; *map, 311*
Bryant, Paul "Bear," 264
    I Am an Arkansan, 456
buckskin, 134, 139
Buffalo National River, 22, 23, 90, 182, 183, 258, 335, 350
Bug Scuffle, AR, 23
Bull Shoals Lake, 183, 373, 412
Bumpers, Gov. and Sen. Dale, 64, 70, 392, 418, 420–21; *photo, 420*
    I Am an Arkansan, 421
Burlington, AR, 226
Burnett, Chester "Howlin' Wolf," 87, 98

Bush, President George H. W., 440, 443, 447; *photo, 422*
Bush, President George W., 389, 442, 443, 447, 449
bushwhackers, 216, 226, 227
businesses, 82–83, 376, 377–78, 417, 428–29, 449, 450
    failure during Great Depression, 331
    furniture, 296, 314
    mining, 296–97
    Progressive Era, 279, 294–96
    recovery, 334
    timber, 294–96

C

cabinet, 54
Cabot, AR, 408
Cache River, 22, 24, 136, 222, 305
Caddos, 116–19, 129, 137; *photos, 117; map, 116*
    removal, 172, 174; *map, 174*
Cadron, AR, 155, 156, 168
Caesar, Augustus, 107
Cahokia (IL), 107
Calhoun, AR, 312
Calhoun County, AR, 451
    County Quest, 310
Calico Rock, AR 153; *photos, 22, 28*
calumet, 124, 131
Camden, AR, 128, 155, 246, 421; *photo, 7*
    "Camden Knights," 217
    Civil War, 225, 226
campaign buttons, *photo, 447*
Campbell, Glen, 141
    I Am an Arkansan, 457
Camp Chafee, 354, 364; *map, 360*
Camp Dermott, 364; *map, 360*
Camp Robinson, 353, 364; *map, 360*
Canada, 130, 132, 134, 135, 141, 159
Cane Creek State Park, 370
Cane Hill, AR, 139
canoeing/canoeists, 25, 194, 200; *photo, 23*
capital (city), 164, 168
    Arkansas Post, 168
    Little Rock, 168
capital (financial), 182, 186
capitalism, 76
capitol (state of Arkansas building), 170, 177; *photo, 177*
    as a symbol of progress, 177
Caraway, Sen. Hattie, 70, 322, 330, 332, 370, 425; *photo, 333*
    I Am an Arkansan, 333
Caraway, Sen. Thaddeus, 333
carpetbaggers, 240, 242
Carroll County, AR, 92, 200, 282, 432
    County Quest, 149
cars. *See* automobiles
"car tags and Cubans," 426
Carter, President Jimmy, 422, 441, 443, 447
Cash, Johnny (John, J. R., John R.), 98, 136, 139, 439
    I Am an Arkansan, 433
Casqui, 124, 127; *photos, 128*
    I Am an Arkansan, 127
casualties, 216, 219
catalyst, 304
catastrophic, 324, 325

Index **469**

catfish, 130, 140, 431; *map,* 140
Catholics, 124, 128, 130, 185, 317, 439
Caulder, Peter
    I Am an Arkansan, 202
cavalry, 216, 217, 232
Cedar Falls at Petit Jean State Park, *photo, 101*
censured, 370, 374
census, 154, 155
Central Baptist College, 406
Central High School, 288, 378, 379, 384–407, 418; *photos,* 387, 388, 389, 394, 406
    National Historic Site, 100, 384, 403, 406; *photo, 407*
    special feature, 384–89
Charleston, AR, 392, 393, 420
charter, 182, 183
Cherokees, 172–73, 175
    Civil War, 220; *illustration,* 222
    Sequoyah (George Guess), 173; *illustration,* 173
    written language, 173
Cherokee Village, AR, 336
Cherry, Gov. Francis, 376
Cherry Valley, AR, 304
chert, 22, 23
Chicago, IL, 306, 311
Chickasaws, 134, 139, 157, 172, 175
Chi Omega, 262
Chicot County, AR, 129, 140, 186, 190, 331, 364; *photo, 28, 322, 325; illustration, 162*
    drought and dustbowl, 328
    County Quest, 56
children, 137, 196, 441, 450; *photo, 450*
    Native Arkansans, 111, 115
    Progressive Era, 291, 292, 297
    World War II, 352, 353, 362, 363; *photos, 361, 363*
China, 123, 124, 349
Choctaws, 163, 172, 175
Christian/Christianity, 107, 109, 125, 130, 175, 193
Chrysler Building (New York City), 311
church bombing, 388
Churchill, Winston, 385
circuit court, 54, 57
citizen, 6, 7, 14, 53, 70
    privilege, 70
    responsibility, 70
citizenship, 53
civic, 53, 278, 279
civil, 194, 197
civil rights, 239, 368, 374, 375, 384–412, 418; *photo, 385; map, 392*
    Central High School, 378, 379, 384–407, 418; *photos, 387, 388, 389, 394, 406*
    Civil Rights Act, 385, 389, 408
    National Historic Site, 100, 384, 403, 406; *photo, 407*
    special feature, 384–89
    World War II, 347
Civilian Conservation Corps (CCC), 334, 335
    projects by, 335
Civil War, 187, 210–32; *photos, 210*
    battles with two names, 223, 232
    ends, 232
    hero, 225
    letter from citizen, 226
    letter from soldier, 221
    major Arkansas battles, *map,* 220
    shortage of food, 228
    spy, 225
    uniforms, *illustrations,* 216, 218
Clarendon, AR, 118
Clark, Gen. Wesley, 442
    I Am an Arkansan, 458
Clark, William (of Lewis and Clark), 146, 147, 150, 152
Clark County, AR, 118, 164, 289, 302, 378
    County Quest, 9
Clarksville, AR, 159, 352
Clay County, AR, 98, 312
    County Quest, 390
Clayton, Gov. Powell, 240, 241, 268
    against KKK, 242–43
Cleaver, Eldridge
    I Am an Arkansan, 398
Cleburne, Gen. Patrick, 217, 218, 449; *photo, 219*
Cleburne County, AR, 77, 90
    Civil War, 221
    County Quest, 449
Cleveland, President Grover, 246
Cleveland County, AR, 433
    Civil War, 226
    County Quest, 374
climate, 22, 26
Climber Company, 310, 314, 318
Clinton, AR, 158
Clinton, Chelsea, 440, 447
Clinton, First Lady and Sen. Hillary Rodham, 91, 427, 440, 446
    elected to Senate (New York), 442
    healthcare controversy, 442
    2008 presidential candidacy, 439
Clinton, Gov. and President William J., 14, 91, 95, 401, 421, 422, 424, 426, 438, 443, 451; *photos, 401, 406, 426, 427, 441*
    accomplishments, 441–42
    autobiography, *My Life,* 442–43
    "bridge to the twenty-first century," 446
    controversies, 426, 438, 439, 442
    elected president/inauguration, 438, 440, 441
    e-mail administration, 442
    governor, 64, 426–28, 432; *photo, 64*
    impeachment, 438, 442, 448
    inauguration, 340, 440
    Lewinsky, Monica, 438, 442
    New York, 442
    presidential campaign, 432
    "travelgate," 442
    "Whitewater," 438, 442, 448
Clinton Presidential Library and Museum, 17, 21, 100; *photo, 438*
    dedication, 439, 443, 446
    special feature, 444–47
Clooney, George, 374
Clover Bend, AR, 6, 339
coal (mining), 25, 86, 296
    Franklin, Johnson, Sebastian counties, 296
    labor strike, 297
Coal Hill, AR, 240, 247, 280

coat of arms, 124, 132; *photo, 133*
Coffin, Frank, 271
cold war, 370, 372, 373, 405, 411
Columbia, AR, *illustration, 162*
Columbia County, AR, 312, 378
    County Quest, 327
Columbine, CO, high-school shooting, 438
Columbus, Christopher, 110, 122, 124, 126
Comet, The, (boat) 176
commencement, 260, 262
commodity, 334, 340
Common School Law, 182, 187
Commonwealth College, 330, 332, 376
communism/communist(s), 306, 372, 373, 411, 416, 426
commuted, 418, 420
compress, 188, 191
Concatenated Order of Hoo-Hoo, 9
concentration camps, 348, 350
Conditionalists, 212, 215
Confederacy, The, 13, 210, 212, 214, 215; *map, 218*
    constitution, 215
Confederates, 257; *photo, 240*
    Arkansas State capitol, 224
    army, 217, 219
    generals, chart, 217
    soldier reunion; *photo, 240*
    uniforms, 218; *illustration, 218*
Confederate States of America. *See* Confederacy, The
confluence, 134, 137
Congressional Medal of Honor, 348, 351, 352
conservation, 334, 340
Conservatives, 240, 244
constituents, 54, 57
Constitution
    Arkansas, 427
    Arkansas 1874, 246, 260
    Arkansas's first (provisions of), 183, 184
    Confederacy, 215
    United States, 70, 123, 164, 239, 283, 444
continent, 22
contraband, 216, 229
convict-lease system, 277, 280, 283, 284
Conway, Henry, 163, 171, 184
    death, 163, 171
    duel, 163, 169
Conway, Gov. Elias Nelson, 202, 203
Conway, Gov. James Sevier, 57, 184, 202, *photo, 185*
Conway, AR, 89, 281, 288, 377, 406
Conways ("The Family"), 185
Conway County, AR, 92, 261, 269, 318, 378; *photo, 101*
    County Quest, 60
Coolidge, President Calvin, 326
co-op, 334, 339
Cooperationists, 212, 215
Corbin, Joseph Carter, 260, 262
corn, 84, 107, 115, 128, 188, 299; *charts, 200, 355*
    as a sugar or starch, 115
Corning, AR, 390
Corporation Commission, 278, 283
corps, 232
Cosmopolitan Magazine, 432
Cossatot Community College, 332

Cossatot River, 82, 263
Cotter Bridge, *photo, 92*
cotton, 84, 166, 188, 189, 190–91, 356, 429; *photo, 193; charts, 200, 355*
    cash crop, 166, 200, 248
    Egypt, 248
    gin, 123, 164, 166; *illustration, 166*
    glut, 248
    prices, 236, 244, 248
    prices during Great Depression, 331, 332
    prices during Progressive Era, 297
Cotton Club, 310, 311
Cotton Plant, AR
    Civil War, 223
Couch, Harvey, 310, 312, 313
counties. *See also county name*
counties, 68; *map, 166*
county government, 68
county seat, 68, 88
court cases
    Aaron v. Cooper, 390, 395
    Brown v. the Board of Education of Topeka, 386, 390, 391, 392, 393, 396, 400
    Dred Scott v. Sanford, 181
    Epperson v. Arkansas, 318
    McLean v. Arkansas, 318
    Plessy v. Ferguson, 264, 265
    Roe v. Wade, 416
courtship, 194, 197
Craighead County, AR, 89, 159, 269
    County Quest, 330
Crater of Diamonds State Park, 11, 14, 94, 141; *photo, 11*
Crawford County, AR, 92, 270
    County Quest, 25
creationism/creationist, 317–18, 417, 427
credit, 182, 186
creed, 8, 11, 12
Creeks (Indians), 172, 175
Crittenden, Robert, 63, 163, 168, 169, 170, 171, 172, 184, 185; *photo, 170*
    death, 171
    duel, 169, 171
    role in Indian Removal, 174–75
Crittenden County, AR, 115, 371, 376, 443
    County Quest, 63
Crockett, Davy, 163, 198, *quotes, 199*
crop duster, photo, 429
Cross County, AR, 115, 128
    County Quest, 304
Crossett, AR, 393
Crowley's Ridge, 18, 21, 23, 25, 78, 98, 330, 424
    state park, 335
Crowley's Ridge Parkway, 98
crude, 124, 190
Crystal Hill, 154, 155; *map, 156*
Cuba/Cubans, 385, 417, 426
culture, 6, 7, 11, 17, 19, 278, 449, 450
    counterculture, 410, 411
    1960s, 410
Cummins Prison Farm, 278, 280, 422; *photo, 281*
Curtis, Gen. Samuel R., 217, 220, 222, 229
Cushman, AR, 296

customs, 123
Czechoslovakia, 350

D

Daffodil Festival, 246
Dallas County, AR, 308
    County Quest, 264
Dallas Cowboys, 412
Dalton Gang, 258
Dalton Period Cemetery, 152
Daly, John, 93, 219; *photo, 93*
    I Am an Arkansan, 93
Danville, AR, 219
Darby, William, 348, 352
Dardanelle, AR, 92, 219
Darrow, Clarence, 318
Darwin, Charles, 181, 316, 317
Darwinism, 427
Daughters of Rebecca, 194, 197
Davis, Herman, 304, 305
Davis, Gov. and Sen. Jeff, 276, 279, 284
    racism, 280
Davis, Jefferson, 212, 214
Dean, Jay Hanna "Dizzy," 354
Declaration of Independence, 123, 444
default, 330, 332
defense plants, 353, 354
DeGray Lake, 94
de la Harpe, Bernard, 123, 137–38
delegate, 164
Delight, AR, 141
delta, 96–98, 110, 305, 306, 365; *photo, 97, 98*
Delta Cultural Center, 24, 96
Deltic Timber, 82
Democrat-Conservatives, 240, 244, 246
democratic (as in a form of government), 54
Democratic Party, 68, 170, 181, 184, 185, 213, 239, 246–47, 249, 250, 251, 334, 373–75, 378, 418–19, 420, 421, 422, 440, 441, 448, 449; *chart, 185*
    Progressive Era, 279, 281, 282
    World War II, 361, 362
DeQueen, AR, 87
Dermott, AR, *photos, 322, 325, 326*
Des Arc, AR, 237, 284
desegregation, 384–402
Desha County, AR, 28
    County Quest, 213
    flood, 325
de Soto, Hernando, 56, 109, 118, 122, 125–30, 131, 140; *photos, 122, 125; map, 129*
    death, 128
    hogs, 125, 126
    journals, 126
    slaves, 125
de Tonti, Henri, 122, 132–36; *photo, 134*
DeValls Bluff, AR, 194, 199, 226, 230, 284
Devil's Den State Park, 91, 335
DeWitt, AR, 5
diamonds, 11, 14, 25, 141
    discovered, 276
Dierks Lake, AR, 440

Dierks Lumber and Coal Company, 295
    sustained yield forestry, 327
Dillard, William T., 77, 428, 440
Dillard's, 82, 83, 426, 428
Ding Dong Daddy Days Festival, 213
dinosaurs, 110
diphtheria, 286, 291
diplomat, 150, 152
discovery and exploration, 122–41
disease, 19, 125, 128, 138, 140, 154, 157, 175, 292, 305
    caused by flood, 326, 327
    Civil War, 228
    dysentery, 216, 228
    immunizations, 420
    influenza, 125
    measles, 125
    Progressive Era, 286–92
    smallpox, 125
district court, 54, 57
districts, 78
diversity, 449
Dodd, David O., 225; *photo, 225*
dogs
    de Soto, 125
    Native Arkansans, 111
    racing, 63, 341, 376
dogtrot, 134, 138, 188; *photos, 138, 139*
domestic workers, 334, 336
dominion, 278, 281
Donaghey, Gov. George, 57, 61, 276, 277, 281–82, 284, 304; *photo, 61*
Don't Stop Believin', 440
Douglas, Stephen A., 213, 214
"downstream people," 8, 118
draft
    Civil War, 216, 217, 218
    Vietnam, 410–11
    World War I, 304
Dred Scott v. Sanford, 181
Drew, Gov. Thomas, 199
Drew County, AR
    County Quest, 280
Driftwood, Jimmy, 98, 428
"dropped out," 410
drought, 327–28
    farmers, 328
    food riot, 328
Duck Gumbo Cook-Off Festival, 5
duel/dueling, 169, 170, 171
Dumas, AR, 213
Dunbar High School, 390, 394
Dunbar, William, 147, 152; *photo, 152*
dustbowl, 324, 327; *map, 328*
dutch oven, 11
Dwight Mission, 170, 175; *illustration, 174*
Dyess, W. R., 335, 337, 339
Dyess, AR, 139, 433
Dyess Colony, AR, 339; *photo, 339*
dynasty, 170
dysentery, 216, 228

E

Earhart, Amelia, 322, 338
early settlement, *map, 156*
earthquake (New Madrid), 147; *map, 158*
East Indies, 110
Ebony (magazine), 213
Eckford, Elizabeth, 386, 398, 399, 403, 404–5; *photos, 386, 399, 405*
economic development, 376, 377–78, 426, 427, 428
economics/economy, 11, 75–86, 181, 185, 186–87, 449
    bank failures, 330–32, 334
    boom/prosperity, 17, 203
    business failures, 330–32
    Civil War, 218
    crisis/panic, 17, 187
    depression, 187
    employers, 85; *map, 83*
    entrepreneurs, 426, 428, 429, 432
    failure, 330–41
    fiscal, 264, 266
    and geography, 17, 28
    global, 75
    global panic, 236
    Great Depression, 330–41
    minimum wage, 336
    other states, 75
    Panic of 1837, 187
    Progressive Era income, 299; chart, 299
    Progressive Era jobs, 294–97
    Reconstruction, 237–51
    reform, 187, 334
    slavery, 166–67
    statehood days, 194–95
    stock market, 330–31
    wage cuts, 331
    World War II, 353–57
Ecore á Fabri. *See* Camden, AR
Edison, Thomas, 254
education, 78–80, 138, 187, 259–65, 420, 426, 431, 441, 448; *map, 79*
    Arkansas, behind in, 374–75, 431
    consolidation, 372
    desegregation, 347
    districts/consolidation, 277, 287
    funding (lack of), 247, 286, 431
    graduation rate, 431
    impact of Great Depression, 331
    improvements, 249, 374, 427, 431
    integration, 375
    job training/vocational tech, 428
    Progressive Era, 286–89, 299; *photos, 286, 287, 289*
    Reconstruction, 243
    reform school for boys, 280
    school districts, 372
    school shooting in Jonesboro, 330
    segregation, 286, 287, 374, 378, 379, 386–406
    teacher pay, 286, 372
    World War II, 346, 353–57
Egypt, 106
    cotton, 248
    hieroglyphs, 162

Eighteenth Amendment, 277, 281–83. *See also* prohibition
Eisenhower, President Dwight, 386, 389, 400
El Dorado, AR, 77, 95, 96, 303, 310, 313, 314, 315; *photos, 96, 314, 315; map, 311*
    County Quest, 111
Elaine, AR, 97, 306–9
Elaine Mercantile, *photo, 307*
Elaine Race Riot, 24, 306–9, 318; *photos, 302, 307, 309; map, 311*
Elders, Joycelyn, 438
elections, 184
    Arkansas gubernatorial (1944), 370, 371
    1860 presidential, 212–14
    1874 gubernatorial, 244–45
    fair, 378
    1966 gubernatorial, 418–19
    1970 gubernatorial, 420
    million-dollar race, 370
    poll tax, 184, 250, 362, 371, 372, 378
    primaries, 250–51, 278, 279, 280
    restrictions on voters, 250–51
Electoral College, 212, 214
electric/electricity, 310, 378; *map, 311*
    lights, 269, 279
    Rural Electrification Agency, 340
Eleven Point, AR, 23
elite, 182, 184
Elizabeth I, Queen of England, 122
Elkhorn Tavern, battle of (at Pea Ridge), 220, 222, 232; *photo, 222*
Ellington, Duke, 311
elocution, 260, 265
e-mail, 442
emancipation, 216, 230
Emancipation Proclamation, 211, 216, 230, 270, 444; illustration, 231
Emerson, AR, 327
England, AR
    food riot, 328
England. *See* Great Britain
enlightenment, 260
entrepreneurs, 426, 428, 429, 432
epidemics, 154, 158
Epperson v. Arkansas, 318
Equal Rights Amendment, 418, 425
equator, 18, 19
era, 108, 109
    modern, 439, 450
Ernst, Tim
    I Am an Arkansan, 20
erosion, 334, 340
Eureka Springs, AR, 92, 282
Europe/European(s), 365
    culture, ideas, 124
    exploration, 122–41
    fashion, 140, 310
    First Arkansans, 109, 110, 113, 115, 119
    musical instruments, 311
    rivalry, 122–41
    ruling power, 122–41
    settlement/settlers, 5, 96, 133, 246, 259
    technology, 125

World War II, 348, 350
Evanescence, photo, 95
   I Am an Arkansan, 95
Evening Shade, AR, 336
Evers, Medgar, 388
evolution, 303, 312, 316–17, 427; *map, 311*
excursion, 194, 195
executive branch of government, 54
Executive Order 8802, 353, 359
exploration/explorers, 122–41; *maps, 129, 131, 132*
expressionism, 310, 311

F

factions, 240, 244
"The Family," 170–72, 185
   during Civil War, 213
Fancher-Baker Train, 200
Farewell to Arms, A, 390
Farm Security Administration (FSA), 339
   farm colonies, 339
fascism, 348
"Father of the Blues," 302
Faubus, Gov. Orval, 63, 194, 369, 376–78, 379, 386, 387, 389, 393, 396, 397, 398, 399
   Central High School Crisis, 400, 418, 420, 421, 431; *photos, 63, 399, 402*
Faulkner, Col. Sanford, 8, 11
Faulkner County, AR, 89, 155, 281, 288, 377; *photo, 186*
   County Quest, 406
Fayetteville, AR, 89, 91, 92, 175, 185, 243, 254, 261, 262, 392, 393, 422, 423, 424, 425, 447; *photo, 92*
   Civil War, 212, 215, 224, 229
federal, 54
Federal, 212, 215. *See also* Union, The
"Federal Catfish Lab." *See* Harry K. Dupree National Aquaculture Research Center
Felsenthal, AR, 27
Felsenthal Wildlife Refuge, 111
Ferdinand, Archduke Franz, 302
Ferdinand, King of Spain, 124
festivals, *map, 90*
   Altus Wine Festival, 93; *photo, 93*
   Armadillo Festival, 288
   Bikes, Blues, and BBQ, 91
   Bradley County Pink Tomato Festival, 241
   Daffodil Festival, 246
   Ding Dong Daddy Days, 213
   King Biscuit Blues Festival, 24, 98; *photos, 98*
   Purple Hull Pea Festival, 327
   Smoke on the Water BBQ Festival; *photo, 97*
   Toad Suck Daze, 406
   Turkey Trot Festival, 183
   War Eagle Crafts Fair, 91
fiddle, 11
Fifteenth Amendment, 236; *illustration, 236*
   excerpt, 242
Fifty Six, AR, 23
Figure Five, AR, 23
"Fine Arkansas Gentleman," 153
fire departments, 269
First Amendment, 318

First Arkansans, 104–19
fiscal, 266, 268
fish/fishing, 68, 130, 140, 183, 263, 284, 332, 336, 373, 428, 431, 449
Fisher, George
   I Am an Arkansan, 443
Five Civilized Tribes, 172–73
Five Themes of Geography, 18, 19, 20, 21; *illustration, 21*
Flanagin, Gov. Harris, 215, 224
flapper, 310, 311
flatboat, 154, 189; *photo, 155*
Fleetwood Mac, 440
Fletcher, John Gould, 173, 323
   I Am an Arkansan, 329
Flippin, AR, 183
flood of 1927, 19, 322, 324–27, 451; *photos, 322, 324, 325; map, 325*
   American Red Cross, 325, 326
   cause, 324
   damage, 325
   disease, 326
   farmers, 324
   starvation, 326
Florida, 130, 135
"flower child," 410
flu. *See* influenza
"Folk Music Capital of the World," 428
folk singers, *photo, 92*
football, 260, 277, 288, 303, 351, 394, 412, 416, 422, 430
   "Game of the Century," 422, 430; *photo, 422*
   1964 championship, 422, 430
   Razorbacks, 422, 430; *photo, 422*
   Super Bowl, 412
Ford's Theatre, 232, 238
Fordyce, AR, 264
Forgotten Expedition, 147
Forrest City, AR, 78, 265
Forrest L. Wood Crowley's Ridge Nature Center, 98, 330
Fort Chaffee, 417, 426
Fort Hindman, *illustration, 224*
Fort Smith, AR, 78, 89, 92, 170, 175, 177, 194, 259, 314, 392, 426; *photos, 268, 290*
   battle of, 209, 224
   flood; *photo, 324*
   National Historic Site, 270, 314
Fort Sumter, 215
Forty-Four, AR, 23
forty-niners, 198, 199
Fountain Hill, AR, 19
Fourche LaFave River, 23
Four Freedoms, 348, 350
Fourteenth Amendment, 236, 238, 239, 240
   excerpt, 239
Foxe, Fannie, 418, 422
France/The French, 8, 9, 13, 146, 148, 149, 246
   Arkansas Post, 134–41
   exploration/explorers, 122–23, 130–37
   fashion, 311
   French and Indian War, 123, 134, 141
   language, 132, 135
   ruling power, 124, 136, 141

trade, 130–40; *photo, 135*
World War I, 304
Franklin County, AR, 26, 92, 305, 392, 420, 421; *photos, 23, 93*
County Quest, 200
free states, 182–84
Freedmen's Bureau, 216, 230, 242; *illustration, 230*
"Freedom Riders," 388
French and Indian War, 123, 134, 141
fugitives, 154, 155
Fuhrer, 348
Fulbright, Sen. J. William, 323, 368, 371, 373, 418, 419, 421, 431
civil rights, 391
Senate Foreign Relations, 411
Fulton, AR, 194
Fulton, Gov. William S., 172, 185
Fulton County, AR, 27, 91, 153, 269
County Quest, 242
fundamentalism, 316, 317
furnish, 294, 298
fuses, 353, 358
Futrell, Gov. Junius, 331, 332, 341
future, 450, 451; *photo, 450*

G

Gaddy's Corner, AR, 226
gallows, 266, 270; *photo, 270*
gambling, 197, 311, 341, 385, 419
Gandhi, 389
gangsters, 341
Garfield, President James
assassination, 236
Garland, Gov. Augustus Hill, 59, 240, 246; *photo, 59*
Garland County, AR, 21, 89, 276, 311, 372, 378, 452; *photos, 94*
County Quest, 396
Garvan Woodland Gardens, 94; *photo, 94*
Gates, Noah, 262
General Assembly, 54, 56. *See also* Arkansas General Assembly
Geneva Convention, 211
geographers, 18, 19
tools, 19, 21
geographic regions of Arkansas, 17, 18, 21, 22
geography, 16–28
dividing Arkansas, 181
economics, 28
human, 18
impact on history, economy, lifestyles, politics, image, reputation, and citizens, 27
industry, 28
physical, 18
racism, 28
geologic fault, 154, 158
Georgia (state), 316
Germans/Germany, 96, 259, 322, 323, 350, 416, 417
in interment camps, 364; *photo, 364*
World War II, 348–50
Gettysburg, PA, 211
G.I., 370, 376
G.I. Bill, 370, 372

G.I. Revolt, 370–71
Gibbs, Mifflin W., 264; *photo, 264*
Gilchrist, Ellen
I Am an Arkansan, 425
glaciers, 110, 112
globalization, 16
global positioning system (GPS), 19
globes, 18, 19
glut, 248
gold, 125, 128, 136, 187
gold rush, 181, 199, 314
trails in Arkansas, 199
Gone With the Wind, 17
Goobertown, AR, 23
Good Night and Good Luck (movie), 374
goods, 19, 76, 189
household, 188, 196
Goodwin, AR, 337
goosefoot, 110, 113
Gore, Vice President Al, 440, 442
government
branches of, 54–55, 57, 68
county, 68
federal, 55
local, 55, 68–69
municipal, 68–69
national, 54–55
state and local, 52–53, 55–57, 184–87
Progressive Era, 279–81, 283–99
US Congressional districts, *map, 57*
governors, Arkansas, *chart, 58*
letters, 66–67
mansion, 447
Gracen, Elizabeth Ward, 354
Grand Prairie, 14, 24, 365
Grangers, 248
Grant, Gen. Ulysses S., 211, 217, 226, 232,
as president, 244
Grant County, AR, 77, 371
Civil War, 226
County Quest, 353
grapes, 86, 156
gravel, 25, 86
graven, 353, 365
Gravette, AR, 305
Great Depression, 294, 297, 374
Great Britain (England), 148, 162, 304, 441
colonies, 130, 135, 141
French and Indian War, 123, 134, 141
ruling power, 124
trade, 139
War of 1812, 162, 168
World War I, 304
World War II, 347, 351
Great Depression, 322–41, 355; *photos, 331*
causing political shifts, 332
causing social unrest, 332–33
cotton prices, 331
impact on farmers, 331
New Deal, 334–41
relief programs, 335
school closings, 331

state government turmoil, 331
Great Red River Raft, 124, 129, 154, 177; *photo, 129*
Great River Road, 96; *photo, 22*
Great Seal of Arkansas, 11
Great Society, 385, 410, 412
Greece, 106, 107
Green, Ernest, 387, 398, 400, 403
Greenback Party, 247
Green, Al
    I Am an Arkansan, 459
Green Forest, AR, 432
Greene County, AR, 269
    Civil War, 221
    County Quest, 152
Greenwood, AR, 314
Greers Ferry Dam, 409, 412, 449
Greers Ferry Lake, 90, 409, 412, 449
Grey, William H., 263
Grice, Geleve, 119
Grider, John, 304, 305
Grisham, John, 98, 202
    I Am an Arkansan, 460
gross state product, 76
Grubb Springs, AR, 23
gruel, 110, 115
guerilla, 216, 223, 226
Guess, George. *See* Sequoyah
Gulf Coastal Plain, 18, 21, 23, 24, 95–96, 111; *photos, 95, 96*
gumbo, 193
Gurdon, AR, 9
gusher, 310, 313; *photo, 315*
gypsies, 348, 350

H

Hamburg, AR, 288
Hampton, AR, 310, 451
Handy, W. C., 302
"Hanging Judge." *See* Parker, Judge Isaac C.
Harding University, 171
Hardman Site, 118
Hardy, AR, 336
    Old Hardy Town, 336
Harlem, NY, 311
Harlem Globe Trotters, 303
Harris, E. Lynn
    I Am an Arkansan, 461
Harrisburg, AR, 202
Harrison, AR, 350
Harry K. Dupree, National Aquaculture Research Center, 5
Harvey, William "Coin," 289; *photo, 285*
    I Am an Arkansan, 285
"Hatchet Carry." *See* Nation, Carry
Hatfield, Ken, 412
hay, 86, 299
Hays, Brooks, 391, 394, 400
Hays, Gov. George W., 281
Hazen, AR, 299
headpot, photo, 108
healthcare, 441, 448

Progressive Era, 279, 286, 291–92, 299
Heber Springs, AR, 90, 449
Heifer International, 82, 228
heinous, 348, 350
Helena, AR, 24, 70, 96, 97, 98, 126, 129, 155, 156, 165, 219, 449; photos, 98
    battle of, 210, 211, 222–23, 224, 229
    Civil War, 230
Helm, Levon, 97, 98; *photo, 97*
    I Am an Arkansan, 97
hematite, 110, 114
Hemingway, Ernest, 98, 311, 312, 390
Hemingway-Pfeiffer Home, 98
hemispheres, 18, 19
    Northern, 22
    Western, 22
hemp, 154, 156
Hempstead County, AR, 95, 164, 194, 198, 448
    County Quest, 14
"Hempstead Hornets," 216
Henderson State University, 9, 289, 378
Hendrix College, 288, 377, 406
heritage, 6, 7, 11, 19, 193, 449, 450
Hickory Ridge, 304
Hilton, Paris, 200
Hindman, Gen. Thomas C., 213, 214, 217, 223; *photo, 223*
    "total war," 223
hippies, 410, 411
Hispanics, 88, 449
history, 107, 108, 450
Hitler, Adolf, 322, 323, 348–50
Hocker, Willie Kavanaugh, 8, 13, 14, 119, 291
Hodges, Kaneaster, 422
Hog Jaw, AR, 23
hogs, 125, 126, 299
"hogs-n-hominy," 188, 292
Hogskin Holidays Festival, 310
Holocaust, 353, 365
Holocaust Museum, 438
Holyfield, Wayland, 8, 11, 12
Homestead Act, 211, 212, 213
hominy, 188
honeybee, 11
hookworm, 286, 292
Hoop Spur, AR, 307, 308; *illustration, 309*
Hoover, President Herbert, 334
Hope, AR, 14, 95, 440, 447, 448
Hopefield, AR. *See* West Memphis, AR
horse racing, 94, 95, 197, 341, 396; *photo, 94*
Horseshoe Bend, AR, 68
Hot Spring County, AR, 302, 372
    County Quest, 125
Hot Springs, AR, 89, 94, 276, 303, 311, 341, 371, 372, 378, 385, 396, 419, 447, 452; *photos, 94*
Hot Springs National Park, 94
hot springs, natural, 21, 129, 130, 147–52
Houston, TX, 306
how a bill becomes a law, 56
Howard County, AR, 77, 226, 298
    County Quest, 440
Hoxie, AR, 6
    civil rights, 384, 392–93, 395, 396

Huckabee, Gov. Mike, 14, 65, 95, 419, 430, 448; *photo, 65*
    Baptist minister, 448
    governor, 448–49
    letter from, 66
    lieutenant governor, 448
    smoking ban, 448
    term limits, 448
    2008 presidential candidacy, 439
Huckaby, Elizabeth, 389
human environmental interaction, 18, 19; *illustration, 21*
    negative, 19
    positive, 19
Hundred Days, 334
Hunt, J. B., 76, 82, 83; *photo, 76*
    I Am an Arkansan, 77
Hunt, Silas H., 262, 368, 370, 374, 390
    I Am an Arkansan, 375
Hunter, George, 152
hunters/hunting, 155
Huntsville, AR, 97, 194, 376
Hurricane Katrina, 439
hushpuppies, 193
Hussein, Saddam, 438
Hutchinson, Cong. Asa, 448
Hutchinson, Sen. Tim, 448

I

Ice Ages, 110
ice plants, 269
Idaho, 150
ideas, 19, 21
Illinois, 150
illiteracy, 278, 279
image, 6, 7
Imboden, AR, 6
impeachment, 240, 442, 448
inaugural, 238, 334
income, 376
    Great Depression, 330–41
    increases, 428
    minimum-wage, 419
    personal, 428, 429
    Progressive Era per capita, 299; *chart, 299*
    Progressive Era wages, 299; *chart, 299*
Independence County, AR, 85, 139, 153, 269, 296
    County Quest, 28
India, 124
Indians. See Native Americans/Native Arkansans
Indian Removal, 163, 172–76; *map, 174*
    Quapaws, *timeline, 174–75*
Indian Territory, 270, 271
Indies, 124, 133
indigo, 154, 156
industry/manufacturing, 8, 257, 374, 376, 378, 428, 429
    automobiles, 314
    food processing, 374
    and geography, 28
    labor unions, 296, 297; *photo, 296*
    mining, 294–96
    poultry, 7
    Progressive Era, 279, 294–97; *photos, 294, 295*
    railroads, 136
    salt, 118, 177
    timber, 111, 125, 294, 314; *photos, 294, 295*
infamy, 348, 351
infantry, 216, 217, 218, 232
influenza, 125, 305
inherent, 53, 54
initiative, 278, 284
insurrection, 212, 215
integration, 384–402
interdependent, 18, 19
International Paper Mills, 119
interned, 353, 362
internment camps, 346, 353, 362–65; *map, 360*
Iowa, 150
Iran, 417
Iranian Revolution, 417
Iraq, 442
Irby, Edith, 368, 366, 370
Ireland, 441
iron-clad oath, 240, 241
Iron Mountain Railroad, 136; *photo, 257*
Isabella, Queen of Spain, 124
Israel, 416, 441
Italians/Italy, 259
    in internment camps, 364
    World War II, 348–50
Izard, Gov. George, 68, 169, 171
Izard County, AR, 28
    County Quest, 68

J

Jackson, President Andrew, 171, 172, 184, 185, 186–87
Jackson County, AR, 194, 449; *photo, 96*
    County Quest, 136
Jacksonport (State Park), 136, 194; *photo, 96*
Jacksonville Air Force Base, 17
James, Jesse, 226
James Gang, 226, 227, 258
Japan/Japanese
    daily life in internment camps, 362–65
    US apology to, 365
    World War II, 346, 347, 350, 351, 362–65
Jasper, AR, 258
jayhawkers, 216, 226, 227
jazz, 311
J. B. Hunt Transport, 187, 426, 429
Jefferson, President Thomas, 119, 123, 146, 147, 148, 149, 398, 406
Jefferson County, AR, 89, 97, 137, 254, 288, 339, 375, 398, 429; *photo, 255*
    Civil War, 226, 230
    County Quest, 119
Jehovah's Witnesses, 35, 365
Jenkins's Ferry Civil War Battlefield State Park, 353
    battle of, 226
Jerome, AR, 346, 353, 362–65; *map, 360*
Jesus, 107, 109
Jews/Jewish, 317, 350
Jim Crow Laws, 248, 250, 251, 267
John Brown University, 187

Johnson, Jimmy, 412
Johnson, John H., 213
   I Am an Arkansan, 413
Johnson, Justice Jim, 393, 395, 396, 418–19, 421; *photo, 393*
Johnson, President Andrew, 238–40
   impeachment, 448
Johnson, President Lyndon, 389, 412
   Civil Rights Act, 385, 389, 408
   Great Society, 385, 410, 412
   Voting Rights Act, 389
   War on Poverty, 410, 412
Johnson County, AR, 200, 247, 280, 352
   County Quest, 159
Johnsons ("The Family"), 185
Joliet, Louis, 8, 122, 130–32; *photo, 131; map, 131*
Jones, E. Fay, 92
Jones, Jerry, 412
Jones, Scipio, 309; *photo, 308, 309*
   I Am an Arkansan, 308
Jones, Wiley, 265; photo, 265
Jonesboro, AR, 89, 330, 333
   school shootings, 439
Jordan, Louis
   I Am an Arkansan, 462
Jordan (country of), 416, 441
journals
   de Soto's men, 126
   Dunbar and Hunter, 157
   Joyner, Al 417
judicial, 54

K

Kansas, 150
Kappa, 116, 118, 132
KATV Television, 429
keel, 154
keelboat, 154, 168; *photo, 169*
Kennedy, President John F., 384, 385, 404, 409, 410, 412, 449
Kennedy, Robert F., 416
Kensett, AR, 377
Kent State University, 416
Kentucky, 159
KFFA, 87
Kindley, Field E., 305; *photo, 305*
King Biscuit Blues Festival, 24; *photos, 98*
King Biscuit Time, 87
King Ferdinand of Spain, 124
King Louis XIV of France, 132
King, Dr. Martin Luther, Jr., 359, 387, 388, 389, 400, 408, 409; photo, 403
   assassination, 389; *photos, 389, 409*
King's Creek bowl, *photo, 114*
Kingsland, AR, 433
Kings River, 22, 23, 194
Klaff, Gary, 8, 11
Korea, 368, 372–73
   World War II, 349
Kosovo, 442
Ku Klux Klan (KKK), 240, 242–43, 254, 267–69, 302, 303, 306, 316, 318, 350; *photos, 268, 316*
Kunzelmann, James, 9

L

Lafayette County,
   County Quest, 57
Lake Catherine, 94, 125, 310, 312, 313, 335, 353
Lake Chicot State Park, 96; *photo, 28*
Lake Dardanelle State Park, 92
Lake De Gray State Park, 9
Lake Dick, AR, 339
Lake Erling, 57
Lake Greeson, *photo, 94*
Lake Hamilton, 94, 310, 312, 313
Lake Village, AR, 56
L'Anguille River, 22, 24, 135, 424
Land of Opportunity, 428
La Salle, Robert, 122, 132–34, 148; *photos, 133; map, 132*
Latinos, 88, 449
latitude, 18
Law, John, 123, 134, 135–36; *photo, 136*
Lawrence County, AR, 164, 339, 392–93; *photo, 267*
   County Quest, 6
laws, 54
lean-to, 194, 197
Lee County, AR, 118, 146, 165, 416, 424
   County Quest, 424
   flood, photo, 325
Lee, Gen. Robert E., 211, 217, 232
Leflar, Robert, 375
legacy, 123, 124, 127, 130, 369, 439
legislative, 54
legislature, 54, 56. *See* Arkansas General Assembly; US Congress
Lepanto, AR, 98, 202, 351
letters, 66–67, 69, 71
   from Clinton's presidency, 445
levees, 19, 240, 243
   flood, 326
Lewinsky, Monica, 438, 442
Lewis, Meriwether (of Lewis and Clark), 146, 147, 150, 152
Lewisville, AR, 57
liberals, 334, 341
Lincoln, President Abraham, 181, 210, 211, 226, 230, 231, 448
   assassination, 211, 232, 236, 238–39; *illustration, 238*
   election of 1860, 213–14
   Reconstruction plan, 238
Lincoln, Sen. Blanche Meyers Lambert, 449; *photo, 70*
   I Am an Arkansan, 70
   letter from, 71
Lincoln County, AR, 280
   County Quest, 370
Lindbergh, Charles, 56
Little Red River, 412, 449
Little Red Schoolhouse, 376
Little River County, AR, 354, 375
   County Quest, 332
Little Rock, AR, 17, 27, 77, 78, 89, 100, 101, 123, 138, 154, 155, 177, 191, 193, 198, 259, 261, 263, 271, 284, 349, 386–402, 408, 428, 429, 446; *photos, 2, 28, 52, 55, 284, 404*
   becomes the capital (1821), 168
   Brooks-Baxter War, 244
   capitol, 21; *photos, 52, 55, 56*
   Civil War, 211, 224, 225, 226, 230

Clinton Presidential Library and Museum, 17, 21
   flood, 326
   governor's mansion, 447
   presidential celebration, 440
   railroads, 194
   River Market, 21
   statehood days, 185
   zoo, 100
Little Rock Central High School. *See* Central High School
Little Rock Nine, 5, 387–92, 394, 396, 397, 398, 400, 402–3, 404, 406, 451; *photo, 406*
   foundation, 406
livestock, 324, 325, 357; *chart, 200*
   cattle, 86, 188, 429
   hogs, 188, 299
lobby, 286, 289
loblolly pine, 11
local government, 68
location, 18, 19; *illustration, 21*
   absolute, 19
   Arkansas's, 22
   relative, 19
loess, 22, 25
Logan County, AR, 27, 92, 292; *photo, 28*
   County Quest, 354
log cabin, 188; *photo, 186*
Long, Sen. Huey P., 332
longitude, 18
Long Shadow of Little Rock, The, 401, 405
Longview, TX, 306
Lonoke, AR, 276, 299, 351, 408
Lonoke County, AR, 88, 276, 299, 328, 351; *photo, 88*
   County Quest, 408
loo, 134, 138
"Lost Year, The," 400–2; *photos, 402*
Louisiana (state), 117
   as a territory, 124, 132, 136, 146, 149, 164, 439
   Orleans, territory of, 164
Louisiana Purchase, 146, 147, 148, 149 152, 164, 165, 167
   Historical Monument/State Park, 96, 118, 148, 165; *photo, 146; map, 149*
Louisville, KY, 159
Lowell, AR, 77, 82, 429
Low's Bridal, 118
loyalty, 211–32
lumber, 294–96
lyceum, 194, 197
lynching, 266, 268; *photo, 317*
Lynn, AR, 6
Lyon, Gen. Nathaniel, 217, 219
Lyon College, 28

M

MacArthur, Gen. Douglas
   I Am an Arkansan, 349
MacArthur Museum of Military History, 100, 186; *photo, 101*
MacArthur Park, 186, 225
Madden, Owney, 311, 341
Madison, President James, 147, 194
Madison, AR, 195

Madison County, AR, 97, 194, 376
   Civil War, 224
   County Quest, 194
Madison County Record, 376
Magic Springs Amusement Park, 94
Magnolia, AR, 327, 378
Maine, 166
maize. *See* corn
malaria, 154, 157, 158, 292, 351
Malcolm X, 389
Malvern, AR, 125, 226, 302, 372; *map, 311*
Mammoth Spring, AR, 27, 150, 153
   State Park, 242
Manifest Destiny, 181, 198; *illustration, 198*
Manila, AR, 305
"man in black," 433
manganese, 294, 296
maps, 18, 19
Marche, AR, 259
Marett, Samuel, 348, 352
Marianna, AR, 416, 424
   flood, *photo, 325*
Marinoni, Rosa, 282, 283
Marion, AR, 63
Marion County, AR, 200, 203
   County Quest, 183
Marked Tree, AR, 158
Mark's Mill
   battle of, 226
Marquette, Father Jacques, 8, 122, 130–32; *photo, 131; map, 131*
Marshall, AR, 182
Marshall, Justice Thurgood, 353, 361, 395
Marshall Islands/Marshallese, 449
marsh elder, 110, 113
martial law, 216, 223
Martin, Mark, 28, 98; *photo, 85*
   I Am an Arkansan, 85
Martineau, Gov. John, 288, 290, 291
Martineau Road Plan, 286, 288, 290–91
masks, *photo, 117*
Masons, 194, 197
Massachusetts, 159, 166
mastodon, 110, 111; *photo, 112*
Matthews, Jess, 389
Maumelle River, 23
McCarthy, Sen. Joseph, 371, 373–74, 375
McCarthyism, 373
McClellan, Sen. John, 370, 373–74, 422, 423; *photo, 372; illustration, 373*
   civil rights, 391
   I Am an Arkansan, 371
McClellan-Kerr Arkansas River Navigation Project/System, 371, 416, 423
McCulloch, Gen. Ben, 217, 219, 220, 222
McDougal, Jim and Susan, 442
McGehee, AR, *photo, 28*
   flood, *photo, 326*
McKennon, Pierce, 348, 352
McKinley, President William
   assassination, 276
McLarty, Thomas F. "Mack," 441
McLean v. Arkansas, 318

McMath, Gov. Sid, 368–71, 372, 376; *photo, 368*
    I Am an Arkansan, 378
McRae, Gov. Thomas, 292
measles, 125, 228
Meatless Tuesdays, 304, 305
medicines/medicinal, 19, 150, 152, 279, 292
Melbourne, AR, 68
Memphis, TN, 126, 194, 302, 389, 403, 409
    Freedman's Bureau, 230; *photo, 230*
Mena, AR, 263, 332
Meredith, James, 388
Mesopotamia, 106
meteorite, 322
Methodist, 159
Mexico, 129, 130, 135, 181, 198–99, 203
Michigan Territory, 182, 184
Microsoft, 416
midwives, 286, 291
Military Road, 170, 176; *map, 176*
militia, 164, 168
milk, 11
milled, 154, 156
Miller County, AR, 295, 375; *photos, 95, 96*
    County Quest, 21
Miller, James (territorial governor), 137, 168; *photo, 170*
Miller, Oscar, 304, 305
million-dollar race, 370
Mills, Cong. Wilbur D., 323, 370, 371, 421, 422
    civil rights, 391
    I Am an Arkansan, 377
Millwood Lake, 332
Mineral Springs, AR, 77
mining, 279, 294, 296–97, 299
Miss America, 354, 385
Mississippi (state), 140, 154, 308, 439; *map, 140*
Mississippi Alluvial Plain (the delta), 18, 21, 23, 24, 25, 26, 96–97, 111, 189
Mississippian Tradition, 100, 107, 114–15
Mississippi County, AR, 108, 158, 159, 269, 305, 335, 339, 433
    County Quest, 139
Mississippi River, 9, 24, 25, 82, 110, 114, 118, 119, 122, 123, 126, 128, 129, 130, 131, 133, 134, 137, 139, 140, 141, 148, 149, 155, 158, 159, 171, 176
    importance in Civil War, 222, 224
    flood, 324–27
Missouri, 114, 119, 150, 167
    Missouri bootheel. *See* bootheel
    territory, 164, 165
Missouri Compromise, 162, 164, 165–67, 182; *map, 167; illustration, 167*
Miss USA, 408
Mitchell, H. L., 337; *photo, 337*
Mitchell, Moses, 230
moats, 110, 114
Mobile, AL, 135
mockingbird, 9
moderate, 212, 213
modifying, 18, 19
"monkey trial." *See* Scopes "Monkey Trial"
monopoly, 278, 280
Monroe, President James, 118, 168
Monroe County, AR, 146, 357

    County Quest, 118
Montana, 150
Monte Ne Resort, 276, 285
Montgomery, AL, 389
Montgomery County, AR, 14
    County Quest, 247
"Montgomery Hunters," 217
Monticello, AR, 280
morale, 238
Mormons, 200–2
morphine, 216, 228
Morrill Act of 1864, 261
Morrill Land Grant Act of 1862, 261
Morrilton, AR, 60, 92, 101, 261
Morris, Susie, 353, 361
Morse code, 225
mortgage, 266
Mosaic Templars of America, 260, 265
mosquitoes, 19, 157, 292, 326
MosquitoFest, 305
Mothershed Wair, Thelma, 398, 403
Mother's League of Central High School, 386, 398
motion pictures (movies), 279, 310, 313
mound builders/mounds, 113–115, 128
Mountain Home, AR, 373
Mountain Meadows Massacre, 181, 200–2
    memorial, 202
Mountain View, AR, 90, 91, 96, 428; *photo, 92*
Mount Ida, AR, 14, 247
Mount Judea, AR, 91
Mount Magazine State Park, 27, 92; *photo, 28*
Mount Nebo, 335; *photo, 74*
    State Park, 92
"Mounted Devils of Arkansas," 199
movement, 18, 19; *illustration, 21*
    goods, 19
    ideas, 19
    people, 19
Mt. St. Mary's Academy, 181, 197; *photo, 197*
MTV, 440
Mudd, Dr. Samuel, 238, 239
"Muddy Bayou Heroes," 217
Mulberry River, 25, 200; *photo, 23*
Mullins, David W., 336
mumps, 228
municipal, 68, 69
munitions, 353, 358
Murfreesboro, AR, 11, 14, 94, 141; *photo, 94*
Murphy, Charles, 77
Murphy, Gov. Isaac, 59, 194, 211, 212, 215, 224, 239; *photo, 59*
Murphy Oil, 77, 82
Murrow, Edward R., 374
Museum of Automobiles, 318
museums, 80–81, 96, 100, 186, 280, 329; *map, 81*
    Antique Car, 60
music/musicians, 11, 12, 13, 18, 24, 93, 97–98, 119, 136, 138, 139, 191, 197, 263, 269, 302, 311, 357, 406, 424, 428, 433, 440; *photos, 92, 260, 261*
    blues, 302
    1960s, 410
Mussolini, Benito, 348–50

N

NAACP, 361, 387, 389, 390, 395, 396, 401, 403, 404; *photo, 396*
    founded, 277
Napoleon, 146, 148, 149, 162
NASCAR, 28, 85, 98
Nashville, AR, 77, 298, 440
Nation, Carry "Hatchet Carry," 282; *photo, 282*
National Archives and Records Administration (NARA), 444–47
national fish hatchery, 449
National Geographic, 325
National Socialist Party (Nazis), 348, 350; *photo, 348*
    death camps, 365
    Holocaust, 365
Native Americans/Native Arkansans, 5, 6, 106–19, 123, 126–33, 138–41, 149, 155, 159, 164, 450
    culture, 125
    removal, 137, 172–76
natural gas, 22, 25, 86
natural resources, 17, 23, 25, 76, *map, 26*
natural selection, 316, 317
"Natural State," 428
Nebraska, 150
Negro School for Industrial Arts, 390, 394
nepotism, 370, 371
Nevada County, AR, 295
    County Quest, 359
New Deal, 322, 334–41, 355, 356, 394
New Madrid, MO, 154, 158, 165
New Madrid Earthquake, 147, 154, 158, 159, 164, 176, 202; *map, 158*
New Orleans, 135, 140, 148, 156, 176, 439
    music, 311
Newport, AR, 136; *photo, 96*
New South, 256, 257
newspapers, 5, 9, 124, 162, 164, 168–69, 172, 202, 269, 302, 305, 360, 397, 401, 417, 426, 431–32, 443; *photo, 169; illustration, 162, 180, 190*
    war, 431–32
Newton County, AR, 91
    County Quest, 258
Nineteenth Amendment, 277, 283, 425. *See also* suffrage
Nisei, 353, 362, 363; *photos, 361, 363*
Nixon, President Richard, 416, 422, 423, 448; *photo, 422*
Nobe Dilbeck Home, *photo, 186*
Nodena headpot, *photo, 108*
Noland, Charles M., 183, 184
Norfork Lake, 353, 373, 412
North America, 110
North American continent, 22
North Arkansas College, 350
North Dakota, 150
North Little Rock, AR, 17, 89, 446; *photos, 55, 100*
Northwest Arkansas Community College, 187
Northwest Ordinance, 123, 164, 165
novaculite, 22, 23, 86, 110, 114
Number Nine, AR, 23
Nuttall, Thomas, 152, 153

O

Oaklawn Park, 94, 95, 396; *photo, 94*
oats, 298
O'Connor, Justice Sandra Day, 417
Odd fellows, 194, 197
Oh, Arkansas, 11
oil, 86, 111
oil boom, 310, 313, 314; *photos, 314, 315; map, 311*
Oil Trough, AR, 134, 139
Okies, 324, 327
Oklahoma, 117, 154, 172, 175
Oklahoma City, OK bombings, 438
Old Main, 262; *photo, 261*
Old Mill, (North Little Rock), 17; *photo, 100*
Old Southwest Trail, 194
Old State House, 163, 440; *photos, 55, 177*
    museum, 100
Old Town Lake, *photo, 22*
Old Washington State Park, 95
"On the Pulse of Morning", 340, 440
oppressed, 316, 318
ordinance, 54, 56
Oregon, 152
Osages, 116, 119, 132, 138, 157, 172, 174, 175; *map, 116*
    removal, *map, 174*
Osceola, AR, 139, 335
Ouachita Baptist University, 9
Ouachita County, AR, *photo, 6*
    Civil War, 226
    County Quest, 246
Ouachita Mountains, 18, 20, 21, 22, 23, 26, 92, 94, 111, 116, 128, 141, 258, 294; *photos, 16, 94*
Ouachita National Forest, 155, 263
Ouachita River, 22, 23, 24, 27, 82, 125, 141, 152, 154, 155, 177, 246, 263
    dams, 313
Our Own Sweet Sounds, 87
outlaws. *See* fugitives
oval office, *photo, 445*
override, 54, 55
overseer, 188, 190
oxbow lake, 56
Ozan Lumber Company, 295
Ozark, AR, 26, 200; *photo, 93*
Ozark Folk Center, 91, 96, 428; *photo, 92*
Ozark Highland Trails Association, 20
Ozark Mountains, 18, 20, 21, 22, 26, 27, 90–92, 111, 113, 159, 258
Ozark National Forest, 27, 182, 428; *photo, 27*
Ozark Natural Science Center, 194
Ozark Plateau, 23
Ozark Trails Association, 285, 289

P

Pacific Islanders, 88
paddlewheels, 170, 176
Painted House, A, 98, 202
Paleo Arkansans/Paleo Indians, 106, 110, 111
Paleo Period, 111, 112
Palestine/Palestinian 416

Index   **481**

Palestinian Liberation Organization (PLO), 441
Panic of 1819, 176
Panic of 1837, 182, 187
Paragould, AR, 152, 322
Paris, AR, 354
parity, 334, 336
Parker, Judge Isaac, 92, 236, 266, 269–71, 314; *photo, 269*
Parkin, AR, 115, 304
Parkin Site, 98, 127, 128
Parks, Rosa, 386
    death, 439
Parnell, Gov. Harvey, 331, 333
passenger pigeons, 154, 156
patronage, 212, 213
Patrons of Husbandry, 248
Pea Ridge, AR, 91
    battle of, 187, 210, 220, 222, 223, 224, 229, 232; *photos, 210, 222; illustration, 222*
peaches, 86, 440
peanuts, 299
Pearce, Gen. N. B., 217, 219
Pearl Harbor, HI, 346, 347, 350–51, 362
pearls, 136
pecans, 86
pellagra, 286, 292, 326
per capita, 82, 86, 87
    personal income. *See* income
period, 108, 109, 111
Perry County, AR
    County Quest, 228
Perryville, AR, 228
Persian Gulf War, 417, 442
Petit Jean Mountain, AR, 335, 378
Petit Jean State Park, 60, 92; *photo, 101*
petroglyph, *photo, 109*
petroleum, 22, 25
Philadelphia, MS, 389
Philander Smith College, 260, 265, 271, 308, 408; *photo, 408*
philanthropy, 418, 419
Phillips County, AR, 70, 87, 96, 97, 118, 126, 146, 165; *photos, 22, 98*
    Civil War, 219, 224, 230
    County Quest, 24
    Elaine race riot, 306–9
photography, 20, 119
Piggott, AR, 98, 312, 390
Pike, (Gen.) Gov. Albert, 172, 185; *photo, 171*
    Arkansas Advocate, 172
    Cherokee regiment, 220; *illustration, 222*
    Civil War, 217, 220, 222, 223
    fighting for Texas, 199
    I Am an Arkansan, 153
    Whig Party leader, 172
Pike County, AR, 11, 94, 276; *photos, 11, 94*
    County Quest, 141
Pine Bluff, AR, 89, 97, 119, 137, 155, 241, 254, 265, 280, 312, 313, 400, 408; *photo, 263*
    Brooks-Baxter War, 244
    Civil War, 226, 230
Pine Bluff Arsenal, 119
Pippen, Scottie, 288
place, 18, 19, 20, 21; *illustration, 21*

Plessy v. Ferguson, 237, 266, 267, 361
plantation(s), 182, 183, 189–93, 194, 229; *photos, 183, 188*
    counties, *map, 191*
planters, 182, 185, 186, 189–93, 246
plow, 11
Pocahontas, AR, 172
poet laureate, 278, 283
Poinsett County, AR, 98, 158, 159, 323, 339, 351
    County Quest, 202
Poison Spring Civil War Battlefield State Park, 359
    battle of, 226
Poke Bayou. *See* Batesville, AR
police action, 370, 373
Poland/Polish, 259
political machines, 170, 370, 371
politicians/politics, 17, 181, 368, 369, 379, 412, 417, 418–25, 440, 450; *photo, 368*
    belief shift due to flood, 327
    belief shift due to Great Depression, 332
    during Civil War, 213
    during the Progressive Era, 279–80, 285
    during Reconstruction, 236–51
    during statehood, *chart, 185*
    "The Family," 170–72
    farmers, 248–51
    governors, Arkansas, *chart, 58*
Polk, President James K., 263
Polk County, AR, 332
    County Quest, 263
    "Polk County Invincibles," 217
pollution, 19
Pope, Gov. John, 171, 177
Pope County, AR
    County Quest, 115
Pope John Paul II, 439
population, 54, 88–89, 269; *map, 89*
    decrease, 376
    diversifying, 449
    geography's impact on, 17
    growth during statehood, 194–95, 202; *chart, 196*
    increase, 44
    slave, *map, 189*
    World War II, *chart, 355*
Populist Movement/Party, 248, 250, 278, 279, 280, 318
Portis, Charles, 219, 288
posse, 306, 307
Possum Trot, AR, 23
pottery, 106, 107, 110, 114–15; *photo, 114–15*
poultry, 6, 332, 357, 428–29, 430, 440
Poverty Point Site, 114
Powell, Louis, 238, 239
Powhatan, AR, 6, 221
Prairie County, AR, 24, 194, 237, 299
    Civil War, 226, 229, 230
    County Quest, 284
Prairie Grove, AR, 91
    battle of, 210, 223–24
Prattsville, AR, 77
precipitation, *maps, 24*
prehistory/prehistoric, 108, 109
Prescott, AR, 295, 359
presidential libraries

special feature, 444–47
Presley, Elvis, 417
Price, Gen. Sterling, 217, 219, 220, 222
pride, 6, 7, 53
primary (elections), 278, 279, 280
prime meridian, 18, 19
primer, 353, 358
Princess Diana
    death, 438
    divorce, 438
printing press, 124, 168; *photo, 169*
prisons, 55, 68, 185, 424; *photo, 281*. *See also* Brickeys, AR; Cummins Prison Farm; Tucker Plantation
    Brubaker, 422
    convict-lease system, 277, 280, 283, 284
    Cummins, 422
    poor conditions, 247, 280
    reform, 419–20
    reform school for boys, 280
privy, 188, 189
Professional Golf Association (PGA), 95
progressive, 278, 279
Progressive Era/Progressive Movement, 277–99, 323
    daily life, 292
Progressive Farmers and Household Union of America, 306, 307
prohibition, 277, 281–83, 310. *See also* Eighteenth Amendment
Protestant, 175, 317
protest movement(s), 250, 384, 387, 388, 410, 411, 412; photos, 387, 388, 389, 395, 411
    Vietnam War, 416
Pryor, Sen. David, 69, 338, 418–20, 421, 422; *photo, 421*
Pryor, Sen. Mark, *photo, 69*
    I Am an Arkansan, 69
    letter from, 69
Pryor, Susan, 69
    I Am an Arkansan, 463
public service, 441
Pueblo dwelling, 107
Pulaski County, AR, 78, 89, 100, 101, 154, 164, 259, 271, 292, 349, 364, 428; *photo, 100*
    Civil War, 211, 224, 225, 226, 230
    County Quest, 17
    flood, 326
Pulitzer Prize, 329
pumpkins, 86
purge, 390, 400
Purple Hull Pea Festival, 327
Putman, Anna, 262

Q

Quapaws, 8, 116–19, 122, 125, 131, 132–33, 136–38, 140; *photo, 118, 119; map, 116*
    downstream people, 118
    naming of Arkansas, 132
    removal, 162, 163, 172, 175; *map, 173, 174; illustration, 173; timeline, 174–75*
quartz crystal, 11, 247; *photo, 11*
Queen Elizabeth I of England, 122
Queen Isabella of Spain, 124

Queen Wilhelmina State Park, 263
quinine, 216, 228
Quitman, AR, 221
quorum court, 68

R

racism/racist, 181, 280, 286, 303, 316, 379, 384–412
    and geography, 28
Radical Reconstruction, 240–46
radio, 310, 313
railroads, 194, 195, 236, 237, 243, 248, 257, 259, 304, 314, 326; *photo, 257; map, 258*
    Arkansas and Missouri Railroad, 92
    Cairo and Fulton Railroad, 194, 304
    regulations, 250, 283
Randolph, Vance
    I Am an Arkansan, 464
Randolph County, AR
    County Quest, 172
Ranger Battalions, 348, 352
Ranger Boats, 84, 183
Rathbone, Maj. Henry, 238, 239
rationed, 348, 352
Ray Karlmark, Gloria, 398, 403
Razorback(s), 6, 126, 262, 412, 422, 430
    basketball national championship, 438
    "Game of the Century," 422, 430; *photo, 422*
    1964 championship, 422, 430
Reagan, President Ronald, 417
Real Estate Bank, 182, 186–87, 201, 202
Rebel Ram "Arkansas," *photo, 227*
receivership, 198, 203
Reconstruction, 236–51, 255, 264, 265; *map, 241*
    economy, 237–51
"recovery, relief, reform." *See* New Deal
recreation, 7
Rector, Elias, 153
Rector, Henry, 213, 214, 215; *photo, 215*
Rectors ("The Family"), 185
Red Cross. *See* American Red Cross
Redeemers, 240, 246, 251
Red River, 22, 24, 57, 116, 129, 172, 177, 189, 194
    AR/TX border, 22, 24, 154, 155
Red Scare, 306
reel, 134, 138
Reelfoot Lake (TN), 159
Reeves, Bass, 266, 270; *photo, 271*
referendum, 278, 284
reform, 278
refrigerators, 310
refugee, 324, 326
regiment, 232
region, 18, 19, 20, 21; *illustration, 21*
regulation, 256, 258
relative, 18, 19
religion, 107, 109, 124–25, 126, 130, 175, 181, 185, 265, 271, 317
    Progressive Era, 279
    statehood days, 197–98
relocation centers, 353, 362
Renaissance, 124

Index **483**

Republican National Convention, 308
Republican Party, 69, 213, 334, 373–75, 376, 378, 379, 416, 418–19, 422, 440, 442, 448
reputation, 6, 7
Revolutionary War, 123, 134, 141, 148
Rex Hancock Black Swamp Wildlife Management Area, 305
rice, 14, 84, 96, 156, 276, 299, 357; *photo, 84; charts,* 200, 355
Riceland Foods, 5, 82, 84, 426, 430
rice producing counties, *map, 84*
Richie, Nicole, 200
Richter Scale, 154, 159
rifle, *photo, 196*
Rison, AR, 374
rivers, 11, 22–24, 25, 27, 194–95; *photo, 23*
    flood, 324–27
    importance to plantations, 189
rivet, 353, 358
roads, 185, 194–95, 372, 374, 427, 428, 448, *map, 176*
    flood, 326
Progressive Era, 285, 286, 288, 289–91; *photos, 290*
    Roaring Twenties, 310
Roberts, Terrence, 398, 406
Rockefeller, Gov. Winthrop, 63, 351, 376, 377–79, 391, 403, 409, 416, 418–20; *photos, 63, 418; illustration, 419*
Rocky Mountains, 9, 23
Roe v. Wade, 416
Rogers, AR, 89, 187, 213
Rohwer, AR, 346, 353, 362–65; *photo, 361; map, 360*
    monument, *photo, 362*
Roman Catholic. *See* Catholic
Roman Empire, 107
Rome, Italy, 106
Roosevelt, President Franklin, 322, 333, 334–41, 348, 350, 351, 358, 362, 365, 444; *photo, 334. See also* New Deal
    quote, 334
Roosevelt, President Theodore, 276, 281, 282
Rose, Terry, 8, 11
Rosetta Stone, 162
Rosie the Riveter, 353, 358, 359; *photo, 346*
Roy, Justice Elsijane T., 416, 418, 424, 425
Rudolph, Wilma, 384
rural, 6, 68, 69, 196, 260, 286, 299, 374
Rush, AR, 296
Russellville, AR, 115, 173, 174, 175
Russia, 110, 304, 306

S

Sainte Genevieve, MO, 154
St. Louis, MO, 134, 135
Salem, AR, 242
Saline County, AR, 11, 452
    bauxite, 177
    County Quest, 177
    salt mines, 177
Saline River, 22, 24, 226
salt, 118, 140
    mines, 177
Saltillo, AR, *photo, 186*

Sam's Throne, *photo, 91*
sanatorium, 286, 292
sand, 25, 86
Sarasin
    I Am an Arkansan, 137
savages, 124, 125
sawmills, 256, 294–95; *photo, 256*
sawyers, 170, 177
saxophone, 440; *photo, 447*
scalawags, 240, 242
scarcity, 76
school shooting, 330, 438, 439
Schoolcraft, Henry R., 152, 153
Scopes, John T., 316, 318
Scopes "Monkey Trial," 303, 316, 318
Scott, Dortha, 8, 14, 247
Scott County, AR
    County Quest, 155
Searcy, AR, 171, 377, 443
Searcy County, AR
    County Quest, 182
Sebastian County, AR, 194, 259, 364, 417; *photo, 259*
    flood, *photo, 324*
    County Quest, 314
secession, 210, 212, 214, 215
secession of the Southern states, *map, 214*
sections, 164; *illustration, 165*
sectors, 76
segregation, 255, 266, 267, 384–409
    in the schools, *map, 391*
segregationists, 384, 387, 390, 395, 396; *photos, 382–83, 393*
Selective Service Act, 348, 350
Selma, AL, 389
Seminoles, 172, 175
Sequoyah (George Guess), 170, 172, 173; *illustration, 173*
    quote about, 173
    written language, 173
settlement, early, *map, 156*
    Arkansas Post, 134–41
    1541–1802, 122–41
    first permanent European, 133
    Law's colony, 136
settlers, 137, 176, 196–97, 259; *photo, 168*
    frontier life, 245
Seven Years' War. *See* French and Indian War
Sevier, Ambrose, 87, 171, 185; *photo, 185*
Sevier County, AR
    County Quest, 87
Seviers ("The Family"), 185
Sex and the Single Girl, 432
Shakespeare, 122
sharecroppers/sharecropping, 240, 246, 257, 264, 265, 266–67, 297–99, 306, 323, 337, 339, 357; *photos, 267*
    daily life, 298–99
Sharp County, AR
    County Quest, 336
Sheridan, AR, 353, 371
Sherman, Gen. William T., 211, 217, 218, 226
Shorter College, 260, 265, 308
short leaf pine, 11
shrapnel, 256, 257
Shreve, Capt. Henry, 177, 194

"Silent Hattie," 333. *See also* Caraway, Hattie
Simon, Charlie May, 329
Simple Life, The, 200
Sioux Indians, 118
Sisters Union Society, 260, 265
sit-ins, 408; *photo, 408*
skirmish(es), 219, 221, 240, 244
slavery/slaves, 122, 125, 140, 141, 163, 164, 165–67, 180–203, 212, 214, 218, 230–31, 232, 255; *illustration, 162, 192*
    Arkansas Post, 140
    Arkansas statistics, *chart, 192*
    auction, *illustration, 190; photo, 193*
    codes (laws/restrictions), 190, 192
    cotton gin, 166
    daily life, 189–93
    de Soto, 125, 140
    economic issue, 166–67
    emancipation/ending, 166, 230–31, 232
    owners, *chart, 192*
    population, *map, 189*
    rebellion, 192
    runaway, *illustration, 190*
    Vermont, first to abolish, 165
slave states, 182–84
Slingblade, 452
Sloan Site, 152
sloth, 110, 111
Smackover, AR, 96, 135, 310, 314
smallpox, 125, 286, 291
Smith v. Allwright, 346, 353, 362
smoking ban, 448
snag boats, 170, 177
socialist, 330, 332
Social Security, 334, 336
Some Jazz a While, 424
sorghum, 294, 299
Soul on Ice, 398
South Carolina
    Fort Sumter attacked, 215
    secession, 181, 210, 214
South Dakota, 150
Southern Arkansas University, 327
Southern consciousness, 212
Southerner, The (airplane), 337
Southern Manifesto, 390, 391
Southern Tenant Farmer's Union, 202, 323, 337, 339; *photos, 337, 339*
    African Americans, 339
    goals, 339
Southland Institute, 260, 265
Southwest Conference, 412
Southwest Trail, 154
Soviet Union, 372
    collapse, 417
    World War II, 347
soybeans, 84, 429
Spain/Spanish, 13, 148, 149
    Arkansas Post, 134
    exploration/explorers, 122–23, 125–30
    kings and queens, 124
    ruling power, 124, 132, 135, 141

trade, 137
speakeasies, 310, 311
special interests, 418, 420
specie, 182, 187
Specie Circular, 182, 187
species, 316, 317
speculate, 330
speculator, 188
spinach/"Spinach Capitol of the World," 25, 86
Springdale, AR, 77, 89, 91, 92, 448
Spring River, 6, 27, 153, 242
spy, 225
square dance, 11
squash, 106, 113
squatters, 188
Stamps, AR, 57, 340
Staples, Nancy Morton, 227
Star City, AR, 370
Starr, Belle, 255
Starr, Kenneth, 442
starvation, 175, 257, 324–28
State Bank, 182, 186–87
statehood, 180–203
    daily life/town life, 194–97
    frontier violence, 195, 200–2
states' rights, 182, 185, 212, 213
state symbols, 9–14; *map, 11*
staves, 294, 295
St. Charles, AR, 98
steamboat(s), 11, 176, 177
Steele, Gen. Frederick, 217, 224, 225, 226
Steenburgen, Mary, 443
    I Am an Arkansan, 465
Stephens, Charlotte, 264, 394; *photo, 262*
    I Am an Arkansan, 259
Stephens, Incorporated, 77, 84, 426, 429
Stephens, Jack, 77
Stephens, Warren, 77
Stephens, Witt, 77
stereotype(s), 6, 7
St. Francis, AR. *See* Helena, AR
St. Francis County, AR, 195, 337
    County Quest, 78
St. Francis National Forest, 424
St. Francis River, 22, 24, 78, 129, 165, 173, 177, 221, 304
    flood, 324–27
Stone County, AR, 90; *photo, 92*
    County Quest, 428
Stop This Outrageous Purge (STOP), 387, 390, 400
strawberries, 86
Strawberry, AR, 6
Strawberry River, 68
Student Nonviolent Coordinating Committee (SNCC) 384, 408
students; *photo, 450*
Stuttgart, AR, 5, 77, 96, 259, 428, 429
suffrage, 266, 268; *map, 283. See also* Nineteenth Amendment; voters/voting
    for African Americans, 246
    for women, 277, 282–83, 310; *photos, 276, 282*
Sultana, 231
"summer of love," 410

sumpweed, 110, 113
sunken lands, 159, 202; *photo, 159*
sunshine law, 418, 419
surplus, 76
Surratt, Mary, 238, 239
surrealism, 310, 311
surveyed, 164
survival of the fittest, 316, 317
sustained yield forestry, 294, 296, 327
Sutton, Ozell, 408, 409
swastika, *photo, 348*
swine, 86
Switzer, Barry, 412

T

Table Rock Lake, 412
tainted, 256, 257
Talimena National Scenic Byway, 263
tapir, 110, 111
tax/taxes, 54, 182–83, 185, 186, 249, 250–51
    business exemptions, 428
    Great Depression, 341
    poll, 184, 237, 362, 371, 372, 378
    reform, 420
    revenue, 420
technology, 269
telephones, 310, 312
temperance, 260–61
temperate, 22, 26
temperatures, drought and dustbowl, 327; *maps, 25,*
tenant farmers, 294, 297–99; *photos, 297. See also* share-
    cropping
    daily life, 298–99
Tennessee, 114, 154, 159, 318
term limits, 448
Terry, Aldolphine Fletcher, 400; *photo, 402*
Texarkana, AR, 21, 295, 375; *photos, 95, 96*
Texas, 117, 129, 133, 134, 154
    Arkansans fight in TX/Mexico war, 199
    independence from Mexico, 198–99
Texas Ranger, 219
Thaden, Louise, 322
    I Am an Arkansan, 338
theaters (of war), 232
Thirteenth Amendment, 211, 231
Thomason, Harry Z.
    I Am an Arkansan, 451
Thorncrown Chapel, 92
Thornton, Billy Bob, 177
    I Am an Arkansan, 452
Till, Emmett, 386
timber (industry), 24, 25, 86, 94, 111, 125, 279, 294–97,
    299, 314; *photos, 294, 295*
    companies, 295
    impacted by flood, 327
    way of life, 294–96
time zones, 237
Titanic, 231, 277
Toad Suck Daze Festival, 406
tobacco, 117, 156; *chart, 200*
Toltec Indians/Mounds, 113

tomato, 86, 241
    South Arkansas Vine Ripe Pink, 11
Tontitown, AR, 135, 259
    Grape Festival, 135
tornadoes, *map, 26*
"total war," 223
tourism, 74–101, 285, 428
townships, 164; *illustration, 165*
tractorette, 353, 359
trade, 86, 124, 130–37, 139, 140, 175; *photo, 135*
    salt, 140
tradition(s), 19, 106, 107, 108, 112–15, 193
Trail of Tears, 172–76; *illustration, 173; map, 175*
    National Historic Trail Memorial, 175
transportation, 19, 86
    statehood days, 194–95
Trapnall, Mrs. Frederick, 212, 215
treaty, 170, 172
    1818, 174; *illustration, 173*
    1824, 174
    1833, 175
Treaty of Versailles, 302
tremors, 154, 159
trout fishing, 428
trucking, 428–29
True Grit, 219, 288
Truman, President Harry S., 346, 372
Trumann, AR, 339
trustys, 418, 419
tuberculosis, 286, 292
    hospitals, 292
Tucker, Gov. Jim Guy, 20, 438, 440, 442
    resignation, 448
    "Whitewater," 448
Tucker Plantation, (prison), 278, 280
Tulip, AR, 308
Tulsa, OK, 306
turkey producing states, *map, 86*
Turkey Scratch, AR, 23
Turkey Trot Festival, 183
Twain, Mark, 255
Twitty, Conway, 136
    I Am an Arkansan, 465
typhoid, 286, 291
Tyronza, AR, 323, 337
"Tyronza Rebels," 216
Tyson, Don, 77
Tyson, John, 77
Tyson Foods, 77, 82, 83, 91, 426, 428, 429, 432

U

unanimous, 212, 215
uniforms, 217; *illustration, 216*
Union, The, 210–32, 257; *map, 218*
    generals, *chart, 217*
    government, 211
    uniforms, *illustration, 216*
Union and the Confederacy, *map, 216*
Union County, AR, 27, 77, 95, 96, 303, 314; *photos, 96, 268,*
    312, 315
    County Quest, 111

Union Labor Party, 248, 249
United Nations, 372
United States, 13
    World War II, 350–65
University of Arkansas Aquaculture Lab (catfish lab), 119
University of Arkansas at Little Rock, 17
University of Arkansas at Monticello, 280
University of Arkansas Community College at Batesville, 28
University of Arkansas–Fayetteville, 70, 91, 254, 255, 260, 261, 262, 288, 323, 351, 370, 394, 395, 410, 412
    students, *photo, 409*
University of Arkansas–Fort Smith, 314
University of Arkansas Law School, 262, 368, 375, 390, 449
University of Arkansas–Pine Bluff (AM & N), 119, 288, 375, 400
University of Arkansas School of Medicine, 283, 291, 368, 375
University of Central Arkansas, 288, 406
University of Mississippi
    civil rights/desegregation, 388
urban, 260, 266, 269, 278, 374
Urban League, 390, 391
US Army, 175, 241, 244, 373
US Army Reserves, 308, 449
US Congress, 54
US Congressional districts, *map, 57*
US House of Representatives, 54
US Senate, 54
US Supreme Court, 54, 318, 361, 365, 386, 387, 391
USS *Razorback*, 100; *photo, 101*
Utley, Terri, 408

V

Van Buren, President Martin, 184
Van Buren, AR, 25, 92, 262, 270
Van Buren County, AR
    County Quest, 158
Van Dorn, Gen. Earl, 217, 220, 222
verdicts, 306, 309
Vermont, 165
veteran's bonus, 164
veto, 54
vice versa, 54, 55
Vicksburg, MS, 211, 222, 224
victory gardens, 348, 352
Vietnam, 140, 416, 419, 423; *map, 140*
    Tet Offensive, 416
    Veterans Memorial, 423
    war, 410–11; *photos, 410, 411*
volunteers, 198
    Civil War, 216, 217, 229
voters/voting, 54–57, 68, 184, 241, 250–51, 310. *See also* Nineteenth Amendment
    African-Americans, 246, 250–51
    restrictions, 250–51
Voting Rights Act, 389

W

Wabbaseka, AR, 398
Waldron, AR, 155
Walk the Line, 433
Walker, Hazel
    I Am an Arkansan, 354
Walker, Judge David, 185, 212, 215; *photo, 215*
Wallace, Gov. George, 388, 418, 419
Walls Lanier, Carlotta, 398, 406
Wal-Mart, 19, 77, 82, 83, 187, 426, 428, 432; *photo, 80*
Wal-Mart Visitors' Center and Museum, 91; *photo, 80*
Walnut Ridge, AR, 6
Walton, Sam, 77, 91, 187, 428; *photo, 80*
Walton Arts Center, 91
war, 341, 348–65, 450. *See also* names of specific wars
    power to declare, 55
    War between the States, 232
    War for States' Rights, 232
    War of 1812, 162, 168
    War of the Rebellion, 232
war bonds, 348, 352
War Eagle Crafts Fair, 187
War Eagle Creek, 194
War Eagle Mill, *photo, 91*
Warren, AR, 241
Warriors Don't Cry, 403
washing machines, 310
Washington (Old), AR, 198
    Confederate Capital, 224
Washington, Booker T., 276, 278, 287; *photo, 281*
    quote from, 281
Washington, President George, 123, 141
Washington County, AR, 77, 89, 91, 135, 175, 243, 254, 259, 261, 262, 283, 392, 424, 425, 429; *photo, 92*
    Civil War, 212, 215, 227
    County Quest, 91
Washington, D.C., 54, 69, 184, 232, 333, 421, 422, 440, 441, 442, 449
    capitol, 284
Washington (state), 150
Watergate Scandal, 416
Wayne, John, 219, 288
weather, 17, 22, 26; *maps, 24, 25*
    drought and dustbowl, 327–28
    flood, 324–27
    records, 27
West Memphis, AR, 63, 155, 194, 376, 443; *map, 156*
West Memphis News, 443
wheat, 11, 86, 299
Wheatless Mondays, 304, 305
wheelwrights, 188, 191
Whig Party, 170, 171, 172, 181, 184, 185, 199; *chart, 185*
    Reconstruction, 242
whiskey runner, 306, 307
White Citizens' Councils, 390, 395, 396
White County, AR, 377, 443
    County Quest, 171
"white flight," 416
White House
    china, 447
    dining table, 447

oval office; *photo*, 445
White River, 5, 22, 23, 24, 28, 68, 82, 91, 118, 128, 136, 139, 153, 155, 171, 177, 183, 194, 284, 285; *photos*, 28, 92
    flood, 324–27
    National Wildlife Refuge, 98
white-tailed deer, 11
Whitney, Eli, 123
Williams Baptist College, 6
Williams, Lucinda, 424
Williams, Miller
    I Am an Arkansan, 424
Williamson, Sonny Boy, 86, 98
    I Am an Arkansan, 87
Wilson, Donald Roller
    I Am an Arkansan, 423
Wilson Plantation, 139
Wilson, President Woodrow, 282
Wilson's Creek, MO
    battle of, 219
wine, 92, 200
Wings over the Prairie Festival. *See* Duck Gumbo Cook-Off Festival
Winrock International, 84
Winslow, AR, 283
Winthrop Rockefeller Foundation, 403
Wisconsin, 114
Withrow Spring State Park, 194
Witt, James Lee, 441
WOK. *See* Workers of Kilowatts
Wolf House, photo, 138
women, 69, 260–61, 262, 264, 310–11, 338, 340, 354, 417, 424, 432, 438, 440, 449, 450
    activists, 282–83; *photos,* 282
    Civil War, 217, 227–28
    Clinton Administration, 441
    education, 287–88
    feminist movement, 424, 432
    jobs/wages, 374, 424
    Peace Day 1983, 425; *illustration,* 425
    role change, 358
    Rosie the Riveter, 353, 358, 359; *photo,* 346
    statehood days, 196
    suffrage/voting, 282–83, 425; *map,* 283
    World War II, 351, 352, 357–58; *photos,* 346, 356
Women's Emergency Committee to Open Our Schools, 387, 390, 400
"Wonder State," 310, 313, 428
Woodland Indians, 113, 114
Woodland Junior High School, Fayetteville, 450
Woodland Tradition/period, 100, 106, 113, 114; *photo,* 109
Woodruff, William, 5, 164, 168–69, 172, 180, 183, 305; *photos,* 169
    salt mines, 177
Woodruff County, AR, 266
    Civil War, 223
    County Quest, 305
Woodstock Music Festival, 410
wool hat boys, 278, 279; *photo,* 279
woolly mammoth, 110
Workers of Kilowatts, 310, 312, 313
World Trade Center
    1993 bombing, 438
    2001 terrorist attacks, 439
World War I, 302, 304–5, 318
World War II, 348–65; *photos,* 346, 347, 356, 358, 359
    Army bases, 354
    defense plants, 353, 354, 358
    end, 365
Worthington, Elisha, 188, 190
Writers' Project (WPA), 336
writers/writing(s), 98, 108–13, 172, 213, 285, 288, 311, 312, 329, 336, 340, 390, 424, 425, 432, 440
written history, 108–13
Wynne, AR, 115, 304

Y

Yankees, 216, 228
Yarnell's Ice Cream, 84, 171
Yell, Gov. Archibald, 183, 184–85, 187, 219; *photo,* 185
    death, 199
    fighting for Texas, 199
Yell County, AR, 92, 371; *photo,* 74
    County Quest, 219
yellow fever, 154, 157, 158
Yellville, AR, 183
yeoman (farmers), 185, 188–89
Young Arkansans, *photo,* 450

Z

zinc mining, 296, 350

Photo Credits

An Arkansas History for Young People
Photo/Illustration Credits

Cover photo, Hawkbill Crag at sunrise, by TimErnst.com.

Front Matter

ix Shay Hopper (all photos), **x** Shay Hopper (all photos), **xiv** Debbie Baldwin, **xv** Arkansas Department of Parks and Tourism, A.C. Haralson (spelunkers)/Arkansas Department of Parks and Tourism, A.C. Haralson (sightseers on cliff)/Official White House photo (Bill Clinton), **xvi** J.B. Hunt Transport Services (trucks)/Hampson Museum, Wilson, Arkansas (head pot), **xvii** Arkansas Department of Parks and Tourism, A.C. Haralson (Caddo drum)/University of Arkansas Museum, Fayetteville, Arkansas (arrowheads), **xviii** University of Arkansas Museum, Fayetteville, Arkansas (Sequoyah)/Arkansas History Commission (Arkansas Traveler), **xix** University of Arkansas Special Collections (newspaper)/Historic Arkansas Museum, Little Rock, Arkansas (rifle), **xx** Library of Congress (all photos), **xxi** University of Arkansas Special Collections (sheet music)/Arkansas History Commission (Rosa Marinoni), **xxii** Richard C. Butler Center for Arkansas Studies, **xxiii** Library of Congress (Franklin Roosevelt)/Arkansas Department of Parks and Tourism, A.C. Haralson (Rohwer marker), **xxiv** University of Arkansas Special Collections, Orval Faubus papers, **xxv** University of Arkansas–Little Rock, Special Collections, **xxvi** University of Arkansas Special Collections (Arkansas banner)/Clinton Presidential Center, Library and Museum, Little Rock, Arkansas (limousine and Clinton presidential seal), **xxxiv** Shay Hopper

Unit One/Chapter 1

1 Arkansas Department of Parks and Tourism, A.C. Haralson, **2** Arkansas Department of Parks and Tourism, A.C. Haralson, **3** Arkansas Department of Parks and Tourism, A.C. Haralson, **4** David Hopper, **7** Arkansas Department of Parks and Tourism, A.C. Haralson, **9** James Konzelmann, **11** Arkansas Department of Parks and Tourism, A.C. Haralson (all photos), **14** Debbie Baldwin

Unit One/Chapter 2

16 Arkansas Department of Parks and Tourism, A.C. Haralson, **20** Tim Ernst, **22** Arkansas Department of Parks and Tourism, A.C. Haralson (all photos), **27** Arkansas Department of Parks and Tourism, A.C. Haralson (all photos), **28** Arkansas Department of Parks and Tourism, A.C. Haralson (all photos)

Unit One/Chapter 3

52 Arkansas Department of Parks and Tourism, A.C. Haralson, **55** Arkansas Department of Parks and Tourism, A.C. Haralson (all photos), **56** Arkansas Department of Parks and Tourism, A.C. Haralson, **59** Arkansas History Commission (all photos), **61** Arkansas History Commission (George Donaghey), **64** Arkansas History Commission (Dale Bumpers)/Official White House photo (William J. Clinton), **65** Office of the Governor, state of Arkansas (Mike Huckabee)/Office of the Governor, state of Arkansas (Mike Beebe), **69** Official photo, United States Senate (Mark Pryor), **70** Official photo, United States Senate (Blanche Lincoln)

Unit One/Chapter 4

74 Arkansas Department of Parks and Tourism, A.C. Haralson, **75** Dr. Stanley Trauth, **76** J.B. Hunt Transport Services (all photos), **80** Arkansas Department of Parks and Tourism, A.C. Haralson, **82** Arkansas Department of Parks and Tourism, A.C. Haralson (all photos), **84** Arkansas Department of Parks and Tourism, A.C. Haralson, **85** Mark Martin, **87** Arkansas History Commission, **88** Arkansas Department of Parks and Tourism, A.C. Haralson, **91** Arkansas Department of Parks and Tourism, A.C. Haralson (all photos), **92** Arkansas Department of Parks and Tourism, A.C. Haralson (all photos), **93** Arkansas Department of Parks and Tourism, A.C. Haralson (all photos) except Banpei (John Daly), **94** Arkansas Department of Parks and Tourism, A.C. Haralson (all photos), **95** Arkansas Department of Parks and Tourism, A.C. Haralson/Julie Camp, Wind-Up Records (Evanescence), **96** Arkansas Department of Parks and Tourism, A.C. Haralson (all photos), **97** Arkansas Department of Parks and Tourism, A.C. Haralson (all photos) except Tony LoBue, Levon Helm Studios (Levon Helm), **98** Arkansas Department of Parks and Tourism, A.C. Haralson (all photos), **100** Arkansas Department of Parks and Tourism, A.C. Haralson, **101** Arkansas Department of Parks and Tourism, A.C. Haralson (all photos)

Unit Two/Chapter 5

104 Arkansas Department of Parks and Tourism, A.C. Haralson, **105** Arkansas Department of Parks and Tourism, A.C. Haralson, **106** Arkansas Department of Parks and Tourism, A.C. Haralson, **108** Hampson Museum, Wilson, Arkansas, **109** Arkansas Archaeological Museum, **111** University of Arkansas Museum, Fayetteville, Arkansas, **112** Arkansas State University Museum, Jonesboro, Arkansas, **113** University of Arkansas Museum, Fayetteville, Arkansas, **114** University of Arkansas Museum, Fayetteville, Arkansas, **117** Arkansas Department of Parks and Tourism, A.C. Haralson (Caddo drum)/Arkansas Department of Parks and Tourism, A.C. Haralson/University of Arkansas Museum, Fayetteville, Arkansas (Caddo mask), **118** University of Arkansas Museum, Fayetteville, Arkansas, **119** Arkansas Archaeological Survey

Unit Two/Chapter 6

122 University of Arkansas Special Collections, **125** University of Arkansas Museum, Fayetteville, Arkansas, **126** Chicago Historical Society, **127** Parkin State Park, Tim Morris, **128** Parkin State Park, Tim Morris, **129** Historic Arkansas Museum, Little Rock, Arkansas, **131** Chicago Historical Society/Chicago Historical Society, **133** University of Arkansas Special Collections/Chicago Historical Society, **134** Arkansas History Commission, **135** Library of Congress, **136** Chicago Historical Society, **138** Illinois State Historical Society/University of Central Arkansas Archives, **139** Historic Arkansas Museum, Little Rock, Arkansas

Unit Three/Chapter 7

144 Library of Congress, **145** Library of Congress, **146** Arkansas Department of Parks and Tourism, A.C. Haralson, **148** Arkansas Department of Parks and Tourism, A.C. Haralson, **152** Library of Congress, **155** University of Arkansas Special Collections, John Hughes Reynolds, *Makers of Arkansas History* (1911), **156** Arkansas History Commission, **159** University of Arkansas Special Collections

Unit Three/Chapter 8

162 University of Arkansas Special Collections, **166** Library of Congress, **168** University of Arkansas Special Collections, **169** Arkansas History Commission/University of Arkansas Special Collections, John Hughes Reynolds, *Makers of Arkansas History,* 1911 (raft), **170** Arkansas History Commission (all photos), **171** Arkansas History Commission, **173** University of Arkansas Museum, Fayetteville, Arkansas (Sequoyah)/Old State House Museum, Little Rock, Arkansas (map)/Woolaroc Museum, Bartlesville, Oklahoma (Trail of Tears), **174** Arkansas History Commission, **177** Old State House Museum, Little Rock

Unit Three/Chapter 9

180 University of Arkansas Special Collections, **183** Arkansas Department of Parks and Tourism, A.C. Haralson, **185** Arkansas History Commission (all photos), **186** University of Central Arkansas Archives, **188** Library of Congress, **190** University of Central Arkansas Archive (newspaper)/University of Arkansas Special Collections ("Sale of Slaves" newspaper), **192** Library of Congress, **193** Library of Congress, **196** Historic Arkansas Museum, Little Rock, Arkansas, **197** Arkansas History Commission, **198** Library of Congress, **201** Arkansas Department of Parks and Tourism, A.C. Haralson

Unit Four/Chapter 10

208 Arkansas Department of Parks and Tourism, A.C. Haralson, **210** Arkansas Department of Parks and Tourism, A.C. Haralson, **215** University of Arkansas Special Collections (Henry Rector)/University of Arkansas–Little Rock, Special Collections (David Walker), **216** University of Arkansas Special Collections, **218** University of Arkansas Special Collections, **219** Chicago Historical Society, **222** University of Arkansas Special Collections (all photos), **223** Library of Congress (Pea Ridge)/Chicago Historical Society (Thomas Hindman), **224**

Photo Credits

University of Arkansas Special Collections (all photos), **225** Arkansas History Commission, **226** University of Arkansas Special Collections, **227** University of Arkansas Special Collections, **229** Arkansas History Commission, **230** Library of Congress, **231** Library of Congress

Unit Four/Chapter 11

236 Library of Congress (all photos), **238** Library of Congress, **239** Library of Congress, **240** University of Arkansas Special Collections, **243** University of Central Arkansas Archives, **244** University of Central Arkansas Archives, **249** Arkansas History Commission, **250** University of Central Arkansas Archives

Unit Four/Chapter 12

254 Arkansas History Commission, **256** University of Arkansas Special Collections, **257** University of Arkansas Special Collections, **259** University of Arkansas Special Collections, **260** University of Arkansas Special Collections, **261** University of Arkansas Special Collections, **262** University of Arkansas Special Collections, **263** University of Central Arkansas Archives, **264** Arkansas History Commission (Charlotte Stephens)/University of Central Arkansas Archives (Mifflin Gibbs) , **265** University of Central Arkansas Archives, **266** University of Central Arkansas Archives, **267** University of Central Arkansas Archives/University of Arkansas Special Collections, **268** University of Arkansas Special Collections, **269** University of Arkansas Special Collections, **270** Arkansas Department of Parks and Tourism, A.C. Haralson, **271** University of Central Arkansas Archives

Unit Five/Chapter 13

276 University of Arkansas Special Collections, **278** University of Arkansas Special Collections, **279** University of Arkansas Special Collections (baby in airplane)/ University of Central Arkansas Archives (mountain man), **281** Arkansas History Commission (prisoners working)/University of Central Arkansas Archives (Booker T. Washington, Scott Bond), **282** Arkansas History Commission (Rosa Marinoni)/University of Arkansas Special Collections (Carry Nation), **284** University of Central Arkansas Archives, **285** University of Arkansas Special Collections, **286** University of Arkansas Special Collections, **287** Arkansas History Commission, **289** University of Arkansas–Little Rock, Special Collections, **290** University of Central Arkansas Archives (all photos), **292** University of Central Arkansas Archives, **294** University of Arkansas–Little Rock, Special Collections, **295** University of Central Arkansas Archives, **296** University of Arkansas Special Collections, **297** University of Arkansas Special Collections (all photos), **298** University of Arkansas Special Collections

Unit Five/Chapter 14

302 Richard C. Butler Center for Arkansas Studies, **305** University of Arkansas Special Collections, **307** Richard C. Butler Center for Arkansas Studies (all photos), **308** University of Central Arkansas Archives, **309** Richard C. Butler Center for Arkansas Studies (all photos), **312** University of Arkansas Special Collections, **313** University of Arkansas Special Collections, **314** University of Arkansas Special Collections, **315** Arkansas Museum of Natural Resources, Smackover, Arkansas, **316** University of Arkansas Special Collections, **317** Richard C. Butler Center for Arkansas Studies

Unit Five/Chapter 15

322 University of Central Arkansas Archives (all photos), **324** Arkansas History Commission, **325** Arkansas History Commission (all photos), **326** Arkansas History Commission, **328** University of Arkansas Special Collections, **329** Arkansas History Commission, **331** University of Arkansas Special Collections (displaced family)/University of Central Arkansas Archives (log cabin), **333** University of Arkansas Special Collections, **334** Library of Congress, **335** University of Central Arkansas Archives, **336** Library of Congress, **338** University of Arkansas–Little Rock, Special Collections, **339** Library of Congress (tenant farmers)/Library of Congress (Dyess home), **340** Dwight Carter, Lordly & Dame

Unit Six/Chapter 16

346 Arkansas History Commission (women with U.S. flag)/University of Arkansas Special Collections (African American soldiers), **348** Library of Congress, **349** University of Arkansas–Little Rock, Special Collections, **351** University of Arkansas Special Collections, **352** University of Arkansas–Little Rock, Special Collections, **356** Arkansas History Commission (women canning)/University of Central Arkansas Archives (WACs), **358** Arkansas History Commission, **359** University of Arkansas Special Collections, **361** University of Central Arkansas Archives, **362** Arkansas Department of Parks and Tourism, A.C. Haralson, **363** Library of Congress, **364** University of Arkansas–Little Rock, Special Collections

Unit Six/Chapter 17

368 University of Arkansas–Little Rock, Special Collections, **372** University of Arkansas Special Collections, **373** Ouachita Baptist University Special Collections, **375** University of Arkansas Special Collections, **379** Arkansas History Commission

Unit Seven/Chapter 18

378 Library of Congress, 379 Arkansas History Commission, **380** University of Arkansas Special Collections, Orval Faubus papers, **382** University of Central Arkansas Archives, **383** Library of Congress (empty school hallway)/Arkansas History Commission (Kennedy at Greer's Ferry)/Library of Congress (segregationist rally), **385** University of Arkansas Special Collections, **386** University of Arkansas – Little Rock, Special Collections, **387** Library of Congress, **388** Library of Congress, **389** Library of Congress (boy observing marchers)/Arkansas History Commission (Daisy Bates), **393** University of Central Arkansas Archives, **394** Library of Congress, **395** Arkansas History Commission (all photos), **396** Arkansas History Commission ("lost year" student)/ University of Arkansas Special Collections (Daisy Bates), **397** Shay Hopper, **399** Library of Congress (boy observing marchers)/University of Central Arkansas archives (Elizabeth Eckford), **400** Arkansas Department of Parks and Tourism, A.C. Haralson, **401** University of Arkansas Special Collections (Bates portrait)/Arkansas History Commission (Bates, Clinton), **402** Arkansas History Commission ("lost year")/University of Arkansas Special Collections (Bates), **403** University of Arkansas Special Collections (King assassination protest)/ Arkansas History Commission (John Kennedy at Greer's Ferry)/Shay Hopper (Brown-Tricky), **404** Arkansas History Commission, **405** University of Arkansas Special Collections, **406** Arkansas Department of Parks and Tourism, A. C. Haralson, **407** Little Rock Central High School National Historic Site and Museum, Little Rock, Arkansas, **408** Arkansas History Commission, **409** Arkansas History Commission

Unit Seven/Chapter 19

University of Arkansas Special Collections, **418** Arkansas History Commission, **419** University of Arkansas Special Collections, **420** Arkansas History Commission, **421** Arkansas History Commission, **422** Official White House photo, **423** Donald Roller Wilson, **425** University of Arkansas Special Collections, **424** University of Arkansas Special Collections, **425** University of Arkansas Special Collections, **426** Arkansas History Commission, **427** Arkansas History Commission, **429** University of Arkansas–Little Rock, Special Collections, **430** University of Central Arkansas Archives, **433** Don Hunstein (all photos)

Unit Eight/Chapter 20

436 Arkansas Department of Parks and Tourism, A. C. Haralson (Little Rock skyline) /University of Arkansas Special Collections (banner), **438** William J. Clinton Presidential Library and Museum, Little Rock, Arkansas, **441** William J. Clinton Presidential Library and Museum, Little Rock, Arkansas, **442** William J. Clinton Presidential Library and Museum, Little Rock, Arkansas, **443** William J. Clinton Presidential Library and Museum, Little Rock, Arkansas (all photos), **445** Official White House photo, **449** Office of the Governor, state of Arkansas, **450** Shay Hopper, **452** Billy Bob Thornton; Rogers & Cowan, Pacific Design Center

Appendix/I Am an Arkansan

454 University of Arkansas Special Collections (Dee Brown), **456** Paul "Bear" Bryant Museum, Tuscaloosa, Alabama, **461** E. Lynn Harris, **464** Arkansas History Commission (Randolph)